PLATO ON KNOWLED

Plato on Knowledge and Forms

Selected Essays

GAIL FINE

CLARENDON PRESS · OXFORD

OXFORD
UNIVERSITY PRESS

Great Clarendon Street, Oxford OX2 6DP

Oxford University Press is a department of the University of Oxford.
It furthers the University's objective of excellence in research, scholarship,
and education by publishing worldwide in

Oxford New York

Auckland Bangkok Buenos Aires Cape Town Chennai
Dar es Salaam Delhi Hong Kong Istanbul Karachi Kolkata
Kuala Lumpur Madrid Melbourne Mexico City Mumbai Nairobi
São Paulo Shanghai Taipei Tokyo Toronto

Oxford is a registered trade mark of Oxford University Press
in the UK and in certain other countries

Published in the United States
by Oxford University Press Inc., New York

© in this volume Gail Fine 2003

British Library Cataloguing in Publication Data

Data available

Library of Congress Cataloging in Publication Data

Data available

ISBN 0–19–924558–4 (hbk.)
ISBN 0–19–924559–2 (pbk.)

1 3 5 7 9 10 8 6 4 2

Typeset by John Waś, Oxford
Printed in Great Britain
on acid-free paper by
Biddles Ltd., Guildford & King's Lynn

To My Parents
Jean and Sidney Fine

PREFACE

This volume contains some of the essays I have written on Plato's metaphysics and epistemology over approximately twenty-five years. (I have, however, omitted some of the articles I have written on these topics, either because they were revised for inclusion in my book *On Ideas: Aristotle's Criticisms of Plato's Theory of Forms* (Oxford: Clarendon Press, 1993), or because they were primarily criticism or analysis of others.) At the urging of several people, I have not substantially revised any of the essays. I have, however, modestly revised some of them, hoping to make various claims clearer, correcting or tightening up some arguments, and trying to make the volume a more continuous whole. I have also corrected typographical errors and incorrect references; I have tried to bring footnote references largely into conformity with OUP house style; and I have occasionally updated the footnotes and introduced cross-references. All Greek has now been transliterated; and I have consistently used (for example) 'form of large' rather than 'Form of large' or 'Form of Large'.

To compensate for the lack of large-scale revision, in the Introduction I outline the main themes of the essays and some connections between them. (In doing so, especially in the sections on metaphysics, I borrow freely from my Introduction to *Plato 1: Metaphysics and Epistemology*, in the Oxford Readings in Philosophy series (Oxford: Oxford University Press, 1999), and from *On Ideas*, chapter 4.) In the Introduction I also attempt to clarify some of my views, to indicate some ways in which they have changed, and to respond to criticisms, though in doing so I am extremely selective.

The chapters that follow record particular debts. Here I should like to single out a few especially important general influences. Some of the essays are revisions of chapters of my dissertation, which I wrote at Harvard under the supervision of G. E. L. Owen. Anyone who reads both his work and mine will see the influence he has had on me. I spent my third year of graduate school at Oxford, where I was fortunate to work with J. C. B. Gosling and J. L. Ackrill; I am grateful for their guidance. I have also learnt a lot from Myles Burnyeat, especially (so far as this volume is concerned) from his work on the *Theaetetus*.

Since 1975, I have had the privilege of being a member of the Sage School of Philosophy at Cornell University. I am deeply indebted to many colleagues for helpful conversations, comments, and friendship over the years. I should especially like to mention the late Norman Kretzmann, Sydney Shoemaker, and Nicholas Sturgeon. I am also grateful to many wonderful students. Many of my ideas were first tried out on them, and I have benefited from their questions and comments.

Much of this volume was conceived, and most of the Introduction was written, in the spring of 2002, while I was the Fowler Hamilton Research Fellow at Christ Church, Oxford. I thank the Dean and Students of Christ Church for awarding me the fellowship, and for making my stay so pleasant. While there, I was able to try out a number of my ideas on various people, whose friendly help I am pleased to acknowledge: Lesley Brown, Christopher Taylor, Michael Frede, Lindsay Judson, Ben Morison, Dominic Scott, and David Sedley.

Karen Nielsen kindly compiled the Bibliography and prepared the Index Locorum.

My single most important debt is to Terry Irwin. For over thirty years, I have been the beneficiary of his numerous comments, both written and oral, on virtually everything I have written or thought. He also remains the best of husbands and the best of friends.

The articles printed here originally appeared as follows. They are reprinted with the kind permission of the relevant publishers.

'Inquiry in the *Meno*', in R. Kraut (ed.), *Cambridge Companion to Plato* (Cambridge: Cambridge University Press, 1992), 200–26.

'Knowledge and Belief in *Republic* V', *Archiv für Geschichte der Philosophie*, 60 (1978), 121–39.

'Knowledge and Belief in *Republic* V–VII', in S. Everson (ed.), *Epistemology* (Companions to Ancient Thought, 1; Cambridge: Cambridge University Press, 1990), 85–115.

'Plato on Naming', *Philosophical Quarterly*, 27 (1977), 289–301.

'Protagorean Relativisms', in *Boston Area Colloquium in Ancient Philosophy*, 10 (Lanham, Md.: University Press of America, 1994), 211–43.

'Conflicting Appearances: *Theaetetus* 153 D–154 B', in C. Gill and M. McCabe (eds.), *Form and Argument in Late Plato* (Oxford: Clarendon Press, 1996), 105–33.

'Plato's Refutation of Protagoras in the *Theaetetus*', *Apeiron*, 32 (1998), 201–34.

'False Belief in the *Theaetetus*', *Phronesis*, 24 (1979), 70–80.

'Knowledge and *Logos* in the *Theaetetus*', *Philosophical Review*, 88 (1979), 366–97.

'Separation', *Oxford Studies in Ancient Philosophy*, 2 (1984), 31–87.

'Immanence', *Oxford Studies in Ancient Philosophy*, 4 (1986), 71–97.

'Relational Entities', *Archiv für Geschichte der Philosophie*, 65 (1983), 225–49.

'Forms as Causes: Plato and Aristotle', in A. Graeser (ed.), *Mathematics and Metaphysics in Aristotle/Mathematik und Metaphysik bei Aristoteles* (Bern: Haupt, 1987), 69–112.

'Plato and Aristotle on Form and Substance', *Proceedings of the Cambridge Philological Society*, 209 (1983), 23–47.

CONTENTS

1. Introduction   1
2. Inquiry in the *Meno*   44
3. Knowledge and Belief in *Republic* V   66
4. Knowledge and Belief in *Republic* V–VII   85
5. Plato on Naming   117
6. Protagorean Relativisms   132
7. Conflicting Appearances: *Theaetetus* 153 D–154 B   160
8. Plato's Refutation of Protagoras in the *Theaetetus*   184
9. False Belief in the *Theaetetus*   213
10. Knowledge and *Logos* in the *Theaetetus*   225
11. Separation   252
12. Immanence   301
13. Relational Entities   326
14. Forms as Causes: Plato and Aristotle   350
15. Plato and Aristotle on Form and Substance   397

Works Cited   426
Index Locorum   439

1

Introduction

I

The *Meno* is the first Platonic dialogue to reflect systematically on some still fundamental issues in epistemology: What is knowledge? How does it differ from true belief? What if anything can we know, and how can we know it? In 'Inquiry in the *Meno*' (Chapter 2) I explore the *Meno*'s answers to some of these important questions.[1]

At the very beginning of the *Meno*, Meno asks Socrates whether virtue

---

[1] Before proceeding, I should say something about the vexed issue of chronology. I follow a common practice of dividing Plato's dialogues into four groups: (1) early or Socratic dialogues—*Apology, Crito, Euthyphro, Charmides, Laches, Lysis, Hippias Minor, Ion, Protagoras*; (2) transitional dialogues—*Gorgias, Meno, Hippias Major, Euthydemus* (?), *Cratylus* (?); (3) middle dialogues—*Phaedo, Symposium, Republic, Phaedrus*; and (4) late dialogues—*Parmenides, Theaetetus, Sophist, Timaeus* (?), *Critias, Politicus* (= *Statesman*), *Philebus, Laws*. For a defence of roughly this dating, and the appropriateness of the labels, see e.g. G. Vlastos, *Socrates, Ironist and Moral Philosopher* (Ithaca, NY: Cornell University Press, 1991), chs. 2–3. The dating of the dialogues whose names are followed by question marks is especially controversial. (I discuss the controversy about the dating of the *Timaeus* in 'Owen's Progress: *Logic, Science, and Dialectic: Collected Papers in Greek Philosophy*. By G. E. L. Owen, ed. by M. Nussbaum', *Philosophical Review*, 97 (1988), 373–99 at 374–83.)

Some scholars favour a tripartite division, into early, middle, and late dialogues. John Cooper has recently argued that, though we may take the *Timaeus, Critias, Sophist, Politicus, Philebus*, and *Laws* to comprise a late group, we should be reluctant to make further chronological claims; see his Introduction to *Plato: Complete Works* (Indianapolis: Hackett, 1997), sect. II. He agrees, however, that the dialogues I've listed in (1), along with some others, have 'certain broad thematic affinities' (xv) that make it appropriate to call them Socratic. He also thinks that the dialogues I've listed in (3), along with some others, constitute a second group, and he says that 'While one might reasonably suppose that, in general, the dialogues of the second group [i.e. my group (3)] were written later than the Socratic group, it is not safe to rule out some chronological overlapping in composition' (xviii). The dating of the dialogues is also discussed by L. Brandwood, 'The Dating of Plato's Works by the Stylistic Method: A Historical and Critical Survey' (diss. Ph.D., University of London, 1958) (available from University Microfilms); see also his 'Stylometry and Chronology', in R. Kraut (ed.), *Cambridge Companion to Plato* (Cambridge: Cambridge University Press, 1992), 90–120.

In some chapters, I contrast Socrates and Plato; in doing so, I generally have in mind the early as opposed to middle dialogues. Here I follow those who think that the early

can be taught. Socrates replies that unless one knows what something is, one can't know anything about it; since he doesn't know what virtue is, neither does he know anything about it (71 A–B). This is Plato's Principle of the Priority of Knowledge What (PKW): to know anything about F, one must know what F is. In some cases, such as virtue, to know what F is is to know the answer to the question 'What is F?', that is, to know the real definition of the nature of F-ness, the one, nondisjunctive property because of which (*di' ho*) all F things are F (72 C 8). This gives us an instance of PKW: the Principle of the Priority of Knowledge of a Definition (PKD). Though PKD governs knowledge of such things as virtue, it doesn't clearly govern all cases. For example, it's not clear that Plato thinks that to know who Meno is (71 B),[2] one must know his definition; perhaps here, PKW can be satisfied in some other way. What it takes to know what F is may vary from case to case, depending on what sort of thing F is.[3]

Despite claiming not to know anything at all about virtue, Socrates claims to be eager to inquire into it. In the early dialogues too, Socrates often claims not to know what something is, yet professes to inquire into it. At

dialogues represent the thought of the historical Socrates. For a defence of this controversial assumption, see Vlastos.

[2] I take it that Plato speaks here not of knowing Meno, but of knowing who Meno is. Even if knowing Meno requires acquaintance with him, knowing who Meno is does not do so. Knowing who Meno is is a piece of propositional knowledge that can be acquired in a variety of ways: not only by interacting with him, but also by reading the appropriate books about him. See ch. 2 n. 42.

[3] It's sometimes thought that Plato takes PKD to be a general condition governing all knowledge. If this were right, and if he doesn't think sensible particulars can be defined, it would follow that he doesn't think they can be known. If, as I am inclined to think, PKD governs only some cases, and PKW is the general condition, then even if sensible particulars can't be defined, it doesn't follow that they can't be known. So far as I can see, the *Meno* leaves open the possibility of knowing sensible particulars, though it doesn't seem to me to take a stand on whether this is because they can be defined, or because knowledge, in their case, doesn't require a definition.

Some commentators deny that Plato here articulates either PKW or PKD. In 'Socratic Intellectualism', *Proceedings of the Boston Area Colloquium in Ancient Philosophy*, 2, ed. J. J. Cleary (Lanham, Md.: University Press of America, 1987), 275–316, repr. in his *Virtues of Authenticity* (Princeton: Princeton University Press, 1999), 27–58 (latter pagination), for example, A. Nehamas argues that Plato makes only 'the modest claim that there are some features of virtue (those which are as disputable as its definition or essentially connected with it) about which he can have no knowledge, or any other cognitive attitude, without first knowing what virtue itself is' (32). I think this is both too strong and too weak. It is too strong, in that it requires *knowledge* of what virtue is for having *any cognitive attitude* towards its disputable features. Yet Socrates has the cognitive attitude of belief towards some of virtue's disputable features, without knowing its definition; for example, he believes that virtue is one (*Meno* 72 A ff.). It is too weak, in that it says that knowledge of what virtue is is necessary only for knowledge of some of its features; whereas, in my view, Plato takes it to be necessary for knowing each of its features.

Meno 80 D, however, Meno asks how one can inquire into something if one doesn't know anything about it. Even if one finds what one was inquiring into, how would one know it was what one was inquiring into? Socrates converts Meno's questions into the form of a constructive dilemma:

(1) For any x, one either knows, or does not know, x.
(2) If one knows x, one cannot inquire into it.
(3) If one does not know x, one cannot inquire into it.
(4) Therefore, whether or not one knows x, one cannot inquire into it.

This paradox of inquiry, as we may call it, challenges Socrates' procedure both earlier in the *Meno* and in the early dialogues; for that procedure assumes that one can inquire even if one lacks knowledge.[4] And yet, the paradox is valid if 'know' is used univocally. And one would be tempted to think it sound if one thought that, for any item, one either has complete knowledge of it or is totally out of touch with it.[5] For if one knows everything there is to know about a thing, there is nothing left to inquire into. And if one is totally ignorant of something—if one's mind is a complete blank with respect to it—then one can't inquire either. For in this case one can't even identify something as what one is inquiring into; one doesn't even have a preliminary description.

Plato, however, doesn't think the paradox is sound. He rejects premiss (3): even if one has no knowledge whatsoever about a thing, one can inquire into it.[6] For complete ignorance is not the only alternative to knowledge: there are also true beliefs. And, Plato argues, if one has and relies on them, one will make progress in inquiry;[7] indeed, one can progress all the way to knowledge. On this view, knowledge is conceived as a high-level cognitive condition, one that goes beyond mere true belief. It is fundamental for understanding Plato's epistemology to see that this is how he conceives of knowledge. Indeed, one of his main projects is to distinguish knowledge both from belief as such (whether true or false) and from true belief in

---

[4] I provide a brief discussion of this issue in connection with the early dialogues in ch. 2; see also my 'Nozick's Socrates', *Phronesis*, 41 (1996), 233–44. Here I focus on the *Meno*.

[5] For speculation about why one might be tempted to think this, see ch. 2 n. 24.

[6] I think he also rejects premiss (2); but that is not the focus of his discussion.

[7] What's required for successful inquiry is having and relying on one's true beliefs; one need not correctly identify them as such, and often one does not do so. Indeed, the slave doesn't always do so, though, to be sure, in this particular case Socrates does so. But that isn't essential to successful inquiry, even if it makes this one go more smoothly. Hence, contrary to P. Dimas in 'True Belief in the *Meno*', *Oxford Studies in Ancient Philosophy*, 14 (1996), 1–32 at 9, I don't think Plato accepts what Dimas calls the True Belief thesis, which says that the slave can inquire, even though he lacks knowledge, only because he has beliefs which Socrates correctly identifies as being true. See ch. 2, Objection 5 and the Reply to it.

particular, and to explain why knowledge is both more valuable and more difficult to achieve.

To explain and defend his rejection of (3), Socrates cross-examines one of Meno's slaves about a geometry problem. At the beginning of the inquiry, the slave lacks knowledge; he has a mixture of true and false beliefs. Upon being questioned by Socrates, contradictions among his beliefs are uncovered. He eventually rejects the false ones and retains the true ones; and, using the latter, he is eventually able to answer Socrates' question. Though the slave now has a true belief about the answer, Plato says that he still doesn't know the answer.[8] Plato also says, however, that if the slave continues to inquire in the same way, he will eventually acquire the knowledge he currently lacks (85 B 8–D 1). Plato has done more than solve the paradox; he has also sketched a view on which, beginning without any knowledge, one may acquire it. Even if knowledge is difficult to acquire, even if we all lack knowledge, it is possible to acquire it because, like the slave, we all have and tend to rely on our true beliefs. This reply to the paradox vindicates Socrates' procedure earlier in the *Meno* and in the early dialogues, where, as we've seen, he claims to inquire even though he lacks knowledge.

In addition to rejecting premiss (3) of the paradox, Plato discusses the theory of recollection, according to which we all have immortal souls and, in a previous discarnate existence, had knowledge of such things as what virtue is. The theory of recollection is often thought to be a theory of innate knowledge. And it is often thought that Plato appeals to it in order to reject premiss (2) of the paradox: though we all have knowledge innate in us, we can none the less inquire by making our innate but tacit knowledge explicit. In my view, however, the theory of recollection is not a theory of innate

---

[8] In ch. 2 I assume that the true belief that the slave articulates at the end of the inquiry is a new true belief, one he acquires only at the end of the discussion with Socrates. If that is right, he must have been relying on different true beliefs while inquiring—for example, his belief about what a square is (82 B 2–4). By contrast, in 'Connaissance et réminiscence dans le "Ménon"', *Revue philosophique*, 181 (1991), 603–19, L. Brown argues that the true belief that the slave articulates at the end of the inquiry was in him all along and guided him in his inquiry.

In 'Socrates and the Jury: Paradoxes in Plato's Distinction between Knowledge and True Belief', *Proceedings of the Aristotelian Society*, suppl. 54 (1980), 173–91 at 187, Myles Burnyeat says that at the end of the inquiry the slave has a justified true belief about the answer; since Plato says that the slave still lacks knowledge, Burnyeat infers that Plato doesn't think knowledge is justified true belief. However, Plato might think that, though the slave has *some* justification for his belief, he doesn't have *enough* justification for satisfying the justification condition on knowledge. To say that knowledge is justified true belief isn't to say that any old justification will do: people differ about what sort or level of justification is necessary. Perhaps Plato has a demanding view about the sort of justification one needs in order to have knowledge, and so would say that the slave isn't justified according to those standards. I return to this issue below.

knowledge. For Plato emphasizes that, though we once knew, and can come to know again, we do not know now. If we do not know now, we do not have innate knowledge.[9] Nor is the theory of recollection introduced as a direct reply to the paradox. Rather, it is meant to explain the remarkable fact that, when faced with contradictions among our beliefs, we tend to favour the true ones over the false ones. It explains how inquiry in the absence of current knowledge is possible, and so it makes Plato's rejection of premiss (3) more plausible.

If Plato solves the paradox of inquiry by distinguishing knowledge from true belief, and by arguing that one can have the latter without having the former, then he owes us an account of how knowledge differs from true belief. He provides one in 98 A, where he says that knowledge is true belief that is bound by an *aitias logismos*. In Chapter 2 (and elsewhere) I say he is defining knowledge as justified true belief;[10] and indeed, the passage is sometimes cited as the first passage in Western philosophy to define knowledge in this now familiar—if now also widely discredited—way. The view that he is so defining knowledge is, however, controversial. Myles Burnyeat, for example, says that 'the *Meno*'s leading condition on knowledge, *aitias logismos*, is Greek for working out the explanation of something, *not* for assembling a justification for it'.[11] On this view, Plato's claim is not that

---

[9] In *Recollection and Experience* (Cambridge: Cambridge University Press, 1995), Dominic Scott says that, though he agrees with nearly everything I say in 'Inquiry in the *Meno*' (=ch. 2 below), he thinks (unlike me) that the theory of recollection in the *Meno* posits innate knowledge (16 n. 4). He cites two passages that he thinks tell against me: *Phaedo* 73 A 9 (which seems to refer back to the *Meno*) and *Meno* 85 D 9. The first passage says that the slave could not have inquired if knowledge were not in him. But Plato doesn't say *when* the knowledge was in him; perhaps it was in him only in a previous, discarnate existence. The second passage is forward-referring, to the time when the slave *will* acquire the knowledge he lacks during his discussion with Socrates. Scott thinks that the present tense and 'now' count against this reading. But when the passage is read in context, I do not think this is so. 85 D 3–4, for example, says that 'if he were repeatedly asked these same questions in various ways, you know that in the end his knowledge about these things would be as accurate as anyone's'; 'now' and the present tense in 85 D 9 refer to this future time, when the slave acquires the knowledge he lacks in the inquiry described in the *Meno*.

[10] However, I enter some caveats in ch. 2 n. 19. See also ch. 10.

[11] 'Socrates and the Jury', 187. In *Names and Natures in Plato's* Cratylus (New York: Routledge, 2001; this is a revised version of her 1996 Princeton Ph.D. thesis), R. Barney argues that Plato thinks that in addition to true belief, knowledge requires 'not a bare propositional content but a *process* of "tying down"—not a *logos* but a *logismos*' (172). In fact, Plato sometimes uses *logismos* to mean no more than *logos* (see e.g. *Tim.* 33 A 6); and I am not convinced that it has its process rather than its product sense in *Meno* 98 A. But even if Barney is right to say that *logismos* has its process sense here, Plato could still (contrary to what Barney may think) favour a version of a justified-true-belief account of knowledge. If her account of *logismos* is right, and Plato favours a justified-true-belief account of knowledge, then his view would be that one isn't properly justified in believing p unless one comes

knowledge is justified true belief; rather, his view is that one's true belief that p counts as knowledge that p just in case one can explain why p is so. I agree that Plato takes knowledge to require explanation. But we shouldn't infer that he doesn't take knowledge to be justified true belief. We should infer instead that the sort of justification he takes to be necessary for knowledge requires explaining why things are so. Otherwise put, even if *aitias logismos* is not best translated as 'justification', it does not follow that Plato rejects a justified-true-belief account of knowledge. Rather, he assumes that knowledge is justified true belief; in saying that knowledge is true belief that is bound by an *aitias logismos*, he is telling us what justification consists in. He takes 'justified true belief' to be the nominal definition of knowledge; 'true belief bound by an *aitias logismos*' is its real definition.[12]

It is sometimes said that Plato's interest in explanation shows that he is interested in understanding rather than in knowledge or, at any rate,

to believe p by reasoning in a certain way. Though this goes beyond some versions of a justified-true-belief account of knowledge, it is similar to other versions of it.

In 'Three Platonist Interpretations of the *Theaetetus*', in C. Gill and M. M. McCabe (eds.), *Form and Argument in Late Plato* (Oxford: Clarendon Press, 1996), 79–103, David Sedley raises a quite different challenge from those suggested by Burnyeat and Barney to the view that Plato is defining knowledge as justified true belief: that Plato, so far from saying that knowledge implies belief, says that it excludes it (93). (He suggests this not in his own right, but as a hypothesis that might appeal to those who favour a unitarian view of Plato and think that in the middle dialogues he takes knowledge and belief to exclude one another.) For Plato says that when true beliefs are tied down, they *become* (*gignontai*) knowledge. When a child becomes an adult, she is no longer a child; perhaps, similarly, when true beliefs become knowledge, they are no longer beliefs. However, *gignontai* need not be so understood: when I become old, I am still me; I just acquire a new property. Similarly, I think, Plato's point is that when true beliefs become knowledge, they are still true beliefs, but they now have the additional property of being tied down, which means that they are no longer *mere* true beliefs, but are now true beliefs plus something, so that they now constitute knowledge. On this interpretation, Plato takes knowledge to be a species of belief. Notice that on the view Sedley suggests, though knowing p at t_1 excludes believing p at t_1, it implies having believed p at some earlier time.

[12] See n. 8. This partly corrects what I say in 'Inquiry'. I say there that Plato thinks that (*a*) every case of knowledge requires justification, but (*b*) only some cases (those relevantly like virtue and geometry) require explanation. I also assumed that (*c*) explaining something is explaining what it essentially is. I still think Plato believes (*a*). But I no longer think he believes (*b*). Rather, he thinks that *every* case of knowledge involves an *aitias logismos*; and so he thinks that every case of knowledge requires explaining why what one knows is so. Nor am I sure he believes (*c*). To be sure, he thinks that to know what virtue is, one needs to know its essence. But he leaves open the possibility that to know the way to Larissa (97 A ff.), one needs to be able to explain, not its essence, but why this, rather than that, is the way. Or, if that is its essence, then perhaps he believes (*c*); but if so, explaining something's essence is less demanding than I originally took it to be. See also n. 3. These corrections to my view in 'Inquiry in the *Meno*' also affect some things I say in 'Knowledge and Belief in *Republic* V–VII' (ch. 4) and in 'Knowledge and *Logos* in the *Theaetetus*' (ch. 10).

Introduction   7

rather than in knowledge as it is conceived of nowadays. But we shouldn't divorce a concern with explanation from a concern with knowledge as it is conceived of nowadays. For though Plato's views are controversial, some contemporary epistemologists agree with him that knowledge is a high-level cognitive achievement, and one that requires grasping explanatory connections. His view has affinities with, for example, some contemporary coherence theories of justification, which likewise take knowledge to require understanding explanatory connections. I explore this theme briefly in 'Knowledge and Belief in *Republic* V–VII' (Chapter 4 below) and in 'Knowledge and *Logos* in the *Theaetetus*' (Chapter 10 below).

In so far as Plato takes knowledge to be true belief bound by an *aitias logismos*, he takes it to be propositional, in the sense that the claim that knowledge is true belief plus something is an account of what it is to know that p.[13] Several commentators have objected that Plato is concerned, not with propositional knowledge, but with knowledge of things.[14] I agree that he is concerned with knowledge of things. In *Meno* 97 A ff., for example, he mentions knowing the way to Larissa.[15] But to say that in 98 A Plato takes knowledge to be propositional isn't to deny that he is interested in knowledge of things; nor is it to say that he confuses the two notions. Rather, he thinks knowing things requires knowing propositions that are true of them. To know virtue, for example, one must know what it is, that is, its definition; to know the way to Larissa requires knowing that this, not that, is the way. So far from confusing propositional knowledge with knowledge of things, and so far from being interested in the latter to the exclusion of the former, Plato has the important insight that knowledge of things requires propositional knowledge.[16]

---

[13] In saying this, I don't assume any particular analysis of propositions.

[14] In 'The Structure of Dialectic in the *Meno*', *Phronesis*, 46 (2001), 413–19, for example, Lee Franklin levels this criticism against 'Inquiry in the *Meno*'. M. Stokes, 'Plato and the Sightlovers of the *Republic*', *Apeiron*, 25 (1992), 103–32, and F. Gonzalez, 'Propositions or Objects? A Critique of Gail Fine on Knowledge and Belief in *Republic* V', *Phronesis*, 41 (1996), 245–75, level the same criticism against my interpretation of *Republic* V; I discuss this below. It's sometimes argued, not that Plato is interested in knowing things *rather than* in propositional knowledge, but that he *confuses* the two notions. See e.g. J. McDowell, *Plato: Theaetetus* (Oxford: Clarendon Press, 1973), 192–3; and D. Bostock, *Plato's* Theaetetus (Oxford: Clarendon Press, 1988), e.g. 268.

[15] Even if, as has been argued, this is an analogy rather than an example, still, it mentions knowing a thing.

[16] I discuss this briefly in ch. 10; see also the next section. I take it that, both in fact and according to Plato, to know what something is is a case of propositional knowledge. I also take it that, both in fact and according to Plato, even if knowing a thing, such as Meno or the way to Larissa, involves more than propositional knowledge, it involves at least that. Hence Plato doesn't countenance any pure *de re* knowledge: in his view, all knowledge at least

II

It is often thought that in the middle dialogues Plato favours the Two Worlds Theory. There are different versions of this general sort of theory. On one familiar version, knowledge and belief have disjoint objects—forms and sensibles, respectively. (I discuss forms below. For now, it will do to say that they are mind-independent objective universals or properties.) Otherwise put, the contents of knowledge and belief—the propositions one can know or believe—are disjoint: the contents of knowledge are exhausted by propositions that are about forms; and the contents of belief are exhausted by propositions that are about sensibles. On this view, knowledge, so far from implying belief, excludes it.[17] Hence Plato is cited not only as the first Western philosopher to say that knowledge is justified true belief, but also as a classic example of someone who takes knowledge to exclude belief. Those who do the first typically focus on the *Meno* and *Theaetetus*; those who do the second typically focus on the *Republic*.

The Two Worlds Theory is at odds with the epistemology of the *Meno*. For there, as we saw, Plato says that knowledge is true belief bound by an *aitias logismos*; on this view, knowledge, so far from excluding belief, implies it.[18] And, as we've also seen, in the *Meno* Plato gives examples of things one can both know and have beliefs about. He says, for example, that although the slave has a mere true belief about the answer to the geometrical question Socrates poses, he can acquire knowledge of it. Plato also says that one may know, or have a mere true belief about, the way to Larissa (97 A ff.). The *Meno* also seems to allow knowledge of sensible particulars as well as beliefs about forms.[19] In 'Knowledge and Belief in *Republic* V' and

requires propositional knowledge, and some knowledge is exhausted by it. For a defence of the view that there is no such thing as pure *de re* knowledge, see M. Dummett, 'Frege's Distinction between Sense and Reference', in his *Truth and Other Enigmas* (Cambridge, Mass.: Harvard University Press, 1978), 116–44 at 123 ff. See also J. Hintikka, 'Knowledge by Acquaintance—Individuation by Acquaintance', in D. Pears (ed.), *Bertrand Russell: A Collection of Critical Essays* (Garden City, NY: Doubleday, 1972), 52–79.

[17] There are other versions of a Two Worlds Theory than the one just described. For example, R. S. Bluck (ed.), *Plato's* Meno (Cambridge: Cambridge University Press, 1961), 34 ff., argues that Plato allows beliefs about forms; and in *An Introduction to Plato's* Republic (Oxford: Clarendon Press, 1981), ch. 8, Julia Annas argues that Plato allows some knowledge of some aspects of some sensibles. I focus here on the version of the Two Worlds Theory described in the text.

[18] But see n. 11. Even if the view Sedley suggests were correct, it would not provide much comfort to friends of the Two Worlds Theory, since it allows knowledge and belief about the same things.

[19] If who Meno is and the way to Larissa are mentioned as literal examples of something

in 'Knowledge and Belief in *Republic* V–VII' (Chapters 3 and 4 below) I ask whether *Republic* V–VII—which is Plato's lengthiest and most systematic discussion of knowledge and belief in the middle dialogues—is committed to the Two Worlds Theory.[20]

At the end of *Republic* V Plato seeks to persuade those he calls sightlovers, on grounds acceptable to them, that they lack knowledge. The argument is therefore governed by what I call the requirement of noncontroversiality, or the dialectical requirement (cf. *Meno* 75 D):[21] it should use premises that are acceptable to the sightlovers. Two central premises are that knowledge is set over what is (*esti*) and that belief is set over what is and is not.[22] It's not immediately clear what these premises mean since, as is well known, *esti* can be used in different ways: for example, veridically, existentially, and predicatively.[23] If *esti* is used veridically here, then the point is that knowledge but not belief implies truth. I call this a *contents analysis*, since it distinguishes knowledge and belief by their propositional contents. If *esti* is used existentially or predicatively, then knowledge and belief are distinguished by their nonpropositional objects; hence I call this an *objects analysis*. On the predicative reading (which is probably the most popular one), Plato would be saying that the objects of knowledge are restricted to

one might know, then the *Meno* explicitly allows knowledge of sensibles. Even if they are analogies rather than literal examples, still, I don't think Plato says anything in the *Meno* that precludes knowledge of sensibles. For example, we've seen that he says that knowledge is true belief that is tied down with an *aitias logismos*. So far as I can see, he leaves open the possibility that one can explain why this is the way to Larissa, or why a given action is (or is not) virtuous: in which case he leaves open the possibility of knowing sensibles. See also nn. 3 and 12. As for beliefs about forms: though Socrates claims not to know what virtue is, he expresses beliefs about what it is (for example, that it is a single nondisjunctive property because of which all F things are F); and virtue is a form (*eidos*: 72 C 6, D 8, E 5). Forms may be conceived of differently in the *Meno* and in the middle dialogues; but however they are conceived of in the *Meno*, they are things one can have beliefs about.

[20] The first article (=ch. 3) was published earlier and, as the title makes clear, it doesn't discuss *Republic* VI–VII. I've none the less included it, because its discussion of *Republic* V is considerably fuller than the discussion in the later article (=ch. 4); it also now seems to me to be right on some issues about which the later article now seems mistaken.

[21] I use the first label in 'Knowledge and Belief in *Republic* V–VII' (ch. 4), and the second in 'Knowledge and Belief in *Republic* V' (ch. 3).

[22] The first claim—that knowledge is set over what is—is an opening premiss. The second claim—that belief is set over what is and is not—is not explicitly mentioned until 478 D, though it is implicit much earlier; and it is argued for, rather than being an independent premiss. I see this in 'Knowledge and Belief in *Republic* V'. But in the later 'Knowledge and Belief in *Republic* V–VII' I mistakenly say that both claims are opening premisses. That the later article is mistaken on this point is noted by Stokes, in 'Plato and the Sightlovers', 123.

[23] It can also be used in yet further ways; but the uses just mentioned are the main ones that have been thought to be relevant in *Republic* V. To say that Plato uses *esti* in different *ways* is not to say that he uses it in different *senses*.

what is F (and not also not F), whereas the objects of belief are restricted to what is both F and not F. I argue, however, that for most of the argument (from the beginning through 478 D 12), *esti* is used veridically, to make the point that knowledge but not belief implies truth. One advantage of this reading is that it, unlike its rivals, satisfies the dialectical requirement.[24]

Though Plato focuses on the veridical use of *esti* for most of the argument, at 479 A ff. he turns to the predicative use, to make the point that the many Fs are both F and not F. The many Fs are sensible properties such as bright colour and circular shape (cf. *Phd.* 100 D). Bright colour is one of the many beautifuls recognized by the sightlovers: one of the many sensible properties in terms of which they define beauty. According to the sightlovers, to be beautiful is sometimes to be brightly coloured, sometimes to be sombre-coloured, and so on. There is no single property, the beautiful, because of which all beautiful things are beautiful. Yet, Plato notes, each of the many beautifuls is both beautiful and ugly. Bright colour, for example, is beautiful in this Matisse painting; but it is merely garish, and so ugly, in that other painting. The claim that each of the many Fs is both F and not F doesn't violate the dialectical requirement. On the contrary, it is precisely because the sightlovers accept it that they take the beautiful to be many rather than one. They see that no single sensible property (and they recognize only such properties: that's why they are *sightlovers*) can explain why all and only beautiful things are beautiful, and so they infer that the beautiful is many.

One might infer that Plato confuses the veridical and predicative uses of *esti*, or that he employs only the predicative use throughout.[25] I argue, however, that he shifts from the veridical to the predicative use, without confusion, in order to persuade the sightlovers that if they define beauty in terms of the many beautifuls, which are beautiful and ugly, they will inevitably have both true and false beliefs about beauty: in which case they lack knowledge of beauty. And that is what Plato wanted to show.

How exactly does he attempt to persuade the sightlovers of this? In Chap-

---

[24] This claim is controversial. Stokes, 'Plato and the Sightlovers', 110, for example, seems to suggest that it is not common ground between Plato and the sightlovers that knowledge but not belief implies truth. And in *Plato on Knowledge and Reality* (Indianapolis: Hackett, 1976), 160 n. 9, N. P. White claims that his version of an objects analysis satisfies the dialectical requirement. A further advantage of my reading of the argument is that on it, the argument is valid. On at least some versions of the existential and predicative readings, by contrast, the argument is invalid. However, not all alternative readings of the argument make it invalid.

[25] For the second suggestion see e.g. Annas, *An Introduction to Plato's Republic*, ch. 8. See also the interesting discussion in L. Brown, 'The Verb "to be" in Greek Philosophy: Some Remarks', in S. Everson (ed.), *Language* (Cambridge Companions to Ancient Thought, 3; Cambridge: Cambridge University Press, 1994), 212–37.

ters 3 and 4 I say he assumes that beauty is one. This, however, can't (or, at any rate, had better not) be right: for that assumption is the central bone of contention between Plato and the sightlovers. If Plato simply assumes that beauty is one, there is an especially egregious violation of the dialectical requirement.[26] But in fact, contrary to Chapters 3 and 4, we need not accuse Plato of reasoning in this way. Instead, he seems to be arguing that if one relies on the sightlovers' definition of beauty in terms of a list of sensible properties, one will inevitably have some false beliefs about what things are, and are not, beautiful, in which case the definition that led to these beliefs must itself be false. He seems to rely, not on the assumption that beauty is one, but on the assumption that reliance on a satisfactory definition shouldn't inevitably issue in false beliefs about what things do, or don't, fall under the definition: this explains his emphasis on the truth condition for knowledge.

I don't think the sightlovers challenge that assumption; hence relying on it doesn't violate the dialectical requirement. But why does Plato think that relying on the sightlovers' definitions will inevitably lead to misclassifications? He doesn't spell out his reasoning, but perhaps he is thinking along the following lines. Suppose I define beauty merely by listing sensible properties such as bright colour, circular shape, and so on. As the sightlovers agree, each such property collects things that are both beautiful and not beautiful: some brightly coloured things are beautiful; others are not. Suppose I encounter a new object, of a sort I've never seen before, and wonder whether it is beautiful. It is brightly coloured, and bright colour figures in my definition of beauty. So I might infer that it is beautiful. But it may not be, as I can come to understand if I study it more carefully. Guided by the sightlovers' definition of beauty, I am led to a false belief about what things are beautiful. Their definition doesn't give me clear guidance about how to classify the object; it isn't suitably explanatory. Plato thinks that once the sightlovers see this, they will abandon their claim that a mere list of sensible properties is adequate as a definition.[27]

Having argued that the sightlovers lack knowledge, Plato goes on to argue that in order to have knowledge, one must know forms.[28] The form of

---

[26] This point is noticed by Gonzalez, 'Propositions or Objects?', 270.

[27] This is just a sketch of how I would now explain this stage of Plato's argument. In coming to think along these lines, I've been influenced by T. Irwin, *Plato's Ethics* (Oxford: Oxford University Press, 1995), §§ 181–5.

[28] I'm not sure whether Plato means to say that (*a*) to have any knowledge at all, one must know forms, or (*b*) to have any knowledge of the sort he is interested in (such as knowledge about beauty or justice), one must know forms. If he intends (*a*), then he goes beyond the *Meno*. For though the *Meno* says that knowledge requires an *aitias logismos*, it does not say that this requirement can be satisfied only by mentioning a definition of a form; it leaves

beauty is, among other things, a single, nondisjunctive, nonsensible property that explains why all and only beautiful things are beautiful. Plato therefore in effect eventually argues that beauty is one; but he doesn't assume that it is in arguing against the sightlovers. Nor, in any case, is this last stage of the argument governed by the dialectical requirement. That requirement governs only the argument for the claim that the sightlovers lack knowledge.[29]

As I construe the argument, Plato is interested both in propositional knowledge and in knowledge of things. That he is interested in propositional knowledge is clear from the fact that he repeatedly emphasizes that knowledge but not belief implies truth. That he is interested in knowledge of things is clear from the fact that he argues that one can have knowledge only if one knows forms. Yet it has been argued that Plato is interested here *only* in knowledge of things: in which case, contrary to what I say, *esti* is not used veridically.[30] Once again, however, the fact that Plato focuses on propositional knowledge doesn't mean that he isn't interested in knowledge of things. Or, to put it the other way around, even though he is interested in knowledge of things, we shouldn't infer that he doesn't focus on propositional knowledge. For in his view, to know a form requires knowing what it is; and that, in turn, is to know its definition, which is a matter of propositional knowledge.

As I interpret the argument, it doesn't imply the Two Worlds Theory. Rather, Plato defends only the weaker view that to have any knowledge at all, one must know forms. This leaves open the possibility that once one has such knowledge, one can know more than forms; it also leaves open the possibility that one can have mere belief (whether true or false) about

open the possibility that different sorts of cases involve different sorts of *aitiai*, some of them bypassing forms. See n. 3. I shall generally write as though the middle dialogues accept (*a*); but it's worth bearing (*b*) in mind.

[29] In chs. 3 and 4 I say that the last stage of the argument—where Plato argues that knowledge requires knowledge of forms—violates the dialectical requirement in assuming that knowledge must be based on knowledge. However, I'm no longer sure the sightlovers object to that assumption. Even if they do, it would be misleading to say that Plato *violates* the dialectical requirement, since this stage of the argument isn't governed by it.

[30] See Stokes, 'Plato and the Sightlovers', and Gonzalez, 'Propositions or Objects?'. Stokes, for example, says that the sightlover denies that beauty exists, but doesn't dispute the truth of any propositions—except the proposition that the F by itself exists (110). But then, even on Stokes's own interpretation, propositions are not irrelevant. At 112 he likewise imports propositions. Stokes also notes that Plato says that knowledge is set over what is, to 'gnow', as he puts it, *hōs ekhei*, how it is or that it is. He says that 'how it is' means 'what its properties are' (128). But knowing what something's properties are involves propositional knowledge: for knowing what x's properties are requires knowing that it has various properties, and that its properties are such and so.

forms. In *Republic* VI–VII, in the famous images of the Sun, Line, and Cave, Plato goes further, and says that there is (or can be) knowledge of sensibles,[31] and that there is mere belief about forms. The *Republic*, then, so far from endorsing the Two Worlds Theory, is incompatible with it.[32]

We have seen that *Republic* V–VII, like the *Meno*, takes knowledge to be truth-entailing. And just as the *Meno* claims that knowledge requires an *aitias logismos*, so *Republic* V–VII says that knowledge requires a *logos* (KL).[33] *Republic* V–VII also seems to assume that knowledge must be based on knowledge (KBK): I can know p only if I know its justification q.[34] The

---

[31] One passage I appeal to is *Rep.* 520 c 4, where Plato says that the philosopher who re-descends to the cave will know (*gignōskein*) the images on the cave wall, which are sensibles. C. Bobonich, *Plato's Utopia Recast* (Oxford: Clarendon Press, 2002), 62 n. 79, objects that (*a*) Plato typically uses *epistasthai*, not *gignōskein*, when he wants to contrast knowledge with belief; it's not clear *gignōskein* means 'knowledge'. Moreover, (*b*) Plato sometimes uses *epistēmē* more weakly than for genuine knowledge. Bobonich doesn't cite any passages in support of (*b*), but he mentions an article by N. Cooper, 'Between Knowledge and Igno-rance', *Phronesis*, 31 (1986), 229–42 at 240–1; and Cooper cites a passage in *Republic* IV which supports (*b*) (this is the only passage Cooper cites as evidence of a weaker use of *epistēmē*). However, that passage comes before the technical discussion in *Republic* V, which clearly uses *epistēmē* for knowledge in particular; hence one would expect subsequent uses of the word to indicate knowledge, at least if they occur in epistemological contexts. As for (*a*), whatever may be true of *epistasthai* and *gignōskein* in general, *Republic* V uses the two words interchangeably, and contrasts both with belief. It would therefore be extremely misleading if *gignōskein* in 520 c 4 were used for anything less than knowledge.

[32] In ch. 3 n. 3, I say that Plato may be more sympathetic to the Two Worlds Theory in *Phileb.* 58 E–59 c. In 'Epistêmê and Logos in Plato's Later Thought' A. Nehamas provides a more plausible interpretation of the passage, on which it allows knowledge of sensibles. (This paper was first published in *Archiv für Geschichte der Philosophie*, 66 (1984), 11–36; it is reprinted in Nehamas's *Virtues of Authenticity*, 224–48.) I was also pleased to see that D. Frede, in 'The Philosophical Economy of Plato's Psychology: Rationality and Common Concepts in the *Timaeus*', in M. Frede and G. Striker (eds.), *Rationality in Greek Thought* (Oxford: Clarendon Press, 1996), 29–58, argues that the *Timaeus* does not accept the Two Worlds Theory.

[33] KL is implicit in *Republic* V; it is explicit in VI–VII. See e.g. 534 B. It's not clear whether the claim that knowledge requires an *aitias logismos* is exactly the same as the claim that it requires a *logos*, but the former at least implies the latter.

[34] The *Meno* may also be committed to KBK. For as we've seen, it says that one can know something about F only if one knows what F is. Hence knowledge about F requires knowledge of something else (of what F is); one can know whether virtue is teachable, for example, only if one knows what virtue is. We've also seen that, at the end of the geometrical inquiry, the slave is said to have true belief but not knowledge. Presumably in order to have knowledge, he needs to master a wider range of geometrical concepts, and be able to answer related questions. That is, he can know the answer to Socrates' question only if he knows a lot of other things as well.

Rather than saying that to know p, one must know its justification q, one might say instead that to know any entities mentioned in p, one must know any entities mentioned in q. I tend to speak in the former way in 'Knowledge and Belief in *Republic* V–VII', and in the latter way in 'Knowledge and *Logos* in the *Theaetetus*'. I don't think the difference

conjunction of KL and KBK raises the threat of the famous regress of reasons: to know something, I must, by KL, provide a *logos* of it. Given KBK, I must know this *logos*. Given KL, I must then provide a *logos* of it which, by KBK, I must also know—and so on, it seems, *ad infinitum*. Plato discusses this regress in detail in the *Theaetetus*; I explore what he says there in 'Knowledge and *Logos* in the *Theaetetus*' (Chapter 10). But the regress is lurking not far below the surface in *Republic* VI–VII. It's sometimes said that discussion of the regress begins with the Hellenistic sceptics (in, for example, the Five Agrippan Modes), or perhaps with Aristotle, in *Posterior Analytics* I. 1–3 and II. 19. But if I'm right, discussion of it is at least as early as Plato.

Plato is often thought to solve the regress by embracing foundationalism. There are many versions of foundationalism, but on one version often associated with Plato, the regress comes to a halt with isolated acts of acquaintance, by which we grasp individual forms; I can know each form in and of itself, by being acquainted with it, by having some sort of direct apprehension of it. On this view, Plato conceives of knowledge atomistically: one can know an individual form on its own, without reference to anything else; hence the regress comes to a halt.

Coherentism provides an alternative response to the regress of reasons. Just as there are many versions of foundationalism, so there are many versions of coherentism. On one version, one can't know an individual entity or proposition on its own; one must be able to relate it appropriately to other connected entities or propositions which, in turn, must be related to other connected entities or propositions including, eventually, the one with which one started. This replaces a linear infinite regress with a circle: accounts circle back on themselves. But, according to coherentists, if the circle is large enough, and explanatorily powerful enough, it is virtuous, not vicious, and it constitutes the right sort of justification for knowledge.

In Chapter 4 I argue that Plato stops the regress by endorsing coherentism:[35] here as elsewhere, he conceives of knowledge holistically. One can't know a single entity or proposition on its own; knowing any given entity or proposition requires knowing related ones as well. One knows more as one can explain more; the best sort of knowledge, which only the dialectician has, involves a synoptic grasp of reality as a whole, one that involves understanding its teleological structure. I call this Plato's interrelation model of knowledge. Though many commentators agree that he favours some such

matters for my purposes. For one thing, we've seen that Plato intends a very tight connection between propositional knowledge and knowledge of things.

[35] Or rather, Plato would solve the regress in this way: as I've said, he doesn't explicitly consider it in the *Republic*.

view in dialogues that post-date the *Theaetetus*, I argue that it is present at least as early as the *Republic*; it is not a new view of the late dialogues. I discuss it further, in connection with the *Theaetetus*, in Chapter 10.

Though a holist model of knowledge is incompatible with foundationalism as I've described it—such that one grasps an individual entity or proposition in and of itself, independently of other things—it isn't incompatible with every version of foundationalism. For example, one might argue that, though Plato thinks one can't know an individual form independently of knowing other forms, one can know forms without knowing sensibles, but not conversely; and one might argue that this asymmetry is a sort of foundationalism, though a different sort from the one I've described.[36] This second sort of foundationalism, however, isn't adequate to stop the regress. Be that as it may, my main concern is to argue that Plato is a holist about knowledge, in the sense that he thinks one can't know any individual entity or proposition on its own; and that view requires him to reject at least certain versions of foundationalism.

Notice that if Plato favours the Two Worlds Theory, there is a sense in which he doesn't think that knowledge of forms is the foundational base in terms of which all other knowledge is justified; for if he accepts the Two Worlds Theory, there is no knowledge other than knowledge of forms. One might argue, however, that knowledge of some forms is necessary for knowledge of others, but not conversely, and that that gives us a sort of foundationalism within the world of forms. Perhaps, for example, one can know the form of the good in and of itself, but can know other forms only if one knows the form of the good? If so, then there is a sense in which the form of the good is a foundational entity. Plato certainly takes the form of the good to be prior to other forms in some sense. But in 'Knowledge and Belief in *Republic* V–VII' I argue that he thinks that one can know it only if one knows other forms (and perhaps only if one knows sensibles too), just as knowledge of them (or, at any rate, the best sort of knowledge of them) requires knowledge of the form of the good.

III

Just as there is dispute about whether Plato is an epistemological atomist, so there is dispute about whether he is a logical or semantic atomist. According to semantic atomism, all words are treated as names; and the

---

[36] Thanks to Lesley Brown for this suggestion.

meaning of a name consists solely in its reference.[37] Accordingly, to grasp
the meaning of a word, one must be acquainted with its referent. So just as
Plato is sometimes thought to believe that knowledge consists in or requires
acquaintance, so he is sometimes thought to believe that understanding the
meanings of words requires acquaintance with their referents. And just as
he is sometimes thought to believe that one knows individual forms in and
of themselves, independently of their connections to other things, so he is
sometimes thought to believe that one learns the meanings of words atomistically, one by one, by being acquainted with their individual referents.
Semantic atomism also treats sentences as though they are just complex
names; and stating is treated as naming. Plato's alleged semantic atomism
has been thought to explain his alleged inability to explain the possibility of
falsehood. For on semantic atomism, a false sentence is just a name without
a referent, in which case it is meaningless.

   Plato is often thought to be in the grip of semantic atomism until the
Sophist, a dialogue in which he is generally thought to reject it decisively.
(This goes along with the view that, until after the *Theaetetus*, he is an epistemological atomist.) The *Cratylus* is one dialogue that has been adduced as
evidence of Plato's alleged semantic atomism. In 'Plato on Naming' (Chapter 5), however, I argue that the *Cratylus* rejects it; indeed, its account of
falsity anticipates the one given in the *Sophist*. (This parallels my claim that
the *Republic* and *Theaetetus* have a holist view of knowledge; holism about
knowledge is not to be found only in post-*Theaetetus* dialogues.) So far
from treating any words as names whose meaning consists solely in their
referents, he treats them all as disguised descriptions.[38] Nor does he confuse
names and sentences, or naming and stating.

   Interestingly enough, it has also been argued that Plato confuses names

---

[37] On a weaker version of this view, basic words, but not all words, are names whose
meanings consist solely in their references. However, G. E. L. Owen, who is a main proponent
of the view that Plato is a semantic atomist, formulates it in the way stated in the text. See e.g.
'Notes on Ryle's Plato', in O. P. Wood and G. Pitcher (eds.), *Ryle: A Collection of Critical Essays*
(London: Macmillan, 1971), 341–72 at points (4) and (17). Moreover, the claim that Plato
can't explain falsity because he treats sentences as names may assume the stronger view.

[38] At *Crat.* 435 E–440 A Plato argues that the best sort of inquiry requires attention to
things, not names. In 'The End of the *Cratylus*: Limning the Real', *Ancient Philosophy*, 21
(2000), 25–43, A. Silverman argues that this shows that, contrary to my view, Plato thinks
that the best sort of knowledge is prior to language and nondiscursive; this is part of Silverman's criticism of ascribing to Plato the sort of epistemological holism I favour. However,
all Plato means is that if we restrict our attention to the structure of language, and to the
ordinary meanings encoded in our names, we won't achieve genuine knowledge; in some
cases we must look at the things themselves. We can't, for example, learn the nature of gold
simply by considering ordinary beliefs about gold. For one thing, many of those beliefs
might be wrong; for another, we must do scientific experiments with gold itself.

and sentences, not by reducing sentences to names, but by treating names as though they are sentences. One argument for this view is that Plato takes names to have descriptive content. However, the view that names have descriptive content does not imply that they are sentences. *Cratylus* 385 B 2–D 1 has also been adduced as evidence for the view that Plato treats names as sentences. For it is sometimes thought that in this passage Plato commits a crude fallacy of division, arguing from the truth and falsity of sentences to the truth and falsity of names, as though the latter are true and false in just the way in which the former are. I argue, however, that rather than committing a fallacy of division, Plato is articulating a plausible principle of compositionality: he explains the truth and falsity of sentences in terms of what their constituent words are true and false of. A sentence of the form 'S is P' is true just in case 'P' is true of what 'S' is true of; and a sentence of the form 'S is P' is false if 'P' is not true of what 'S' is true of.[39]

IV

Chapters 6–10 are devoted to the *Theaetetus*, one of the richest Platonic dialogues for anyone interested in his epistemology. Indeed, it is the only Platonic dialogue structured around the question 'What is knowledge?' The first answer Plato considers in detail is Theaetetus' suggestion that know-

---

[39] This is essentially the account I give in 'Plato on Naming', though I don't there use the label 'principle of compositionality'. I have been able to make my point more clearly here as a result of having read J. L. Ackrill, 'Language and Reality in Plato's *Cratylus*', in his *Essays on Plato and Aristotle* (Oxford: Clarendon Press, 1997), 33–52, repr. in G. Fine (ed.), *Plato 1: Metaphysics and Epistemology* (Oxford: Oxford University Press, 1999), 125–246; and Barney, *Names and Natures*. At one point Barney formulates the principle of compositionality as follows: 'for a property to belong to (or be capable of belonging to) a whole of parts such as a complex linguistic expression, it must belong (or be capable of belonging) to those parts individually' (32; contrast 181). If Plato is relying on this version of a principle of compositionality, then he would be committed to saying that words are true and false in the same sense in which sentences are. On my formulation, by contrast (a formulation Barney at times also uses), Plato is committed only to the view that the truth and falsity of a sentence depend on something about its parts: in particular, on what its constituents (or some of them) are true and false of.

In 'Plato on Naming' I say that 385 B–D is the only place in the *Cratylus* in which Plato says that names are true and false; elsewhere, I claim, he says instead that they are correct or incorrect. However, as Barney, 188 n. 13, points out, he seems to call names true and false at both 437 D 5–6 and 438 D 7–8. The first passage seems to use 'true' and 'correct' interchangeably. If so, presumably 'false' and 'incorrect' are also interchangeable. The second passage says that true names are those that 'express the truth about the things that are'. So perhaps correct names are just names that are true of things, in virtue of correctly describing them.

ledge is perception (T).[40] Plato doesn't discuss this proposal in isolation. Rather, he links it to Protagoras' measure doctrine (P), according to which 'man is the measure of all things, of those that are that they are, and of those that are not, that they are not' (151 E 1–3), and to a Heraclitean flux doctrine (H), according to which 'all things change, like streams' (160 D 7–8). At 160 D 6 he says that these three theses 'come to the same'. I take him to mean that each of them best supports, and is best supported by, the others. Though there are no strict logical implications among them, they form a sort of 'package deal', such that anyone who accepts part of it is well advised to accept the rest. Having described the three theses and their interrelations, Plato turns to the offensive: in 169–71 (cf. 177 C 6–179 D 2) he refutes the measure doctrine; in 181–3, he refutes a Heraclitean flux doctrine; and in 184–6 he argues that knowledge is not perception.

This part of the *Theaetetus* is a remarkable example of Plato's dialectical sensitivity. In many of the early dialogues an interlocutor proposes a definition of some virtue, which is then tested against examples and general principles. A contradiction among the claims to which the interlocutor has committed himself is uncovered and then, usually, the definition is rejected. The first part of the *Theaetetus* fits this general pattern, in so far as Theaetetus proposes that knowledge is perception, and Socrates then tests this definition against examples and general principles. However, rather than quickly rejecting the definition when a contradiction is uncovered, they retain the definition and reject the examples; they also retain the Principle of Noncontradiction. For example, the claim that knowledge is perception might seem to be refuted by alleged cases of misperception. But rather than rejecting the claim that knowledge is perception, Plato describes a view of the world and of perception on which we can dismiss such purported counter-examples without threat to the Principle of Noncontradiction. The price of doing so is accepting a Protagorean epistemology and a Heraclitean ontology. It's only after giving the definition a long run for its money that Plato turns to the offensive, and rebuts it: though actually, the 'stage directions'[41] that make Theaetetus' commitments clear constitute an indirect criticism of the view that knowledge is perception. For in making

---

[40] Before considering this suggestion, Plato asks whether knowledge is knowledge of shoemaking and the like.

[41] The phrase is Burnyeat's, in 'Idealism and Greek Philosophy: What Descartes Saw and Berkeley Missed', *Philosophical Review*, 91 (1982), 3–40 at 6 n. 2. As anyone who reads both his work and mine will realize, my views about the *Theaetetus* are deeply indebted to his work, though we differ in various ways. For example, our views of the stage directions are not exactly the same; and our accounts of Protagoras, and of Plato's refutation of him, are very different.

Theaetetus' commitments clear, Plato also makes it clear how implausible his view is, by showing how high the price of acceptance is.

Protagoras' measure doctrine is introduced as a solution to the Problem of Conflicting Appearances. In Plato's example (153 D–154 B) the wind appears cold to the one who shivers, but not to the one who doesn't. The Protagorean infers that the wind is cold to the first person but not to the second; he thinks we can infer from how things appear, to how they are (to one). Eventually Plato extends Protagoreanism beyond perceptual appearances to all appearances, so that any belief whatsoever is true, or true to the one who believes it. We therefore need to distinguish narrow from broad Protagoreanism. According to narrow Protagoreanism, things are, and are only (to one), however they perceptually appear to one to be. That is, things are, and are only (to one), however one believes them to be on the basis of perception. According to broad Protagoreanism, things are, and are only (to one), however one believes them to be; hence, all beliefs (not merely perceptual ones) are true (to the one who believes them).

How exactly should we understand the measure doctrine?[42] Plato tells us that Protagoras 'means [*legei*] something along these lines: everything is, for me, the way it appears to me, and is, for you, the way it appears to you' (152 A 6–8). What exactly does this mean? There are many interpretations, but I focus primarily on two, which I call relativism about truth and infallibilism.[43] On the first, Protagoras believes that no propositions are flat-out true, or true *simpliciter*; rather, all propositions are true only to, or for, those who believe them.[44] On the second, Protagoras believes that all beliefs are true *simpliciter*; and so we are infallible in the sense that whatever we believe is guaranteed to be true. In Chapters 6–8 I argue that Protagoras is an infallibilist.[45]

---

[42] See chs. 6–8 for discussion of further details about how to understand the measure doctrine.

[43] I consider relativism about truth because it is such a familiar interpretation; I consider infallibilism because it is the interpretation I favour. In ch. 6 I consider two further positions, which I call perceptual relativism and relationalism. Other commentators consider yet further positions, and use yet further labels. In 'Protagoras and Inconsistency', *Archiv für Geschichte der Philosophie*, 59 (1977), 19–36, for example, S. Waterlow distinguishes what she calls relativism of fact from relativism about truth; she argues that Protagoras is a relativist of the first, but not of the second, sort.

[44] This is one interpretation of Protagoras that Burnyeat defends; see especially his 'Protagoras and Self-Refutation in Plato's *Theaetetus*', *Philosophical Review*, 85 (1976), 172–95, repr. in S. Everson (ed.), *Epistemology* (Companions to Ancient Thought, 1; Cambridge: Cambridge University Press, 1990), 39–59; and his Introduction to *The* Theaetetus *of Plato* (Indianapolis: Hackett, 1990). This is broad relativism about truth; there is also narrow relativism about truth. Similarly, we may distinguish broad from narrow infallibilism.

[45] Contrary to A. Silverman, 'Flux and Language in the *Theaetetus*', *Oxford Studies in Ancient Philosophy*, 18 (2000), 109–52, however, I do not say that on infallibilism all beliefs

The first stage of my argument is in Chapter 6, where I distinguish among different positions, all of which have been called 'relativism', despite the fact that they are actually quite different from one another, though the differences have often gone unnoticed. Having settled on an appropriate understanding of the term—as relativism about truth—I go on to argue that Plato portrays Protagoras, not as a relativist about truth, but as an infallibilist. Here I deploy two main strategies. First, in Chapters 6 and 7, I argue that if Protagoras is an infallibilist, he fits well into the dialectical context in which Plato situates him; whereas, if he is a relativist about truth, he does not fit into that context. Infallibilism, but not relativism about truth, therefore satisfies what I call the connection criterion: it connects Protagoras in the right way both to Theaetetus' claim that knowledge is perception and to Heracliteanism.[46] Secondly, in Chapter 8, I argue that Plato's arguments against Protagoras in 169–71 are aimed against infallibilism rather than against relativism about truth; I also argue that they succeed against infallibilism but not against relativism about truth. This is one reason, though not a decisive one, to suppose that infallibilism is his target. If I am right, then (contrary to what is often said) this famous passage is not the first attempt to show that relativism about truth is self-refuting: though it is not the less interesting for that.[47] If I am right, moreover, Plato's discussion satisfies what I call the univocity criterion: he understands Protagoras in the same way both when he is introduced and when he is refuted. This is as it should be. For if Plato refutes only a version of Protagoreanism that is not at issue in discussing the three theses, he would commit the fallacy of irrelevance.[48]

---

are true 'because the belief of the agent makes her world the way that the belief says it is or represents it as being' (125); though infallibilism says that all beliefs are true, it doesn't say that believing makes it so. Nor do I say that, on infallibilism, 'there are no appearances or propositions in common' (125); roughly speaking, on my interpretation that holds for narrow but not broad infallibilism.

[46] More precisely, narrow infallibilism does so.

[47] It is generally thought that in this passage Plato aims to refute relativism about truth but fails to do so; see e.g. McDowell, *Plato: Theaetetus*, notes ad loc; and Bostock, *Plato's Theaetetus*, 84–99. Though McDowell thinks that Plato's argument fails from a logical point of view, he thinks that Plato none the less raises some telling points against relativism; see 171. In 'Protagoras and Self-Refutation in Plato's *Theaetetus*' Burnyeat interestingly argues that Plato aims to refute, and succeeds in refuting, relativism about truth. In 'Relativism and Self-Refutation: Plato, Protagoras, and Burnyeat', in J. Gentzler (ed.), *Method in Ancient Philosophy* (Oxford: Clarendon Press, 1998), 138–63, I argue that his rescue attempt fails. On my view, however, no such attempt is needed, since Plato aims to refute infallibilism and succeeds in doing so.

[48] This is too quick, since 169–71 refutes only broad Protagoreanism, though it is narrow Protagoreanism that is connected to (T) and (H). However, if Protagoras, up to this point, has been portrayed just as an infallibilist, it would be odd were Plato suddenly to

In arguing against Protagoras that things aren't always just as they appear to be, Plato defends realism, the view that there is an objective, person-independent world.[49] This view is clear in earlier dialogues too. But there, he tends to assume it, and devotes himself to defending a particular version of it. So, for example, in the argument in *Republic* V explored in Section II above, he argues that genuine knowledge requires the existence of forms; merely countenancing sensible properties won't do. Though the sightlovers reject Plato's view of how the world is—unlike him, they don't think it contains forms—they don't dispute that there is a way the world is. In the *Theaetetus*, Plato digs deeper, and defends realism; but in contrast to the *Republic*, he does so without intruding forms. This isn't to say that he no longer believes there are forms. It's just to say that here, he undertakes to defend realism without mentioning them.

V

Having refuted Protagoras, Plato goes on to refute the Heraclitean view that, at every moment, everything is changing in every respect (181–3). He also refutes the view that knowledge is perception (184–6).[50] He then asks whether knowledge is, not all belief, but true belief. Before addressing this question directly, he embarks on a lengthy discussion of whether false belief is possible. This is surprising for at least three reasons. First, throughout the dialogues, and earlier in this one, Plato assumes that there are false beliefs; yet here he questions whether there are any. Secondly, it seems to be a digression to consider false belief when the topic at hand is whether knowledge is

turn to relativism about truth. On my view, he first refutes a broad view of which narrow Protagoreanism is an instance; showing that broad infallibilism is self-refuting makes us wonder whether even the narrow version could be correct. Plato then goes on to refute it in turn. There would, of course, be nothing wrong were Plato to discuss both infallibilism and relativism about truth; and Aristotle may do so in *Metaphysics* Γ 5. But it is not clear, dialectically speaking, why Plato should suddenly shift to relativism about truth in 169–71. By contrast, there is a clear point to his turning to broad infallibilism. Moreover, on some views, Plato refutes *only* relativism about truth. If that were the case, then the dialectical structure of this part of the *Theaetetus* would be broken-backed, since that is not how Protagoreanism is conceived when it is connected to (T) and (H).

[49] He also defends realism elsewhere in the *Theaetetus*: e.g. in 181–3, in arguing against a version of Heracliteanism; and in 184–6, in arguing that knowledge is not perception. In a way the discussion of false belief, to be explored in the next section, also defends it, in so far as certain versions of anti-realism deny that there are false beliefs, whereas Plato continues to insist that there are false beliefs.

[50] I discuss 184–6 briefly in 'Plato on Perception', *Oxford Studies in Ancient Philosophy*, suppl. vol. (1988), 15–28.

true belief. Thirdly, the puzzle of false belief on which I focus assumes that, for any item, one either has complete knowledge of it or is totally ignorant of it; and this view, in turn, seems to rest on a strong acquaintance model of knowledge.[51] The view that, for any item, one either has complete knowledge of it or is totally ignorant of it, is familiar from the *Meno*'s paradox of inquiry. Yet, we saw earlier, Plato rejects that view by arguing that there are knowledge-independent true beliefs; here, by contrast, he seems to accept it.

In 'False Belief in the *Theaetetus*' (Chapter 9) I suggest that these three problems may be solved in the same way. Though the puzzle of false belief that I focus on does indeed assume that, for any item, one either has complete knowledge of it or is totally ignorant of it, Plato is not committed to that view. He introduces it because he is trying to defend Theaetetus' suggestion that knowledge is true belief; and it is a sufficient condition for the truth of that suggestion. For since true belief plainly isn't total ignorance, it must be complete knowledge, since, in the context, that is the only alternative. Just as Plato supports the suggestion that knowledge is perception by linking it to Protagoreanism and to Heracliteanism, so he initially supports the suggestion that knowledge is true belief by showing how it may be derived if we assume that there is an exclusive and exhaustive dichotomy between complete knowledge and total ignorance. And just as Plato doesn't in the end accept the view that knowledge is perception, so he doesn't in the end accept the view that knowledge is true belief. Just as attention to the dialectical setting shows that he isn't committed to Protagoreanism or to Heracliteanism, so it shows that he isn't committed to the view that complete knowledge and total ignorance are exhaustive options.[52]

[51] In 'False Belief in the *Theaetetus*' (ch. 9 below) I associate the acquaintance model of knowledge that underlies the puzzles of false belief with Russell's technical notion of knowledge by acquaintance. This is misleading in at least one respect: Russellian knowledge by acquaintance is supposed to be nonpropositional; but the sort of complete knowledge I discuss is propositional. For this point, see T. Barton, 'The *Theaetetus* on How We Think', *Phronesis*, 44 (1999), 163–80. However, even though Russell's notion of acquaintance doesn't by itself imply the dichotomy between complete knowledge and total ignorance, it might be part of a fuller story that leads to that dichotomy. Such a story seems to be told by McDowell, *Plato*: Theaetetus, 197. I was assuming something like his reconstruction of the argument. We differ, however, in that he thinks Plato is committed to the view he describes, whereas I think he introduces it for dialectical purposes only. That some sort of acquaintance plays some role in the argument is suggested by Plato's comparison between belief, on the one hand, and seeing and touching, on the other.

[52] In *Plato's* Theaetetus, David Bostock interprets the logic of my argument as follows: 'she holds that the difficulties [in explaining false belief] all stem from the premiss that knowledge is the same as true belief, and of course Plato does not accept this premiss. But I do not understand why she supposes that, if you do think that knowledge is just true belief, then you will also be bound to say that if one knows anything about an object then one must know everything about it, which is her explanation of the fallacy' (198). However, I did not

Attention to the dialectical setting also allows us to see that the discussion of false belief is not a digression. Rather, it is an indirect criticism of the view that knowledge is true belief: if we take knowledge to be true belief, we pay the intolerably high price of precluding the possibility of false belief. At least, that is so if the view that knowledge is true belief is defended in the way in which Plato defends it.

Plato supplements his indirect refutation of the claim that knowledge is true belief with a direct one (201 A–C). This too mirrors his discussion of the claim that knowledge is perception; for after an indirect criticism of it (which shows the implausibility of its best support), he proceeds to a direct criticism of it (in 184–6). These direct refutations are, in turn, indirect refutations of the views that make the claims that knowledge is perception, or true belief, seem plausible. These two parts of the dialogue are therefore structurally very similar.

VI

Having refuted the claim that knowledge is true belief, Plato next asks whether it is true belief plus an account (*meta logou*).[53] This is the last

claim that if you think knowledge is true belief, then you are bound to think that if one knows anything about an object, one must know everything about it. My argument was that if one assumes that, for any item, one either has complete knowledge of it or is completely ignorant of it (is completely out of touch with it), then (*a*) false belief is impossible, and (*b*) knowledge may be identified with true belief. Both the puzzles of false belief and the claim that knowledge is true belief follow from that assumption. It is a sufficient condition both for generating the puzzles and for identifying knowledge with true belief; it is not a necessary condition. For an example of someone who understands the logic of my argument correctly (though he defends an interesting alternative), see H. Benson, 'Why is There a Discussion of False Belief in the *Theaetetus?*', *Journal of the History of Philosophy*, 30/2 (1992), 171–99.

[53] In '*Epistêmê* and *Logos* in Plato's Later Thought' Nehamas notes that *meta logou* 'occurs, in connection with knowledge and outside the *Theaetetus*, only in two instances in the *Timaeus*' (*Virtues of Authenticity*, 236; the two passages are 28 A 1–2 and 51 E 3). He makes this point in the course of discussing what he calls the additive model of knowledge, which he thinks I take Plato to hold. I'm not entirely sure what the additive model is, but at one point Nehamas says that according to it, 'the justification that is necessary to transform a belief into knowledge is thought to be added to the belief in question. That is, each belief is identifiable quite independently of its justification' (229; cf. 231). If this means that one can have the true belief that p without being able fully to specify its justification, then I do indeed take Plato to accept the additive model. For in his view, we all have true beliefs but lack knowledge-conferring *logoi*. But Nehamas seems to think that if one accepts the additive model, one is committed to thinking that every true belief can become knowledge; whereas, in his view, Plato restricts knowledge to true beliefs about the essential properties of things (and perhaps to what follows from the essential properties: 228). I'm not sure Plato restricts knowledge

definition of knowledge that he considers in the *Theaetetus*.[54] It is reminiscent of the *Meno*'s claim that knowledge is true belief bound with an *aitias logismos*, and of the *Republic*'s claim that knowledge requires a *logos*.[55] Yet at the end of the *Theaetetus*, he seems to reject the view that knowledge is true belief plus an account; and the dialogue ends aporetically. I consider this part of the dialogue in 'Knowledge and *Logos* in the *Theaetetus*'.

Plato first discusses a dream Socrates says he has had. The 'dream theory' is sometimes thought to be a version of semantic atomism. I argue that it isn't, though it does describe a sort of epistemological atomism. We shouldn't infer, however, that he is therefore an epistemological (or semantic) atomist. For just as he believes that false belief is possible, so he rejects the dream theory. Nor should we infer that the dream theory describes an epistemological theory to which he was once wedded. At least, I've argued that in the *Republic* he is an epistemological holist; I also believe that he is also an epistemological holist in other dialogues that both pre-date and post-date the *Theaetetus*, though I haven't defended that belief here. And in

in this way. For example, at *Meno* 71 A he seems to allow that one can know whether Meno is rich or handsome. These aren't essential properties of his, nor do they seem to follow from his essential properties. (Nehamas, however, takes knowing who Meno is and knowing the way to Larissa to be mere analogies.) In any case, I take Plato's view to be that every true belief that is properly justified constitutes knowledge. I'm not sure whether this is what Nehamas means by the additive model. Be that as it may, the view that every true belief that is properly justified constitutes knowledge doesn't imply that every true belief can be known. For as we've seen, Plato has demanding views about proper justification. Perhaps he thinks that some true beliefs can't be properly justified: in which case neither can they be known.

[54]   At least, I take it to be a definition of knowledge. In '*Epistêmê* and *Logos* in Plato's Later Thought', however, Nehamas argues that 'Plato is not here concerned with our concept of knowledge, but with our concept of understanding' (*Virtues of Authenticity*, 231; as he notes, he is following Burnyeat, 'Socrates and the Jury'). His main argument is that Plato restricts *epistēmē* to essences (and perhaps to what follows from essences); but as knowledge is usually conceived of nowadays, we can know accidental features of things as well (228). Rather than saying that Plato has implausible conditions on knowledge, we should say instead that he is concerned with understanding; for his claims are plausible if, and only if, they are so read. He presses a similar argument in connection with the *Meno* in his 'Meno's Paradox and Socrates as a Teacher', e.g. at 20. (This article was originally published in *Oxford Studies in Ancient Philosophy*, 3 (1985), 1–30; it is reprinted in his *Virtues of Authenticity*, 3–26, and I have used the latter pagination.) I've already said that I'm not convinced that Plato restricts *epistēmē* in the way Nehamas suggests. But even if he does, I don't think we should say he is discussing understanding rather than knowledge. Rather, we should in this case say that he has a demanding view about what can be known, as do some contemporary epistemologists. Nor do I think such a view is as implausible as Nehamas takes it to be. Nor do I think knowledge and understanding are as distinct as Nehamas takes them to be. For example, in 'Meno's Paradox' he suggests that understanding, but not knowledge, requires explanation (20). But, as I've noted, some coherentists about justification think that knowledge requires a grasp of explanatory connections.

[55]   Which is not to say that all these claims are exactly the same; see n. 33.

the *Theaetetus*, though he doesn't explicitly endorse the interrelation model of knowledge, he adverts to it. If he endorses it elsewhere, both before and after the *Theaetetus*, and mentions it here as well, it is reasonable to think he endorses it here as well: especially when, as we shall see, it solves various problems he raises. It's just that the dialectical strategy of the dialogue makes it more appropriate for him to hint, rather than to say outright, that this is so: he is a midwife, and wants us to give birth to the truth ourselves.

One problem the interrelation model of knowledge solves is posed by the dream theory, which says that there are simples that are unknowable, yet are that in terms of which complexes are known. The dream theory accepts KL. It also assumes that an account of something consists in enumerating its elements (EE). The dream theorist uses KL and EE to argue that simples can't be known; for, being simple, they have no elements. Hence, by EE, they lack accounts; and so, by KL, they are unknowable. Yet if unknowables are the basis of all knowledge, KBK is violated. Plato replies by retaining both KBK and KL, and by replacing EE with the help of the interrelation model of knowledge. That model allows him to argue that if there are any simples which lack elements, they none the less have accounts: we provide accounts of them by explaining their place in the complex systems of which they are parts.[56]

The dream theory refuted, Plato turns more directly to the question of what exactly it means to say that knowledge is true belief plus a *logos*. He considers three accounts of what a *logos* might be: that is, of the sort of account that converts true belief into knowledge. According to the third account of 'account', having a knowledge-conferring account is 'being able to state some mark by which what was asked about differs from everything else' (208 c 7–8). On this view, to know x is to have a true belief about it, and to be able to say, when asked, how it differs from everything else. Plato raises the following dilemma for this account of 'account': being able to say how x differs from other things is necessary for belief; hence it isn't sufficient for knowledge. If we attempt to avoid this difficulty by saying that to know something, one must not just say but must also know how it differs from other things, the account of knowledge is circular (209 e 6–210 a 9).

---

[56] In '*Theaetetus*: Knowledge and Definition, Parts, Elements, and Priority', *Proceedings of the Aristotelian Society*, 94 (1994), 229–42, Lesley Brown argues that at the end of the *Theaetetus* Plato suggests that elements are prior to compounds; she thinks this contrasts with the interrelation model that I defend, according to which, she thinks, there is no priority of knowledge between elements and compounds, at least in so far as both may be known and both have accounts. Others who challenge my claim that the *Theaetetus* accepts the interrelation model of knowledge include Nehamas, '*Epistêmê* and *Logos* in Plato's Later Thought', and Bostock, *Plato's* Theaetetus, 243–50.

Plato doesn't explicitly reply to this dilemma; but what he says earlier provides a response. When he initially explained the third account of 'account', he said that to have a *logos* is to have an *ability*: the ability to say, when asked, how x differs from other things. This allows us to eliminate the second occurrence of 'know': we can say that one knows x when one has a true belief about x and is able, when asked, to explain how x differs from other things.[57] This defuses the second horn of the dilemma: it shows that the proposed account of knowledge isn't ultimately circular. But aren't we now impaled on the first horn of the dilemma? For didn't Plato say that being able to provide a distinguishing mark is necessary for belief? If being able to provide a distinguishing mark is necessary for belief, it doesn't distinguish knowledge from belief. Here, however, the interrelation model of knowledge is again helpful. To have a belief about x, one must be able, in some way or other, to distinguish x from other things. But to know x, one must have a true belief about x, and so be able to distinguish x from other things, not just in some way or other, but in a very particular way: by being able to explain x's place in the system or field or domain of which it is a part. Though true belief requires one to have *a* distinguishing mark, it doesn't require the sort of distinguishing mark the interrelation model demands.

One might argue that even if one has a true belief about x, and is able to say how x is related to other things in the same field, that isn't sufficient for knowledge. For one might memorize an account of the complex interrelations in which x stands to other things without having knowledge.[58] It's true that simply mentioning x's place in some system isn't sufficient for knowledge. But this objection ignores the fact that Plato says that to have a *logos* is to have the *ability* to say, *when asked*, how x differs from other things. What's needed for knowledge is an ability to respond to different sorts of questions; that, in turn, requires a sort of flexibility that can't be programmed or simply memorized. Being able to explain x's place in some system requires sensitivity to new evidence, and an ability to explain the same phenomenon in different ways, depending on the questions asked. We might say that formally speaking, it's the reference to an ability that solves the circularity problem; but when we add that the relevant ability is not just the ability to mention any old distinguishing mark, and not just something that can be memorized, but the ability to explain x's connections to other entities in a way that involves sensitivity to new evidence, and flexibility in

---

[57] See ch. 10, § vii. Cf. C. Shields, 'The Logos of "Logos": The Third Definition of the *Theaetetus*', in M. McPherran (ed.), *Recognition, Remembrance and Reality* (Apeiron, 32; Kelowna, BC: Academic Printing and Publishing, 1999), 107–24.

[58] For this objection to my account, see Bostock, *Plato's* Theaetetus, 250; cf. Barney, *Names and Natures*, 172–4.

the face of different questions, then the definition is not only noncircular but also plausible.

One might argue that if Plato relies on the notion of an ability in this way, he doesn't conceive of knowledge as justified true belief. As before, however, I think it is better to say that his view is that one isn't properly justified in believing p unless one has the ability to explain why p is so. He has a rich notion of what it is to be justified. That differentiates his version of a justified-true-belief account of knowledge from some versions of it, but not from all versions of it.

Even if the definition avoids the dilemma—even if it is not ultimately circular, and even if it allows us to distinguish knowledge from true belief—it may be vulnerable elsewhere. For the *Theaetetus*, like other Platonic dialogues, accepts KBK: I can know a given object or proposition only if I know other related objects or propositions. Given KL, I can know them only if I can provide a *logos*.[59] Given KBK, I must also know this *logos*.[59] Given KL, this requires further accounts which, given KBK, requires knowledge of yet a further *logos*—and so on, it seems, *ad infinitum*. We seem to be launched on the familiar regress of reasons, which we considered earlier in looking at *Republic* VI–VII. I suggested there that Plato's holism provides a way out: to know a given object or proposition, one must be able to explain its connections with other related objects or propositions which, given KBK, one must also know, which requires being able to explain their connections to other related objects or propositions. Eventually, we will mention the initial objects or propositions. As we've seen, this replaces a linear infinite regress with a circle: accounts circle back on themselves.[60] But, according to coherentists, the circle is virtuous, not vicious. I think Plato hints at this same solution in the *Theaetetus*: we can solve the aporia with which the dialogue ends by again invoking his interrelation model of knowledge, a model of knowledge that he favours at least from the *Republic* on, and that he describes earlier in the *Theaetetus* as well.

On the general account of Plato's epistemology that I've suggested, he favours a version of a justified-true-belief account of knowledge. On this view, he takes knowledge to be propositional; at least, the sort of knowledge he focuses on, the sort he is interested in and repeatedly discusses, is propositional. This doesn't mean that he isn't interested in knowledge of things, or that he confuses knowledge of things with propositional knowledge. Rather, he has the deep insight that knowing things requires knowing

---

[59] See n. 34.

[60] This is a different circle from the one discussed a moment ago. That was circularity in the definition of knowledge. This is circularity in justificatory accounts.

truths about them. On Plato's view, moreover, knowledge is a type of belief. Plato couldn't consistently take knowledge to be a type of belief if, as is
often thought, he were committed to the Two Worlds Theory, according to
which knowledge excludes belief. But I argued that even in the *Republic*, he
rejects the Two Worlds Theory; he allows knowledge of sensibles and belief
about forms. Though Plato takes knowledge to be justified true belief, he
has an unusually rich conception of justification, or of being justified. In
particular, one is justified in believing p, in the way necessary for satisfying
the justification condition on knowledge, only if one can explain why p is
so, where this involves being able to explain how p is connected to other
propositions in the same domain or field; for the best sort of knowledge,
one must be able to explain the teleological structure of reality as a whole.
On this view, Plato is a holist about knowledge: knowledge of a given object or proposition requires knowledge of related objects or propositions.[61]
The knowledge Plato thinks we have is knowledge of an objective, person-
independent world. Though he sometimes simply assumes this view, he
also sometimes defends it, especially, we've seen, in the *Theaetetus*. Some of
those who agree with Plato that knowledge of an objective world is possible
think we can have such knowledge only if we have direct, nonpropositional
access to such a world. It is to Plato's credit that he sees that we can have
knowledge of an objective world even if knowledge is propositional, and
even if it is conceived of holistically.

VII

We have seen that Plato thinks knowledge is possible. In his view, this has
metaphysical implications. For as we saw in looking at the *Meno*, he thinks
that to know anything about F, one must know what F is; this is his Principle of the Priority of Knowledge What (PKW). He also thinks that in
some cases, such as virtue, to know what F is is to know the answer to the
question 'What is F?', that is, to know the real definition of the nature of
F-ness, the one, nondisjunctive property because of which (*di' ho*) all F
things are F (72 c 8). This is his Principle of the Priority of Knowledge of a
Definition (PKD). In the middle dialogues, virtue and so on—the referents
of 'F' in 'What is F?' questions—are forms (*eidē*).[62] Hence, in at least some

[61] I argued that the *Republic* and *Theaetetus* have a holist view of knowledge; I haven't argued that other dialogues do so, though I've said that I believe they do. If the first paragraph
of n. 34 is correct, the *Meno* may well be sympathetic to a holist conception of knowledge,
though more argument would be needed.
[62] Virtue and so on are also called forms in the *Meno*: 72 c 7, d 8, e 5. There is controversy

phases of his career, Plato takes the possibility of knowledge, or at least of some knowledge, to require the existence of forms. This is an epistemological argument for the existence of forms; and it posits forms as objective, mind-independent explanatory properties or universals.[63]

In Chapters 11–15 I explore (among other things) some aspects of Plato's theory of forms as it figures in the middle dialogues. Doing so is complicated by the fact that Plato never sets out a theory of forms in systematic detail.[64] However, in various dialogues he offers arguments, or fragments of arguments, whose conclusion is that there are 'forms' (*eidē*) or 'ideas' (*ideai*), or whose conclusion is that forms or ideas (which are assumed to exist) have various features. He also sometimes simply describes, or says various things about, forms or ideas. Yet there is considerable dispute about what sort of entities forms are, and about how exactly Plato conceives of them. So, for example, I said a moment ago that Plato's epistemological

about whether the *Meno* and middle dialogues conceive of forms in the same way. I focus here on the middle dialogues; but for some discussion of forms in earlier dialogues see my 'Vlastos on Socratic and Platonic Forms', in T. H. Irwin and M. Nussbaum (eds.), *Virtue, Love and Form* (Edmonton, Alberta: Academic Printing and Publishing, 1992), 67–83; and *On Ideas*, esp. ch. 4, § 4. It is conventional for those writing in English to use an initial upper-case letter in 'Form' (or, sometimes, 'form of (e.g.) Equality' or 'form of the Equal') in discussing Plato's allegedly distinctive forms, and an initial lower-case in discussing the forms of the early dialogues and forms whose status is unclear. This was not, however, a convention in ancient Greek or in Latin. Nor is it a convention in German, which always uses an initial upper-case for nouns. I think it best not to follow the convention. For one thing, those who follow the convention sometimes disagree about when an initial lower- or upper-case is appropriate. For another, it is partly motivated by the view, which I reject, that the forms of the early and middle dialogues are different entities (rather than the same entities differently described). Accordingly, throughout this volume I use an initial lower-case (except, of course, when quoting someone who uses an initial upper-case, or when the word 'form' begins a sentence). This involved revising several of the articles included in this volume, which, in their original versions, designated forms in various ways, not always consistently.

[63] I use 'property' and 'universal' interchangeably. The distinction between universals and particulars has been drawn in different ways. On one view, universals are abstract entities, whereas particulars are concrete. However, it's sometimes thought that there are abstract particulars, e.g. numbers. On another view, particulars but not universals are perceivable. But it's sometimes thought that some particulars, e.g. numbers or God, are not perceivable. It's also been argued that some universals, e.g. redness, are perceivable. According to Aristotle, 'some things are universals [*katholou*], others are particulars [*kath' hekasta*]. By "universal" I mean what is naturally predicated of more than one thing; by "particular", what is not. Man, for instance, is a universal, Callias a particular' (*De int.* 17ᵃ38–ᵇ1). Plato doesn't himself use the word 'universal'. But in *Meno* 77 A 6 he uses the adverbial phrase *kata holou*, according to the whole. To examine virtue *kata holou* is to examine what's common to all virtues. See *On Ideas*, ch. 2.

On whether Plato takes all or some knowledge to require knowledge of forms, see n. 28.

[64] This has led some commentators to deny that he has a theory of forms at all. I use 'theory' more broadly.

argument for the existence of forms conceives of them as explanatory properties or universals: knowledge requires explanation; explanation requires
a definition; and a definition must be of a real entity, in particular, of a universal. In saying this, I agree with Aristotle, who, in three key passages in the
Metaphysics (A 6, 987^{a}29–^{b}8; M 4, 1078^{b}12–32; M 9, 1086^{a}32–^{b}13), describes
the origins of the theory of forms; and he says (among other things) that
according to Plato, knowledge requires a definition, and definitions require
the existence of real universals.[65] However, it's been thought that some of
the ways in which Plato describes forms make it difficult to see how they
can nonproblematically be properties or universals. According to Aristotle,
for example, forms are—impossibly—both universals and particulars.[66]
On another view, forms are not any sort of property or universal, but just
perfect particulars.

This dispute arises, at least in part, because there is dispute both about
what features forms have, and about how to understand the features Plato
ascribes to them. It's generally agreed that in the middle dialogues he takes
forms to be everlasting, unchanging, and unobservable or unperceivable;
these descriptions pose no threat to forms being just properties or universals. But Plato also occasionally says that forms are paradigms; and there
is controversy about how to understand paradigmatism. There is also controversy about whether he accepts self-predication, the thesis that any form
of F is itself F, so that the form of beauty is itself beautiful, and the form
of justice is itself just, and so on. Among those who think he accepts self-
predication, there is controversy about how it should be understood. There
is also controversy about whether forms are separate and/or immanent,
and about how these notions should be understood; about whether forms
are causes; and about how forms are related to particulars.

On one view, forms are separate, self-predicative paradigms in a way that
precludes their nonproblematically being either universals or immanent in
particulars, and in a way that leaves Plato with an implausible account of
property possession. Chapters 11–14 in effect argue that, though forms
are separate, self-predicative paradigms, this doesn't lead to the suggested
difficulties. In particular, these features of forms pose no threat to forms

---

[65] I discuss these three passages in ch. 11; cf. *On Ideas*, ch. 4.

[66] See e.g. *Metaph. M* 9, 1086^{a}32–^{b}13, where he says not only that positing forms as objects of knowledge and definition requires them to be universals, but also that in separating
forms, Plato makes them into particulars. Yet, Aristotle believes, nothing can be both a particular and a universal. This is the point Aristotle has in mind in saying, for example, that
'it is evident that nothing that belongs universally is a substance and that what is predicated
in common signifies this sort of thing, not a this' (*Metaph. Z* 13, 1038^{b}34–1039^{a}2). See also
Metaph. M 9, 1086^{b}5–13.

being either universals or immanent in particulars. Nor do they give Plato an implausible account of property possession; at least, contrary to what is sometimes said, his account of property possession is no more implausible than Aristotle's allegedly superior account. On the view I defend, forms are just universals, conceived as real, mind-independent, objective explanatory properties; they are not also or instead particulars.[67] As in his epistemology, so in his metaphysics: Plato's views, this time about forms, have much to recommend them still.

VIII

I begin, in 'Separation' (Chapter 11), by asking various questions related to the central notion of separation: What is separation? Does Plato take forms to be separate? If so, why does he do so? Is separation as problematical as Aristotle and others have taken it to be? Is Aristotle right, for example, to say that if (as he thinks) forms are separate, they are thereby particulars?

Some of the dispute about separation—about whether forms are separate; about why Plato takes them to be separate, if he does so; and about whether separation is absurd—stems from the fact that there is no agreed use of the term. Accordingly, I try to fix one. Since Aristotle initiated the debate, it seems reasonable to use 'separation' as he does, and then ask various questions about separation when it is so understood. Separation is a relational notion: to be separate is to be separate *from* something. Aristotle claims that Plato takes forms to be separate from sensible particulars. Separation is also a modal notion: to say that forms are separate is to say that they *can* exist whether or not some range of other entities exists. When Aristotle says that forms are separate, he means that the form of F can exist whether or not any F sensible particulars exist. To say that the form of justice is separate, for example, is to say that it can exist whether or not there are any just people, actions, or institutions.[68]

---

[67] One might argue that I achieve this result only by not considering everything Plato says about forms. In particular, it's sometimes thought that Plato posits forms not just for the epistemological reasons on which I focus here, but also for semantic reasons, to explain how we can understand the meanings of terms. And it's sometimes thought that Plato's alleged semantic argument for the existence of forms posits them as perfect particulars, acquaintance with which confers linguistic understanding. In *On Ideas*, however, I argue that, in the middle dialogues, Plato doesn't posit forms for semantic reasons, but only for epistemological and metaphysical reasons, none of which requires them to be particulars.

[68] In ch. 11, as well as in various other chapters, I sometimes say that separation is the capacity for independent existence, sometimes that it is independent existence. The seeming

If, as Aristotle and I believe, forms are universals, then to say that they are separate is to say that they can exist uninstantiated by sensible particulars.

Or so I argue in Chapter 11. But there is a problem here. For the view that universals can exist uninstantiated by sensible particulars is insufficient for the view that they can exist uninstantiated by particulars as such. Suppose, for example, that no human beings, actions, or institutions are just. In that case, the form, or universal, of justice is uninstantiated by sensible particulars; and so it is separate, if separation is separation from sensible particulars. It might none the less be instantiated by something else: for example, by god. In that case, it is not uninstantiated by particulars as such.

Now, Aristotle thinks that the separation of forms turns them into particulars. This is because he thinks that universals cannot exist uninstantiated as such (i.e. from all particulars). But even if all forms can exist independently of, are separate from, sensible particulars, that shouldn't, by Aristotle's lights, turn them all into particulars. For perhaps some forms can exist only if they are instantiated by a nonsensible particular. Yet Aristotle tends to say both that forms are separate from sensible particulars (though, to be sure, he often enough speaks simply of 'separation', omitting 'from sensible particulars') and that their separation turns them into particulars. Perhaps one of his reasons is that, in at least many cases, sensible particulars are the only sorts of particulars that could instantiate a given form or universal; in many cases, there is no suitable nonsensible particular available. He is also, of course, especially interested in Plato's conception of the sensible world, and so he often focuses on it. Like Aristotle, I sometimes ask whether Plato thinks forms are separate from sensible particulars, sometimes whether he thinks they can exist uninstantiated as such.

The view that universals can exist uninstantiated is controversial. But it is not clearly absurd; and it certainly doesn't imply that forms, or universals,

inconsistency is due to the fact that I use 'independent existence' in two ways, which are captured by two natural parsings of the sentence 'Jane is independent': (*a*) Jane is the sort of person who could live on her own; and (*b*) Jane does live on her own. When 'independent existence' is understood in the first way, 'capacity for independent existence' involves a double modality that I did not intend. For in my view, to say that A is separate from B is to say that A can exist without B, that is, A can exist whether or not B exists. For criticism of my account of separation, see D. Morrison, 'Separation in Aristotle's *Metaphysics*', *Oxford Studies in Ancient Philosophy*, 3 (1985), 31–49. I reply in 'Separation: A Reply to Morrison', in the same volume, 159–65. He replies in turn in 'Separation: A Reply to Fine', in the same volume, 167–73. To say that the form of F is separate from F sensible particulars is in some respects vague. For example, is the claim that the form of F can exist at t_1 whether or not F sensible particulars exist at t_1? Or is the claim that it can exist whether or not the corresponding sensible particulars ever exist? I discuss this issue briefly in my reply to Morrison. My reply also clarifies and corrects other claims made in 'Separation', which, however, I have let stand for this volume.

thereby become particulars. Yet Aristotle says that the separation of forms turns them into particulars. From this point of view, the puzzling question isn't why Plato takes forms to be separate, if he does, but why Aristotle thinks that separation makes forms particulars. I suggest that Aristotle has the deep-seated view that only particulars can be separate (that is, only they can exist whether or not some range of entities exists); universals, in his view, are not the sorts of things that can exist uninstantiated. He thinks universals exist when and only when they are instantiated. Accordingly, if forms are separate, as Aristotle thinks Plato takes them to be, they must, in Aristotle's view, be particulars.

Does Plato accept the controversial view that forms, universals, can exist uninstantiated? If so, why does he do so? It's difficult to answer these questions. For one thing, it's a striking fact that none of Plato's arguments for the existence of forms implies that they are separate. For example, we've seen that he thinks that the possibility of knowledge requires the existence of forms, that is, of objective, mind-independent universals. He also argues that such universals must be nonsensible: they are not identical to any observable particulars or properties, nor are they definable in terms of them. This shows that forms must be *different* from sensible particulars (and from sensible properties).[69] But to say that forms are *different* from sensibles falls short of saying that they are *separate* from them: A can be different from B, without being able to exist without it. Or again, Plato is often thought to argue from the flux of sensibles to the separation of forms. He certainly argues that the flux of sensibles requires the existence of stable, nonsensible forms that escape flux.[70] But this again shows only that forms are different from sensibles; it doesn't show that forms are separate from sensibles. Nor does Plato invalidly infer separation from the 'flux argument', or from the more general claim that knowledge requires the existence of nonsensible forms. He takes such arguments to establish no more than that forms are different from sensibles. Nor does Aristotle accuse Plato of arguing invalidly for separation; he thinks separation rests on other grounds, which give Plato a valid (but, in Aristotle's view, unsound) argument for separation.

So Plato's explicit arguments for the existence of forms do not imply that forms are separate; nor, as Aristotle agrees, does Plato invalidly infer separation from them. Nor, in the middle dialogues, does he even explicitly

[69] An example of a sensible particular is the Parthenon; an example of a sensible property is bright colour (*Phd.* 100).

[70] There is considerable controversy about what sort of flux Plato appeals to: compresence, succession, or both. My own view is that in arguing for the existence of forms, the only sort of flux he relies on is compresence. See *On Ideas*, chs. 5, 10, 11.

say that forms exist separately (*chōris*).[71] None the less, I think Plato accepts separation. Just as Aristotle seems to assume without argument that universals cannot be uninstantiated, so Plato seems to assume without argument that forms are separate, that is, can exist uninstantiated. Interestingly, his commitment to this view emerges in unexpected ways and in unexpected cases. For example, one piece of evidence stems from his account of artefact forms. Plato may countenance different ranges of forms at different periods of his career; and he characterizes them in different ways at different times. But at least in the *Cratylus* and *Republic* X, he countenances artefact forms. We've seen that a given form is separate just in case it can exist uninstantiated. The form of shuttle is separate, then, if it can exist whether or not there are any particular sensible shuttles. Presumably particular shuttles have not always existed; and it seems reasonable to assume that the form of shuttle, whether or not it has always existed, at least antedates the existence of particular shuttles. If this is so, it existed uninstantiated, which is sufficient (but not necessary) for separation. Similarly, the form of name, which is also countenanced in the *Cratylus*, seems to have existed before actual names existed, in which case it too is separate.

Plato probably accepts separation, then; and Aristotle certainly rejects it. If Plato accepts it but Aristotle rejects it, then Plato but not Aristotle thinks that universals can exist uninstantiated. This particular debate between them is a debate that is still with us.[72] Whichever side we favour, if the separation of forms is just their ability to exist uninstantiated, it isn't the obviously absurd thesis that it has sometimes been taken to be. It doesn't, for example, turn forms into particulars.

---

[71] Though Plato never says, in the middle dialogues, that forms exist *chōris*, he does say this in the later *Parmenides* (130 B 2–5). But there he doesn't use the word in the relevant sense; I discuss this in 'Vlastos on Socratic and Platonic Forms'. In *Socrates, Ironist and Moral Philosopher*, Vlastos argues that Plato's claim in the *Phaedo* that forms are *auta kath' hauta* implies that they are separate; see ch. 2 and Additional Note 2.5. See also D. Devereux, 'Separation and Immanence in Plato's Theory of Forms', *Oxford Studies in Ancient Philosophy*, 12 (1994), 63–90, § III, repr. in Fine, *Plato 1*, 192–214. In ch. 11 I provide an alternative explanation of the phrase '*auto kath' hauto*'.

[72] For contemporary discussion of whether universals can exist uninstantiated see e.g. D. Armstrong, *Universals and Scientific Realism* (2 vols.; Cambridge: Cambridge University Press, 1978); and his *Universals: An Opinionated Introduction* (Boulder, Colo.: Westview Press, 1989). His own view is that a universal must be instantiated at some point for it to exist at all, though he allows that a universal can exist at t_i even if it is not instantiated at t_1. So he accepts separation in so far as he allows that a universal need not be instantiated at t_1 in order to exist at t_1. But he rejects separation in so far as he thinks that there cannot be universals that are never instantiated. I discuss Armstrong on universals in 'Armstrong on Relational and Nonrelational Realism', *Pacific Philosophical Quarterly*, 62 (1981), 262–71.

IX

Just as there are debates about separation, so there are debates about immanence. Are forms immanent? If so, does this lead to absurdities? I explore these issues in 'Immanence' (Chapter 12). Once again, some of the dispute stems from the fact that there is no agreed use of the term: forms might be immanent in one sense but not in another, just as they might be separate in one sense but not in another. Accordingly, I again try to fix a relevant sense of the term; in doing so, I again use Aristotle as a guide, focusing on passages in which he argues that the immanence of forms would issue in absurdities. Following Aristotle's lead, I suggest that for the form of F to be immanent in F sensible particulars is simply for it to be the property of F in virtue of which they are F; it is the property of F that sensibles 'have'.

In Chapter 12 I argue that, at least in the *Phaedo*, Plato says that forms are immanent.[73] Accordingly, we need to ask whether they can nonproblematically be immanent. If immanence and separation are understood as I suggest, then the latter poses no threat to the former. For as we've seen, to say that the form of F is separate is just to say that it can exist whether or not any F sensible particulars exist. To say that the form of F can exist whether or not any F sensible particulars exist doesn't imply that it is not the property in virtue of which F sensible particulars are F, the property they 'have'.

Even if separation poses no threat to immanence, there might be other obstacles to it. Plato himself raises various difficulties in the *Parmenides*, as does Aristotle in the *Peri ideōn*. They argue, for example, that if the form of F is in each F thing, either the whole form is in each F thing or else a part of the form of F is in each F thing; they then argue that both options are problematical. Here Plato and Aristotle raise fundamental questions about how to conceive of universals, and about how universals are related to particulars. They also ask how forms can be in things if they are self-predicative paradigms. I explore these objections to immanence, and argue that they can be answered.

For example, I give an account of self-predication that allows forms to be immanent. Self-predication is the thesis that any form of F is itself F, that is, has the property of being F. It's sometimes argued that Plato isn't committed to self-predication; but, like many commentators, I think he

[73] For criticism of 'Immanence' (=ch. 12), see D. Devereux, 'Separation and Immanence in Plato's Theory of Forms', repr. in Fine (ed.), *Plato 1*, 192–214. Though 'Immanence' argues that, at least in the *Phaedo*, forms are immanent, in ch. 13 I consider the view that unit properties, rather than forms themselves, are in things. And in ch. 14 I am agnostic about whether forms are immanent, and I consider the implications of various views.

accepts it. It's more difficult, however, to say precisely how to understand it. I find it helpful to distinguish narrow from broad self-predication. On narrow self-predication, 'large', for example, has its intuitive, pre-analytic sense, such that only things with determinate sizes can be large. If forms are self-predicative in this sense, then obvious difficulties arise. For example, the form of large, being incorporeal, has no size. I argue, however, that Plato accepts only broad self-predication. On broad self-predication, the form of large isn't large in virtue of exceeding other things in size; it has no size at all. Rather, it is large because it is the property of largeness in virtue of which large things are large. This isn't to say that it is large in a different *sense* of 'large' from that in which sensible particulars are large. Rather, it is large in a different *way* from the way in which sensible particulars are large. Plato encourages us to revise our beliefs about the extension of the predicate, and about the ways in which things can be large. In his view, not only things like Mt. Everest, but also the property of largeness, are large, though they are so in very different ways: by exceeding some range of other things in size, on the one hand, and by being the property of largeness, on the other. This is admittedly an odd way of speaking, and I'm not inclined to defend it. Be that as it may, self-predication, so conceived, is not absurd; nor does it preclude immanence.[74]

X

Yet another central issue about forms is whether they are causes. I explore this issue in 'Forms as Causes: Plato and Aristotle' (Chapter 14). In the *Phaedo* Plato sets out to discover the *aitiai* of why things are as they are and come to be as they do. '*Aitia*' can mean 'cause', 'explanation', or 'reason'.[75] I find it useful to reserve 'cause' for events sufficient for bringing about change; and I take an event to be an ordered triple consisting of an object, a property, and a time. If, for example, at 2:00 p.m. I put pen to paper, I am a constituent object of that event, 2:00 p.m. is its constituent time, and the relation of putting is a constituent property of it. An explanation, on

[74] In *On Ideas*, chs. 15 and 16, I argue that broad self-predication is adequate as the self-predication thesis in the famous Third Man Argument. This is not to say that Plato is vulnerable to that argument; and in *On Ideas* I argue that he is not vulnerable to it.

[75] We looked at the word '*aitia*' earlier in considering the *Meno*'s claim that knowledge is true belief bound with an *aitias logismos*. In that context, I translated it as 'explanation'. For Plato's idea is that the sort of justification needed for knowledge involves explaining why things are so. Some explanations may be causal explanations, but not all of them are. For example, the discussion with the slave in the *Meno* focuses on a geometrical problem; it has an explanation but not a cause. Hence 'explanation' is better than 'cause' in this context.

the other hand, is an answer to a 'Why?' question. Why did you eat that sandwich? Because I was hungry. Why is Fermat's last theorem true? Here is its proof, which explains why it is true. In the first case, the explanation is a causal explanation: we explain why a particular event came about. In the second case, the explanation is noncausal. Fermat's last theorem has an explanation; we can explain why it is true. But it isn't the kind of thing that has a cause: it's not an event; it doesn't involve change.

Plato says he wants to discover the *aitiai* of things, where this includes discovering why things are as they are and come to be as they do. To discover why things come to be as they do involves discovering their causes. Hence it seems reasonable to think that Plato is looking for causes, or for causal explanations. He goes on to say that forms are, or are constituents of, *aitiai*. As he puts it, 'if anything is beautiful other than the beautiful itself, it is beautiful because of nothing else than that it participates in that beautiful, and I say so with everything' (100 c 4–6; cf. c 9–e 3). This is the so-called safe *aitia*, according to which x is F if and only if it participates in the form of F.[76] Later Plato also describes the so-called clever *aitia*, which mentions not only forms but also other explanatory entities. For example, we can explain something's being hot by saying that it is occupied by fire (the physical stuff), which brings on the form of heat (105 b 6–c 6). We might infer that Plato takes forms to be causes; and this view has been defended. Yet forms don't seem to be the kinds of things that can be causes; for one thing, they aren't events. Hence, according to another view, Plato means only that forms are 'logical explanations'. If so, however, he doesn't seem to answer his initial question: he wanted to know the causes of things; instead, he turns to 'logical explanations'. On yet another view, he confuses the two notions. Once again, these issues can't be profitably discussed without a clear account of what causes and explanations are. Forms might nonproblematically be causes on some accounts of cause, but not on others. Having settled on a particular account of causes and explanations (outlined briefly above), I ask whether, in the *Phaedo*, Plato views forms as causes.

Before doing so, I consider Aristotle's account of *aitiai*. As is well known, he thinks there are four sorts of *aitia*: formal, final, efficient, and material.[77]

---

[76] This is not quite accurate since, as phrased, it commits Plato to the existence of a form corresponding to every property; but it's not clear that, in the middle dialogues, he countenances such a broad range of forms. See *On Ideas*, ch. 8.

[77] These are now conventional labels; they are not precisely Aristotle's own. For Aristotle's account of *aitiai* see e.g. *Physics* II. 3 and 7. In these two chapters Aristotle tends to use *aition* (neuter singular; plural = *aitia*), though he occasionally uses *aitia* (feminine singular; plural = *aitiai*). In the *Phaedo*, by contrast, Plato tends to use *aitia* (feminine singular), though he sometimes uses the neuter. I will not ask here whether Plato marks a systematic

Are these causes, explanatory factors, or something else again? I argue that the efficient *aitia* is a cause.[78] But none of the other *aitiai* is a cause, that is, an event sufficient for bringing about change. However, each of them can be, and on some occasions is, a constituent of a cause. So all of Aristotle's four *aitiai* are, in certain circumstances, causally relevant, though three of them are also relevant outside of causal contexts. Though only the efficient *aitia* is sufficient for bringing about change, the other *aitiai* are not irrelevant to causation; for in certain circumstances, they are constituents of causes, and so are causally relevant.

I then turn to the *Phaedo* and ask whether Platonic forms are causes. Clearly it would be problematical if Plato viewed forms as causes in the sense I've specified: the form of justice can't, all by itself, bring it about that Socrates is just. But it doesn't follow that forms are irrelevant to causation, that they are mere logical explanations instead. For we can say something similar to what we said about Aristotle. An event, I suggested, is an ordered triple consisting of an object, a property, and a time; and forms, we've seen, are properties. They (or some of them, on some occasions) are therefore constituents of events that are causes. In such cases, though forms aren't causes in the sense of being events that bring about change, they are causally relevant, by being constituents of events that are causes.[79] For example, the event of something's becoming hot may be caused by the event of fire's occupying it, and fire 'brings on' the form of heat; that is, the form of heat is a constituent property in the event of fire's occupying something.[80] To be sure, forms are also relevant outside of causal contexts—for example, in mathematical contexts. Here they function as noncausal explanations; that is, they answer a 'Why?' question that isn't causal. But that is compatible with forms also, in some cases, being constituents of causes, in which case they are causally relevant. We can, then, steer between the horns of the dilemma (forms are either causes, or mere logical explanations), without imputing confusion to Plato: forms are properties, which in some cases are causally relevant.

We may also draw a connection between the *Meno* and *Phaedo*. As we've seen, the *Meno* says that knowledge is true belief tied down with an *aitias*

distinction through the use of the feminine and neuter. For the sake of simplicity, whenever I discuss Plato and Aristotle on this topic (whether in this chapter or elsewhere in this volume), I use just the feminine forms; in quoting them, I use whatever form they use.

[78] More precisely, what Aristotle calls an actual, as opposed to a potential, efficient *aitia* is a cause.

[79] At least, this is so if they are immanent in things. Even if they aren't immanent in things, they can be causally relevant, if in a more indirect fashion. I discuss this in ch. 14.

[80] This is an example of the clever *aitia* mentioned above.

logismos. I suggested that this implies that to know something, one must be able to explain why it is so. But the *Meno* doesn't say much about the nature of the relevant explanations. The *Phaedo*, however, makes it clear that forms are at least among the relevant explanatory factors;[81] for forms figure in both the safe and the clever *aitiai*. If these are the only two sorts of *aitiai* there are, then the *Phaedo* seems to say more strongly that all knowledge requires knowledge of forms. As we've seen, Plato develops this theme in detail in the *Republic*. At the end of *Republic* V, for example, he argues that only philosophers have knowledge, because only they know forms, which is a necessary condition for having any knowledge at all;[82] he develops this idea in more detail in the Sun, Line, and Cave images. This is just one example of the close connection Plato sees between metaphysics and epistemology.[83]

XI

So far in discussing Plato's metaphysics, I've focused largely on his views about forms. I've suggested that they are objective, mind-independent properties; that they are separate, that is, that they can exist uninstantiated by the corresponding sensible particulars; for all that, they are, and nonproblematically can be, the properties of particulars; and though they are not themselves causes, they are causally relevant. But Plato's metaphysical reflections range beyond forms to sensible particulars and to the relation between forms and sensibles. We've already considered some things he says about the relation between sensibles and forms. For example, we've seen that he thinks that forms are *aitiai*, or are constituents of them. I turn now to another, though related, issue. It's sometimes thought that Plato has a relational account of property possession: sensibles are as they are by being related to forms.[84] Aristotle, by contrast, is often thought to have a nonrelational account of property possession. On this view, Plato, but not Aristotle,

[81] Actually, this point is implicit in the *Meno* as well. For 98 A requires an *aitia* for knowledge; and 72 c 8 makes it clear that forms are among the *aitiai* (*di' ho*) there are (or are constituents of them). However, this point receives less emphasis in the *Meno* than in the *Phaedo*.

[82] Though see n. 28.

[83] That Plato sees a close connection here is rightly emphasized by N. P. White in, among other places, 'Plato's Metaphysical Epistemology', in R. Kraut (ed.), *Cambridge Companion to Plato* (Cambridge: Cambridge University Press, 1992), 277–310. Though we agree about the general point, we disagree about some of the specific connections Plato draws.

[84] This inference may seem to rest on the controversial assumption that Plato thinks there are forms corresponding to every property or predicate; for discussion of this assumption, see *On Ideas*, ch. 8. But even if the assumption is false, one might still argue that Plato has a relational analysis of property possession. For one might argue that he thinks that whenever x is F, it is F by being related to the property of F, whether or not the property of F is a

thinks that for Socrates to be a man, or to be rational, is for him to stand in some relation to the form, or property, of man, or of rationality.[85] Aristotle's alleged account is often preferred. For it's been argued that a relational account of property possession is vulnerable to an awkward dilemma: either particulars are 'bare particulars' (either in the sense that they have no properties, or in the sense that they have no essential properties); or else they are mere 'relational entities' (in the sense that they have at least one of their essential properties relationally). Both disjuncts have been found problematical. I discuss this issue in 'Relational Entities' (Chapter 13).[86]

It's generally agreed that Aristotle takes sensible particulars to have essential properties; but it's disputed whether Plato does so. I argue that he does. If I'm right, then neither Plato nor Aristotle is vulnerable to the first horn of the dilemma: neither treats particulars as bare particulars in either of the senses just mentioned. Even if I'm wrong about Plato, he plainly thinks sensible particulars have properties, so they are at least not bare particulars in the sense of lacking all properties.[87] It's disputed whether there are essential properties. So even if, contrary to my view, Plato doesn't think sensible particulars have essential properties, one might argue that his view is correct or, at any rate, not as obviously implausible or unsatisfactory as it is sometimes taken to be.

But suppose that I am right, and that both Plato and Aristotle take sensibles to have essential properties. Are they then both vulnerable to the second horn of the dilemma? Do they treat sensible particulars as essentially relational entities? On what I call a crude relational analysis, they do so. On a crude relational analysis, x is F in virtue of being related to something distinct from x. Both Plato and Aristotle, in my view, think that x is F, whether it is essentially or accidentally F, in virtue of being related to something distinct from x. For Plato, Socrates is a man in virtue of participating in the form of man; or, if there is no such form, in virtue of being in some way related to the property of man, or the property of being human; or, at least, in virtue of his place in a teleological system organized around the form of the good. And in the *Categories* Aristotle suggests that an individual man is what he is in virtue of (among other things) being a member

form. Alternatively, if every *aitia* involves a form, then perhaps whenever x is F, it is F, at least in part, by being related to some form or other, even if there is no form of F. For example, perhaps everything is what it is, at least in part, by being related to the form of the good; Plato suggests just this in *Republic* VI, in discussing the role of the form of the good.

[85] Or to stand in a relation to some relevant form or forms: see previous note.
[86] I discuss some related issues in 'Armstrong on Relational and Nonrelational Realism'.
[87] Though even this has been disputed. I discuss this briefly in ch. 13.

of the species man, which is distinct from any individual man. Hence both Plato and Aristotle think that x is F, even when it is essentially F, in virtue of a relation to another thing—a species or form or property. They may invoke different relata—Platonic forms as opposed to Aristotelian species, say—but that doesn't alter the fact that two different things are involved in x's being F, even when x is essentially F. So on a crude relational analysis, both Plato and Aristotle are committed to sensible particulars' being relational entities. But I am not troubled by this result; for I don't find this horn of the dilemma implausible. On the contrary, the view that things are what they are in virtue of their place in some system is an appealing form of ontological holism. It goes along well with the sort of epistemological holism (which I also find appealing) that I take Plato to favour. Indeed, at least one reason for his epistemological holism is his ontological holism: it's at least partly because he thinks the natures of things are essentially interconnected that he also thinks we can know one thing only if we know other connected things as well. Once again, there is a deep connection between his metaphysical and epistemological views.

I suggest, then, that neither Plato nor Aristotle is committed to the existence of bare particulars. On a crude relational analysis, they both treat sensible particulars as relational entities; but doing so is plausible, not implausible. It emerges, then, that on this as on some other issues, Plato and Aristotle are closer to one another than they are sometimes taken to be.[88]

XII

As the above makes clear, in considering Plato's metaphysics, I often make use of Aristotle's account of it; I also sometimes compare their views. I do so for various reasons. First, Aristotle is the first person to discuss Plato's metaphysics systematically and in detail.[89] Secondly, his discussion sets the stage for most future discussions. Thirdly, I find it illuminating to look at Plato's metaphysics through Aristotelian lenses. And finally, though Aris-

[88] One might argue that on some other account of a relational analysis, Plato but not Aristotle has one. In ch. 13 I formulate a second account of a relational analysis (which I call a refined relational analysis), and I ask whether, on it, Plato but not Aristotle has a relational analysis of property possession. But the account I give there now seems to me unsatisfactory, nor have I been able to formulate an alternative that seems satisfactory. But I'm not tempted to keep trying to find one since, as I've said, I'm not troubled by the thought that both Plato and Aristotle have relational analyses in the sense explained above.

[89] Or rather, he is the first person other than Plato to do so: in the *Parmenides* Plato subjects a theory of forms to searching criticisms. Presumably Speusippus and Xenocrates also discussed Plato's metaphysics; but no detailed account of their views survives.

totle's and Plato's metaphysics are often thought to be radically different,
they in fact agree on a variety of issues. I explore some connections in
Chapter 14, in comparing Aristotle's doctrine of the four *aitiai* with the
way in which, in the *Phaedo*, Plato takes forms to be *aitiai* or constituents
of them. I also explore some connections in Chapter 13, in asking whether
Plato and/or Aristotle has a relational analysis of property possession. The
last essay in this volume, 'Plato and Aristotle on Form and Substance',
considers further comparisons.

Plato and Aristotle give different answers to the question 'What are the
substances [*ousiai*]?' To call something a substance (an *ousia*) is to bestow
an honorific title on it; it is to say that that entity is a basic being. Plato and
Aristotle propose different *candidates* for the role of basic being: Plato proposes forms, whereas Aristotle, at least in the *Categories*, argues that the
primary substances are particulars such as an individual man or horse or
tree, not universals like the form of man or of justice. It's sometimes thought
that in the later *Metaphysics* Aristotle is more sympathetic to Plato on the
status of universals. I argue, however, that the *Metaphysics* is if anything less
sympathetic to Plato on this score. For in the *Categories* some universals (for
example, man and animal—the species and genera of primary substances)
at least count as secondary substances. In the *Metaphysics*, by contrast, no
universals count as substances. (In other respects, however, the *Metaphysics*
does indicate increased sympathy for some aspects of Platonism.)

In addition to having different candidates for the role of substance, Plato
and Aristotle have some different *criteria* for deciding what the basic beings are. Indeed, Aristotle argues (if only implicitly) that one reason Plato
favours the wrong candidates is that he has the wrong criteria. I look at
Plato's and Aristotle's criteria for being the basic substances; and I ask how
well their respective candidates fare on these various criteria. Though Plato
and Aristotle have some different criteria for being a substance, their criteria
overlap. In particular, both Plato and Aristotle think that substances must
be basic, or prior, in knowledge and definition—though Aristotle presses
these criteria for substantiality more clearly in the *Metaphysics* than in the
Categories. I argue that on these criteria, Platonic forms fare better than do
the primary substances of the *Categories*. However, secondary substances—
indeed, universals quite generally, including nonsubstance universals such
as red and colour—may be as basic in knowledge and definition as Platonic
forms are. That, however, doesn't yield the result Aristotle wants. It's true
that where Plato's and Aristotle's criteria diverge, the *Categories*' primary
substances fare better than Platonic forms do. But it's not clear what justifies Aristotle's new criteria for substantiality. None the less, in the end I

urge an irenic solution: that even though Aristotle doesn't succeed in de-throning Platonic forms from the ranks of substances, he at least succeeds in showing that particulars are worthy of the same honorific.[90]

[90] Thanks to Lesley Brown, Terry Irwin, and Chris Shields for helpful comments.

2

Inquiry in the *Meno*

In most of the Socratic dialogues, Socrates professes to inquire into some virtue.[1] At the same time, he professes not to know what the virtue in question is. How, then, can he inquire into it? Doesn't he need some knowledge to guide his inquiry? Socrates' disclaimer of knowledge seems to preclude Socratic inquiry.[2] This difficulty must confront any reader of the Socratic dialogues; but one searches them in vain for any explicit statement of the problem or for any explicit solution to it. The *Meno*, by contrast, both raises it explicitly and proposes a solution.

The first version of this chapter was written while I was on leave in Oxford in the spring of 1987. Since then, various versions have received helpful comments. I am especially indebted to Jyl Gentzler, both to discussions with her and to her writings, and also to Lesley Brown, David Brink, Terry Irwin, and Richard Kraut.

[1] As I note in the Introduction, n. 1, Plato's dialogues are often divided into four groups: early or Socratic; transitional; middle; and late. The *Meno* is generally taken to be a transitional dialogue. Among the reasons for so classifying it are the following: it is more self-conscious about methodology than the so-called early or Socratic dialogues; it also explicitly defends more positive doctrines than they do. (For example, it defends the theory of recollection, and it explicitly says what knowledge is and how it differs from true belief.) On the other hand, the theory of forms that is prominent in the so-called middle dialogues is muted in the *Meno*; some would argue that forms are described differently in the *Meno* and in the middle dialogues.

[2] There are actually two questions here: (*a*) Does Socrates need to have some knowledge in order to inquire? (*b*) Does he need to believe he has some knowledge in order to be subjectively justified in inquiring? If Socrates believes he lacks knowledge but in fact has knowledge, then (*b*) but not (*a*) arises. If he believes he has knowledge but does not in fact have any knowledge, then (*a*) but not (*b*) arises. I shall generally ignore the difference between (*a*) and (*b*), though see my Reply to Objection 5 in sect. 3.

I take inquiry to be a directed, intentional search for knowledge one lacks. Hence, perceiving, happening upon an object one is looking for, and being told are not forms of inquiry. Ordinary scientific research, on the other hand, is an example of inquiry. Inquiry can take various forms. In the Socratic dialogues (and, I shall suggest, in the *Meno*), it takes the form of elenchus, on which see further below.

1. The Priority of Knowledge What (PKW)

Meno begins the dialogue by asking whether virtue is teachable (70 A 1–2). Socrates replies that he doesn't know the answer to Meno's question; nor does he at all (*to parapan*, 71 A 7) know what virtue is. The latter failure of knowledge explains the former; for 'if I do not know what a thing is, how could I know what it is like?' (*ho de mē oida ti estin, pōs an hopoion ge ti eideiēn?*, 71 B 3–4). None the less, he proposes to inquire with Meno into what virtue is. Here, as in the Socratic dialogues, Socrates both disclaims knowledge and proposes to inquire. Socrates' disclaimer rests on his belief that he satisfies the antecedent of the following conditional, when 'virtue' is substituted for x:

(PKW) If one doesn't at all know what x is, one can't know anything about x.

I shall call this claim the Principle of the Priority of Knowledge What (PKW). There is considerable dispute about how to interpret PKW. One suggestion is that it means:[3]

(A) If one has no idea what x is—has no beliefs at all about x—then one can't (intend to) say anything about x.

(A) is independently plausible; but it is difficult to believe it is what Socrates intends. For the self-confident way in which he examines Meno about virtue suggests he satisfies neither the antecedent nor the consequent of (A): he appears to have some ideas, some beliefs, about virtue; and he proceeds to say various things about it. Moreover (focusing for the moment on the antecedent of PKW), Socrates doesn't say he has no ideas or beliefs about virtue; he says he doesn't *know* [*oida*] *what virtue is*.[4] Here there are two

---

[3] See A. Nehamas, 'Meno's Paradox and Socrates as a Teacher', *Oxford Studies in Ancient Philosophy*, 3 (1985), 1–30 at 5–6.

[4] Unfortunately, many translations obscure this crucial point. For example, although W. K. C. Guthrie (*Plato:* Protagoras *and* Meno (Harmondsworth: Penguin, 1956)) translates 71 B 3–4 accurately enough, he mistranslates similar passages in the surrounding context. He translates 71 A 5–7 as: 'The fact is that far from knowing whether it can be taught, I have no idea what virtue itself is.' Here 'I have no idea' should be rendered as 'I do not know [*eidōs*]'. He translates 71 B 4–6 as: 'Do you suppose that somebody entirely ignorant who Meno is could say whether . . .', when he should have: 'Do you suppose that someone who does not at all know [*gignōskei*] who Meno is could know [*eidenai*] whether . . .' Nehamas ('Meno's Paradox and Socrates as a Teacher', 8) translates 80 D 5–6 as 'in what way can you search for something when you are altogether ignorant of what it is?'; but the last clause is better rendered by 'when you don't at all know what it is'.

points: first, he claims to lack *knowledge*, not all beliefs or ideas; second, he claims to lack knowledge about *what virtue is*. This second claim, taken in context, suggests that the knowledge he (believes he) lacks is knowledge of the definition of virtue, of its nature or essence; he doesn't know the answer to the Socratic 'What-is-F?' question, where F is virtue. We might then try altering the antecedent of (A) so as to yield (B):[5]

(B) If one doesn't at all know the definition of x, one can't (intend to) say anything about x.

In contrast to (A), (B)'s antecedent is one Socrates seems to satisfy (believe he satisfies). However, unlike (A), (B) seems self-defeatingly strong. For if it is a precondition of saying anything (intending to say anything) about x that one know what x is, and one does not know what x is, then it is difficult to see how one can inquire into x. How can one inquire into something if one can't even (intend to) say anything about it? Moreover, we have seen that Socrates acts as though he doesn't satisfy the consequent of (B), for he says quite a lot about virtue. If he is committed to (B), and (believes he) doesn't know what virtue is, yet continues to talk about virtue, then his theory and practice conflict.

There is an alternative to (B) that is worth considering. Just as Socrates says, not that he lacks *beliefs* about what virtue is, but that he lacks *knowledge* of what virtue is, so he says that such knowledge is necessary, not for *saying* (intending to say) anything about virtue, but for *knowing* anything about virtue:[6]

(C) If one doesn't at all know the definition of x, one can't know anything about x.

---

[5] See P. T. Geach, 'Plato's *Euthyphro*: An Analysis and Commentary', *Monist*, 50 (1966), 369–82.

[6] What he literally says is that one needs to know what x is (*ti*) to know what x is like (*poion*). But I take the present contrast between *ti* and *poion* to be exhaustive. (In the case of things like virtue, this will be the exhaustive contrast between the essence of x (*ti*) and its nonessential properties (*poion*); cf. the contrast at *Euphr.* 11 A–B between *ti* and *pathos*.) Hence, if one needs to know what x is to know what x is like, then one needs to know what x is to know anything at all about x.

Strictly speaking, I would prefer to say that (C) is an instance of, rather than a version of, PKW. That is, PKW claims quite generally that in order to know anything about x, one must know what x is. But I think Plato believes that the relevant knowlege-what differs from case to case: to know anything about virtue, one must know its definition; but to know, for example, who Meno is, one need not know his definition—here, the relevant knowledge-what consists in something other than knowing a definition. Hence, even if Meno cannot be defined, it does not follow that he cannot be known. I focus on definitions in this chapter, since I shall not be discussing Plato's views about knowledge of such things as Meno; but see nn. 19, 21, and 26.

In contrast to (B), (C) uses 'know' in both clauses; so too does Socrates. What he *says* is that one needs to *know* what virtue is, not in order to say anything about virtue, or in order to have any beliefs about virtue, but in order to *know* anything about virtue. This claim leaves open the possibility that one could have beliefs about virtue, and (intend to) say various things about virtue, without knowing what it is; and, if beliefs that fall short of knowledge are adequate to guide inquiry, then even if Socrates lacks all knowledge about virtue, he can still inquire if he has and relies on suitable beliefs.

Although (B) and (C) can thus be read so as to be quite different, it does not follow that Plato is alive to, or exploits, their difference. For him to do so, he must be clear, among other things, about the difference between knowledge and belief. Yet it has been argued that he is unclear about their difference, at least in the Socratic dialogues.[7] We shall need to see, then, whether Plato is able to exploit the difference between (B) and (C) that their phrasing leaves open.

Whether we read PKW as (B) or (C), Socrates claims not to know what virtue is, in the sense of not knowing the definition of virtue.[8] One might wonder why he does so. Does not his ability to pick out examples of virtuous actions, to use virtue terms coherently, and the like, show that he knows the definition of virtue? If to know the definition of virtue were simply to know the meaning of the term 'virtue', in the sense of knowing something like a dictionary or lexical definition of it, then it would indeed be odd for Socrates to claim not to know the definition of virtue.[9] But for Socrates, to know the definition of virtue is not simply to know the ordinary meaning of the term 'virtue'; it is to know what the thing, virtue, really is, its explanatory properties. Knowing what virtue is, for Socrates, is more like knowing a Lockean real than nominal essence—more like knowing, say, the inner constitution, the atomic number, of gold, than like knowing, or having some idea of, the surface, observable features of gold, such as that it

---

[7] See e.g. J. Beversluis, 'Socratic Definition', *American Philosophical Quarterly*, 11 (1974), 331–6.

[8] I assume PKW is not to be read as (A), and so I shall not consider it further here.

[9] This might be disputed. David Bostock, for example, in *Plato's* Phaedo (Oxford: Clarendon Press, 1986), 69–72, argues that knowing the meanings of terms is actually quite difficult. That is no doubt true on some views about meanings; but if we take meanings simply to articulate ordinary usage, then even if not everyone can readily state them, it would be odd for Socrates to believe that knowledge is as difficult to come by as he seems to assume it is. In other respects too, it is unlikely that Socrates is searching for knowledge of the meanings of terms. For some brief considerations against the meaning view, see my 'The One over Many', *Philosophical Review*, 89 (1980), 197–240, and my *On Ideas: Aristotle's Criticism of Plato's Theory of Forms* (Oxford: Clarendon Press, 1993), esp. chs. 4 and 8. See also n. 10.

48   *Inquiry in the* Meno

is yellow and shiny.[10] If this is right, then Socrates' claim not to know what virtue is is reasonable; for as the progress of science reveals, real essences are difficult to discover.

Even if it's reasonable for Socrates to disclaim knowledge of the real essence of virtue, one might wonder whether it's reasonable for him to claim that such knowledge has the sort of priority he accords it. Here (B) and (C) demand different verdicts.[11] It certainly doesn't seem reasonable to say, as (B) does, that such knowledge is necessary for *saying* (intending to say) anything about virtue. Surely most of us lack knowledge of the real essence of virtue, but have some reliable beliefs about virtue. Socrates seems to agree; at least, in the Socratic dialogues, certain beliefs about virtue— for example, that it is admirable (*kalon*), good (*agathon*), and beneficial (*ōphelimon*)—are regularly relied on.[12] But (C) seems more reasonable; it says that knowledge of the real essence of virtue is necessary for *knowing* anything else about virtue. If we place strong conditions on knowledge, and clearly distinguish knowledge from belief, then it is reasonable if con- troversial to claim that knowledge of the nonessential properties of a thing must be suitably rooted in knowledge of its nature.[13]

PKW raises a prima facie problem. For it says that if one doesn't know what x is, one can't know anything about x. Socrates claims not to know what virtue is, yet he proposes to inquire into what virtue is. How can he inquire, or be justified in inquiring, given his disclaimer of knowledge? Doesn't inquiry demand some initial knowledge?

On some interpretations of his disclaimer and his project, there is no difficulty. One interpretation, for example, is that (*a*) Socrates is not really inquiring into virtue, at least, not in the sense of seeking knowledge of what virtue is; he seeks only to expose the ignorance of others, and this less demanding aim does not require moral knowledge. Hence, his dis-

---

[10] For Locke on real vs. nominal essences, see John Locke, *An Essay concerning Human Understanding*, ed. P. Nidditch (Oxford: Clarendon Press, 1975) (originally published in 1690), III. iii; III. vi; III. x; IV. vi. 4–9; IV. xii. 9. For a defence of the claim that Socrates is more interested in something like the real essence of virtue than in the meaning of virtue terms, see T. Penner, 'The Unity of Virtue', *Philosophical Review*, 82 (1973), 35–68; T. Irwin, *Plato's Moral Theory* (Oxford: Clarendon Press, 1977), esp. ch. 3; and my *On Ideas*, chs. 4 and 8.
[11] At least, this is so if (B) and (C) are taken to differ in the way described above.
[12] See e.g. *Chrm.* 159 C 1, 160 E 6; *La.* 192 C 5–7; *Prt.* 349 E 3–5, 359 E 4–7. See also *Meno* 87 E 1–3. Socrates also seems to believe that his, and his interlocutors', beliefs about examples of virtuous actions are generally reliable.
[13] In *Posterior Analytics* I. 1–10 Aristotle defends a version of (C), claiming that one can know the nonessential properties of a thing only by deducing certain propositions about them from its real definition.

claimer does not conflict with his project after all.[14] Another view is that
(*b*) although Socrates wants to know what virtue is, he is hypocritical or
ironical in disclaiming moral knowledge or, more charitably, he disclaims
knowledge only in an effort to force interlocutors to think for themselves.
If Socrates does not intend the disclaimer seriously, then, again, there is no
difficulty in squaring his project with his disclaimer.[15]

Yet a third view is that (*c*) both the disclaimer of knowledge and the desire
to know what virtue is are genuine—but the disclaimer is less sweeping than
it is sometimes thought to be. On one version of this view (*c*1), Socrates
disclaims knowledge in the sense of 'certainty', but not in the different
sense of 'justified true belief'; and knowledge in this latter sense can guide
inquiry. On another version of this view (*c*2), Socrates disclaims knowledge
of *what virtue is*—of its essence or nature—but not of *what virtue is like*; he
does not, for example, disclaim knowledge of instances of virtuous action,
and his knowledge of them can guide inquiry.[16]

If any of these interpretations is correct, then the problem disappears.
Unfortunately, however, none of them works for the *Meno.*[17] Plato claims
in what follows that inquiry can achieve knowledge (85 c 9–d 1). It would
be perverse to suggest that although he believes it can achieve knowledge,
its true goal is only to perplex interlocutors; rather, as we shall see, he elicits

[14] For (*a*), see G. Vlastos, 'Introduction', in *Plato:* Protagoras (New York: Bobbs-Merrill,
1956), esp. xxvi–xxx; contrast Vlastos, 'The Socratic Elenchus', *Oxford Studies in Ancient
Philosophy*, 1 (1983), 27–58, esp. 45 ff. In 'Elenchus and Mathematics', *American Journal of
Philology*, 109 (1988), 362–96, Vlastos rejects (*a*) for the Socratic dialogues; but he argues
that in the *Meno* Plato believes that elenchus (the form of inquiry favoured in the Socratic
dialogues) can do no more than detect contradictions.
[15] For (*b*), see e.g. R. Robinson, *Plato's Earlier Dialectic*, 2nd edn. (Oxford: Clarendon
Press, 1953), ch. 2.
[16] (*c*1) distinguishes between two types or kinds of knowledge (certainty and justified
true belief); (*c*2) distinguishes between different ranges of things known or not known (what
virtue is, what it is like). For (*c*1), see G. Vlastos, 'Socrates' Disavowal of Knowledge', *Philosophical Quarterly*, 35 (1985), 1–31. For (*c*2), see R. Kraut, *Socrates and the State* (Princeton:
Princeton University Press, 1984), ch. 8. There are traces of (*c*2) in Vlastos's article, though
he focuses on (*c*1). Alexander Nehamas, in 'Socratic Intellectualism', *Proceedings of the
Boston Area Colloquium in Ancient Philosophy*, 2, ed. J. J. Cleary (Lanham, Md.: University
Press of America, 1987), 275–316, esp. 284–93, also seems to endorse a version of (*c*2). One
might try to defend (*c*1) by appealing to two types of knowledge other than those Vlastos
appeals to; for such an attempt, see P. Woodruff, 'Plato's Early Theory of Knowledge', in S.
Everson (ed.), *Epistemology* (Companions to Ancient Thought, 1; Cambridge: Cambridge
University Press, 1990), 60–84. The consideration I adduce below against Vlastos's version
of (*c*1) applies to other versions of it as well.
[17] It is of course possible that one or more of them is adequate for one or more of the
Socratic dialogues. Kraut, for example explicitly defends (*c*2) only for some of the Socratic
dialogues; he agrees that it is inadequate for the *Meno.*

perplexity only as an interim stage in a journey whose ultimate destination is the acquisition of moral knowledge. Conception (*a*) is thus inadequate.

(*b*) is also inadequate. As Irwin argues, Socrates' 'repeated disclaimers of knowledge are too frequent and emphatic to be dismissed as ironical without strong reason; Aristotle takes them seriously (*Soph. El.* 183b6–8), and so should we'.[18]

Nor is (*c*1) adequate. At *Meno* 98 A, Plato offers just one definition of knowledge—as justified true belief (true belief bound by an *aitias logismos*)—and it is presumably knowledge of this sort that he disclaims. Yet it is just this sort of knowledge that, according to (*c*1), Socrates (believes he) possesses.[19]

Nor is (*c*2) adequate. For Socrates claims not to know what virtue is; given PKW, it follows that he knows nothing at all about virtue. He can't then, as (*c*2) proposes, know some things about virtue.

Our problem remains, then. On the one hand, Socrates professes not to know what virtue is; given his affirmation of PKW, it follows that (he

---

[18] Irwin, *Plato's Moral Theory*, 39–40.

[19] Even if one denies that 98 A defines knowledge as justified true belief, the fact remains that Plato offers only one definition of knowledge, and that would be odd if he intended his disclaimer to apply only to some other sort of knowledge. Hence we should be reluctant to endorse any version of (*c*1).

It is sometimes denied that 98 A defines knowledge as justified true belief. For example, it is sometimes said that (i) what Plato believes must be added to true belief to get *epistēmē* is not justification but explanation, so that (ii) *epistēmē* is not knowledge but understanding. (Further arguments have also been offered in support of (ii). For various versions of this view, see e.g. Nehamas, 'Meno's Paradox', esp. 24–30; M. F. Burnyeat, 'Socrates and the Jury: Paradoxes in Plato's Distinction between Knowledge and True Belief', *Proceedings of the Aristotelian Society*, suppl. 54 (1980), 173–91, esp. 186–8; and Burnyeat, 'Wittgenstein and Augustine *De Magistro*', *Proceedings of the Aristotelian Society*, 61 (1987), 1–24, esp. 17–24.) However, (i) does not imply (ii); for Plato might believe that knowledge requires explanation. I also doubt that (i) is true. Although Plato believes that in many cases, adequate justification consists in explaining the natures of the entities one claims to know, he doesn't believe that it always does so. One can adequately justify one's claim to know, for example, who Meno is, or the road to Larissa, without explaining their essences; here some less demanding sort of justification will do. (Hence, contrary to Nehamas, if we take *epistēmē* to be knowledge, Plato does not have an impossibly demanding conception of knowledge; this removes one reason for wanting to believe (ii).) Plato focuses on explanation, not because he thinks it is necessary for *epistēmē* as such, but because he thinks it is necessary for knowledge of things like virtue, which are his primary concern here. See also nn. 6, 21, and 26.

G. Vlastos, '*Anamnesis* in the *Meno*', *Dialogue*, 4 (1965), 143–67 at 154–5, believes that Plato's definition of knowledge as true belief 'bound' by an *aitias logismos* is meant to restrict knowledge to necessary truths. But this is too narrow, nor are Vlastos's arguments convincing. He appeals, for example, to Presocratic usage of *anankē*, a word the *Meno* does not at this stage even use. He himself notes that *logismos* is often used for rational thought in general, and it is of course well known that *aitia* can be used quite broadly.

believes) he knows nothing at all about virtue. How, then, can he inquire into virtue? As we shall see, this is just the question Meno asks him.

2. Meno's Paradox

Although Socrates claims not to know what virtue is, and so not to know anything about virtue, he proposes to inquire into what virtue is. Meno valiantly offers several suggestions; but Socrates rebuts him at every turn, using his familiar elenctic method. He asks an interlocutor a What-is-F? question—What is courage (*Laches*)? or friendship (*Lysis*)? or piety (*Euthyphro*)? He cross-examines the interlocutor, appealing to various agreed examples and principles. Eventually the interlocutor discovers that, contrary to his initial beliefs, he does not know the answer to Socrates' question. For it emerges that he has contradictory beliefs about the matter at hand and so lacks knowledge about it; if I have contradictory beliefs about x, then I lack knowledge about x.[20] The Socratic dialogues typically end at this stage, with the interlocutor at a loss (in a state of aporia). In the *Meno*, however, matters are carried further. Meno turns to the offensive, challenging Socrates' ability to question him when Socrates himself lacks knowledge. He poses a paradox, generally known as the eristic paradox or as Meno's paradox:

How will you inquire into something, Socrates, when you don't at all know what it is? Which of the things that you don't know will you suppose it is, when you are inquiring into it? And even if you happen upon it, how will you know it is the thing you didn't know? (80 D 5–8)

Socrates reformulates the paradox as follows:

I understand what you mean, Meno. Do you see what an eristic argument you're introducing, that it isn't possible for one to inquire either into what one knows, or into what one doesn't know? For one wouldn't inquire into what one knows—for one knows it, and there's no need to inquire into such a thing; nor into what one doesn't know—for one doesn't know what one is inquiring into. (80 E 1–6)

Meno poses three questions:

(*a*) How can one inquire into something if one doesn't at all know what it is?

[20] It might be argued that having contradictory beliefs does not automatically debar one from having any knowledge about the subject matter; for this argument, see e.g. A. Goldman, *Epistemology and Cognition* (Cambridge, Mass.: Harvard University Press, 1987); and G. Harman, *Change in View* (Cambridge, Mass.: Bradford Books, 1986). However, the contradictions Socrates uncovers are so blatant that it seems reasonable to conclude that his interlocutors lack knowledge.

(*b*) Which of the things one doesn't know is one inquiring into?

(*c*) How will one recognize the object of one's inquiry, even if one finds it?

Socrates recasts Meno's paradox into the form of a constructive dilemma:[21]

(1) For any x, one either knows, or does not know, x.

(2) If one knows x, one cannot inquire into x.

(3) If one does not know x, one cannot inquire into x.

(4) Therefore, whether or not one knows x, one cannot inquire into x.

The argument seems valid. (1) is a harmless instantiation of the law of the excluded middle—one either does, or does not, know p; *tertium non datur*. (2) and (3) tell us that whichever of these exclusive and exhaustive options obtains, inquiry is impossible. (4) then validly concludes that inquiry is impossible.

Although the argument seems valid, one might question its soundness.[22] (1) is harmless; but what about (2) and (3)?

In defence of (2), Socrates says only that if one already knows, there is no need to inquire. This is not a very good defence of (2); I don't need another meal at Lutèce but, for all that, I might still go there. Nor is it clear why, if one knows x, one cannot inquire into it. I might know who Meno is, but seek to know where he is; I might know something about physics, but seek to know more about it. Of course, if I know *everything* there is to know

[21] For this point, see N. P. White, 'Inquiry', *Review of Metaphysics*, 28 (1974), 289–310 at 290 n. 4.

Some differences between Meno's and Socrates' formulations are worth noting: (*a*) (2) has no analogue in Meno's formulation. (*b*) Conversely, Socrates' formulation ignores Meno's third question. (*c*) Meno asks how one can inquire into what one does not know at all (*to parapan*, 80 D 6; cf. 71 A 7, 71 B 3, 5); Socrates asks only how one can inquire into what one does not know. (For further discussion of (*c*), see n. 29.)

Some details about the scope of the paradox are also worth noting. The paradox does not ask whether, in general, one can acquire knowledge; it asks only whether one can come to know things like virtue through inquiry. Hence Meno's paradox does not question one's ability to come to know things quite unlike virtue (e.g. the road to Larissa); nor does it question one's ability to come to know things in some way other than through inquiry (e.g. through perception, or by being told). Correspondingly, Plato's reply does not address the question of whether it is possible to know things unlike virtue, nor does it say whether it is possible to know things in some way other than through inquiry. It does not follow that Plato restricts knowledge to things like virtue, or restricts the method of achieving knowledge to inquiry. For what it is worth, I think the *Meno* leaves open the possibility of knowing, for example, who Meno is and the road to Larissa; I also think it leaves open the possibility of achieving knowledge by means other than inquiry. I shall not defend these claims in any detail here, but see nn. 6, 19, and 26.

[22] The argument can be read so as to be invalid, through equivocation on 'know'. But since Socrates' reply seems to attack only its soundness, I shall assume it is valid.

about Meno, or physics, *then* there is no need—or possibility—of inquiring about them. But surely not all knowledge of a thing is tantamount to complete or total knowledge of it; generally, one has only partial knowledge. (2) thus seems false.[23]

(3) also seems false. To be sure, if I do not know x in the sense that my mind is a complete blank about it, if I am totally ignorant about it, have no ideas whatsoever about it, then I cannot inquire into it. But being totally ignorant about x is not the only way to lack knowledge about it. I might lack all knowledge about x, but have some (true) beliefs about it; and perhaps they are adequate for inquiry. Having (true) beliefs that fall short of knowledge is one way of lacking knowledge; but it is not a way of lacking knowledge that seems to preclude inquiry. (3) thus also seems false.[24]

Notice that in arguing that (3) is false, I appealed to the sort of distinction I mentioned above, in distinguishing between two readings, (B) and (C), of PKW. I suggested earlier that PKW (if it is read as (C), and (C) is carefully distinguished from (B)) is controversial but not outrageous. It is not outrageous, I suggested, because, although one might need to *know* what x is to *know* what x is like, one need not *know* what x is to have *beliefs* about what

---

[23] (2) can be read so as to be more plausible than I have made it seem. It is more plausible, for example, if it is read to say that if I know that p, then there is no need to inquire whether p. One reason to favour a plausible reading of (2) is that although Socrates (I shall argue) goes on to argue that (3) is false, he does not explicitly reject (2). Though rejecting (3) is sufficient for showing that the paradox is unsound, one might expect him to reject (2) as well, if it is indeed false. Perhaps the fact that he does not do so suggests that (2) should be read so as to be true. On the other hand, there are good reasons for him to be especially troubled about (3), and so it is not surprising that he focuses on it. Moreover, if (2) is read so as to be plausible in the way just suggested, it does not fit as well into the overall argument as it does if it is read in the way suggested in the text; see n. 24.

[24] Although (2) and (3) seem false, they would seem true to anyone who believed that there was an exclusive and exhaustive dichotomy between complete knowledge and total ignorance, such that if one has any knowledge at all about a thing one has complete knowledge of it, and such that if one lacks any knowledge at all about a thing one is totally ignorant of it. And someone who accepts a certain sort of acquaintance model of knowledge would believe just this. (This perhaps provides some reason to read (2) as I read it in the text, rather than in the more plausible way suggested in the previous note.) For a lucid account of how one might be seduced by the paradox in virtue of accepting such a model, see J. McDowell, *Plato: Theaetetus* (Oxford: Clarendon Press, 1973), 194–7. He is explaining a puzzle about false belief raised in *Tht.* 188 A–C which, like the eristic paradox, begins from the assumption that for all x, one either knows, or does not know, x. However, McDowell believes Plato *accepts* the underlying acquaintance model. If he were right, then Plato might well be seduced by the eristic paradox. In 'False Belief in the *Theaetetus*' (ch. 9 below), however, I argue that Plato does not accept the underlying acquaintance model in the *Theaetetus*. The account I go on to give here suggests he does not accept it in the *Meno* either, but I cannot defend this view in detail here. The similarity between the eristic paradox and the puzzle at *Tht.* 188 A–C, and the possible connection to some sort of acquaintance, are also noted by Irwin, *Plato's Moral Theory*, 315 n. 12.

x is like, and perhaps beliefs can guide inquiry. If, however, one speaks of a lack of knowledge without differentiating between total ignorance (being a blank) and having beliefs that fall short of knowledge, then this way of distinguishing between (B) and (C) will not be available. One might expect, then, that if Plato is aware of the falsity of (3), he can also distinguish between (B) and (C); if, however, he is not aware of the falsity of (3), then perhaps, equally, he will not be able to distinguish between (B) and (C).

I have argued so far that the eristic paradox is unsound, since both (2) and (3) are false. But how does Plato view the matter?

We might expect him to be especially troubled by (3). At least, we should expect him to be especially troubled by (3) if he takes Socrates' disclaimer of knowledge seriously, thinks Socrates was genuinely inquiring, through the elenchus, in an effort to find moral knowledge, and also wants to defend Socrates. For if (3) is true, Socrates cannot, as he claims to, inquire in the absence of knowledge. (3) thus threatens the core of Socratic inquiry. However, the *Meno* is a transitional dialogue—transitional between the thought of the Socratic dialogues, on the one hand, and that of the middle dialogues, on the other—and one might think that it is transitional in part because it finds fault with Socrates' claim to be able to inquire in the absence of knowledge.[25] Let us see, then, whether Plato attempts to dislodge (3), and so to vindicate Socrates; or, alternatively, whether he abandons the Socratic procedure—a procedure that requires the falsity of (3)—in favour of some other epistemological programme.

3. The Elenctic Reply to the Paradox

In reply to Meno's paradox, Socrates initially describes a priests' and priestesses' story, according to which:

Since the soul is immortal and has been born many times, and has seen [*heōrakuia*] all the things both here and in Hades, there is nothing it has not learnt. Hence it is no wonder if it can recall virtue and other things which it previously knew. For since all nature is akin, and since the soul has learnt all things, there is nothing to prevent it, when it has recollected one thing—which men call learning—from discovering all the other things, if he is brave and does not tire of inquiring. For inquiring and learning are just recollection. (81 c 5–d 5)

This is Plato's famous theory of recollection, according to which the soul is immortal and, in a prior life, knew 'virtue and other things', so that what

---

[25] For the dating of the dialogues, see n. 1; and the Introduction, n. 1.

is called learning is really just recollection of things previously known.[26] Meno professes not to understand what it means to say that learning is just recollection, and so he asks Socrates to teach him that it is (81 E 3–5). Socrates points out that, since learning is just recollection, there is no such thing as teaching, and so he cannot teach him that learning is just recollection; but, he says, he will show (*epideixomai*, 82 B 2) Meno that it is. He then embarks on a standard Socratic-style elenchus, along with a running commentary, with one of Meno's slaves (82 B–85 D). He then reverts to the theory of recollection (85 D–86 C). There are, then, two accounts of the theory of recollection; sandwiched in between, there is a sample elenchus.[27]

How do the elenchus and the theory of recollection fit together? How does either reply to the paradox? I begin by considering the elenctic reply.

Socrates draws a square with sides two feet long, and asks the slave how long a side is needed for a square with double the area of the original square (82 C–E). The slave replies that we need a side with double the length of the original side (82 E). Like most of Socrates' interlocutors in the earlier dialogues, and like Meno at the beginning of this one, the slave thinks he knows the answer to Socrates' questions, though he does not. Socrates then questions him further, until the slave realizes that he doesn't know what he thought he did; he is then puzzled and confused (84 A–B). This aporetic result is often reached in the Socratic dialogues too, as it was earlier in the *Meno*. The Socratic dialogues typically end at this point, which is one reason Socrates is often thought to be purely negative and destructive in his use of the elenchus. Here, however, Plato defends him against that charge. Initially the slave thought he knew the answer to Socrates' geometrical question, but

---

[26] At 81 C 6–7 (cf. D 1) Socrates says that (*a*) the soul has seen 'all things', which might suggest omniscience. However, at 81 C 8 he talks instead of (*b*) 'virtue and other things'; and at 81 D 4–5 he talks about (*c*) all *zētein kai manthanein* ('inquiry and learning'). I assume that (*b*) and (*c*) restrict the scope of (*a*), which makes it reasonable to assume that recollection is restricted to general truths about such things as virtue and geometry. Hence there is no implication that our discarnate souls knew truths falling outside the scope of such disciplines, or even particular (as opposed to general) truths within such disciplines. One might argue that if such truths are not recollected, then they cannot be known. For at *Meno* 98 A Plato says that this—working out a suitable *aitias logismos*—is recollection, and having a suitable *aitias logismos* is necessary for knowledge. However, Plato means only that working out a suitable *aitias logismos* is, in certain cases, a case of recollection. He does not mean that every case of working out an *aitias logismos* involves recollection, or that working out an *aitias logismos* is all there is to recollection. Hence he leaves open the possibility that one can have a knowledge-constituting *aitias logismos* of, for example, the way to Larissa, but one that does not involve recollection. See Irwin, *Plato's Moral Theory*, 316–17 n. 17; contrast Nehamas, 'Meno's Paradox', 10–11.

[27] See Irwin, *Plato's Moral Theory*, 139, 315–16, for a lucid and detailed defence of the claim that the whole of the demonstration with the slave is a standard Socratic elenchus. For a different view, see Vlastos, 'Elenchus and Mathematics', esp. 375. See also n. 28.

he didn't; he then realizes that he doesn't know the answer. But realizing this is not merely destructive; it makes (or ought to make) him more willing and able to inquire (84 B–C). The exposure of ignorance is thus of positive value.

Plato also points out that although the Socratic dialogues typically end aporetically, elenchus need not end in aporia; the elenctic method can take one all the way to knowledge. To show this, Socrates questions the slave further, until the slave eventually states the right answer (84 D–85 B); this further stage of questioning involves the elenctic method no less than does the initial stage, and so Plato shows that the elenchus can go beyond the exposure of ignorance to the articulation of true beliefs.[28] For although the slave still lacks knowledge, he 'has in himself true beliefs about the things he does not know' (85 C 2–8). Not only that, but 'if someone asks him the very same [sorts of] questions [*alternative translation*: 'asks him questions about the very same things'] often and in different ways, you can see that in the end he will know these things as accurately as anybody' (85 C 10–D 1).

Now if the slave can inquire about geometry in the absence of knowledge then so too, Socrates assumes, can we all. Nor is there anything special about geometry; inquiry in the absence of knowledge is likewise possible for 'every other subject' (85 E 2–3), including virtue, and so, Socrates concludes, they ought to resume their inquiry into virtue, even though they don't know what it is (86 C).

Plato has just rejected (3) of the paradox. Contrary to (3), one can inquire even if one lacks all knowledge of the subject, for the slave has just done so. The slave can inquire, although he entirely lacks knowledge, because he has both true beliefs and the capacity for rational reflection and revision of his beliefs, and these are adequate for inquiry.[29] Similarly, Socrates was

---

[28] Vlastos, 'Elenchus and Mathematics', 375, agrees that the negative stage of the inquiry involves the elenchus, but he argues that the positive stage does not: 'Elenchus is good for this, and only this [i.e. only for "convicting him of error"]. It does not begin to bring him to the truth he seeks.' However, his reasons for this claim are weak. They seem to be that (*a*) in the positive stage of inquiry, Socrates sheds his adversarial role; and that (*b*) the inquiry concerns geometry rather than morality. But as against (*a*), elenchus does not require anyone to play an adversarial role in the sense Vlastos seems to intend. As to (*b*), the initial stage of inquiry equally involves geometry, yet Vlastos allows that it involves elenchus. See also the replies to objections at the end of this section for a defence of the claim that geometrical and moral inquiries are (for Socrates) quite similar. For cogent criticism of Vlastos's view, see J. Gentzler, 'Knowledge and Method in Plato's Early through Middle Dialogues' (diss. Ph.D., Cornell University, 1991).

[29] I pointed out above (n. 21, difference (*c*)) that one difference between Meno's and Socrates' formulations of the paradox is that Meno asks whether one can inquire into what one doesn't *at all* know, whereas Socrates asks only whether one can inquire into what one doesn't know. This difference is sometimes thought to suggest that Plato believes that one can't inquire into what one doesn't *at all* know, but can inquire into what one doesn't know

justified, in the Socratic dialogues and earlier in the *Meno,* in claiming to be able to inquire into virtue in the absence of knowledge. For although he disavows all moral knowledge, he never claims to lack true moral beliefs; and, indeed, he seems to believe he has them.[30] Moreover, in clearly distinguishing between knowledge and (true) belief, and in insisting that inquiry requires only the latter, Plato shows that PKW is not self-defeatingly strong, that he can distinguish between (B) and (C), and accepts only (C).[31]

Various objections to Plato's claims about the powers of the elenchus might be raised, however; let us consider some of them, along with some possible replies.

Objection 1: I am over-optimistic about the force of 85 c 6–7, where Plato distinguishes between knowledge and true belief. Alexander Nehamas, for example, argues that the passage is merely an intermediate step in Plato's resolution of the paradox, not his final conclusion.[32] Even if it is true that using the elenchus can take us all the way to knowledge, and that knowledge and true belief differ, surely 85 c 6–7 is not the core of Plato's reply to the paradox?

Reply: It is true that there is more to come: we have not yet looked at the theory of recollection. But there is reason to believe that, whatever the importance of the theory of recollection, the distinction Plato draws between knowledge and true belief is of vital importance,

---

in a way (so long as one knows it in some different way); see e.g. J. M. E. Moravcsik, 'Learning as Recollection', in G. Vlastos (ed.), *Plato*, i. *Metaphysics and Epistemology* (Garden City, NY: Doubleday Anchor, 1971), 53–69 at 57. On my account, however, Plato allows that one can inquire into what one doesn't at all know, in any way, and so his omission of 'at all' is not significant, at least, not in the suggested way. Plato is cavalier in his use of *to parapan* elsewhere too: despite its occurrence in 71 A 7 and B 3, 5, it is omitted in the statement of PKW at 71 B 3–4.

[30] For a justification of this claim, see Irwin, *Plato's Moral Theory*, ch. 3. The frequency with which Socrates relies on various claims in the dialogues (see n. 12) also supports this view. It is sometimes wrongly thought that Irwin's view is that Socrates identifies knowledge and true belief; see e.g. Woodruff, 'Plato's Early Theory of Knowledge', 64. Vlastos, in 'Socrates' Disavowal of Knowledge', 6 n. 12, on the other hand, wrongly suggests that Irwin's view involves conflating knowledge and certainty. Irwin's view is that for Socrates, knowledge is justified true belief (which does not involve certainty); Socrates disavows all moral knowledge, but he thinks he has (not moral knowledge but) true beliefs about virtue.

[31] Further, in noting that knowledge and total ignorance are not exhaustive options, that (true) belief is a *tertium quid*, Plato says something that is incompatible with the acquaintance model on which the paradox arguably rests; see n. 24. This suggests that, at least in the *Meno*, he does not accept that sort of acquaintance model of knowledge.

[32] Nehamas, 'Meno's Paradox', 29.

not only to Plato's epistemology generally, but also to his resolution
of the paradox. For at the close of the dialogue, he returns to, and
elaborates on, the distinction between knowledge and true belief
(97 A–98 C). He argues first that true belief is as good a guide for
right action as knowledge is. This re-emphasizes the present point
that one can inquire on the basis of true belief; knowledge is not
necessary for inquiry. None the less, he insists, knowledge is more
valuable. For although both knowledge and true belief are truth-
entailing, knowledge is true belief tethered with an *aitias logismos*,
an explanatory account. He also insists that the process by which
one works out an explanatory account is recollection. Hence the
difference between knowledge and true belief is not a mere aside;
Plato returns to it later, and connects it to the present context.[33]

Objection 2: Socrates has not shown that inquiry is possible in the absence
of knowledge. For even if the slave lacks knowledge, Socrates, in this
case if not in the moral case, has the relevant knowledge, and that
is what makes progress possible.

Reply: Socrates does not claim that he *knows* the answers to the questions
he asks, and it is not clear that (he believes) he does; perhaps he
only has a correct belief about the answers. In just the same way,
Socrates can guide elenchi in the Socratic dialogues, not because he
knows the answers, but because he has and relies on true beliefs.[34]

But even if Socrates knows, or believes he knows, the answers,
the point of the elenctic demonstration is not undermined. For although Socrates asks the slave leading questions, he does not feed
him the answers. On the contrary, Socrates emphasizes that the
slave should not rely on Socrates' authority, but should say what
he believes (83 D); this point is brought home by the fact that the
slave twice offers wrong answers by relying uncritically on what
Socrates says. The slave's progress—from initial misguided confidence, to a realization of his ignorance, to the discovery of the right
answer—ultimately comes from his own independent reflection. At

[33] On Plato's account of knowledge as true belief bound by an *aitias logismos*, see n. 19.
For his claim that working out an account is recollection, see n. 26.

[34] Socrates (believes he) has, not just true beliefs, but also true beliefs that are better
justified than are those of his interlocutors (though not well enough justified to count as
knowledge—justification comes in degrees). Hence, Socrates belongs at the second stage of
the Line; he has *pistis*, whereas his interlocutors have only *eikasia*, about morality. See ch. 4,
esp. pp. 103–4.

each stage he decides to resolve a conflict in his beliefs by discarding those beliefs that seem less reasonable, or less well entrenched— just as other interlocutors do in moral inquiry. Socrates' geometrical knowledge (or true belief) makes the elenchus proceed more quickly and smoothly; but it is not what makes it possible. What makes it possible is the slave's own true beliefs and his capacity for reflection and revision.[35]

Objection 3: The slave can make progress in the geometrical case because geometry is a deductively closed system, consisting of necessary, a priori truths; since morality is not like this, progress cannot be achieved in the same way in its case.

Reply: If the objector concedes that one can inquire in the absence of knowledge in the geometrical case, then he concedes that the paradox has been disarmed; for that concession involves abandoning (3). Still, the objector has a point; for we want to be able to vindicate Socratic moral inquiry in the absence of moral knowledge. But are the geometrical and moral cases so different? To be sure, geometry (unlike morality) may well be a deductively closed system, consisting of necessary, a priori truths. But these are not the facts about it that Socrates emphasizes. He describes the mathematical inquiry in much the same way that we would describe scientific inquiry. We begin with a variety of beliefs about, say, gold. Some of these are true, others false; we gradually refine our beliefs—discovering, for example, that fool's gold is not gold—until we arrive at knowledge of the real essence of gold, its atomic constitution. We have moved from belief about gold to knowledge of its real essence, not by rigorous deduction, but by trial and error; in just the same way, we can make progress in the moral sphere.

Objection 4: The scientific analogy is unhelpful. After all, one thing that enables us to make progress in the scientific case is the availability of samples or examples of gold; but what samples or examples are available in the moral case?

Reply: The answer is: examples of virtuous behaviour. Although Socrates denies that we know what virtue is, he never denies, but in fact as-

---

[35] See Vlastos, '*Anamnesis* in the *Meno*', esp. 158–9, and 'Elenchus and Mathematics', 374 n. 42.

sumes, that we have fairly reliable beliefs about virtue.[36] To be sure, sometimes we make mistakes—we falsely believe, for example, that lions are courageous (*La.* 196 E 1–197 C 4). But then, people once believed that fool's gold was gold. We also correctly believe that returning a sword to a madman is not just (*Rep.* 331).

But doesn't Socrates insist, contrary to my suggestion, that there are irresoluble disputes in the moral cases? Well, he does believe there is great dispute about the correct definition of virtue terms, and of course there is *some* dispute about particular moral cases. But there is also considerable agreement, enough agreement to secure the reference of the terms and so to ground inquiry.

Objection 5: How can we know which of our beliefs are true, which false? Beliefs don't come neatly labelled 'true' and 'false'; what's to stop us from relying on the false ones instead? The mere fact that I have true beliefs is not sufficient to ground inquiry.[37]

Reply: Plato's claim is that one can inquire, even if one lacks knowledge, so long as one *in fact* relies on one's true beliefs; he does not claim that one can inquire, even if one lacks knowledge, only if one *knows* that one is relying on true beliefs. Of course, from a first-person perspective, I will be subjectively justified in inquiring only if I believe that I am relying on true beliefs. But I do not need to be able to identify my true beliefs as such in order to be able to inquire. We need to distinguish the question of what makes inquiry possible from the question of what subjectively justifies one in thinking one is in a position to inquire. In neither case, however, do I need to know (or even have true beliefs about) which of my beliefs are true, which are false. In the first case, I need to rely on some beliefs that are in fact true; in the second case, I need to believe I have some true beliefs. Neither

[36] See nn. 12 and 30. One might argue that although we have fairly reliable beliefs about the nature of virtue and about what sort of behaviour and what sort of person would count as virtuous, there are no actual examples of virtuous actions or of virtuous people available for us to rely on. For Socrates thinks that knowledge of what virtue is is necessary for being a virtuous person; since no one knows what virtue is, no one is virtuous, and so, one might also think, neither are there any virtuous actions, although, of course, some people and actions might none the less be better than others. (A can be better than B even if neither is good.) If this is so, then we could not say, in reply to Objection 4, that examples of virtuous behaviour play the role in moral inquiry that examples of gold, for example, play in scientific inquiry into the nature of gold. However, reliable moral intuitions and beliefs could still guide inquiry.

[37] For something like this objection, see Nehamas, 'Meno's Paradox', 16–17.

of these ways of appealing to true beliefs requires one to know (or have true beliefs about) which of one's beliefs are in fact true.[38]

Of course, someone might rely on false, rather than on true, beliefs. As in science, one can follow a false track; progress requires luck. Socrates seems to assume, however, that everyone, or at least everyone rational, will, if they inquire systematically, progress in the same direction. That's because he also seems to assume that some important true beliefs are better entrenched than are various false beliefs (or will seem more reasonable to us when we first consider them) so that, in cases of conflict, we tend, upon reflection, to reject the false beliefs.[39] This is a substantial, and optimistic, claim about human nature—one that requires and, as we shall see, receives further explanation.

4. The Theory of Recollection

The elenctic reply disarms the paradox by arguing that, contrary to (3), inquiry is possible in the absence of knowledge. It seems to be a good, and complete, reply. Why, then, does Plato supplement the elenctic reply with the theory of recollection? What role does it play in replying to the paradox?

I suggest that the theory of recollection is introduced, not as a direct reply to the paradox (the elenctic reply plays that role),[40] but to explain

[38] See n. 2. One might argue that it is not necessary to have true beliefs in order to inquire; all that is necessary is that one's use of a term be on a suitable causal chain; see S. Kripke, *Naming and Necessity* (Cambridge, Mass.: Harvard University Press, 1980) (originally published in 1972); and H. Putnam, 'The Meaning of "Meaning"', in *Philosophical Papers* (2 vols.; Cambridge: Cambridge University Press, 1975), ii. 215–71.

[39] See Irwin, *Plato's Moral Theory*, 41–2, 66–70.

[40] It is sometimes thought that the theory of recollection is the direct reply, and that it replies by denying (2): the slave can inquire because he has knowledge; more generally, everyone can inquire, because everyone has some relevant knowledge. If Plato does claim that everyone now knows, then he contradicts his claim at 85 B–D, that the slave does *not* now know. But Plato does not claim that everyone (or the slave) now knows; all of his references to knowledge are either forward-referring (to the time when, by further questioning, the slave will acquire knowledge) or backward-referring (to our previous lives, when we did know). The passage that seems most difficult to square with this claim is 86 A 8; but it too can be accommodated, for all it says is that the slave's soul 'has for all time been in the state of having once been [in a] learned [condition]'—that is, it is always true of him (and so it is now true of him) that he was once in a learned condition, i.e. once had knowledge. To claim that it is always (and so is now) true of him that he once had knowledge is not to claim or imply that it is now true of him that he now knows. (For a similar suggestion, see Vlastos, '*Anamnesis* in the *Meno*', 153 n. 14.) I count 85 D 1, 3–4 (*epistēsetai*), D 6, 9 as forward-referring; 81 C 9 as backward-referring. 86 B 1 says that the truth about the things that are is

certain facts assumed in the elenctic reply. For example, the elenctic reply assumes that in inquiring, we tend to favour true over false beliefs. Plato believes that this remarkable tendency cannot be a brute fact, but requires further explanation; the best such explanation, in his view, is the theory of recollection. We can all inquire, and tend towards the truth in doing so, because, although we now lack the relevant knowledge, we once had it, in a prior life. Like advocates of innate knowledge, Plato believes that certain remarkable features of human beings require explanation in terms of prior knowledge—though for Plato, in contrast to the innatists, the knowledge is had not from birth, but only in a previous existence.

Even though the theory of recollection is thus not a theory of innate knowledge,[41] its motivation is similar to the motivation for innatist theories

always in the soul, but that is not to say that *knowledge* is; perhaps we always have the truth in our souls in that we once knew, can come to know again, and indeed are predisposed to the truth though we do not now know it. Similarly Leibniz says that innate ideas are in us in something like the way in which Hercules is in rough marble before it has been carved, because its veins make it easier to carve a Hercules shape than various other shapes; the use of 'in' is very weak. See G. W. Leibniz, 'Meditations on Knowledge, Truth, and Ideas', in *Philosophical Essays*, trans. R. Ariew and D. Garber (Indianapolis: Hackett, 1989), 23–7 at 27.

N. P. White, *Plato on Knowledge and Reality* (Indianapolis: Hackett, 1976), 47 ff., attempts to disarm the seeming contradiction by claiming that in those passages where Plato says that the slave has belief but not knowledge, he is speaking with the vulgar. Given the importance the *Meno* attaches to the difference between knowledge and (true) belief, this seems unlikely.

If Plato nowhere claims that anyone now knows, then he nowhere replies to the paradox by denying (2). I do not think he believes (2) any more than he believes (3)—at least, that is so if (2) is construed as I construed it in the text above, rather than as it is construed in n. 23. But he focuses only on (3), and does not address (2)—because, I take it, he wants to vindicate Socrates' claim to be able to inquire in the absence of knowledge, and to encourage us (who, in his view, lack knowledge) to inquire. Aristotle, by contrast, disarms the paradox by denying (2): we can inquire into what we know in one way, so long as we do not know it in some other way; indeed, Aristotle suggests that inquiry requires some prior knowledge. See *Posterior Analytics* I. 1.

[41] Contrast Leibniz, *New Essays on Human Understanding*, ed. and trans. P. Remnant and J. Bennett (Cambridge: Cambridge University Press, 1981), bk. I, ch. i; and D. Scott, 'Platonic Anamnesis Revisited', *Classical Quarterly*, NS 37 (1987), 346–66, esp. 351–3. Nor, contrary to Moravcsik, 'Learning as Recollection', 59, 61–2, is the theory of recollection a theory of innate beliefs or concepts. The theory of recollection does accord us innate abilities, and it is sometimes suggested that concepts or beliefs are abilities. But as Aristotle points out (*De An.* II. 1), there are two different ways of construing abilities. A child is able to be a general in that she might become one under certain circumstances when she grows up (this is what Aristotle calls a first potentiality); and I am able to study Greek, even though I am not doing so now, because I can do so immediately if I choose (a second potentiality). If one construes abilities as first potentialities, then concepts and beliefs are not abilities; but that is the only way in which the theory of recollection postulates innate abilities.

Nor is the theory of recollection a theory of concept acquisition. It explains, not how one acquires concepts, but how one can move from concepts and beliefs to knowledge, how, given our various beliefs (however they are acquired in the first place, a question Plato does

of knowledge. As such, it is vulnerable to similar objections. Many would prefer to say that even if a given tendency is remarkable, still, it is just a brute fact that we have it; there is no further explanation. Or, if there is a further explanation, it consists not in immortal souls that had knowledge in some previous life, nor in innate knowledge, but in, for example, evolution.

In claiming that we once had the relevant knowledge, Plato inevitably invites the question of how we acquired it. If the answer is 'through inquiry', then we can raise Meno's paradox again, and we might then seem to be launched on a vicious infinite regress. But there is no regress, vicious or otherwise; for Plato does not commit himself to the claim that we *acquired* the previous knowledge at all. He seems to think we simply had it at some previous stage, without having gone through any process of acquiring it.[42]

not address), we tend to favour the true ones over the false ones. For this point, see further my 'The Object of Thought Argument', *Apeiron*, 21 (1988), 105–45, esp. 137–42; and Scott, 'Platonic Anamnesis Revisited'.

For some discussion of innatist theories, see S. P. Stich (ed.), *Innate Ideas* (Berkeley: University of California Press, 1975).

[42] As I noted (in n. 40), 86 A 8 says that the soul is always in a state of once having been in a learned condition; the perfect tense leaves open the possibility that there was no process of learning (contrast Vlastos's translation of the passage, '*Anamnesis* in the *Meno*', 153 n. 14). Even if the soul did go through an initial process of learning, a vicious regress can be avoided—even if the process was simply (elenctic) inquiry all over again. Plato might argue, for example, that when the soul was discarnate, it was not hampered by perception and bodily desires; without such distractions, it could acquire knowledge through inquiry even if it did not know in some still earlier life. On this account, the theory of recollection would be introduced to explain not how inquiry is in general possible, but how inquiry is possible in this life, or when incarnate.

Plato's claim that the soul 'saw' various things is sometimes thought to suggest that the soul acquired its previous knowledge through some sort of acquaintance; see e.g. R. S. Bluck (ed.), *Plato's Meno* (Cambridge: Cambridge University Press, 1961), 286–7; Vlastos, '*Anamnesis* in the *Meno*', 164–5; H. Cherniss, 'The Philosophical Economy of the Theory of Ideas', *American Journal of Philology*, 57 (1936), 445–56. However, I take it that we saw all things in that we saw their point, i.e. understood them; for this sort of interpretation of Plato's visual vocabulary, see J. C. B. Gosling, *Plato* (London: Routledge & Kegan Paul, 1973), ch. 8; Burnyeat, 'Wittgenstein and Augustine *De Magistro*', esp. 19–21.

Other attempts to argue that in the *Meno* Plato accepts some sort of acquaintance model of knowledge are similarly weak. For example, at 71 B 4–7 Plato illustrates PKW by saying: 'Does it seem to you possible for one who does not at all know who Meno is [*Menōna mē gignōskei to parapan hostis estin*] to know whether he is fine or wealthy or well-born or the opposites of these?' It is sometimes inferred that for Plato, all knowledge is like knowledge of persons, which, it is assumed, consists in or involves acquaintance; see e.g. Bluck, *Plato's Meno*, 213–14. But Plato speaks here, not of knowing Meno, but of knowing who Meno is, and it is not at all clear that I need to be acquainted with Meno to know who he is—I know who he is from having read Plato's dialogues. (The syntax is 'know Meno who he is'; but the natural sense of the phrase is 'know who Meno is'. White seems to agree, though he also argues that for Plato, one can know who Meno is only if one knows Meno, by being acquainted with him; see *Plato on Knowledge and Reality*, 36–7, 54 n. 8.) Or again, at 97 A

Notice that whatever account one favours of how the soul once knew, the theory of recollection (in contrast to the elenctic reply) does not by itself provide a sufficient answer to the paradox—for if one once knew, but now lacks the ability to inquire, the prior knowledge is idle. We should therefore be reluctant to put the whole weight of Plato's reply to the paradox on the theory of recollection; and on my account of its role, we need not do so. It is also important to be clear that, no matter what account one favours of how the soul once knew, Plato's introduction of the theory of recollection does not show that he has abandoned the elenchus as the sole method of inquiry (in this life). The demonstration with the slave is just a standard elenchus; and in it, Socrates claims that if one follows it long enough one will achieve knowledge. The theory of recollection goes beyond Socrates, not by replacing the elenchus with an alternative route to knowledge, but by explaining how something he took for granted (the possibility of inquiry in the absence of knowledge, and the remarkable fact that in so inquiring we tend towards the truth) is possible. To say that p is best explained by q, or is possible because of q, is not to abandon p. The theory of recollection is introduced to vindicate, not to vitiate, Socrates' claims about the powers of the elenchus.

However one spells out the details of the theory of recollection, few nowadays are likely to believe it. The elenctic reply, however, remains convincing, and it can be accepted even by one who rejects the theory of recollection; one can accept Plato's claim that one can inquire in the absence of knowledge, because of one's capacity for reflection and because of one's true beliefs, without accepting his account of what explains the capacity and the beliefs. It is thus pleasing to see that Plato himself seems to place less weight on the theory of recollection than on the elenchus. He introduces the theory as something said by priests and priestesses and by Pindar and other poets (81 A 5–6, A 10–B 2); later he makes it plain that he thinks such

---

9–B 3, Plato seems to suggest that someone can know the road to Larissa only if she travels along it (although he does not actually quite say so); this too is sometimes thought to suggest that all knowledge involves some sort of acquaintance. But even if one in some sense needs to be acquainted with a route to know it, it does not follow that knowledge in general requires acquaintance. Plato's point is that in order to know something, one must have some sort of first-hand understanding or experience. In the case of a route, this first-hand understanding may require travelling along it (a not implausible claim in Plato's day, when there were no detailed road maps), and so in some sense it may require being acquainted with it; but in other cases, understanding will be gained by independent thought and reflection, which does not involve acquaintance in any interesting sense. For this point, see Burnyeat, 'Socrates and the Jury' and 'Wittgenstein and Augustine *De Magistro*'. Further, if, as I suggested, Plato's reply to the eristic paradox presupposes a rejection of an acquaintance model of knowledge (see nn. 24 and 31), then we should be reluctant to saddle him with it elsewhere in the dialogue; and there is no need to do so.

people lack knowledge (99 c). Socrates says he would not like to take an oath on all that he has said (86 B), but later he says that if he were to claim to know anything, one of the few things he would claim to know is that knowledge differs from true belief (98 B 1–5).[43] And it is of course the difference between knowledge and true belief that is crucial to the elenctic reply.

At least in the *Meno*, then, Plato replies to the eristic paradox by re-affirming the powers of the elenchus and by vindicating Socrates' claim to be able to inquire, through the elenchus, in the absence of knowledge. At least in this respect, the *Meno* does not depart from, but is continuous with, the project begun in the Socratic dialogues.

---

[43] The passage can be read to say that one of the few things Socrates actually claims to know is that knowledge and true belief differ, in which case it provides even stronger support for my view. But if the passage is taken that way, then Socrates would be claiming, contrary to PKW, that he knows something about knowledge and true belief (that they differ) without knowing what they are. Although, on my view, Socrates does not flatly claim to know that knowledge and true belief differ, he expresses considerable confidence in that claim, saying that he does not issue it on the basis of *eikasia*. Perhaps he thinks he has *pistis* about it. (On the differences between *eikasia* and *pistis*, see *Republic* VI–VII and my 'Knowledge and Belief in *Republic* V–VII' (ch. 4).) I am indebted to Hannes Jarka for discussion of this passage.

3

Knowledge and Belief in *Republic* V

It is often said that Plato distinguishes knowledge and belief by reference to their objects, so that one can have knowledge, but not beliefs, about forms, and beliefs, but not knowledge, about sensibles. If I know, I can know only a form; and if I have a belief, it must be directed to sensibles. Call this the Two Worlds Theory (TW).[1]

It is clear that Plato does not always subscribe to this view. Both at *Meno* 98 A and at *Theaetetus* 201 A–C he clearly allows knowledge and belief to be about the same objects; and he may also there allow knowledge of sensibles. Still, the theory of forms is not prominent in either of these dialogues, and so it might be argued that even if Plato did not always accept the Two Worlds Theory, he at least did so in the middle dialogues, especially in the *Republic*. Not even this claim is true as it stands: at *Republic* 520 C Plato says that the philosopher who redescends to the cave will have knowledge of the things there,[2] and at 506 C he claims to have beliefs, but not knowledge, about the form of the good. But although these are things Plato sometimes says, it might none the less be maintained that his explicit theory does not allow these claims, and that that theory commits him to

---

[1] TW is defended by J. Brentlinger, 'Particulars in Plato's Middle Dialogues', *Archiv für Geschichte der Philosophie*, 54 (1972), 116–52; F. M. Cornford, *The Republic of Plato*, translated with introduction and notes (Oxford: Clarendon Press, 1941), 180–1; R. C. Cross and A. D. Woozley, *Plato's Republic: A Philosophical Commentary* (London: Macmillan, 1964), 164–5; R. E. Allen, 'The Argument from Opposites in *Republic* V', *Review of Metaphysics*, 15 (1961), 325–35 at 325; G. Vlastos, 'Degrees of Reality in Plato', in R. Bambrough (ed.), *New Essays on Plato and Aristotle* (London: Routledge & Kegan Paul, 1965), 1–20, repr. in G. Vlastos (ed.), *Platonic Studies*, 2nd edn. (Princeton: Princeton University Press, 1981), 58–75; J. Hintikka, 'Knowledge and its Objects in Plato', in J. M. E. Moravcsik (ed.), *Patterns in Plato's Thought* (Dordrecht: Reidel, 1973), 1–30; and by G. Santas, 'Hintikka on Knowledge and its Objects in Plato', in Moravcsik, *Patterns in Plato's Thought*, 31–51. By 'the Two Worlds Theory' I do not mean only the thesis that there are forms as well as sensibles (a thesis I do not dispute) but especially the epistemological claim that there is knowledge only of forms and belief only about sensibles (a claim I shall dispute). I use 'belief' merely as a counter for *doxa*; 'opinion' or 'judgement' are equally possible translations.

[2] Plato's claim is that the philosopher will 'know each of the images, what they are and of what'; *gnōsesthe* plus the *hatta* clause suggests he means 'know' and not merely 'recognize'.

the Two Worlds Theory, that there is no knowledge of sensibles and no belief about forms.

A crucial passage often adduced in support of this view occurs at the end of *Republic* V (473 c 11–480 a 13), Plato's only lengthy attempt to distinguish knowledge from belief, and it is that passage I shall discuss in what follows. I do not deny that the text can be read so as to support TW. But if it is, it not only contradicts Plato's explicit claims elsewhere, but also is a very bad argument. Plato might, of course, have offered us such an argument. But if we can find a better argument consistent with the text, we should prefer it, and I think such a better reading is available. The best argument consistent with the text, however, fails to support TW.

I shall argue that although Plato in some way correlates knowledge with forms, and belief with sensibles, he does not say that there is knowledge only of forms or belief only about sensibles. All he argues is the weaker claim that to know, one must, first of all, know forms; restricted to sensibles, one cannot achieve knowledge. This makes forms the primary objects of knowledge, but not necessarily the only ones; knowledge begins, but need not end, with knowledge of forms. This also leaves open the possibility of having only beliefs, and not knowledge, about forms.

If this is right, *Republic* V does not commit Plato to TW. He might still be committed to it elsewhere, of course, and I do not dispute that claim here. But if this central passage does not commit Plato to TW, we should at least be more careful in ascribing it to him elsewhere.[3]

I

The general context is Plato's claim that only philosophers should rule, since only they have knowledge, and knowledge is necessary for good ruling. Only philosophers have knowledge, he argues, because only they know forms, a knowledge without which no other knowledge is possible. He argues this claim twice over—once, briefly, to Glaucon, on the assumption that the theory of forms is true,[4] and once, at greater length, to certain opponents

---

[3] *Phil.* 58 e–59 c (although see also *Phil.* 61 d 10–e 4, 62 a 2–d 7) and *Ti.* 28 a–29 c may support TW; but I do not think the *Republic* is committed to TW.

[4] One might think that the first argument, since it assumes the theory of forms at the outset, supports TW; but it does not. Plato argues only that the sightlovers, since they do not recognize forms, cannot achieve knowledge and so have only belief. This of course does not imply that no one can ever have knowledge of sensibles, or that every claim about a form is tantamount to knowledge of it (cf. 476 c 9–d 3 with 520 c). Plato argues only that there is no knowledge without knowledge of forms—that is, all knowledge begins with forms. So

called sightlovers (*philotheamones*, 475 D 2; cf. 476 A 10, B 4), who do not accept the theory of forms (476 C 2–7); they recognize that there are many beautiful things, but not that there is one form, the beautiful.[5]

In the second argument, Plato wants to persuade the sightlovers, on grounds acceptable to them (476 E 4–8, 478 E 7–479 B 2), that they do not have knowledge but only belief. If his argument is to rest on genuinely noncontroversial premisses, as he claims it does, it cannot assume the theory of forms, or any esoteric theory unacceptable to the sightlovers, at the outset. I shall ask later whether or not Plato satisfies this condition of noncontroversiality.[6]

Plato's general strategy is to correlate knowledge with what is (knowledge is *epi tō(i) onti*), belief with what is and is not (*epi tō(i) onti te kai mē*), and ignorance[7] with what is not (*epi tō(i) mē onti*). He then draws out various implications of these correlations, and concludes that only those who know forms have knowledge at all; the sightlovers, who are restricted to the world revealed by their senses, can at best have belief.

The force of this argument in large part depends on the reading of 'is' ('*esti*'); but a decision here is not at all easy. Plato's opening moves illustrate the difficulty:

(1) Whoever knows knows something (*ti*) (476 E 7–9).
(2) Whoever knows knows something that is (*on ti*); for one could not know a thing that is not (*mē on ti*) (476 E 10–11).
(3) What completely is is completely knowable; what in no way is is in no way knowable (477 A 2–4).
(4) If anything is and is not, it lies between what really is and what in no way is (477 A 6–7).
(5) Knowledge is set over (*epi*) what is; ignorance (*agnōsia*) is set over what is not (477 A 9–10).
(6) Something between knowledge and ignorance is set over what is and is not (477 A 10–B 1).

(1) might mean:

read, the conclusion of the first argument exactly matches that of the second, although the arguments leading there are very different.

[5] For discussion of the sightlovers, see N. R. Murphy, *The Interpretation of Plato's* Republic (Oxford: Clarendon Press, 1951), 100–5; J. C. B. Gosling, '*Republic* V: *Ta Polla Kala*, etc.', *Phronesis*, 5 (1960), 116–28 at 121–3. I discuss the sightlovers in § IV below.

[6] See J. C. B. Gosling, '*Doxa* and *Dunamis* in Plato's *Republic*', *Phronesis*, 13 (1968), 119–30 at 120–2; Murphy, *The Interpretation of Plato's* Republic, 105. It may be, of course, that Plato's conclusion is controversial; but his opening premisses should not be. Cf. n. 22.

[7] I use 'ignorance' to translate '*agnoia*'; see § III below.

(1a) Whoever knows knows some existent thing; or
(1b) Whoever knows has some content of his knowledge.

On (1a) Plato is correlating knowledge with features of the world. I shall call this reading an objects analysis. On (1b) Plato is only claiming that if one knows, there is an answer to the question 'What do you know?'; he is correlating knowledge with certain sorts of propositions, saying that there is some content of the cognitive condition. No conclusions about what objects these propositions are about need follow. I shall call this reading a contents analysis; in what follows I defend it.[8]

A decision between (1a) and (1b) depends on the readings endorsed for (2)–(6), where difficulties again emerge. As is well known, '*esti*' can be used in several ways.[9] Three of its standard uses, and the only ones we will consider here, are (*a*) the existential (*is-e*), (*b*) the predicative (*is-p*), and (*c*) the veridical (*is-v*). (2), for example, could thus read:

(2a) Whoever knows knows something that exists.
(2b) Whoever knows knows something that is (really) F.
(2c) Whoever knows knows something that is true.

Here (1a) goes naturally with (2a) or (2b), and (1b) goes naturally with (2c). On either of the first two alternatives, Plato simply repeats the claim made at (1a), that knowledge is correlated with objects. On the third reading, he claims not only that knowledge has content (1b) but also that that content is always true or, in other words, that knowledge entails truth.

Applying these three readings to the rest of the opening steps reveals the outlines of the interpretations I shall consider here. TW has focused on is-e and is-p, yielding a degrees-of-existence (DE) and a degrees-of-reality

---

[8] I use 'contents' where I. M. Crombie, *An Examination of Plato's Doctrines* (2 vols.; London: Routledge & Kegan Paul, 1962–3), ii. 57, uses 'internal accusative' and where Gosling, '*Doxa* and *Dunamis* in Plato's *Republic*', uses 'formal object'. '*Epi*' can range over contents as well as objects, as Crombie recognizes (ii. 58). The point is missed by Allen, 'The Argument from Opposites in *Republic* V', 166, and by Cross and Woozley, *Plato's Republic*, who assume '*epi*' must range over objects. For a clear Platonic use of what I call contents, see *Phil.* 37 A. Cf. also *Phd.* 75 D 4, 76 A 4, 76 C 15, with D. Gallop, *Plato:* Phaedo (Oxford: Clarendon Press, 1975), 230.

[9] For general discussion of '*esti*', see C. H. Kahn, *The Verb Be in Ancient Greek* (Dordrecht: Reidel, 1973). G. E. L. Owen, 'Plato on Not-Being', in G. Vlastos (ed.), *Plato*, i. *Metaphysics and Epistemology* (Garden City, NY: Doubleday Anchor, 1971), 223–67 at 223–6, Vlastos, 'Degrees of Reality in Plato', 1–7, and M. Furth, 'Elements of Eleatic Ontology', *Journal of the History of Philosophy*, 6 (1968), 111–32 at 114–16, argue that Plato uses, fuses, or confuses various uses of '*esti*' in this and other arguments. Although Plato does not explicitly discuss different uses of '*esti*' until the *Sophist*, this does not entail that he was confused about them earlier. In what follows, I try to see if we can ascribe to Plato an argument that does not require confusion; if such an argument is available, surely it is to be preferred.

(DR) interpretation.[10] For DE, the claim is that knowledge is of what exists, that belief is of what half exists or what both exists and does not exist, and that ignorance is of what does not exist or is not anything at all. For DR, knowledge is of what is really F (for some predicate F), belief is of what is F and not F, and ignorance is of what is not F.

Although they are possible readings of the text, both DE and DR provide inappropriate starting premisses, by violating the condition of noncontroversiality. DE sharply separates the objects of knowledge and belief, and consigns the objects of belief to the realm of 'half-existent'. Even though no specific objects are so construed at this stage, it would be inappropriate to assume that whatever the relevant objects turn out to be, they cannot be both known and believed, or that they merely half exist.

DR also separates the objects of knowledge and belief. But its characterization of the objects of belief might seem more promising. At least, as we shall see, the sightlovers agree that their objects of concern, the many beautifuls, for example, are beautiful and not beautiful. Moreover, a version of (2b) seems to occur at the close of the argument (479 E 10–480 A 4; cf. step (36)). But this is a conclusion Plato argues for, and so it should not be a starting premiss. Moreover, if we take (3) to mean that whoever knows knows only what is fully F, and not also what is F and not F, then it violates the condition of noncontroversiality. For why can I not know of a particular action, for example, that it is just and not just? There is no intuitive reason for the sightlovers to accept this claim. DR, like DE, provides Plato with inappropriate starting premisses.

Readings focusing on is-v are more promising. Plato's claim is then that knowledge is of what is true, that belief is of what is and is not true, and that ignorance is of what is false. This claim states familiar conditions on knowledge and belief that the sightlovers can be expected to agree to: knowledge, but not belief, implies truth. And unlike DE and DR, this claim does not force a separation of the objects of knowledge and belief, but only of their contents. But this claim does not imply TW: although knowledge and belief differ in their truth implications, the claims that are known or believed can be directed to the same objects.

The is-v reading allows two interpretations of belief. Plato might be claiming that each token belief is 'true and not true', in the sense of being partly true and partly false, or near the mark. Call this the degrees-of-

---

[10] For a defence of DE, see Brentlinger, 'Particulars in Plato's Middle Dialogues', 149 ff., and Cross and Woozley, *Plato's Republic*. For a defence of DR, see Vlastos, 'Degrees of Reality in Plato'; Gosling, '*Doxa* and *Dunamis* in Plato's *Republic*'.

truth reading (DT).[11] Alternatively, Plato might be characterizing the set of beliefs covered by the capacity, claiming that it contains true as well as false members: some of my beliefs are true, others false. Call this reading T.

For DT, 'belief' acquires a specialized sense, not elsewhere accorded it, as being 'near the mark'; false beliefs are not beliefs at all. Moreover, the contents of knowledge and belief will be irreducibly different: knowledge will range over truths, and belief over partial truths. T avoids these unintuitive results. It allows false as well as true beliefs (*Grg.* 454 D), and it allows that the same proposition can be the content of belief and of knowledge—at least not all propositions are such that they can be only believed or only known, for you might know a proposition about which I have only belief (*Meno* 97 A–98 B; *Tht.* 201 A–C).

T is the most intuitively plausible of the suggested readings, and in what follows I see how far Plato's argument fits it. I do not claim that T is ever required; but I do claim that it is a possible reading of the text, and that it provides Plato with a more plausible argument than do any of the proposed alternatives. But in providing Plato with a plausible argument, we also avoid TW. For Plato now distinguishes knowledge and belief not by reference to their objects, but by reference to the truth implications of their contents. This need not rule out every version of TW; Plato might claim that the contents of knowledge and belief are always about different objects. But the argument he presents here, as we shall see, neither requires nor suggests any version of TW.

II

Plato argues next that belief is the middle state between knowledge and ignorance; this entails, by (6), that it is set over what is and is not, but Plato does not reach this conclusion until much later.

His next steps simply state what is to be proved:

(7) Belief is a different capacity (*dunamis*) from knowledge (477 B 3–6).
(8) Therefore, belief and knowledge are set over different things, each according to its capacity (477 B 7–8).
(9) Knowledge is set over what is, to know how what is is (*gnōnai hōs esti to on*) (477 B 10–11).

(7) introduces belief explicitly for the first time; later stages of the argument

---

[11] For a defence of DT, see Gosling, '*Doxa* and *Dunamis* in Plato's *Republic*'; Crombie, *An Examination of Plato's Doctrines*.

look for an analogue to (9) for belief, in accordance with (8). (7) also shows that the capacities of knowledge and belief, and not necessarily every token act of knowing or believing, are being distinguished. Were token acts being considered, Plato might be pressed to DT; the emphasis on capacities at least allows T. Plato can now claim, not that every content of belief is only partially true, but that the set of beliefs collected by the capacity of belief contains both true and false members.

(10) Capacities are a kind of thing by which we are able (*dunametha*) to do what we are able to do, and by which everything else can do what it can do (477 c 1–4).

(11) Capacities are distinguished by (*a*) what they are set over (*epi*) and by (*b*) what work they accomplish. What is set over one thing and what accomplishes one thing is one capacity; those things which are set over different things and accomplish different things are different capacities (477 c 6–d 5).

(12) Knowledge is a capacity (477 d 7–9).

(13) Belief is a capacity, since it is that by which we are able to believe (477 e 1–3).

(14) Knowledge and belief are different capacities, since knowledge does not err (*anhamartēton*) but belief may err (477 e 6–7).

(15) Therefore each of them, being capable of something different, is set over something different (478 a 3–4).

(16) Knowledge is set over what is, to know how what is is (*to on gnōnai hōs echei*) (478 a 6).

(17) Belief believes (478 a 8).

(18) Since knowledge and belief are different capacities, and are set over different things, what is known (*gnōston*) and what is believed (*doxaston*) cannot be the same (478 a 12–b 2).

(19) Since what is known is what is, what is believed must be something other than what is (478 b 3–5).

(10) provides a general account of what a capacity is. (11) expands upon (10) by providing two conditions for capacity individuation. It follows from (10), in (12) and (13), that knowledge and belief are capacities. Applying (11), it then follows, in (14), that knowledge and belief are different capacities. (15) follows from (11) and (14). (16) then specifies (11a) and (11b) for knowledge; and this restates (9). (17) states (11b) for belief. It then remains, as (18) and (19) acknowledge, to find what belief is set over (the correlate of belief), in satisfaction of (11a), and this occupies Plato in the final stage of his argument.

These steps may well arouse our suspicions. (11) claims that if two purported capacities satisfy its two conditions in the same way, they are in
fact one capacity; and if they satisfy them differently, they are two different
capacities. This apparently leaves open two additional possibilities, however: (i) x and y do the same thing to different things, and (ii) x and y do
different things to the same thing.

Now at (14) Plato seems to infer from the fact that knowledge and belief
satisfy (11b) differently that they are different capacities; that is, he seems
to assume that because knowledge and belief satisfy (11b) differently, they
also satisfy (11a) differently and hence, by (11), are different capacities.
But given (ii) above, Plato does not seem to be justified in assuming that
knowledge and belief satisfy (11a) differently, just from the fact that they
satisfy (11b) differently, even if he is justified in assuming that they are
different capacities. For why should knowledge and belief not be different
capacities with different work on the same things? Husbandry and butchery,
for example, do different work, even if both are set over domestic animals,
and so have the same objects or sphere of operation; a difference in their
work does not imply a difference in their objects.

To see whether or not this suspicion of unfairness is warranted, we need
to examine (11a) and (11b) more carefully. (11b) is explained, at least
in part, by (14): knowledge, but not belief, does not err. That is to say,
knowledge knows and belief believes (cf. (13) and (17)), and the result of
this work is that knowledge will collect only truths, because only they can
be known, whereas belief will collect both truths and falsehoods, since both
can be believed. The result of the different work of knowledge and belief
is that knowledge, but not belief, includes only truths, but belief contents
include both truths and falsehoods.[12]

Our reading of (11a) depends on our interpretation of '*epi*'. For TW,
'*epi*' ranges over objects. Plato is then assuming that different capacities
(*dunameis*) must have different objects. Not only is this untrue in general,
as the earlier example of husbandry and butchery makes clear, but if it is
what Plato means here, then his argument is indeed invalid. For, as we have

---

[12] This interpretation of '*anhamartēton*' is adequate for the argument, whether or not it
is all Plato has in mind. Truth is, of course, only a necessary, and not also a sufficient, condition on the content of knowledge. Plato elsewhere also endorses an explanation condition
(see e.g. *Meno* 98 A); but that condition need not be invoked here, since the set of contents collected by the capacities of knowledge and belief can be distinguished by the truth
condition alone. I follow Crombie, *An Examination of Plato's Doctrines*, ii. 67, and Santas, 'Hintikka on Knowledge and its Objects in Plato', 45–6, in correlating '*anhamartēton*'
with (11b).

seen, (11b) does not imply (11a), so interpreted. On the TW reading, then, this argument is invalid.[13]

The contents analysis, however, can avoid this result. As we have seen, '*epi*' can range over contents as well as objects, and was most plausibly so read in earlier stages. Retaining that reading here has the further advantage of rendering Plato's argument valid. For Plato now claims only that when one knows (11b) one knows a piece of knowledge (11a); and when one believes (11b) one believes a belief (11a). That is how (11b) determines (11a). So read, the argument simply elaborates earlier, and noncontroversial, claims; and the trivial move from (11b) to (11a) does not illicitly preclude (i) and (ii), as TW does. To say that knowledge is set over pieces of knowledge, and that belief is set over beliefs, does not restrict the objects these propositions are about; husbandry and butchery are concerned with different sorts of facts, but these different facts could equally well be about the same domestic animals. The objects of knowledge and belief need not be separated; indeed, they are not relevant to the argument at all. Ascribing to Plato a valid argument, then, goes hand in hand with rejecting TW.

Plato has not only allowed there to be knowledge and belief about the same objects ((ii) is left open); he has also left open the possibility that your token piece of knowledge could be my token belief. A given proposition is a belief when it is believed, and a piece of knowledge when it is known; that is how (11b) determines (11a).[14]

III

Plato has now specified both what knowledge is set over and what work it does (16). He has claimed that belief is a distinct capacity from knowledge (14), and he has specified what work it does (17). He must now specify what it is set over. First, however, he distinguishes belief from ignorance; this is in order, given (5) and (6).

(20) Whoever believes believes some one thing (478 B 9–10).
(21) What is not is not one thing, but nothing (478 B 12–c 1).

---

[13] This problem for TW is also noted by Crombie, *An Examination of Plato's Doctrines*, ii. 57, and our alternative accounts of the argument are the same.

[14] This is of course consistent with (18). For (18) does not discuss *token* contents but only the *set* of belief contents and of knowledge contents. It says that the set of belief contents is not the same as the set of knowledge contents, since it has one different property: containing true and false members, and not only true members. This of course does not prevent your knowing that justice is psychic harmony while I only believe it.

(22) We assign ignorance to what is not, and knowledge to what is (478 c
      3–4).
(23) Therefore, belief is not set either over what is or over what is not
      (478 c 6).

By (19) it has been shown that belief is not set over what is, and this
conclusion is repeated at (23), along with the claim that it is not set over
what is not, either. That claim evidently implies that belief is not the same
capacity as ignorance, since ignorance is said to be set over what is not
((22), (5)).

Now we might expect this argument to be parallel to (14)–(19). There
Plato claimed that belief is not set over what is because it does not imply
truth as knowledge does. 'What is' is not an adequate account of the content of belief. Similarly here, Plato claims that neither is 'what is not' an
adequate account of the content of belief, since belief does not imply falsity as ignorance does. Still, particular beliefs might be false just as, earlier,
they could be true. The claim is only that belief implies neither truth nor
falsity.

But the argument seems to say rather more than this. (20) and (21)
seem to claim not that all beliefs are false, but that the contents of belief
contain no false beliefs. If false beliefs are now assigned to ignorance, belief
will no longer be set over true and false beliefs. It then either collapses
into knowledge, if it is simply set over what is—a collapse the previous
argument had tried to avoid—or is correlated with partial truths, as DT
suggests.

But neither does this seem to account for all that occurs here. For (20)
and (21) also seem to shift away from is-v to is-e (what does not exist) or to
a strong version of is-p (what is not anything); they mention the availability
of content, not the truth or falsity of particular contents.

So read, (20) may seem plausible: it supplies an analogue to (1) for belief.
Belief, like knowledge, has content; when one believes, there is some content
of the mental condition. Considering (20) along with (21), however, leads
to other problems. For Plato may now seem to be denying the possibility
of false belief, along familiar lines; as Crombie suggests, he 'seems to argue
from the premise that every belief must have content to the conclusion
that the content of a belief cannot be a nonentity, or in other words a
falsehood'.[15] Retaining is-v above seemed to restrict the content of belief to
true beliefs; ignorance was set over false beliefs. Now, if Plato equivocates
between is-v and is-p, he seems to deny that there are any false beliefs.

[15] Crombie, *An Examination of Plato's Doctrines,* ii. 59.

Either way, belief will not be set over true and false beliefs as I claimed it would.

But the argument need not be read in either of these two ways. We can easily avoid the equivocation Crombie suggests by using only is-p here. Plato's claim in (20), as we have seen, is that belief has content; it does not happen that one believes and yet believes nothing. But then (21) may, instead of shifting illegitimately to is-v, simply draw out this consequence of (20). In assigning what is not to *agnoia*, Plato assigns not false beliefs but nothing to it. *Agnoia* is then something like blank ignorance, and there is no determinate content of the mental condition. True and false beliefs are still the correlate of belief, as we claimed; *agnoia* consists not of false beliefs but of ignorance or lack of awareness. If one is ignorant of p, one cognizes nothing true of p; there is no content of the mental condition.

The chief difficulty with this reading is that (22) is then strikingly unparallel to (5), despite their apparent similarity; for (5) uses is-v, whereas (22) uses is-p. Another reading is possible, however, and it will preserve the parallelism. Suppose I claim that justice is a vegetable. Plato might argue that my claim does not amount to a belief about justice at all; it displays total ignorance of justice. We might then read (21) with is-v, after all, while still avoiding the equivocation Crombie suggested. It claims that if what I say is not at all true of justice, it says nothing—that is, it says nothing true about justice. So read (22) and (5) both use is-v. Nor is this line of argument DT. Plato's claim is now only that totally false beliefs are assigned to ignorance, and not that all false beliefs are. If one has *agnoia*, one will have a totally false belief, or ignorance. But Plato has not asserted that every false belief is a content of ignorance. Although ignorance has as its contents only very false beliefs, not every false belief need be assigned to ignorance.

Plato has now proved that:

(24) Belief is neither knowledge nor ignorance (478 c 8).

This makes belief a candidate for being the middle state, set over what is and is not, and he next argues that it satisfies the conditions for being the middle state:

(25) Belief is neither clearer than knowledge nor more obscure than ignorance; it is more obscure than knowledge, but clearer than ignorance (478 c 10–14).
(26) Belief lies between knowledge and ignorance (478 d 1–4).
(27) We said before (in (6)) that what is and is not will be between what

is and what is not, and will have some state between ignorance and knowledge set over it (478 D 5–9).

It follows that belief is set over what is and is not; (6) can now be filled in appropriately. If the argument we have sketched is Plato's, he has, as promised, distinguished knowledge and belief on noncontroversial grounds, acceptable to the sightlover. He has argued that knowledge, but not belief, implies truth; there may be false beliefs, but there is no false knowledge. We need not appeal to is-e or is-p to understand Plato's main claims; nor need we appeal to a peculiar 'degrees of truth' doctrine. The first two options were ruled out on grounds of general plausibility; the argument could be read without them, and was effective only without them. DT, although it may seem plausible initially, is less attractive once Plato makes it clear that he is discussing the set of beliefs covered by the capacity; he can then say, as we would like, that although any particular belief is determinately true or false, the set of beliefs contains some true and some false members.

But the argument is not yet complete. The sightlover could accept it so far, and still see no reason to conclude that he has only belief; but showing this was Plato's main aim. In the final stage of his argument he goes further, and argues that the particular claims of the sightlover are at best beliefs.

IV

The final stage of Plato's argument raises more severe problems for my interpretation T than any encountered so far. The first problem arises with the next step:

(28) It remains, then, to find what partakes of what is and is not so that we may say it is believed (478 E 1–4).

(28) is problematic, for it seems to say that every token belief is true and not true, or only partially true, as DT, but not T, holds. Nor are the next steps of Plato's argument encouraging:

(29) Each of the many Fs is no more F than not F (478 E 5–479 B 8).
(30) Therefore, each of the many Fs is and is not (479 B 9–10).
(31) The many Fs, therefore, are between being and not being (479 C 6–D 1).

(29)–(31) seem to shift away from DT no less than from T, towards one or another version of TW; for it is clear that here 'is' cannot be 'is-v', but must be 'is-e' or 'is-p'. Moreover, (28) claims quite generally that whatever is between being and not being is what is believed; (31) asserts that the many Fs are between being and not being. The conclusion seems clear: belief is set over the many Fs. And this implication is in fact explicitly drawn in the last step:

(32) We have found, then, that the many *nomima* of the many about the beautiful and the rest roll about between what is not and what fully is (479 D 3–5).

(33) We agreed that if any such thing appeared it would be assigned to the intermediate capacity and be something believed and not known (479 D 7–9).

(34) Therefore, those who look only on the many Fs have belief, not knowledge (479 E 1–5).

(35) Those who look on the Fs which always stay the same have knowledge (479 D 7–8).

(36) Knowledge is set over forms; belief is set over the many Fs (479 D 10–480 A 4).

But it now looks as if Plato has specified forms and sensibles as the correlates of knowledge and belief; he seems to be concerned with objects and not, as we thought, with contents. This leaves us with two options: either Plato consistently intended one or another version of the objects analysis, so that T is just irrelevant; or else Plato began with the noncontroversial assumptions we have elicited, and now shifts, legitimately or not, to a claim about objects.[16]

I argue first that if we use DE or DR here, Plato's argument is either fallacious or unfair. I then argue that although (29)–(31) shift away from is-v, they explain, and do not controvert, T.

(29) clearly uses is-p; the predicate term is in fact explicitly specified ('is no more F than not F'). The claim is the familiar Platonic one, pressed in the first argument addressed to Glaucon, as well as elsewhere, that any observable property adduced to explain what makes something beautiful, for example, is no more beautiful than ugly.[17] In some cases, bright colouring explains something's beauty; in other cases, an appeal to bright colouring explains something's ugliness. But then bright colouring is no more beautiful than ugly. Any observable property F is both F and not F, since it

---

[16] It is of course possible that Plato just confuses these various uses so that 'shift' is inappropriate; but I do not think this assumption is necessary. Cf. n. 9.

[17] See e.g. *Phd.* 66 A, 74 B, 100 B; *H. Ma.* 289 C–D; *Rep.* 623–4. For discussion, see Gosling, 'Republic V', and T. H. Irwin, 'Plato's Heracleiteanism', *Philosophical Quarterly*, 27 (1977), 1–13.

collects F as well as not-F cases. The sightlovers can be expected to agree, and so (29) does not violate the condition of noncontroversiality: no one explanation of beauty, phrased in terms of sensibles, will account for all cases of beauty; and it is for just this reason that the sightlovers insist on many accounts. No one account will do.

Now (30) and (31) differ from (29) in omitting the predicate 'is no more F than not F'. For DE this indicates that Plato has moved from 'is no more F than not F' to 'does and does not exist'. But the move is of course fallacious, since is-p does not carry existential import in this way. One cannot infer from the fact that x is not F that x does not (fully) exist. The paper on which I am now writing is not green; none the less, it exists. Yet DE seems to rest largely on the supposition that Plato is guilty of this crude error.[18]

This does not imply, of course, that Plato does not endorse DE. But if we can find a more plausible interpretation, we should prefer it; and it is not difficult to find one. (30) and (31) are easily taken as ellipses of (29); (29) licenses us to read (30) and (31) correspondingly. Is-p is then the only use of '*esti*' we need see here.[19]

But now one may wish to argue that, since is-p is relevant here, all preceding unsupplemented uses of '*esti*' be read correspondingly, and that DR therefore best represents Plato's argument. Plato's claim is then that one can know only what is really and fully F, or the forms; one can at best have beliefs about sensibles, which, as (29) explains, are F and not F. As Gosling writes, 'Socrates is going to argue that the offerings of the *philotheamones* are and yet are not just, beautiful, etc. and so must be *doxasta*.'[20]

This line of argument, however, either violates the condition of noncontroversiality, or is invalid. We might agree to read (2) as (2b), so that (2), taken together with (3), claims that I can know only what is fully F, and not also what is F and not F. So read, Plato's argument is valid, but in beginning with this assumption, he violates his condition of noncontroversiality. For why should I not be able to know, for example, that sensibles are F and not F? Surely by itself the claim that sensibles are and are not just provides no reason for precluding knowledge of them. Of course, I can know that x is fully F only if x is fully F. But, similarly, I can know that x is F and not F only if x is F and not F. Read this way, Plato's argument is invalid: it begins with the plausible (2c) reading of (2), that knowledge implies truth, but then

---

[18] At least, Cross and Woozley, *Plato's Republic*, 145 and 162, cite no other evidence in favour of DE (aside from the undefended assumption that Plato systematically confuses is-e and is-p).

[19] Cf. Gosling, '*Republic* V', 123–4; Vlastos, 'Degrees of Reality in Plato', 6 n. 4.

[20] Gosling, '*Doxa* and *Dunamis* in Plato's *Republic*', 126. Vlastos, 'Degrees of Reality in Plato', also defends this view.

draws an illegitimate conclusion about the unknowability of sensibles. The underlying reasoning seems to go something like this:

(i)   Necessarily (if A knows that x is F, then x is F).
(ii) If x is a sensible, x is F and not F.
(iii) There are sensibles, and therefore things that are F and not F.
(iv) One cannot know that x is F, if x is a sensible, since, by (iii), x is (also) not F.

'Is F and not F' is, however, a perfectly good substitution instance, in (i), for 'is F'; and since sensibles are F and not F, Plato has not shown why one cannot know that they are. This line of defence, then, leaves Plato with an invalid argument. Of course, one might wish to buttress the argument with additional premises that yield the desired conclusion validly. But the fact remains that no such premises are specified here. Again, if a more plausible argument can be found, it is to be preferred.

I agree, then, that (29)–(31) use is-p; but I resist interpreting the preceding argument to suit. Instead, I think Plato uses is-v in preceding stages, and shifts to is-p here. If this is so, we face a problem of a different sort: does Plato simply confuse is-v and is-p? Or is there a plausible connecting link between the two uses of '*esti*'? I think a link between is-v and is-p can be found, and it preserves the veridical reading.

Note first that (32) says not that the many Fs, the concern of (29)–(31), are between being and not being, but that *nomima* about the many Fs are between being and not being. (33), correspondingly, implies that *nomima* are among the correlates of belief. What are these *nomima*? '*Nomimon*' is a general word for anything one can *nomizein*; it also conveys a notion of generality, and of custom or convention. It can be complemented with is-p or is-v, depending on whether we take it to mean 'customary rules' or 'customary beliefs'. Although '*nomimon*' can in general be complemented with is-p, the present context suggests is-v. It is the beliefs of the many about justice and the like—that justice is paying one's debts, for example (*Rep.* 331 c)—that are being criticized; since the sightlovers restrict themselves to sensible properties in attempting to say what justice is, they are led to various claims that will be unsatisfactory. Plato's claim is that the sightlovers' beliefs about beauty, justice, and the like are among the correlates of belief; (32) then uses is-v.[21]

---

[21] Many translators use is-v for translating '*nomima*' here: 'beliefs' (Bloom), 'conventional opinions' (H. D. P. Lee, G. M. A. Grube), 'conventional notions' (F. M. Cornford). J. Adam, *The* Republic *of Plato*, ed. with critical notes, commentary and appendices, 2nd edn., intr. D. A. Rees (2 vols.; Cambridge: Cambridge University Press, 1963), ii. 167 (cf. i. 343),

Now to say that (32) assigns only certain beliefs to belief does not yet answer all our worries. For it is still true that (29)–(31) use is-p, and that (36) assigns the many Fs to belief; even if *nomima* are among the correlates specified for belief, Plato's claim seems to go beyond this. Also, we have not yet answered an earlier question, raised about (28), of whether the present use of is-v better fits DT or T. Both problems can, I think, be answered in favour of T.

The sightlovers do not acknowledge forms; all their accounts or explanations of beauty, justice, and the like, are phrased in terms of sensibles. They define beauty, for example, as the brightly coloured; their accounts refer to and are based on such observable properties. But we know from earlier steps, and from elsewhere, that such properties are F and not F; some cases of bright colouring are beautiful, others are not. But if 'bright colouring' picks out cases of ugliness no less than of beauty, no belief like 'the beautiful is the brightly coloured' can amount to knowledge—or, in general, no belief based on observable properties can amount to knowledge. The connection between is-p and is-v is then this: reliance on observable properties that are F and not F (is-p) issues in the unsatisfactory *nomima* (is-v); the *nomima* are based on observable properties, and that basis prevents them from being knowledgeable accounts.

This connection also explains (34)–(36). The sightlovers, since they look only to the many Fs, can at best have belief; no account phrased in terms of sensibles can yield knowledge, and so in that sense belief is set over the many Fs. Now this leaves open two possibilities: either there is no knowledge, since there are no entities beyond the many Fs by reference to which one could acquire knowledgeable accounts; or else there is knowledge and, hence, there are other entities beyond the many Fs, that make this knowledge possible. In first explicitly mentioning forms in these concluding steps, Plato endorses the second option.[22]

says that '*nomima*' refers to 'popular canons or opinions'. This reading seems suggested by the sense of the argument, although the syntax does not, of course, require it. For other occurrences of '*nomima*', see *Rep.* 484 D 2, 589 A 7, *Grg.* 488 D 9, A 4, *H. Ma.* 294 C 4. I should make it clear that my interpretation of *nomima* is not also an interpretation of *ta polla kala*, which I take to be sensible properties, as I explain above. As I read the argument, Plato talks about certain sorts of opinions as well as about certain sorts of objects. Although these concerns are connected in the way I explain above, they are distinct concerns.

[22] It may seem that he is not justified in doing so, however, given the first possibility, so that his argument becomes invalid at this stage. I think this is a plausible line to take. But the strategy is a familiar one in Plato (see e.g. *Prm.* 135 A–C, *Ti.* 51 D, where Plato also infers that forms must exist if knowledge does) and so does not affect my interpretation. In any case this line of argument need not violate the principle of noncontroversiality; if the sightlovers will agree that there is knowledge, they will now accept the existence of forms. Plato will

This reference to forms and sensibles does not play into the hands of TW. Plato is not claiming that all knowledge concerns only forms, or that all beliefs concern only sensibles. He does claim that all knowledge requires knowledge of forms. But this leaves open the possibility that one could be aware of forms in less than a knowledgeable way; and it also leaves open the possibility that once one has knowledge of forms, it can be extended beyond forms to sensibles. All knowledge begins with knowledge of forms, but it need not end with them, too; nor need every grasp of a form amount to knowledge of it. To understand Plato's claims, the appropriate restrictive clauses must be assumed: restricted to the many Fs, the most one can attain is belief; for knowledge, one needs an account in terms of forms. But the content of this account need not be restricted to forms, nor need every claim about a form constitute knowledge.

I have argued so far that the shift to is-p does not upset, but rather explains, T. But we are still left with another problem: (32) assigns only *nomima* to belief. This supports an is-v reading, but it may seem to support DT rather than T. A *nomimon*, such as that the beautiful is the brightly coloured, is, presumably, simply false. *Nomima*, although false, are not, however, contents of ignorance, since they are not totally false; but since they are not true, neither can they be contents of knowledge. But once it is spelt out this way, it looks as if we have supported DT: *nomima* are the contents of belief, since they are only partially true.

I do not think we need to read Plato in this way. There are at least two alternatives. First, although any *nomimon* is simply false, it collects other beliefs, some of which are true, others of which are false. For example, the *nomimon* that courage is endurance leads to the true belief that Socrates is courageous and to the false belief that lions are (cf. *La.* 196 E). 'Is and is not' then applies disjunctively to members of a set of beliefs collected by a *nomimon*; but every member of the set is determinately true or false.

Second, it may be that '*nomima*' need not be restricted to the general accounts offered by the sightlovers, but applies as well to the beliefs such accounts collect; that is, not only 'courage is endurance' but also 'Socrates is courageous' may count as a *nomimon*. In that case, we still consider sets of beliefs clustered about a general account, and 'is and is not' still applies disjunctively; but since each member of the set is a *nomimon*, (32) and (33) are not elliptical, as they are on the first reading.

If we do not take 'is and is not' disjunctively in either of these suggested ways, but instead take it to apply conjunctively to each *nomimon*, then

then have committed them to the existence of forms on grounds they have accepted. His argument then follows the standard elenctic procedure.

Plato's description of *nomima* does indeed seem close to DT. For he then seems to say that although any *nomimon* is just false, none is false enough to count as a content of ignorance (since, for example, each leads to some true beliefs). But although *nomima*, interpreted this way, do fit DT's specifications for beliefs, we need not interpret the preceding argument to suit. Instead, what Plato does at (32), I think, is to restrict the scope of his argument. His claim there is not that all beliefs are like *nomima*, but only that *nomima* are at best beliefs. That is, being a *nomimon* is a sufficient but not a necessary condition for being a content of belief.

Plato prepares us for the shift. His avowed strategy is to show that, given a general and noncontroversial account of belief, the sightlovers can at best have belief. To show this, of course, he must provide not only the general account but also a description of sightlovers' beliefs. It is not surprising that the specialized account is narrower: it attempts to classify only one sort of claim. Other claims might count as beliefs for other reasons; but what is of immediate concern is *nomima*.

Plato's claim, then, is that *nomima* are not contents of knowledge, since they are not true and knowledge implies truth; but although false, they are not contents of ignorance either, for they are not totally false. If we want to consider other beliefs, the explanation of their status might differ; not all beliefs are like *nomima*. All Plato has argued here is that *nomima* (*inter alia*) are contents of belief. But the final narrowing of his argument need not infect preceding stages.[23]

VI

On the traditional two-worlds interpretation of Plato's argument in *Republic* V, knowledge and belief are distinguished by reference to their special objects: knowledge is only of forms, and belief is only of sensibles. One

---

[23] This alternative is not wholly satisfactory, however. For on it, Plato does equivocate on 'is and is not'. Until (32) it seemed to apply disjunctively to contents collected by the capacity of belief, so that any belief was determinately true or false; but at (32) and (33) 'is and is not' seems to apply conjunctively to a particular *nomimon*. I do not know if Plato does equivocate in this way, or consistently advocates DT, or endorses one of the two more satisfying explanations I suggest above. Any of these alternatives is possible; I prefer the third largely on grounds of plausibility, and because it fits well with the earlier argument, where Plato seems clearly to be considering sets of beliefs collected by the general capacity of belief. Even if we are pressed to DT or to the equivocation interpretation, however, we still avoid TW. For Plato still at most claims that any partially true content is a content of belief; but such contents could be about sensibles or forms. Nor has Plato said that every claim about a sensible is at best partially true.

84

Knowledge and Belief in Republic *V*

cannot know sensibles or have beliefs about forms. If this is Plato's argument, it violates his starting condition of noncontroversiality, by requiring strong and implausible premises that his opponents cannot be expected to agree to. Moreover, Plato misuses his criteria for capacity-individuation, and, on at least some of the current interpretations, equivocates on uses of '*esti*'.

I suggested that Plato's argument could be interpreted in another way, so that it is free of controversial premises, involves no equivocation on '*esti*', and is valid. On this interpretation, knowledge and belief are distinguished not by their different sets of objects, but by their truth implications. Knowledge, but not belief, implies truth. The argument resulting from this claim is valid; but it does not support the Two Worlds Theory. On our reading, Plato has precluded neither knowledge of sensibles nor beliefs about forms. He does argue, at the close of the passage, that whoever knows will know forms, since it is only by reference to them that correct accounts are forthcoming; if, like the sightlovers, one is restricted to sensibles, the most one can attain is belief. But though all knowledge begins with forms, it need not end with them and one may fail to acquire knowledge of forms, and have only beliefs about them.

The price of ascribing to Plato a valid argument whose premises are noncontroversial is the loss of the Two Worlds Theory. It is a price I am quite willing to pay.[24]

[24] I am especially indebted to T. H. Irwin for many helpful criticisms of several drafts of this chapter. Earlier versions have also been read and helpfully criticized by J. L. Ackrill, J. C. B. Gosling, A. Nehamas, N. Kretzmann, and G. E. L. Owen.

4

Knowledge and Belief in *Republic* V–VII

The *Meno* tells us that knowledge is true belief bound by an *aitias logismos*, an explanatory account (98 A); the *Phaedo* tells us that all *aitiai* refer to forms (96 ff.).[1] It follows that knowledge of forms is necessary for any knowledge at all. But though the *Meno* explains what knowledge is, it does not connect this account to forms; and though the *Phaedo* tells us quite a lot about the metaphysics of forms, it does not tell us much about their epistemological role. We must wait until the middle books of the *Republic* (V–VII) for the details of how forms figure in knowledge. Here there are two crucial stretches of text: first, a difficult argument at the end of *Republic* V; and, second, the famous images of the Sun, Line, and Cave in books VI and VII. Both passages are often thought to show that Plato subscribes to the Two Worlds Theory (TW), according to which there is no knowledge of sensibles, but only of forms, and no belief about forms but only about sensibles.[2]

If Plato is committed to TW, there are, arguably, some consequences of note. First, the objects of knowledge and belief are then disjoint; one cannot move from belief to knowledge about some single thing. I cannot first believe that the sun is shining, and then come to know that it is. Second, Plato then radically rejects the *Meno*'s account of knowledge, according to which knowledge implies true belief. For on TW, knowledge excludes true belief.[3]

---

[1] I take forms to be nonsensible properties, properties not definable in observational or perceptual terms—the property, for example, of beauty, as opposed both to particular beautiful objects (such as the Parthenon) and to observable properties of beauty (such as circular shape or bright colour). I discuss forms in details in chs. 11–15. See also *On Ideas*; and T. H. Irwin, 'The Theory of Forms', in G. Fine (ed.), *Plato 1: Metaphysics and Epistemology* (Oxford: Oxford University Press, 1999), 143–70.

[2] It is sometimes thought to follow from TW that Plato restricts knowledge to necessary truths; for, it is thought, all truths about forms are necessary truths. See e.g. G. Vlastos, 'Socrates' Disavowal of Knowledge', *Philosophical Quarterly*, 35 (1985), 1–31, repr. in Fine (ed.), *Plato 1*, 64–92 at 78. If, as I shall argue, Plato allows knowledge of sensibles, then (on the reasonable assumption that some of the knowable truths about them are contingent) he does not restrict knowledge to necessary truths.

[3] This consequence of TW is clearly noted by D. M. Armstrong, *Belief, Truth and Know-*

Third, Plato is then quite sceptical about the limits of knowledge; although at least philosophers can know forms, no one can know items in the sensible world. No one can know, for example, what actions are just or good; no one can know even such mundane facts as that they're now seeing a tomato, or sitting at a table.

Fourth, this sceptical result would be quite surprising in the context of the *Republic*, which aims to persuade us that philosophers should rule, since only they have knowledge, and knowledge is necessary for good ruling. If their knowledge is only of forms—if, like the rest of us, they only have belief about the sensible world—it is unclear why they are specially fitted to rule in this world. They don't know, any more than the rest of us do, which laws to enact.

Fifth, the text of the *Republic* seems to contradict TW. At 506 c Plato says that he has beliefs about, but no knowledge of, the form of the good; and at 520 c he says that the philosopher who returns to the cave will know the things there, i.e. sensibles.[4] Contrary to TW, then, one can have beliefs about forms, and know sensibles.

I shall argue that we can avoid these unattractive consequences. For *Republic* V–VII is not committed to TW. (If I had more space, I would argue that Plato is never committed to TW: the *Republic* is no anomaly.)

Plato does, to be sure, in *some* way correlate knowledge with forms, and belief with sensibles—but not in a way that involves TW. He argues only that all knowledge requires (not that it is restricted to) knowledge of forms; and that, restricted to sensibles, one can at most achieve belief. This, however, leaves open the possibility that, once one knows forms, one can apply this knowledge to sensibles so as to know them too; the philosopher's knowledge of forms, for instance, helps him to know (although it is not, all by itself, sufficient for knowing) which laws ought to be enacted.

In addition to arguing against TW, I shall also, in looking at *Republic* VI–VII, argue that Plato is a coherentist, rather than a foundationalist, about justification. That is, he believes that all beliefs, to be known, must be justified in terms of other beliefs; no beliefs are self-evident or self-justified. I shall also suggest that knowledge, for Plato, is always essentially articulate;

---

ledge (Cambridge: Cambridge University Press, 1973), 139–41. Unlike me, however, he believes the *Republic* endorses TW.

[4] Plato says that the philosopher 'will know each of the images, what they are and of what'; his use of *gnōsesthe* plus the *hatta* clause suggests he means 'know' and not merely 'recognize'. Plato arguably explicitly admits knowledge of sensibles elsewhere too. See e.g. *Meno* 71 B, 97 A 9–B 7; *Tht.* 201 A–C.

knowledge does not consist in any special sort of vision or acquaintance, but in one's ability to explain what one knows.

1. *Republic* V

The difficult argument at the end of *Republic* V is Plato's lengthiest, most sustained, systematic account in the middle dialogues of how knowledge differs from belief.[5] It is offered in defence of the 'greatest wave of para- dox' of the *Republic*: that, in the ideally just *polis*, philosophers—those who know forms—must rule (472 A 1–7, 473 C 6–E 5). Plato advances this strik- ing claim because he believes that the best rulers must know what is good; but one can know what is good only if one knows the form of the good; and only philosophers can achieve such knowledge. He is well aware that his claim will not meet with general favour. In order to defend it, he offers a long and tangled argument, designed gently to persuade the 'sightlovers'— people who rely on their senses and do not acknowledge forms.

This provides us with an important constraint governing an adequate interpretation of the argument. The argument occurs in a particular dialec- tical context, designed to persuade the sightlovers. If it is to be genuinely di- alectical, then, as Plato explains in the *Meno* (75 D), it should only use claims that are (believed to be) true, and that the interlocutor accepts; this is Plato's *dialectical requirement* (DR). Plato's opening premises should not, then, appeal to forms; nor, indeed, should he begin with any claims the sightlovers would readily dispute, or that they're unfamiliar with. His conclusions may of course be controversial, but the opening premises should not be.

The opening premises, however, are difficult to interpret. The crucial ones are these:[6]

(1) Knowledge is set over what is (*epi tō(i) onti*) (477 A 9–10).
(2) Belief is set over what is and is not.

Esti (like 'is' in English) can be used in a variety of ways: existentially (is-e), predicatively (is-p), and veridically (is-v). (It can be used in yet fur- ther ways too—for example, for identity—but such further uses are not relevant here.) Hence (1) might mean any of (1a–c):

(1a) Knowledge is set over what exists.

[5] I discuss this argument in more detail in ch. 3. Here I offer a brief summary of the main points. The present account occasionally differs from, and so supersedes, my earlier account.
[6] Plato also discusses *agnoia*, ignorance, correlating it with what is not (477 A 9–10). For some discussion, see ch. 3.

    (1b) Knowledge is set over what is F (for some predicate 'F' to be determined by context).

    (1b) Knowledge is set over what is true.

Premiss (2), correspondingly, might mean any of (2a–c):

    (2a) Belief is set over what exists and does not exist.

    (2b) Belief is set over what is F and not-F.

    (2c) Belief is set over what is true and not true.

On the (a) and (b) readings, (1) and (2) specify the *objects* of knowledge and belief. On the (a) reading, one can only know what exists (there is no knowledge of, for instance, Santa Claus); and one can only have beliefs about objects that exist and don't exist (that is, on the usual interpretation, about objects that somehow 'half-exist').[7]

On the (b) reading, (1) claims that one can only know objects that are F and (2) claims that one can only have beliefs about objects that are F and not-F. (That is, on the usual interpretation, every object of belief is itself both F and not-F—both beautiful and ugly, for example, or just and unjust.)[8]

On the (c) reading, by contrast, (1) and (2) specify the propositions that are the *contents* of knowledge and belief. One can only know true propo-

---

[7] (1a) can be interpreted in more than one way. It might mean that (i) I can only know x when x exists; or (ii) I can only know x if x at some point exists; or (iii) I can only know x if x always exists. My own view is that of (i–iii), Plato at most believes (ii); but whatever his belief about (1a), I do not think he intends to assert any version of (1a) at this stage of the argument. (2a) is ambiguous between (i) every object of belief both exists and doesn't exist, i.e. half-exists, and (ii) the set of objects about which one can have beliefs includes some that exist and others that don't (e.g. Santa Claus) (and perhaps some that both exist and don't exist, or that half-exist). Since (i) is the usual is-e reading, I restrict myself to it. For a defence of an is-e reading see e.g. A. C. Cross and A. D. Woozley, *Plato's Republic: A Philosophical Commentary* (London: Macmillan, 1964). For criticism of an is-e reading, see my 'Knowledge and Belief in *Republic* V' (=ch. 3); G. Vlastos, 'Degrees of Reality in Plato', in R. Bambrough (ed.), *New Essays on Plato and Aristotle* (London: Routledge & Kegan Paul, 1965), 1–20, repr. in G. Vlastos (ed.), *Platonic Studies*, 2nd edn. (Princeton: Princeton University Press, 1981), 76–110; J. Annas, *An Introduction to Plato's* Republic (Oxford: Clarendon Press, 1981), 196–7; C. H. Kahn, 'Some Philosophical Use of "to be" in Plato', *Phronesis*, 26 (1981), 119–27.

[8] (2b) is ambiguous between (i) belief is about objects, each of which is F and not-F; and (ii) belief is about objects, some of which is F and others of which are not-F (and perhaps some of which are both). Since (i) is the usual interpretation, I shall not try to see how the argument goes if we assume (ii) instead. A predicative reading is favoured by Vlastos, 'Degrees of Reality in Plato', and by Annas, *An Introduction to Plato's* Republic, ch. 8. Annas correctly points out that even if Plato restricts knowledge to what is F, and precludes knowledge of anything that is F and not-F, TW does not follow; we could still know, for example, that this is a table, or that Socrates is a man, even if we could not know that returning what one owes is sometimes just, sometimes unjust. (Vlastos, by contrast, conjoins is-p with a defence of TW.) On the account I shall provide we can know things that are F and not-F.

sitions; one can believe both true and false propositions. Knowledge, but not belief, entails truth.

The (a) and (b) readings of (1) and (2) seem to violate DR. For both of them sharply separate the objects of knowledge and belief. But why should the sightlovers agree to this at the outset of the argument? Plato may end up concluding that the objects of knowledge and belief are disjoint; but it would violate DR to assume so at the outset.

The (a) reading violates DR in further ways too. To be sure, if, for example, one takes knowledge to involve some sort of acquaintance, (1a) might seem plausible: I cannot know, in the sense of be acquainted with, Santa Claus, or even Socrates, given that he is now dead. But it is unclear why we should assume at the outset that knowledge consists in or requires acquaintance with what is known. Moreover, (2b) introduces the difficult notion of 'half-existence'. But why should the sightlovers agree at the outset that every object of belief only half-exists?

The (b) reading also violates DR in ways peculiar to it. For it claims that one can only know what is F; one cannot know what is F and not-F. But it is unclear how this could be a noncontroversial starting premiss. Why can I not know that this pencil, say, is both equal (to other things of the same length) and unequal (to everything of any different length)? There seems no intuitive reason to suppose that Plato begins by denying the possibility of knowing that something is both F and not-F. Of course, he may end up concluding this (although I shall argue that in fact he does not); but our present task is to find suitably noncontroversial *starting* premisses.

Premiss (1c), by contrast, satisfies DR. For it says only that knowledge implies truth, a standard condition on knowledge the sightlovers can be expected to accept, and one Plato himself has clearly articulated before (*Meno* 98 A; *Grg.* 454 D 6–7).

There are, however, at least two possible veridical readings of (2c):[9]

(2ci) Every proposition that can be believed is both true and false.
(2cii) The set of propositions that can be believed includes some truths and some falsehoods.

Premiss (2ci) is controversial, since it introduces the difficult notion of a *single* proposition's being both true and false. We might be able to make sense of this notion: perhaps, for example, the claim is that all believed propositions are complex, and part of what each says is true, part false. But why should the sightlovers agree that all beliefs are partly true, partly

---

[9] (2ci) is endorsed by J. C. B. Gosling, '*Doxa* and *Dunamis* in Plato's *Republic*', *Phronesis*, 13 (1968), 119–30. I endorse (2cii) both here and in ch. 3.

false? If we can find a more intuitively acceptable reading of the opening premisses, it should be preferred.[10]

Premiss (2cii) is such a reading. In contrast to (2ci), it does not say that each token proposition that can be believed is both true and false, but only that the set of propositions that can be believed contains both true and false beliefs. Belief implies neither truth nor falsity; there are both true and false beliefs. We cannot infer from the fact that p is believed that p is true, or that it is false, although we can infer from the fact that p is known that p is true.

If we read (1) as (1c), and (2) as (2cii), then all we have been told so far is that knowledge but not belief implies truth. This of course leaves open the possibility (although it does not require) that there is knowledge and belief about the same objects (including sensibles), indeed of the same propositions. The readings of the opening premisses that best satisfy DR are thus also the least congenial to TW. Of course, later premisses might tell in favour of TW; we shall need to see. The point for now is only that at least (1–2) (if read as (1c) and as (2cii)) do not at all suggest it.

From 477 B–478 B Plato argues that knowledge and belief are different capacities. First he argues that capacities are distinguished by (*a*) what they are set over (*epi*) and (*b*) what work they do (477 C 6–D 5). Two capacities are the same if they satisfy both (*a*) and (*b*); they differ if they are set over different things and do different work. Plato then seems to argue that since knowledge and belief satisfy (*b*) differently, they are different capacities; and that since they are different capacities, they satisfy (*a*) differently as well.

The first inferences seems warranted; even if x and y satisfy only one of (*a*) and (*b*) differently, they seem to be different capacities. But the second inference does not seem warranted; why can't knowledge and belief do different work (and so be different capacities) even if they are set over the same things? Husbandry and butchery, for instance, do different work; but they are both set over the same objects—domestic animals.

If we favour the objects analysis, so that knowledge and belief are set over different objects, then Plato does seem to argue invalidly here. Just as the objects analysis seems to require Plato to violate DR, so it seems to require him to argue invalidly. If, however, we favour the contents analysis, so that knowledge and belief are not set over different objects but only over different contents, then not only are Plato's starting premisses noncontro-

[10] Notice, though, that (2ci) does not support TW; for there is no reason in principle why I cannot believe a proposition that is both true and false (however we ultimately explain that notion) about a form, or know a true proposition about sensibles. On (2ci), the *propositions* one can believe and the propositions one can know constitute disjoint classes; but they could be about the same *objects*, and so TW would not yet be in the offing.

versial, but also, as I shall now argue, the present argument about capacity individuation is valid.

Knowledge and belief do different work, Plato tells us, in that knowledge but not belief is infallible (*anhamartēton*; 477 E 6–7). This might only mean that knowledge but not belief implies truth: that's one way (the only correct way) to read the slogan 'if you know, you can't be wrong'; and it's the only reading of the slogan that the argument requires.[11]

But how can we legitimately infer from this difference of work to a difference in what knowledge and belief are set over? My reading of (1) and (2) provides the answer: knowledge is set over true propositions; belief is set over true and false propositions. It follows from the fact that knowledge but not belief implies truth that they are set over different (though not necessarily disjoint) sets of propositions—the set of propositions one can know (true propositions) is a subset of (and so is different from) the set of propositions one can believe (true and false propositions).

Plato's inference from (*b*) to (*a*) is thus warranted after all—if we assume that knowledge and belief are set over different sets of propositions, rather than over different objects. Moreover, if we read the argument this way, then Plato leaves open the possibility (although, again, he does not require) that one can know and have beliefs about the same objects, even of the same propositions. A valid, suitably noncontroversial argument goes hand in hand with avoiding TW.

To be sure, Plato claims that what is known (*gnōston*) and what is believed (*doxaston*) cannot be the same (478 A 12–B 2). This, however, might only mean that the set of propositions one can believe is not coextensive with the set of propositions one can know—for one can believe but not know false propositions. More weakly still, Plato might only mean that the properties of being known and of being believed are different properties. Either claim is plausible, and all that the argument, at this stage, requires.

All of the argument to 478 E can be read as emphasizing this crucial point, that knowledge but not belief entails truth. At 479 A ff., however, Plato shifts to another point:

(3) Each of the many Fs is both F and not-F.

The many Fs are sensible properties of the sort recognized by the sight-lover—bright colour, for instance, or circular shape.[12] (3) claims that each

---

[11] For quite a different interpretation of 'infallibility', see Vlastos, 'Socrates' Disavowal of Knowledge', 74–5.

[12] For a defence of this claim, see e.g. J. C. B. Gosling, '*Republic* V: *Ta Polla Kala*, etc.', *Phronesis*, 5 (1960), 116–28.

such property is both F and not-F. Bright colour, for example, is both beautiful and ugly in that some brightly coloured things are beautiful, others ugly;
returning what one owes is both just and unjust in that some token actions
of returning what one owes are just, others unjust. Any sensible property
adduced to explain what it is to be F (at least, for a certain range of predicates) will be both F and not-F, in that it will have some F, and some not-F,
tokens. Here, in contrast to (1) and (2), 'is' is used predicatively, for 'is F'
rather than for 'is true'. One might think that therefore (1) and (2) also use
'is' predicatively; or that Plato is confused about the differences between the
predicative and veridical 'is'. But neither hypothesis is necessary. Plato shifts
from a veridical to a predicative use of 'is'; but he does so without confusion.
There is instead a connecting link between the two uses, as we shall see.

Plato expects the sightlovers to accept (3); he is still speaking in terms
acceptable to them. Indeed, it is because they accept (3) that they deny that
'Beauty is one' (479 A 4). They deny, that is, that beauty is a single property,
the same in all cases; there are, rather, many beautifuls—many different
properties, each of which is the beautiful. In this painting, the beautiful is
bright colour; in that one, it is sombre colour, and so on.

Plato, however, accepts the One over Many assumption: there is just one
property, the F, the same in all cases, in virtue of which all and only F
things are F. If we build this assumption into the argument, then we can
see how Plato finally denies the sightlovers knowledge, and argues that all
knowledge requires knowledge of forms.[13]

The next steps in the argument are:

(4) The sightlovers' beliefs (*nomima*) about the many Fs are and are not
     (479 D 3–5).
(5) Therefore, the sightlovers have belief, not knowledge, about the
     many Fs (479 E 1–5).

Now if Plato were still concerned with the predicative reading of 'is', as
in (3), one might expect him next to say:

(4′) Belief is set over the many Fs, which are F and not-F.

But instead of (4′), Plato says (4). Premiss (4) does not say that the many
Fs are and are not; it says that the sightlovers' *beliefs* (*nomima*) about the
many Fs are and are not.[14] If we are now dealing with beliefs, however,
then we are back at the veridical reading of 'is'. Plato is claiming that the

---

[13] The One over Many assumption, however, might well be thought to violate DR.

[14] *Nomimon* is a general word for anything one can *nomizein*; it also conveys a suggestion
of generality, and of custom or convention. It can be complemented with is-p or with is-v. In

sightlovers' beliefs about the many Fs are and are not true—that is, some of them are true, some of them are false. The sightlovers have some true, and some false, beliefs about beauty; and this is so precisely because they rely on the many Fs, on the many sensible properties. Why should this be so?

Knowledge, Plato has told us, implies truth; it also requires an account (*Meno* 98 A; *Phaedo* 76 B; *Republic* 531 E, 534 B). The sightlovers define beauty, at least in this painting, as, for instance, 'bright colour'. But no such definition can be correct; for some brightly coloured things are ugly, not beautiful. The sightlovers cannot then know what beauty is, since their account of what beauty is—that it is bright colour—is false. Since their account is false, they lack any knowledge of beauty at all; for Plato also believes that one can know something about F only if one knows what F is.[15]

Although the sightlovers thus lack any knowledge about beauty, they have belief, not ignorance, about it. For although beauty should not be defined in terms of bright colour, many brightly coloured things are beautiful; and so, guided by their false definition, they will be led to some true beliefs about beauty, such as that this brightly coloured painting is beautiful. These true beliefs cannot constitute knowledge, since they are not adequately explained; but the fact that the sightlovers have them shows that they are not ignorant about beauty, even if they do not know anything about beauty.

The sightlovers thus have some true beliefs (about what things are beautiful) and some false beliefs (at least about what beauty is). Each of their beliefs is determinately true or false; Plato is not using 'belief' in a special technical sense for 'approximately correct'. Nor is he claiming that everyone who has belief, as opposed to knowledge, has some true, and some false, beliefs. As it happens, the sightlover has some true, and some false, beliefs; but other believers could have all false, or all true, beliefs.

There is, then, a well-argued connecting link between is-v and is-p. The claim is that restricted to the many Fs (is-p), which are F and not-F, one can at best achieve belief (is-v); for accounts phrased in terms of the many Fs (is-p), i.e. in terms of sensibles, will inevitably be false (is-v), thereby depriving one of any knowledge of the matter to hand.

If the sightlovers lack knowledge, then either there is no knowledge, or knowledgeable accounts must be phrased in terms of nonsensible proper-

the former case it generally means something like 'customary rules or laws or conventions'; in the latter case it means something like 'customary beliefs'. That the veridical reading is intended here receives additional support from 508 D 8, where Plato makes a parallel point, using *doxa* (which in context clearly means 'belief') rather than *nomimon*.

[15] This is Plato's Priority of Knowledge of a Definition claim (see e.g. *Meno* 71 B); like the One over Many assumption, it seems controversial.

ties that are not both F and not-F. Plato rejects the first option and so completes the argument as follows (479 E 7–480 A 5):

(6) Knowledge is possible.
(7) There must, then, be nonsensible objects of knowledge.
(8) Therefore, there are forms.
(9) Those who know forms have knowledge; those who are restricted to the many Fs at best have belief.
(10) Therefore knowledge is set over (*epi*) forms, and belief is set over the many Fs (480 A 1).

Conclusion (6) might seem to violate DR; the sightlovers might protest that if they lack knowledge, so does everyone else. The inference to (7) seems to depend on the unstated assumption that knowledge requires the existence of certain sorts of objects.[16]

Is the inference to (8) warranted? That depends on how much we read into the word 'forms'. If (as I believe) the form of F is the nonsensible property of F, which is F and not also not-F, in that it explains the Fness of all and only the F things there are, then (8) is validly inferred. If we take Plato, in (8), to be arguing for forms in some other sense, or for further features of forms than their nonsensible, unitary, and explanatory nature, then the inference to (8) might be unwarranted. But there is no need to assume any other sense, or any further features of forms, in order to understand any part of the argument. If we do not, then (8) is validly inferred.

Conclusion (9) simply summarizes conclusions that have already been validly argued for. (10), however, might seem worrying. For here Plato says that knowledge is set over—not, as we might expect, true propositions, but—forms, certain sorts of objects; and that belief is set over—not, as we might expect, true and false propositions, but—the many Fs. Does not this suggest either that, at this last stage of the argument, Plato falls into an objects analysis and embraces TW; or that he intended an objects analysis all along (in which case, earlier stages of the argument are invalid, and he begins by violating DR)?

---

[16] This is not to play into the hands of the existential interpretation of the argument discussed at the outset. First, no occurrence of 'is' needs to be read as 'exists'; an existential claim is only *tacit* in the argument. (Though the use of is-e is tacit rather than explicit, Aristotle highlights it in his accounts of the theory of forms: cf. the flux arguments recorded in *Metaphysics A* 6, *M* 4, and *M* 9; and the second of the Arguments from the Sciences in the *Peri Ideōn* (Alexander of Aphrodisias, *Commentary on Aristotle's Metaphysics* 79. 8–11 Hayduck).) Second, Plato is not now claiming that knowledge is restricted to what exists—which is what (1) would claim if it were interpreted existentially—but only that knowledge requires the existence of certain sorts of objects This reflects a realist bias about knowledge, but not one that tells in favour of TW.

We need not endorse either option. Plato has explained carefully and in detail what connection he intends between knowledge, truth, and forms, on the one hand; and belief, truth and falsity, and sensibles, on the other. At the close of the argument he offers us an elliptical way of expressing a more complex claim. To say that knowledge is set over forms is shorthand for the claim that all knowledge requires knowledge of forms; to say that belief is set over the many Fs is shorthand for the claim that if one is restricted to sensibles, the most one can achieve is belief.

I have provided an account of Plato's argument on which at least its opening premisses satisfy DR; and on which it is valid and involves no equivocation on 'is'. Though it explicitly uses both is-v and is-p, and tacitly relies on an existential claim at one stage as well, there are systematic, explanatory connections between the different uses, and no crude slides or equivocations.

Nor does the argument commit Plato to TW. He argues only that, to know anything at all, one must know forms; for knowledge requires an account, and it is only by reference to forms that adequate accounts are forthcoming. This leaves open the possibility that once one has these accounts, one can apply them to sensibles in such a way as to know them too. Plato does not—here—explicitly say that knowledge of sensibles is possible. But his argument leaves that possibility open; so too, we shall see, does his account in books VI and VII.

2. *Republic* VI–VII

Republic V distinguishes between knowledge and belief as such; *Republic* VI–VII distinguishes between two sorts of knowledge and two sorts of belief. *Republic* V tells us that knowledge requires knowledge of forms; *Republic* VI–VII adds that the best sort of knowledge requires knowledge of the form of the good. *Republic* V considers knowledge and belief statically: it tells us how they differ, but says nothing about how to improve one's epistemological condition. In the Cave allegory in *Republic* VII, Plato considers knowledge and belief dynamically: he explains how to move from a lower to a higher cognitive condition.

Much of the epistemology of VI–VII is presented in the three famous images of the Sun, Line, and Cave. Plato apologizes for this fact; he resorts to imagery, he tells us, because he lacks any knowledge about the form of the good (506 c), whose epistemological and metaphysical role he now wishes to explain. When one has the best sort of knowledge, he later claims, one can dispense with images and speak more directly and literally (510 B). Though many people are not unnaturally moved by Plato's haunting and beautiful images, it is important to bear in mind that he himself insists that he offers them only because he lacks knowledge; the best sorts of explanations and arguments, in his view, should be couched in more straightforward terms.

The Sun

Plato begins by repeating book V's distinction between the many Fs which are perceivable, and the form of F, which is grasped by thought (507 A 7–B 10). He then likens the form of the good to the sun; as the sun is in the visible world, so is the form of the good in the world of thought (*en tō(i) noētō(i) topō(i)*; *ta nooumena*; 508 B 12–C 2). The sun is the cause (*aitios*)[17] of vision and of the visibility of visible objects: when one looks at visible objects in the light of the sun, one sees them; when one looks at them in the dark (unilluminated by the sun), one cannot see them, at least not well (507 C–508 D). Similarly, the form of the good is the cause of knowledge and of the knowability of knowable objects (*nooumena*).[18] When one thinks about a knowable object illuminated by the form of the good, one knows it best; when one thinks about sensibles unilluminated by the form of the good, one at best has belief about them. The form of the good is also the cause of the being of knowable objects,[19] just as the sun causes objects to come into being and to grow.

[17] *Aitios/aitia* are variously translated as 'cause', 'reason', and 'explanation'. 'Cause' is sometimes thought to be a misleading translation, on the ground that causes are entities productive of change, whereas *aitiai* are not so restricted. For discussion of the connection between *aitiai* and contemporary accounts of causation, see ch. 14. See also G. Vlastos, 'Reasons and Causes in the *Phaedo*', *Philosophical Review*, 78 (1969), 291–325, repr. in G. Vlastos (ed.), *Platonic Studies*, 2nd edn. (Princeton: Princeton University Press, 1981), 76–110; and J. Annas, 'Aristotle on Inefficient Causes', *Philosophical Quarterly*, 32 (1982), 311–26.

[18] It is striking that throughout this passage, Plato uses *nooumena*, rather than 'forms'. Section 507 B 9–10 might seem to suggest that *nooumena* refers just to forms. But it is tempting to believe that he deliberately uses *nooumena* in order to suggest, or at least to leave open the possibility, that more than forms can be known. This suggestion is fortified by the fact that the image part of the Sun (s1 + s2: see below) contrasts two ways of looking at some one sort of entity (visible objects); this suggests that one can have different cognitive attitudes towards a single entity. Perhaps the application part of the Sun (S3 and S4), then, also means to contrast (among other things) two ways of considering sensibles, with knowledge or with mere belief. Even if *nooumena* refers only to forms, TW still does not follow. The point would be that one needs to know the form of the good to have (the best sort of) knowledge about forms. This point does not imply that one can have (the best sort of) knowledge only about forms.

[19] 509 B 7–8 *to einai te kai tēn ousian*. I take *kai* to be epexegetic, and both *to einai* and *tēn ousian* to refer to the being, the essence, of knowable objects.

The Sun presents an image along with its application.[20] The image contrasts two ways of looking at visible objects:

(s1) Sight looks at visible objects in the dark, unilluminated by the sun.
(s2) Sight looks at visible objects illuminated by the sun.

(s1) illustrates (S3), and (s2) illustrates (S4):

(S3) The soul is aware only of sensibles unilluminated by the form of the good (or by other forms), and so has belief.
(S4) The soul considers knowable objects illuminated by the form of the good, and so has (the best sort of) knowledge.

The image (s1 and s2) contrasts two ways of looking at some one sort of entity—visible objects. The application (S3 and S4) contrasts two cognitive conditions, knowledge and belief. They are described in terms familiar from *Republic* V: restricted to sensibles, one can at best achieve belief; in order to know, one must know forms (and, for the best sort of knowledge, one must know the form of the good). As in *Republic* V, Plato does not explicitly mention two further possibilities: (*a*) knowledge of sensibles; and (*b*) belief about forms. Neither, however, does he preclude (*a*) and (*b*). More strongly, he seems to believe they are possible. For as we have seen, he introduces the Sun image by claiming to have only belief about, and no knowledge of, the form of the good (506 E); and he says that the philosopher who returns to the cave knows sensibles (520 C 2).[21]

Although the Sun distinguishes between the same two conditions as *Republic* V, it adds to *Republic* V the claim that the best sort of knowledge requires knowledge of the form of the good (505 A, 508 A 5).[22]

Plato seems to believe this new claim because he seems to believe that the form of the good is both a formal and a final cause of every knowable object. That is, it is part of the essence of every knowable object, and in some

[20] I follow T. H. Irwin, *Plato's Moral Theory* (Oxford: Clarendon Press, 1977), 334 n. 43, in using initial small letters (e.g. 's1', 'c1') for states which illustrate other states, and initial capital letters (e.g. 'S3', 'L1') for the states illustrated; and in using 'Sun' etc. for the name of the image, and 'sun' etc. for the entities mentioned in the images. My account of the Sun, Line, and Cave is indebted to his in more substantial ways as well: see his ch. 7, §§ 13–14.

[21] Moreover, (*a*) may be tacitly included in (S4), if I am right to suggest that *nooumena* may be used more broadly than for forms; see n. 18.

[22] Sometimes Plato seems to suggest instead that all knowledge—not just the best sort of knowledge—requires knowledge of the form of the good: see e.g. 507 D 11–E 2, 508 E 3. On the interpretation assumed in the text, the Sun fits better with the Line; and Plato makes it plain that he takes the Line to be elaborating the Sun (509 D 1–510 A 3). Perhaps the unclarity arises partly because Plato has not yet explicitly distinguished between the two sorts of knowledge.

sense what knowable objects are for. Since knowledge of a thing requires knowing its causes, full knowledge of anything requires knowing the form of the good.

It is easy to see why Plato should believe that the form of the good is the formal and final cause of the virtue forms. A full account of any virtue—of justice or temperance, for instance—will explain its point, what is valuable or choiceworthy about it; and that is to explain its contribution to, its relation to, the form of the good.

But Plato also believes that the form of the good is the formal and final cause of all knowable objects, not just of the virtue forms. We can best understand why if we turn for the moment to Plato's puzzling claim that the form of the good is in some way greater or more important than other knowable objects (504 c 9–e 3, 509 b 6–10), even though, unlike other forms, it is not an *ousia*, a being (509 b 9–10). Usually, to call something an *ousia* is to accord it special importance. One might then expect Plato to claim that the form of the good is the most important *ousia* of all; instead he claims that it is not an *ousia* at all.

The best explanation of this puzzling claim is that the form of the good is not a distinct form, but the teleological structure of things; individual forms are its parts, and particular sensible objects instantiate it.[23] Just as Aristotle insists that the form of a house, for example, is not another element alongside the bricks and mortar, but the organization of the matter, so Plato views the form of the good as the teleological organization of things. If we so view the form of the good, we can explain why Plato claims both that the form of the good is more important than other knowable objects, and also that it is not an *ousia*.

This view also helps to explain why Plato believes that full knowledge of a thing requires knowing its relation to the form of the good. Consider forms first. To know a form's relation to the form of the good is to know its place in the teleological system of which it is a part. Each form is good in that it has the function of playing a certain role in that system; its goodness consists in its contribution to that structure, to the richness and harmonious ordering of the structure, and its having that place in the system is part of what it is. Plato believes, then, that each form is essentially a good thing— not morally good, but, simply, good—in that it is part of what each form is that it should have a certain place in the teleological structure of the world.

A similar account explains why knowledge of the form of the good is also

---

[23] For this view, see esp. H. W. B. Joseph, *Knowledge and the Good in Plato's* Republic (Oxford: Clarendon Press, 1948), in particular ch. 3; J. C. B. Gosling, *Plato* (London: Routledge & Kegan Paul, 1973), 57–71; and Irwin, *Plato's Moral Theory*, 225.

necessary for fully knowing sensible objects. In the later *Timaeus* Plato explains that the sensible world was created by the demiurge (27 D ff.). Since the demiurge is good, he wanted the world to be as good as possible; hence he tried to instantiate the form of the good (and so the teleological structure of forms generally) as widely as possible. Fully to understand his creations, then, we need to refer to the form of the good which they instantiate.[24]

All of this embodies a crucial point to which we shall recur: Plato is a holist about knowledge. Full knowledge of anything requires knowing its place in the system of which it is a part, or which it instantiates; we do not know things in the best way if we know them only in isolation from one another.[25]

The Line and Cave

Plato introduces the image of the Divided Line in order to elaborate the application part of the Sun image (S3 and S4). He tells us to divide each of the Sun's two conditions—knowledge and belief—into two (509 D 6),[26] thus yielding two kinds of belief and two kinds of knowledge. The two sorts of belief—corresponding to the two lower stages of the line (L1 and L2)—are *eikasia* (imagination) and *pistis* (confidence). The two sorts of knowledge—corresponding to the higher stages of the line (L3 and L4)—are *dianoia* (thought) and *nous* (knowledge or understanding).[27]

Plato initially explains each stage of the line by means of illustrative examples. L1 is explained in terms of images of physical objects, L2 in terms of physical objects. At L3 one uses hypotheses, and the sensible objects imaged

[24] I discuss Plato on teleology in somewhat more detail, though still briefly, in ch. 14 below.
[25] It is often agreed that Plato endorses a holist conception of knowledge in various later dialogues; but some believe that that represents a change of view from an earlier atomism. See e.g. G. E. L. Owen, 'Notes on Ryle's Plato', in O. P. Wood and G. Pitcher (eds.), *Ryle: A Collection of Critical Essays* (London: Macmillan, 1971), 341–72, repr. in G. Fine (ed.), *Plato 1: Metaphysics and Epistemology* (Oxford: Oxford University Press, 1999), 298–319. On the account I propose, Plato is a holist in the *Republic* no less than in later dialogues. See ch. 10 below, and the Introduction.
[26] Plato may tell us to divide the line into two unequal parts; but the text is uncertain. If the inequality claim is made, the two likeliest explanations seem to be that (*a*) the belief part is bigger, because more people have belief; or (*b*) the knowledge part is bigger, because knowledge is more valuable.
[27] Plato's terminology is not fixed. At 510 A 9, L3 + L4 are collectively called *to gnōston*; at 511 A 3, B 3 they are collectively called *to noēton* (cf. 533 E 8–534 A). When *to noēton* is used for L3 + L4 collectively, *epistēmē* is sometimes used for L4 (cf. 533 E 2). Nothing should be made of these terminological variations; Plato tells us (533 D 7–E 2) not to dispute about the use of words.

in L1 are in their turn used as images of forms; mathematical reasoning is offered as a characteristic example. At L4 one uses dialectic (511 B, 533 C) in order to 'remove' or 'destroy' (533 C 8) the hypotheses of L3—not by proving them false, but by explaining them in terms of an unhypothetical first principle so that they cease to be mere hypotheses. Although Plato does not say so explicitly, this first principle is plainly the form of the good (or a definition of, and perhaps further propositions about, it).[28] At L4 one also reasons directly about forms without, as in L3, relying on sensible images of them.

Whereas the Line corresponds to the application part of the Sun, the Cave corresponds to its image part (s1 and s2), dividing each of its two parts into two (c1–4). It is an allegory, designed primarily to explain ways of moral reasoning (514 A). Plato begins with a haunting description of prisoners who have been bound since birth so that all they have ever seen are shadows on a cave wall—shadows of artificial objects illuminated by a fire internal to the cave (c1). Strange though the image is, Plato insists that the prisoners are 'like us' (515 A 5). Plato then imagines one of these prisoners being released,[29] so that he can see not only the shadows but also the artificial objects that cast the shadows. When asked to say what each of the artificial objects is, he is at first confused, and thinks the shadows are 'more real' than the objects. Eventually, though, he is able to discriminate systematically between the shadows and the objects, and to see that the latter are 'more real' (c2). He learns to distinguish between the appearance or image of an object and the object, between appearance and reality.

Next the prisoner is led out of the cave. At first he sees only shadows of natural objects, then the natural objects themselves (c3), and finally the sun (c4). He learns to distinguish between appearance and reality outside the cave, just as he previously learnt to distinguish between them inside the cave.

Each of Plato's three images is distinctively different from the others. The Sun describes both image and application; the Line explains the application further, while the Cave explains the image further. The Line is illustrated

---

[28] Like Aristotle, Plato speaks of both propositional and nonpropositional entities as being principles; I shall follow their lead. This double usage involves no confusion. One explains, or justifies one's belief in, a proposition by appealing to other propositions; but these propositions refer to, are about, various sorts of entities, which are explanatory factors one can know.

[29] I assume Plato uses the singular in order to suggest that very few people will ever undergo the transformation he describes (although he seems to believe that everyone could in principle undergo it). I hope it is not too obvious to be worth saying that Plato's picture of the release of the prisoner is an early illustration of the biblical saying 'the truth will set you free'—except that Plato believes that even the prisoners (us) can have by and large true beliefs; what the Cave really illustrates is rather the thesis that 'knowledge will set you free'.

with literal examples of its cognitive conditions; the Cave is an allegory primarily about ways of moral reasoning. The Sun and Line (like *Republic* V) describe conditions statically; the Cave explains them dynamically. Each image offers details not to be found in the others; if we interpret them in the light of one another, we can achieve a better grasp of their underlying thought than if we consider each on its own.[30]

Plato, then, distinguishes between two sorts of belief—imagination (L1) and confidence (L2)—and between two sorts of knowledge—thought (L3) and understanding (L4). One familiar way of explaining the differences between these conditions relies on an *objects analysis*: each condition is individuated by reference to its unique sort of object. Just as some argue that in *Republic* V there is belief only about sensibles and knowledge only of forms, so some argue that in *Republic* VI–VII each cognitive condition has its own unique objects. On this view, one is in a belief state (L1 or L2), for instance, if and only if one is confronted with a certain sort of sensible object (images are the usual candidates for L1, and ordinary physical objects for L2). As in *Republic* V, an objects analysis goes naturally with TW.[31]

Just as I rejected an objects analysis of *Republic* V, so I shall reject one of *Republic* VI–VII, defending again a *contents analysis*. On the contents analysis, L1–L4 are individuated, not by their unique objects (no state has unique objects), but by their distinctive sorts of reasoning (by their cognitive content). What state one is in is determined by the sort of reasoning one engages in, whatever sort of object it is about. To be sure, as in *Republic* V, one needs to know forms to know anything at all. Hence in a way, objects are relevant to determining cognitive level; but as we shall see, they are not relevant in a way congenial to TW.

L1: Imagination

Plato's initial characterization of L1 is quite brief. He says only that 'one section of the visible world [is] images. By images I mean, first, shadows, and then reflections in water and on surfaces of dense, smooth, and bright

---

[30] Plato plainly means there to be some correspondence between the three images; at 517 B, having completed his initial account of the Cave, he tells us to apply that account 'as a whole to all that has been said', i.e. to the Sun and Line. He supplies a brief account of how to do this; but different commentators carry out his directions in different ways, and not everyone would agree with the connections I have claimed obtain. Nor would everyone agree with the account I have provided of the intrinsic nature of each image.

[31] At least, most objects analyses preclude knowledge of sensibles. However, some allow knowledge of more than forms. For it is sometimes thought that L3 is correlated with special mathematical entities that are not forms but which one can know. See n. 35.

texture, and everything of that kind' (509 E 1–510 A 3). Similarly, at c1 the prisoners are bound, and have always been so, so that all that they have ever seen are shadows of artificial objects.

Plato might seem to be suggesting that one is at L1 if and only if one is confronted with an image of a sensible object—just as the objects analysis would have it. But if so, various difficulties arise. First, most of us don't spend much time looking at images and reflections of physical objects;[32] nor will most people in the ideal city do so. Yet Plato says that most of us are at L1 (515 A 5); and that most people in the ideal city would be too (517 D 4–E 2, 520 C 1–D 1).

Second, contrary to the objects interpretation, looking at images doesn't seem to be either necessary or sufficient for being at L1. It's not necessary because the prisoner who is released in the cave and then looks at the artificial objects (not just at their images) is at first confused; he is still at L1, even though he is confronted with an object, not just with its image. It's not sufficient because, as we noted before, Plato says that the philosopher who returns to the cave will know the images there (520 c); he does not lapse back into L1 when he looks at images.

We can avoid these difficulties if we turn to the contents analysis—and also understand the nature of and interconnections between Plato's three images in the way I have suggested.

The prisoners are at L1 about physical objects not because they see, are confronted only with, images of physical objects, but because they cannot systematically discriminate between images and the objects they are of. Even if they were confronted with a physical object, they would remain at L1, so long as they could not systematically discriminate between images and their objects, and could not tell that the objects, are 'more real' than the images, in that they cause the images. They are at L1, not because of the objects they are confronted with, but because of the ways in which they reason about them. Similarly, the philosopher who returns to the cave does not lapse back into L1 about images. For he, unlike the prisoners, can systematically discriminate between objects and their images; he knows that the images are mere images, caused and explained by the physical objects. One is at L1 about physical objects, then, not just in case one is confronted only

---

[32] Contrast N. P White, *A Companion to Plato's* Republic (Indianapolis: Hackett, 1979), 185–6, who argues, on the basis of book X, that most of us do, in Plato's view, spend a great deal of time looking at images of sensible objects, in that we focus only on aspects or appearances of objects, without, for example, correcting for the effects of perspective. It is also sometimes suggested that we are restricted to appearances of objects in that we are restricted to their surface features (e.g. their colour and macroscopic size) and do not know their inner structure (e.g. their atomic constitution).

with images of physical objects, but just in case one cannot systematically discriminate between physical objects and images of them.

Moreover, one can be at L1 in other areas. When Plato says that most of us are like the prisoners (are at L1), he does not mean that most of us literally see only images of physical objects. He means that our moral beliefs are relevantly like the prisoners' beliefs about physical objects; we are at L1 in our moral beliefs (not in our physical-object beliefs), just as they are at L1 about their physical-object beliefs. Thus, for instance, he talks about people who 'fight one another for shadows and wrangle for office as if it were a great good' (520 c 7–d 1)—about people, that is, who take seeming goods to be real goods, and lesser goods to be greater goods than they are. Or again, at 517 d–e Plato speaks about contending 'about the shadows of justice'—about, that is, ordinary, unreflective beliefs about justice (cf. 493 a 6–c 8, 515 b 4–c 2). We uncritically accept what seems just or good as being really just or good.[33]

To be sure, the Line (unlike the Cave) is not an allegory. It describes literal examples of cognitive conditions—but they are only illustrative, not exhaustive, examples. The Line illustrates L1 reasoning about physical objects; but one can be at L1 in other areas, e.g. about morality. Plato does not believe we are at L1 about physical objects (so he illustrates L1 with an example that is not characteristic of us); but we are at L1 in our moral reasoning.

Objects are relevant to the line in a way, then: if one cannot make certain sorts of distinctions between kinds of objects, the most one can achieve is a certain level of understanding about those sorts of objects. This, however, plainly allows one to have different cognitive attitudes to the same sorts of object. L1, then, when properly understood, does not suggest an objects analysis or TW.

L2: Confidence

The prisoners advance to L2 when they are released from their bonds and gradually learn to distinguish between the images and the objects they are of. This represents the first application of elenchus or dialectic. At first the prisoners believe they know that the images exhaust the whole of reality. Then, when they are exposed to the objects the shadows are of, and are asked to say what those objects are, they become confused and frustrated; they

---

[33] Many of our moral beliefs are not only unreflective, but also false. What is crucial about L1, however, is not that one's beliefs are false, but that they are accepted uncritically. Even in Plato's ideally just city, most people will be at L1, even though their beliefs are by and large true (517 d 4–e 2, 520 c 1–d 1).

are at a loss. In just the same way, interlocutors in the Socratic dialogues at first believe they know the answers to Socrates' 'What is F?' questions; when cross-examined, they too are quickly at a loss. Most of the Socratic dialogues end at this aporetic stage—and so it is sometimes concluded that the elenchus is purely negative and destructive (or at best plays the modest positive role of getting people to recognize their own ignorance). Here, however, the elenchus is carried further—and so Plato shows how the Socratic elenchus can enable one to move beyond aporia to better-based beliefs (and, in L3 and L4, to knowledge). For the released prisoner gradually learns to discriminate between images and their objects; his beliefs become more reliable. Similarly, in the *Meno* the elenchus with Meno's slave advances beyond aporia, until the slave improves his beliefs. Like the prisoner, he moves from L1 to L2, from *eikasia* to *pistis*—though in his case, of course, about a mathematical, not about a moral, belief: he (like most of us, in Plato's view) remains at L1 about morality. Because he cannot give a satisfactory account, an *aitias logismos* of the sort necessary for knowledge (98 A), however, he remains at a belief state, though at a better one than he was in before.[34] Perhaps the Socrates of the Socratic dialogues would place himself at L2 about morality. He disclaims knowledge about morality, but clearly believes he is in some way better off in his moral reasoning than his interlocutors are; the difference between L1 and L2 allows us to see how this could be so. His ability to make certain sorts of systematically correct discriminations puts him in a better epistemic position than his interlocutors, even though he (believes he) lacks knowledge.

Just as L1 does not support an objects analysis, neither does L2. Plato does not mean that one is at L2 if and only if one is confronted with a physical object. He rather means that one is at L2 *about physical objects* if one can systematically discriminate between physical objects and images of them, but cannot explain their difference. This, however, allows one to be at L2 about physical objects even if one is not confronted with a physical object. Further, one can be at L2 in other areas—so long as one's reasoning is relevantly like the prisoner's reasoning about physical objects when he has reached L2.

L3: Thought

One moves from L2 to L3—from a kind of belief to a kind of knowledge—when one emerges from the cave, from a preoccupation with sensibles, and

---

[34] Though Plato adds (*Meno* 85 C) that if the slave continues practising the elenchus, he *will* eventually reach knowledge. This claim is not further explained or defended in the *Meno*; but it is illustrated in the Cave, in showing how elenchus, dialectic, enables us to move not only from L1 to L2, but also from L2 to L3 and L4.

turns one's attention to nonsensibles, i.e. to forms. As in *Republic* V, here too one needs to be suitably aware of forms in order to have any knowledge at all (although—again as in *Republic* V—it does not follow that knowledge is restricted to knowledge of forms).

Plato initially distinguishes L3 from L4 as follows:

in one section [L3], the soul is compelled to inquire [*a*] by using as images the things imitated before [at L2], and [*b*] from hypotheses, proceeding not to a first principle but to a conclusion; in the other [L4], it [*b*] advances from a hypothesis to an unhypothetical first principle, [*a*] without the images used by the other section, by means of forms themselves, progressing methodically through them. (510 B 4–9; cf 511 A3–C 2)

When Glaucon professes not to understand this very abstract account, Socrates provides a mathematical illustration of L3:

students of geometry, calculation, and such studies hypothesize the odd and the even and shapes and three kinds of angles and other things akin to these in each branch of study, regarding them as known; they make their hypotheses, and do not think it worth while to give any further [*eti*] account of them to themselves or to others, thinking they are obvious to everyone. Beginning from these, and going through the remaining steps, they reach a conclusion agreeing [*homologoumenōs*] [with the premises] on the topic they set out to examine. (510 C 2–D 3)

He adds:

They also use the visible forms, and make their arguments [*logos*] about them, although they are not thinking [*dianooumenoi*] of them, but of those things they are like, making their arguments for the sake of the square itself and the diagonal itself (510 D 5–8)

Plato cites two key differences between L3 and L4: (*a*) at L3 one uses sensibles as images of forms, although one is thinking of forms, not of sensibles; at L4 one thinks of forms directly, not through images of them; (*b*) at L3 one proceeds from a hypothesis to various conclusions; at L4 one proceeds from a hypothesis to an unhypothetical first principle (510 B)— that is, to (a definition of, and perhaps also further propositions about) the form of the good.

L3 poses a threat for the objects analysis. For Plato makes it plain that the square itself etc. can be known in both an L3- and an L4-type way (511 D); contrary to the objects analysis, then, the same objects appear at two distinct stages of the line.[35] Moreover, L3 uses sensibles as images of forms; but

---

[35] There is dispute about whether 'the square itself' etc. (510 D) are forms; I assume they

sensibles are also in some way correlated with L2. So just as mathematical entities appear at both L3 and L4, so sensibles appear at both L2 and L3.[36]

Although Plato provides a geometrical illustration of L3, L3 is not restricted to geometry or even to mathematical disciplines more generally; any reasoning that satisfies the more general features (*a*) and (*b*) belongs at L3. Indeed, it seems reasonable to suggest that although Socrates (in the Socratic dialogues and *Meno*) places himself at L2 in his moral reasoning, Plato in the *Republic* places himself at L3.[37]

The *Republic* is peppered with images used self-consciously to illustrate something about forms: the Sun, Line, and Cave are cases in point. Similarly, Plato partially explains the nature of justice in the soul through the analogies of health and of justice in the city; he uses the analogy of the ship to illustrate the nature of democracy, and so on. So the *Republic*'s moral reasoning satisfies (*a*).

It also satisfies (*b*). Plato claims that the account of the virtues in book IV is a mere outline that requires a longer way (435 D, 504 C 9–E 3). That longer way involves relating the virtues to the form of the good (a task not undertaken in book IV); and (a definition of) the form of the good is the unhypothetical principle one advances to when one moves from L3 to L4. Similarly, Plato offered accounts of the virtues, and justified them in terms of their explanatory power; but the accounts were partial, and not justified in terms of anything more fundamental.[38]

---

are, but others take them to be mathematical entities that are distinct from forms. For some discussion of this matter, see J. Annas, 'On the Intermediates', *Archiv für Geschichte der Philosophie*, 57 (1975), 146–66; A. Wedberg, *Plato's Philosophy of Mathematics* (Stockholm: Almquist & Wiskell, 1955), ch. 3, and 'The Theory of Ideas', in G. Vlastos (ed.), *Plato*, i. *Metaphysics and Epistemology* (Garden City, NY: Doubleday Anchor, 1971), 28–52, esp. app. D. The difficulty I pose for the objects analysis arises whether or not they are forms; for the crucial point is that, whatever they are, they can be known in both an L3- and an L4-type way.

[36] Moreover, if Plato, in saying that L3 uses sensibles, means to suggest that sensibles can be objects of L3 as well as of L2 epistemic attitudes, then, contrary to TW, Plato explicitly allows one to have at least L3-type knowledge of sensibles. Even if, in saying that L3 uses sensibles, Plato does not mean to say thereby that sensibles can be known in at least an L3-type way, we shall see that he none the less leaves open the possibility that one can have L3- (and L4-)type knowledge of sensibles.

[37] For this suggestion, see also D. Gallop, 'Image and Reality in Plato's *Republic*', *Archiv für Geschichte der Philosophie*, 47 (1965), 113–31; 'Dreaming and Waking in Plato', in J. E. Anton and G. L. Kustas (eds.), *Essays in Ancient Greek Philosophy* (Albany, NY: State University of New York Press, 1971), 187–220; and Irwin, *Plato's Moral Theory*, 222–3.

[38] Cf. the account of the hypothetical method in *Phaedo* 100 ff. (which is plainly not restricted to mathematical reasoning), which the account of L3 clearly recalls. Plato's account of L3 also recalls the *Meno*. There too Plato uses a geometrical example to illustrate a point about our capacity for reaching moral knowledge; he again uses diagrams, but in order to make a point about nonsensibles (diagonals); he insists that in a dialectical, as opposed to

Plato is often said to favour a mathematical model of knowledge. He does, to be sure, count mathematics as a type of knowledge; and mathematical studies play an extremely important role in the philosophers' education. But he places mathematics at L3—it is the lower form of knowledge. Moreover, it is just one example of L3-type reasoning—Plato's moral reasoning in the *Republic* is another example of it. Further, the higher type of knowledge—L4—is not mathematical but dialectical.

Nor does Plato praise mathematics for the reasons one might expect. To be sure, he emphasizes its value in getting us to turn from 'becoming to truth and being' (525 c), that is, in getting us to acknowledge forms. But he adds in the same breath, as though it is of equal importance, that mathematics is also of value in the practical matter of waging war (525 b–c; cf. 522 e, 526 d). Nor does he praise mathematics for using necessary truths or for conferring some special sort of certainty. On the contrary, he believes that even if mathematical truths are necessary, they cannot be fully known until they, like all other truths, are suitably related to the form of the good. Mathematics is not invoked as a paradigm of a discipline consisting of self-evident truths standing in need of no further justification or explanation.[39] Moreover, although mathematical reasoning may be deductive, L3 is not restricted to deductive reasoning; it includes other ways of explaining the less general in terms of the more general. Platonic moral argument, for instance, also belongs at L3, although it is not deductive in character.

It can appear puzzling that Plato counts L3 even as an inferior type of knowledge. To see why, I first need to say a bit more about what he thinks knowledge in general involves.

We have seen that Plato believes that in addition to true belief knowledge requires an account or *logos* (*Meno* 98 a; *Phaedo* 76 b; *Republic* 531 e, 534 b). Call this KL.

It is tempting to infer that Plato is offering a version of the justified-true-belief account of knowledge; and many have succumbed to the temptation.[40] Recently, however, some have argued that the temptation ought to

---

eristic, context, one should use claims the interlocutor agrees he knows (75 d), just as here he says that the mathematicians assume that their hypotheses are obvious to everyone; and, of course, he again uses the hypothetical method.

[39] For an interesting and provocative discussion of this matter, see C. C. W. Taylor, 'Plato and the Mathematicians: An Examination of Professor Hare's Views', *Philosophical Quarterly*, 17 (1967), 193–203 at 202–3.

[40] See e.g. R. Chisholm, *Theory of Knowledge* (Englewood Cliffs, NJ: Prentice Hall, 1966), 5–7; Armstrong, *Belief, Truth and Knowledge*, 137; and ch. 10 below.

be resisted.[41] For, it is argued, KL requires, not a *justification* for believing that something is so, but an *explanation* of why it is so.[42]

I agree that the sort of account Plato at least typically has in mind is an explanation. Often, for instance, he speaks, not of knowing propositions but of knowing things. To know a thing, he believes, usually involves being able to say what it is, in the sense of articulating its nature or essence; doing this explains what the entity in question is. Even when Plato speaks instead of knowing a proposition, the sort of account he generally has in mind is an explanation of why it is so; sometimes this involves proving it, or explaining the natures of any entities it mentions.

But though Platonic accounts are typically explanations, we should not infer that he therefore rejects or bypasses a justified-true-belief account of knowledge. His view is rather that justification typically consists in, or at least requires, explanation. For Plato, I am typically justified in believing p only if I can explain why p is so; I am typically justified in claiming to know some object only if I can explain its nature or essence.

In addition to KL, Plato also believes that knowledge must be based on knowledge (KBK): I know a thing or proposition only if I can provide an account of it which I also know. Stating an account of something is not sufficient for knowing it; in addition, I must know the account.[43]

The conjunction of KL and KBK raises the threat of the famous regress of justification: to know something, I must, given KL, provide an account of it. Given KBK, I must know this account. Given KL, I must then provide an account of it which, given KBK, I must also know—and so on, it seems, *ad infinitum.* Plato discusses this regress in some detail in the *Theaetetus;* but it is lurking not far below the surface here as well.[44]

---

[41] See esp. M. F. Burnyeat, 'Aristotle on Understanding Knowledge', in E. Berti (ed.), *Aristotle on Science: The* Posterior Analytics (Padua: Editrice Antenore, 1981), 97–139, esp. 134–5; and 'Socrates and the Jury: Paradoxes in Plato's Distinction between Knowledge and True Belief', *Proceedings of the Aristotelian Society,* suppl. 54 (1980), 173–91. We have seen before that if Plato accepts TW, that too precludes a justified-true-belief account of knowledge since, on TW, knowledge precludes belief. At the moment, however, I am concerned with a different challenge to attributing a justified-true-belief account of knowledge to Plato.

[42] This is also sometimes used as part of an argument for the claim that Plato is not so much concerned with knowledge as with understanding. I consider this argument briefly below, in discussing L4.

[43] KBK is most explicitly discussed and defended in the later *Theaetetus;* but *Republic* 533 c (quoted and discussed below) may endorse it as well.

[44] I discuss the regress as it emerges in the *Theaetetus* in ch. 10. I argue there that Plato avoids the infinite regress by allowing justifications to be circular, if the circle is sufficiently large and explanatory. As we shall see, this is also the resolution I believe Plato favours in the *Republic.* In this respect as in others, Plato's epistemology remains relatively constant, whatever the fate of the theory of forms.

Plato also believes, as we know from *Republic* V, that if one knows anything at all, one knows forms.

Can one satisfy these three conditions for knowledge—KL, KBK, and knowing forms—within the confines of L3? And if so, how does Plato respond to the regress KL and KBK seem to give rise to? I begin by looking at KL and KBK in the abstract; I leave until later the question of whether everyone at L3 provides accounts of forms.

Plato says that at L3 one offers hypotheses, which are then used in order to derive various conclusions. Are the hypotheses or the conclusions known at L3? At 510 c 7 Plato says that mathematicians offer hypotheses without giving any further (*eti*) account of them. Later he says that mathematicians can't 'see [forms] clearly so long as they leave their hypotheses undisturbed and cannot give an account of them. For if one does not know [*oide*] the starting point [*archē*], and the conclusion and intervening steps are woven together from what one does not know [*oide*], how ever could this sort of agreement [*homologia*] be knowledge [*epistēmē*]?' (533 c 1–5). Both passages may seem to suggest that KL cannot be satisfied for the hypotheses at L3. But if KL is not satisfied for the hypotheses at L3, then the hypotheses are not known at L3, since KL is a necessary condition for knowledge. Moreover, if KL is not satisfied, then neither is KBK; for one certifies that one knows something by producing an account of it.

KL might be satisfied in the case of the conclusions. For the hypotheses and proofs used to derive the conclusions might reasonably be thought to constitute an account of—an explanation of, and so an adequate justification for believing—them. But if the hypotheses are not themselves known, then KBK seems to be violated in the case of the conclusions; and so, since KBK is also a necessary condition for knowledge, the conclusions seem not to be known either.

It is thus initially unclear why Plato counts L3 as a type of knowledge. For KL, and so KBK, seem to be violated for the hypotheses; and at least KBK seems to be violated for the conclusions.

I suggest the following resolution of this difficulty. In saying that no (further) account of the hypotheses is given at L3, Plato does not mean that KL cannot be satisfied for them at L3. He only means, first, that no account can be given of them at L3 in terms of something more fundamental, such as the form of the good; and, second, that at L3 they are used in an enquiry, in order to derive various results, before their assumption has been justified. The mathematician says, for instance, 'Let a triangle be a plane figure enclosed by three straight lines', and then goes on to derive various conclusions about triangles, without first giving us any reason to accept his account of a triangle.

None of this, however, precludes the possibility of justifying the hypotheses *in the course of* the enquiry. And it is clear how this can be done. For in using them in order to reach various results, one displays their explanatory power, shows what results one is able to achieve by using them; and showing this is one way of providing an account. In just the same way, scientists often offer speculative hypotheses, which become confirmed when they are shown to explain some variety of phenomena. One can, then, even within the confines of L3, satisfy KL for the hypotheses.

Does one then know the hypotheses? Only if KBK is also satisfied. For KBK to be satisfied, however, the conclusions must be known, for the hypotheses are justified in terms of the conclusions. But we said before that the conclusions might not be known because, although KL seemed satisfied in their case, KBK was not, because the hypotheses were not known. We seem locked in a vicious circle: we can provide accounts of the hypotheses in terms of the conclusions, and of the conclusions in terms of the hypotheses; but we do not yet seem to have reached anything that is known.

But though there is a circle here, it is not a vicious one. The hypotheses are justified in terms of the conclusions, and the conclusions in terms of the hypotheses. In providing these mutually supporting accounts, one comes to know both hypotheses and conclusions. One does not *first* know the hypotheses, and *then* the conclusions; one comes to know both simultaneously, in seeing how well the hypotheses explain the conclusions. Instead of a vicious circle, there are mutually supporting, interlocking claims.

I suggest, then, that both KL and KBK can be satisfied for conclusions and hypotheses alike, within the confines of L3. One satisfies KL for the hypotheses by appealing to their explanatory power; and one satisfies KL for the conclusions by deriving them from the hypotheses. In thus denying the conclusions, and seeing how well the whole resultant system fits together, one acquires knowledge of both conclusions and hypotheses, and so satisfies KBK for both as well.

Now I said before that the conjunction of KL and KBK threatens a regress: to know p, I must know q; to know q, I must know r, and so on, it seems, *ad infinitum,* There are many different responses to the regress but two of the most popular are *foundationalism* and *coherentism.* Foundationalism claims that the regress halts with basic beliefs that are not themselves justified in terms of any further beliefs; they are self-justified, or self-evident. Coherentism claims that the regress is finite but has no end; accounts can circle back on themselves. I explain p in terms of q, and q in terms of r, and so on until, eventually, I appeal again to p; but if the circle is sufficiently large and explanatory, then it is virtuous, not vicious.[45]

Plato has typically been counted a foundationalist. At least for L3, however, he seems to be a coherentist. For he counts L3 as a type of knowledge, and so believes that KL and KBK are satisfied at L3. But the best explanation of how this could be so appeals to circular accounts, in the way I have suggested.

One might argue that the passage cited above from 533 c (cf. *Cratylus* 436 c–d) shows that Plato rejects coherentism,[46] but it does not. The passage does seem to commit Plato to KBK; if one does not know the starting point, neither does one know the conclusions derived from it, because knowledge must be based on knowledge. That, however, does not show that one cannot come to know the starting point through deriving conclusions from it, and then come to know the conclusions by deriving them from the starting point. The passage may also suggest that consistency or agreement is insufficient for knowledge; but any self-respecting coherentist would agree. For, first, the relevant sort of coherence involves more than consistency or agreement; in addition, the consistent beliefs must be mutually supporting and explanatory, and form a sufficiently large group. And, second, not even such coherence is sufficient for knowledge, but only for justification; knowledge also requires truth.

I have suggested that if Plato is a coherentist about justification, at least for L3, then both KL and KBK can be satisfied at L3, for hypotheses and conclusions alike. One further problem remains, however. If L3 is a type of knowledge, then at L3 one must know forms. Now Plato (who seems to place himself at L3 in his moral reasoning) seems to believe that he has at least partial knowledge of some forms; so at least one person he places at L3 knows some forms. But he also places the mathematicians at L3 about mathematics; yet it may seem unclear that they know mathematical—or any—forms. At least, it seems unlikely that mathematicians explicitly recognize forms at all; there are no entities in their ontology that they call 'forms'. If they do not explicitly admit forms into their ontology, is it appropriate to say that they know forms?

---

[45] There are, of course, many different versions of foundationalism and coherentism. Not all foundationalists, for example, require self-evident beliefs, as opposed to, for example, initial warrant or credibility. Those who view Plato as a foundationalist, however, typically believe that his version invokes self-evident beliefs. For one good recent defence of coherentism about justification, see L. Bonjour, *The Structure of Empirical Knowledge* (Cambridge, Mass.: Harvard University Press, 1985), pt. 2, esp. chs. 5 and 7.

[46] See e.g. N. P White, *Plato and Knowledge and Reality* (Indianapolis: Hackett, 1976), 113 n. 50.

This problem too can be resolved. The mathematicians offer hypotheses. These hypotheses include accounts, or partial accounts, of, for example, the square itself;[47] and the square itself etc. are forms. So the mathematicians offer accounts of forms. To be sure, they do not know that the entities they are defining are forms. It does not follow, however, that they do not know the entities they are defining; it follows only that there are some facts about these entities that they do not know. But one can know an object even if one does not know everything about it. And Plato makes it plain that mathematicians know some crucial facts about the entities they define. Not only do they offer hypotheses, partial definitions of them. But they also know, for instance, 'that the unit should never appear to be many parts and not to be one' (525 E)—the one the mathematician is concerned with is one, and not also not one; it does not suffer compresence of opposites. They may also know that mathematical entities are nonsensible (e.g. 511 D, 525 D–E, 526 A 1–7). Perhaps this shows that mathematicians treat mathematical entities *as* forms, even though they do not recognize that that is what they are doing.

None the less, if one can know a form without knowing that what one knows is a form, then the conditions for knowing forms might seem weaker here than they did in *Republic* V. At least, the philosopher described there seems explicitly to countenance forms in a way mathematicians do not. Still, perhaps that is only sufficient, and not also necessary, for knowledge. Mathematicians still differ significantly from anyone at L1 or L2. For such people do not have any *de dicto* beliefs about forms (although they may of course have some *de re* beliefs about them); but mathematicians do have some *de dicto* beliefs about forms, as expressed in their hypotheses, even if they lack the *de dicto* belief that what they are defining is a form.

L4: Understanding

At L4 one reaches an unhypothetical first principle, (a definition of, and perhaps further propositions about) the form of the good. When one can suitably relate the hypotheses of L3 to the form of the good, the hypotheses are removed or destroyed (533 C 8)—that is, they cease to be mere hypotheses, they lose their hypothetical status and become known in an L4-type way (511 D) and not merely, as before, in an L3-type way. Moreover, at L4 one no longer uses sensibles but only forms.

In saying that at L4 one no longer uses sensibles, Plato does not mean that there is no L4-type knowledge of sensibles. He means only that at

---

[47] This is sometimes disputed; but for a good defence of the claim, see Taylor, 'Plato and the Mathematicians'.

L4 one no longer needs to explain the nature of forms through images of them; one can speak of them directly, as they are in and of themselves. But once one has done this, one can apply these accounts to sensibles, in such a way as to have L4-type knowledge of them. In just the same way, Aristotle believes that one can define various species and genera without reference to particular instances of them; but, once one has done this, one can apply the definitions to particulars in such a way as to have knowledge of them.

L4 raises the following problem. At L4 one explains the hypotheses by relating them to something more fundamental (the form of the good), which is itself known. But how is the form of the good known? It cannot be explained in terms of something yet more fundamental—for there is nothing more fundamental (and if there were, we could raise the same question about how it is known, and then we would be launched on an infinite regress). Are not KBK and KL then violated at this later stage? The same difficulty that arose for L3 seems to arise for the form of the good at L4.

One answer—popular historically—is to say that both the route to L4 and what L4-type knowledge consists in are some sort of vision or acquaintance. One knows the form of the good, not by explaining it in terms of something more fundamental, but by a self-certifying vision, which is also what the knowledge consists in.[48] The threatened regress thus halts with a self-certifying vision that confers knowledge. This answer essentially abandons KL; for it claims that knowledge does not require an account after all, but only a vision.

However, Plato repeatedly stresses that the route to L4 (as to L2 and L3) is dialectic (511 B–C, 533 A–D)—the Socratic method of cross-examination, of critically testing beliefs against general principles and examples.[49] Moreover, Plato asks rhetorically, 'do you not call the person who is able to get an account of the essence of each thing "dialectician"? And will you not say that someone who cannot do this, in so far as he cannot give an account to

[48] An acquaintance view is favoured by, for example, F. M. Cornford, 'Mathematics and Dialectic in the *Republic*, VI–VII', in R. E. Allen (ed.), *Studies in Plato's Metaphysics* (London: Routledge & Kegan Paul, 1965), 61–95. See also the discussion in R. Robinson, *Plato's Earlier Dialectic*, 2nd edn. (Oxford: Clarendon Press, 1953), 172–9, for a critical assessment of the acquaintance view (or, as he calls it, the 'intuition' theory).

[49] There is one difference in the practice of dialectic at L4 and at earlier stages, however: at L4 dialectic is practised *kat' ousian*; at earlier stages it is practised *kata doxan* (534 C 2). By this Plato means that at L4 dialectic is practised on accounts of forms—i.e. on the hypotheses of L3 (although, of course, when one begins, these are not fully satisfactory accounts—otherwise one would already be at L4); at L2 and L3, on common beliefs that fall short of knowledge and are not (except perhaps *de re*) about forms. The method is the same, although what it is applied to differs.

himself and others, to that extent lacks knowledge [*nous*] about the matter?'
(534 B 3–6).

Dialectic, not acquaintance, is thus the route to L4; and since L4 cru-
cially involves the ability to provide an account, neither does it consist in
acquaintance alone. KL is thus not abandoned at L4. Even if acquaintance
is necessary for L4, it is not sufficient; an account is also needed. And so
our problem remains: what is there in terms of which we can justify our
beliefs about the form of the good?[50]

An alternative—and I think preferable—solution appeals again to coherence: one justifies one's claims about the form of the good, not in terms
of anything more fundamental (there is nothing more fundamental), but
in terms of its explanatory power, in terms of the results it allows one to
achieve; and one justifies one's acceptance of the hypotheses of L3 by explaining them both in terms of their results and in terms of the form of the
good. The form of the good, we have seen, is the teleological structure of
the world; other forms are its parts, and sensibles instantiate it. We justify
claims about other forms and about sensibles by relating them to this general structure; and we justify claims about the form of the good by showing
how well it allows us to explain the natures of, and interconnections between, other forms and sensibles. There is again a circle; but, again, it is a
virtuous, not a vicious, circle.

But how, it might be asked, could this be so? For didn't we propose a
moment ago that L3 was an inferior type of knowledge precisely because
it relied on coherence? If so, how could L4's justifications also be rooted in
coherence?

The answer is that it is not coherence as such that makes L3 inferior to
L4, but the degree and kind of coherence. Both L3 and L4 rely on coherence
for justification; but their coherentist accounts differ. The justifications at
L3 are piecemeal, restricted to individual branches of knowledge—one justifies mathematical beliefs, for example, solely in terms of mathematical
claims, and so on (*mutatis mutandis*) for morality and the like. At L4, by

---

[50] Although I have argued only that acquaintance is not sufficient for knowledge, I do
not believe it is necessary either. The chief reasons for introducing acquaintance seem to
be (*a*) that it is needed to halt the regress; and (*b*) that Plato's visual metaphors suggest it.
Reason (*a*), however, is false; coherence is another way of halting the regress and, as I go
on to explain, I believe it is Plato's way of halting the regress at L4 as at L3. As to (*b*), even
if Plato's visual metaphors suggest some sort of acquaintance, they do not require it. The
metaphors can as easily be interpreted in terms of understanding; when I say that I finally
see the point of what you have said, I do not mean that I have had some special vision
that confers knowledge, but that I now understand what you have said. For this point, see
Gosling, *Plato*, esp. ch. 8; and M. F. Burnyeat, 'Wittgenstein and Augustine *De Magistro*',
Proceedings of the Aristotelian Society, 61 (1987), 1–24; see also ch. 10.

contrast, one offers more synoptic accounts, integrating every branch of reality into a synoptic whole, in terms of the form of the good (531 c 6–E 5, 537 B 8–C 7)—that is, in terms of the teleological structure of reality. The mathematician, for instance, provides some sort of account of the square itself; the dialectician provides an account of *each* thing (534 B), and relates each thing to the form of the good. The mathematician restricts himself to mathematical connections; the dialectician provides 'a comprehensive survey of their affinities with one another and with the nature of things' (537 c)—his accounts are not restricted to individual branches of know-ledge, but interrelate them, by means of the form of the good. He shows the point and interconnection of all things.

L4 thus relies on coherence no less than does L3; but its coherentist ex-planations are fuller and richer, and that is why L4 counts as a better sort of knowledge. Not every sort of coherentist account is equally good; L4 is an improvement on L3, not because it appeals to something different from coherence, but because its coherentist accounts are more explanatory.

This account also helps to explain how L4-type knowledge of sensibles is possible. The teleological structure of the world is stated in general terms, in terms of properties and natural laws, without reference to sensibles. However, once this general structure is articulated, one can have L4-type knowledge of sensibles by seeing what properties and laws they instantiate, and by seeing how they contribute to the goodness of things.

Indeed, Plato's coherentism may require that L4-type knowledge of sen-sibles be possible. At least, it seems reasonable to suppose that Plato believes that one eventually needs to refer back to sensibles in order to justify one's belief that one has correctly articulated the world of forms—for part of one's justification for believing one has correctly articulated the world of forms is that it allows one to explain sensibles so well. If Plato accepts KBK, and believes one needs to refer to sensibles to justify one's beliefs about forms, then he must allow knowledge of sensibles.

On the account I have proposed, one knows more to the extent that one can explain more; knowledge requires, not a vision, and not some special sort of certainty or infallibility, but sufficiently rich, mutually supporting, explanatory accounts. Knowledge, for Plato, does not proceed piecemeal; to know, one must master a whole field, by interrelating and explaining its diverse elements.

It is sometimes argued that if this is so, we ought not to say that Plato is discussing knowledge at all; rather, he is discussing the distinct phenome-non of understanding. For, it is said, understanding, but not knowledge, requires explanation and interrelated accounts; and knowledge, but not understanding, requires certainty, and allows one to know propositions individually, not only collectively. A more moderate version of this general sort of view claims that Plato is discussing knowledge—but an older concept of knowledge, according to which knowledge consists in or requires understanding, in contrast to 'knowledge as knowledge is nowadays discussed in philosophy'.[51]

Now I agreed before that, for Plato, knowledge typically requires explanation; but I argued too that this is only to say that, for him, justification typically requires explanation. Similarly, I agree that, for Plato, knowledge does not require any sort of vision or certainty, but does require interrelating the elements of a field or discipline or, for L4, interrelating the elements of different disciplines in the light of the form of the good. But once again, I do not think this shows that he is uninterested in knowledge, We can say, if we like, that he believes knowledge consists in or requires understanding. But I would then want to add that this is not so different from 'knowledge as knowledge is nowadays discussed in philosophy'. To be sure, some contemporary epistemologists focus on conditions for knowing that a particular proposition is true, or believe that knowledge requires certainty, or that justification does not consist in or require explanation. But that is hardly characteristic of all contemporary epistemology. Indeed, concern with certainty is rather in disfavour these days; and many contemporary epistemologists defend holist conceptions of knowledge, and appeal to explanatory connections to explicate the sort of coherence a justified set of beliefs must exhibit. Plato does indeed explicate *epistēmē* in terms of explanation and interconnectedness, and not in terms of certainty or vision; but we should resist the inference that he is therefore not talking about knowledge, or that, if he is, he has an old-fashioned or unusual notion of knowledge. On the contrary, in this as in other matters Plato is surprisingly up to date.

[51] Burnyeat, 'Socrates and the Jury', 188. A similar view is defended by Annas.

5

Plato on Naming

I

Plato is sometimes criticized for having failed to distinguish names and sentences, and naming and stating, until the *Sophist*, and this failure is thought to underlie both his supposed perplexity about false belief in the *Cratylus*, *Theaetetus*, and elsewhere, and his claim, in the *Cratylus*, that names can be true and false. Interestingly enough, the charge has been pressed from two quite different directions.

Owen and others have argued that the assimilation of names and sentences, and of naming and stating, is one mark of Plato's semantic atomism. On this view, sentences are treated either as 'very long complex words'[1] or as strings of nouns;[2] and all words are treated as names: 'words are given their purchase on the world by being used to name parts of it, and names, or the basic names to which the rest are variously reducible, are simple proxies for their nominees'.[3]

Moreover, just as sentences are reduced to (strings of) names, so stating

---

[1] I. M. Crombie, *An Examination of Plato's Doctrines* (2 vols.; London: Routledge & Kegan Paul, 1962), ii. 481, cf. 489. See also D. Wiggins, 'Sentence Meaning, Negation, and Plato's Problem of Non-Being', in G. Vlastos (ed.), *Plato*, i. *Metaphysics and Epistemology* (Garden City, NY: Doubleday Anchor, 1971), 268–303 at 278.

[2] G. E. L. Owen, 'Notes on Ryle's Plato', in O. P. Wood and G. Pitcher (eds.), *Ryle: A Collection of Critical Essays* (London: Macmillan, 1971), 341–72 at 365. Cf. Crombie, *An Examination of Plato's Doctrines*, ii. 476; J. H. McDowell, *Plato:* Theaetetus (Oxford: Clarendon Press, 1973), 233. Obviously, the view that sentences are names and the view that they are strings of names are different, perhaps even incompatible, views. Both have been attributed to Plato, sometimes by the same person without notice of the difference, as part of Plato's alleged atomism. I shall ignore the important differences between the two views here, since for our purposes they are unimportant; what is important is that on either view all one can do with a sentence is to name, i.e. to refer, point, or touch.

[3] Owen, 'Notes on Ryle's Plato', 365. Cf. Crombie, *An Examination of Plato's Doctrines*, ii. 476; K. W. Mills, 'Some Aspects of Plato's Theory of Forms: *Timaeus* 49 E ff.', *Phronesis*, 13 (1968), 145–70 at 145–9. As stated, Owen's claim only commits him to the view that certain basic names, and not necessarily all words, function in this way; for some discussion directed specifically against this view, see n. 24 below.

is reduced to naming. Plato is alleged to be ignorant of syntax, and so treats speaking as 'stringing nouns together', whereas, in fact, 'learning to speak is not, as the *Cratylus* had implied, a piecemeal business of correlating atoms of the world with atoms of language'.[4]

Semantic atomism is in turn thought to explain why Plato cannot accommodate falsity. For 'falsehood had appeared an abortive attempt to mention something, like an unsuccessful attempt to touch or to hear; and this confused the conditions for naming with the conditions for truth'.[5]

Robinson, by contrast, has argued, not that Plato reduces sentences to names, or naming to stating, but, rather, that Plato thinks of names as little sentences, and accords them the same complexity and descriptive functions as properly belong only to sentences. 'The most fundamental falsehood' of Plato's theory of names in the *Cratylus,* Robinson urges, is 'that it assumes that the business of a name is to describe its nominate, whereas it is merely to refer to that nominate'.[6] This view, Robinson argues, explains or underlies Plato's claim in the *Cratylus* that names can be true and false, since truth and falsity normally attach only to sentences.

On either view, Plato fails to distinguish names and sentences, and naming and stating. But, obviously, the source of error is quite different. On Owen's semantic-atomism view, sentences are divested of their proper complexity and reduced to simple names; and, since all we can do with names, either singly or in strings, is to name (i.e. to refer, point, or touch), stating is similarly reduced to naming. For Robinson, on the other hand, names are accorded the same complexity as sentences are, and naming is treated as stating.

A main source of evidence for these views is the *Cratylus*, Plato's only full treatment of names (*onomata*). But a careful examination of its claims will reveal that he is not committed to the suggested views. Although Robinson is right in thinking that, for Plato, all words have descriptive content, this does not by itself show that Plato thinks names are little sentences, since, obviously, not all descriptions are sentences; but there is no further evidence in favour of Robinson's view. If Robinson is right this far, however, it is at least clear that Plato does not treat all words as simple names. This does not imply that Plato is clear about the differences between names and sentences; but we shall at least find that there is no evidence committing him to any confusion here. Nor, as we shall see, does Plato conflate stating and naming, in either of the alleged ways. Finally, we shall see that neither his account of

    [4] Owen, 'Notes on Ryle's Plato', 365.
    [5] Owen, 'Plato on Not-Being', in Vlastos (ed.), *Plato*, i. 223–67 at 245.
    [6] R. Robinson, *Essays in Greek Philosophy* (Oxford: Clarendon Press, 1969), 133.

true names nor his account of false belief in the *Cratylus* rests on the crude views ascribed to him. The account of true names says no more than that names are true or false of things, and that correct assignments of names depend upon the descriptive content of names. The account of false belief, so far from depending on the atomist 'hit or miss' model, in fact matches the *Sophist*'s later, supposedly more mature, account.

II

Although I shall primarily be concerned with the *Cratylus*, it will be helpful to begin obliquely by looking at the *Sophist*, where, both parties claim,[7] Plato overcomes the earlier crude account. In the *Sophist* Plato provides an account of sentence constitution, and he uses it to explain how falsity is possible. A sentence (*logos*) is said to be a weaving together of *onomata* and *rhēmata* (262 D 2–6); it then not only names but also 'goes further' (*ti perainei*) and says something. It is by combining *onomata* with *rhēmata*, grammatical expressions of different types, that one can go further than naming, and also say something.

It is well known that Greek contains no separate word corresponding to our 'word'; '*onoma*' does service for both 'name' and 'word'. It is then striking that here Plato tries to narrow the scope of '*onoma*' to something like our 'name', and introduces '*rhēma*' as another sort of grammatical expression. An *onoma* indicates (*sēmeion*, 262 A 6) agents; a *rhēma* shows (*dēlōma*, 262 A 4) actions performed by agents. So '*onoma*' is restricted to, roughly, nouns, and '*rhēma*' is introduced to do service for verbs or, more generally, for predicate expressions. Plato can then no longer believe, if he ever believed, that all words are names, or function like nouns, since *rhēmata* are words expressly distinguished from names.

Moreover, Plato's account of sentence constitution in the *Sophist* clearly distinguishes names and sentences. Sentences require a combining of different sorts of syntactic elements; in that case, names and sentences no longer differ only in degree of complexity, but also in type. Finally, Plato also clearly distinguishes naming from stating; a *logos* goes beyond mere naming and also says something.

Plato uses this general account to explain truth and falsity. True and false sentences are alike in being about something (262 E 5–6). Both 'Theaetetus is sitting' and 'Theaetetus is flying', for example, are about Theaetetus, or

[7] Owen, 'Notes on Ryle's Plato', 365; 'Plato on Not-Being', 263–5; Robinson, *Essays in Greek Philosophy*, 123, 134.

refer to him, even though only the first sentence is true. The first sentence is true because it says what-is about Theaetetus; the second is false because it says what-is-not about him.[8] The importance of the initial account is now clear: in any sentence, the *onoma* secures a reference, and indicates what the sentence is about. Truth and falsity then occur when a *rhēma* is applied to the referent, and the *logos* then says either what-is or what-is-not about it. Falsity does not consist in simple misreference, in a failure to hit something; if no reference is secured, no truth or falsity occurs, since no statement has been made.

The same account shows that Plato does not here hold the earlier putative doctrine of true and false names. For truth and falsity are clearly attached to sentences; names are below the threshold of truth and falsity.

In the *Sophist*, then, Plato seems to reject semantic atomism by recognizing that not all words are names, that names are not sentences, and that naming is not stating. This in turn dispels the paradox of false belief. For a false sentence, although false, none the less secures a reference: falsity does not collapse into misreference. This is incompatible with the 'little sentences' theory, for truth and falsity are firmly attached to sentences; and so Plato can no longer (if he ever did) believe that names are true, a crude assumption generated by his supposed earlier assimilation of names to sentences.

I do not now wish to challenge this familiar picture of the *Sophist*. Instead, I want to deny that its claims contradict those made in earlier dialogues, in particular in the *Cratylus*. I press this claim on two fronts: first, seemingly significant verbal differences in fact prove nothing; and, second, the positive theory of names in the *Cratylus* is a good deal more sophisticated than is usually supposed.

III

The distinction between *onomata* and *rhēmata* does not decisively show that Plato has abandoned the view that all words are, in some sense, names. For the distinction in the *Sophist* is produced as one among *onomata*. At

---

[8] Here I ignore several difficulties and differing interpretations. For some discussion, see D. Keyt, 'Plato on Falsity: *Sophist* 263b', in E. N. Lee, A. P. D. Mourelatos, and R. M. Rorty (eds.), *Exegesis and Argument: Studies in Greek Philosophy Presented to Gregory Vlastos* (Assen: Van Gorcum, 1973), 285–305; J. P. Kostman. 'False Logos and Not-Being in Plato's *Sophist*', in J. M. E. Moravcsik (ed.), *Patterns in Plato's Thought: Papers Arising out of the 1971 West Coast Greek Philosophy Conference* (Dordrecht: Reidel, 1973), 192–212; Owen, 'Plato on Not-Being'; and Wiggins, 'Sentence Meaning, Negation, and Plato's Problem of Non-Being'.

261 E 5 the Eleatic Stranger claims that all *onomata* reveal being (*peri tēn ousian dēlōmatōn*; cf. *Cra.* 422 D–E, 428 E); but there are still two sorts of *onomata*, *onomata* and *rhēmata*, as defined above. In this broad sense of '*onoma*', *rhēmata* are *onomata*; and so even in the *Sophist* Plato maintains that, in some sense, all words are names.[9] Nor does he there consistently employ its distinction among *onomata*, as he might if that distinction were a self-conscious advance over earlier views. At 226 B, for example, 'winnow', 'spin', and 'thresh' are all called *onomata*; yet they are *rhēmata* by the later criterion.[10]

But is the claim that all words are names troubling? Surely by itself it tells us nothing until we know what names are. If all words are treated as some have treated proper names, as mere tags for their nominees, devoid of descriptive content, then the claim is troubling. And it is clearly this view of names that Owen has in mind in calling Plato a semantic atomist: names 'are simple proxies for their nominees'.

Now it is true that Plato uses proper names, in the *Cratylus*, as examples in explaining his theory of names. But this will tell us nothing either, until we know how he treats proper names. As we shall see, he analyses names into their etymological roots, and assesses their adequacy in terms of the descriptive appropriateness of the roots. Hector's son, for example, is said to be correctly named 'Astyanax', since 'Astyanax' means 'ruler', and Hector's son was expected to be a ruler (392–3). I shall be returning to this theory later; but it is worth noting here that if Plato treats even proper names as disguised descriptions, the temptation to say he treats all words as 'simple proxies for their nominees' should be severely weakened. Instead, Plato's assumption that all words are names more nearly amounts to the assumption that all words, including proper names, have descriptive content.

IV

However one treats names, there should, of course, be a distinction between names and sentences. The *Sophist*, in defining a sentence as a weaving

---

[9] The point is recognized by G. Vlastos, in 'The Unity of the Virtues in the *Protagoras*', in his *Platonic Studies*, 2nd edn. (Princeton: Princeton University Press, 1981), 221–65 at 239 n. 49.

[10] There are many other similar examples: at *Sph.* 237 D 2 'something' is called a *rhēma*. At *Ti.* 50 A 'this' and 'that' are called *onomata*; just a few lines earlier they are called *rhēmata*. *Tht.* 199 A calls 'know' and 'learn' *onomata*, yet they satisfy the *Sophist*'s test for being *rhēmata*. These examples are cited by M. F. Burnyeat in his unpublished paper 'The Simple and the Complex in the *Theaetetus*' (1970), in making a similar point. I am indebted to this fine paper both here and elsewhere.

together of *onomata* and *rhēmata*, seems to draw one; is it a distinction obscured in earlier contexts? The linguistic evidence might suggest this. For example, in the *Theaetetus* a *logos* is said to be a weaving together of *onomata*—no mention of *rhēmata* (202 B 4–5). It is then natural to suppose that here Plato 'seems to regard the difference between an account and a name as lying fundamentally in the fact that an account consists of several names'. Plato 'makes no distinction among the constituents which . . . [here] . . . constitute accounts, *viz.*, names'.[11] But that this conflicts with the *Sophist* is questionable. For, as I have already noted, the *Sophist*'s distinction of *onomata* and *rhēmata* is a distinction among *onomata*; *rhēmata* are, in the broad sense of '*onoma*', a kind of *onoma*. But in that case, the *Theaetetus*' formulation could simply be elliptical for the *Sophist*'s. This suggestion is strengthened when we note that at *Theaetetus* 206 D, shortly after the troublesome passage, Plato uses the *Sophist*'s phraseology, and says that in one sense of '*logos*' a *logos* consists of *onomata* and *rhēmata*. Although he does not explicitly tell us what *onomata* and *rhēmata* do, at least the *Sophist*'s formula is not new and so does not, on its own, imply that any new theory is in the offing. Moreover, its use in the *Theaetetus* suggests that the alternative formulation at 202 B need not be a significant one.

There is another way of reading *Theaetetus* 202 B. It may be that Plato is not discussing sentences, but accounts. This is suggested by the fact that knowledge is said to be true belief conjoined with a *logos* (202 B–C); and as Plato remarks later, to say that knowledge is conjoined with a sentence will not distinguish knowledge from true belief (206 D–E). Since not all accounts are sentences, however, this would show, not that the *Theaetetus* conflicts with the *Sophist*, or makes the same claim elliptically, but rather that it is simply addressed to a different issue. Some accounts might be sentences, of course; but even so, the *Theaetetus* and *Sophist* need not conflict. If the broad use of '*onoma*' is in play, the claim is again compatible with the *Sophist*; and even if the narrow sense is intended, as seems likely, Plato is not committed to the claim that accounts consist *only* of names. The names could be conjoined with suitable binding variables. Not too much weight should be put on the passage in any case, however, since Plato goes on to argue against the position it defends.

The *Sophist* terminology also occurs at *Cratylus* 431 B 5–C 7. Although Plato does not there tell us how *onomata* and *rhēmata* function, he does tell us this earlier in the dialogue. At 421 D–E he describes his procedure

<hr>

[11] McDowell, *Plato:* Theaetetus, 233. Cf. also Crombie, *An Examination of Plato's Doctrines*, ii. 116–17.

of uncovering the descriptive content of names as one of analysing names into their associated *rhēmata*. To be sure, '*rhēma*' can easily mean 'phrase' or even 'sentence' here; it need not mean 'verb' or 'predicate'. None the less, although the *grammatical* role specified is different, the *logical* role is quite similar: in both cases, *rhēmata* supply descriptions additional to the name, and show us something true or false of what the name names.[12]

Plato's account of *logos* in the *Sophist*, then, is not obviously new: verbally similar claims occur elsewhere, where the background reasoning may be the same. Whether or not any serious differences are in the offing can only be decided by close attention to particular contexts and arguments.

V

In Sections III and IV I considered terminological evidence seeming to support Owen's view, and I argued that it was indecisive. I turn now to Robinson's claim, that Plato treats names as little sentences. That Plato holds this view is suggested to Robinson in part by the *Cratylus*' claim that names may be true or false, a claim ordinarily made only about sentences. That Plato gives up the supposed view in the *Sophist* is in turn suggested by the fact that there truth and falsity are ascribed only to sentences; names are not said to be true or false.

To show that the *Sophist* abandons the *Cratylus* account of true names, one of course needs more than the *ex silentio* argument that in the *Sophist* only sentences are said to be true: after all, the *Sophist* does not say that names are not true. But a stronger case can be made. For Plato suggests that nothing true or false can be said until names have been combined with verbs to form sentences. If a name cannot say anything, and the occurrence of truth and falsity requires that something be said, then names cannot be true or false.

But before concluding that the *Sophist* drops a hopelessly muddled earlier claim,[13] we should see what that claim amounts to. It occurs as part of an

---

[12] Cf. Crombie, *An Examination of Plato's Doctrines*, ii. 495. McDowell has argued that 'the *Cratylus* has not yet mastered the *Sophist*'s distinction' (*Plato:* Theaetetus, 236). However, his argument is not persuasive. All Plato says is that a *logos* can go wrong as *onomata* and *rhēmata* can, since any logos is a combination of them. This does not imply that the whole sentence has a purely referential function, as McDowell assumes, especially since, as I argue below, Plato does not think *onomata* go wrong by a simple failure of reference. Cf. sect. vii below.

[13] It is unlikely in any case that the *Sophist* drops the claim; for it reappears in a later dialogue, the *Politicus* (281 A 12–B 1). There Plato says one would 'say a false name' if one

argument against Hermogenes, who, like Protagoras, had denied that there is falsity:

   (i)   there is such a thing as speaking truly and speaking falsely;
  (ii)   true speaking is speaking of things that are as they are; false speaking is speaking of things that are as they are not;
 (iii)   in a true sentence, the whole as well as all the parts is true; in a false sentence the whole as well as a part is false;[14]
 (iv)   therefore, names, being the smallest (significant) parts of sentences, may be true or false;
  (v)   therefore, it is possible to say a true or a false name (385 B 2–D 1).[15]

Robinson argues that 'this argument is bad; for names have no truth-value, and the reason for saying they do is a fallacy of division . . . We find that the proper function of a name is hardly recognized at all, and instead the name is thought of as if it were a little statement and had the same descriptive function as a statement'. But 'statements are true or false because they describe and assert; and names are neither true nor false, because they do not assert or describe, but name or refer'.[16]

Now it is true that (v) concludes that names can be true and false. None the less, Robinson's analysis can be resisted. Plato explains (v) later in the *Cratylus* (430 D, 431 B). There, as elsewhere in the *Cratylus* apart from the argument of 385, he avoids saying that names are true or false; instead he says that names are correct or incorrect, and can be truly or falsely applied to things.[17] Plato's talk of truth in assignment suggests he means, not that names are true or false in the same way as sentences are, the conclusion for which Robinson argues, but rather that names are true or false of things

called the art of warping and woofing weaving. Of course, the *Politicus* could be as confused as earlier contexts.

[14] M. Schofield, 'A Displacement in the Text of the *Cratylus*', *Classical Quarterly*, NS 22 (1972), 246–53, thinks Plato claims that every part of a false sentence is false (246). C. H. Kahn, 'Language and Ontology in the *Cratylus*', in Lee, Mourelatos, and Rorty (eds.), *Exegesis and Argument*, 152–76 at 160–1, argues that only a part need be false. He is supported by the fact that the '*panta*' at 385 c 5–6 is not repeated here.

[15] The Greek is ambiguous; it could also read 'It is possible for a name to say something true or false', taking '*onoma*' as the subject, rather than as the object. But my reading is supported by the parallels at 385 E 7–8, 10, D 2, where '*onoma*' is clearly the object.

[16] Robinson, *Essays in Greek Philosophy*, 123, 131.

[17] Robinson incorrectly claims that 431 B 'makes the converse mistake of composition' (*Essays in Greek Philosophy*, 123); but all Plato says is that names can be applied truly or falsely, not that they are true or false. McDowell (*Plato: Theaetetus*, 236) and Kahn ('Language and Ontology in the *Cratylus*', 161) also incorrectly suppose that at 431 Plato says that names are true and false. Jowett's translation constantly uses 'true' and 'false' where the Greek has 'correct' and 'incorrect'.

and can be rightly or wrongly applied to them. Plato claims that the truth and falsity of sentences is to be assessed in terms of the adequacy of their components: he does not assume that names are little sentences, or are true and false just as sentences are.[18]

Plato's explanation of (v) shows that his conception of true names or, more accurately, of correct names is not the one Robinson describes, but is instead a plausible and perfectly respectable claim. None the less, this does not show that the present argument is valid. For Plato's argument to be effective, 'true' must be used in exactly the same sense for sentences and for names. But if my explanation of (v) is correct, this is not the case; for Plato does not claim that names are true in the same way as sentences are, but only that names can be correct or incorrect and truly or falsely applied to things. In that case, the argument appears to equivocate, by using 'true' of names where it should use 'correct' or 'true of'. Despite the fact that the argument remains a bad one, however, it at least does not commit Plato to the view that names are little sentences. To decide whether or not this is Plato's view we need to look at his positive theory of names, and not at this one brief, and unrepresentative, argument.

VI

I turn now to Plato's own theory of names. At *Cratylus* 388 B 10–11, Plato assigns two tasks to names: they are instruments for teaching or conveying information to one another, and for distinguishing things or natures (*ousiai*) as they are. And just as any instrument can perform its tasks well or ill, so not all names are equally apt or correct. What counts as a correct name, as a name apt for teaching and discriminating natures? Plato suggests two conditions of adequacy: first, a name must segregate a real natural kind. If, for example, our language contains the word 'trock', to be applied indifferently to trees and rocks, yet trees and rocks are distinct natural kinds, 'trock' is an incorrect name; it does not divide up reality correctly. As Kretzmann notes, 'according to Plato's general theory we are capable of avoiding incorrect names . . . to the extent to which science and

---

[18] W. V. Quine, *Methods of Logic* (New York: Holt, 1950), § 12, explains the 'is true of' idiom. My account here is similar to the accounts of Kahn ('Language and Ontology in the *Cratylus*', 160) and of K. Lorenz and J. Mittelstrass, 'On Rational Philosophy of Language: The Programme in Plato's *Cratylus* Reconsidered', *Mind*, 76 (1967), 1–20 at 5–9. However, unlike me, they assume that Plato's argument is valid. My alternative is perhaps strengthened by the fact that Hermogenes does not see the relevance of the argument to the correctness of names; his perplexity is in order if Plato has equivocated by using 'true' where he should, and elsewhere does, use 'correct'.

philosophy ... have provided us with a correct conceptual schema'.[19] Plato
writes, for example, that

it is fitting ... to call a lion's offspring a lion and a horse's offspring a horse ...
I am not speaking of prodigies, such as the birth of some other kind of creature
from a horse, but of the natural offspring of each species after its kind ... If a
horse, contrary to nature, should bring forth a calf, the natural offspring of a cow,
it should be called 'calf', not 'colt' ... The same applies to trees, and to everything
else (393 B–C) ... Then to those things that come into being according with nature
the same names are to be given. (394 D)

Now it is true that Plato focuses on a name–thing correlation; he discusses how words refer to things and not, say, how names are parts of
sentences, or how sentences purport to describe the world. This might
suggest that Plato is a semantic atomist, that he thinks, for example, that
speaking is just 'a piecemeal business of correlating atoms of the world with
atoms of language'. However, all Plato has said so far is that some of our
words are, or should be, true of things; and surely this is a necessary part of
any respectable theory of language. It cannot by itself commit Plato to any
theory about the nature of language in general. The claim that words are
sometimes true of things does not reflect an atomist theory of language,
but is compatible with a variety of theories; nor has Plato yet said anything
stronger that could be used to support the claim that he is an atomist.

We should note in any case that Plato's interest here is not in providing
a complete theory of language, but rather in assessing the adequacy of
conceptual schemes. He is asking what natural kinds there are and how
divisions among words should match them. This alternative focus should
forestall the temptation to interpret his name–thing correlations as part of
an atomist theory.

Although the first condition of adequacy, the name–nature principle,
is consistent with (although it does not entail) the claim that names are
just tags for things, Plato's second condition shows that he does not treat
names as simple tags, with no descriptive content, but, quite the contrary,
assesses the correctness of names in terms of their descriptive adequacy.
Plato argues first that not all names for the same things are equally apposite.
Even if 'rock' picks out a natural kind, it might not be a perspicuous name
for that kind. 'Astyanax', for example, is a correct name for Hector's son,
since it means 'ruler', and Hector's son was expected to be a ruler. But, he
claims, 'Scamandrius' would not have been equally apt (392 B–393 B). He

---

[19] N. Kretzmann, 'Plato on the Correctness of Names', *American Philosophical Quarterly*, 8 (1971), 126–38 at 132. My discussion of this theory is brief; I refer the reader to
Kretzmann's article for a fuller, and excellent, discussion.

does not dispute that both names referred to, or picked out, Hector's son; he says only that the first name is more correct because it, unlike the second name, is descriptively accurate. A name is correct, then, not just so far as it picks out a natural kind, but only if it also reveals the nature of that kind, or correctly describes it: a name is correct if 'the essence of the thing remains in force and is revealed in the name' (393 D 1–4; cf. 394 E 3, 7–8; 395 B 6; 396 E 5).

Plato allows some latitude here. For example, 'Atreus' can mean 'fearless', 'stubborn', or 'destructive'; the analyses are not synonymous, but Plato allows that each is correct, since Atreus is fearless, stubborn, and destructive (395 B 7–C 5). Or, again, he says we all refer to the same nature, justice, in using its name, even though our beliefs about justice vary widely (412 E 6–413 D 2).

These claims are explained later, with the aid of a picture analogy (432 B– 433 B). No picture is exactly like its original, otherwise there would be two originals, not one original and its copy. Instead, pictures fall short of their originals; and different pictures can equally well be of the same thing, even if they are in many ways dissimilar to one another. So long as they reveal enough of the essence of the thing, or preserve its outline (*tupos*), they are pictures of it. Similarly, different names for the same thing convey different sorts of information about it. But so long as the *tupos* or outline of the thing's essence is revealed by the name, the name is correct.[20]

Plato's *tupos* theory of names rejects any causal theory of names. Plato will not allow 'n' to be a name of x just in case there is an appropriate causal connection between 'n' and x. Nor is a picture a camera took of me really of me, if it does not look like me. Instead, for 'n' to name x, it must reveal the *tupos* or outline of the essence of x; that is to say, it must correctly describe x's essence. Only a picture that looks like me, whatever its causal history, is really of me. The correctness of names consists, then, in their descriptive adequacy.[21]

Now if this is Plato's theory of names, it clearly counts against the view that, for Plato, all words are 'simple proxies for their nominees'. It may be

[20] Cf. D. Kaplan, 'Quantifying In', in L. Linsky (ed.), *Reference and Modality* (London: Oxford University Press, 1971), 112–44, for an interestingly similar use of a picture analogy to explain the of-relation (although Kaplan's theory, unlike Plato's, is a causal one).

[21] Searle's theory is in some ways similar to Plato's. Searle argues that we all attach different descriptions to, say, 'Aristotle', and therefore mean something different by the name. None the less, we all refer to the same man, Aristotle, since (or so we believe) enough of our descriptions are true. His argument resembles Plato's, that we all refer to the same nature, justice, in using the name '*dikaiosunē*', despite the differences in our beliefs, since enough of those beliefs, even if nonoverlapping, are true. Cf. J. Searle, 'Proper Names', in P. F. Strawson (ed.), *Philosophical Logic* (London: Oxford University Press, 1967), 89–96.

true that Plato treats all words as he treats proper names. But this is only to say that for Plato all words, including proper names, have descriptive content.

It might be thought that my argument applies only to what Plato calls secondary or derived names, and that what he calls first names (*prōta onomata*: 422 c–d, 424 b, 425 b, etc.) resist such analysis and function as simple names. However, Plato is clear that even the latter, like other names, reveal being (422 c–d). It is true that he specifies an alternative way in which they do so: by sounding appropriate. But Plato views the onomatopoeic theory as an alternative method of description, not as a substitute for it; he nowhere suggests that *prōta onomata* directly refer us to things or are mere tags, as atomism requires. To be sure, first names are not composed of other names; but this does not at all entail that they are devoid of sense.[22]

To say that Plato treats words as having descriptive content is not to say, with Robinson, that words are little sentences. 'The tall blond man with one black shoe' is a description, but not a sentence. To show that Plato assimilates words to sentences, we need more evidence than that he ascribes descriptive content to words; yet Robinson adduces no additional evidence. Again, this does not imply that Plato does not make the alleged error; but the available evidence does not commit him to it.

VII

At the end of the *Cratylus* Plato presents an account of false belief. It has seemed to some that, whatever the earlier theory of the *Cratylus* amounts to, here Plato shows that he is unclear in some of the suggested ways. Thus Runciman, for example, argues that Plato endorses an

atomistic analysis of error. That is to say, a mistake is taken to be to perform a bad piece of naming, or to miscouple a particular name to a particular object . . . Moreover, it confuses description and reference; and meaning becomes on this analysis no more than a mere set of nominata. There is no hint in any of this of a distinction between the proposition, or meaning, expressed by a statement, and its nominatum, or truth-value.[23]

Thus, it is alleged, Plato here reduces stating to naming, and thereby also confuses referring and saying something. In the mature theory of the

---

[22] For further discussion and defence, see my unpublished Ph.D. dissertation, 'Plato and Acquaintance' (Harvard, 1975), ch. iii.

[23] W. G. Runciman, *Plato's Later Epistemology* (Cambridge: Cambridge University Press, 1962), 32–3. Cf. also Owen, 'Plato on Not-Being', 245, and see n. 42 for a partial retraction; Crombie, *An Examination of Plato's Doctrines*, ii. 487–92.

Sophist Plato sees that falsity consists in a two-part process: a sentence must first secure a reference and then say something false about the referent; in the *Cratylus*, however, falsity is collapsed into one stage: it consists in simple misreference.[24]

I argue that falsity here does not consist simply in misreference; instead, Plato's account exploits his *tupos* theory and, in so doing, presents the same crucial distinctions as the *Sophist*. Moreover, I shall also argue that his account, rightly understood, prevents a possible misunderstanding of the *Sophist*.

Plato presents an account of falsity to combat Cratylus' view that no falsity is possible. Cratylus argues that any name or sentence purports to pick out a situation in the world. If there is such a situation, the name or sentence is about it; if there is no such situation, nothing has been said. For example, if I address Cratylus saying, 'Hello, Hermogenes, son of Smicrion', what I have said is either true or meaningless. If there is someone correctly named Hermogenes who is the son of Smicrion, what I have said is true; if no one is correctly named 'Hermogenes', I have said nothing, but just uttered meaningless noises (429 e 8–9; 430 a 4–5).

Plato dismantles this theory by invoking his analogy between names and pictures. Suppose I approach a man and say 'This is your picture', and then show him a likeness of him. In that case, my attribution is correct. If, on the other hand, I had shown him the likeness of a woman, my attribution would have been incorrect. But exactly the same procedure is possible with names. I might approach the man, indicating I will say his name, and then do so; in that case what I have said is true. But if I supplied the name 'woman', what I said would be false. Falsity is therefore possible in the misapplication of a name.

Now in the *Sophist* names only secure a reference, and do not themselves account for falsity. For example, in the sentence 'Theaetetus is flying', 'Theaetetus' picks out Theaetetus, but only when 'flying' is added to the name has something false been said about Theaetetus. There are thus two distinct stages, one securing a reference and one saying something about the referent; the conditions for naming and the conditions for truth are sharply separated. In the *Cratylus*, however, falsity seems to occur in the misapplication of a name; but then, does falsity not consist in misreference, since names secure references?

---

[24] Runciman and others give similar explanations of Plato's discussions of false beliefs elsewhere. But I do not think he is anywhere committed to the atomist underpinnings, or that his discussions of false belief are defective. For my view of the *Republic*, see chs. 3 and 4; for my view of the *Theaetetus*, see ch. 9.

This interpretation looks plausible only if one ignores part of the situation Plato describes. Saying 'woman' is only one part of that situation, and it is not the part that secures a reference. Rather, as in the *Sophist*, two distinct stages are marked. The subject of discourse is indicated, correctly, by the preamble 'This is your name', together with an ostensive device such as pointing (430 E 5–7; cf. *Sph.* 263 A 8). One then goes on to assign a name, and it is only then that truth or falsity results, *after* the referent has been otherwise indicated. The word 'woman' does not both name and say something.

Now one may still feel dissatisfied, for two different reasons. First, even if the *Cratylus* draws the same distinctions, it does not present them intra-linguistically. That is to say, although Plato does distinguish referring and saying something, he does not explain these distinctions in terms of sentences and their constituents; the failure to focus on the importance of sentences might suggest latent unclarity. Second, in the *Cratylus* it appears that the utterance of an *onoma*, such as 'woman', is what is responsible for falsity; yet in the *Sophist* Plato seems to restrict *onomata* to a referring role.

I do not think either point is evidence of Plato's confusion here. It is true that the *Cratylus* does not present its distinctions intralinguistically; none the less, the *Sophist* does not present any new claims. The importance of the *Sophist*'s focus on sentences can, in any case, be overrated. As Wiggins notes, even there Plato 'retains the idea of analysing what is said into a structure of individually describable parts'.[25] Looked at one way, the *Sophist* simply repeats the *Cratylus*' claim that sentences are true only if their constituent parts are correctly applied (385); and the present discussion of falsity explains in what correct application consists.

The second point may seem more troubling. In the *Sophist* 'Man learns' is used as a sample sentence. 'Man' is an *onoma* and secures a reference; 'learns' is a *rhēma* which shows something about the referent. Only when the two words are conjoined is something said. In the *Cratylus*, however, *onomata* seem shunted into predicate position: addressing Socrates as 'woman', for example, is responsible for falsity.

This may seem troubling if we suppose that the *Sophist*'s distinction between *onomata* and *rhēmata* is absolute, that all words are either *onomata* or *rhēmata* and that no word can be both. But surely the *Sophist*'s distinction is context-relative. In (the English) 'Theaetetus is sitting', 'sitting' is a *rhēma*; in 'Sitting is pleasurable when one is tired', 'sitting' is an *onoma*. In the first case, 'sitting' is true or false of Theaetetus, just as 'is pleasurable when one is tired' is true or false of sitting in the second case—and just as

---

[25] Wiggins, 'Sentence Meaning, Negation, and Plato's Problem of Non-Being', 303.

'woman', in the *Cratylus* example, is true or false of Socrates. What in one sentence serves as a name might in another sentence serve as a predicate. If this is right, the *Cratylus'* use of 'woman' in predicate position betrays no confusion, especially when, as we have noted, the reference is otherwise indicated.

At the same time, the fact that the *onoma–rhēma* distinction is context-relative forestalls a possible misreading of the *Sophist*. It may seem tempting to suppose that in making that distinction Plato is suggesting that *onomata* only refer and do not describe, and that *rhēmata* only describe and do not refer.[26] But we must recall that Plato's distinction of *onomata* and *rhēmata* is one among *onomata*: all *onomata*, in the broad sense, reveal being; that is to say, as the *Cratylus* has argued, all words describe essences. What the *onoma–rhēma* distinction shows is not that some words lack descriptive content, but that in different sentences words function, or display their descriptive content, in different ways. Viewing the distinction as context-relative allows us to see that Plato is not giving up his claim that all words have descriptive content. And surely Plato is right here. Surely it is incorrect to suppose that referring and describing are incompatible or mutually exclusive. Rather, as Plato and others have argued persuasively, names refer *through* their descriptive content. The *Cratylus* is clear on this point; and with its aid we can see that the *Sophist* need not be, and should not be, abandoning it.[27]

---

[26] This seems suggested, and commended, by Robinson. He argues that 'a name does not describe its nominate' (*Essays in Greek Philosophy*, 130), as Plato began to see when he distinguished *onomata* and *rhēmata* (ibid. 134).

[27] I am indebted to T. H. Irwin and N. Kretzmann for helpful comments on earlier drafts.

6

Protagorean Relativisms

I

In the first part of the *Theaetetus* (151 E–186 E), Plato considers three theses: Theaetetus' claim that knowledge is perception (T) (151 E 1–3); Protagoras' measure doctrine (P), according to which 'man is the measure of all things, of those that are that they are, and of those that are not that they are not' (*Tht.* 152 A 2–4);[1] and Heracleitus' claim (H) that 'all things change, like streams' (160 D 7–8).[2] These theses are not considered in isolation; on the contrary, Plato takes them to be intimately connected. There is considerable dispute, however, both about the precise content of each of the theses and about how they are connected (both in fact and in Plato's view). These two disputes are related. For we can know how the three theses are connected only if we know what each of them says. But at the same time, since they do not readily interpret themselves, Plato's indications about their connections impose some prima facie constraints on plausible interpretations; for we should aim to interpret each of the theses in a way that makes it intelligible that Plato connects them as he does. In this chapter I shall focus on Plato's account of Protagoras, asking what interpretation of him best fits the complex dialectical structure of the first part of the *Theaetetus*.[3]

Protagoras' measure doctrine is often thought to be one of the first formulations of relativism, and indeed the phrase 'Protagorean relativism'

[1] This is generally agreed to be a quotation from Protagoras. For further occurrences of the quotation, see Plato, *Cra.* 385 E 6–386 A 3; Sextus Empiricus, *M.* 7. 60–1; Diogenes Laertius, *Lives* 9. 51.

[2] This is clearly an allusion to Heracleitus' alleged claim that 'one can't step into the same river twice'. There is dispute as to whether Heracleitus did say this. Plato thinks he did: *Cra.* 402A 8–10 (=DK A 6; cf. B 91).

[3] Though my focus is Plato's account of Protagoras in the *Theaetetus*, there may be implications for the interpretation of the historical Protagoras. At least, M. F. Burnyeat claims that Plato's account has 'by far the best claim to authenticity' ('Protagoras and Self-Refutation in Later Greek Philosophy', *Philosophical Review*, 85 (1976), 44–69 at 45). However, since Protagoras' own works are not extant, Burnyeat's claim is difficult to assess.

is common currency. But does Plato portray Protagoras as a relativist? A quick answer is 'yes, of course, he does': after all, relativism has been understood in a variety of ways, and no doubt an account of it can be found according to which Plato portrays Protagoras as a relativist. But this simple answer is unsatisfactory. For we want to know precisely what sort of relativist Plato takes Protagoras to be, if indeed that is how he describes him at all. And here matters become more difficult. For although Plato is often thought to portray Protagoras as a relativist, many different—indeed incompatible—doctrines have been made to shelter under this label.

In Section II I make some general remarks about Protagoras' measure doctrine. In Section III I say something about Protagoras' place in the *Theaetetus*, and suggest two criteria an adequate interpretation of Protagoras should satisfy.[4] In subsequent sections I consider two interpretations of Plato's Protagoras that have not been adequately distinguished from one another, and that fail the two criteria. I then propose an alternative account of Plato's Protagoras that satisfies them. On this interpretation, Plato's Protagoras is not best characterized as a relativist.

II

Plato tells us that Protagoras' measure doctrine (P) 'means [*legei*] something on these lines: everything is, for me, the way it appears to me, and is, for you, the way it appears to you' (*Tht.* 152 A 6–8).[5] In the context of the measure doctrine, to say how things *appear* to me is to say how I *believe* things are,[6] and to say how things *are* for me—to say, for example, that the wind is cold for me—is to say that it is true for me that the wind is

---

[4] An earlier version of sect. II and of part of sect. III may be found in my 'Conflicting Appearances: *Theatetus* 153 D–154 B' (ch. 7 below).

[5] There is some dispute as to whether this passage is a quotation from Protagoras, or Plato's own explanation of what Protagoras means. McDowell translates '*legei*' as 'means', which suggests he thinks that Plato is offering his own explanation (J. McDowell, *Plato: Theaetetus* (Oxford: Clarendon Press, 1973)); but in his notes ad loc. he says that *Cra.* 386 A 1–3 suggests that Plato is quoting Protagoras.

[6] 'Appears' (*phainesthai*) can be veridical or nonveridical: I can say 'It is apparent that the wind is cold', where this means that it obviously, evidently is cold; but I can also say 'The wind appears to be cold', where this means that I believe that it is cold. In Greek, the first use is indicated by an accusative plus participle, the second by an accusative plus infinitive. But sometimes, as in (P), the second verb is omitted and so one has to decide from the context which construction is intended. I take it that (P) involves the second use. In the present context, the usual terminology—veridical and nonveridical—is somewhat awkward: the second use is called nonveridical since it is normally supposed that one cannot infer from how one believes things are to how they are. Protagoras, of course, in some sense licenses the inference and so there is a sense in which, although 'appears' indicates belief in

cold. So Protagoras claims that if I believe the wind is cold, then it is true for me that the wind is cold. He also seems to accept the 'converse rule' that if it is true for me that the wind is cold, then I believe that it is.[7] If so, then (P) is a biconditional: it claims that p is true for A if and only if A believes p.

In discussing (P), Plato considers two different ranges of appearances or beliefs. 'Appears' statements can be used in statements about perceptual appearances, to say how one believes things are on the basis of perception (e.g. 'It appears red to me'). But they can also be used in statements about what one believes about any matter whatsoever (e.g. 'The argument appears sound to me').[8] So we need to distinguish between what I shall call *Narrow Protagoreanism* (NP) and *Broad Protagoreanism* (BP). According to Narrow Protagoreanism, each thing is, for any person, the way he perceives it as being. According to Broad Protagoreanism, each thing is, for any person, the way he believes it is. The distinction between Narrow and Broad Protagoreanism is that between two different substituends for 'each thing'. According to Narrow Protagoreanism, only perceptual predicates are appropriate substituends; according to Broad Protagoreanism, any term whatever is an appropriate substituend. The *Theaetetus* considers both Narrow and Broad Protagoreanism. In his initial discussion of Protagoras (152 A–169 D), for example, Plato focuses on Narrow Protagoreanism. But in the self-refutation argument (169 D–171 D), he focuses on

the measure doctrine, it is none the less used veridically. But that is not to say that 'appears' *means* 'obviously, evidently is'. Rather, to say how things appear to one is to say how one believes things are; Protagoras then insists that one can move from how one believes things are to how they really are (to one).

[7] For a defence of the claim that Protagoras accepts what Burnyeat calls the 'converse rule', see M. F. Burnyeat, 'Protagoras and Self-Refutation in Plato's *Theaetetus*', *Philosophical Review*, 85 (1976), 172–95 at 178–9. The claim is criticized by R. Ketchum, 'Plato's "Refutation" of Protagorean Relativism: *Theaetetus* 170–171', *Oxford Studies in Ancient Philosophy*, 10 (1992), 73–105 at 77–9, and by N. P. White, 'Plato on the Contents of Protagorean Relativism' (unpublished). I thank White for letting me read and refer to his paper. Although I find their criticisms persuasive, I am none the less inclined to accept Burnyeat's conclusion, if only because (as White remarks) it seems intuitively plausible to assume that it is a necessary condition of p's being true for A that A believe p.

[8] Of course, it is not easy to determine the range of perceptual predicates. The discussion that follows is indebted to McDowell, *Plato:* Theaetetus, 119–20. See also Burnyeat, 'Protagoras and Self-Refutation in Plato's *Theaetetus*', 178 n. 9. (This note erroneously refers back to n. 2 of 'Protagoras and Self-Refutation in Later Greek Philosophy'; however, I cannot find a note in the latter paper that makes the relevant point, though the point is made on p. 45, where n. 2 also occurs.) Although Burnyeat agrees that the measure doctrine sometimes uses 'appears' to cover all beliefs, he thinks that extending 'appears' beyond perceptual appearances 'may have little but bluff to support it' ('Protagoras and Self-Refutation in Later Greek Philosophy', 45).

Broad Protagoreanism.[9] In the present paper, I focus on Narrow Protagoreanism.

III

In interpreting Plato's Protagoras, it is vital to bear in mind that he is not discussed in isolation. Rather, as noted above, the first part of the *Theaetetus* is a complex and subtle dialectical investigation of the connections among three theses. Initially Theaetetus defines knowledge as perception; his definition is then quickly associated both with Protagoras' measure doctrine and with Heracleitus' claim that the world is in constant flux or change. At 160 D 6, Plato says that these three theses coincide.

There is considerable controversy about precisely how Plato takes the three theses to coincide. On the account I favour, Plato argues that Theaetetus' definition of knowledge as perception commits him to a Protagorean epistemology which, in turn, commits him to a Heracleitean ontology. He also argues that Theaetetus' definition is best supported by a Protagorean epistemology which, in turn, is best supported by a Heracleitean ontology.[10] (More precisely, Plato argues that (T), (H), and *Narrow* Protagoreanism

[9] For places where Plato adverts, at least implicitly, to the distinction between Narrow and Broad Protagoreanism, see 152 c 1–2 ('that which is hot and everything of that sort'), 171 E, and 178 B 5.

[10] This view has been well defended by M. F. Burnyeat, 'Idealism and Greek Philosophy: What Descartes Saw and Berkeley Missed', *Philosophical Review*, 91 (1982), 3–40, esp. 5–7; see also Burnyeat, *The Theaetetus of Plato* (Indianapolis: Hackett, 1990). Plato gives various 'stage-directions', as Burnyeat calls them, to indicate the connections he has in mind. Here are just a few of them. When Theaetetus proposes that knowledge is perception, Socrates tells him that 'what you've said about knowledge is no ordinary theory, but the one that Protagoras too used to state' (151 E 8–152 A 1). This suggests that Plato takes (T) and (P) to be equivalent. He then describes Protagoras' 'secret doctrine' (152 c 10), which, among other things, involves a Heracleitean flux ontology; the point of calling it a secret doctrine is presumably to indicate that it is an unnoticed implication of (P) (so McDowell, *Plato: Theaetetus*, 121–2), and so of (T). At 160 D 5–E 2, Plato says that since all things change (H), and since man is the measure of all things (P), knowledge is perception (T). So (H) and (P) jointly imply (T). We have already seen, however, that (P) implies (T) quite independently of (H). And that (H) implies (P) is suggested by, for example, 156 A 3–5, where Plato tells us that everything that's been said depends on the assumption that everything is change: so the defence of (P), among other things, depends on (H); that is, I assume, (H) is the basis for (P), and in that sense implies it. Cf. 183 A 2–3: (H) was introduced in order to establish (T); that is, it was taken to imply (T).

Despite my phrasing in the preceding paragraph, I do not think Plato takes the three theses literally to imply one another; rather, his idea is that each of them best supports and is best supported by the others. Even this overstates the case a bit; for the connections among the three theses are forged only with the aid of various ancillary premises. So, for example, Plato doesn't argue that (T) and (NP), on their own, imply one another or are,

are connected in these ways. Obviously the claim that knowledge is perception, for example, is neither committed to nor best supported by Broad Protagoreanism, since the latter allows knowledge to range outside the perceptual sphere.[11]) Once the connections among the three theses have been established, Plato turns to the offensive, rejecting each in turn.[12]

On this account of the structure of the first part of the *Theaetetus*, Plato is not propounding his own views about knowledge and perception; rather, he is asking what Theaetetus, and then Protagoras, are committed to, and how they are best supported. His strategy is the same as that pursued in many of the Socratic dialogues: an interlocutor proposes a definition, which Socrates then tests against various principles and examples; eventually the interlocutor is caught in contradiction. Faced with contradiction, the interlocutor can reject his initial definition, or he can reject the principles or examples. In the Socratic dialogues, the definition is generally rejected; and in the *Theaetetus* too, this is the eventual outcome. First, however, a different strategy is pursued: Theaetetus holds on to his definition, and revises his beliefs about the nature of the world to suit.[13]

If Plato's dialectical strategy is to succeed, various criteria must be satis-

---

on their own, one another's best support. Rather, he secures their connection only with the aid of the additional assumption that for A to perceive x as F is for x to appear F to A (152 B 9–12).

Note that to say that each of the three theses best supports, and is best supported by, the others is not to say that any of the three theses provides very good support for any of the others: the best available support might not be very good, and I take it that in his refutations, Plato argues just this.

Though I believe Plato connects the three theses in the way just described, it is sufficient for my purposes in this chapter that he envisages some close connection between (NP) and (H).

[11] One might argue that (BP)'s claim that all beliefs are true (to the believer) does not imply that all beliefs constitute knowledge, on the ground that being true (to the believer) is not sufficient for being knowledge. However, being true is necessary for being knowledge, and this is the condition on knowledge that Plato focuses on in assessing (T). One might also argue that (BP) does not conflict with (T), on the ground that (BP) does not say that beliefs can range outside the perceptual sphere. But as Plato conceives (BP), it does have this broader scope. (McDowell, *Plato: Theaetetus*, 168, however, thinks that 167 A 8 might restrict beliefs to perceptual beliefs.)

[12] He criticizes (P) primarily in 169 D–171 D and in 177 C 6–179 D 2; (H) in 181–3; and (T) in 184–6. Plato also levels other criticisms; and his criticisms of each of the three theses has implications for all three. Moreover, although 151–60 is ostensibly aimed at supporting Theaetetus' suggestion, it also in effect contains various criticisms. For example, Plato makes it plain that Theaetetus is committed to a very strong sort of Heracleiteanism; to the extent that that sort of Heracleiteanism is implausible, it counts against Theaetetus' suggestion.

[13] Not that Theaetetus is deeply wedded either to the definition or to the beliefs about the world that he endorses: he seems simply to play along with Socrates' development of various views. Here I am indebted to Lesley Brown.

fied. Here I shall mention just two of them. The first is the *univocity crite-rion*: it says that each of the three theses must be interpreted in a univocal way both when it is connected to the other two and when it is refuted. (P), for example, must be interpreted in some one way, both when it is connected to (T) and (H) and when it is refuted. If Plato were to refute a version of (P) quite different from the version earlier connected to (T) and (H), he would commit the fallacy of irrelevance.[14]

The second criterion is the *connection criterion*: we should aim to inter-pret each of the three theses in a way that makes it plausible to suggest that each of them is committed to and best supported by the others. In particu-lar, for our purposes here, we should aim to provide an interpretation of (NP) on which it is committed to and best supported by (T) and (H). If we find ourselves interpreting (NP) in such a way that (H), for example, is quite irrelevant to it, then we should think again.[15]

[14] There is a complication here. In connecting (P) to (T) and (H), Plato focuses on (NP); yet in refuting (P), he focuses on (BP). However, this does not show that univocity is violated. For although Plato's refutation of (P) focuses on (BP), I think he takes 181–6, coupled with the refutation of (BP), to constitute a refutation of (NP). If this is so, then univocity could be satisfied as follows: Protagoras holds (BP). In assessing (BP), Plato begins by considering a defence of an instance of it, namely (NP). He then returns to the original thesis, (BP), and refutes it. He realizes, however, that his argument leaves (NP) intact. Accordingly, he then returns to and criticizes it. Alternatively, Plato might think Protagoras believes (NP). In this case univocity could be satisfied as follows: Plato first defends (NP) by linking it to (T) and (H). He then considers and refutes a broader Protagorean doctrine, namely (BP). Having refuted it, he then returns to the original thesis, (NP), and refutes it. If Plato reasons in either of these ways—on both of which (NP) is a genuine instance of (BP)—then univocity is satisfied. If, however, (NP) is not an instance of (BP), if the two are quite different sorts of doctrine, then the structure of the first part of the *Theaetetus* would be very awkward at best. For in this case, Plato would have sandwiched a seemingly irrelevant discussion of (BP) in between his initial account of (NP) and its refutation. On the alternative account(s) I prefer, by contrast, the first part of the *Theaetetus* is quite smoothly organized. Of course, we cannot conclude that (NP) is an instance of (BP) without a full discussion of (BP) and its refutation. I take steps in this direction in ch. 8. See also my 'Relativism and Self-Refutation in Plato's *Theaetetus*: Plato, Protagoras, and Burnyeat', in J. Gentzler (ed.), *Method in Ancient Philosophy* (Oxford: Oxford Clarendon Press), 138–63.
A further complication in deciding whether the univocity criterion is satisfied is that the account of Heracleiteanism develops in various ways. I discuss this below.
[15] One might argue that we do not need to find an account of (P) and (H) on which they are *in fact* related as Plato suggests; all we need to do is to find an account that makes it plausible to suggest that *Plato* takes them to be so related. If he holds misguided philosophical views, then he might take them to be related in ways in which they are not in fact related. However, I hope to provide an account of (P) and (H) on which they are in fact related as Plato takes them to be; this, in turn, makes it reasonable to suppose that that is why Plato so links them.
Alternatively, one might argue that *Protagoras* links (P) and (H) in a way in which they are not in fact related. However, it is not clear what grounds we have for assuming that the historical Protagoras actually linked his doctrine to (H) at all; and even if he did, it would

In what follows, my main focus will be on the connection criterion. But the univocity criterion will concern us at a couple of junctures.

IV

These preliminaries out of the way, we can now ask how Plato interprets the measure doctrine. Various accounts have been proposed. According to one familiar account, Plato takes Protagoras to be a relativist about truth. In 'Protagoras and Self-Refutation in Later Greek Philosophy' and 'Protagoras and Self-Refutation in Plato's *Theaetetus*',[16] for example, Myles Burnyeat argues that Plato portrays Protagoras as 'a relativist who maintained that every judgment is true *for* (in relation to) the person whose judgment it is' (p. 172). He contrasts this with a view he calls subjectivism, according to which 'every judgment is true *simpliciter*—true absolutely, not merely true for the person whose judgment it is' (p. 46). Burnyeat believes that 'Aristotle, Sextus Empiricus, and the later sources generally' take the historical Protagoras to be a subjectivist; but he thinks that Plato—in his view correctly—takes Protagoras to be a relativist about truth instead (p. 46).[17]

Though many commentators claim that Plato portrays Protagoras as a

be reasonable to assume that, however the historical Protagoras defended himself, Plato is, perhaps among other things, aiming to provide what he sees as the best possible defence of Protagoras, whether or not the historical Protagoras offered it. If all he does is refute a weak defence offered by the historical Protagoras, without pointing out that a stronger one is available, we would have reason to be disappointed.

Note that even if one rejects my particular view of how Plato connects the three theses, one should still accept a version of the connection criterion. For it is clear that Plato envisages *some* fairly close connection between (NP) and (H).

Just as my account of the univocity criterion is limited (see previous note), so too is my account of the connection criterion. For to know that it is satisfied would require a full account not only of (P), but also of (T) and (H), whereas in this chapter I focus on (P), taking certain claims about the interpretation of (H) more or less for granted, and leaving (T) almost entirely to one side. (I am grateful to Gary Matthews for pointing this out to me.) But to the extent that the general picture I sketch allows us to satisfy the connnection criterion, that is some evidence in favour of the interpretations I suggest of the theses. Moreover, even if my account of (H) is not entirely uncontroversial, it is by no means idiosyncratic. I shall be content if I can show that on that account, we have reason to question the adequacy of some familiar interpretations of Protagoras.

[16]　For references to these two articles, see nn. 3 and 7. Subsequent references to them will generally be given by page reference alone, and they will generally be given in the text.

[17]　The view that Plato portrays Protagoras as a relativist about truth is also (independently) accepted by C. C. W. Taylor, who says that Protagoras 'held that in general what each man believes is true for him, which I take to imply that the notion of impersonal truth, according to which a belief is true or false *simpliciter*, is an empty one ... no one view can be said to be just true or false' (Taylor, *Plato: Protagoras*, 2nd edn. (Oxford: Clarendon Press, 1991), 83). (Though Taylor is discussing the *Protagoras* rather than the *Theaetetus*, he seems

relativist about truth, there are different accounts of precisely what this view amounts to. It is common ground that the view denies that there are any absolute truths—it denies, that is, that there are any propositions that are true *simpliciter*, just flat-out true.[18] But what does it mean to say that all beliefs are merely relatively true, that is, are true only for those who hold them?

It seems generally agreed that p's being true for A is equivalent to A's believing p. On the account I favour, there is an even stronger connection: 'true for A' means the same as 'believed by A'. This view is sometimes rejected on the ground that, as Burnyeat puts it, 'If the equivalence were mere synonymy, [(P)] would reduce to the bare tautology' that it appears to A that p if and only if it appears to A that p; but 'it is not likely that a clever man like Protagoras was merely waffling'.[19] But this is not a decisive reason for rejecting the synonymy interpretation. First, there can, of course, be informative synonymies, and perhaps this is one of them. Indeed, that the synonymy would have to be an informative, or deep, one is indicated

to believe that Plato describes Protagoras in the same way in both dialogues; see e.g. pp. 61, 101.) Unfortunately, Taylor sometimes calls this view subjectivism, sometimes relativism; contrast pp. 61 and 83 with p. 101. Further, Taylor speaks interchangeably of impersonal truth, truth *simpliciter*, and being just true. But if an impersonal truth is a truth that obtains independently of what anyone believes, then impersonal truth and truth *simpliciter* are not the same. For example, according to what Burnyeat calls subjectivism, if I believe p, then p is true *simpliciter*; but subjectivism does not countenance the existence of any impersonal truths in the sense of propositions that are true independently of being believed. Relativism about truth, on the other hand, denies not only that there are any impersonal truths but also that there are any propositions that are true *simpliciter*.

Or again, R. M. Dancy, 'Theaetetus' First Baby: *Theaetetus* 151e–160e', *Philosophical Topics*, 15 (1987), 61–108, says that he accepts Burnyeat's account of Plato's portrayal of Protagoras, which he describes as 'the doctrine that truth is relative to the individual' (103 n. 36). Though Dancy says that he accepts Burnyeat's view of how Plato portrays Protagoras, he calls this view subjectivism. This is unfortunate, given that Burnyeat claims that Plato's Protagoras (like the historical Protagoras, according to Burnyeat: see above with n. 3) is *not* a subjectivist.

D. Bostock, *Plato's* Theaetetus (Oxford: Clarendon Press, 1988), 88–92, also seems to think that Plato takes Protagoras to be a relativist about truth, at least in the self-refutation argument.

[18] At least, it is relatively (!) common ground. Those who favour a relativist reading, however, disagree as to whether Plato's Protagoras takes the statement of relativism itself to be an absolute truth. If he does, then he allows the existence of at least one absolute truth. For the sake of simplicity, I shall generally assume here that relativism about truth denies that there are any absolute truths whatsoever. I do not think the substance of any of my arguments depends on this assumption. But if one takes the statement of relativism to be an absolute truth, then many of my claims would need to be rephrased.

[19] Burnyeat, 'Protagoras and Self-Refutation in Plato's *Theaetetus*', 180–1; see Ketchum, 'Plato's "Refutation" of Protagorean Relativism', 82. Bostock, *Plato's* Theaetetus, 91 n. 6, notes the objection but responds to it in something like the way I do.

by the fact that there is dispute about what 'true for A' means.[20] Further, one might argue that the phrase 'true for A' is a technical one, and that as such it is reasonable to suppose that it is linked to 'believed by A' in order to provide a stipulative definition.[21] If there is a mere equivalence, we have not been given enough guidance for understanding what the novel locution means.[22] Moreover, even if the synonymy were uninformative, Protagoras would not be 'merely waffling' in offering it. For relativism about truth is a conjunctive thesis: it involves not only some connection between being true for A and being believed by A, but also the claim that there are no absolute truths; and this second claim is far from being a tautology.

So my own view is that relativism about truth should be construed as a conjunctive claim: that (i) 'true for A' means the same as 'believed by A', and that (ii) there are no absolute truths.[23] This particular explanation of relative truth would not be accepted by everyone. But however we interpret 'true for A', relativism about truth claims that there are no absolute truths; and this claim is often ascribed to Plato's Protagoras.[24]

---

[20] Here I am indebted to Nicholas Sturgeon and Lesley Brown.

[21] Even if 'believed by A' is a stipulative definition of 'true for A', there are, I think, constraints on what it could mean; in particular, the definition should make it clear why 'true' occurs in 'true for A'. I hope my account of relativism satisfies this constraint. J. Meiland, 'Concepts of Relative Truth', *Monist*, 60 (1977), 568–82 at 574, by contrast, does not seem to accept the constraint just mentioned. In his view, 'one can no more reasonably ask what "true" means in the expression "true-for-W" than one can ask what "cat" means in the word "cattle"'.

[22] One might argue that it is unreasonable to demand a definition of 'true for A'; after all, we often use terms quite well even when we cannot define them. But what is at issue here is not just whether we can use the phrase, but whether the claim that relative truth is the only sort of 'truth' there is is plausible; to be able to answer this question, we need to know what the claim amounts to, and here it is reasonable to suppose that we need to know what 'relative truth' means. But if (unlike me) one is moved by the objection, then I should still want to say that, in order to assess the view, we at least need to know what truth for a person consists in; on the account I favour, it consists in being believed by a person.

It is worth noting that at least some relativists accept the demand that 'true for A' be defined. Meiland, 'Concepts of Relative Truth', 580, for example, although he denies that 'true for A' means 'believed by A', agrees that he needs to provide an alternative account of what the phrase means. He suggests that 'true for A' means 'corresponds to reality for A'. He then imagines someone asking what 'corresponds to reality for A' means. He admits that this is an 'embarrassing question'; he replies only that nonrelativists, for their part, have found it difficult to explain their notion of truth.

[23] Again, one might exempt the statement of relativism, holding that it, at any rate, is an absolute truth.

[24] Nihilism is sometimes explained as the view that there are no absolute truths; so one might ask how, on my account, relativism differs from nihilism. The answer is that whereas the nihilist simply claims that there are no absolute truths, so that people who take themselves to be asserting them are simply making a mistake, the relativist about truth says that, though people do not succeed in asserting absolute truths (since there are none),

The claim that Protagoras believes that there are *no* absolute truths is a claim about how to interpret Broad Protagoreanism. Obviously Narrow Protagoreanism does not claim that there are *no* absolute truths. If Protagoras is a relativist about truth, then Narrow Protagoreanism should say that there are no absolute truths in the perceptual sphere; rather, propositions about what one perceives are merely relatively true.

V

Does Plato portray Protagoras as a relativist about truth, in the sense just explained? There is a good reason to hope that he does not do so. For relativism about truth violates the connection criterion: it is not committed to, nor does it best support, Heracleitus' claim that the world is in constant flux or change. This can be seen as follows.

Protagoreanism is initially explained as a possible solution to the problem of conflicting appearances: the wind seems cold to me, but not to you (152 B 1–7). What should we infer? Plato's Protagoras suggests we should infer that the wind is cold for me but not for you. On relativism about truth, this should mean that neither of our beliefs is absolutely true (or false), since there are no absolute truths (or falsehoods) (either *tout court* or in the perceptual sphere); but they are both relatively true. Hence both of our beliefs are in a sense right, but not in a sense that involves contradiction. There might be a contradiction if our beliefs were both absolutely true.[25] But since relativism about truth denies that there are any absolute truths (in the perceptual sphere, or *tout court*), it can allow all (perceptual) beliefs to be true (for the one who believes them) without sanctioning contradictions. The problem of conflicting appearances is therefore dissolved by denying that any beliefs conflict, since none of them is absolutely true.

Having explained Protagoras' solution to the problem of conflicting appearances, Plato introduces Protagoras' 'secret doctrine' (152 C 8–E 10). Presumably it is called a secret doctrine to indicate that it is an unnoticed

still, they do succeed in asserting something—relative truths. (Or at least they succeed in uttering relative truths: it is not clear that relativists think people *assert* anything.) The relativist tries to make the denial of absolute truth more palatable by allowing that there are, at any rate, relative truths. Here I am indebted to comments by Nicholas Sturgeon; see also Sturgeon, 'Moral Disagreement and Moral Relativism', *Social Philosophy and Policy*, 11 (1994), 80–115.

[25] Then again, there might not be. If, for example, we make our remarks at different times, and the wind changes between our utterances, then there would be no conflict even if both our beliefs were absolutely true.

consequence of Protagoras' view. The secret doctrine is, to say the least, complex, and its interpretation is controversial. However, one of its key components is the claim that 'nothing ever is, but all things are always coming to be' (152 D 8–E 1); 'all things are the result of flux and change' (152 E 8).

This suggests that the Protagorean solution to the problem of conflicting appearances implies something about change. But if Protagoras is a relativist about truth, he is not committed to an ontology of change; nor is he best supported by one. If Protagoras said that both our beliefs were *absolutely* true, so that the wind really is both cold and not cold, then we could see intuitively how Heracleitus might enter the picture. The idea (in this case) would be that Heracleitus supports Protagoras by showing how seemingly conflicting appearances that occur at different times can be absolutely true without contradiction. For if the wind changes from being cold when I believe it is, to being not cold when you believe it is not, then our beliefs can be absolutely true without conflicting. Similarly, if both our beliefs are absolutely true, then, if they occur at different times, and if we are pronouncing on the same wind, Protagoras is committed to Heracleiteanism, in so far as he would (in this case) have to say that the wind has changed from being cold to not cold.

But if Protagoras denies that there are any absolute truths, either *tout court* or in the perceptual sphere, then there is no need for him to appeal to an ontology of change to resolve the problem of conflicting appearances. For denying that there are any absolute truths dissolves the problem all on its own: the seeming conflict disappears once it is explained that the seemingly conflicting utterances are merely relative truths. So the relativist about truth does not need to appeal to an ontology of change, or to any ontology, to solve the problem of conflicting appearances; relativizing truth solves the problem all by itself. Nor does relativism about truth carry with it a commitment to a Heracleitean ontology, or to any other ontology. Indeed, so far from being committed to a view about how the world is, relativism about truth denies that there is an absolute truth about how the world is.

Not only, then, does relativism about truth not imply (H), and not only does it not need to appeal to (H) in its support, but, more strongly, (H) actually seems to conflict with relativism about truth. For (H) takes it to be an absolute truth that the world is in constant change, whereas relativism about truth denies that there are any absolute truths.[26]

---

[26] At least, relativism about truth, as we are conceiving it, denies that there are any absolute truths except, perhaps, for the statement of relativism itself. But even if one takes the statement of relativism to be an absolute truth, that does not alleviate the conflict just

One might argue that although this shows that (H) conflicts with an *unrestricted* relativism about truth, it does not show that (H) conflicts with a version of relativism about truth that is restricted to the perceptual sphere; for it might be argued that although Heracleiteanism is a claim *about* the perceptual sphere, it is not itself a perceptual claim.[27] But even if this is so, (H) still conflicts with a relativism about truth that is restricted to the perceptual sphere. For this more limited version of relativism denies that any perceptual claims are absolutely true; rather, according to it, all such claims are merely relatively true. (H), by contrast, says that there are some absolute truths about particular changes in the world. If (H) says, but a restricted version of relativism about truth denies, that there are some absolute truths in the perceptual sphere, then the two views conflict.

If, as I have argued, relativism about truth (broad or narrow) actually conflicts with (H), then if Plato portrays Protagoras as a relativist about truth, he violates the connection criterion.

Now it is true that the account of Heracleiteanism develops; one version gives rise to another in the face of various objections. Initially Heracleitus posits intersubjectively available if changing objects. But he eventually replaces them with private changing objects. Indeed, in the end he argues that neither objects nor perceivers persist; rather, there is a series of momentary objects and perceivers. On this view, no two people ever see the same

mentioned. That relativism about truth conflicts with (H) in something like the way just mentioned is also suggested by R. Waterfield, *Plato:* Theaetetus (Harmondsworth: Penguin Books, 1987), 151; see also Dancy, 'Theaetetus' First Baby', 62 and § 4. Dancy (p. 75) resolves the conflict by modifying (P) so that it says that 'everything is subjective [i.e. relative: cf. n. 17 above] *except* the changes that (H) alleges to be out there'. This resolution seems to abandon the view that (NP) involves relativism about truth. Hence although Dancy initially says that he agrees with Burnyeat that Plato's Protagoras is a relativist about truth, he eventually seems to reject this interpretation of (NP). But if he thinks that (BP) but not (NP) involves relativism about truth, then he violates the univocity criterion.

Gary Matthews and Lesley Brown have urged that (H) doesn't explicitly mention truth, absolute or otherwise, in which case the claim that (H) and relativism about truth conflict might seem too strong. I agree that (H) doesn't explicitly claim that it is an absolute truth that the world is in constant change; it simply says that the world is in constant change. But I take it that, though (H) doesn't explicitly say that it is intended as an absolute truth, that is how it should be understood: it purports to tell us how the world really is. And if it purports to tell us how the world really is, then it conflicts with relativism about truth, even if the conflict is not apparent at first glance.

One might argue that if the conflict is not apparent at first glance, perhaps it escaped Plato's notice. Of course, this possibility can't simply be ruled out without argument. But if we can provide an interpretation of (P) and (H) on which Plato is not confused, that is to be preferred; later I try to provide such an interpretation.

[27] I owe this suggestion to Sydney Shoemaker.

thing twice, nor can any one person ever see the same thing twice.[28] When public changing objects are replaced by private objects, Protagoras solves the problem of conflicting appearances as between different observers not by saying that some one wind has changed between our utterances, but by saying that we have not pronounced on the same wind: the wind I perceive is cold, whereas the one you perceive is not.

But neither is this solution to the problem of conflicting appearances appropriately related to relativism about truth, whether restricted to the perceptual sphere or not. First, just as relativism about truth's resolution of the problem of conflicting appearances does not commit it to an ontology of change, so it does not commit it to an ontology of private objects.

---

[28] So, for example, in the initial example of the wind at 152 B–C, it seems to be assumed that we are pronouncing on the same object. Then, in the development of the theory of perception at 153 D ff., various 'secondary' qualities such as the colour of a stone are said to be private (*idion*, 154 A 2) to each perceiver (so that what we strictly speaking see are not colours conceived as general properties but what are sometimes called tropes). It is then argued that no two perceivers can perceive the same object, e.g. a stone, nor can the same perceiver do so twice. I take this to be the upshot of the perplexing argument at 158 E 5–160 D. Though we differ on many points, my view is in this respect close to Burnyeat's; see Burnyeat, 'Protagoras and Self-Refutation in Plato's *Theaetetus*', 181–3. In saying that Protagoras is eventually committed to the view that objects like stones are private to perceivers, I mean to leave open the possibility that there is some bare matter that 'isn't anything (in itself)' that is not thus private. Sextus may ascribe this view to Protagoras; see *PH* 1. 216–19. M. Matthen, 'Perception, Relativism, and Truth: Reflections on Plato's *Theaetetus* 152–60', *Dialogue*, 24 (1985), 33–58, denies that Protagoras endorses an ontology of private objects; see also L. Brown, 'Understanding the *Theaetetus*', *Oxford Studies in Ancient Philosophy*, 11 (1993), 199–224 at 206.

Although I think the account of Heracleiteanism develops, I do not think Plato is merely considering a family of loosely related Heracleitean doctrines, as is suggested by R. Bolton, 'Plato's Distinction between Being and Becoming', *Review of Metaphysics*, 29 (1975), 66–95 at 70 n. 15. Nor do I think Plato confuses the notion of an intersubjectively changing object with that of a private object, as is perhaps suggested by Bostock, *Plato's* Theaetetus, 47–8. Rather, Plato initially supports Protagoras with a moderate version of Heracleiteanism, according to which there are intersubjectively available objects that, however, change according to appearance. He then points out that this moderate Heracleiteanism does not allow Protagoras to provide a satisfactory account of seemingly conflicting appearances that occur at some one time. In an effort to provide him with a better account, the initial version of Heracleiteanism is replaced with a new one, according to which there are only private objects, each of which changes according to its perceiver's changing appearances. Plato then argues that Protagoras is committed to an even stronger version of Heracleiteanism, according to which neither objects nor perceivers persist. We begin, then, with a moderate version of Heracleiteanism, which is gradually refined and revised in the face of various objections; as befits a dialectical discussion, Protagoras' commitments are uncovered only gradually. On this interpretation, the account of Heracleiteanism satisfies univocity even though more than one Heracleitean doctrine is considered. For the task is to find an account of Heracleiteanism that plays its assigned role, of being the best support for (T) and (NP), and such that they, in turn, are committed to it. Naturally, enough, then, different doctrines are auditioned for the part, until the most satisfactory candidate is found.

Relativizing truth solves the problem of conflicting appearances without commitment to *any* ontology. Secondly, relativism about truth is not best supported by an ontology of private objects. Indeed, just as taking it to be absolutely true that there are changing objects conflicts with relativism about truth, so too does taking it to be absolutely true that there are private objects.[29]

One might argue that, contrary to what I have been assuming, an ontology of private objects is incompatible with absolute truth. Wittgenstein, for example, famously remarks that, given an ontology of private objects, 'whatever is going to seem right to me is right. And that only means that here we can't talk about "right"' (*PI* 1. 258). I myself don't agree. But no one who agrees should think this makes advocating an ontology of private objects consistent with relativism about truth. For if Wittgenstein's argument succeeded, it would equally well show that there are no relative truths, for he is arguing that a private language is impossible; yet though the relativist about truth denies that there are absolute truths, she believes that there are meaningful relative truths. (Whether she is entitled to this claim is of course another question.) So if one argues along Wittgensteinian lines that an ontology of private objects is incompatible with absolute truths, one should concede that it is equally incompatible with relativism about truth.

Even if one at this point agrees that Protagoras is not portrayed as a relativist about truth when he is initially discussed in connection with Heracleitus, one might none the less wish to argue that he is so viewed in the self-refutation argument; and indeed, just this sometimes seems to be assumed.[30] However, if Plato portrays Protagoras as a relativist about truth in the self-refutation argument, but not in linking him to Heracleitus, then

[29] Bostock, *Plato's Theaetetus*, 91, also notes that the view that all beliefs are true about private objects is quite different from relativism about truth. None the less, he seems to think that Protagoras espouses both views. For, as we have seen (n. 17), he seems to view Protagoras as a relativist about truth in connection with the self-refutation argument; yet in discussing the 150s, he seems to suggest that Plato sometimes ascribes to Protagoras an ontology of private objects. See pp. 47–51; although in this passage the doctrine of private objects is suggested merely as a possible solution to the problem of conflicting appearances, Bostock appears to believe that Plato at some stages takes Protagoras to endorse it.

It is worth emphasizing that the contradiction I have alleged between relativism about truth and Heracleiteanism does not depend on the synonymy account of relativism. All my argument requires is the claim that relativism about truth denies the existence of absolute truths (either *tout court* or in the perceptual sphere). But Heracleiteanism (whether about intersubjectively available changing objects or about private objects) claims that there are such truths. If one view denies the existence of absolute truths, but the other view claims that there are such truths, then the two views conflict. On whether (H) claims that there are such truths, see n. 26.

[30] This may be Bostock's view, though he does not say so explicitly (see previous note). It may also be Dancy's view; see nn. 17 and 26 above, with pp. 74 and 96 of his article.

he violates the univocity criterion.[31] So if I am right to say that Protagoras should not be viewed as a relativist about truth in the 150s, on the ground that that would violate the connection criterion, then we have reason to hope that he is not portrayed as a relativist about truth *anywhere* in the *Theaetetus*. For if he were so portrayed at some stage, either the connection or univocity criteria, or both, would be violated.

VI

Accordingly, I now turn to a second account of Plato's Protagoras that has also been proposed, to see whether it does a better job of satisfying our criteria. It is sometimes argued that Plato's Protagoras resolves the problem of conflicting appearances, at least in the perceptual sphere, by relativizing properties to perceivers. Burnyeat, for example, says that Protagoras 'allows the honey to be both sweet and bitter, subject to the qualification that it is sweet *for* (in relation to) some palates and bitter *for* others. By relativizing the attributions of sweet and bitter Protagoras avoids the contradictions embraced by Heraclitus.'[32] Or again, B. A. O. Williams says that what Protagoras 'relativized were the perceptual terms, such as "hot" '.[33] And David Bostock ascribes to Protagoras what he calls 'the solution by relativity', according to which 'our judgements do concern the same object, but say quite compatible things about it, for the predicate of the judgement should in each case be regarded as relativized to the person making it'.[34] Let us call this view *perceptual relativism*.[35]

According to perceptual relativism, 'There is no such thing as (being)

---

[31] I mentioned above that the account of Heracleiteanism develops, yet this does not violate univocity. One might then wonder: why can't Plato consider different Protagorean doctrines without violating univocity? The answer is that he can in principle do so (and does do so in so far as he considers both (NP) and (BP)), but that, given the structure of his discussion, univocity would be satisfied only if (NP) were an instance of (BP). See above, n. 14.

[32] M. F. Burnyeat, 'Conflicting Appearances', *Proceedings of the British Academy*, 65 (1979), 69–111 at 71. Burnyeat is here talking about the historical Heracleitus, not about Heracleitus as he is portrayed in the *Theaetetus*. It is interesting to note that although Burnyeat believes that Plato's account of Protagoras in the *Theaetetus* is historically accurate (see above, sect. 1), he does not seem to think that his account of Heracleitus in the *Theaetetus* is historically accurate.

[33] See his Introduction in *Plato: Theaetetus* (Indianapolis: Hackett, 1992), p. xiii.

[34] Bostock, *Plato's Theaetetus*, 47–8.

[35] Burnyeat uses this phrase for Protagoras' position in 'Conflicting Appearances', 71; see also Burnyeat, *The Theaetetus of Plato*, 15. For further discussion of his defence of the view that Protagoras is a perceptual relativist, see my 'Conflicting Appearances' (ch. 7 below). Burnyeat's account of what he calls perceptual relativism may not be identical in all its

white *simpliciter*, only white for you and white for me.'[36] That is, whiteness is a relational rather than an intrinsic property: objects are not white on their own, independently of perception; rather, they are white only in relation to perceivers.[37]

Now it is clear that Plato's Protagoras in some sense relativizes properties to perceivers. But perceptual relativism has a special account of the way in which he does so: it says that an object can appear different without itself genuinely changing. Suppose, for example, that the wind appears cold to me but not to you. As Bostock explains, it 'may very well be that this appearance has changed, not because there has been any change in the wind, but because there has been a change in me. (I have got colder.)'.[38] Or again, in 'Conflicting Appearances' Burnyeat discusses *Theaetetus* 153 D–154 B in some detail. He argues that this passage aims to establish perceptual relativism. And he claims that Plato makes 'absolutely explicit the important point that . . . the argument [on behalf of perceptual relativism] only applies on the assumption that the thing we are talking about remains unchanged'.[39]

According to perceptual relativism, then, 'change' of colour can be a mere Cambridge change in the object.[40] For perceptual relativism says that an

details with Bostock's account of what he calls the solution by relativity; but, so far as I can tell, the two views are the same on the points I discuss here. (Williams does not develop his suggestion in any detail.)

[36] Burnyeat, 'Conflicting Appearances', 78.

[37] As I have described perceptual relativism, it allows that objects are, for example, white, so long as this is correctly understood, as claiming that perceptual properties are relational. Burnyeat seems to suggest this view in the passage quoted from him just above, since he says there that Protagoras 'allows the honey to be both sweet and bitter', so long as we understand that it is so only in some relation or other. Sometimes, however, Burnyeat seems to say instead that, on perceptual relativism, objects are not really white. (He says, for example, that whiteness is 'not a distinct thing existing anywhere at all': 'Conflicting Appearances', 77, cf. 78.) When he speaks in this way, however, he seems to allow that whiteness-tokens, or what are sometimes called tropes, none the less exist. I discuss this further in ch. 7 below. In this chapter, I shall assume that on perceptual relativism objects can be, for example, white, though their whiteness is a relational rather than an intrinsic feature of them, and though the whiteness of an object is a trope rather than a general, shared property.   [38] Bostock, *Plato's* Theaetetus, 48; cf. 59.

[39] Burnyeat, 'Conflicting Appearances', 79. The claim that the passage assumes that the object does not change seems to be generally accepted. See e.g. McDowell, *Plato's* Theaetetus, 132; Dancy, 'Theaetetus' First Baby', 79; Bostock, *Plato's* Theaetetus, 59; F. M. Cornford, *Plato's Theory of Knowledge: The* Theaetetus *and the* Sophist *of Plato*, translated with a running commentary (London: Routledge & Kegan Paul, 1935), 40–1 n 1.

[40] P. T. Geach, *God and the Soul* (London: Routledge & Kegan Paul, 1969), 71. Geach introduces a criterion for change that he calls the 'Cambridge criterion': 'The thing called "x" has changed if we have "F(x) at time t" true and "F(x) at time t'" false, for some interpretations of "F", "t", and "t'".' On this criterion, I undergo a Cambridge change if I grow from being 5′1″ to 5′2″; I also undergo one if I come to be shorter than Theaetetus

object is red, in a given relation, if and only if it appears red to the perceiver in that relation. So if an object no longer appears red to that perceiver, it no longer is red in that relation. But an object can cease to appear red to me if I am suddenly struck blind. In this case, perceptual relativism says that the object ceases to be red, in relation to me, without itself genuinely changing; its ceasing to be red is a mere Cambridge change in it.

Perceptual relativism is obviously an account of Narrow rather than of Broad Protagoreanism—of the view, that is, that things are (to one), and are only (to one) however one believes them to be on the basis of perception. And it is usually offered as an interpretation of the early 150s, where private objects have not yet been introduced; at this point objects are still taken to be intersubjectively available.

I suspect that, like relativism about truth, perceptual relativism will appeal to many people. Certainly Locke sometimes seems attracted to it.[41] But is Protagoras a perceptual relativist?

VII

Before answering this question, I attempt to answer another, related question: what, if any, connection is there between perceptual relativism and relativism about truth? Burnyeat appears to believe that they are the same position.[42] In a passage part of which was quoted above, for example, he says:

in virtue of his growth. 'Mere Cambridge changes' are the subclass of Cambridge changes that are not intuitively taken to be genuine changes.

[41] Locke says, for example, that colours and so on are powers in objects to produce certain sorts of sensations in perceivers. (See e.g. *An Essay concerning Human Understanding* II. viii. 10: secondary qualities 'are nothing in the objects themselves but powers to produce various sensations in us'.) This makes them relational: objects have the colours they do partly in virtue of their relation to perceivers. Locke also says that only a thing's primary qualities are its real qualities. (See e.g. *Essay*, II. viii. 17.) So Locke seems to hold that colours are in some sense not real properties of objects (perceptual relativism is sometimes taken to claim this: see n. 37). Locke also seems to be committed to the view that an object can change colour without itself undergoing a genuine change. For he takes it to be essential to an object's being red that it appear red to someone. (See *Essay*, IV. iii. 15. I owe this reference to Nicholas Sturgeon.) So if an object no longer appears red to someone because the person is struck blind, the object no longer is red (in that relation). Locke is then committed to the view that change of secondary qualities can be a mere Cambridge change in the object.

[42] The two views may also be assimilated by E. Schiappa, *Protagoras and Logos: A Study in Greek Philosophy and Rhetoric* (Columbia, SC: University of South Carolina Press, 1991): on e.g. p. 126 he speaks of Protagoras' relativism; on p. 128, of his view that perception is relational. (However, p. 130 suggests that he might view the attempt to be precise about Protagoras' view as anachronistic.) Williams, by contrast, seems to deny that the two views

Protagoras' doctrine that man is the measure of all things recommends a relativistic account of truth which allows the honey to be both sweet and bitter, subject to the qualification that it is sweet *for* (in relation to) some palates and bitter *for* others. By relativizing the attributions of sweet and bitter Protagoras avoids the contradictions embraced by Heraclitus. ('Conflicting Appearances', 71)

Burnyeat initially says that Protagoras is a relativist about *truth*; but he explains this by saying that Protagoras relativizes *perceptual properties*.[43] Is Burnyeat right to assimilate the two views?

Perceptual relativism is clearly quite different from a completely general relativism about truth. For the former view concerns only sensible qualities, whereas the latter view is more wide-ranging. But is perceptual relativism the same as a relativism about truth that is restricted to the perceptual sphere?

It is important to see that the mere view that perceptual properties are relational does not involve relativism about truth (restricted or unrestricted), as the latter notion has been explained. Consider, for example, the analogy of a good diet. No one diet is good for everyone, so we may say that there is no such thing as a good diet as such; there are only diets that are good for A, good for B, and so on. We can put this by saying that the notion of a good diet is relational. But this sort of *relationalism* (as we might call it) does not import *relativism* about truth. On the contrary, it is an absolute truth that (say) a high-fibre diet is good for Jane but not for Joe. Nor do facts about what constitute good diets for particular people have anything

are equivalent. For he says that 'Protagoras' formulae did not rely on deploying a relativized sense of "true"' (Introduction to *Plato: Theaetetus*, p. xii); and he then goes on to say, in the remark quoted from him above, that Protagoras relativized perceptual terms instead. This suggests that he views relativizing truth as an alternative to relativizing properties. (If this is his view, however, then I am not sure why he goes on to say that '"*It is hot* is true for me" got its content by meaning "It is hot for me".')

[43] Perhaps Burnyeat uses 'relativism about truth' differently in 'Conflicting Appearances' from how he uses it elsewhere, so I would not want to rely on the mere occurrence of the phrase here in order to argue that he takes relativism about truth (as I have explicated it) to be the same as perceptual relativism. However, we have seen that he sometimes understands relativism about truth as I have explicated that notion; and we have also seen that in 'Conflicting Appearances' he ascribes perceptual relativism to Protagoras. So even if the passage just cited does not by itself show that Burnyeat takes relativism about truth and perceptual relativism to be the same, I hope to have shown that he ascribes both views to Protagoras; nor do I know of any place where he suggests that the two views differ (except in so far as perceptual relativism is restricted to perceptual properties, whereas relativism about truth ranges more widely). Similarly, in *The Theaetetus of Plato*, 21, Burnyeat says that although initially the Protagorean formula 'x appears F to A' restricts substituends for 'x' and 'F' to sensible objects and perceptual properties, respectively, beliefs and truth eventually count as substituends. This too suggests that Burnyeat views perceptual relativism as an instance or type of relativism about truth.

to do with people's beliefs; a given diet is good for Jane quite independently of whether Jane or anyone else believes that it is.[44]

But even if relationalism as such does not involve relativism about truth, a given version of relationalism might involve it. So we need to ask more precisely what sort of relationalism is involved in perceptual relativism. If the claim is that an object is red if and only if a person's sense organs are stimulated in a certain way, then we still do not have relativism about truth. For this is not to say that there is no absolute truth, no truth *simpliciter*, as to when an object is red. Rather, the claim is that it is absolutely true that an object is red—if and only if a given perceiver's sense organs are stimulated in a given way. Moreover, that a perceiver's sense organs are stimulated in a given way is a wholly objective matter, in the sense that how one's sense organs are stimulated is independent of what anyone believes.[45]

But perceptual relativism claims more than that objects have perceptual properties if and only if a perceiver's sense organs are stimulated in a given way. It also claims that an object is red, in relation to a perceiver, if and only if it *appears* red to that perceiver; and, as we have seen (in Section II), as appearance is understood here it includes (or is a kind of) belief. So perceptual relativism claims that an object is red, in relation to a given perceiver, if and only if that person believes, on the basis of perception, that he is seeing something red. But not even this view involves relativism about truth. Relativism about truth says something about the nature of truth, in particular, that there are no absolute truths—either at all (BP) or in the perceptual domain (NP). So it says that it is not absolutely true, but is at best true for a given person, that an object is red (in relation to a given perceiver). Perceptual relativism, by contrast, says something about the nature of perceptual properties, in particular, that they are relational. According to perceptual relativism, when a perceiver believes, on the basis of perception, that he is seeing something red, it is absolutely true that he is doing so. This conflicts with the claim that it is merely relatively true that he is doing so. Of course, if perceptual relativism is true, then only certain claims are true. But this says that perceptual relativism has implications for which propositions are true. It does not say—and it is

[44] For these points, see Taylor, *Plato: Protagoras*, 133–4. Taylor says that those who find an allusion to Protagoreanism (which, as we saw in n. 17, he takes to be relativism about truth) in the view that 'good' is a relational predicate, such that things are good only in some relation or other, are involved in 'sheer confusion' (p. 134). See also P. Railton, 'Facts and Value', *Philosophical Topics*, 14 (1986), 5–31 at 10–11.

[45] We might, however, say that this account none the less makes perceptual properties subjective, in so far as perceivers are one of the relata. If this is right, then not every sort of objectivity excludes every sort of subjectivity.

not true—that perceptual relativism implies that any beliefs are merely relatively true.

Perhaps the conflict between the two views can be seen more clearly by contrasting the following two sentences:

(1) It is absolutely true that this apple is red, in relation to a given perceiver, if and only if it appears red to that perceiver.
(2) It is not absolutely true that this apple is red; rather, it is true only for the person who believes it.

Perceptual relativism asserts (1);[46] relativism about truth asserts (2). But (1) and (2) are incompatible, since (1) takes a given proposition to be absolutely true, whereas (2) denies that it is.[47]

Here it might be useful to distinguish between *objective* and *absolute* truth. Let us say that an objective truth is one that obtains independently of belief,[48] and that an absolute truth is one that is true *simpliciter*, that is simply flat-out true rather than being merely relatively true, i.e. merely

[46] Gary Matthews has objected to me that perceptual relativism doesn't explicitly say that it is absolutely true that objects have perceptual properties only in relation to perceivers; it doesn't explicitly make any claims about the nature of truth. Doesn't this show that it is less clear than I make it out to be that perceptual relativism conflicts with relativism about truth? I agree that perceptual relativism doesn't explicitly mention absolute (or any other sort of) truth. But I think that, as Burnyeat and others conceive it, perceptual relativism is intended to be a metaphysical thesis about the real nature of perceptual properties; it is intended to explain how things really are, even if it doesn't explicitly say that that is the status of its claims. (And that it doesn't say anything about the status of its claims is hardly surprising: when I say 'It's raining' (or whatever), I don't usually trouble to add: 'By the way, I think it's really true that it's raining'.) If this is right, then the two views do conflict in the way I suggest, even if perceptual relativism doesn't explicitly claim to be an absolute truth. See above, n. 26, for a parallel discussion in connection with (H). (In *The* Theaetetus *of Plato*, 16–17, Burnyeat contrasts what he calls a physical and a metaphysical interpretation of the theory of perception, and seems to endorse the latter. Later, however, he contrasts instead a literal and metaphorical interpretation (p. 48). These are not the same contrast. Nor do we need to choose between saying that the theory of perception provides a description of the physical process of perception and saying that it presents a certain metaphysical picture.)

[47] (1) and (2) are both different from:

(3) 'It is true for me that the apple is red' is absolutely (relatively) true.

(3) is a higher-order statement than (1) or (2). Perceptual relativism says nothing about the status of propositions like 'It is true for me that p'. Of course, unrestricted relativism about truth takes such propositions to be merely relatively true. I am not sure whether such higher-order propositions about perceptual appearances fall within the scope of relativism about truth when it is restricted to the perceptual sphere. But it doesn't matter, since it is only (1) and (2) that are relevant at this point.

[48] As Sydney Shoemaker has pointed out to me, this account of objectivity is not quite right, since some propositions about what people believe are objectively true. But I hope the account none the less suffices for present purposes.

believed true by someone. Perceptual relativism and relativism about truth both deny that there are any objective truths in the perceptual domain. But the two views none the less conflict, since relativism about truth denies that there are any absolute truths (in the perceptual domain, or *tout court*), whereas perceptual relativism claims that there are such truths. Perceptual relativism is a metaphysical thesis about the conditions that have to obtain in the world for it to be the case that an object has a perceptual property; it is a thesis about how the world really is. But relativism about truth denies that there is a way the world really is.[49]

One might argue that, contrary to what I have said, perceptual relativism does not countenance absolute truths, propositions that are true *simpliciter*. For, as we have seen, perceptual relativism says that there is no such thing as being white *simpliciter*. Does it not then follow that perceptual relativism denies the existence of absolute truths, at least in the perceptual sphere? No, it does not. For, as we have seen, to say that there is no such thing as being white *simpliciter* is to say that whiteness is a relational property. But to say that whiteness is a relational property does not imply that there are no absolute truths as to when an object is white in a given relation.[50]

One might also claim that perceptual relativism is tantamount to a restricted version of relativism about truth, on the ground that in making perceptual properties relative to perceivers, it makes them private: the redness that I perceive can be seen only by me; each person perceives numerically distinct perception tokens, indeed, as Plato makes clear (154 A 6–8), qualitatively different ones as well. But, as we have seen, privacy does not import relativism about truth.[51] Even if a given redness-token is accessible

---

[49] As I mentioned above (n. 37), perceptual relativism is sometimes described as the view that objects in some sense do not really have perceptual properties. On this characterization, perceptual relativism does deny that it is flat-out true that objects have perceptual properties, and this might make it seem closer to relativism about truth. But if perceptual relativism denies that it is flat-out true that objects have perceptual properties, it does not do so because it denies that there are absolute truths. Rather, it is because (on this interpretation) it claims that it is absolutely, flat-out false that objects have such properties. But such a claim is still incompatible with relativism about truth, since the latter denies that there are absolute falsehoods.

[50] As we have seen, to deny that anything is white *simpliciter* may also be to say that there is no general property whiteness, but only whiteness-tokens or tropes. But neither does this mean that there are no absolute truths as to when things have such tokens or, at least, as to when they exist: they exist when and only when they are perceived to exist.

[51] Earlier we saw that countenancing private objects doesn't get one to relativism about truth, either because, on my view, there are absolute truths about such objects or because, on a Wittgensteinian view, there can be neither absolute nor relative truths about such objects. Perceptual relativism doesn't introduce private objects. But it might seem to make perceptual properties private. My point then is that just as countenancing private objects

only to me, and even if its existence is dependent on my perceiving it, it might none the less be absolutely true that it exists.[52]

I have been arguing that perceptual relativism, so far from being a sort of relativism about truth, actually conflicts with it. For the former purports to tell us the real nature of perceptual properties—it is offered as an absolute truth about their nature—whereas the latter denies that there are any absolute truths. Even if one rejects my argument, one should none the less, I think, agree that the two views are at least different, in so far as relativism about truth denies that there are any absolute truths (*tout court* or in the perceptual sphere), whereas perceptual relativism does not deny this.

But suppose that even this weaker view is wrong, and that perceptual relativism is a sort of relativism about truth. Then we already have reason to hope that Plato does not portray Protagoras as a perceptual relativist. For if he does so, and if perceptual relativism is a sort of relativism about truth, and if I was right to argue that relativism about truth violates the connection criterion, then perceptual relativism would also violate it. If, however, I am right to say that perceptual relativism conflicts with (or at least differs from) relativism about truth, then we still need to ask whether it is adequate as an interpretation of Narrow Protagoreanism. So let us now turn to the adequacy of perceptual relativism on the assumption that it conflicts with (or at least differs from) relativism about truth in the way in which I have suggested.

VIII

Even if perceptual relativism is conceived as I have conceived it, so that it conflicts with (or at least differs from) relativism about truth, we still have reason to hope that Plato does not portray Protagoras as a perceptual relativist; for like relativism about truth, perceptual relativism violates the connection criterion. This can be seen as follows.

Perceptual relativism allows an object to appear different without changing. Indeed, we have seen that, according to Burnyeat, the argument on its behalf, in 153 D–154 B, depends on the assumption that an object remains the same when it appears different. So according to Burnyeat Plato supports Protagoras, at least at one stage, not with a Heracleitean ontology

does not import relativism about truth, neither does countenancing private properties do so.

[52] It would in this case not be objectively true that it exists; but we have seen that one can deny that there are any objective truths yet countenance absolute truths.

of changing objects, but with an ontology of stable objects. That sort of support would indeed be appropriate for perceptual relativism. But that very fact shows that perceptual relativism is the wrong sort of doctrine to import here. For Plato says that Protagoras is best supported by Heracleiteanism, yet perceptual relativism is not best so supported since in contrast to Heracleiteanism it allows objects to remain stable even when they appear different.

It is true, as we have noticed, that the relevant version of Heracleiteanism develops. Perhaps in 153–4 Heracleiteanism is weak enough to allow objects to remain the same when they appear different? This is, of course, in principle possible. But in Chapter 7 I argue that the text of 153–4 does not in fact assume that objects can remain the same when they appear different, and hence the requisite support for perceptual relativism is not in fact in place.[53] Nor is it invoked later. Indeed, as Heracleiteanism develops it becomes increasingly clear that it cannot support, but indeed conflicts with, perceptual relativism. At 156 A 1–3, for example, Plato says that 'everything that's been said depends on the assumption that the universe is change and *nothing else*'. The claim that the universe is change and nothing else conflicts with perceptual relativism, according to which objects are sometimes stable.

Not only is perceptual relativism not best supported by Heracleiteanism as it is described in the *Theaetetus*, but neither is it committed to it. Perceptual relativism can dissolve the problem of conflicting appearances by saying that perceivers have changed; it need not posit changes in objects and, in fact, it declines to do so in at least some cases, which it claims are mere Cambridge changes in objects. Yet positing genuine changes in objects is precisely what Heracleiteanism does.[54] As Bostock remarks, 'if one sticks firmly to the approach in terms of relativity, there is no obvious temptation

---

[53] Perceptual relativism has several components, and I think Plato's Protagoras accepts some of them. For example, he clearly thinks that perceptual properties are in some sense relational. But the crucial question here is whether he thinks they are relational in the particular way described by perceptual relativism, such that objects can remain unchanged when they appear different. My claim here is only that this particular aspect of perceptual relativism is not involved even in 153 D–154 B.

[54] Again, one might argue that the relevant version of Heracleiteanism develops. Perhaps at an early stage, changes in perceivers will do; one need not posit corresponding changes in objects. But see above. We have seen, of course, that at a later stage of discussion, seemingly conflicting appearances between different observers, or between a 'single' observer over time, are dissolved by appealing not to a single changing object but to different objects. But neither does this view fit with perceptual relativism since it does not allow objects to remain unchanged while appearing differently; on the contrary, each new occasion of perception (appearance) is the perception of a different object, which is only as it appears to be.

to be led from these considerations to anything resembling the doctrine of Heraclitean flux, as that appears in our dialogue'.[55]

IX

I have argued so far that Plato's Protagoras is not satisfactorily interpreted either as a perceptual relativist or as a relativist about truth; for both views violate the connection criterion. Nor should Plato attribute first one view, then the other, to Protagoras; for then the univocity criterion would be violated.[56] Fortunately, however, another and better interpretation of Plato's Protagoras is available—one that satisfies the connection criterion.[57]

We saw above that Burnyeat contrasts relativism about truth (the view he thinks Plato ascribes to Protagoras) with subjectivism (a view he thinks Plato does not ascribe to Protagoras, though he thinks that all ancient commentators aside from Plato interpret Protagoras in this way). According to subjectivism, again, all beliefs are true—true *simpliciter*, not merely true for the one who holds them. Though Burnyeat calls this view subjectivism, I shall call it *infallibilism*.[58]

[55] Bostock, *Plato's* Theaetetus, 49.

[56] At least, this is so if, as I have argued, perceptual relativism is not a version of relativism about truth.

[57] I believe that the view I go on to describe also satisfies the univocity criterion—that is, I believe that Plato construes both (NP) and (BP) along infallibilist lines. For a defence of the view that (BP) should be interpreted along infallibilist lines, see ch. 8; see also n. 14.

[58] I do so partly because 'subjectivism' is used in so many different ways that its use here would only add to the confusion. We saw above (n. 17), for example, that Taylor and Dancy use 'subjectivism' for the view that Burnyeat calls 'relativism'. Moreover, 'subjectivism' might misleadingly suggest that all objects and properties are mental entities. But infallibilism does not claim this. It claims that things are—really are—(and are only, since (P) is a biconditional: see sect. 11) however they are believed to be, where at least many objects and their properties are extra-mental, though the existence of all objects and properties depends on their being perceived or believed to be as they are. (I say 'many' because infallibilism does not deny the existence of mental objects and properties.) The label 'infallibilism' avoids the difficulties the label 'subjectivism' gives rise to, and it also captures the fact that we are all infallible as to how things really are.

S. Waterlow, 'Protagoras and Inconsistency', *Archiv für Geschichte der Philosophie*, 59 (1977), 19–36, at e.g. 32, distinguishes between what she calls relativism about truth and relativism about fact; and she argues that Plato portrays Protagoras as a relativist about fact. So like me, she denies that Plato takes Protagoras to be a relativist about truth; and relativism about fact is in many ways like infallibilism. However, her article focuses on the self-refutation argument, which I do not discuss here; hence our defences of our alternative to relativism about truth likewise differ. We also differ in further ways, some of which I explore in ch. 8.

Just as we earlier distinguished between narrow and broad versions of relativism about truth, to correspond to the difference between Narrow and Broad Protagoreanism, so we need to distinguish between narrow and broad infallibilism. Narrow infallibilism says that all perceptual beliefs are absolutely true; broad infallibilism says that all beliefs whatever are absolutely true. Since (P) is a biconditional,[59] infallibilism says that objects are, and are only, as they appear to be; so, all (perceptual) beliefs are true, and there are no (perceptual) truths that are not believed.

Infallibilism differs from both perceptual relativism and relativism about truth. For example, infallibilism holds that all beliefs (either *tout court* or in the perceptual sphere) are absolutely true, whereas relativism about truth denies the existence of absolute truths (either *tout court* or in the perceptual sphere). And in contrast to perceptual relativism, infallibilism holds that objects cannot appear different without genuinely changing. For infallibilism says that objects are—really are—however they appear to be. But then, if an object appears first green, then not green, it was green, then not green—it was really green, then really not green—and so it must have changed. Even if the object no longer appears green to me because I have been struck blind, still, according to infallibilism the object none the less undergoes a genuine change, from being green to not being green.[60]

It might seem that infallibilism is so implausible that we should, if possible, avoid importing it into the text. Burnyeat, for example, claims that infallibilism 'is in clear violation of the law of contradiction'.[61] But this claim is too quick. It would be true if the world were populated by stable, intersubjectively available objects. But that is precisely why Plato has Protagoras reject this view of the world in favour of Heracleiteanism.

---

[59] See sect. II.

[60] Alternatively, when private momentary objects are on the scene, the object ceases to exist when there is a different case of perception. At this stage, every case of perception involves the perception of a numerically distinct object by a numerically distinct perceiver. But there is still constant change in so far as neither objects nor perceivers persist from one moment to the next; and each object is exactly as it is perceived. Hence at no stage do objects merely Cambridge change according to perception.

[61] Burnyeat, 'Protagoras and Self-Refutation in Later Greek Philosophy', 46. One might also ask why, if Plato's Protagoras is an infallibilist, Plato uses the qualifier 'to one' in describing his position. I cannot provide a full reply here. But, briefly, if (P) is a biconditional, then one role the qualifiers play is to indicate that a proposition can be true only if it is believed true, and so in that sense every truth is true for someone. Secondly, we have seen that at least (NP) is eventually supported by means of, and is committed to, an ontology of private objects; such objects exist only for a particular person. So the qualifiers play at least two roles on infallibilism. It is also important to note that Plato does not consistently include the qualifier either in refuting or in reporting Protagoras; and when it is included, it does not always (or even usually) qualify truth.

This, in turn, shows that whatever the intrinsic implausibility of in-fallibilism, it has a big advantage over both relativism about truth and perceptual relativism, considered as an interpretation of Protagoras as he is portrayed in the *Theaetetus*: unlike these latter two views, infallibilism makes Protagoras' Heracleitean connections clear. Unlike relativism about truth and perceptual relativism, that is, infallibilism satisfies the connection criterion. For if objects are, and are only, as they appear, then, given that objects constantly appear different, objects are constantly changing; and so infallibilism is committed to Heracleiteanism.[62]

It is also clear how Heracleiteanism supports narrow infallibilism.[63] Nar-row infallibilism says that all perceptual beliefs are true. But then suppose that at one time you believe the wind is cold, and at another time I be-lieve it is not. Infallibilism says that both our beliefs are true; as we have seen, Heracleiteanism explains how this can be so without violating the law of noncontradiction. It describes a world in which Protagoras can main-tain that at least many seemingly conflicting beliefs are all true without contradiction. Whether infallibilism in the end violates the law of non-

[62] I noted above (n. 10) that Plato does not argue that the three theses 'imply' one another all on their own; rather, their connections are secured only with the aid of additional assumptions. An additional assumption used in connecting (P) and (H) is the one just mentioned: that objects constantly appear different. Bostock, *Plato's* Theaetetus, 49, asks why we should assume this. There are at least two replies. One is that it is a plausible assumption given that, as Plato plausibly says at 154 A 3–8, conditions are never exactly the same. A second reply is that Protagoras must allow that it is at least possible that things never appear the same; and so Plato asks what the world would be like if something Protagoras takes to be possible were actual. In this latter case, his claim is that Protagoras must allow that the most extreme sort of Heracleiteanism is at least possible. If Plato can show that it is not possible (as he aims to do in 181–3), then this counts against Protagoreanism.

Gary Matthews has objected to me that since infallibilism on its own does not 'imply' (H) (since we need the additional assumption that objects constantly appear different), it does not satisfy the connection criterion. I agree that infallibilism on its own does not 'imply' (H); but neither does relativism about truth or perceptual relativism do so. But, as I have said, Plato connects the three theses only with the aid of additional assumptions. Hence, to see whether the connection criterion is satisfied, we need to see whether (P) and (H) are appropriately connected once these additional assumptions are made clear. I am suggesting that the crucial assumption used in order to link (P) and (H) is that objects always appear different. I think that when this assumption is coupled with infallibilism, we get an appropriate connection to (H); but coupling it with relativism about truth or perceptual relativism does not yield an appropriate connection.

[63] In 181–3 Plato agues that an extreme Heracleiteanism cannot be sustained, and so there is clearly a sense in which it does not support Protagoras. But there is an intuitive sense in which Heracleiteanism is the sort of doctrine Protagoras needs to appeal to to support his position, to allow all seemingly conflicting beliefs to be absolutely true without conflict. We again need to bear the dialectical context in mind. Plato initially shows how Heracleiteanism supports Protagoras; he then goes on to argue that, though this is the best support available to Protagoras, it isn't good enough.

contradiction, especially when it strays outside the perceptual sphere, or for seemingly conflicting beliefs that occur at some one time, is another question.[64] The present point is that even if it violates the law of noncontradiction at some stage, Heracleiteanism is introduced to show that it is not as vulnerable on this score as it initially seems to be. Once we bear the dialectical structure of this part of the dialogue firmly in mind, and keep the connection criterion in view, we can see how Heracleitus allows Protagoras to hold on to the law of noncontradiction in at least many cases.

An account of Protagoras is available, then, on which the connection criterion is satisfied; and that, in turn, gives us some reason to favour the account.[65] Of course, a full defence of the claim that Plato portrays Protagoras as an infallibilist would require a more detailed account than I have provided both of Plato's complicated arguments linking the three theses and of his characterization of each of them. Nor have I asked whether infallibilism satisfies the univocity criterion. Some of these gaps are filled in the next two chapters. In Chapter 7 I argue that infallibilism fits the text of the 150s better than perceptual relativism does. And in Chapter 8 I argue that Plato's refutation of Protagoras is aimed against infallibilism.[66]

Suppose that Plato does portray Protagoras as an infallibilist. Does he, in so doing, portray him as relativist as well—that is, is infallibilism a kind of relativism? It depends, as I said in the beginning, on how we choose to use the term 'relativism'. If we reserve it for views that deny the existence of absolute truths in some domain, as I should like to do, then Plato does

[64] Note that when Protagoras moves to private objects, he eliminates further seeming conflicts between different people: if at t₁ we both say 'The wind is cold', we do not contradict one another, since we are speaking about different winds. This is, of course, part of the reason the move is made, to allow more seemingly conflicting beliefs all to be true without contradiction. Infallibilism therefore also does a good job of explaining why the first version of Heracleiteanism—which posits changes in intersubjectively available objects—gives way to another version, according to which there are private objects. Further, making the private objects and perceivers momentary eliminates the possibility of a single person contradicting herself over time. See n. 28.

[65] Note that if Plato portrays Protagoras as an infallibilist, then his account meshes with that of other ancient commentators, for, as Burnyeat notes ('Protagoras and Self-Refutation in Later Greek Philosophy', 46; the relevant passage is quoted above), that is how they portray Protagoras. That might give us yet another reason to suppose that Plato so portrays Protagoras. For example, Aristotle's account of Protagoras in *Metaphysics* Γ is so deeply indebted to Plato's that I cannot believe that they have fundamentally different interpretations of Protagoras. Burnyeat, by contrast, views their allegedly different accounts of Protagoras as a 'historical puzzle' ('Protagoras and Self-Refutation in Later Greek Philosophy', 46).

[66] Further, in 'Relativism and Self-Refutation in Plato's *Theaetetus*' I argue that if Plato's refutation of Protagoras were aimed against relativism about truth, it would fail.

not portray Protagoras as a relativist.[67] But however we use the word, we need to be clear what position Plato ascribes to Protagoras. We also need to distinguish among different views that have been misleadingly assimilated. In this chapter, I hope to have taken some preliminary steps in this direction.[68]

[67] On this account, perceptual relativism is not a version of relativism either. R. Bett, 'The Sophists and Relativism', *Phronesis*, 34 (1989), 139–69, argues that, with the possible exception of Protagoras, none of the sophists was a relativist in any deep or interesting sense. If my argument in this chapter is correct, and if Burnyeat is right to say that Plato's account of Protagoras is the most authoritative, then the historical Protagoras is not an exception. But (see n. 3) it is difficult to be sure whether Plato's account is accurate. One might think that it is more likely to be correct if, as on my account, it meshes with that given by other ancient commentators, than if, as on Burnyeat's, it diverges from them. But, on the other hand, one might argue that other ancient commentators are indebted to Plato's, possibly erroneous, account; or perhaps the historical Protagoras did not hold a view as determinate as the view Plato makes it out to be. So even if ancient commentators are unanimous in their interpretation of Protagoras, we could not infer that they are all correct.

[68] Earlier versions of this chapter were read at Harvard University in March 1994, under the auspices of the Boston Area Colloquium in Ancient Philosophy; and at Amherst College in April 1994, at a conference organized by Jyl Gentzler. I thank the audiences on both occasions—especially Gary Matthews, my commentator at Amherst—for helpful comments. I should also like to thank Lesley Brown, Jyl Gentzler, Terry Irwin, Sydney Shoemaker, Nicholas Sturgeon, and Nicholas White for helpful comments.

7

Conflicting Appearances:
Theaetetus 153 D–154 B

I

Ancient and modern philosophers alike have been fascinated by the so-called problem of conflicting appearances. The problem is simply this. There are, or at least seem to be, conflicting appearances: the wind seems cold to me, but not to you; the honey seems sweet to me, but not to you; abortion seems right to me, but not to you. What should we infer? Numerous answers have been proposed. In this essay, I consider the answer Plato attributes to Protagoras in *Theaetetus* 153 D–154 B. The passage has been analysed in detail by Myles Burnyeat, in his fascinating and stimulating paper 'Conflicting Appearances';[1] and I shall accordingly spend some time exploring his account, as well as proposing my own.

Burnyeat ascribes to Protagoras a position he calls perceptual relativism. Now, as Burnyeat would readily agree, in deciding about the content of Protagoreanism, we need to be guided by the context in which it is embedded; and I shall argue that perceptual relativism does not fit the context. Plato argues that Protagoras is best supported by, and is in turn committed to, a Heracleitean doctrine of flux. Perceptual relativism, however, is not best supported by, nor is it committed to, a Heracleitean doctrine of flux. I therefore ascribe to Protagoras a different position, which I call infallibilism, on which his Heracleitean associations are clearer.

II

I begin with some general preliminary remarks about Protagoras and his place in the dialogue. Protagoras claims that 'man is the measure of all

[1] M. F. Burnyeat, 'Conflicting Appearances', *Proceedings of the British Academy*, 65 (1979), 68–111. Subsequent references to this article will generally be given by page reference alone, and they will generally be cited in the text.

things, of those that are that they are, and of those that are not that they are not' (*Tht.* 152 A 2–4). Plato tells us that Protagoras' measure doctrine (P) 'means [*legei*] something like this [*pōs*]: everything is, for me, the way it appears to me, and is, for you, the way it appears to you' (*Tht.* 152 A 6–8).[2] 'Appears' (*phainetai*) can be veridical or nonveridical: I can say, 'It is apparent that it is cold', where this means that it obviously, evidently, is cold. But I can also say, 'It appears to be cold', where this means that I believe it is cold.[3] (P) uses 'appear' in the second way; that is, 'appears', in (P), indicates belief. (P) then makes the striking claim that, however I believe things are, so they in fact are (for me).[4]

In discussing (P), Plato considers two different ranges of appearances or beliefs. 'Appears' statements can be used in statements about perceptual appearances, to say how one believes things are on the basis of perception (e.g. 'It appears red to me'). But they can also be used in statements about what one is inclined to believe about any matter whatever (e.g. 'The argument appears sound to me').[5] So we need to distinguish between what I shall call *Narrow Protagoreanism* and *Broad Protagoreanism*. According to Narrow Protagoreanism, each thing is, for any person, the way he perceives it as being. According to Broad Protagoreanism, each thing is, for any

---

[2] The first passage is generally agreed to be a quotation from Protagoras; there is some dispute as to whether the second passage is also a quotation or Plato's own explanation of what Protagoras means. J. H. McDowell, *Plato:* Theaetetus, trans. with notes (Oxford: Clarendon Press, 1973), translates '*legei*' as 'means', which suggests he thinks that Plato is offering his own explanation; but in his notes ad loc. he says that *Cra.* 386 A 1–3 suggests that Plato is offering a second quotation from Protagoras. For further occurrences of the undisputed quotation, see *Cra.* 385 E 6–386 A 3; Sextus Empiricus, *M.* 7. 60–1; Diogenes Laertius, *Lives* 9. 51.

[3] In Greek, the first use is indicated by an accusative plus participle, the second by an accusative plus infinitive. But sometimes, as in (P), the relevant accusative or participle is omitted, and so one has to decide from the context which construction is intended.

[4] 'Appears' can also be used both nondoxastically and doxastically: I can say that the oar appears (looks) bent in water, where I do not mean to commit myself to the belief that it is bent in water; or I can say that the wind appears cold, where I do mean to express my belief about how it is. If, as I have suggested, (P) uses 'appears' to express beliefs, then it uses 'appears' doxastically.

[5] However, it is, of course, difficult to determine the range of perceptual predicates. The discussion that follows is indebted to McDowell, *Plato:* Theaetetus, 119–20. See also M. F. Burnyeat, 'Protagoras and Self-Refutation in Plato's *Theaetetus*', *Philosophical Review*, 85 (1976), 172–95 at 178 n. 9. (This note refers back to n. 2 of 'Protagoras and Self-Refutation in Later Greek Philosophy', *Philosophical Review*, 85 (1976), 44–69, though I cannot find any note in this latter paper that makes the relevant point; the point is, however, made on p. 45 of that paper, where n. 2 also occurs.) Although Burnyeat agrees that (P) sometimes uses 'appears' to cover all beliefs, he thinks that using 'appears' for more than perceptual appearances 'may have little but bluff to support it' ('Protagoras and Self-Refutation in Later Greek Philosophy', 45).

person, the way he is inclined to think it is. The distinction between Narrow and Broad Protagoreanism is that between two different substituends for 'each thing'. According to Narrow Protagoreanism, only perceptual predicates are appropriate substituends; according to Broad Protagoreanism, any term whatever is an appropriate substituend.[6] The *Theaetetus* considers both Narrow and Broad Protagoreanism. In the famous self-refutation argument (169 D–171 D), for example, Plato focuses on Broad Protagoreanism. But in his initial discussion of Protagoreanism (152 A–169 D), he focuses on Narrow Protagoreanism.[7] In this chapter I focus on Narrow Protagoreanism. In the next chapter, I consider Plato's refutation of Broad Protagoreanism.

III

These brief remarks underdetermine the precise content of (P). In attempting to arrive at a deeper understanding, it is vital to consider Protagoras' place in the dialogue. For he is not discussed in isolation. Rather, the first part of the *Theaetetus* (151 E–186 E) is a complex and subtle dialectical investigation of the connections among three theses: Protagoras' measure doctrine (P), Theaetetus' claim that knowledge is perception (T) (151 E 1–3), and a Heracleitean ontology (H) according to which 'all things change, like streams' (160 D 7–8)—clearly an allusion to Heracleitus' claim that 'one can't step into the same river twice'.[8] At 160 D 6 Plato says that the three theses coincide.

There is considerable controversy about precisely how Plato takes the three theses to coincide. On the account I favour, Plato argues that Theaetetus' claim that knowledge is perception commits him to a Protagorean

[6] Jonathan Barnes, in *The Presocratic Philosophers* (2 vols.; London: Routledge & Kegan Paul, 1979), ii. 240–2, distinguishes between phenomenological and judgemental seeming, where an example of the first is 'The oar seems bent in water' (it presents itself to the senses as being bent in water, whether or not I believe that it is bent in water) and the second expresses any belief whatsoever. What Barnes calls judgemental seeming corresponds to Broad Protagoreanism. But what he calls phenomenological seeming does not correspond to Narrow Protagoreanism. Narrow Protagoreanism involves judging that things are as they appear to the senses to be; Narrow Protagoreanism, that is, is a sort of judgemental seeming. Barnes's phenomenological seeming corresponds instead to nondoxastic appearances in the perceptual realm; but, in my view, nondoxastic appearances are not at issue in (P) (see n. 4 above).

[7] For places where he distinguishes, at least implicitly, between Broad and Narrow Protagoreanism, see 152 C 1–2 ('that which is hot and everything of that sort'), 171 E, and 178 B 5.

[8] There is dispute as to whether Heracleitus did say this. But Plato thinks that he did: *Cra.* 402 A 8–10 (=DK A 6; cf. B 91).

epistemology which, in turn, commits him to a Heracleitean ontology. He also argues that Theaetetus' definition is best supported by a Protagorean epistemology which, in turn, is best supported by a Heracleitean ontology.[9] (More precisely, Plato argues that (T), (H), and Narrow Protagoreanism are connected in these ways. Obviously, the claim that knowledge is perception, for example, is neither committed to nor best supported by Broad Protagoreanism, since the latter allows knowledge to range outside the perceptual sphere, since it takes all beliefs, not merely perceptual beliefs, to be true (to the believer).)[10] Having articulated the connections among the three theses, Plato proceeds to the offensive, arguing against each of the three theses in turn.

On this account of the structure of the first part of the *Theaetetus*, Plato is not propounding his own views about knowledge and perception; rather, he is asking what Theaetetus, and then Protagoras, are committed to, and how they are best supported. His strategy is the same as that pursued in many of the Socratic dialogues: an interlocutor proposes a definition, which Socrates tests against various principles and examples; eventually the interlocutor is caught in contradiction. Generally, the definition is then

[9] This view has been well defended by Burnyeat; see e.g. his 'Idealism and Greek Philosophy: What Descartes Saw and Berkeley Missed', *Philosophical Review*, 91 (1982), 3–40, esp. 5–7; and *The* Theaetetus *of Plato*, trans. M. J. Levett, rev. and intro. M. F. Burnyeat (Indianapolis: Hackett, 1990), esp. 7–19. Plato gives various 'stage-directions', as Burnyeat calls them, to indicate the connections that he has in mind. Here (ignoring several complications) are just a few of them. When Theaetetus proposes that knowledge is perception, Socrates tells him that 'what you've said about knowledge is no ordinary theory, but the one that Protagoras too used to state' (151 E 8–152 A 1). This suggests that Plato takes (T) and (P) to be equivalent. He then describes Protagoras' 'secret doctrine' (152 C 10), which, among other things, involves a Heracleitean flux ontology. The point of calling it Protagoras' secret doctrine is presumably to indicate that he is unwittingly committed to it (so McDowell, *Plato:* Theaetetus, 121–2). So (P), and therefore also (T), implies (H). That (H) implies (P), and so (T), is suggested by, for example, 156 A 3–5, where Plato tells us that everything that's been said depends on the assumption that everything is change, in which case (P), and so (T), depends on (H). That is, I assume, (H) is the basis for, and in that sense implies or supports, (P), and so (T). Cf. 183 A 2–3: (H) was introduced in order to establish (T); that is, it was taken to imply or support (T). (Strict implication is not in view here; the idea is, rather, that each of the three theses best supports and is best supported by the others. Note that the best available support might not be very good. I take it that Plato argues just this in refuting the theses.)

[10] Of course, to say that all beliefs are true (to the believer) is not to say that all beliefs constitute knowledge, since being true (to the believer) is not sufficient for being knowledge. However, it is necessary for knowledge, and it is the condition on knowledge that Plato focuses on in assessing (T). One might argue that to say, as Broad Protagoreanism does, that all beliefs are true (to the believer) does not conflict with (T), since Broad Protagoreanism does not say that beliefs can range outside the perceptual sphere. But, as Plato conceives Broad Protagoreanism, it does have this broader scope. (McDowell, *Plato:* Theaetetus, 168, however, thinks that 167 A 8 might restrict beliefs to perceptual beliefs.)

rejected, just as here Theaetetus' definition of knowledge as perception is eventually rejected (184–6). In all this, Socrates is exploring, not his own views, but those of his interlocutor. In just the same way, this part of the *Theaetetus* investigates Theaetetus' claim that knowledge is perception. But here, rather than proceeding quickly to criticism, Plato begins by asking how far the initial thesis can be supported: he constructs an elaborate defence of Theaetetus' claim before dismantling it.

It is often difficult to figure out precisely what position is being ascribed to, say, Heracleitus. Commentators sometimes try to decide about this by asking what interpretation best corresponds with views Plato expounds in his own right elsewhere. But the right question to ask here is not 'What does Plato himself believe?' Rather, the right questions to ask are 'What version of Heracleiteanism best supports Protagoras?' and 'What version of Heracleiteanism is Protagoras committed to?'[11]

Of course, it might turn out that a Protagorean epistemology is best supported by, or is committed to, one of Plato's own views. Similarly, in the Socratic dialogues, Socrates might agree with one of his interlocutors on a given point. However, we should not come to the text aiming to find agreement. Nor does it count in favour of an interpretation that, on it, this part of the *Theaetetus* meshes with views Plato expresses in his own right elsewhere. The best interpretation is one that makes it as clear as possible why Plato takes the three theses to be related as he does. We have no reason to suppose that such an interpretation will involve importing Platonic views (except in the sense mentioned in n. 11).

Once we are clear about Plato's strategy, we can also guard against another mistake. Some of the arguments attributed to, say, Protagoras appear to be confused. Commentators sometimes then search for alternative interpretations on which there is less, or no, confusion, in the belief that this will make Plato look better. However, the mere fact that Plato attributes a confused argument to Protagoras does not by itself show that Plato is confused. Of course, he might be. But before concluding this, there is an alternative worth considering: perhaps Plato is suggesting that the confused

---

[11] Of course, asking these questions involves asking about Plato's views, in so far as we need to ask, for example, what version of Heracleiteanism Plato thinks best supports Protagoras, and what version of Heracleiteanism he thinks Protagoras is committed to. But we should not assume in advance that Plato believes that Protagoras, say, is committed to or best supported by any view Plato himself accepts. A full discussion should answer not only the questions raised in the text, but also the question of what version of Protagoreanism and Heracleiteanism are required in connection with Theaetetus' claim that knowledge is perception; but in this chapter I focus on the connections between Protagoras and Heracleitus.

argument is the best that Protagoras, given his views, can do. If we can see why Plato might argue in his way, then that is some reason to suppose that the confusion is Protagoras' rather than Plato's.[12]

IV

These preliminaries out of the way, I turn now to *Theaetetus* 153 D–154 B. I begin by quoting it in full:

soc. Well, then, you must think like this. In the case of the eyes, first, you mustn't think of what you call white colour as being some distinct thing outside your eyes, or in your eyes either—in fact, you mustn't assign (153 E) any place to it; because in that case it would, surely, be at its assigned place and in a state of rest, rather than coming to be.

THT. Well, how can I think of it?

soc. Let's follow what we said just now, and lay it down that nothing is one thing (153 E 5) itself in itself. On those lines, we'll find that black, white, or any other colour will turn out to have come into being from the collision of the eyes with the appropriate motion. What we say a given colour (154) is will be neither the thing which collides nor the thing it collides with, but something which has come into being between them, something private to each one. Or would you be prepared to insist that every colour appears to a dog, or any other living thing, just the way it appears to you? (154 A 5)

THT. Certainly not.

soc. And what about another man? Is the way anything appears to him like the way it appears to you? Can you insist on that? Or wouldn't you much rather say that it doesn't appear the same even to yourself, because you're never in a similar condition to yourself?

THT. Yes, I think that's nearer the truth than the first alternative.

soc. (154 B) Surely then, if what we measure ourselves against or touch was large, white, or hot, it would never have become different by bumping into a different perceiver, if it itself didn't undergo any change. And on the other hand, (154 B 5) if what does the measuring or touching was any of those things, then, again, it wouldn't have become different when another thing came up against it, or the thing which came up against it had something to happen to it, if it itself hadn't had anything happen to it.[13]

[12] Of course, Plato might be wrong to think that Protagoras is confused in some way; so saying that he takes Protagoras to be confused does not automatically absolve Plato from confusion. But if he does turn out to be confused, it would be because he has misunderstood what, for example, Protagoras is committed to, and not because he himself necessarily accepts the content of the confused argument he thinks Protagoras must accept.

[13] I follow Burnyeat's translation (in his 'Conflicting Appearances'), with some modifi-

The general aim of the passage is clear enough: Plato is explaining Protagoras' solution to the problem of conflicting appearances in the case of sensible qualities. But precisely what solution does he ascribe to him? I begin by considering Burnyeat's explanation. He suggests that Plato's aim 'is to establish on behalf of Protagoras that sensible qualities like hot and cold, white and black, are essentially relative to the individual perceiving subject' (p. 77). On this view, 'Neither the object seen nor the perceiving subject is in itself white (154b)' (p. 77).[14] Burnyeat takes this to show that

no sentence of the form 'x is white' is true as it stands, without a qualifying clause specifying a perceiver for whom it is true. This gives us the result that the colour white is essentially relational . . . there is no unqualified predicate 'white' to be abstracted from its predicative position and made the subject of the definitional question 'What is white?'. There is no such thing as (being) white *simpliciter*, only white for you and white for me. (pp. 77–8)

It follows, Burnyeat suggests, that 'white is not a distinct thing existing in the subject or in the object of perception' (p. 78); indeed, it is 'not a distinct thing existing anywhere at all' (p. 77).

Burnyeat's idea seems to be as follows. We know that Protagoras thinks that all appearances are true for those who have them. But appearances seem to conflict. Must Protagoras then violate the law of noncontradiction, counting conflicting appearances as true? On Burnyeat's account, Protagoras avoids this result by relativizing sensible properties to perceivers. The appearance that there are conflicting appearances therefore turns out to be deceptive, at least in the case of sensible qualities; and so seemingly conflicting appearances can all be true (for those who have them) without violating the law of noncontradiction.

This, then, is the solution that Burnyeat finds in the passage. How does he think it is defended? He suggests that 'The argument for the relativity of

cations. His translation is in turn based on McDowell's. M. J. Levett, by contrast, translates 154 b 1–2 as 'supposing such things as size or warmth or whiteness really belonged to the object'; but the Greek contains nothing corresponding to 'really'. She translates 154 b 3 as 'without any change in itself'; but '*auto*' merely indicates the object, not anything about what the object is in itself. (Her translation was originally published in 1928, by the University of Glasgow Press. A version that has been somewhat revised by Burnyeat is contained in his *The Theaetetus of Plato*. He unfortunately did not correct her translation in these two places.) F. M. Cornford, *Plato's Theory of Knowledge: The* Theaetetus *and the* Sophist *of* Plato, translated with a running commentary (London: Routledge & Kegan Paul, 1935), also mistranslates the passage in these two ways. As we shall see, these differences are significant.

[14] In his translation of 154 b in 'Conflicting Appearances', Burnyeat correctly refrains from translating '*auto*' as 'in itself' (see n. 13 above). However, the passage just quoted in the text shows that he, none the less, takes the passage to be discussing what objects are in themselves.

sensible qualities is entirely general, and its leading premiss is the conflict of sensible appearances' (p. 78). In particular, Socrates claims that sensible appearances vary;[15] and he 'asserts at 154b that this is incompatible with attributing sensible qualities either to the object or to the subject of perception' (p. 78). Burnyeat continues:

We may elucidate his claim as follows. Take, as before, an event of the kind we would ordinarily describe as the seeing of a white stone ... Then, first, the stone cannot be white in itself or else, so long as it suffered no change, it would appear white to any other perceiver ... More generally, if sensible qualities inhere in the objects of perception, they ought to make themselves apparent to every perceiver alike, regardless of differences between perceivers or changes in the condition of a single perceiver ... But it is a fact of experience familiar to us all that sensible appearances vary with differences and changes on either side of the perceptual encounter. So we are invited to draw the desired conclusion: sensible qualities are essentially relative to the individual perceiver. (p. 79)

This argument, according to Burnyeat, rests on the striking premiss that:[16]

(1) If something appears F to some observers and not-F to others, then it is not inherently/really/in itself F.

But, as Burnyeat points out, (1) is equivalent to:

(2) If something is inherently/really/in itself F, then it appears F to all observers or it appears not-F to all.[17]

Furthermore, Burnyeat claims, Plato makes 'absolutely explicit the important point that with either formulation [i.e. with either (1) or (2)] the argument applies only on the assumption that the thing we are talking about remains unchanged' (p. 79). The view that the passage assumes that the object does not change is not unique to Burnyeat; on the contrary, it seems to be generally accepted.[18]

We can summarize Burnyeat's interpretation of the argument as follows:

[15] As Burnyeat notes, Socrates 'actually implies the strongest possible claim, that no two colour appearances are alike'; but it is 'sufficient for the argument Socrates has in view to start from the more modest claim that variations do occur' (p. 78).

[16] R. M. Dancy, 'Theaetetus' First Baby: *Theaetetus* 151e–160e', *Philosophical Topics*, 15 (1987), 61–108 at 79, also believes that Plato's argument assumes this premiss.

[17] Since the second disjunct is irrelevant to our discussion, I shall follow Burnyeat in ignoring it.

[18] See e.g. Cornford, *Plato's Theory of Knowledge* 40–1 n. 1; McDowell, *Plato:* Theaetetus, 132; Dancy, 'Theaetetus' First Baby', 79; and D. Bostock, *Plato's* Theaetetus (Oxford: Clarendon Press, 1988), 59. I discuss McDowell's interpretation further below.

(A) There are, or at least seem to be, conflicting appearances; for example, the stone appears white to me, but not to you.

(B) If the stone is really, or in itself, white, then (unless it changes) it will appear white to everyone.[19]

(C) The stone hasn't changed between the different appearances.

(D) Therefore the stone is not really, or in itself, white; rather, sensible qualities are relative to perceivers.

Let us call this position *perceptual relativism*.[20] Two points about perceptual relativism are worth making before proceeding further. First, as Burnyeat conceives it, it claims not only that perceptual properties are relational but also that objects do not really have them. This is clear from (1), which speaks indifferently of being inherently or in itself F, and being really F.[21]

Secondly, according to perceptual relativism, 'change' of colour can be what Geach calls a mere 'Cambridge change' in the object.[22] Perceptual relativism says that an object is red in a given relation if and only if it appears red to a perceiver. So, if the object no longer appears red to a perceiver, the object no longer is red in relation to that perceiver. But an object can cease to appear red to me if I am suddenly struck blind. Perceptual relativism says that, in this sort of case, the object ceases to be red in relation to me without itself genuinely changing.[23]

---

[19] This involves assumption (1) mentioned just above.

[20] Burnyeat uses this label on p. 71; see also Burnyeat, *The* Theaetetus *of Plato*, 15.

[21] See Burnyeat's discussion of (1) on pp. 74 and 91. See also pp. 78–9. (On the other hand, on p. 71 Burnyeat says that Protagoras 'allows the honey to be both sweet and bitter, subject to the qualification that it is sweet *for* (in relation to) some palates and bitter *for* others'. Depending on the force of the qualification, this seems to allow honey to be sweet and so on.) I am not claiming that Burnyeat himself believes that things really have only intrinsic properties; but he does say that that is Protagoras' view. Dancy also seems to assume that something is really F if and only if it is intrinsically, in itself, F; see e.g. p. 66, which moves freely between the two claims. (Perhaps Dancy assumes this only on Protagoras' behalf; I am not sure.) Levett's insertion of 'really' into the text encourages this view; see n. 13 above.

[22] See P. T. Geach, *God and the Soul* (London: Routledge & Kegan Paul, 1969), 71. Geach introduces what he calls the 'Cambridge criterion' for change: 'The thing called "x" has changed if we have "F(x) at time t" true and "F(x) at time t'" false, for some interpretations of "F", "t", and "t'".' On this criterion, I undergo a Cambridge change if I grow from being 5′1″ to 5′2″; I also undergo one if I come to be shorter than Theaetetus in virtue of his growth. As Geach uses the phrase, real or genuine changes are a subclass of Cambridge changes; mere Cambridge changes are the subclass of Cambridge changes that are not intuitively taken to be genuine changes.

[23] Perceptual relativism is, or is close to, a view Locke sometimes seems to hold. Locke says that colours and so on are powers in objects to produce certain sorts of sensations in perceivers. (See e.g. *An Essay concerning Human Understanding* II. viii. 10: secondary qualities 'are nothing in the objects themselves but powers to produce various sensa-

V

Now that we have seen how Burnyeat interprets 153–4 we can ask whether his account is correct. Let us note, first, that there is a good reason to hope that it is not. As we have seen, Plato does not discuss Protagoras in isolation, but as part of a dialectical investigation of Theaetetus' claim that knowledge is perception. He argues that Theaetetus is committed to a Protagorean epistemology which, in turn, is both committed to and best supported by a Heracleitean ontology according to which the world is in constant flux or change. In our passage, Plato is explaining Protagoras' solution to the problem of conflicting appearances. He should do so in a way that appeals to, or at least prepares us for the appeal to, Heracleiteanism.

Yet, according to Burnyeat, 'the argument [on behalf of (P)] applies only on the assumption that the thing we are talking about remains unchanged' (p. 79). This is very surprising: if Plato thinks that (P) is best supported by (H), why would he here support (P) with an argument that assumes that the object doesn't change? On Burnyeat's account, (P) is supported by a doctrine of stability rather than one of change. Nor, on Burnyeat's account, does Protagoras seem to be committed to Heracleiteanism. In Burnyeat's interpretation, Protagoras solves the problem of conflicting appearances by relativizing sensible properties in a way that, at least in some cases, does not require any change in the object.

On Burnyeat's account, then, Protagoras, so far from being supported by Heracleiteanism, is initially defended by an ontology that looks incompatible with Heracleiteanism. Nor does Protagoras seem to be committed to Heracleiteanism, in so far as he allows objects to appear different without changing. Perceptual relativism therefore seems to be the wrong sort of theory to secure Protagoras' Heracleitean associations. Given the gap

tions in us'.) This makes them relational: objects have the colours they do partly in virtue of their relation to perceivers. Locke also says that only a thing's primary qualities are its real qualities (e.g. *Essay* II. viii. 17). So he seems to hold that colours are in some sense not real properties of objects. Locke also seems to be committed to the view that an object can change colour without undergoing a genuine change. For it is essential to an object's being red that it appear red to someone. (In *Essay* IV. iii. 15, Locke seems to say that an object is red just in case it appears red to someone. I owe this reference to Nicholas Sturgeon.) So, if an object no longer appears red to someone because the person is struck blind, the object no longer is red (in that relation). Locke is then committed to the view that 'change' of secondary qualities can be a mere Cambridge change in the object. I would not claim that this is Locke's only view of the nature of secondary qualities; but it does seem to be a view that he is sometimes committed to.

between perceptual relativism and Heracleiteanism, it is not surprising that Burnyeat does not mention the latter here at all.[24]

Now it is true that the account of Heracleiteanism develops. Plato begins with a moderate sort of Heracleiteanism. He then points out that Protagoras is committed to, and requires, a stronger version; and so on, until his final position has been fully articulated. So perhaps 153 D–154 B assumes that objects can remain unchanged in the face of conflicting appearances, and it is only later passages that abandon that assumption? This is, to be sure, a theoretical possibility. I argue below, however, that the text does not require us to endorse it; and, on the alternative reading that I propose, the dialectical unfolding of Protagoras' position proceeds more smoothly.

VI

Still, to say that Heracleiteanism is irrelevant to perceptual relativism is not to say that Protagoras is not a perceptual relativist: perhaps Plato ascribes to Protagoras a position that sits ill with his view about Protagoras' Heracleitean connections. So we need to press further.

As Burnyeat construes the argument (A–D above), it is valid. Moreover, premiss (A)—that there are, or at least seem to be, conflicting appearances—seems obviously true. But premiss (B) involves the false and surprising claim that if x is really, in itself, F, it will appear F to everyone.[25] Burnyeat agrees that this assumption is false; indeed, exposing its falsity is one of his main aims. But it contains a defect he does not mention: it takes

[24] Later in his article Burnyeat says that 'Socrates makes the very strong suggestion that no two colour appearances are alike. The theory he is elaborating is committed to the view that, if this were so, each appearance should still yield knowledge of a real state of affairs. If the theory is to hold good, it must be able to take in its stride the most extreme variation imaginable in the course of appearances. So we had better suppose, for the sake of the argument, that extreme variation actually obtains. Each appearance is independent of every other appearance, yet each is knowledge. But now, if each appearance is independent of every other, yet each is knowledge, there must be a matching variation in the states of affairs which correspond' (p. 86). *Here* Burnyeat says that, if appearances vary, so too do the objects of perception. But this seems to conflict with his claim that 153–4 assumes that the objects need not change when they appear different. Perhaps Burnyeat would say that Protagoras abandons the assumption of 153–4, according to which objects need not change when they appear different—his initial support is later overturned. But he nowhere explicitly says this; nor does everything he says fit well with this suggestion. And, in any case, I shall suggest that the text reads more smoothly on my alternative.

[25] Although the assumption is obviously false, Burnyeat believes that many philosophers have, perhaps unwittingly, relied on it. He mentions Democritus, Berkeley, and Russell as examples. It is easier to think that 154 B involves this assumption if we follow Levett in inserting 'really' into the text, and if we take '*auto*' to mean 'in itself'; see nn. 13, 21 above.

being really F, and being F in itself, to be the same. However, if to be really F is to be truly (i.e. in fact) F, and if to be F in itself is to be intrinsically (i.e. non-relationally) F, then the two are not the same. For objects can really (in fact) have relational properties. This is so even if the relational property is subjective, in the sense of being relational to a perceiver.[26]

I agree with Burnyeat that Protagoras takes perceptual properties to be in some sense relational. (However, as will become clear, we have different accounts of what this involves.) But, unlike Burnyeat, I do not think that Protagoras denies that objects really have perceptual properties. Burnyeat seems to favour his view partly because he takes 153 D 9–E 1 to say that whiteness, for example, is not in the object. It is true that Protagoras says that 'white colour is not some distinct thing outside your eyes, or in your eyes either'. But the reason he gives for this is that, if it were, then 'it would be at its assigned place and in a state of rest, rather than coming to be'. This suggests that Protagoras means only that whiteness is not *stably* in the object—or, more precisely, that no whiteness-token is stably in any object.[27] And it is clear why he believes this, since otherwise Heracleiteanism would be violated.

That Protagoras believes that objects are genuinely coloured, even if they have any given colour-token only for a moment and only in relation to a given perceiver, is also suggested by 156 E 5–7, where he says that, when an eye and a suitable object generate a whiteness-token, the object 'comes to be not whiteness but, again, white—a white log or stone or whatever happens to have that sort of colour'. Here he speaks clearly of an object's actually being white. So, although Protagoras takes perceptual properties to be relational, he does not think that this shows that objects do not really have them.[28]

Moreover, although Protagoras takes perceptual properties to be in some sense relational, that point does not seem to be stressed in 154 B. Burnyeat thinks that it is, partly because he takes the passage to say that 'Neither the object seen nor the perceiving subject is *in itself* white (154b)' (p. 77,

---

[26] For this point, see C. McGinn, *The Subjective View* (Oxford: Clarendon Press, 1983), 119.

[27] Protagoras seems to believe that we do not see general properties, but property-tokens, or what are sometimes called tropes; he also seems to believe that no two perceptual encounters involve numerically the same property-token. Indeed, as our passage makes clear, he also believes that, since conditions are never exactly the same, no two property-tokens are ever exactly alike.

[28] McDowell, *Plato: Theaetetus*, 139–40, seems to agree with me about this (though contrast pp. 132–3). I discuss McDowell further below. Burnyeat, p. 77 with n. 3, seems to think that 156 E says how 'we would ordinarily describe', for example, a white stone; but he thinks that Protagoras would view this description as inaccurate.

emphasis added), where, in his view, we are meant to understand that colours and so on are relational rather than intrinsic. However, 154 B does not say that the object is not *in itself* white; it says that if the object is white, then it will not become different, when it appears different, unless it changes. Nothing corresponding to 'in itself' occurs in the text at 154 B: Plato says something about what will happen if the object is white, not about what will happen if it is white in itself.[29]

Nor, so far as I can see, does Plato say or assume that the object does not change; he does not, that is, assert premiss (C) of the above argument. He says only that if the object is white, then it will not become different, when it appears different, unless it changes. The argument, that is, offers us disjunctive options: when the object appears different, either it was not previously F, or else it became different and so it changed (from being F to being not-F). But the passage does not tell us which disjunct is the favoured one. To know which disjunct Protagoras favours, we need to look elsewhere.[30]

In place of Burnyeat's (A)–(D), therefore, all we have so far is the following:

(A) There are, or at least seem to be, conflicting appearances; for example, the stone appears white to me, but not to you.

(B′) If the stone is white, then it will not become different, when it appears different, unless it changes.

(C′) Therefore, either it is not white, or else it becomes different and so changes (from being white to not being white).[31]

---

[29] As McDowell, *Plato: Theaetetus*, 135, remarks, if 154 B were concerned to stress the relational nature of properties, then we should expect it to say 'if what we measure ourselves against or touch had been *on its own* large, white, or hot . . .'. In Burnyeat's paraphrase of 154 B, the passage says just this; but this is not what the text actually says. It is true that 'in itself', *kath' hauto*, occurs *earlier* in our passage: at 153 E 4–5, they 'lay it down that nothing is one thing itself in itself'. But 'in itself' does not occur at 154 B. Moreover, the force of 'in itself' is of course disputed.

[30] In seeing that this is all that the present passage says, I have been helped by a paper by Christie Thomas. Previously, I took the passage to say that, since the object appeared different, it was different and so it must have changed, from being white to not being white. But Thomas has convinced me that the passage is neutral as between Burnyeat's reading and my earlier reading.

[31] I have wondered whether the passage could instead be taken to say: (A); (B′); and then 'The stone became different; and so either it was not white or else it changed'. On this reading, it would be being assumed that since the stone appeared different, it became different, and the question then is whether becoming different requires change. On the reading suggested in the text, it is assumed that the object appeared different but not that it thereby became different.

Of course, perhaps the ensuing discussion will show that Plato does assume, on Protagoras' behalf, that the object did not change and was not white (in itself). That is, perhaps Burnyeat's general account of Protagoras is correct, even if he should not read it into the present passage. So we need to see what happens next in the text.

VII

Before doing so, however, it will prove interesting and instructive to compare McDowell's interpretation of our passage with Burnyeat's. McDowell suggests that the argument relies on the following principle:[32]

> (P) If something is f and does not itself change, then it does not come to be other than f.

He then says:

By (P), if something is white and does not itself change, it does not come to be other than white. But (Socrates implies) anything of which one might be inclined to say that it is white does, without itself changing, come to be other than white, by coming into contact with a different person. . . . Therefore it cannot be true of any such thing that it is white.

Like Burnyeat, then, McDowell thinks the argument assumes that the object does not change. However, he derives a different moral from the passage from the one Burnyeat draws. Burnyeat thinks the moral we are meant to draw is that colours and so on are relational. McDowell argues, as I have done, that the passage does not emphasize the relational nature of properties. He then concludes that the argument says, not that nothing is white in itself, but that nothing is white, period.[33] One reason McDowell favours this interpretation is that he thinks that the passage assumes that the object does not change; I have already challenged this assumption. But McDowell also has another reason for favouring his interpretation. He thinks, rightly, that we should read the passage in accordance with Protagoras' 'secret doctrine', adumbrated at 152 c–153 d. As he notes (p. 123), on one interpretation of the secret doctrine, its main concern is the relational nature of sensible properties. But he rejects this interpretation. One of his reasons for doing

---

[32] The two quotations that follow are from McDowell, *Plato: Theaetetus*, 132.

[33] In a sense, Burnyeat also derives this moral, in so far as he says that objects do not really have relational properties; but the main point Burnyeat wants to stress is the relational nature of sensible properties, whereas McDowell argues that this point is not stressed.

so is that it pays 'too little attention to a striking parallelism' between the secret doctrine and some passages in the *Republic* and *Timaeus*.[34] So he endorses a second account of the secret doctrine on which (he thinks) it meshes with these passages.

But, as we have seen, this is the wrong strategy for interpreting our passage; the mere fact that the secret doctrine sounds like passages in the *Timaeus* and *Republic* is not a good reason to interpret them in the same way. Our guiding concern should not be finding Platonic parallels, but discovering what Protagoras is committed to, and how he is best supported.[35] McDowell's method of interpretation is, at this point, not sufficiently sensitive to Plato's dialectical strategy.

I agree with McDowell, against Burnyeat, then, that our passage does not emphasize the relational nature of properties. I also agree with McDowell that *if* the passage assumes that the object does not change, we should conclude that the object is not white—not merely that it is not intrinsically white. But I do not agree with McDowell, Burnyeat, and others that the passage assumes that the object does not change; nor do I think we should follow McDowell in looking for Platonic parallels in attempting to interpret our passage.

All we know so far, then, is that our passage says that either the object was not previously white, or else it changed (from being white to not being white). Which disjunct do later passages favour?

VIII

Having said that, if an object is F, it does not become different, when it appears different, unless it changes, Plato says: 'As things are, however, we carelessly get ourselves committed to saying things which are extraordinary and absurd: so Protagoras, and anyone who sets out to state the same doctrines as he does, would say' (154 в 6–8). Plato is quite clear about his strategy: he is going to tell us, not what he thinks, but what Protagoras thinks. Protagoras believes that we say things that are extraordinary and absurd. To explain why Protagoras believes this, Plato introduces what

[34] McDowell also gives other reasons for rejecting the first interpretation. One of them is that 'it leaves unexplained the fact that the secret doctrine is taken to imply radical instability in the perceptual world' (ibid. 123). This is the right sort of reason for rejecting the first interpretation; but it sits unhappily with looking for Platonic parallels. One reason appeals to the dialectical demands of the context, the other assumes that Plato is speaking in his own voice.

[35] Nor are the passages as parallel as McDowell suggests. See my 'Plato on Perception', *Oxford Studies in Ancient Philosophy*, suppl. vol. (1988), 15–28.

Cornford calls 'some puzzles concerning size and number' (p. 41). Socrates begins with a 'small example' (154 c 1): 'Take six dice. If you put four beside them, we say they're more than the four, in fact one and a half times as many; and if you put twelve beside them we say they're fewer, in fact half as many' (154 c 2–4). Theaetetus agrees that this is what we say. Socrates then says: 'Well, now, suppose that Protagoras, or anyone else, asks you this: "Theaetetus, is there any way in which something can become larger or more numerous, other than by undergoing increase?" What will you answer?' (154 c 7–9). Theaetetus is unsure. On the one hand, focusing on the example of the dice, he is inclined to say that there is; on the other hand, focusing on the question just asked, he is inclined to say that there is not.

It is obvious what the correct answer is; that is, leaving Plato and Protagoras to one side for now, it is obvious what we ought in fact to say here. We ought to say that the six dice are more than the four and fewer than the twelve, and that they are so without undergoing any genuine change. Of course, six dice cannot become more than they are—cannot become a group of more than six dice—without genuinely changing. But six dice can 'become' more than a group of four dice, and fewer than a group of twelve dice, without genuinely changing. Similarly, they can appear more (than the four) and fewer (than the six) without really changing. Appearances might seem to conflict here; but we can resolve the conflict, and we can do so without invoking change.

Not only is this the correct solution to the puzzles, but it is also the solution Plato ought to offer Protagoras, if the latter is a perceptual relativist. On this account, Plato would be explaining Protagoras' alleged view that, since perceptual properties are relational, objects can appear different without changing—just as six dice can appear more (in relation to four dice) and fewer (in relation to twelve dice) without really changing. As Burnyeat explains, 'the new puzzles are explicitly about relative predicates (e.g. six dice are more *than four* and less *than twelve*). Their solution can thus serve as a perspicuous model for the thoroughgoing relativization which Protagoras recommends. When you add an explicit specification of the different relations in which opposite predicates hold of the same thing, the contradiction disappears.'[36] Protagoras' idea, on this interpretation, is

---

[36] *The* Theaetetus *of Plato*, 13. Unfortunately, Burnyeat nowhere discusses the puzzles in detail. The passage just cited suggests that he favours the same interpretation of the puzzles as that favoured by Cornford (discussed further below). However, Burnyeat goes on to say that 'relativization is not the complete answer to our problem', since Heracleiteanism enters the picture as well. He suggests that 'objects cannot have a continuing identity through time if every feature they manifest is relativized to a single perceiver and to the time of their perception' (ibid. 17). This claim, however, sits awkwardly with his interpretation of 153 D–

that, once we are clear about relational properties, we will see that conflicting appearances can all, in a sense, be true without contradiction and without positing change.[37]

Cornford thinks that this is Protagoras' solution to the puzzles. He says:

It is clear that the difficulty here exists only for one who thinks of 'large' as a quality residing in the thing which is larger than something else, with 'small' as the answering quality residing in the smaller thing. If that is so, then, when the large thing is compared with something larger instead of something smaller, he will suppose that it has lost its quality 'large' and gained instead the quality 'small'. He will be puzzled when we point out that the thing has not altered in size. (pp. 43–4)

Cornford goes on to argue that, in the *Phaedo*, Plato 'shares the ordinary view and thinks of tallness as an internal property on the same footing as "hot" or "white", not as standing for a *relation between* the taller person and the shorter' (p. 44). However, by the time of the *Theaetetus*, Cornford believes, Plato has abandoned this view. He no longer believes that 'any of these qualities—hot, white, large—is an instance of a Form residing in an individual thing' (p. 45). We can now see, therefore, that 'The six dice will *appear* more than twelve, but they have not become more or fewer in themselves. This will help us to understand how a thing can appear or become white for me, without that implying that whiteness in it has replaced some other colour' (p. 45). According to Cornford, then, although in the middle dialogues Plato viewed colours and so on as intrinsic rather than as relational, in the *Theaetetus* he sees that they are relational properties, such that an object can be or appear white to me, but not to you, without contradiction and without genuinely changing.

On Cornford's account of the puzzles, the extraordinary and absurd thing that we non-Protagoreans do is to treat relational properties as though they were intrinsic; and this, in turn, leads us to view mere Cambridge changes as though they were real changes. Protagoras then rescues us from our error, by pointing out that these properties are relational; and this,

154 B, according to which the relational nature of properties is established by assuming that objects can appear different without changing. Nor does Burnyeat provide any explanation of why objects cannot persist if all their features are relativized.

[37] However, as McDowell remarks (*Plato*: Theaetetus, 135), the claim that objects have properties only in relation to perceivers is not really very similar to the claim that predicates such as 'smaller' need to be supplemented with a 'than' clause. So if Protagoras' solution to the puzzles means to emphasize the relational nature of various properties, as part of an effort to explain perceptual relativism, the explanation is not very helpful. This gives us one reason to suppose that this is not Protagoras' solution; below, I give another reason for thinking that it is not his solution. We have also seen that 154 B does not stress the relational nature of properties.

in turn, allows us to see mere Cambridge changes for what they are. So Protagoras has the correct view, and we have the wrong view. Nor is it only Protagoras who has the correct view of relational properties. Cornford thinks that Plato is describing his own solution to the puzzles; and he commends Plato for (as he thinks) finally seeing, as he allegedly did not before, that properties like largeness and so on are relational rather than intrinsic. But, as we have seen, Plato is not expounding his own solution to the puzzles about the dice; he is saying how Protagoras would resolve them. Plato is quite clear about this (154 B 6–8, c 6, 155 D 5–7, 156 A 2 ff.).[38]

Of course, one might argue that Plato attributes the correct solution of the puzzles to Protagoras; and one might then argue that this is a philosophical advance, in so far as, earlier, Plato did not see that this was the correct solution. On this interpretation, however, we once again have to wonder why Protagoras is committed to a Heracleitean ontology; for once again, Protagoras is being offered a solution to the problem of conflicting appearances on which they are all in a sense true without contradiction and without change. But then Heracleiteanisn is simply irrelevant.

Cornford's account of the puzzles therefore seems to ignore the dialectical structure of the passage, both in assuming that Plato is articulating his own views, and in interpreting Protagoras in such a way that Heracleitus has no role to play. But is Cornford's solution none the less correct? Does Plato ascribe to Protagoras the view that some seemingly conflicting appearances can be true, without contradiction and without change, simply by recognizing the relational nature of various properties? I shall now argue that this is not the solution that Plato attributes to Protagoras.

IX

Theaetetus is understandably perplexed by the difficult discussion of the puzzles about size and number (155 D 5–8), so Socrates undertakes to elucidate it (155 D 9–E 1). He goes on to say that 'Their starting point, on which everything we've just been saying depends, too, is this: the universe is change and nothing else' (156 A 3–5). Here Plato says quite clearly

[38] My own view is that, in the middle dialogues, Plato is well aware that, for example, Socrates can be taller than one person and shorter than another without genuinely changing. That is, he is well aware, in the middle dialogues, of how the puzzles about size and number should be resolved. But in the *Theaetetus*, he does not advert to his own preferred, and correct, solution; at this stage he is not articulating his own views, but Protagoras'. Roughly speaking, the account that Cornford finds in the *Theaetetus*, I find in the middle dialogues; and (as will become clear shortly) the account he finds in the middle dialogues, I find in the *Theaetetus* (minus the reference to forms).

that Protagoras' solution to the puzzles about size and number—and so also Protagoras' solution to the problem of conflicting appearances proposed in 153–4—in some way involves change: *everything* that's been said depends on the assumption that everything is constantly changing.[39] If this is so, then Burnyeat's account of 153–4, and Cornford's account of the puzzles, cannot be right, since, on their accounts, Protagoras explains seemingly conflicting appearances without invoking change, but simply by noting the relational character of certain properties. Or again, Burnyeat says that, in 153–4, the argument on behalf of Protagoreanism assumes that the object doesn't change; but 156 tells us that everything that's been said assumes that there is constant change.[40]

I suggest the following alternative solution. Plato's idea seems to be that, according to Protagoras, if an object appears different, then it becomes different and so it changes. Since the dice appear first more, then fewer, they were more, then fewer. Since the object appears first red, then green, it was red, then green. Protagoras does not believe that an object can appear different without changing. This is what *we* believe, but it is not what Protagoras believes. On the contrary, he believes that if an object appears different, it is different in a sense that involves change—real change, not mere Cambridge change. Since the dice appear more, then fewer, they change from being more to being fewer. If the wind appears warm, then cold, it changes from being warm to being cold.

Earlier, we saw that 154 B offered us disjunctive options: either the object was not previously white, or else it became different and so changed. We now know that the object became different, when it appeared different,

---

[39] 156 A 5 actually says, not that everything is *changing*, but that everything is *change*. This is sometimes taken to mean that there are no things, only processes; see e.g. Burnyeat, *The* Theaetetus *of Plato*, 16. An alternative is that there are things, but that they are processes.

[40] Burnyeat says: 'Finally, at 155d–156a the Heracleitean explanation of all this is at last announced. It becomes clear that relativization is not the complete answer to our problem, for Socrates proceeds to a complicated account (156a ff.) of perception, perceivers, and sensible things which spells out Protagorean relativity in the language of becoming' (ibid. 13); and, as Burnyeat agrees, this account involves change. But, again, it is not as though perceptual relativism and Heracleiteanism can sit happily side by side: the first assumes that different appearances need not involve change in the object that appears different; Heracleiteanism assumes that objects are always changing. Or again, having said that the solution to the puzzles about size and number does not involve change but only relativization, Cornford goes on to consider the theory of perception. He sees that the two passages are connected: 'light on the puzzles here is to be drawn from the theory of sense-perception' (p. 44). He also sees that on this theory 'properties, whatever they are, are always changing' (p. 51). Yet how, in that case, does the theory illuminate the solution to the puzzles which, on Cornford's view, assumes that objects are not always changing?

and so we can conclude that it must have changed. So the above argument, (A)–(C′), should be completed as follows:

(D′) The object became different and so it changed.

What about the other disjunct: was the object white? McDowell, we saw, took 154 B to deny that the object was white; I argued that 154 B neither denied nor affirmed this. But we can now see that it is affirmed, if not in 154 B then elsewhere. After all, Protagoras tells us that things are (for one) just as they appear to be. So, since the object appeared white, it was white; when it then appeared not white, it must have become not white, and so it must have changed, from being white to not being white. This suggests that, in the case described in 154 B, Protagoras argues as follows:[41]

(1) There are, or at least seem to be, conflicting appearances; for example, the stone appears white at t_1, then not white at t_2.
(2) Things are however they appear to be.
(3) Therefore, the stone was white, then not white.
(4) Therefore it changed, from being white to being not white.

In the case of the dice, similarly, Protagoras argues as follows:

(1′) There are, or at least seem to be, conflicting appearances; for example, the dice appear more (than the four) at t_1, then fewer (than the twelve) at t_2.
(2′) Things are however they appear to be.
(3′) Therefore, the dice were more, then fewer.
(4′) Therefore, they changed, from being more to being fewer.

Notice, in support of this interpretation, that Plato carefully describes the dice example in terms of conflicting appearances at different times: someone first places four dice next to six, at which time the six seem more (than the four); he then puts twelve dice next to the six, at which time they seem fewer (than the twelve). Plato doesn't ask what we should say about six dice, right now, being more than the four and fewer than the twelve. He asks what we should say when someone first sees six dice placed next to four, and then sees them placed next to twelve, so that they appear different on the two occasions of comparison. If his point were that the puzzles could be solved simply by noting that various properties are relational, he would not

---

[41] I do not mean that 154 B itself says this; we have seen that it does not say whether the object has changed, though it leaves this possibility open. I mean that Protagoras goes on to say that this possibility is actual.

emphasize that we are concerned with conflicting appearances that occur at different times.[42] Likewise, 154 B assumes that we are talking about different times; it is only on that assumption that the question arises of whether the object changed in between the seemingly conflicting appearances.[43]

If this is Protagoras' solution to the puzzles, then he is not a perceptual relativist, since he believes that whenever objects appear different, they genuinely change. Even if the reason that the object no longer appears red to me is that I have been struck blind, still, if it no longer appears red, it no longer is red, and so it must genuinely have changed, from being red to not being red. Protagoras, that is, believes that objects are—really are—however they appear to be. I shall call this position *infallibilism* since it takes us to be infallible about how things are.[44]

Infallibilism is like perceptual relativism in some ways. In particular, both views take perceptual properties to be both relational and subjective, in so far as both views claim that, for an object to be, say, white, it must stand in a suitable relation to a perceiver. However, on infallibilism, Burnyeat's striking premiss (1)—that if something appears F to some observers and not-F to others, then it is not really F—is irrelevant to the argument. For on infallibilism, whiteness and so on are not relational *because* they appear F only to some observers rather than to all. Even if they appeared F to everyone, they would still be relational.[45] Moreover, unlike perceptual relativism, infallibilism claims that, though perceptual properties are both relational and subjective, objects really have them. And unlike perceptual relativism, infallibilism claims that change of colour is never a mere Cambridge change in the object; even if an object appears different because of a change in a perceiver, the object itself undergoes a genuine change.

If Protagoras is an infallibilist, he cannot solve the puzzles as we would.

[42] Invoking change provides a solution only for seemingly conflicting appearances that occur at different times. So, at this point, Protagoras is offering only a limited solution to the problem of conflicting appearances; later he takes up the question of seemingly conflicting appearances that occur at the same time. As befits a dialectical discussion, his commitments are uncovered only gradually.

[43] That this is the situation that Plato envisages in 153 D–154 B is also suggested by the fact that he says that 'you are never in a similar condition to yourself'. It eventually emerges, then, that since appearances are always different, things are always different, and so there is constant change.

[44] Broad infallibilism says that all our beliefs are infallible; narrow infallibilism says that all our perceptual beliefs are infallible.

[45] As we have seen, Protagoras claims that colour appearances are never the same, so he cannot allow any object to appear precisely the same shade of, say, white to everyone. However, he can allow a given object to appear white (a generic shade) to everyone; and, in this case, he would still want to say that whiteness is relational (or that whiteness-tokens are relational; see n. 27 above).

We would say that the six dice are more in relation to the four, and fewer in relation to the twelve, and that these facts do not involve the dice changing. *We* can solve the puzzles by distinguishing between mere Cambridge and genuine change and by pointing out that differences in certain relational properties do not involve genuine change. But Plato is arguing that Protagoras cannot do this: in his view, Protagoras is committed to saying that, in every case in which things seem different, they are really different, and so they genuinely change. Since the dice seem different, they are different, and so they must have changed. On Burnyeat's view, Protagoras says that objects can appear different without changing—indeed, Burnyeat thinks that the argument in 154 B depends on this assumption. On my account, this is precisely what Plato says that Protagoras *cannot* say. So on my account, it is *we* who solve the puzzles about the dice without invoking change, simply by noting that the properties at issue are relational. Protagoras thinks that this—the correct view—is extraordinary and absurd; he thinks that genuine change is involved. If this is right, then it is not our view, but Protagoras', that is extraordinary and absurd. But that is Plato's point. He is offering an indirect argument against Protagoras; he is suggesting that Protagoras cannot distinguish between genuine and mere Cambridge change, and so has to resolve the puzzles by invoking genuine change.

Why does Plato think that Protagoras must offer this solution? I cannot provide a full answer to this question here. But, roughly, his idea seems to be that we can distinguish between genuine and mere Cambridge change only if an object is something in itself; since Protagoras claims that nothing is anything in itself (153 E 4–5), he cannot distinguish between genuine and mere Cambridge change. Plato then commits him to the view that every case of appearing different involves a genuine change in the object that appears different. This is one reason that Protagoras is committed to Heracleiteanism.[46]

---

[46] Bostock, *Plato's* Theaetetus, 45–6, notices that the puzzles are phrased in terms of perceivers viewing the dice at different times, and he wonders whether this involves confusion on Plato's part, since the correct solution to the puzzles does not require any reference to change or perceivers. (Perhaps Bostock is raising only a prima facie difficulty here; I am not sure.) McDowell, *Plato: Theaetetus*, 136–7, also thinks that Plato's failure to provide the correct solution shows that he is unclear about it. But this again ignores the dialectical strategy of the passage. It is not Plato himself, but Protagoras, who requires a reference to change. Of course, one might argue that Plato himself mistakenly accepts Protagoras' incorrect solution. But if the suggestion made in the text is correct, then we need not convict Plato of confusion on this score. That Plato is arguing that Protagoras cannot distinguish between genuine and mere Cambridge change is also suggested by T. H. Irwin, 'Plato's Heracleiteanism', *Philosophical Quarterly*, 27 (1977), 1–13 at 5–6. See also P. L. Gottlieb, 'Aristotle and the Measure of All Things' (diss. Ph.D., Cornell, 1988), 21–9. As we have seen (nn. 24, 36), Burnyeat also claims that, if all features of an object are relativized, so that the object

X

We have now looked at part of Plato's argument for the claim that Protagoras is committed to Heracleiteanism. The argument involves the suggestion
that Protagoras cannot distinguish between genuine and mere Cambridge
change. Though the argument committing Protagoras to Heracleiteanism
involves Protagoras in confusion, we can also see why Protagoras should
none the less welcome Heracleitus' support. For Protagoras believes that
all beliefs are true, true *simpliciter*. According to Burnyeat, infallibilism
'is in clear violation of the law of contradiction, since it allows one person's judgment that something is so and another person's judgment that
it is not so both to be true together'.[47] But we should not conclude so
quickly that infallibilism violates the law of noncontradiction: whether it
does so depends on what the world is like. If the world is populated by
stable, intersubjectively available objects, then infallibilism violates the law
of noncontradiction. But if the world is constantly changing to accommodate our different appearances, then it is not so clear that infallibilism
violates the law of noncontradiction.[48] This is precisely why Plato sug-

is nothing in itself, then Protagoras is committed to a very strong sort of Heracleiteanism.
However, again, it is not clear that that suggestion of his fits very well with his account of
153 D–154 B. Moreover, we construe the nature of the relevant relativizations differently,
since I take Protagoras to be an infallibilist, whereas Burnyeat denies that Protagoras is an
infallibilist (see n. 47).

[47] Burnyeat, 'Protagoras and Self-Refutation in Later Greek Philosophy', 46. More precisely, Burnyeat says that the view that he calls subjectivism violates the law of noncontradiction. But 'subjectivism' is just his label for the view I call infallibilism. I prefer my label
largely because 'subjectivism' has been used in so many different ways that its use here would
be liable to misinterpretation. In particular, it might suggest, misleadingly, that for Protagoras colours and so on are purely mental entities. On infallibilism, colours and so on do not
exist unperceived, but they are genuine features of extra-mental objects. Burnyeat rejects the
infallibilist reading of Protagoras in favour of a relativist reading, according to which 'every
judgement is true *for* (in relation to) the person whose judgement it is' ('Protagoras and
Self-Refutation in Plato's *Theaetetus*', 176). Although Burnyeat, in his two papers on the self-
refutation argument, denies that Protagoras is an infallibilist, elsewhere he sometimes seems
to conceive of him as an infallibilist. In, for example 'Idealism and Greek Philosophy', he says
that 'Protagoras' book was called *Truth* precisely because it offered an account of the conditions under which things really are as they appear. The Greek use of the predicates "true"
and "false" embodies the assumption of realism on which I have been insisting all along'
(p. 26). Earlier in the same article, he says that Protagoras 'demands a state of affairs for every
appearance, rendering that appearance true' (p. 8); and that 'every perception will be the
unerring apprehension of a particular state of affairs' (p. 9). Here Burnyeat says that things
change whenever they appear different. This is what infallibilism says. According to perceptual relativism, however, things can appear different without undergoing a genuine change.

[48] Conversely, if objects are as they appear, then, given the assumption that objects con-

gests that Heracleitus is Protagoras' best support: he tries to buttress at least Narrow Protagoreanism by showing that it can eliminate a number of seeming contradictions, at least in the perceptual sphere, by embracing a Heracleitean ontology. Whether infallibilism in the end violates the law of noncontradiction, especially when it strays outside the perceptual sphere (or for conflicting appearances that occur at some one time), is another question, which I take up in the next chapter. The present point is that, even if it violates the law of noncontradiction at some stage, Heracleiteanism is introduced to show that it is not as vulnerable on this score as it initially seems to be.

This, in turn, shows that Protagoras should have mixed feelings about his Heracleiteanism. On the one hand, it allows him to argue that many seemingly conflicting appearances do not in fact conflict. To this extent, invoking Heracleiteanism makes infallibilism look more plausible than it might initially seem to be. On the other hand, Protagoras is committed to being a Heracleitean, to invoking genuine change, in cases that in fact involve mere Cambridge change. So Protagoras' best support also involves him in some confusion. This, no doubt, is Plato's point. But we can see that this is his point only if we are clear about the complex dialectical character of his discussion.[49]

stantly appear different, they are constantly changing. Bostock, *Plato's* Theaetetus, 49, asks why we should assume that objects always appear different. I can think of two replies. One is that the assumption is quite reasonable; for since, as Plato says at 154 A 3–8, conditions are never exactly alike, how things appear from one moment to the next is never exactly the same. (Contrast Bostock's intuitions, p. 61.) Another is that Protagoras must allow that things can always appear different, in which case he is committed to allowing that the most radical sort of Heracleiteanism is at least possible. On either view, Plato then asks whether something Protagoras takes to be possible is in fact possible. (On the first view, he explores whether something Protagoras takes to be actual, and so possible, is in fact possible; on the second view, he explores whether something Protagoras views as possible, even if not actual, is in fact possible.) When he argues, at pp. 181–3, that the most extreme sort of Heracleiteanism is after all impossible, that undercuts Protagoreanism as well.

[49] I should like to thank Terry Irwin, M. M. McCabe, Gisela Striker, and Nicholas Sturgeon for helpful written comments; and the members of a graduate seminar held in Cornell in the autumn of 1992 for many stimulating discussions. Some of the ideas presented in this chapter are developed further in ch. 6 above.

8

Plato's Refutation of Protagoras in the *Theaetetus*

I

According to Protagoras, 'a man is the measure of all things, of those that are that they are, and of those that are not that they are not' (*Tht.* 152 A 2–4).[1] In *Theaetetus* 169 D–171 D, Plato argues that Protagoras' measure doctrine (P) is in some sense self-refuting.[2] It is unclear, however, precisely how we are to understand the measure doctrine, and so it is also unclear whether Plato succeeds in refuting it.

Plato is often thought to portray Protagoras as a relativist, according to whom no beliefs are absolutely true, or true *simpliciter*; rather, all beliefs are true only *for* those who hold them.[3] It is well known, however, that if

---

[1] This is generally agreed to be a quotation from Protagoras. For other occurrences of it, see Plato, *Cra.* 385 E 6–386 A 3; Sextus Empiricus, *M.* 7. 60–1; Diogenes Laertius, *Lives* 9. 51. I should note that my concern throughout this chapter is primarily with Plato's portrayal of Protagoras, not with the historical Protagoras. However, since Plato is one of our main sources of information about the historical Protagoras, looking at how he portrays Protagoras presumably gives us some indication of Protagoras' views: though one of course can't rule out the possibility that Plato misinterpreted him.

[2] Sextus Empiricus, *M.* 7. 389–90, calls the argument a *peritropē*, literally a turn about or around, hence a refutation, though Sextus generally uses the term for a *self*-refutation in particular. For detailed discussion, see M. F. Burnyeat, 'Protagoras and Self-Refutation in Later Greek Philosophy', *Philosophical Review*, 85 (1976) 44–69. (As Burnyeat explains, to say that p is self-refuting needn't be to say that p, all by itself, implies not-p; rather, p plus at least one ancillary premiss implies not-p, where there are constraints on what sorts of ancillary premisses are appropriate.) Plato doesn't himself call his argument a *peritropē*. But at 169 E 7–8, he says that he aims to refute the measure doctrine from Protagoras' own words (*ek tou ekeinou logou*). Cf. *Euthd.* 286 B–C, where he says that the Protagorean view, that it is not possible to contradict, 'always seems remarkable to me, turning both other theses and also itself upside down [*anatrepein*]' (286 C 3–5); I take it that *anatrepein*, like *peritrepein*, indicates a self-refutation.

[3] See e.g. Burnyeat, 'Protagoras and Self-Refutation in Later Greek Philosophy'; and 'Protagoras and Self-Refutation in Plato's *Theaetetus*', *Philosophical Review*, 85 (1976) 172–95, repr. in S. Everson (ed.), *Epistemology* (Companions to Ancient Thought, 1; Cambridge: Cambridge University Press, 1990), 39–59 (original pagination). I shall from now on generally cite these two papers by page number alone, and references to them will generally be given in the text. I discuss the second of these papers in detail in 'Relativism and

Plato takes Protagoras to be a relativist, various difficulties arise. First and foremost among them is that Plato's arguments do not seem to succeed in refuting relativism. In particular, at several crucial junctures he omits the qualifier 'for one' in places where the relativist would insist on it. As Gregory Vlastos puts it:[4]

Protagoras is very fussy about adding 'for . . .' after 'true' or 'is' or 'real', while his thickheaded interlocutor keeps ignoring the difference. Even Plato himself is not as strict as he should be on this point. While he puts in the 'for . . .' almost invariably while *reporting or describing* Protagoras's doctrine (not only at 170a, but at 152bc, 158a, and all through 166c–167c, where the repetition gets almost tiresome, and then again at 171e–172a; also at *Crat* 385e–386d), he sometimes drops it in the course of *arguing* against Protagoras (e.g., in the 'exquisite' argument at 171a), thereby vitiating his own polemic.

Actually, Vlastos overstates the extent to which Plato includes the qualifiers in reporting Protagoras' position. Even here he often omits them, representing Protagoras as holding that all beliefs are *true*, not that they are true *for those who hold them.*[5] This, of course, is another count against a relativist reading: the text often fails to describe Protagoras in the requisite way.

Self-Refutation in Plato's *Theaetetus*: Plato, Protagoras, and Burnyeat', in J. Gentzler (ed.), *Method in Ancient Philosophy* (Oxford: Clarendon Press, 1998), 138–63.

Others who seem to understand the measure doctrine in roughly the same way as Burnyeat include J. McDowell, *Plato:* Theaetetus, trans. with notes (Oxford: Clarendon Press, 1973), 169–73; D. Bostock, *Plato's* Theaetetus (Oxford: Clarendon Press, 1988), 89–92; K. M. Sayre, *Plato's Analytic Method* (Chicago: University of Chicago Press, 1969), 87–90; R. Waterfield, *Plato:* Theaetetus (Harmondsworth: Penguin Books, 1987), 172–6; C. C. W. Taylor, *Plato:* Protagoras, 2nd edn. (Oxford: Clarendon Press, 1991), at e.g. p. 83; R. M. Dancy, 'Theaetetus's First Baby: *Theaetetus* 151e–160e', *Philosophical Topics*, 15 (1987), 61–108. There are some differences among these authors which need not concern us here; see ch. 6 above.

I follow Burnyeat in using 'absolutely true', 'true *simpliciter*', and 'true period' interchangeably.

[4] G. Vlastos, 'Introduction', in *Plato:* Protagoras (Indianapolis and New York: Bobbs-Merrill, 1956), xiv n. 29. Though Vlastos thinks that the omission of the qualifiers vitiates Plato's argument, I'm not sure that he takes Protagoras to be a relativist, as I understand that position here; see 'Relativism and Self-Refutation in Plato's *Theaetetus*', n. 18.

Commentators who take Protagoras to be a relativist, and who agree with Vlastos that Plato fails to refute Protagoras, include McDowell, Bostock, Sayre, and Waterfield. Though all these authors believe that Plato fails to refute relativism from the logical point of view, some of them believe that he none the less raises serious difficulties for Protagoras; see e.g. McDowell, *Plato:* Theaetetus, 171.

Of course, even if Plato fails to refute relativism, it does not follow that he was not trying to refute it. Nor does everyone agree that he fails to refute it; Burnyeat, for example, believes that he succeeds. I challenge his interpretation in 'Relativism and Self-Refutation in Plato's *Theaetetus*'.

[5] For places where the qualifiers are omitted, see (in addition to the self-refutation pas-

There are also further difficulties for a relativist reading. For example, other ancient commentators do not view Protagoras as a relativist; rather, they view him as what I shall call an *infallibilist*, according to whom all beliefs are absolutely true, or true *simpliciter*. This is how Aristotle and Sextus, for example, view him.[6] It would be surprising if Plato were the only ancient commentator to view Protagoras as an infallibilist. Moreover, not only do other ancient commentators portray Protagoras as an infallibilist, but they also use against him an argument quite like Plato's. Yet, as Burnyeat remarks, it would be 'curious' (p. 46) if the same argument were brought to bear against two such different—indeed incompatible—positions.

On the interpretation that I shall propose, we do not face these difficulties. For I shall argue that Plato, like other ancient commentators, portrays Protagoras as an infallibilist: he is not the odd man out. Moreover, his arguments fare far better against infallibilism than they do against relativism. We shall also see that the text is quite naturally read as I shall read it. A further bonus of my interpretation is that, as I argue in Chapters 6 and 7, Plato portrays Protagoras as an infallibilist in *Theaetetus* 151–60;[7] and surely it is desirable that he interpret Protagoras in the same way both when he initially articulates his position and when he refutes it.[8]

---

sage that we shall come to) 161 c 2–3, 161 d 5–7, 162 a 1, 167 b 1, 167 c 2 (on which see McDowell's note ad loc.), 172 b 6, 179 c 2, 179 c 4, 179 b–d. It's important to note that in some of the places where a qualifier occurs, the point is to express, not relativism about truth, but the relational nature of some properties, which is quite a different matter. I discuss this in ch. 6.

[6] See Aristotle, *Metaph.* *Γ* 5, *K* 6; Sextus Empiricus, *M.* 7. 60–4; *PH* 1. 216–19; cf. Diogenes Laertius, *Lives* 9. 51. It's worth noting that, although Aristotle and Sextus portray Protagoras as holding that all beliefs are true, they also associate *pros ti* with him. Burnyeat, 'Protagoras and Self-Refutation in Later Greek Philosophy', 46 n. 3, thinks this shows that they ascribe both infallibilism and relativism to Protagoras. My own view is that they do not use '*pros ti*' to indicate relativism, as I understand that notion here.

I use 'infallibilism' to capture the fact that, on this view, we are all infallible in our beliefs, in the sense that, if A believes p, p is true. Burnyeat uses 'subjectivism' for this view. There are of course interpretations of Protagoras, and of Plato's portrayal of him, besides relativism and infallibilism. I none the less focus on these two interpretations because (i) relativism is such a familiar interpretation, yet (ii) I favour infallibilism.

[7] I summarize the essential argument on behalf of this claim below, in describing the role of Heracleitus.

[8] That is, it is desirable that Plato satisfy what, in ch. 6, I call the univocity criterion. Univocity does not mean that Plato cannot or should not canvas more than one interpretation of Protagoras. (That he does so is argued by R. Ketchum, 'Plato's "Refutation" of Protagorean Relativism: *Theaetetus* 170–171', *Oxford Studies in Ancient Philosophy*, 10 (1992), 73–105.) Rather, the point is that if he portrays Protagoras as an infallibilist in the 150s, then, when he argues against Protagoras, he should argue against infallibilism.

II

It will help, to begin with, to provide a more detailed account of relativism and infallibilism. Relativism has, of course, been understood in many different ways, both in general and in connection with the *Theaetetus*. I shall generally focus here on what I take to be the best recent account, that proposed by Burnyeat. According to Burnyeat, Protagoras is a relativist about *truth*; he offers a theory of truth, according to which all truth is relative.[9] In particular, Burnyeat argues that Protagoras accepts a biconditional: p is true for A if, and only if, A believes p. What, on this view, does 'p is true for A' mean? Burnyeat argues that the phrase is equivalent to, but not synonymous with, 'A believes p' (pp. 181–2). I think it's difficult to be sure precisely what 'p is true for A' means, if not 'A believes p'; but I shall not press that point here. For present purposes, the crucial point is that on Burnyeat's interpretation the qualifier 'for one' indicates that Protagoras denies that any propositions are absolutely true or true *simpliciter*. On a variant of this view (though not one endorsed by Burnyeat), 'for one' indicates a novel understanding of the truth predicate: 'true' *means* 'true-for-a-person'.[10] On both views, the qualifiers are ineliminable; one cannot move from 'p is true for A' to 'p is true'. For the whole point of relativism is to say that no propositions are flat-out true.[11]

On the view I favour, by contrast, Protagoras is an infallibilist. He claims

---

[9] See e.g. 'Protagoras and Self-Refutation in Plato's *Theaetetus*', 181. In what follows, I shall generally simply speak of relativism, meaning thereby relativism about truth, as I explain that notion here.

[10] For this interpretation, see e.g. T. D. J. Chappell, 'Does Protagoras Refute Himself?', *Classical Quarterly*, NS 45 (1995), 333–8. On yet another view, the claim is that 'true' as ordinarily understood is meaningless (and not just uninstantiated). McDowell, *Plato: Theaetetus*, 171, may hold this view; see also S. Tigner, 'The "Exquisite" Argument at *Theaetetus* 171a', *Mnemosyne*, 4th series, 24 (1971), 366–9.

[11] Here there are two complications. First, there is dispute as to whether (P) is itself a merely relative truth or is exempted from its scope. In the latter case, Protagoras admits the existence of one absolute truth, viz. (P) itself. As I explain in 'Relativism and Self-Refutation in Plato's *Theaetetus*', I think Burnyeat vacillates between these two views. In this chapter I shall assume that, whether (P) is to be understood along relativist or infallibilist lines, it falls within its scope. (None the less, I shall occasionally indicate what difference it makes to Plato's argument if (P) does not fall within its scope.) I do so because this seems to be Plato's view; see Argument II (3) and note ad loc. (In 'Relativism and Self-Refutation in Plato's *Theaetetus*', by contrast, I assumed that (P) does not fall within its own scope.) Secondly, Burnyeat argues that in one special case, where 'p' is the measure doctrine, it is legitimate to drop the qualifier in arguing against relativism. I criticize this argument in 'Relativism and Self-Refutation in Plato's *Theaetetus*', and I shall assume here that, even where 'p' is the measure doctrine, it is not legitimate to drop the qualifier in arguing against relativism.

that (i) all beliefs are absolutely true, and (ii) there are no truths that are not believed: p is true if and only if it is believed.[12] On this view, Protagoras does not deny that any statements are absolutely true; nor does he have a novel understanding of the truth predicate. Rather, he thinks that all beliefs are guaranteed to be true—absolutely true, or true *simpliciter*. He offers, not a theory of truth, but an account of the conditions under which statements are true: they are true if and only if believed. On this view, 'for one' doesn't block the implication that any statements are absolutely true; on the contrary, the move from 'p is true for A' to 'p is true' is always legitimate.

We can already see one outstanding advantage of the infallibilist reading: on it, Plato is entitled to omit the qualifiers, as he so often and conspicuously does; whereas he is not entitled to omit them if he is arguing against relativism. Of course, it doesn't follow that Plato therefore succeeds in refuting infallibilism: his arguments could fail for other reasons. Still, it's an important advantage of my reading that Plato is entitled to omit the qualifiers.

One might think that this advantage needs to be set against the following disadvantage: Burnyeat believes that infallibilism is an 'arid' view that 'no one is likely to defend', but he takes relativism to be an 'intriguing' view 'which some think is still unrefuted' (p. 46). For consider Plato's initial example of a case of seemingly conflicting appearances: the wind seems cold to me but not to you (*Tht.* 152 B 1–C 3). According to the relativist, we should infer that the wind is cold for me but not for you, in the sense that we are both right in a way, though not in a way that involves contradiction, since neither of our beliefs is true (or false) *simpliciter*. Burnyeat argues that infallibilism, by contrast, 'is in clear violation of the law of contradiction, since it allows one person's judgment that something is so and another person's judgment that it is not so both to be true together' (p. 46). If infallibilism but not relativism is in clear violation of the principle of noncontradiction (PNC), then relativism might well seem to be the more plausible view.

---

[12] N. Denyer, *Language, Thought and Falsehood in Ancient Greek Philosophy* (London and New York: Routledge and Kegan Paul, 1991), considers but rejects something like this interpretation of Protagoras; see e.g. p. 87. Note that (i) and (ii) mean that p is true if and only if *someone* believes p. In saying that Protagoras accepts this biconditional, I retract a claim made in 'Relativism and Self-Refutation in Plato's *Theaetetus*', where I suggested that Protagoras only accepts the conditional, that if A believes p, then p is true. Though I therefore now agree with Burnyeat that Protagoras accepts a biconditional, we differ over what the relevant biconditional is. This difference is at least partly due to the fact that I take Protagoras to be an infallibilist, whereas Burnyeat takes him to be a relativist.

However, Burnyeat is too quick in claiming that infallibilism is in *clear* violation of PNC. To be sure, he is correct if the world is as we ordinarily take it to be, if it consists of stable, intersubjectively available objects. But in the first part of the *Theaetetus* (151–60), Plato defends Protagoras by means of a Heracleitean ontology; this allows him to argue that seemingly conflicting perceptual beliefs do not conflict.[13] How this can be so is explained in different ways as the dialectic unfolds: initially it is suggested that the wind changes between our two utterances. Eventually it is suggested that we are talking about different winds: I was talking about a cold one, and you were talking about one that is not cold.[14] In either case, both of our beliefs are true—true *simpliciter*—and they are so without contradiction. Infallibilism is therefore not in *clear* violation of PNC, and so it is not *as* 'crude' (p. 46) a view as one might initially take it to be.

The fact that Plato defends Protagoras with a Heracleitean ontology indicates two things. First, it shows that Protagoras *wants* to preserve PNC; he would be worried if it could be shown that he is committed to violating it. If he didn't care about preserving PNC, there'd be no need to introduce a Heracleitean ontology. Protagoras could just say: 'Of course (P) violates PNC, given that people hold conflicting beliefs. But what do I care?' It's precisely because he *does* care that Plato troubles to offer him Heracleitus' support.[15]

[13] In my view, Heracleiteanism is invoked only in connection with first-order perceptual beliefs, such as 'The wind is cold', 'The wine is sweet'. (However, Protagoras has quite a broad view of what can be perceived. At 156 B 4–6, for example, he counts 'pleasures, pains, desires, fears, and others' as perceptions. None the less, there seem to be some limits, which are never clearly specified, on what counts as a perception.) Bostock, *Plato's* Theatetus, 90, seems to agree. McDowell, *Plato:* Theaetetus, 168 n. (d), may disagree. S. Waterlow, 'Protagoras and Inconsistency', *Archiv für Geschichte der Philosophie*, 59 (1977), 19–36, definitely disagrees. (My view is in many ways close to Waterlow's, but this is one central difference between us. See n. 15 for another one.) On this issue, see also G. Kerferd, 'Plato's Account of the Relativism of Protagoras', *Durham University Journal*, 42 (1949), 20–6.

[14] There is dispute as to whether Plato eventually (on Protagoras' behalf) introduces private objects, or only public objects with relational properties. I think 159 A–160 C suggests that private objects are on board; but contrast M. Matthen, 'Perception, Relativism, and Truth: Reflections on Plato's *Theaetetus* 152–160', *Dialogue*, 24 (1985), 33–58. The issue is also discussed by Kerferd.

[15] Similarly, I take it that if Protagoras said that it is impossible to contradict (*ouk estin antilegein, Euthd.* 286 B–C; cf. Diogenes Laertius, *Lives* 9. 53), it was because he wanted to preserve PNC, yet, if all beliefs are true, and it is possible to contradict (in the strict logical sense), then PNC breaks down. Contrast Waterlow, who thinks that, for Protagoras, 'respect for those [logical] laws is no more than an idle fetish' ('Protagoras and Inconsistency', 25, cf. 23). I'm not sure whether Waterlow thinks that Protagoras' views in fact violate PNC. The first complete paragraph on p. 26 says that 'the views which Plato ascribes to Protagoras in the *Theaetetus* entail the same denial', viz. of 'the law of non-contradiction'. But the second complete paragraph says that it would be 'ineffective' to argue that Protagoras' position is

Secondly, the fact that Plato supports Protagoras with a Heracleitean on-tology is evidence, independent of the self-refutation argument, in favour of infallibilism. For if Protagoras is an infallibilist (who cares about PNC), then it's clear why he welcomes Heracleitus' support: Heracleitus offers an ontology that allows seemingly conflicting appearances, at least in the per-ceptual sphere, to be true—absolutely true—without contradiction. Rela-tivism, by contrast, does not need to appeal to any ontology in order to resolve the problem of conflicting appearances. It resolves the problem, not by introducing a special ontology, but by interpreting the truth pred-icate in a novel way, or by denying that any propositions are flat-out true. Infallibilism does not have an unusual understanding of the truth pred-icate, nor does it deny that any propositions are flat-out true. Rather, it has an unusual understanding of the conditions under which objects have properties, or under which propositions are true: a proposition is true if and only if it is believed.

III

These preliminaries out of the way, we can now turn to the details of the text. Discussions of Plato's refutation of Protagoras generally focus on 171 A 6 ff. This is perhaps not surprising, given that Plato himself says that it is 'especially clever' (*kompsotaton*, 171 A 6). But it is important to see that this passage is not self-standing. Rather, it is the culmination of an intricate series of arguments, the first of which occurs in 170 A–C. There are, in fact, three linked passages: 170 A–C; a transitional passage (170 C 5–E 6); and then a third passage (170 E 7–171 D 8), of which the 'especially clever' argument is one part. I shall explore each of these passages in turn, beginning with the first.

inconsistent, since Plato 'provides his Protagoras with the means to avoid ever being caught in self-contradiction'; nor, she thinks, does Plato's Protagoras allow that two people can ever contradict one another. See also pp. 20–1. On her view, if no one can contradict himself, and if no two people can contradict one another, then PNC doesn't break down.

One might argue that *Protagoras* doesn't care about PNC; rather, *we* do and so, since Plato wants us to take Protagoras' position seriously, he tries to give it a run for its money by showing that, whether or not Protagoras cares about preserving PNC, he can in fact do so, at least for first-order perceptual beliefs. However, Plato often puts the relevant points in Protagoras' mouth. That is, he doesn't merely say that this is what *we* could say; he says that this is what *Protagoras* would say. Of course, one might argue that Protagoras says this merely to assuage us and not because he believes it. Such hypotheses are difficult to refute, but neither is there any reason to accept them.

Plato first argues as follows (170 A 3–C 5):[16]

soc. He says, doesn't he, that what seems [*to dokoun*] to anyone actually is for the person to whom it seems [*dokei*]?

THEO. Yes.

soc. Well, now, Protagoras, we too are talking about the beliefs [*doxai*] of a man, or rather of all men, when we say that there isn't anyone who doesn't think [*hēgeisthai*] that he's wiser than others in some respects, whereas others are wiser than him in other respects. In the greatest of dangers, when people are in trouble on campaigns, or in diseases, or at sea, they treat the leading men in each sphere like gods, expecting them to be their saviours, because they're superior precisely in respect of knowledge. The whole of human life is surely full of people looking for teachers and leaders for themselves and other animals, and for what they do; and, on the other hand, of people who think themselves capable of teaching and capable of leading. Now what can we say, in all these cases, except that men themselves think [*hēgeisthai*] that there is wisdom and ignorance [*amathia*][17] in them?

THEO. Nothing.

soc. And they think that wisdom is true thinking [*dianoian*] and that ignorance is false belief?

THEO. Of course.

soc. Well then, how are we to deal with your theory, Protagoras? Should we say that people always believe things that are true? Or that they sometimes believe things that are true and sometimes things that are false? Because from both alternatives it follows, I think, that they don't always believe things that are true, but believe both ⟨truths and falsehoods⟩.

We may formulate this reasoning as follows:

Argument I

   (1) (P): As things seem to one, so they are to one.

   (2) Each person thinks that he is wiser than others in some respects, and that others are wiser than him in other respects, where wisdom involves having true beliefs and ignorance involves having false beliefs.

   (3) Either (a) all beliefs are true, or (b) some beliefs are false.

[16] Here and elsewhere I generally follow McDowell's translation. However, I generally use 'belief' and its cognates for '*doxa*' and its cognates (McDowell uses 'judgement'), 'think' for '*hēgeisthai*' (McDowell uses 'believe'), and 'judge' for '*krinein*' (McDowell uses 'decide'). So far as I can tell, Plato uses these terms interchangeably.

[17] In the present context, '*amathia*' means something more like stupidity or folly than simply not knowing, as is clear from the fact that Plato goes on to say that *amathia* involves false beliefs. 'Ignorance' can be used both for stupidity and for simply not knowing; I use it rather than e.g. 'stupidity', simply because this often makes for smoother prose.

(4) If (3a) is true, then the belief expressed in (2) is true, in which case there are some false beliefs.

(5) If (3b) is true, then there are some false beliefs.

(6) Therefore whether or not all beliefs are true, there are some false beliefs.

(7) Therefore there are some false beliefs.

(8) Therefore not-(P).

(1) simply states (P), and so it is obviously acceptable to Protagoras— although there is of course controversy about precisely what (P) says.

(2) is complex and requires careful scrutiny.[18] First, it contains an analysis of wisdom and ignorance: wisdom involves having true beliefs; ignorance involves having false beliefs. Secondly, it makes a comparative claim: each person thinks that he is *wiser* than others in some respects, and that others are wiser than him in other respects. Now, one might think that A can be wiser than B without A's being wise, just as one person can be richer than another without either's being rich. However—and this is a third point—Plato seems to intend not just the comparative claim but also the corresponding categorical claim. That is, each person thinks that he is *wise* about some matters (and so has true beliefs about those matters) on which others are ignorant and so have false beliefs. Similarly, each person thinks that he is ignorant about some matters (and so has false beliefs about those matters) on which others are wise and so have true beliefs. Hence Plato says that 'men themselves think that there is wisdom and ignorance in them'. It follows that everyone believes that there are genuinely conflicting beliefs, in the sense that everyone believes that there are cases in which A believes p and B believes not-p, and one of p and not-p is true, the other false. Finally, it's important to be clear that (2) *doesn't* say that *there are* false beliefs, or conflicting beliefs in the sense just explained. Rather, it says that people *believe* these things.

Various aspects of (2) will be important to us at different stages. However, in Argument I, which is our present concern, the main crucial feature is the claim that people believe that there are false beliefs. Hence I shall focus on this aspect of (2) for the remainder of this section.

It's clear why (2) says, not that there are false beliefs, but that people believe that there are. For it would beg the question against both relativism and infallibilism to assume that there are false beliefs, since both positions

---

[18] In thinking about (2), I have been helped by N. P. White, 'Plato on the Contents of Protagorean Relativism' (unpublished). I thank White for showing me his paper and for allowing me to discuss it.

deny that there are.[19] Accordingly, (2) says instead that everyone *believes* that there are false beliefs.

But even once this point is understood, (2) still appears to be at any rate false since, again, neither relativists nor infallibilists believe that there are false beliefs, and so not *everyone* believes it.[20] However, we can easily avoid this difficulty by replacing 'each person' with 'everyone but Protagoras and his followers' or, for short, 'some people'; nor does this affect the validity of the argument. Accordingly, let us replace (2) with:[21]

> (2′) Some people believe that each person is wiser than others in some
> respects, and that others are wiser in other respects, where wisdom
> involves having true beliefs and ignorance involves having false
> beliefs.

Is (2′) acceptable to relativists or infallibilists? McDowell seems to think that it is acceptable to relativists. For he takes Protagoras to be a relativist, and he says that 'It is, arguably, in the spirit of [(P)] to assume that people are authoritative, not just about the truth of their own judgements, but about what judgements they are.'[22] McDowell seems to make two points: first, that according to Protagoras there is a fact of the matter about the contents of beliefs; and second, that each person is authoritative about the contents of their beliefs. The first point, however, so far from being acceptable to an extreme global relativist, begs the question against him by admitting that

---

[19] As we have seen (n. 11), some relativists exempt the statement of relativism from its scope. Hence one might say that some relativists think that there can be one false belief, namely, the belief that relativism is false; and (2) might be acceptable to such a relativist. However, as we've also seen (n. 11), this doesn't seem to be the version of relativism that Plato assumes here. Moreover, 170 a–c emphasizes that people think there are many false beliefs, including first-order beliefs about, for example, how to navigate or heal someone.

[20] To be sure, Plato eventually concludes that everyone, including Protagoras, believes that there are false beliefs (at e.g. 171 d 5–7). But he is not entitled to assume this yet; on the contrary, it is something he is trying to prove.

[21] One might argue that Plato never intended (2), but only (2′). In support of this suggestion, see *phamen* in 170 a 7, with *phēsei* in 170 a 3. Note too that in 170 b 5–6 Plato just says that 'men' (170 b 5–6) believe this. 170 c 5–8 speaks of Protagoras and his followers.

[22] McDowell, *Plato:* Theaetetus, 171. He believes that, though this is in the spirit of (P), it none the less leads to a difficulty for (P). For if people are authoritative about the contents of their beliefs, and if Protagoras' opponents believe that there are absolutely false beliefs, then Protagoras will have to admit that the notion of absolute truth makes sense. For this point, see also Tigner, 'The "Exquisite" Argument at *Theaetetus* 171a'. In my view, however, Plato never suggests that Protagoras denies that the notion of absolute truth makes sense. Though Burnyeat thinks that Plato portrays Protagoras as a relativist rather than as an infallibilist, he seems to agree with me on this point.

there is a fact of the matter about the contents of beliefs.[23] Here, then, is one strike against a relativist reading.

It does not, however, beg the question against infallibilism to assume that there is a fact of the matter about the contents of beliefs, at least insofar as the infallibilist admits the existence of absolute truths.[24] So Plato is entitled to (2′) if he is arguing against infallibiism, but not if he is arguing against extreme global relativism.

(3) is also problematical in an argument against relativism but not in one against infallibilism. For (3) omits the qualifiers on which the relativist insists.[25] In place of (3), the relativist favours:

(3′) All beliefs are true for those who hold them.

But from (3′), it is not clear how to mount a valid argument against relativism. For example, in place of (4), we seem to be entitled only to:[26]

(4′) If (3′) is true, then the belief that some people have—namely, that each person is wiser than others in some respects, and that others are wiser in other respects, where wisdom involves having true beliefs and ignorance involves having false beliefs—is true for those who hold that belief.

[23] This point is also made by White. Unlike me, however; White thinks that Protagoras is an extreme global relativist; he then argues that Plato (perhaps unwittingly) begs the question against him in just this way. Of course, (2′) would not beg the question against a more moderate version of relativism that exempts the contents of beliefs from its scope. But Burnyeat, for one, at some points takes Protagoras to hold an extreme form of relativism, according to which *all* truth is relative to belief ('Protagoras and Self-Refutation in Plato's *Theaetetus*', 179), in which case truths about the contents of beliefs ought to be thus relative as well. (2′) would also beg the question against a version of relativism that exempts only the statement of relativism from its scope.

[24] However, infallibilism also says that there are no truths that are not believed. So if it's true that A believes p, A (or someone) must believe that A believes p; and if it's true that A (or someone) believes that A believes p, then someone must believe that too, and so on, it seems, *ad infinitum*. This might seem to be a vicious infinite regress. Still, it is hardly a defect in Plato's argument if he assumes a premiss that Protagoras is committed to but that leads him into trouble. (And perhaps one might argue that, on some accounts of belief, the premiss does not lead to a vicious infinite regress.) In thinking about this issue, I have benefited both from White's paper and from questions by Victor Caston.

[25] One might argue that if Protagoras is a relativist who believes that the statement of relativism is absolutely true, then he accepts (3b); and if he accepts (3b), he accepts (3). But if the relativist accepts (3) in virtue of accepting (3b), then she can say that even though she is in this sense committed to (7), the inference to (8) fails, since all that has been shown is that there can be one false belief, namely, the belief that relativism is false, and that is something the relativist (on this interpretation) is happy to agree with.

[26] I have weakened 'everyone' in (4) to 'some people' in (4′), to correspond to my weakening of (2) to (2′).

But (4′) seems perfectly compatible with relativism.

Hence, if Plato's argument is aimed against relativism, it is either question-begging or invalid. It begs the question as written, since (3) omits the qualifiers. If they are added in, as in (3′), the argument becomes invalid.

Though (3) is uncceptable to the relativist, it is acceptable to the infallibilist. For the infallibilist accepts (3a); indeed, (3a) simply states infallibilism.[27] If she accepts (3a), she accepts (3).[28]

If we assume for the moment that Protagoras is an infallibilist, then we can see how the rest of the argument goes. If, as (3a) says (i.e. if, as infallibilism says), all beliefs are true, then the belief that some people have—namely, that each person is wiser than others in some respects, and that others are wiser in other respects, where wisdom involves having true beliefs and ignorance involves having false beliefs—is true, and so there are false beliefs. If (3b) is true, then again there are false beliefs; for that is simply what (3b) says. Hence, whether (3a) or (3b) is true, there are false beliefs. And if there are any false beliefs, then infallibilism is false; for infallibilism says that all beliefs are true.

On the infallibilist reading, then, Plato has a valid and, in my view, neat and elegant argument. It is in the form of a dilemma, one horn of which is a self-refutation or, to use Sextus' label, a *peritropē* of infallibilism.[29] This horn derives the falsity of infallibilism by assuming infallibilism, along with the empirical premiss that people believe that there are false beliefs. The overall idea of the dilemma is that whether or not (3a) is true, there are false beliefs, given that people believe that there are.

We have seen, then, that if Argument I is aimed against relativism, it seems to be either question-begging or invalid, whereas it succeeds against infallibilism.[30] We have also seen that the text is quite naturally read as I have read it. These are good reasons for supposing that Plato aims to refute

---

[27] Or perhaps we should say that infallibilism implies but is not equivalent to (3a). For infallibilism says not only that all beliefs are true but also that there are no truths that are not believed; this latter claim is not explicit in (3a).

[28] This is so whether (3) is of the form (p or not-p), or of the form (p or q). For whichever of these forms (3) takes, (3b) implies the falsity of infallibilism, and that is the crucial point for my purposes. Alternatively, one might rewrite (3) as follows: 'Either (a) all beliefs are true, or (b) not all beliefs are true'. This clearly puts (3) in the form of (p or not-p), and allows Plato's argument to go through.

[29] See n. 2.

[30] We've seen, though, that (2) is too strong; but this is easily remedied by replacing (2) with (2′). This difficulty is neutral as between relativism and infallibilism. Denyer, *Language, Thought and Falsehood in Ancient Greek Philosophy*, 95–6, briefly considers something like my interpretation of Argument I, but he is less impressed with it than I am.

infallibilism rather than relativism.[31] Still, let us press further and see what happens in the next stages of the argument.

IV

We next get a transitional passage which, as the opening *gar* ('for') suggests, aims to elucidate Argument I. Plato writes (170 c 5–8):[32]

For [*gar*] consider, Theodorus, whether you, or any of Protagoras' followers, would be willing to contend that no one ever thinks of another that he's ignorant and believes falsely.

Theodorus replies: 'No, that's incredible [*apiston*], Socrates' (170 c 9), to which Socrates replies in turn: 'Still, that's what the theory that a man is the measure of all things is necessarily committed to' (*eis touto ge anankēs hēkei*, 170 D 1–2).

Why so? Well, according to Argument I, we can refute (P) by assuming (P), along with the additional premiss (=I (2)) that people believe that

---

[31] Burnyeat takes Argument I to be the most difficult passage to square with a relativist reading ('Protagoras and Self-Refutation in Plato's *Theaetetus*', 189). Unfortunately, he does not discuss it in any detail, saying 'I do not wish to undertake these further exegetical inquiries here' (189). But he does discuss it briefly in n. 19, where he says that it is cryptic, that Theodorus accordingly asks for clarification, and that the clarification fits the relativist account. He seems to think this licenses us to supply the qualifiers in the necessary places. I suggested above that if we do so, the argument becomes invalid. Burnyeat does not say how he would overcome this objection, but perhaps he thinks that Argument I can be read in something like the way in which he reads Argument II. (But if so, I am not sure why he thinks that Argument I is the *most* problematic for him: why, on this suggestion, is it any more problematic than Argument II?) If Burnyeat thinks that Argument I can be understood in something like the way in which he explains Argument II, then perhaps the argument so read is vulnerable to the same objections I bring to bear against his reading of Argument II (for which see 'Relativism and Self-Refutation in Plato's *Theaetetus*').
   In this same note, Burnyeat says that it is 'possible . . . to understand the text as stating or implying . . . the following variant of the *peritropē* argument'—and he then lays out what seems to me to be a *peritropē* of infallibililsm. So he seems to agree with me that the text *can* be read as I have suggested it *should* be read, though he says that this reading is 'not obligatory'.

[32] 170 A 6–9 (=I (2)) claims not only that people take *others* to have false beliefs, but also that they take *themselves* to have false beliefs; yet Plato does not mention (here) that, to preserve (P), Protagoras will have to abandon this latter claim as well. One might think he fails to mention this on the ground that no one can coherently take oneself to have a false belief. However, although it might be incoherent to say 'I believe p, and I believe that p is false', one can coherently think that one has some false beliefs or other, even if one doesn't think, of any particular belief one holds, that it is false. (Cf. 'Any remaining errors are my own'.) And Plato does later consider the first-person case (of taking oneself to have a false belief). Indeed, as we'll see, he thinks that the third-person case (of taking others to have false beliefs) has implications for the first-person case.

everyone has (and so others have) false beliefs.[33] Since (P) plus this premiss imply not-(P), Protagoras has to reject that premiss if he is to preserve (P).[34] But this is not a result he is happy with. On the contrary, it's 'incredible' to suppose that Protagoras, any more than anyone else, would deny that people take others to have false beliefs. None the less, he can't allow this consistently with maintaining (P).

Theodorus understandably asks for clarification, whereupon Socrates says (170 D 4–E 6):

soc. When you've judged [*krinein*] something by yourself, and express a belief about it to me, let's grant that, as Protagoras' theory has it, that's true for you. But what about the rest of us? Is it impossible for us to get to make judgements about your judgement? Or do we always decide that your beliefs are true? Isn't it rather the case that on every occasion there are countless people who have beliefs opposed to yours and contend against you [*machontai antidoxazontes*], thinking that what you judge and think is false?

THEO. Good heavens, yes, Socrates, countless thousands, as Homer puts it; they give me all the trouble in the world.

soc. Well now, do you want us to say that what you believe on those occasions is true for you but false for those countless people?

THEO. It looks as if we must, at any rate as far as the theory is concerned.

The reasoning seems to go as follows:

Transitional Passage

(1) A believes p.
(2) (P).
(3) Therefore, p is true for A.
(4) Countless others believe that A's belief that p is false.
(5) Therefore p is false for countless others.
(6) Therefore p is true for A but false for countless others.

Protagoras favours (4); that is, he allows that people take others to have false beliefs. However, in context this leads to (6). And Protagoras is not happy about having to accept (6). Yet, to avoid it, he has to reject (4), and say instead that no one ever takes others to have false beliefs. Plato suggests

[33] As we've seen, I (2) claims more than that people believe that everyone has some false beliefs, but since this is the crucial aspect of I (2) for present purposes, I shall continue to focus on it for now. I shall from now on generally use '(2)' rather than '(2′)'.

[34] That this is Plato's point is noticed by McDowell, *Plato:* Theaetetus, 169–70. (But McDowell says that 170 C 5–D 2 denies that 'all men believe that some judgements are false'. What it denies, however, is that anyone ever takes others to have false beliefs.) See also Burnyeat, 'Protagoras and Self-Refutation in Plato's *Theaetetus*', 189 n. 19; and Ketchum, 'Plato's "Refutation" of Protagorean Relativism', 98 n. 36.

two ways of circumventing (4): one might say that no one has access to anyone else's beliefs (or, at least, no one has any attitude, one way or the other, to the beliefs of others); or one might say that everyone takes others' beliefs to be all of them true (170 D 6–8). But Plato suggests that Protagoras would be unhappy at having to accept either of these views; he prefers to say that people have access to one another's beliefs, and sometimes take others to have false beliefs.[35] Yet if he continues to say this, he must say that there are cases in which p is true for A but false for B; and he is not happy about having to say that either.

If Protagoras is a relativist, it's difficult to see what the point of the present passage is. For Plato suggests that Protagoras *objects* to (6). Yet the relativist, so far from objecting to the claim that, in some cases, p is true for A but false for others, insists on this way of speaking; it is the locution he introduces in order to dissolve the problem of conflicting appearances. Perhaps the best one can do, on behalf of a relativist reading of the present passage, is to say that, although it is unclear *at this stage* why Protagoras should object to (6), later stages make it clear.[36] We will need to see, then, whether they do so.

It's already absolutely clear, however, why (6) is objectionable to Protagoras if he's an infallibilist; for on infallibilism, we may drop the qualifiers and infer that p is true and false, in which case it's necessarily false. On this reading, Plato is hinting that infallibilism, coupled with the fact that people take others to have false beliefs, leads to necessary falsehoods, and so is to be rejected.[37]

---

[35] This is quite interesting. One might think that Protagoras would be quite happy to say that 'we always decide that your beliefs are true': after all, Protagoras is an infallibilist, so he thinks that all beliefs are true. If everyone thinks that others' beliefs are all of them true, then, it might seem, everyone else is an infallibilist too (unless they take themselves to have false beliefs). Yet Plato seems to think that Protagoras would prefer to say that people sometimes take others to have false beliefs. But if Protagoras says this, he seems to admit that others aren't infallibilists. Why should he be anxious to *deny* that others are infallibilists? Denyer in effect suggests one possibility (though he is not addressing my worry): that Protagoras accepts 'our everyday standards for telling who believes what' (*Language, Thought and Falsehood in Ancient Greek Philosophy*, 90); and by those standards, people do take others to have false beliefs. (But why should he accept those standards? Elsewhere he shows himself quite willing to reject ordinary beliefs. Why would he baulk here?) Cf. the discussion below, of Argument II (10)–(11).

Notice that another way in which Protagoras might in principle seek to evade (6) is by rejecting the inference from (4) to (5). Waterlow seems to think that that is what Protagoras would do; see 'Protagoras and Inconsistency', 29 ff. (Here, however, she is discussing not the present passage, but what I call Argument II. I touch on her view below.)

[36] I owe this suggestion to Gisela Striker.

[37] Waterlow, 'Protagoras and Inconsistency', 23, argues that if Plato tries to refute Protagoras by showing that his position is necessarily false, he 'flagrantly begs the question

Although we can thus see how an infallibilist reading of the present passage goes, there might seem to be a problem for it. For in contrast to Argument I (and, as we shall see, Argument II), the present passage uses the qualifiers precisely where the relativist would want them (170 D 5–6, E 4–5). This might be thought to show that Protagoras is being portrayed as a relativist after all.[38]

However, whether the qualifiers support relativism depends on how they are understood. They would presumably support relativism if they introduced a special concept of relative truth, being-true-for-a-person, or if they were meant to block the implication that any propositions are true *simpliciter*. But I do not think that is how they should be understood. Rather, to say that p is true for A but false for others is only to say that p is true in A's view, but false in the view of others; that is, A thinks that p is true, whereas others think that it is false. The dative is the dative of 'person judging';[39] it is not meant to block the implication that any propositions are absolutely true or true *simpliciter*.[40] On this view, the qualifiers do not indicate relativism.

against Protagoras. For the issue is, precisely, whether opinions can be false'. (She is discussing 171 A 6–C 7, but the issue is relevant here.) I agree that Protagoras claims that all beliefs are true. However, as we've seen, he also wants to hold on to PNC. Hence if it can be shown that his position leads to a breakdown of PNC, in virtue of being necessarily false, then he will abandon (P). (This assumes that, if forced to choose between PNC and (P), he will retain PNC.) My disagreement with Waterlow here therefore stems from our different views about Protagoras' attitude to PNC. See above, sect. I, and n. 15.

[38] So Burnyeat believes: see 'Protagoras and Self-Refutation in Plato's *Theaetetus*', 189.

[39] Waterlow understands the dative in 170 D 5 in this way, and so she too denies that it indicates 'a special concept of relative truth' ('Protagoras and Inconsistency', 34). (At p. 31 n. 16 she cites A. W. Matthiae, *A Copious Greek Grammar*, trans. E. V. Blomfield, 2nd edn. (2 vols.; Cambridge: Murray, 1820–1), vol. ii, § 389, for this usage. Matthiae writes that 'The dative is often put, especially with *hōs*, in order to show that a proposition is affirmed, not as generally true, but as valid only with respect to a certain person, consequently relatively and subjectively'; 'it expresses the opinion or judgment of a person'. His two explanations are not clearly equivalent. The first suggests relativism; the second does not do so. Whatever Matthiae intended, I use 'dative of person judging' to mean only that the person making the judgement takes it to be true.) However, Waterlow thinks that the datives in 170 E 4–5 are more congenial to a special concept of truth ('Protagoras and Inconsistency', 35). In the end she concludes that they need not be interpreted this way; but she doesn't seem to think that they are datives of person judging either. I'm not sure why. My own view is that the datives in the two passages should all be understood in the same way, as datives of person judging.

[40] One might object to this reading of the datives on the ground that 170 D 4–6 seems to say that Protagoras' theory licenses us to move from the claim that A believes p to the claim that p is true for A; on my reading of the datives, we don't need Protagorean licence for this move. However, although it is true that, on my reading, the inference is not *specially* licensed by (P), it is licensed by (P); so perhaps Plato is emphasizing that, as promised, he is not begging the question against Protagoras.

Still, one might wonder why, on infallibilism, the qualifiers are so conspicuously highlighted here. The point, I take it, is to emphasize that there are cases in which beliefs do genuinely conflict (*machontai antidoxazontes*, 170 D 8–9). That there are such cases is not to be taken for granted. On the contrary, as we've seen, Protagoras' strategy in the first part of the *Theaetetus* is to emphasize that what seem to be conflicting appearances in fact are not. Rather, with Heracleitus' support, he argues that the wind (for example) has changed between our seemingly conflicting utterances, or that we were talking about different winds. That's how, despite being an infallibilist, he was able to hold on to PNC (as he wants to do) in at least some cases.

Though this explains the presence of the qualifiers, and in a way congenial to an infallibiist interpretation, it raises a difficulty: Argument I assumes that people *believe* that beliefs conflict, in the sense that one is true, the other false.[41] Plato now goes further and says that beliefs *do* conflict in this sense—in which case some beliefs *are* true and others false. Is Plato entitled to say this? Doesn't it unfairly ignore Protagoras' Heracleitean strategy?

I'm not sure. But one possible answer is quite simple: (P) claims that all beliefs are true. Argument I makes it clear that one belief people have is that there are conflicting beliefs. Given (P), their belief must be true, and so there are conflicting beliefs. The present claim, that there are conflicting beliefs, therefore just draws out a point implicit in Argument I.

I've offered a simple explanation of why Plato feels entitled both to ignore Protagoras' Heracleitean strategy and to assume that there are after all cases of conflicting appearances. There are also further explanations worth considering. For example, in the first part of the *Theaetetus*, the Heracleitean strategy is used only in connection with first-order perceptual beliefs.[42] Perhaps Plato thinks that, although this strategy works (or is at any rate initially plausible) in such cases, it doesn't work elsewhere. Although the present passage doesn't say what belief is at issue here, perhaps Plato assumes that it is not a first-order perceptual belief, and that that is why the beliefs countenanced here can genuinely conflict.

---

[41] I mentioned this aspect of I (2) when the premiss was first discussed, but then left it to one side since it was not crucial in Argument I. Now, however, it becomes important. That Argument I uses as a premiss not the claim that there are false beliefs, but that people believe that there are, whereas the transitional passage says that there are genuinely conflicting beliefs, is also emphasized by White. However, our explanations of how this move is effected are quite different.

[42] See above, n. 13.

That this is Plato's view is suggested by a comment he makes later. At 179 c he says that there are many ways in which one could refute Protagoras 'and show that not every judgement of every person is true. But when it's a question of each person's present experience, from which there come to be his perceptions and the judgements which conform to them—well, it's harder to refute these latter and show that they're not true.' So Plato thinks that the self-refutation passage shows that not *all* beliefs are true (notice, in support of infallibilism, the absence of the qualifiers); but he doesn't think it shows that not all *perceptual* beliefs are true.[43]

But this leads to another question: *why* does Plato think that the Heracleitean strategy is restricted to the perceptual sphere? Once again, I'm not sure. But perhaps he thinks that, although someone *could* extend it further, *Protagoras* would not do so. After all, Protagoras sets himself up as a teacher, in which case he must allow the possibility of communication. But surely, if I can communicate my beliefs to you, you might sometimes disagree with me and think that some of my beliefs are wrong.[44] Perhaps an infallibilist need not allow communication, in which case perhaps Plato doesn't refute that version of infallibilism. Still, perhaps he can refute Protagoras' version of infallibilism.

Or perhaps he thinks that the Heracleitean strategy can't really be deployed outside the perceptual sphere; it's not just a quirk of Protagoras' to restrict it in this way. Here the thought might be that, although we can make intuitive sense of the wind's changing and perhaps even of our having access to different winds, it's much more difficult to say how we might hope to resolve a dispute as to whether, say, $2+2=4$ along similar lines.

Whichever of these interpretations we favour (and no doubt there are others worth considering),[45] the fact remains that, for whatever reason,

---

[43] I take it that 181–3, coupled with 184–6, defends the further claim that neither are all perceptions, or all perceptual beliefs, true. So first Plato argues that not all beliefs whatsoever are true; then he argues that neither are all perceptual beliefs true.

[44] However, that Protagoras denies the possibility of interpersonal disagreement is argued by D. Glidden, 'Protagorean Relativism and the Cyrenaics', in N. Rescher (ed.), *Studies in Epistemology* (Oxford, Clarendon Press, 1975 = *American Philosophical Quarterly* Monograph Series, 9), 113–40 at 115, 120–1. See also Burnyeat, 'Protagoras and Self-Refutation in Plato's *Theaetetus*', 181–2: 'Protagoras' contention that genuine disagreement is impossible'.

[45] Here is one of them. Suppose one agrees with me that our present passage aims to refute Protagoras without giving him the benefit of the Heracleitean strategy (outside the perceptual sphere). Still, one might argue, in 181–3 Plato *does* consider how Protagoras fares if he is allowed to deploy that strategy more widely. On this view, 181–3 argues that,

Plato at this point ignores Protagoras' Heracleitean strategy, and assumes that there are genuinely conflicting beliefs between different people. Given this assumption, it is clear how he can refute Protagoras—if Protagoras is an infallibiist.

V

Plato next argues as follows (170 E 7–171 C 7):

SOC. And what about Protagoras himself? Isn't it necessarily the case that, if he didn't himself think a man is the measure, and if the masses don't either, as indeed they don't, then that *Truth* which he wrote wasn't ⟨the truth⟩ for anyone? Whereas if he did think so himself, but the masses don't share his view, then, in the first place, it's more ⟨the case⟩ that it isn't ⟨the truth⟩ than that it is: more in the proportion by which those to whom it doesn't seem ⟨to be the case⟩ outnumber those to whom it does.

THEO. That must be so, if it's indeed going to be or not be ⟨the case⟩ according to each individual belief.

SOC. And secondly, it involves this especially clever [*kompsotaton*] result: Protagoras agrees that everyone believes the things which are. In doing that, he's surely conceding that the opinion of those who have opposing beliefs [*antidoxazontōn*] about his own belief—that is, their belief that what he thinks is false—is true.

THEO. Certainly.

SOC. So if he admits that their opinion is true—that is, the opinion of those who believe that what he thinks is false—he would seem to be conceding that his own opinion is false?

THEO. He must be.

SOC. But the others don't concede that what they think is false?[46]

if Heracleiteanism is thus extended, language breaks down—in which case Protagoras can't even articulate, let alone defend, his position. So 170–1, taken together with 181–3, in effect constitutes a dilemma: if Heracleiteanism is restricted to the perceptual sphere, as in 170–1, then (P) (plus a further premiss) violates PNC and so is to be rejected. If, as in 181–3, we seek to avoid this result by extending Heracleiteanism further, then (P) can't even be coherently stated, and so it is again to be rejected. In formulating this alternative, I am indebted to an audience at Ohio State University, especially Allan Silverman.

I myself do not think that 181–3 countenances an expanded role for Heracleiteanism; rather, it is still restricted to the perceptual sphere (see n. 43). I none the less mention this alternative interpretation, since it allows one to argue that even if (contrary to my view) Plato at some stage considers an expanded role for Heracleiteanism, he would not be at fault in ignoring that fact in 170–1. Rather, on this interpretation one could say that he first rebuts Protagoras on the assumption that Heracleiteanism is restricted, and then on the assumption that it is not.

[46] In 171 B 4–5, I follow W and read *heautous*, rather than BT's *heautois*.

THEO. No.

soc. And Protagoras, again, admits that that belief of theirs is true, too, according to what he has written.

THEO. Evidently.

soc. So his theory will be disputed by everyone, beginning with Protagoras himself; or rather, Protagoras himself will agree that it's wrong. When he concedes that someone who contradicts him [*tanantia legonti*] believes truly, he will himself be conceding that a dog, or an ordinary man, isn't the measure of so much as one thing that he hasn't come to know. Isn't that so?

THEO. Yes.

soc. Well, then, since it's disputed by everyone, it would seem that Protagoras' *Truth* isn't true for anyone: not for anyone else, and not for Protagoras himself.

We may formulate the argument as follows:[47]

Argument II

(1) If no one believes (P), then (P) isn't ⟨true⟩ for anyone. (170 E 7–171 A 1)

(2) Only Protagoras believes (P); no one else shares his view. (171 A 1)

[(3) (P). (171 A 4–5)][48]

(4) [Therefore] it depends on each individual belief whether (P) is or is not ⟨true⟩. (171 A 4–5)

(5) Therefore it's more ⟨the case⟩ that (P) is not ⟨true⟩ than that it is ⟨true⟩. (171 A 1–3)

(6) Protagoras believes that all beliefs are true. (171 A 8–9)

(7) Everyone but Protagoras believes that Protagoras' belief—that (P) is true—is false. (171 A 6–8)[49]

---

[47] I have supplied the steps enclosed in square brackets. The material enclosed in angle brackets indicates how I think the elliptical Greek should be expanded. In some cases I have altered the order in which Plato introduces various premisses, in order to clarify the logical structure of his argument.

[48] Plato doesn't explicitly mention (P) as a premiss in his argument. However, 171 A 4–5 seems to assume it.

[49] The text at this point actually only speaks of 'those' (e.g. 171 B 4) who believe that Protagoras' belief—that (P) is true—is false: it isn't explicitly said that everyone but Protagoras believes that his belief is false. However, 171 B 9–10 says that (P) is disputed by everyone; for this conclusion to follow, 'the others' must include everyone but Protagoras. A similar problem arises with 170 E 7–171 A 2: Plato says that 'the many' (*hoi polloi*, 170 E 8; cf. *to plēthos*, 171 A 1) do not believe (P); he then infers that, if Protagoras doesn't either, then the *Truth* wasn't true for anyone (*mēdeni*, 170 E 9). For this conclusion to follow, 'the many' must include everyone but Protagoras, just as, in this passage, 'the others' must include everyone but Protagoras.

(8) Therefore Protagoras believes that everyone else's belief—that his belief, that (P) is true, is false—is true. (171 A 6–8; B 1–2)

(9) Therefore Protagoras believes that his belief, that (P) is true, is false. (171 B 1–2)

(10) The others won't concede that their belief—that Protagoras' belief, that (P) is true, is false—is false. (171 B 4)

(11) Protagoras agrees that everyone else's belief—i.e. their belief that Protagoras' belief, that (P) is true, is false—is true. (171 B 6–7)

(12) Therefore [whether or not Protagoras believes (P),] everyone believes that (P) is false. (171 B 9–C 2, C 5)

(13) Therefore (P) isn't true for anyone. (171 C 5–7)

Let's look first at (1). Like the transitional passage, (1) uses the qualifiers where a relativist would want them. Does this support a relativist reading? As before, that depends on how the qualifiers are understood. I favour the same account here as the one I proposed earlier: 'true for one' means 'true, in one's view'.[50] Once again, the dative does not indicate a special sense or kind of truth, being true-for-someone; nor is it meant to block the implication that any propositions are true *simpliciter*. To say that p is not true for A is simply to say that p is not true in A's view, i.e. according to A. On this interpretation, (1) makes the perfectly correct but seemingly innocuous point that, if no one believes (P), then (P) isn't true in anyone's view, that is, no one takes it to be true, no one believes it.[51]

I take it that Protagoras is happy to accept the *conditional* expressed in (1); but, at least initially, he thinks that its *antecedent* is false, for he thinks that *he* believes (P). (2)–(5) temporarily concede this to Protagoras. But, Plato argues, no one else shares his view: that is, everyone else

---

[50] The Greek literally says that Protagoras' '*Truth* isn't for anyone': 'is' (*einai*) is not explicitly complemented. As is well known, *einai* can be understood in a variety of ways. So a further question about (1) is how to understand *einai* here. Waterlow takes it to be existential. She argues that Plato means that 'What Protagoras in his book asserted to be the case would be the case (or: would be a fact or reality) for no one'; she concludes that 'the point concerns relativity of fact', not of truth ('Protagoras and Inconsistency', 34–5). I agree that Plato is not adverting to a special concept of relative truth. But the overall structure of the passage, coupled with the parallel passage in 171 A 6 (which explicitly supplies *alēthēs*), suggests that we are meant to supply *alēthē* in 170 E 9. So I take Plato to be saying that if no one believes (P), (P) isn't true for anyone. Hence we need to ask what 'true for one' means in the present context.

[51] Contrast Burnyeat, 'Protagoras and Self-Refutation in Plato's *Theaetetus*', 177, who thinks that (1) is an argument against Protagoras. Although (1) *seems* innocuous, we'll see later that it raises difficulties for Protagoras.

thinks that (P) is false.[52] Plato infers that (given (P)) (P) is more false than true.[53]

(2)–(5) are—with one notable wrinkle to be discussed shortly—an instance of the transitional passage just discussed. In the transitional passage, Plato considers the abstract case in which A believes p, and others believe that A's belief is false; he infers that p is true for A but false for others. Plato now considers the case in which A = Protagoras, p = (P), and then there is everyone else. That is, Protagoras believes (P), but everyone else thinks that his belief is false. As I've said, Plato infers that (given (P)) (P) is more false than true.

The wrinkle is obvious: in the transitional passage, Plato explicitly infers only that p is true for A but false for others: the qualifiers are in place. Here he infers, not that (P) is true for Protagoras but false for others, but that (P) is more false than true. Why are the qualifiers omitted here, but in place in the transitional passage?

If one favours a relativist reading, one might reply that Plato intended the qualifiers; the omission is inadvertent. In this case, all Plato is saying here is that (P) is false for more people than it is true for. He is perfectly entitled to this claim; but it has no anti-relativist force. Another possibility, again on the assumption that Plato aims to refute relativism, is that he intentionally omitted the qualifiers, in the false belief that he is entitled to do so. In this case, (2)–(5) do constitute an argument against Protagoras, but one that fails in a by now familiar way.

We noted earlier that it was difficult to see what the point of the transitional passage is, if Protagoras is a relativist; but, it was suggested, perhaps later passages will make the point clear. (2)–(5) do not do so; or, at any

---

[52] The claim that no one shares Protagoras' view—that is, that no one else believes (P)—might mean either that (i) everyone else thinks that (P) is false, or that (ii) everyone else either thinks that (P) is false, or has no views about it one way or the other. (7) explicitly says that everyone but Protagoras thinks that (P) is false (or, more precisely, that everyone but Protagoras thinks that his belief, that (P) is true, is false); and that passage seems to be taking up the present claim. So I take (2) likewise to mean that everyone else thinks that (P) is false. I ask later about the connection between not believing (P), on the one hand, and believing that it is false, on the other.

One might argue that the claim that only Protagoras believes (P) is too strong: surely there are other Protagoreans about? If so, (2) should be altered to: (2′) Only Protagoras and his followers believe (P). With (2′), we can infer (5) only if there are fewer Protagoreans than non-Protagoreans. But Plato seems to assume just that: see n. 54.

[53] Plato doesn't explicitly say that (P) is more false than true. He says that 'it's more ⟨the case⟩ that it is not than that it is'. One might argue, as Waterlow does in connection with (1), that we shouldn't supply 'true' (see above, n. 50). I would give similar reasons for supplying 'true' here to those I gave for supplying it in (1). The connection with the transitional passage, which I go on to discuss, also supports this interpretation.

rate, if they aim to do so, they fail in their purpose. For either they do not argue against relativism at all, or else they advance a fallacious argument against it.

Suppose, however, that Plato aims to refute infallibilism. In that case, the present passage follows on quite nicely from the transitional passage. As we've seen, Plato says that there are cases in which p is true for A but false for others, where this was a result that was unwelcome to Protagoras. Plato didn't explain there why this was unwelcome to Protagoras. But if Protagoras is an infallibilist, the reason is clear; for we can then drop the qualifiers and infer that p is both true and false, in which case it is necessarily false. The present passage supplements the transitional passage by making this point explicit.[54] Indeed it rubs the point in, by showing that (P) in particular turns out to be both true and false, and so necessarily false: it's not just any old belief that suffers this unfortunate fate, but Protagoras' belief in (P).

On this reading, (2)–(5) constitute another *peritropē* of (P), one that draws on the transitional passage: given (P), and the empirical assumption that only Protagoras believes (P), whereas others believe that it is false, it follows that (P) is both true and false, and so it is necessarily false.[55]

This *peritropē* is, not surprisingly, quite closely related not only to the transitional passage but also to Argument I.[56] In Argument I, (P), plus the belief that there are false beliefs, implies not-(P). In II (2)–(5), (P), plus

[54] More exactly, Plato says that (P) is more false than true. Why does he speak in this latter way, rather than saying that (P) is both true (because believed by Protagoras) and false (because believed false by everyone else)? Perhaps he means that (P) is false on more occasions than it is true on. Consider, for example, Plato's discussion of the compresence of opposites in *Republic* V, where he at one point asks: 'Is any of the manys what someone says it is, then, any more than it is not what he says it is?' (479 B 9–10). Though the issue is complicated, I take him to mean that some sensibles are both beautiful and ugly, just and unjust, etc. That something is no more beautiful than ugly, or just than unjust, means that it is not one to the exclusion of the other, since it is both. By parity of reasoning, then, perhaps in saying that (P) is more false than true, Plato means that it is both true and false—but false on more occasions, or more often, since it is more often taken to be false. See the last paragraph of n. 52. Contrast Ketchum, 'Plato's "Refutation" of Protagorean Relativism', 100.

[55] Hence I disagree with McDowell, *Plato:* Theaetetus, 170, who thinks that (5) 'is clearly incidental. Its derivation is suspect'. Burnyeat says that (5) is 'ambiguous: it is not clear whether Socrates wants to infer simply that the doctrine is false for more people than it is true for . . . or whether he tries to go beyond this to the conclusion that it is more false than true in some absolute sense' ('Protagoras and Self-Refutation in Plato's *Theaetetus*', 183). He seems to think that in the latter case, Plato 'is to be censured', and that the move is 'questionable'. On the interpretation I've defended, however, the move is not questionable, and Plato is not to be censured.

[56] Not surprisingly because, as we've seen, the transitional passage aims to elucidate Argument I.

the belief that (P) is false, implies not-(P). To be sure, the two ancillary premisses differ: Argument I supplies the premiss that people believe that there are false beliefs (where the beliefs in view seem to be primarily first-order beliefs about how, for example, to navigate or to heal); whereas here the additional premiss is that people believe that (P) is false. However, these two premisses are closely related: presumably any clear-headed person who believes that there are false beliefs also believes that (P) is false, for (P) says that all beliefs are true.[57]

VI

At this point, (P) has been refuted twice over: once in Argument I and then again in II (2)–(5). What, then, is the point of the especially clever argument that follows (=(1), (6)–(13))? Let us turn, finally, to it.

We might note, to begin with, that (7) seems too strong: perhaps not everyone but Protagoras believes that (P) is false. But we can easily accommodate this point by taking (7) to mean 'Everyone but Protagoras and his followers . . .' (cf. 170 c 5–7); this is, moreover, all Plato needs for his argument.[58] But let us leave this difficulty to one side and turn to some other issues.

It has often been noted that, like the other arguments we have explored, this one too seems to fail if it is aimed against relativism. For example, if Protagoras is a relativist, he would reject (6) in favour of:

(6′) Protagoras believes that all beliefs are true for those who hold them.

Similarly, if Protagoras is a relativist, he would reject (8) in favour of (8′):

[57] Burnyeat, 'Protagoras and Self-Refutation in Plato's *Theaetetus*', 189 n. 19, criticizes McDowell for assimilating Argument I to Argument II; he does so on the ground that McDowell doesn't distinguish between the two ancillary premisses. Though I agree that the two premisses differ, they are more closely related than Burnyeat seems to allow.

[58] See n. 49; and also the parallel discussions of premiss (2) in Argument I and of premiss (2) in Argument II. (Indeed, II (7) basically restates II (2); Plato is now going to use it to prove another point.) If we alter (7) in this way, then we will of course also need to make corresponding adjustments in some other premisses. (8), for example, would become: 'Therefore Protagoras and his followers believe . . .'.

Even if we alter (7) in the way suggested, one might still find it too strong. For one might think that there are many people who are not in any obvious sense followers of Protagoras who do not believe that (P) is false, for the simple reason that they have never heard of it, or who have no attitude to it one way or the other. Perhaps Plato assumes that they are tacitly committed to believing that (P) is false since, as Argument I points out, they believe that there are false beliefs; see further below. See also Ketchum, 'Plato's "Refutation" of Protagorean Realtivism', 77–8.

(8′) Therefore Protagoras believes that everyone else's belief—that his belief, that (P) is true, is false—is true for them.

(6) and (8), that is, omit the qualifier, 'for one', on which the relativist insists. Once again, then, either Plato begs the question against relativism by omitting the qualifiers, or else he wrote carelessly and really intended (6′) and (8′). In this latter case, he still fails to refute relativism, since it is not clear how we can proceed beyond (8′) to (9). Hence neither does this passage explain why a relativist should mind saying that there are cases where p is true for A but false for others; or, if it aims to do so, it fails in its purpose.[59]

Once again, however, the argument fares far better if it is aimed against infallibilism. (2)–(5) allow that Protagoras (though no one else) believes (P). Plato now argues that in fact no one, not even Protagoras, believes (P). For suppose that Protagoras, but no one else, believes (P). Well, if Protagoras believes (P), he believes that all beliefs are true. But in that case, as (8) points out, he believes that the belief that everyone else has—that his belief, that (P) is true, is false—is true. But if he believes that that belief of theirs is true, then he believes that his belief—that (P) is true—is false (9). For if one believes that A's belief that p is true, then one believes that p is true.[60] Hence, since Protagoras believes that the belief that others have— that his belief, that (P) is true, is false—is true, he believes that his belief,

---

[59] Hence neither does the especially clever argument fulfil the promise of explaining why a relativist should, after all, mind having to say that there are cases in which p is true for A but false for others; see sect. iv. In 'Relativism and Self-Refutation in Plato's *Theaetetus*', I provide a fuller account of *why* I think the especially clever argument fails to refute relativism.

[60] Waterlow, "Protagoras and Inconsistency', 31, agrees that 'The fact that someone agrees with an opinion would normally be taken as ground for ascribing the opinion *to him*'. But, she adds, 'the normal rules do not apply in Protagoras' case' (ibid.). Her reason seems to be that she thinks Protagoras will deploy his Heracleitean strategy even here, and say that his opponents' belief is true of a reality private to them; but, for Protagoras to have to endorse their belief in his own right, there would also have to be a corresponding reality private to him, but he need not admit this (cf. p. 30). If, however, I'm right to suggest that Protagoras invokes Heracleiteanism only to defuse seemingly conflicting appearances in the perceptual sphere, then 'the normal rules' do apply in the case currently under discussion, and Plato is entitled to move from (8) to (9). (The same is true of the transitional passage's move from (4) to (5); see above, n. 35.)

Here it may be significant that Plato doesn't simply say that Protagoras believes (P), whereas others believe that (P) is false. Rather, he says that others believe *that Protagoras's belief, that (P) is true, is false*; and that Protagoras believes that *their belief* is true. Perhaps he speaks in this latter way to make it clear that there is some one belief (Protagoras' belief that (P) is true) about which Protagoras and his opponents initially have genuinely conflicting views ('initially', because Plato argues that that conflict leads Protagoras to abandon his view). The former way of speaking might leave it open that the appearance of conflict is not genuine, on the ground that they are speaking about different things.

Once Plato has made this point, however, he feels free to speak, not just of Protagoras

that (P) is true, is false. If he believes that his belief, that (P) is true, is false, then he believes that (P) is false.

In the transitional passage, Plato contents himself with pointing out that sometimes appearances genuinely conflict: there are cases in which A believes p, and others believe that p is false, and one of these two beliefs is true, the other false. In II (2)–(5), he focuses on a specific case of conflicting appearances, one in which A = Protagoras, and p = (P). Given (P), it follows that (P) is true (since Protagoras believes it) and false (since others believe that it is false). Plato then argues that Protagoras will have to accept the results just described. But in accepting the claim that *others* believe that (P) is false, he has to accept that it is false, given his view that all beliefs are true. This leads to a different and more striking case of conflicting appearances: for Protagoras himself is now the subject of conflicting appearances. On the one hand, he believes (P); on the other hand, he's just been forced to believe that (P) is false. Plato begins with a case of *interpersonal* conflicting appearances: Protagoras believes (P), whereas others believe that it is false. He then shows that this leads to a case of *intrapersonal* conflict: Protagoras initially believes (P); but given the argument just rehearsed, he is forced to believe that (P) is false.[61]

Protagoras could avoid this unhappy result if he could get others to abandon their belief that his belief, that (P) is true, is false. However, this is not empirically possible: 'the others don't concede that what they think is false' (10); that is, they will continue to think that their belief is true.[62]

and others having conflicting beliefs about *his belief that* (P) *is true*, but also of their having conflicting beliefs about *the truth of* (P). Hence I shall sometimes speak in this latter way as well.

[61] Cf. Aristotle, *Metaph.* Γ 4: 'Further, it follows that all would then be right and all would be in error, and *our opponent himself confesses himself to be in error*' (1008ᵃ28–30). Cf. also Γ 5, 1009ᵃ7–12: 'For on the one hand, if all opinions and appearances are true, all statements must be at the same time true and false. For many men hold beliefs in which they conflict with one another, and all think those mistaken who have not the same opinions as themselves; so that the same thing must be and not be.'

If Protagoras were to invoke his Heracleitean strategy here, perhaps he could argue that we do not have a case of intrapersonal conflict; rather, Protagoras-at-t_1 believes (P) and a different person, Protagoras-at-t_2, believes that (P) is false. In this case, what might seem to be intrapersonal conflict turns out to be another case of interpersonal conflict. Cf. *Tht.* 166 B 5–C 2, and Waterlow, 'Protagoras and Inconsistency', 26–7. But it's not clear to me that Protagoras-at-t_1 can't have conflicting beliefs at t_1.

[62] Recall that the transitional passage says that, to save (P), Protagoras will have to say that no one ever believes that others have false beliefs; but it's *apiston* to suppose that Protagoras would say that. As in the transitional passage, so here: Plato assumes that Protagoras will not abandon the view that people take others to have false beliefs. He acknowledges the fact that they think this; and they can't be brought to think otherwise.

Protagoras has to admit that this belief of theirs is also true (11). (10)–(11) therefore block a possible escape route.[63]

But in that case it follows that everyone, including Protagoras, believes that (P) is false (12) ('his theory will be disputed by everyone, beginning with Protagoras himself', 171 B 9–10; cf. 171 B 10–C 5).

Having argued that everyone, including Protagoras, believes that (P) is false, Plato infers that (P) isn't true for anyone (171 C 5–7 = premiss (13)). Is this inference justified? (1) says that if no one believes (P), then (P) isn't true for anyone. One might think that, to infer the consequent of (1)—that (P) isn't true for anyone—Plato has to establish its antecedent, that no one believes (P). But what he has established is that everyone believes that (P) is false. One might argue that it doesn't follow from the fact that everyone believes that (P) is false that no one believes (P). For people can, after all, have contradictory beliefs, and perhaps this is one of them.

Perhaps Plato would reply as follows. According to Argument I, everyone but Protagoras and his followers believes that there are false beliefs.[64] This commits them to believing that (P) is false. For though it's reasonable to say that people don't believe all the consequences of their explicit beliefs, it's also reasonable to say that they believe their obvious consequences. And if someone believes there are false beliefs, then it's reasonable to say that she believes that (P) is false. To be sure, she might not have heard of (P); the content of her belief might not be '(P) is false'. None the less, she is committed to believing that not all beliefs are true, and that commits her to believing that (P) is false. So, everyone but Protagoras and his followers believes that (P) is false. Nor, Plato assumes, do they believe anything that commits them to believing (P) simultaneously. Hence, although people can have contradictory beliefs, Plato assumes that non-Protagoreans, at any rate, don't have this one. (This is an empirical assumption of Plato's, one that might or might not be true.)

---

[63] For a quite different explanation of the point of (10)–(11), one along relativist lines, see E. Emilsson, 'Plato's Self-Refutation Argument in *Theaetetus* 171 AC Revisited', *Phronesis*, 39 (1994), 136–49. I find the objections he raises for his interpretation on p. 143 more troubling than he does.

Protagoras might try saying that people don't *really* believe that his belief, that (P) is true, is false; but in this case, it would appear that they falsely believe that they have this belief, and so by a different route it can be proven that there are false beliefs. One route derives the falsity of (P) by relying on the premiss that people take others to have false beliefs; the other route relies on the premiss that people have false beliefs about what their own beliefs are. (In this latter case, people would not be authoritative about what their beliefs are. In a sense, perhaps the first route shows this too.)

[64] Strictly speaking, Argument I says that *everyone* believes this; but see the discussion of I (2) and (2′).

What, however, about Protagoras and his followers? Mightn't *they* agree that (P) is false, yet continue to believe (P)? Not if I have been right to say that Protagoras is eager to hold on to PNC. For if he continues to believe (P), yet agrees that it is false, then (given that he is an infallibilist) he'll have to conclude that it's true and false. Once he is brought to believe that (P) is false, he'll have to abandon his belief in (P), if he is to hold on to PNC.[65]

VII

Why is this passage highlighted as being especially clever? The explanation can't, or at any rate shouldn't, be that it is only here that (P) is refuted. For (P) was refuted long ago, in Argument I, and then again in II (2)–(5). I think Plato uses the label to capture two points. First, consider again the overall structure of our three passages (Argument I, the transitional passage, and Argument II). Argument I assumes (P), along with the obvious empirical fact that people believe that there are false beliefs, and genuinely conflicting beliefs. This allows us to infer that there are false beliefs, in which case (P) is false. The transitional passage reiterates that if we assume (P), then not only do people *believe* that there are genuinely conflicting beliefs, but in fact *there are* genuinely conflicting beliefs and so false beliefs. Once again, then, (P) is false. II (2)–(5) describes a particular case of conflicting beliefs: Protagoras believes (P), whereas everyone else believes that it is false. Given (P), these conflicting beliefs must be true, and so (P) is both true and false, and so it is false. This proves the falsity of (P) by appealing to a striking case of *interpersonal* conflict. The especially clever passage goes one step further. It shows how the case of interpersonal conflicting appearances just considered leads to a case of *intrapersonal* conflicting appearances. In particular, Protagoras himself believes (P); but at the same time, he is forced to believe that it is false. It's not just, as before, that Protagoras believes (P) whereas others believe that it is necessarily false.

Secondly, once Protagoras is forced into this uncomfortable position, he has to abandon (P). Indeed, the main focus of the especially clever passage isn't so much on the direct refutation of (P), as on showing that Protagoras

---

[65] This again assumes that, if forced to choose between PNC and (P), Protagoras will opt for PNC. What about infallibilists who don't care about PNC? Perhaps here Plato would follow Aristotle's lead and say that 'what one says need not be what one supposes to be true' (*Metaph.* 1005^{b}25–6), and no one can really believe not-PNC; hence any purported infallibilist will in fact be one who believes PNC, and so one who will accept Plato's argument. Alternatively, perhaps here one would have to say that Plato refutes only Protagoras' brand of infallibilism, and not all possible versions of it.

accepts the previous arguments, with the result that he can no longer believe (P). Plato is here commenting, not just on the logic of the situation, but on Protagoras' acceptance of it. So the argument is also especially clever in that it is a double *peritropē*: it is a *peritropē* both of (P) and of the claim that Protagoras believes (P). By assuming (P), we can again (given certain empirical facts) prove that (P) is false. By assuming that Protagoras believes (P), we can show (given certain empirical facts) that Protagoras does not believe (P).

Plato's label therefore seems to me to be justified. But we can best appreciate his cleverness by seeing the passage in its overall context. For it is not an independent argument, but one that builds on preceding results. Indeed, all three of the passages that we have explored seem to me to be quite clever. Moreover, Plato's arguments are not just clever but also largely successful[66]—if, that is, he aims to refute not relativism but infallibilism.[67]

---

[66] Along the way we've registered a couple of worries. For example, some premisses seem too strong; and I've asked whether Plato is entitled to move from the claim that everyone thinks that (P) is false to the claim that no one believes (P). There are also questions to be raised about whether the fact (as it seems to me) that Plato restricts the Heracleitean strategy to the perceptual sphere is unfair to Protagoras—though I've suggested, without pursuing the point fully, that it is not.

[67] Earlier versions of this chapter were read at Harvard University, Ohio State University, and the Classical Seminar in Corpus Christi College, Oxford. I thank the audiences on these occasions—especially Gisela Striker, Victor Caston, Lindsay Judson, and Lesley Brown—for helpful comments. I am also grateful to Christopher Taylor (my commentator at Corpus) for helpful written comments and for many helpful discussions.

9

False Belief in the *Theaetetus*

I

It is often supposed that Plato regards knowledge as some kind of acquaintance, so that knowing consists in some sort of grasping or hitting, the only alternative to which is not hitting, or missing. Knowledge is an all or nothing, hit or miss affair. It is also often assumed that this model of knowledge underlies or explains Plato's supposed inability to accommodate false belief in dialogues prior to the *Sophist*. Either one 'hits' what one is talking about, and so has knowledge, not false belief; or else one fails to grasp, and so has said nothing, and hence again does not have false belief.[1]

A major source of evidence adduced in support of this view is the *Theaetetus*' discussion of false belief. That discussion ends at an impasse, and it is often alleged that Plato fails to explain in what false belief consists because of an underlying acquaintance model.[2] With this claim I shall not quarrel. I shall argue, however, that Plato is not committed to the underlying acquaintance model that occurs here. Rather, he uses it to buttress Theaetetus' suggestion, presented just before the discussion of false belief (at 187 B), that knowledge is true belief. When, at the end of the discussion, Socrates rejects Theaetetus' suggestion (201 A–C), he also rejects the acquaintance model that had made Theaetetus' suggestion look plausible and that also precludes a satisfactory explanation of false belief. This strategy, in addition to freeing Plato from any commitment to the acquaintance model here, also shows that the discussion of false belief is not, as is usually supposed, an irrelevant digression, awkwardly sandwiched between Theaetetus' definition and its refutation.[3] Rather, the discussion is an integral part of Plato's

---

[1] For this view, see G. E. L. Owen, 'Plato on Not-Being', in G. Vlastos (ed.), *Plato*, i. *Metaphysics and Epistemology* (Garden City, NY: Doubleday Anchor, 1971), 223–67, esp. 245, 262–5; J. H. McDowell, *Plato*: Theaetetus, trans. with notes (Oxford: Clarendon Press, 1973), and 'Identity Mistakes: Plato and the Logical Atomists', *Proceedings of the Aristotelian Society*, 70 (1970), 181–96; W. G. Runciman, *Plato's Later Epistemology* (Cambridge: Cambridge University Press, 1962).   [2] See n. 1.

[3] For this view, see McDowell, *Plato*: Theaetetus, 194; F. M. Cornford, *Plato's Theory of*

attack on that definition. I shall return to these general morals at the close of the chapter. First, however, it is necessary to understand Socrates' general procedure.

Socrates presents two puzzles designed to show that false belief is impossible, and three models that attempt, but fail, to overcome the puzzles. I shall here consider only the first puzzle, what I shall call K, and the first model of false belief, *allodoxia* or otherjudging.[4] I argue first that K rests on a strong acquaintance view. I then argue that *allodoxia* is not defective in any of the ways usually proposed, but that it matches Plato's account of falsity in the *Sophist*. It fails here only because of its reliance on K. But since Plato is not committed to K, this does not show that he cannot handle the subtleties of *allodoxia*. Rather, *allodoxia*'s failure to explain in what false belief consists is an indirect argument that Theaetetus' definition of knowledge as true belief is faulty, since that definition requires K in its support, and K in turn precludes a satisfactory account of false belief.

II

I turn first to the first puzzle (188 A–C), what I call K. Socrates argues that:

(1) For any x, either one knows x or one does not know x.
(2) For any x such that one has a belief about x, either one knows x or one does not know x.
(3) It is impossible for one both to know and not to know the same thing.

He then argues that (1)–(3) rule out false belief:

(4) If one has a false belief that x is y, either

Knowledge: The Theaetetus *and the* Sophist *of Plato*, translated with a running commentary (London: Routledge & Kegan Paul, 1935), 110. McDowell does suggest two rather tenuous links, (*a*) that the discussion considers knowledge, the central topic of the *Theaetetus*, and (*b*) if there is to be true belief, there must also be false belief with which it can be contrasted. (*b*) is also suggested by F. A. Lewis, 'Two Paradoxes in the *Theaetetus*', in J. M. E. Moravcsik (ed.), *Patterns in Plato's Thought* (Dordrecht: Reidel, 1973), 123–49 at 123. (*a*) does not explain why false belief should be considered at *this* point in the dialogue, rather than elsewhere. (*b*) gets Plato's argument back to front. At 200 D he claims that they must know what knowledge is *before* they can know what false belief is. The link I suggest later preserves this priority.

[4] The second puzzle (188 C 9–189 B 8) is essentially the same as K. The second and third models of false belief (the wax tablet and the aviary), like *allodoxia*, fail because of their reliance on K. For further defence of these claims, see my unpublished PhD. thesis, 'Plato and Acquaintance' (Harvard, 1975).

      (a) one knows x and y; or

      (b) one knows x or y, but not both; or

      (c) one knows neither x nor y.

(5) None of (4) (a)–(c) is possible.

(6) Therefore there is no false belief.

Two questions arise immediately. First, why is none of the cases described in (4) possible? (1)–(3) seem simply to be instances of logical laws, (1) and (2) of the law of the excluded middle, and (3) of the principle of noncontradiction; it is then difficult to see how they could rule out false belief.[5] Second, even if (5) follows, why does (6) follow? (5) seems at most to rule out false identity beliefs; (6) rules out all false beliefs.[6]

Socrates defends (5) in this way: if one believes that x is y, but x is not y, then one is ignorant of x and y (188 в 3–5). But if one is ignorant of x and y, one cannot have any beliefs about them, and hence no false beliefs about them (188 в 6–c 4). Otherwise put, whichever option in (2) obtains, false belief is impossible. If one does not know x, one cannot have any beliefs about x; but if one does know x, one cannot have any false beliefs about x, since knowledge precludes error. If one is to have a belief about x, then, one must know x:

(2a) For any x such that one has a belief about x, one knows x.

Read one way, (2a) is innocuous enough. If I have a belief about something, I must know it in at least the minimal sense that I could identify or recognize it; I do not have beliefs, for example, about persons I have never met or heard of. (2a) then suffices to rule out (4b) and (4c); in them I do not know, that is, could not identify or recognize, one of the items in a purported belief. If I am totally ignorant of one of these items, it is reasonable to suppose that I cannot hold the belief in question.

But this still leaves (4a). Suppose I know Gerald Ford; I've heard him, seen pictures of him, could easily recognize him, and so forth. Still, I might have the false belief about him that he was born in Boston; (2a) is not strong enough to yield (5).

Other readings of (2) are possible, however. We might note, first, that Plato's substitutions for 'x' are all of persons. We might then suppose he has in mind some sort of acquaintance principle:

---

[5] Lewis, 'Two Paradoxes in the *Theaetetus*', defends this view; I reject it.

[6] Lewis, 'Two Paradoxes in the *Theaetetus*', 124, McDowell, *Plato:* Theaetetus, 185–95, id., 'Identity Mistakes', 181–2, and J. L. Ackrill, 'Plato on False Belief: *Theaetetus* 187–200', *Monist*, 50 (1966), 383–402 at 385–7, agree that (5) considers only identity beliefs; I argue later that this restriction is unnecessary, and that (5) does entail (6).

    (2b) For any x such that one has a belief about x, one is acquainted with x.

However, if 'acquaintance' is taken in the ordinary sense in which I can 'know' a person or thing (*connaître*), it is still not strong enough. I may have met Gerald Ford, and so 'know' him or be acquainted with him; none the less, I might still think he was born in Boston. *Connaître*-acquaintance will not rule out false belief, as Plato attempts to do.[7]

Russell once held a principle like (2b), claiming that 'whenever a relation of judging or supposing occurs, the terms to which the supposing or judging mind is related by the relation of supposing or judging must be terms with which the mind in question is acquainted'.[8] Russell explained further that 'We shall say we have *acquaintance* with anything of which we are directly aware . . . no further knowledge of [such a thing] is even theoretically possible.'[9] Acquaintance, in this sense, confers total knowledge; it is, moreover, a hit or miss, all or nothing, affair. Either one is acquainted with something, and so knows all there is to know about it, or else one is not acquainted with it, and so has total ignorance. (2b) then becomes:

    (2c) For any x such that one has a belief about x, one either knows everything about x or is totally ignorant of x.

And (2c) does yield (5). If I am ignorant of x, I have no beliefs about x, as (2a) plausibly claimed; but if I know everything about x, I can have no false beliefs about x. Although (2c) yields (5), (1)–(3) are now no longer innocuous.

---

    [7] McDowell, 'Identity Mistakes', argues that *connaître* is all that is involved. He considers the stronger claim I later press, but rejects it on the grounds that it rules out all false beliefs and not merely identity beliefs. The stronger view does have that consequence, but I think it is a consequence Plato intends. In his book, McDowell vacillates between endorsing the *connaître* interpretation ('Acquaintance is a relation of the ordinary sort', p. 197) and the stronger view ('there would seem to be nothing between blank ignorance . . . and the unqualified or complete obtaining of knowledge', ibid.); but these views are obviously quite distinct.

    [8] B. Russell, 'Knowledge by Acquaintance and Knowledge by Description' (1910–11), repr. in *Mysticism and Logic, and Other Essays* (London: Allen & Unwin, 1917), 202–24 at 220–1. The parallel is noticed and pressed by McDowell, *Plato:* Theaetetus, 196, and 'Identity Mistakes', *passim.*.

    [9] B. Russell, *The Problems of Philosophy* (New York: Oxford University Press, 1912), 46–7. Cf. Russell, 'Knowledge by Acquaintance and Knowledge by Description', 202–3, and 'The Philosophy of Logical Atomism' (1918), *Logic and Knowledge: Essays 1901–1950*, ed. R. C. Marsh (London: Allen & Unwin, 1956), 177–281 at 204.

III

The answer to our second question, of why Plato moves from (5) to (6), emerges from a consideration of the first model of false belief, *allodoxia* or otherjudging. Socrates suggests that a false belief occurs when one 'says in his thought that something of the things that are is, having interchanged some other thing for it. For then he always judges something that is, but one thing in place of another, and since he misses what he was aiming at, he can rightly be said to be judging falsely' (189 C 1–4). Theaetetus suggests as an example 'whenever one thinks ugly in place of beautiful, or beautiful in place of ugly' (*hotan gar tis anti kalou aischron ē anti aischrou kalon doxazē(i)*, 189 C 5–6).

Theaetetus' example is an instance of the general schema 'thinking that x is not x but something else, y'. But there are at least four ways in which this schema can be read and, correspondingly, at least four ways in which Theaetetus' example can be parsed. One difficulty arises over Plato's use of such phrases as 'the beautiful' (*to kalon*). The phrase can refer to the property of beauty; but it can also be used as an adjective, as 'the beautiful ———', with a proper or common name filling the blank. A second difficulty arises when we note that Theaetetus' example can be taken to be either an opaque or a transparent representation of a belief; it might be a verbatim report of a belief, or it might be a description of a belief that does not report it verbatim.[10] Thus one way we might read Theaetetus' example is:

(7) Theaetetus thinks that ugliness is beauty.

In (7) 'ugliness' refers to the property of ugliness, and Theaetetus' example is taken to be an opaque representation of a belief—the terms it contains also occur explicitly in the believer's belief, and the example is a direct report of that belief. The belief is also an identity belief, involving a mix-up of concepts or properties.

Now (7) is a reading often proposed for *allodoxia*.[11] But if (7) is the right reading of Theaetetus' example, it is unclear why Theaetetus needs such lengthy persuading that *allodoxia* is implausible—for on (7) *allodoxia* is obviously implausible and unintelligible. Nor is it plausible to suppose that *allodoxia*, so construed, is a *general* model for false belief; it is not at all

[10] C. J. F. Williams, 'Referential Opacity and False Belief in the *Theaetetus*', *Philosophical Quarterly*, 22 (1972), 289–302, also distinguishes the opaque from the transparent readings of *allodoxia*. He argues, however, that Plato confuses the two readings, whereas I go on to argue that he does not.

[11] See e.g. Ackrill, 'Plato on False Belief', 388–9.

obvious that every false belief involves the explicit mix-up of concepts or properties that occurs in (7). Yet Socrates introduces *allodoxia* as though it is a general model of false belief, and, moreover, as though it is a plausible one.

As Ackrill notes, we should be justly disappointed if (7) is all *allodoxia* discusses.[12] Other readings of *allodoxia* are possible, however. Theaetetus' example can be read transparently rather than opaquely, as a description, rather than as a verbatim report, of Theaetetus' belief:

(8) Theaetetus thinks of ugliness that it is beauty.

In (8) 'ugliness' is still taken to refer to the property of ugliness. But now Theaetetus does not explicitly say 'ugliness is beauty'. Rather, he is described as believing that ugliness is beauty, but his actual belief would be, for example, 'gaudiness is beauty'. Now some instances of *allodoxia*, construed on the model (8) provides, may be unintelligible. Theaetetus' belief might be so far wrong that we would say, not that he has a false belief about beauty, but that he fails to have the concept at all (for example, he might believe 'what disgusts the beholder is beauty'). But aside from this limiting case, many instances of the allodoxastic schema, construed as in (8), will be intelligible. For example, 'being brightly coloured is beauty' is false but intelligible; and so (8) is an instance of the allodoxastic schema that is not unintelligible.

(7) and (8) restrict themselves to consideration of properties. But the schema Socrates provides can also accommodate beliefs concerning particulars:

(9) Theaetetus thinks that the ugly thing (for example, Socrates) is beautiful.
(10) Theatetus thinks of the ugly thing (for example, Socrates) that it is beautiful.

In (9) and (10) 'ugly' functions as an adjective, and some particular thing is affirmed to be beautiful. (9), like (7), is an opaque representation of the belief, and it is similarly unintelligible. Theaetetus here explicitly affirms something like 'ugly Socrates is beautiful', and it is difficult to construe this belief so that it is intelligible.[13] (10), like (8), is a transparent representation of the belief, and it is a prima facie plausible subject–predicate sentence. Theaetetus' explicit belief would be, for example, 'Socrates is beautiful'.

---

[12] Ibid.

[13] Although not impossible. The early and middle dialogues, for example, often consider cases of the compresence of opposites; Socrates might be beautiful in one way and ugly in another. But that view does not seem to be relevant here.

This belief is still allodoxastic, since Theaetetus has substituted 'beautiful' for 'ugly'; but the belief, though false, involves no mix-up of concepts or properties.

(8) and (10) together show how *allodoxia* can be a plausible model of false belief, and one that is perfectly general. They show that instances of the general schema are restricted neither to identity beliefs nor to beliefs involving only properties nor to opaque representations of beliefs; rather, the schema will even accommodate ordinary subject–predicate judgements. Correspondingly (8) and (10) show how Plato can move from (5) to (6). For although the beliefs described in K may appear to be restricted to identity beliefs, (8) and (10) show that the restriction is unnecessary there, too. For K's schema for false belief is also 'thinking that x is not x but something else, y' (see e.g. 188 B 3–5), and (8) and (10) show that instances of this schema are not restricted to identity beliefs. (8) and (10) also match the *Sophist*'s account of falsity, where false statements are analysed as cases where one says of something something other than what is true of it (see e.g. 263 B 7–13). (8) and (10) are then prima facie plausible false beliefs; they show how *allodoxia* can accommodate all false beliefs; they explain K's seeming restriction to identity beliefs; and they match Plato's account of falsity in the *Sophist*.[14] But though they are possible readings of the allodoxastic formula for representing false beliefs, this does not by itself show that they are the readings Plato intends. All I have argued so far is that *if* (8) and (10) are the readings Plato intends, *allodoxia* is more general and more plausible than on any other reading; but does Plato intend *allodoxia* to be general and plausible?

Theaetetus' opening comments suggest that he does. But Socrates' concluding comments, in which *allodoxia* is rejected, rather suggest (7) or (9). Socrates asks Theaetetus to 'try to recall whether you have ever said to yourself that assuredly what is ugly is beautiful or that what is unjust is just. Or again, in general, consider whether you have ever tried to persuade yourself that assuredly one thing is another thing . . .' (190 B 2–8). The attempt is taken to be absurd; but since neither (8) nor (10) is absurd, (7) or (9) should be assumed here.

Now it is usually supposed that since Socrates clearly invokes (7) or (9) in his rejection of *allodoxia*, either they are all he considers here, or, alternatively, he somehow confuses them with (8) or (10).[15] The first alternative

---

[14]   This paragraph largely agrees with Williams, 'Referential Opacity and False Belief in the *Theaetetus*'. McDowell, *Plato: Theaetetus*, 203, considers two purported differences beween *allodoxia* and the *Sophist*'s later account; but if the analysis of *allodoxia* I offer here is correct, neither of these purported differences is relevant.

[15]   For a defence of the first claim, see Ackrill, 'Plato on False Belief', 388–9; for a defence

is unattractive. For if (7) or (9) are all Plato considers, it is, as I have already noted, difficult to understand why Theaetetus initially takes *allodoxia* to be a plausible model of false belief, or why he needs such lengthy persuading that it is not. Perhaps, then, Plato confuses the various possibilities, trading on the plausibility of (8) and (10) to secure Theaetetus' agreement, but using (7) or (9) to show the absurdity of *allodoxia*. An equally plausible interpretation that avoids attributing confusion to Plato is to be preferred, however, and I think such an interpretation is available. I shall argue that Socrates begins with the plausible (8) or (10)—and hence Theaetetus accepts *allodoxia* as a plausible model of false belief—but that Socrates then argues that (8) or (10) can be reduced to (7) or (9), respectively; the argument he presents is valid, however, and does not trade on any confusion.

The key to this interpretation lies in the intervening discussion between Theaetetus' initial example and Socrates' criticism of it, where Socrates proposes that thinking is a sort of silent speech, 'speech the mind goes through with itself about whatever it is considering' (189 E 6–7). In likening belief to speech, Socrates is saying that they are equally propositional, or involve a complete sentence for their expression. Uttering 'beautiful' alone, for example, is not the expression of a belief, but 'Socrates is beautiful' is.

Socrates then insists that in any belief 'both things' (189 E 1–2) must be involved, and uses this claim to turn all cases of otherjudging into cases of (7) or (9). Now 'both things' clearly refers to 'beautiful' and 'ugly'; but as (7)–(10) make clear, there are different ways in which both things might be in the mind. For example, Socrates might be insisting that when one judges of an ugly thing that it is beautiful, one's belief must explicitly contain the terms 'ugly' and 'beautiful', so that even (10) involves an explicit mix-up of concepts. If this is meant, it will be difficult to acquit Socrates of foul play.

But another reading of the requirement that 'both things' be in the mind is possible. Socrates might only be insisting that any judgement affirming one thing to be another must involve both items in some way, so as to yield a complete sentence in satisfaction of the *logos* model of belief. But the ugly can be in the mind without being there under the description 'the ugly' if Socrates, for example, is an ugly thing and is in the mind. Both things, on this view, might be Socrates (who is the ugly thing) and beautiful. Taken this way, Socrates' requirement does not illicitly require self-contradiction (as in (7)) in every belief, but only insists, plausibly, that

of the second claim, see Williams, 'Referential Opacity and False Belief in the *Theaetetus*', 291 ff., and McDowell, *Plato:* Theaetetus, 204 ff. Ackrill's view is well criticized by Williams. From now on I shall largely focus on (10); but most of my remarks apply equally well to (8).

complete sentences represent beliefs: something must be affirmed to be beautiful. The requirement, then, is consistent with (8) and (10).

Using this plausible claim, however, Socrates can now validly reduce (10) to (9)—given K.

If 'Socrates' and 'beautiful' figure in one's judgement, one must, by (2c), know Socrates and beautiful. But if one knows Socrates, one knows that he is ugly. If one does not know this, one is ignorant of Socrates, and so cannot have any beliefs about him. If, though, one knows that Socrates is ugly, yet claims that he is beautiful, it is as if one said that ugly Socrates is beautiful. And such a belief is absurd.

We can schematize Plato's argument like this:

(11) Theaetetus thinks that Socrates is beautiful (10).
(12) Socrates is ugly.
(13) Therefore Theaetetus thinks that ugly Socrates is beautiful.

The move from (11) and (12) to (13) can be validated with the aid of K:

(14) Theaetetus knows Socrates and beauty, since they figure in his judgement (2c).
(15) Theaetetus, since he knows Socrates, knows that he is ugly.
(16) Theaetetus thinks (a) Socrates is ugly (15), and (b) Socrates is beautiful (11).
(17) Therefore Theaetetus thinks that ugly Socrates is beautiful (13).

Plato has not simply confused (10) and (9); he has argued validly that, given K, (10) reduces to (9).

IV

I have argued so far that otherjudging is a plausible model of false belief, endorsed by Plato in the *Sophist*; it fails here not because of any of its intrinsic features, nor because Plato cannot yet handle its subtleties, but because, given K, it can be reduced to absurdity. But this pushes our problem back a step: why endorse K?

K offers us, with (2c), a purportedly exhaustive dichotomy of knowing all about or being totally ignorant of a thing, a dichotomy generated by a particular model of acquaintance. The way to dispel K is simply to attack that acquaintance model, or to point out that the dichotomy is not genuinely exhaustive. It is not the case that, for any x, either I know everything about x or am totally ignorant of it; I might be in the intermediate position of having knowledge-independent beliefs.

Why does Plato not mention this simple refutation of (2c)? We might think the answer is that he endorses K, that he believes that any grasp of a thing confers total knowledge of it, and that the only alternative is total ignorance. Knowledge is a hit or miss, all or nothing affair. There is a better explanation of K's presence here, however, if we recall the context within which K is offered.

Theaetetus proposes that knowledge is true belief; Socrates then turns to a discussion of false belief and, when he fails to explain it, argues that Theaetetus' definition is faulty; 'it is impossible to know what [false belief is] until one knows what knowledge is' (200 D). This suggests that the discussion of false belief is relative to Theaetetus' definition and that, since the discussion ended in failure, the definition that guides it is defective.

Now the failure to explain false belief resulted from K's strong acquaintance model, which precluded any distinction beween true belief and knowledge: on that model, any grasp of a thing amounts to knowledge, and so true belief, since it involves a grasp of a thing, is knowledge. But of course Theaetetus should welcome this result, since he suggests that there is no distinction between knowledge and true belief. Thus, the underlying acquaintance model, although it precludes a satisfactory explanation of false belief, supports Theaetetus' suggestion, by obliterating any distinction between knowledge and true belief.[16] K occurs here, then, not because Plato is vulnerable to it, but because it follows from the acquaintance model introduced in support of Theaetetus' suggestion.

I do not claim that Theaetetus' definition entails the conundrums of K. Rather, I claim that the acquaintance model that underlies K is a sufficient condition of Theaetetus' definition. If the acquaintance model of knowledge is accepted, Theaetetus' definition follows. The discussion of

---

[16] This line of reasoning shows that there cannot be knowledge-independent true beliefs; but could there not be false belief? I think Plato would say that if, for any x, I have only false beliefs about x, then I in effect have ignorance, as described here. If a false belief is to be about x, it cannot be all we intend to say about x; for a false belief to attach to a referent, it must be linked to other true beliefs. If all I can say of justice is that it is a vegetable, this does not count as a belief about justice at all; it displays ignorance of justice. To count as a false belief about x, a claim must be linked to other beliefs that manage to refer to x. In this sense, false beliefs require there to be true beliefs, but K does not allow this sort of interdependence. For, by (3), one cannot both know and not know the same thing. Our only options, then, are all true beliefs, which here amount to knowledge, or all false beliefs, which then plausibly reduce to ignorance. Plato thus rejects the Kripkean view that all my beliefs about something could be false.

false belief thus explores the consequences of accepting the support used to make Theaetetus' definition look plausible.[17]

But there is a problem: the acquaintance model used to support Theaetetus generates the conundrums of K, and prevents us from accommodating false belief. The support used for Theaetetus' definition leaves no room for false belief. But since there is false belief, there must be something wrong with Theaetetus' definition; as Plato says, their inability to explain false belief shows that they do not know what knowledge is, either. If the result of pressing Theaetetus' definition, through its support of acquaintance, is to preclude false belief, then that is an indirect argument that that definition is faulty.

Looked at in this way, the discussion of false belief is not an irrelevant digression; rather, it reveals the difficulties created by acceptance of Theaetetus' definition. Since these difficulties are intolerable, Theaetetus' definition is to be rejected.

Plato thus has a two-pronged strategy against Theaetetus' suggestion that knowledge is true belief. At 201 A–C he refutes it directly. In the discussion of false belief he criticizes it indirectly, by showing that its support leads to intolerable results. The discussion of false belief is then an integral part of the consideration of Theaetetus' definition, not a mere digression.

V

If this is right, there is another point worth making. It is often claimed that Plato endorses K, that he thinks of knowledge as a sort of grasping, or acquaintance. But if what I have said so far is right, at least this passage does not support that view. For the same two-pronged strategy Plato used against Theaetetus works as well against K. First, K's inability to accommodate false belief is an indirect argument that it is faulty. Second, 201 A–C rejects K by a simple application of Modus Tollens. Plato argues there that knowledge is not true belief, and so Theaetetus' definition is wrong. But if K entails Theaetetus' definition, the rejection of Theaetetus' definition carries with it the rejection of K.

To be sure, those who ascribe an acquaintance model of knowledge to Plato can appeal to other passages. But if the Modus Tollens argument just sketched is right, they should be wary: for Plato consistently denies that

---

[17] I have suggested so far that the acquaintance model is *sufficient* to support Theaetetus; but is it *necessary*? Plato seems to place the burden on the defender of Theaetetus to find an account of knowledge which (*a*) unlike the acquaintance model, does not entail K, and (*b*) supports Theaetetus' failure to distinguish knowledge and true belief.

knowledge is true belief (see e.g. *Meno* 98 A; *Grg.* 454 D; cf. *Rep.* 477 A). If the rejection of that view here counts against acquaintance, it may do so elsewhere as well.[18]

[18] An earlier version of this chapter was read at the meetings of the APA Eastern Division, December 1976. I wish to thank Donald Zeyl for his helpful comments on that version. The present version was accepted for publication by the editor of *Phronesis* in May 1977.

10

Knowledge and *Logos* in the *Theaetetus*[1]

I

At least as early as the *Meno*, Plato is aware that true belief, though necessary for knowledge, is not sufficient. In addition, he claims, true belief must be 'fastened with an explanatory account [*aitias logismos*]' (98 A). Plato's claim has often been linked to modern accounts of knowledge, according to which S knows that p if and only if p is true, S believes that p, and S has adequate justification or grounds for believing that p.[2] In the end I believe this linkage is correct, but it is as well to issue a caveat at the outset. In the modern account, the definiendum concerns one's knowledge that a particular proposition is true. Plato tends instead to speak of knowing things (virtue, knowledge, Theaetetus, and the sun are among the examples he gives of things one may know or fail to know). But this difference should not be pressed too far. First, the account that certifies that one knows a particular thing will itself be a proposition: one knows a thing through or by knowing certain propositions to be true of it. Knowledge of things,

[1] The original stimulus for this chapter was M. F. Burnyeat's rich and exciting paper 'The Simple and the Complex in the *Theaetetus*' (read at the Princeton Conference on Plato's Philosophy of Language, 1970). Unfortunately, this paper is still unpublished, although some parts of it appear in his 'The Material and Sources of Plato's Dream', *Phronesis*, 15 (1970), 101–22. I acknowledge particular points of agreement and disagreement along the way. Some of the terminology I use later (KL, AL, AK, WP) is derived from his paper. I also wish to thank Carl Ginet, Terence Irwin, and Nicholas Sturgeon for their helpful comments on earlier drafts. Parts of the chapter (especially sects. v–vii) were read at the APA Eastern Division meetings, Washington, December 1977; I thank Alexander Nehamas for his comments on that occasion. Nehamas, '*Epistêmê* and *Logos* in Plato's Later Thought', *Archiv für Geschichte der Philosophie*, 66 (1984), 343–74, is a revised and expanded version of those comments.

[2] See e.g. R. Chisholm, *Theory of Knowledge* (Englewood Cliffs, NJ: Prentice Hall, 1966), 5–7; D. M. Armstrong, *Belief, Truth and Knowledge* (Cambridge: Cambridge University Press, 1973), 137 (where *Meno* 97–8 is miscited as 87–8). N. P. White, *Plato on Knowledge and Reality* (Indianapolis: Hackett, 1976), 176–7, issues a caveat like the first one I mention; unlike me, however, he takes this difference to show that comparisons between Plato's account and the modern one are therefore 'misleading'. See also J. H. McDowell, *Plato: Theaetetus*, trans. with notes (Oxford: Clarendon Press, 1973), 232.

for Plato, is description-dependent, not description-independent. Second, Plato tends to speak interchangeably of knowing x and knowing what x is (see e.g. *Meno* 79 c 8–9; *Tht.* 147 B 2–5).[3] Thus a sentence of the form 'A knows x' can always be transformed into a sentence of the form 'A knows what x is'; and the latter, in turn, is readily transformed into 'A knows that x is F'. Hence even if Plato's primary concern is knowledge of objects, this concern can readily be phrased in the modern idiom as knowledge that a particular proposition is true.

A second difference between Plato's account and the modern one is also worth noting. The modern tradition has the broad interest of justifying one's claim to know that p, for any true proposition p. Plato, however, focuses only on a subset of such cases; he is concerned only with accounts specifying the nature of entities one claims to know, and knowledge of such accounts provides something like philosophical insight or understanding, not merely good grounds for believing that a particular proposition is true. But this narrower focus does not divorce Plato's concern from the modern one; and in particular, as we shall see, his account of knowledge leads to problems which also confront the modern one.

Plato's *logos* condition on knowledge concerns the content of one's claim to know: a *logos* must be suitably explanatory. In addition, Plato claims, one counts as knowing a particular object only if one also knows the referents of any terms contained in its *logos*. If my definition of x is in terms of y and z, I count as knowing x only if I also know y and z (*Meno* 75 c 8–D 7). Knowledge, Plato believes, must be based on knowledge (KBK): if I utter some true and even explanatory account which, however, I do not understand (I've accidentally uttered an appropriate Russian sentence, or learnt some answer by rote that I could not explain), I do not have knowledge.

When we put KBK together with Plato's initial claim, that all knowledge requires a *logos* or account (KL), a familiar regress ensues: to know an object o, I must, by KL, produce a true account of o. But I must in addition, by KBK, know any objects mentioned in the account. Given KL, this requires further true accounts, which, given KBK, in turn requires knowledge of any objects mentioned in them, and so on. Does the ensuing regress have an end or not? And if not, is the regress linearly infinite, or circular? Plato does not explicitly consider these questions in the *Meno*. But he does consider them in some detail in the last pages of the *Theaetetus*.

---

[3] McDowell, *Plato: Theaetetus*, 115 and elsewhere, notes the equivalence but draws a different moral.

II

Having argued earlier in the *Theaetetus* that knowledge is neither perception nor true belief, Plato returns to the *Meno*'s claim that knowledge is true
belief with an account (201 c 9–d 1). The rest of the *Theaetetus* contains
a two-pronged analysis of that claim: in the first stage, Socrates considers
a dream he says he has had, according to which there are no accounts of
some things, which are therefore unknowable. In the second stage he turns
to the general thesis and investigates three interpretations of '*logos*'.

Each of these stages considers a familiar response to the regress outlined
above. According to Socrates' dream, the regress is finite: it halts with
basic elements that lack accounts. Given KL, these basic elements must be
unknowable, and so the dream theorist argues. Given KBK, however, no
knowledge can be founded on unknowables; and it is by insisting on KBK
that Plato ultimately rejects the dream theory. With KL and KBK intact,
this leaves two options: the regress is either linearly infinite or circular. In
the second stage of the discussion, Plato explores these options.[4]

Many philosophers have believed that there are fundamental objections
to all of the suggested responses to the regress. It is not, then, surprising
that the *Theaetetus* appears to end aporetically: 'So it would seem, Theaetetus, that knowledge is neither perception, nor true belief, nor an account
added to true belief' (201 b). Since the regress is engendered by the joint
endorsement of KL and KBK, it is often suggested that Plato abandons at
least one of them. Perhaps the most familiar line of argument is that he
rejects KL, and maintains instead that knowledge requires some sort of
intuitive, nondiscursive access to objects known.[5]

I shall argue instead, however, that Plato retains at least a modified version

---

[4] Aristotle considers the regress problem in the *Posterior Analytics*, 1. 3; his response is
different from any we shall find in the *Theaetetus*. He argues, with the dream theorist, that if
knowledge is to be possible, accounts must end somewhere. But unlike the dream theorist,
he does not think they end with unknowables: he argues instead that one grasps basic
elements by an intuitive apprehension (*nous*) of them; and *nous*, he believes, does provide
knowledge of elements or, at least, something cognitively just as good. Aristotle's position
is discussed by T. H. Irwin, 'Aristotle's Discovery of Metaphysics', *Review of Metaphysics*, 31
(1977), 210–29. For some comparison of Plato and Aristotle, see G. R. Morrow, 'Plato and
the Mathematicians', *Philosophical Review*, 79 (1970), 309–33.

[5] See e.g. I. M. Crombie, *An Examination of Plato's Doctrines* (2 vols.; London: Routledge
& Kegan Paul, 1962–3), ii. 113–14; W. G. Runciman, *Plato's Later Epistemology* (Cambridge:
Cambridge University Press, 1962), 40. R. Robinson, 'Forms and Error in Plato's *Theaetetus*',
Philosophical Review, 59 (1950), 3–30, repr. in his *Essays in Greek Philosophy* (Oxford:
Clarendon Press, 1969), 39–73 (latter pagination) at 52–5, argues that KL is abandoned,
but he does not explicitly invoke acquaintance in its stead. Burnyeat also argues that KL is

of the thesis that knowledge is true belief with an account, a view advanced not only in the *Meno* but also throughout the middle dialogues (see e.g. *Phd.* 76 B, 78 D; *Rep.* 534 B). He argues that knowledge involves mastery of a field, an ability systematically to interrelate the elements of a particular discipline.[6] If this interrelation model of knowledge, as I shall call it, carries with it any criticism of the claim that knowledge is true belief with an account, the criticism is only that knowledge involves true belief with *several* accounts, explaining the interrelations among the elements of a discipline. But this criticism neither abandons the basic commitment to a *logos*-based epistemology nor requires its supplementation with any sort of nondiscursive access to objects known. In fact, as we shall see, Plato insists very strongly, perhaps too strongly, on descriptions as the only relevant factor in determining not only the objects of knowledge but also those of belief.

In defending the interrelation model of knowledge, Plato accepts one of the responses to the regress mentioned above: he endorses the view that there is no basic terminus towards which our justifications or explanations converge, no basis consisting of objects themselves knowable without appeal to further justification or explanation. Justification or explanation instead proceeds circularly, within a particular discipline or field. Plato thus retains KL and KBK, and outlines a theory of knowledge compatible with them.

In Section III, I consider the dream theory; in Section IV, Plato's criticism of it. Subsequent sections explore the three interpretations of '*logos*' and the development of Plato's interrelation model of knowledge.

III

The dream theorist distinguishes between primary elements (*ta prōta stoicheia*, 201 E 1) and the compounds (*hai sullabai*, 202 B 7) formed from them. Compounds, but not elements, are knowable, although elements are nameable and perceivable. This asymmetry in knowability (AK) between

abandoned, but rejects the view that acquaintance is thereby invoked. Some of these views are discussed below.

[6] G. E. L. Owen, 'Notes on Ryle's Plato', in O. P. Wood and G. Pitcher (eds.), *Ryle: A Collection of Critical Essays* (London: Macmillan, 1971), 341–72 at 365, urges that such later dialogues as the *Sophist* and *Philebus* advocate some such view, but he denies that the *Theaetetus* does. McDowell, *Plato:* Theaetetus, 254, 258, and Burnyeat see at least the germs of the interrelation model here. Burnyeat, however, thinks this shows that Plato has abandoned KL; I argue instead that it is a way of defending that thesis. See below, nn. 16, 22, 30.

elements and compounds results from the dream theorist's view that all knowledge requires a *logos* (KL), coupled with the claim that compounds, but not elements, have accounts.[7] The asymmetry in *logos* (AL) between elements and compounds results from his interpretation of '*logos*': he suggests that a *logos* is a weaving together of the names of the elements of a thing. This *logos* model I call enumeration of elements (EE). Since elements, *ex hypothesi*, are not composed of further elements, it follows that they have no accounts. Thus KL and AL entail AK; and AL is in turn entailed by the dream theorist's *logos* model, EE.

The dream theorist's claim that elements are unknowable because they have no *logos* can be explained in two quite different ways, depending upon how we interpret '*logos*'. '*Logos*' can mean either 'sentence' or 'statement' (what I shall call logos$_s$); it can also mean something like 'explanation' or 'account', of the sort that produces or evidences knowledge (what I shall call logos$_k$). If '*logos*' here is logos$_s$, AL says that there are no sentences true of elements; elements are then unknowable because a necessary condition on knowledge of a thing is that that knowledge be expressible in a proposition. If no sentences or propositions are true of any element, no element is knowable. If, on the other hand, '*logos*' here is logos$_k$, then AL need not mean that there are no sentences of any sort true of elements, but only that there are no knowledge-producing accounts true of them. Elements are not knowable, not because they are indescribable, but because they are unanalysable: no sentence true of an element—and there may be some—tells us what it is or, therefore, yields knowledge of it. To be sure, on the logos$_s$ interpretation it is also the case that elements are unanalysable: for since analysis is propositional, the unavailability of logos$_s$ entails the unavailability of logos$_k$. None the less, the reasons for which elements are unanalysable differ on the logos$_s$ and logos$_k$ interpretations.[8]

---

[7] Some elements might have accounts, viz. those that themselves contain further elements. Thus syllables might be thought to be among the elements (or, at least, parts) of words, but to have accounts in terms of their elements, letters. But these are not the sorts of element that interest the dream theorist: he is concerned with *primary* elements, those that are not further decomposable. Syllables are thus compounds just as much as words are, and Plato in fact later uses the example of syllables in explicating the dream theorist's notion of a compound.

[8] One might argue that this way of phrasing the difference between logos$_s$ and logos$_k$ credits the dream theorist, or Plato, with too much sophistication, in so far as it presupposes clarity about the notion of a sentence or proposition. For the view that Plato does not evidence this sort of clarity, see McDowell, *Plato: Theaetetus*, 232 ff. But this would not affect the distinction I draw. One could still, using McDowell's terminology, simply distinguish between various ways of putting elements into words. Logos$_s$ then involves putting elements into words in some way or other; logos$_k$ involves putting elements into words in such a way as to express something's essence or nature. Hence if logos$_s$ is unavailable, one cannot put

On the first view, a view championed by Ryle and others, the dream theorist is arguing that

> knowledge requires for its expression not just a name but a sentence or statement. And what a sentence or statement expresses always contains a plurality, at least a duality of distinguishable elements or factors. Knowledge, as well as true or false belief and opinion, cannot be expressed just by a proper name or demonstrative for some simple object, but only by a complex of words which together constitute a sentence.[9]

Ryle's interpretation may seem supported by at least the following considerations. First, in denying that elements have accounts, the dream theorist says that 'the only thing that is possible for [an element] is for it to be named, because a name is the only thing it has' (202 A 8–B 2). Surely the contrast here is between a name and a logos$_s$? Moreover, the dream theorist also says that elements, although unknowable, are perceivable, whereas compounds are 'knowable and expressible and believable with true belief' (202 B 6–7). He does not say explicitly that there are no true beliefs about elements, but surely that is a natural conclusion from what he does say? But we should be justly surprised if logos$_s$, but not true beliefs, were available for elements; for true beliefs are expressed in a logos$_s$. If there are no true beliefs about elements, it is unlikely that there is any logos$_s$ about them either. Finally, in the *Sophist* Plato defines *logos*—and his concern there is clearly logos$_s$—as a combination of names (*onomata*) and verbs or predicates (*rhēmata*) (261 D 4 ff.): a sentence possesses a special sort of complexity involving elements of different syntactic types. A name on its own does not 'complete the business' (*perainein ti*) or achieve a truth-value (262 B 9–C 7);[10] what is further necessary is the absorption of the name into a certain syntactic framework, containing not only names but also verbs or predicates (*rhēmata*). Surely the dream theorist's explanation of '*logos*', as a weaving together of names, is addressed to the same issues?

If so, the dream fits neatly into a familiar picture of Plato's development:

elements into words at all. If logos$_k$ is unavailable, one cannot put elements into words in such a way as to express essence.

[9] G. Ryle, 'Plato's *Parmenides*', *Mind*, NS 48 (1939), 129–51 and 302–25, repr. in R. E. Allen (ed.), *Studies in Plato's Metaphysics* (London: Routledge & Kegan Paul, 1965), 97–147 at 136–7. Ryle's interpretation of the dream is followed, at least in part, by Crombie, *An Examination of Plato's Doctrines* (e.g. ii. 117), and by McDowell, *Plato:* Theaetetus (e.g. 248 and *passim*). The alternative I propose is defended by Burnyeat as well, and my argument is indebted to his.

[10] For this interpretation, and for the felicitous rendering of *perainein ti*, see G. E. L. Owen, 'Plato on Not-Being', in G. Vlastos (ed.), *Plato*, i. *Metaphysics and Epistemology* (Garden City, NY: Doubleday Anchor, 1971), 223–67 at 264.

in his early and middle periods, he is alleged to believe that forms, his primary objects of knowledge, are 'simple nameables', known by direct acquaintance, independently of associated descriptions. The *Theaetetus* now sees that, on the contrary, such simple elements, if only nameable, are not also knowable: all knowledge requires a *logos*. But the *Theaetetus*, unlike the *Sophist*, is not quite free from the old view. Although it sees that the mere utterance of one name does not 'complete the business', it locates the relevant difference in complexity alone, as if a list of several names would do. And it is easy to see how this crude conception could lead to difficulties. For if the mention of one name does not amount to saying something, neither will the mention of several names. In the *Theaetetus* Plato sees that sentences are important; but it is not until the *Sophist* that he sees how they are to be construed.

I think this general picture of Plato's development is ill-drawn. Here, however, I content myself with arguing that the dream theory does not fit into the picture in the suggested way. (I do not deny, of course, that in the *Theaetetus* Plato thinks knowledge requires propositional expression; indeed, I think Plato always assumes that knowledge is essentially articulate, and it is for this reason, among others, that I reject Ryle's picture of Plato's development.[11])

Whether the dream theorist's account of '*logos*' is of logos$_s$ can only be decided by close attention to surrounding context and argument. '*Logos*' and '*onoma*' are used too variously in Greek to force any interpretation on us by themselves, and verbal similarities with the *Sophist* prove nothing.[12] The details of the dream and its context, however, suggest that logos$_k$, not logos$_s$, is at issue.

First, the dream theorist's claim that one can have true beliefs about compounds no more implies that one cannot have true beliefs about elements than his claim that elements are perceivable implies that compounds are not also perceivable. All he says explicitly by way of contrasting elements and compounds is that the latter, unlike the former, are knowable and admit of *logos*. Our interpretation need assume no more.

Nor does the dream theorist explicitly say that one cannot utter sentences true of elements—only that no such sentence says what an element is, or, therefore, yields knowledge of it. If we interpret '*logos*' as logos$_k$, this claim is readily intelligible. 'A name is the only thing [an element] has', not in

---

[11] One need not assume, of course, that Plato is always as enlightened as he is in such later dialogues as the *Sophist*; the question is whether he is ever as unenlightened as to fall into the sort of view Ryle ascribes to him.

[12] For some discussion of Plato on *onomata* and *logos*, see ch. 5.

the sense that it is all one can say of an element, but rather in the sense that it is all one can say of an element *towards saying what it is*, towards analysing or fully explaining it. Other words may be applicable to elements, but none results in a logos$_k$. Thus the dream theorist does not deny that 'this is x' (a complete sentence) is applicable to an element just as much as the mere name 'x' is; what he denies is that the addition of 'this' or 'is' gets us any further towards understanding what x is than 'x' alone does. An account, he argues, should be proprietary (*oikeios*, 202 A 7) to the thing it is of; 'this' and 'is', however, apply equally well to things other than x, indeed, to everything that is, and so are of no help in explaining what x in particular is—they are not *oikeios* to x. It is this special restriction on suitable accounts which precludes elements having accounts, and not any claims about the availability of sentences as such.

There is further evidence of logos$_k$ as well. The dream is introduced, after all, to explain or support Theaetetus' claim that knowledge is true belief with a '*logos*'. '*Logos*' here must be logos$_k$; for Plato later argues that *logos* in the sense in which it does no more than express a belief will not differentiate knowledge from belief (206 D–E). But as we have defined logos$_s$, it does no more than that; hence logos$_s$ does not differentiate knowledge from true belief. Plato's alternative suggestion is that a *logos* says what a given thing is by listing its elements (206 E 6–207 A 1). The claim that a *logos* says what something is ties the dream to the standard Socratic–Platonic 'What is it?' question, a request for a logos$_k$, for an account yielding knowledge of a thing; and that request is clearly echoed in the dream's mention of 'giving and receiving an account' (202 B 8–C 5). The general context thus demands logos$_k$, and the dream theory meets that demand: EE is a certain model for knowledge-producing accounts, that they consist in an enumeration of a thing's elements, and not a model for sentence constitution as such.

On both the logos$_s$ and logos$_k$ interpretations, then, the dream theorist denies that elements are knowable; indeed, on both interpretations he denies that they are analysable, too. But the reasons for these denials differ. With logos$_s$ the explanation is that elements cannot be described in propositions but only named; since an analysis is a particular sort of proposition, it follows that elements are unanalysable. With logos$_k$ it is not denied that there are propositions true of elements; the claim instead is that no such sentence ever amounts to a logos$_k$, to an analytical account of a thing. For something to be known, the dream theorist believes, it must be fully analysed; and a complete analysis consists in listing all the elements of a thing. For this project to yield knowledge, there must be basic elements that themselves lack accounts, that are not themselves composed of further elements. For otherwise, no list could be completed; no account could then be a complete analysis or, therefore, yield knowledge.

So read, the dream is still connected to atomism, as Ryle urged, although not quite in the way he suggested. Thus Russell, for example, says that 'I confess it seems obvious to me (as it did to Leibniz) that what is complex must be composed of simples';[13] and the obviousness stems from the fact that Russell, too, thought knowledge required analysis, which in turn required a breakdown of the complex into its simple constituents: if simples are not postulated as the limit of analysis, no knowledge is possible. The view stretches back from Russell to Descartes, who claims that there are certain simple natures of which all else is composed, and that 'the whole of human knowledge (*scientia*) consists uniquely in our achieving a distinct perception of how all these simple natures contribute to the composition of other things'.[14] On this view, knowledge of a compound consists in reducing it to, or analysing it into, simpler constituents. To halt a regress of accounts, Descartes, Russell, and the dream theorist posit a simple base that cannot be further decomposed, that is unanalysable and without account.

But although this similarity between the dream theorist and others is striking and important, a dissimilarity is even more noteworthy: for Descartes and Russell, simples are postulated not only as the limit of analysis, but also as what is most knowable and certain. To be sure, their simples are unanalysable. But they argue that we have a firmer grasp of them than any account, or any proposition, could provide. Rather than proceeding through the intermediary of propositions of any sort, even of a logos$_k$, we apprehend simples directly: we have an 'intuitive apprehension' of them (Descartes), or know them by some special sort of acquaintance (Russell). Despite the fact, perhaps because of the fact, that simples are known non-propositionally, they provide a firm foundation to knowledge. And here is where the dream theorist disagrees: for his simples, although they, too, are the limit of analysis, are unknowable. He does not, to be sure, deny us all access to them, for he concedes that they are at least nameable and perceivable; but neither naming nor perceiving amounts to knowing. If

---

[13] B. Russell, 'Logical Atomism' (1924), repr. in *Logic and Knowledge: Essays 1901–1950*, ed. R. C. Marsh (London: Allen & Unwin, 1956), 321–43 at 337. The passage is also cited by McDowell, *Plato:* Theaetetus, 231.

[14] R. Descartes, *Rules for the Direction of the Mind*, in *The Philosophical Writings of Descartes*, trans. J. Cottingham, R. Stoothoff, and D. Murdoch (2 vols.; Cambridge: Cambridge University Press, 1985), i. 49. It is worth noting that Descartes's simple natures include not only things he takes to be simple (such as extension, figure, motion) but also various purportedly simple truths and propositions; for the latter way of speaking, see e.g. Rules v, xi.

the requisite sort of propositions—accounts—are unavailable, knowledge is unavailable, too.

It is not difficult to pinpoint the basis of the disagreement: the dream theorist is firmly wedded to the view that all knowledge requires a propositional account. That is a commitment Descartes and Russell are willing to abandon, at least in the case of simples.

We might find the dream theorist's view perplexing or peculiar: the usual point of postulating simples is not just to halt accounts somewhere, but to ground them in certain, secure knowledge. The dream theorist provides a foundation to knowledge, all right, but its utility is questionable, if the base is itself unknowable.

We might wish to dismiss the dream theory as an epistemological oddity, of no special interest or importance, a crude first approximation to views better articulated later on. But this would be a mistake. For the dream theory raises a crucial problem for anyone attracted to the view that analysis can't go on for ever, but must eventually reach bedrock. For what is the cognitive status of the basic elements? If they are unknowable, as the dream theorist believes, the project of analysis looks defeated rather than completed: far from leading us to a secure base, it has led us to unknowables. But if simples are knowable, as we would like, we face the not so easy task of specifying a sort of knowledge that can yield the requisite certainty, yet bypasses accounts. It will not do to say that we know them through propositions that fail to amount to accounts, for such propositions could at best yield true beliefs; but true belief without an account does not amount to knowledge. And so the task has usually been to specify a cognitive relation to simples that bypasses propositions altogether, yet yields the desired certainty. And here is where the trouble begins: for what sort of relation could there be that in itself provides knowledge while bypassing propositions? The ordinary *connaître* will not, as Ryle and others have mistakenly supposed, provide us with a handle on the notion: to say one knows (*connaître*) something is not at all to imply that one knows it independently of truths about it. On the contrary, one does not *know* (*connaître*) a person or thing, unless one also knows various truths about the person or thing; *connaître*-knowledge is always knowledge under a description, or acquaintance with something *as* being something. To count as knowing something, I must not merely have seen it; I must also be able to identify and recognize it, say various things about it. *Connaître*-knowledge is linked to, not divorced from, propositional knowledge. To be sure, '*connaître*' implies something more than descriptive ability; it also implies that one has met the object in question. But because *connaître*-knowledge essentially involves knowledge of truths, it cannot be invoked as an alternative to propositional knowledge, as bypassing it altogether; yet only such a notion would do here.

Russell's technical notion of knowledge by acquaintance is intended to bypass propositions: 'We shall say we have acquaintance with anything of which we are directly aware, without the intermediary of any process of inference or any knowledge of truths.'[15] We may, for the sake of argument, allow that sometimes one is directly confronted with an object without the intermediary of any truths about it. But if one is not aware of the object as anything—if one cannot identify or recognize it or say anything about it—then neither does one know it. So long as the acquaintance relation is direct, it does not amount to knowledge; once it amounts to knowledge, it ceases to be direct and immediate. To be sure, the direct relation may allow one, as it were, to read various truths off the object; and the obtaining of this relation may be independent of propositional knowledge. But this is not to say—as Russell needs to—that the presentation itself constitutes knowledge. The acquaintance relation, construed as a direct confrontation between person and object, is not mediated by truths; but for this very reason it fails to be knowledge. Knowledge obtains only when knowledge of truths is available. Russellian acquaintance thus either fails to be knowledge—if it proceeds without the aid of propositions—or else requires associated descriptions and beliefs. In neither case does it provide a certain epistemic access to simples that bypasses propositional knowledge altogether.

The dream theorist thus sees, as others have not, that all knowledge requires accounts. But although his firm linkage of knowledge and accounts is laudable, it highlights a central difficulty for the view that accounts must end somewhere: for now it emerges that the final resting place will be with unknowables—hardly a satisfying end to the project of analysis.

It is against this awkward result of the dream theory—that compounds are knowable although the elements of which they are composed and in terms of which they are analysed are not—that Socrates launches his attack.

IV

The dream theorist has endorsed the view that knowledge is true belief with an account (KL). He has also provided a particular model of what an account is: enumeration of elements (EE). Given the assumption that there are elements, EE entails that there is an asymmetry of *logos* (AL) between

---

[15] B. Russell, *The Problems of Philosophy* (New York: Oxford University Press, 1912), 46.

elements and compounds. Coupled with KL, this entails an asymmetry of knowledge (AK) between elements and compounds.

Socrates launches his attack initially against AK, the dream's 'most subtle point' (202 D 10–E 1). KL, EE, AL, and not-AK are jointly inconsistent, however, and so Socrates must reject at least one of KL or AL. (Obviously the rejection of EE alone will not resolve the inconsistency.) On one view of the matter, Socrates rejects KL. Robinson, for example, suggests that Plato's point is that some '*aloga* must be knowable if there is any knowledge at all'.[16] If this is the moral to be drawn, we might expect Plato to endorse a refurbished version of the dream, one closer to Descartes's and Russell's dreams: elements or simples are knowable, after all, but without the intermediary of accounts. And so Crombie suggests that Plato's point is that 'knowledge must go beyond the ability to describe';[17] as Runciman puts it somewhat more picturesquely, 'the philosopher's realm cannot be attained without that extra intuition which in the *Republic* was declared to be the reward of the consummate dialectician alone'.[18]

For those fond of Descartes's or Russell's versions of the dream, this interpretation might seem attractive. For it seems to allow us suitable access to simples—unlike the dream theorist's lame concession of perceivability—while still avoiding the regress resulting from continued application of KL. Moreover, it is often thought that Plato proposes no alternative to EE which would allow elements to have accounts; perhaps his silence is best explained on the supposition that he has no need to propose such an alternative, since AL remains intact.

I shall argue that this interpretation is incorrect. Plato retains KL, insisting, along with the dream theorist, that all knowledge requires accounts. Instead, he rejects AL and EE. There may, to be sure, be simples or basic elements that are not themselves composed of further elements. None the less, they have accounts, and so AL is false. But since one cannot, *ex hypothesi*, enumerate their elements, EE is false as well. The conviction that led to simples—that analysis must end somewhere—is, anyway, misplaced, and Plato abandons it in due course.

---

[16] Robinson, 'Forms and Error in Plato's *Theaetetus*', 55. He does not say how he thinks Plato believes *aloga* are known. Burnyeat also argues that KL is abandoned, and replaced with the interrelation model (whereas I argue that the interrelation model explicates, and does not replace, KL). Alexander Nehamas has also tried to persuade me that the interrelation model replaces, rather than explicates, KL.

[17] Crombie, *An Examination of Plato's Doctrines*, ii. 114.

[18] Runciman, *Plato's Later Epistemology*, 40. For a similar view, see also J. H. Lesher, '*Gnōsis* and *Epistēmē* in Socrates' Dream in the *Theaetetus*', *Journal of Hellenic Studies*, 89 (1969), 72–8.

Socrates begins by tacitly endorsing KL: 'what knowledge could there be without an account and correct belief?' (202 D 6–7). He wants instead to attack AK (202 D 8–E 1). The endorsement of KL, coupled with the rejection of AK, suggests that AL and, correspondingly, EE are also to be rejected: since elements are as knowable as compounds, and since all knowledge requires accounts, there must be accounts of elements.

This, I shall argue, is Socrates' eventual conclusion; but the ensuing discussion may seem to cast doubt on it. For Socrates seems next to endorse both AL and EE—the very assumptions we would expect him to reject, having endorsed KL and questioned AK. Using the model of letters and syllables for elements and compounds, Socrates suggests that the first syllable of his name, 'SO', has an account, since it is readily decomposed into its elements: 'SO' is 'S' and 'O'. In so describing 'SO' one has provided an account of it satisfying EE. But one cannot satisfy EE for the elements S and O, since there are no further elements into which they can be decomposed. As Theaetetus says, ' "S" is an unvoiced consonant, only a noise, which occurs when the tongue hisses' (203 B 2–7).

Now Theaetetus may seem to accept AL. He does, at the least, claim that EE is unavailable for S and O, and concludes on that basis that elements have no accounts of any sort (203 B 7). But notice what Theaetetus has done: although he has not satisfied EE, he has classified S, locating it within a certain phonetic system. In the *Cratylus* (424 C ff.), which precedes the *Theaetetus*, and again in the *Philebus* (18 B–D), which follows it, Plato also provides such classificatory accounts of letters; and there it is clear that he takes such accounts to yield knowledge. But since they do not satisfy EE, EE is implicitly rejected. Theaetetus' description of S is at least an inadvertent concession that AL and EE are, after all, mistaken. We shall soon see further evidence that this is the moral we are meant to draw.

Socrates' main attack on the dream theory is launched against AK. He presents a dilemma based on purportedly exhaustive alternative accounts of what a syllable is: a syllable is either (i) its letters, or else (ii) a single entity with its own distinct form, arising out of, but different from, its letters. Either way, he claims, AK is false: (i) entails that letters and syllables are equally knowable, (ii) that they are equally unknowable. (The resultant falsity of AK does not by itself show, of course, that AL rather than KL is to be abandoned, but evidence that this is Socrates' conclusion will be forthcoming shortly.)

Neither argument that Socrates offers appears satisfactory at first glance, but a second look softens this appearance somewhat. Consider Socrates' argument under (i) first. If one knows the syllable 'SO', he claims, one must know its letters, S and O, since, on (i), a syllable just is its letters. It follows that letters and syllables are equally knowable and so AK is false. This argument might seem to involve an invalid substitution into an intensional context, falsely assuming that if one knows x, and x is identical to y, then one also knows y. But Socrates' argument is not invalid in this way. According to the dream theorist, to know the syllable 'SO' one must decompose it into its elements, S and O, which, he believes, are unknowable. But this violates a plausible condition on knowledge we have seen Socrates endorsing before: that knowledge must be based on knowledge (KBK). If one claims to know a syllable 'SO' by referring to its elements, S and O, one must, by KBK, know each of S and O. But this is just what the dream theorist denies, in insisting on AK, the claim here under attack. Socrates insists, against AK, that if the adduced support is unknowable, no appeal to it justifies one's claim to knowledge.

If this is the force of Socrates' argument, his argument is not fallacious. None the less, the argument, even so construed, will hardly persuade the dream theorist, who, after all, assumes that KBK is false. It will hardly do, in arguing against him, simply to insist that it is true. None the less, Plato rejects (i) on the strength of that conviction, and his own alternative, soon to be sketched, endorses KBK.

Next consider (ii). Socrates now argues that if a syllable is not its parts, as (i) assumes, then it has no parts at all. In that case, syllables are as incomposite, and so as unknowable, as elements are alleged to be. AK is again false.

It is certainly true that the dream theorist must conclude that if syllables, like elements, are incomposite, they are unknowable. But how does it follow from the fact that syllables are not their letters (i) that they are partless, incomposite (ii)? Even if the argument under (ii) is successful, we may object that (i) and (ii) are not exhaustive alternatives, and so AK has not yet been shown to be false. As a third possibility, consider the following: a syllable is not just its letters, as (i) assumes (it is not reducible to or fully explicable in terms of them); nor yet is it partless. A syllable is its parts in that it is composed of them; it does not follow that it is identical to them. Once we thus distinguish the 'is' of identity from the 'is' of composition, the move from (i) to (ii) is resistible.[19]

Socrates invokes a principle designed to make (i) and (ii) genuinely exhaustive. He argues that if a thing has parts, it is its parts (WP; 204 A 7–8). Read one way, WP is innocuous enough: if a thing has parts it is

---

[19] Burnyeat also invokes the 'is' of identity and the 'is' of composition in discussing this passage.

(composed of) its parts. So read, however, the rejection of (i) does not yield (ii). WP can be read another way, however: if a thing has parts, it is (identical to) its parts. So read, WP is false; but so read, the rejection of (i) does commit us to (ii), by a simple application of Modus Tollens. Socrates' argument for WP suggests that the second reading is the intended one.

Not only is WP false, but Plato also seems to reject it in the earlier *Parmenides*.[20] If so, either he unfairly uses against the dream theorist a principle he knows to be false, or else the dream theorist is committed to WP. In the latter case, there is of course no unfairness in using it against him. But is the dream theorist committed to WP? The following considerations lend some support to the view that he is. According to the dream theorist, to know something is to enumerate all its elements. Now if such enumeration may include mention of the order in which the elements are enumerated, then EE does not entail or presuppose WP. But if EE precludes appeal to order, then EE does entail WP. For in this second case, appeal to elements alone must be sufficient for knowledge, since EE is sufficient for knowledge. In that case, no appeal to anything other than elements is necessary in producing an account, and order is not an element.[21] Now if a mere list of elements is sufficient for knowledge, then a thing's elements must exhaust all there is to the thing, at least, all that is essential to knowledge of the thing. If a thing is something more than its elements, listing its elements will not specify what the thing completely is, and so satisfying EE is not sufficient for knowledge.

This shows that the dream theorist is committed to WP if he construes EE in such a way as to preclude appeal to order. Is EE so construed? It is, first of all, significant that neither Socrates nor the dream theorist ever explicitly appeals to order in elucidating the dream theory. Second, although it may seem a minimal concession to the dream theorist to allow appeal to order to distinguish between, for example, the syllables 'SO' and 'OS', the concession looks much more striking for another example Plato mentions: a wagon (207 A). Here 'wheels, axle, yoke' is no more appropriate than 'axle, yoke, wheels'. If EE may mention order, it will need, to accommodate this case,

---

[20] See esp. *Parm.* 157 C 4–E 2, and McDowell, *Plato:* Theaetetus, 243–4.

[21] Plato does sometimes use '*meros*' (part) broadly enough to cover the referent of any predicate true of something; on this broad view, order counts as a part (although whether or not it counts as an element (*stoicheion*) might be another question). But this broad view does not seem in play here. For one thing, the dream theorist never mentions such candidates as order for parts; for another, at 205 B 8–13 it seems agreed that if a syllable has parts, its parts can only be letters. Even if this is not correct, however, it is still true that merely adding a mention of order on to a list is not the right way in which to specify something's order; cf. Aristotle, *Metaph. Z* 17. See further below.

to specify all the complex interrelations of a thing's parts—and this no longer even looks like a doctrine for which 'enumeration of elements' is an appropriate label. Nor does the dream theorist ever so much as hint that such interrelations are appropriate. And it is easy to see, on reflection, why the dream theorist might have so restricted EE. An account, he believes, must be proprietary (*oikeios*) to what it is of (202 A 7). Once one begins appealing to principles of arrangement, composition, and the like, one can no longer so easily provide accounts mentioning just the thing itself: principles for concatenating letters into words govern the production of all words and are proprietary to none; principles for linking wheels to yokes apply to all sorts of conveyances, not merely to wagons.

One might object to this suggestion along the following lines. Surely the *oikeios*-requirement on accounts states only that an account as a whole must be *oikeios* to what it is of, not that each of its parts must be. Hence the fact that principles of arrangement are common to other things does not entail that the *oikeios*-requirement has not been satisfied.

But this objection misfires. For the stronger reading of the *oikeios*-requirement is the one the dream theorist intends. As we have seen, he argued that since 'is', 'that', and so on are common to all things, they are *oikeios* to nothing, and so go no way towards providing accounts. This claim is explained only by the stronger reading of the *oikeios*-requirement. As the dream theorist intends the *oikeios*-requirement on accounts, then, it precludes accounts from mentioning order, arrangement, and the like.

Not only does the dream theorist intend the stronger reading of the *oikeios*-requirement; he also requires it if he is to maintain AL. For just as specifying the arrangements of a thing's parts provides a *logos* of the whole, so it provides a *logos* of the parts: 'O' is that letter which belongs here; wheels are that part of a wagon that do thus and so, and the like. Once appeal to order is allowed in accounts, the dream theorist can no longer maintain that elements can only be named: for they can also be located and interrelated. Once this is conceded, however, it will be difficult for the dream theorist to deny that elements are knowable: for why should not the ability to locate and interrelate them—which, on the more generous construal of EE, should count as providing a *logos*—provide knowledge of them?

Hence only if EE is construed so as to entail WP can the dream theorist maintain both AL and his conviction that accounts must be *oikeios* to what they are of. Socrates' argument is thus a plausible *ad hominem* attack on the dream theorist, highlighting the difficulties he encounters in attempting to explain compounds in terms of elements alone, and in terms of unknowable elements at that.

Socrates initially launched his attack ostensibly only against AK (203 c), but his conclusion rejects AL as well: 'So if, on the one hand, the compound is many elements and a whole, and these are its parts, then compounds and elements are *similarly knowable and expressible,* since it was clear that all the parts are the same as the whole. If, on the other hand, it's one and partless, then an element and a compound are *similarly without account and unknowable;* for the same explanation will make them thus' (205 D 7–E 4, emphasis added). If a compound is knowable, so too will its elements be. But then, given KL, there must be accounts of them too. If AK is rejected, AL goes with it. No special defence of KL, or independent argument against AL, has been advanced. But Socrates' remarks none the less clearly show that KL remains intact, and that AL is to be rejected.[22] It follows that EE is to be rejected as well. EE is false because, among other things, elements have accounts, but not all elements consist of further elements. Moreover, as the argument against (ii) hinted, and as Socrates urges in detail later, no appeal to elements alone conveys the special complexity characteristic of wholes like syllables.

He presses home his attack by now insisting that knowledge of elements, so far from being impossible, is in fact the fundamental case (206 A–C). In learning to spell, he argues, one learns to discriminate letters from one another, so as to be able to avoid confusion when they occur in various combinations. Similarly, one has learnt music perfectly when one can 'follow each note and say to which string each belongs' (206 A 10–B 3). In music, as in grammar, attention to elements is essential; if one claimed to know musical or grammatical compounds—chords or syllables, say—but not elements—notes or letters—one would 'be making a joke' (206 B 9–11).

Plato has sometimes been taken to be saying that 'the whole business of learning letters is the effort to pick out each one by itself'.[23] But this is not his point. Learning musical notes, for example, involves not merely the ability to identify each in isolation, but also, and especially, saying 'to which string each belongs'; analogously, and as Plato argues later, learning letters involves learning what words they combine to form. Nor is the resultant knowledge simply an elementary grasp of notes or letters, a halting first

---

[22] The only alternative I see to my conclusion is that Socrates is being ironical in the cited passages, in an effort to highlight the absurdity of KL; this is, in effect, the view defended by Burnyeat. But I see no absurdity in defending KL; and if I am right, Plato does propose an alternative to EE that shows that elements do have accounts. In that case, the passage is perfectly straightforward.

[23] Owen, 'Notes on Ryle's Plato', 365. Cf. also White, *Plato on Knowledge and Reality,* 178.

step on the way to more complicated knowledge of compounds. Rather, Plato says that when one has the ability to handle elements in these diverse ways, one knows music or words perfectly: knowledge of a complex system such as music consists in the ability to identify and interrelate its elements. One does not understand a discipline's elements until one understands the system to which they belong; conversely, understanding any system consists in understanding how its elements are interrelated.

This shows more than that there is some knowledge of elements (of perhaps a weak or halting sort—'elementary' in its sense of 'simple-minded' rather than of 'fundamental'); it also rejects EE. First, Socrates has now explicitly provided an alternative to EE that is available for elements: accounts of elements consist in locating them within a systematic framework, interconnecting and interrelating them. Second, Socrates claims that an interrelation account is necessary for knowledge of compounds as well. It is not just a special sort of account available for recalcitrant elements, but fundamental to knowledge of any sort of entity, elementary or compound. Knowledge always requires the ability to interrelate—not merely to list— the parts of a thing (if it has parts) to one another, and to relate one entity, elementary or compound, to others within the same systematic framework.

In replacing EE with his interrelation model of knowledge, Socrates has insisted that KL is to be retained at every stage of analysis. Analysis does not end with *logos*-lacking elements. Rather, one knows compounds, at least in part, by knowing their constituents, and knowledge of constituents, in turn, consists in relating them to one another and to various compounds. Accounts proceed in a circular fashion, relating the elements covered by a discipline to one another in a systematic way. Plato thus abandons the dream's conviction that accounts end somewhere; instead, they continue on circularly within a given field.

Socrates says there are other proofs of his claim (206 c 1–2). We shall, at the least, find him defending the interrelation model just outlined, both against the rival claims of EE and also against various problems it might seem to engender.

V

In arguing against the dream theory, Socrates attacked its special claim that there are *logos*-lacking elements. His rejection of that claim carried with it endorsement of the general thesis that knowledge is true belief with an account, and so it is appropriate that he turns next to a more detailed investigation of that thesis, and defends again his interrelation model of knowledge.

Three interpretations of 'account' are proposed and criticized: that to have an account of x is (1) to be able to express one's thoughts about x verbally (206 D 1–5); (2) to be able to enumerate all of x's elementary parts (206 E 6–207 A 1); and (3) to be able to state a mark by which x differs from everything else. (1) is quickly rejected on the plausible ground that it will not distinguish knowledge from true belief (or, indeed, from any beliefs one might happen to hold), since anyone can say what he thinks, but not all thoughts are true (206 D 7–E 2). (1) will not concern us further in what follows.[24] The more detailed arguments against (2) and (3), however, are of some interest.

(2) corresponds to the dream's interpretation of 'account', and Socrates' criticism follows familiar lines. Reverting to the example of spelling, he considers a child who spells the name 'Theaetetus' correctly. EE then certifies that he knows the name, since its letters have been correctly listed. Suppose, however, he then goes on to misspell 'Theodorus' as 'Teodorus'. This shows, Socrates argues, that he did not know the first syllable of Theaetetus' name since, on another occasion, he misspelt it. It has already been argued that one cannot know a compound if one does not know its elements; hence, since the child does not know the first syllable of Theaetetus' name, he does not know the name either. Spelling a name correctly, then, is not sufficient for knowledge, and so EE is false.

Plato has not argued that the child does not know 'Theaetetus' because he sometimes misspells that word.[25] Were that Plato's point, he might mean no more than that spelling a word correctly on one occasion is not sufficient for knowledge, although spelling it correctly on several occasions is. The problem is rather that the child misspells *other* words, containing the same letters and syllables. Enumeration of elements is not sufficient for knowledge since it might not issue, as knowledge must, from the proper understanding. To know a word involves not just spelling it correctly some number of times, but also the ability to handle its constituents in a variety of contexts; one must be able to display a grasp of the combinatorial powers of letters and the like. Knowledge of words requires knowledge of their constituents, and knowledge of constituents requires an ability to use them in different contexts. As Plato claims in the *Philebus* (18 C), one does not

[24] The rejection of (1) again suggests, however, that '*logos*' in the dream means 'account' or logos$_k$, not merely 'sentence' or logos$_s$.

[25] The point is noticed by White (*Plato on Knowledge and Reality*, 178, 196 n. 53) and by McDowell (*Plato:* Theaetetus, 253–4).

know one letter until one knows them all: knowledge does not consist in isolated acts of recognition, but in an ability systematically to interrelate the elements of a discipline. And this ability, as Plato has already argued, confers knowledge of elements no less than of compounds. EE thus remains firmly rejected, replaced by the interrelation model of knowledge.

VI

The third and final interpretation of 'account' considered here is that to give an account of a thing is to state some mark by which the thing differs from everything else (208 c 7–8). On this interpretation, one knows the sun, for example, when one can say that it is the brightest of the heavenly bodies that go around the earth (208 d 1–3). A true belief about the sun that does not amount to knowledge would presumably be something like 'the sun is a bright star'. This claim is true of the sun, but of other things as well. Knowledge, but not true belief, it is suggested, requires the ability to provide a uniquely referring definite description.

Plato presents a dilemma for this interpretation of 'account': it either fails to distinguish knowledge from true belief, or else is circular. In presenting the first horn of the dilemma, Plato insists on the importance of descriptions for having beliefs, just as, earlier, he insisted on *logos* as the crucial factor in knowledge. In presenting the second horn, he shows that the circularity resulting from his interrelation model is virtuous, not vicious. I consider the first horn of the dilemma first.

Socrates agrees with the third suggestion to this extent: accounts must at least involve uniquely referring descriptions. But he emphasizes that they are not sufficient for knowledge, since they are also necessary for true belief. In that case, they cannot be what distinguishes knowledge from true belief. Plato's claim contains an important truth: that one must be able to identify descriptively the objects of one's beliefs no less than the objects of one's knowledge. But the particular way in which he presses the claim is obscure, and perhaps not fully consistent.

The argument proceeds in three stages. Socrates first considers the sentence 'Theaetetus is the one who is a man, and has a nose, eyes, and mouth.' He argues that this sentence cannot express a belief about Theaetetus in particular, let alone knowledge of him, since it is equally true of Socrates, Theodorus, and perhaps even the meanest of the Mysians (209 b 8).[26] I do

---

[26] One might argue that the use of a proper name forestalls this worry. To this Plato would

not express even a belief about just Theaetetus until I provide a description true of him alone.

In the second stage Socrates considers a sentence containing a more finely honed description: 'Theaetetus is the man with a snub nose and prominent eyes.' But since the description this sentence contains may be true of other people, it is no more satisfactory than the first.

So far Socrates has insisted that a sentence that expresses a belief about just one object must be true of that object alone; and the only sorts of descriptions he has mentioned concern intrinsic features of a thing. Generalizing, one might suppose that Plato believes that to express a belief about x, one must specify unique intrinsic features of x.

But the third stage may weaken the conditions for having beliefs. At 209 c 4–9 Plato writes: 'In fact it won't, I think, be Theaetetus who figures in a judgement in me until precisely that snubness has imprinted and deposited in me a memory trace different from those of the other snubnesses I've seen, and similarly with the other things you're composed of. Then if I meet you tomorrow, that snubness will remind me and make me judge correctly about you.'

Unfortunately, the claim is ambiguous, depending on how the memory trace of Theaetetus' snubness is 'different'. On one interpretation, the claim is that the memory trace of Theaetetus is qualitatively different from all my memory traces of other snubnesses. Now from this it of course does not follow that my description of Theaetetus' snubness will not also fit the meanest of the Mysians. Perhaps, then, Plato now claims that although suitable referring descriptions may only mention intrinsic features of a thing, they need not distinguish the thing from everything else, but only from everything else within one's experience. If so, Plato now relaxes the initial condition that a sentence that expresses a belief about x must contain descriptions true of x alone. On this construal, although 209 c 4–9 may seem more plausible than the preceding two stages, it is incompatible with them.

A second interpretation preserves compatibility with the first two stages: Plato may believe that having seen and studied Theaetetus enables one to acquire a description of his snubness that is in fact finely honed enough to distinguish him from everything else. On this interpretation, one has a description of Theaetetus' snubness that qualitatively distinguishes it from all other snubnesses, not merely from those within one's experience. In support of this view is the following consideration: Plato suggests that

object that the use of a proper name is worthless without descriptive backing; in that case, the content of the sentence falls back onto the description it contains, and it is clear why that description is unsatisfactory. See n. 12.

the description I acquire will be sufficient for recognizing Theaetetus on another occasion. If the description also fits the meanest of the Mysians, however, and he comes to greet me tomorrow along with Theaetetus, this would not be the case. And in the first two stages, Plato argued that this possibility shows that I do not yet have a belief about just Theaetetus.

There is a third possibility. Plato may mean that my belief is about Theaetetus alone, not because I have a description of his unique snubness, but because I stand in a unique causal relation to him. My memory trace may not be qualitatively different from all others; but it has different causal relations from all my other memory traces; and this in turn provides a uniquely referring description: Theaetetus is the only person so related to me. This view retains the initial claim that, to have a belief about x, I must have available a description true of x alone; but it allows that such descriptions may specify causal connections. This view is compatible with the initial claim if we are not meant to generalize from Plato's initial examples to the conclusion that only intrinsic features of a thing are appropriate in expressing a belief about it.

I do not see how to decide between these three views. But on each of them, 209 c 4–9 seems to accord memory some role in belief. We might suppose the point of doing so is to show that

nothing propositional (whether you call it belief or knowledge) can ever be strictly about *x* unless the person who makes the proposition is directly acquainted with *x*, and retains in his memory an impression of *x* which transcends his ability to describe it. For one can only describe by attaching predicates, and however many predicates I string together, it is always logically possible that there is something else, *y*, to which they apply equally well.[27]

We have already seen reason to doubt that Plato relies on acquaintance in his account of knowledge. But perhaps he believes that acquaintance of some sort is necessary for belief? Plato's recognition of the importance of memory to belief—or, for that matter, to knowledge—supports no such view. It is, surely, plausible to suppose that only creatures with memories can have knowledge or beliefs; without memory, there is no knowledge or belief (see Aristotle, *Metaphysics A* 1). To have beliefs I must have some experiences and be able to retain memories of them; and experiences of course include acquaintance with objects in the world. But this does not

---

[27] Crombie, *An Examination of Plato's Doctrines*, ii. 114. The sort of reason Crombie suggests for his interpretation ('For . . .') is criticized by P. F. Strawson, *Individuals* (London: Methuen, 1959), 6–19. Aristotle discusses problems about descriptions couched in general terms at *Metaph. Z* 15. Plato seems to believe that a description that is finely enough honed is in principle (if not in fact) always available.

imply that the objects about which I have beliefs must themselves figure in any direct way in my experience: if I read about DNA in a reliable textbook, I acquire beliefs about DNA that register in my memory, even though I am not directly acquainted with DNA itself; this is because DNA is suitably linked to experiences I have had, although I have not experienced DNA directly. Nor does an appeal to memory imply that my belief defies linguistic expression: to say that one needs experience and memories to have beliefs is not to say that one cannot fully express the content of these beliefs propositionally; it is at most to say that belief is context-dependent.

The point of primary interest to Plato, however, is not so much the relevance of context *per se* as that one must be able descriptively to identify the objects of one's beliefs—whatever sorts of descriptions such identifications will involve. It is because Plato insists on uniquely referring descriptions—unique within my experience or unique *tout court*—that he finds fault with the third account of *logos*: for on this third account, knowledge of x is true belief about x, plus having x's differentness in mind. But since true belief about x also requires having x's differentness in mind, the suggestion will not distinguish knowledge from true belief. If having something's difference in mind is necessary for true belief no less than for knowledge, having something's difference in mind cannot be what distinguishes knowledge from true belief.[28]

---

[28] Even if uniquely referring descriptions are necessary for true belief no less than for knowledge, one might think that there are relevant differences among sorts of distinguishing phrases, such that some, but not others, are necessary for knowledge; if so, Plato's first objection to the third account of *logos* fails. Thus, for example, I might initially distinguish Theaetetus from everyone else by reference to his peculiar nervous twitch; since I have his differentness in mind, this certifies that I have a true belief about Theaetetus. But perhaps I do not know Theaetetus until I can add to the initial description another one specifying his essence. If this is right, the following objection of McDowell's fails: 'it is surely absurd to suppose that if one distinguishing judgement does not constitute knowledge of a thing, two such judgements do. Why should mere weight of numbers have that sort of effect?' (*Plato: Theaetetus*, 257; see also White, *Plato on Knowledge and Reality*, 187 n. 58). McDowell is right to say that *weight* of numbers does not matter; but perhaps the *sort* of description does—if, for example, we can distinguish among accidental and essential descriptions. The cogency of this suggestion, of course, depends on what it is to specify a thing's essence. If a thing's essence may be completely specified by reference to intrinsic features of a thing, say Theaetetus' special character traits, then the suggestion is helpful. However, Socrates has already argued, in criticizing the second sense of *logos*, that no description of an isolated entity ever amounts to knowledge. In that case, no description of Theaetetus, on his own, will provide knowledge of him. None the less, it would still be wrong to say, as McDowell does, that there are *no* important differences among types of uniquely referring descriptions, even though, in the end, this fact may not help to rescue the third account of *logos* from Plato's first criticism.

VII

This still leaves the second horn of the dilemma, however. Socrates argues next that, to avoid the first horn of the dilemma, the definition should be revised to read 'knowledge of x is correct belief about x with knowledge of x's differentness' (210 A 3–5). This avoids the first horn of the dilemma by building a reference to knowledge into the definiens so that the definition now distinguishes knowledge from true belief, as the first horn, it was argued, did not—for obviously, true belief does not require *knowing* something's difference.

Socrates' criticism of the revised definition is disappointingly brief. He says only that 'when we're investigating knowledge, it would be very silly to say it's correct belief with knowledge of difference or of anything at all' (210 A 7–9). This time it is not the notion of difference as such that causes the difficulty, but the mention of knowledge in the definiens, for the revised definition is circular. Commentators have generally matched Socrates' brevity, and simply dismissed this option.[29] Then, since the first line of attack was successful, it is concluded that the third account of *logos* fails. Socrates' brief criticism merits more attention than it has received.

It is true that the definition as initially stated—'knowledge of x is correct belief about x with knowledge of x's difference'—is circular, for 'knowledge' occurs in both the definiens and definiendum. This result is not troubling, however, if the second occurrence of 'knowledge' can be eliminated; for in that case, the definition is not ultimately circular. We need to ask, then, what it is to have knowledge of something's difference. Happily, Plato has

---

[29] White, for example (*Plato on Knowledge and Reality*, 180), dismisses this option cursorily in a parenthesis. McDowell does discuss the problem of circularity (*Plato:* Theaetetus, 254, 256–7). But he does not suggest that Plato proposed a way out of the difficulty, and instead suggests that perhaps the problem of circularity accounts for the aporetic conclusion of the *Theaetetus*.

Interestingly enough, the issue of circularity is also broached at the beginning of the *Theaetetus*. At 146 D Theaetetus suggests that (1) knowledge is the art of shoemaking; Socrates objects that (2) the art of shoemaking is knowledge of how to make shoes, which in turn is equivalent to (3) knowledge is knowledge of shoemaking; but (3) is circular. Plato does not fault (3) simply because it is circular, however. His point is rather that (3) violates KBK: if you ask me what knowledge is, and I tell you that it is knowledge of how to make shoes, you won't thereby understand what knowledge is, since I've used 'knowledge', the term you didn't know, in the definiens (147 B). The point is the same as that made at *Meno* 75 C 8–D 7. For some discussion, see M. F. Burnyeat, 'Examples in Epistemology: Socrates, Theaetetus, and G. E. Moore', *Philosophy*, 52 (1977), 381–98. Burnyeat believes that Plato's argument is invalid; I am inclined to think KBK renders it valid.

already answered this question for us, and in such a way as to show that the definition is not ultimately circular.

In presenting his interrelation model of knowledge, Plato argued that one knows a given object o just in case one can properly relate o to other objects in the same field. One never knows just one object in isolation from others to which it is connected; knowledge always requires the ability systematically to interconnect the elements covered by a particular discipline via a series of interlocking true accounts. Thus, a person P knows an object o just in case o belongs in a single discipline such that P has the ability properly to relate each of the objects contained in the discipline to all the others. An object is known only if it belongs to a suitably large set of objects each member of which is known. Now to know any object, Plato has already told us, is to be able to provide an account of it relating it to other objects in the same field, objects whose interrelations, in turn, can also be suitably specified. This view allows us to eliminate the occurrence of 'knowledge' in the definiens, as follows: 'Knowledge of x is correct belief about x with the ability to produce accounts properly relating x to other suitably interrelated objects in the same field.' This revised definition is not circular. However, one may well raise other problems for it; I turn to one of these below. But it is at least clear that the interrelation model of knowledge allows us to rewrite the initial definition noncircularly in the way just specified. And in that case, the second horn of Plato's dilemmatic argument against the third account of *logos* fails—for reasons Plato has himself already provided.

To be sure, he does not draw this conclusion for us explicitly himself; instead, he ends the dialogue aporetically, as though his criticism is successful. But we need not take this aporia seriously. Just as Plato's conclusion to the *Protagoras* does not show that he doubts whether virtue is really knowledge and so teachable, so his ostensible conclusion here does not indicate genuine loss. Indeed, the prevalence of the interrelation model of knowledge in such later dialogues as the *Sophist, Politicus,* and *Philebus* shows that it is along such lines that Plato was thinking.[30]

---

[30] Burnyeat has objected to me that the prevalence of the interrelation model in later dialogues does not by itself show that Plato retains KL; indeed, Burnyeat argues that the interrelation model *replaces* KL. He suggests it is a difficulty for my view that nowhere in the later dialogues does Plato explicitly say that specifying interrelations provides a *logos* of an element. Of course, the absence of such explicit textual evidence would no more vitiate my view than it would prove Burnyeat's; defence of either view, with respect to the later dialogues, must involve a detailed study of them. But it is not entirely clear to me that there is no textual evidence for my view. See e.g. *Sph.* 253 B 10 (*dia ton logon*); Cornford translates 'on the voyage of discourse', implying logos$_s$, but logos$_k$ seems more appropriate here, where the context explicitly concerns knowing interrelations. At 252 C, it is said that one cannot help but include 'is', 'that', and the like in one's *logoi*, when speaking of elements; there

So far I have argued that Plato's interrelation model of knowledge allows us to rewrite the definition of knowledge noncircularly. The revised definition, however, may seem to raise other problems of its own. Plato has argued that to know a given object o, one must be able suitably to relate o to other objects in the same field, say m and n. Moreover, such interrelations count as knowledge only if m and n are themselves known: knowledge must be based on knowledge (KBK). Given KL, however, one counts as knowing m and n only if one can produce true accounts of them properly relating them to yet further objects in the same field, say a and b, which must themselves, given KBK, also be known. But now it looks as though either an infinite regress, or else a regress that is finite but circular, ensues. In the first case, to know anything, one will need to know infinitely many things. In the second case, a new sort of circularity has emerged—not, as initially, in the definition of knowledge but rather in the account-giving process: to know o one will need to appeal to, say, m and n, and so on, back again to o.[31]

Plato began by considering the view that accounts end with primary elements that themselves lack accounts. Given KL, such elements are unknowable. He then argued, correctly, that no appeal to unknowable elements will explain our purported knowledge of compounds: knowledge must be based on knowledge (KBK). Nor will it do to suggest that elements are known in some way other than through accounts: all knowledge requires a propositional account (KL). Plato then argued that there are suitable accounts for elements: one knows elements by locating and interrelating them in a systematic framework. But in thus retaining KL, along with KBK, at every stage of analysis, Plato commits himself to the view that accounts do not halt at any terminus; they continue on either linearly or circularly. It is a prospect anyone who maintains KL, along with KBK, must face. But is this result as unfortunate as Aristotle and others have supposed?

The view that the regress is infinite and linear need not concern us further here, for Plato's interrelation model of knowledge avoids it: on his view, one does not continue supporting claims to knowledge linearly *ad infinitum*, but only within the confines of a particular framework, music or

are clear echoes of the dream theory here. To be sure, '*logos*' here might be logos$_s$; but as the ensuing argument makes clear, admitting that 'is' and so on are applicable to elements involves conceding more than this: some set of statements involving 'is' will say what an element is, that is, will provide a logos$_k$ of it. See also the pun at *Phil.* 17 E 4–6. At *Pol.* 277 B 7–8 *ho logos* clearly means account; to be sure, the account at issue is of a statesman, which may from some points of view be a compound; but it is also an element, e.g. in statecraft.

[31] The regress problem is clearly set out, and related to the *Theaetetus*, by Armstrong, *Belief, Truth and Knowledge*, 153.

medicine, say.[32] Still, this leaves us admitting that accounts will circle back on themselves, within a particular discipline. I agree that this sort of circularity results from Plato's interrelation model. But it is not an unfortunate problem. Rather, it is one of Plato's significant contributions to epistemology to have seen that we do not possess bits of knowledge in isolated, fragmented segments. One never knows a single entity, in isolation from its ties to other things; all knowledge involves systematic interconnecting. Correspondingly, that one knows a particular object cannot be ascertained solely by looking at what one says about it, in isolation from one's general epistemic repertoire; one might have uttered an appropriate account by accident, without the proper understanding, and so not know the object at hand. But when one can expand one's claims beyond an isolated description of one object to a description of its interconnections in a systematic framework, such doubts are dispelled, for it would be unreasonable to suppose that that ability could also be exercised in the absence of knowledge. If the circle of our beliefs is sufficiently large, and the interconnections suitably comprehensive, the links in the circle are transformed from true beliefs into pieces of knowledge.[33]

[32] At least, this is so for L3-type knowledge (see ch. 4). It's true that the best sort of knowledge, L4, is more synoptic: it involves understanding the teleological structure of reality as a whole, seeing how various disciplines are related to one another and how they are organized around the form of the good. Still, there is no reason to suppose that one can have L4-type knowledge only if one actually provides infinitely many accounts; nor, as we've seen (in ch. 4), does such knowledge proceed in linear fashion. This is not to say that the *Theaetetus* agrees with everything the *Republic* says about knowledge. The point is just that even if its interrelation model of knowledge implies that, for the best sort of knowledge, one must be able to explain not only connections within a single discipline but also connections among various disciplines, it doesn't follow that explanation is entirely linear, or that one can know one thing only if one knows infinitely many things.

[33] Burnyeat also praises Plato for focusing on interrelations rather than on conditions for knowing an isolated entity. Armstrong, by contrast, considers but rejects the sort of position I have attributed to Plato, asking 'what criterion can be given to show that a circle of true beliefs is "sufficiently comprehensive"? It is not easy to say. And might there not be a sufficiently comprehensive circle of true beliefs which was arrived at so irregularly and luckily that we would not want to call it knowledge?' (*Belief, Truth and Knowledge*, 156). I agree that it is not easy to say what exactly sufficient comprehension consists in; but this does not show that the general approach is misguided. As to Armstrong's second question, I think Plato's answer would be 'no'. He allows that an isolated claim to know does not qualify as knowledge since it may be arrived at haphazardly or accidentally: that is the point of KBK. But if one's accounts are sufficiently comprehensive, one has knowledge and satisfies KBK. Plato may believe that in fact one can provide suitably interrelated accounts only by engaging in dialectic. But the criterion of knowledge, like the criterion of belief, focuses on what one can say—although one needs to say rather more on Plato's view than on some other views to count as knowing. Interestingly enough, Armstrong criticizes Plato in the *Meno* for rejecting what he calls a 'reliability' theory of knowledge; see p. 159. KBK explains Plato's rejection of such a theory as well.

11

Separation

Chōrismos is the only doctrine we can with certainty attribute to Plato.

(J. D. MABBOTT[1])

1. Introduction

At *Metaphysics M* 4, 1078^{b}30–1, and *M* 9, 1086^{b}32–^{b}5, Aristotle says that Plato, but not Socrates, separated (*echōrise*, 1086^{b}4) forms[2] or universals; at 1086^{b}6–7 he says that separation is responsible for the difficulties in Plato's theory of forms. What exactly is separation? Did Plato, but not Socrates, separate forms? And if so, is this for the reasons Aristotle suggests? Is Aristotle right to find separation so objectionable?

Answers to these questions are disputed. Some believe that to say that the form of F is separate is to say only that it is *different* from any or all F sensible particulars;[3] others believe it is to say that it *can exist independently* of *any given* F sensible particular;[4] yet others believe it is to say that it can exist independently of *all* F sensible particulars—the form of F can

---

[1] J. D. Mabbott, 'Aristotle and the *Chōrismos* of Plato', *Classical Quarterly*, 20 (1926), 72–9 at 72.

[2] [Here I delete a footnote concerning capitalization conventions, which is not relevant to the present edition. See Introduction, n. 62.]

[3] W. D. Ross, for example, in his *Aristotle's* Metaphysics (2 vols.; Oxford: Clarendon Press, 1924), vol. i, p. xliii, writes that 'to distinguish the universal from its particulars is in a sense to "separate" it. It is to think of it separately, and if the thought is not merely mistaken, this implies that the universal is a different entity from the particulars.' Ross goes on, however, to suggest that Aristotle has more in mind in saying that Plato separated forms. D. R. Morrison, 'Three Criteria of Substance in Aristotle's *Metaphysics*: Unity, Definability, and Separation' (diss. Ph.D., Princeton, 1983), suggests that what Aristotle means by 'separation' (*chōristos*) is 'numerical distinctness'; see his ch. IV.

[4] R. E. Allen, *Plato's* Euthyphro *and the Earlier Theory of Forms* (London: Routledge & Kegan Paul, 1970), 132. Allen believes that more than this sort of independent existence is involved in separation; he also believes, for example, that it is part of Aristotle's meaning that forms are particulars or individuals. However, although Aristotle seems to believe that particularity *follows* from separation, it is not part of what separation *consists in*.

exist whether or not any F sensible particulars ever do.[5] Others explicate separation spatially; the form of F is separate from F sensible particulars just in case it exists in a different place from them (or in no place).[6] Still others explicate separation in terms of a thesis about definability; forms are not definable in sensible terms alone.[7]

It is surprising and disheartening that the central term in the debate about separation is not fixed. But given that it is not, it is not surprising that there are different accounts of whether, and if so of why, Plato but not Socrates separated forms. Some argue that Aristotle is correct to say that Plato but not Socrates separated forms.[8] Others argue that Socrates and Plato both separate forms,[9] others claim that neither does.[10] There is genuine disagreement here, of course, only if the disputants use 'separation' univocally; but this is unfortunately far from clear.

Among those who believe Plato separates forms, accounts of his reasons vary. Some argue that he grounds separation on the flux of sensibles;[11] others point to the alleged facts that forms are paradigms,[12] or are non-

---

[5] W. F. R. Hardie, *A Study in Plato* (Oxford: Clarendon Press, 1936), 73; T. H. Irwin, *Plato's Moral Theory* (Oxford: Clarendon Press, 1977), 154. Actually, as Irwin defines separation there, it is a stronger notion, involving as well the claim that sensibles cannot exist independently of forms. This corresponds, not to Aristotle's notion of separation, but to his stronger notion of ontological priority; see below, sect. 2 and n. 19.

[6] G. F. Else, for example, in 'The Terminology of the Ideas', *Harvard Studies in Classical Philology*, 47 (1936), 17–55 at 55, writes: 'This exaltation of the true seat of the Ideas to a "place beyond heaven" is the transcendence of which Aristotle speaks.'

[7] Thus, Irwin, *Plato's Moral Theory*, 154, speaks of two doctrines of separation; one involves independent existence, but one involves forms not being definable in sensible terms alone. This latter is the thesis Irwin calls 'non-reducibility' (NR); see further below, sect. 6. In an earlier article, 'Plato's Heracleiteanism', *Philosophical Quarterly*, 27 (1977), 1–13, Irwin seems to conceive of separation primarily in terms of a thesis about definability, although he occasionally slides into talk about independent existence (see e.g. p. 2).

[8] e.g. Irwin, *Plato's Moral Theory*, ch. vi.

[9] e.g. Allen, *Plato's Euthyphro and the Earlier Theory of Forms*, 133–6.

[10] Thus A. E. Taylor, for example, under the mistaken impression that whatever a character called 'Socrates' in the dialogues says represents the thought of the historical Socrates, argues that in none of the early or middle dialogues are forms separated. Of course, he takes this partially to vindicate, rather than to undermine, Aristotle's claim that Socrates but not Plato separates forms. But if one believes that the middle dialogues represent Plato's thought, and that forms there are not separate, then the conclusion to draw is that Aristotle is wrong about Plato. See Taylor, *Varia Socratica* (Oxford: J. Parker & Co., 1911). That Plato did not separate forms is also argued by P. Natorp, *Platos Ideenlehre* (Leipzig: F. Meiner, 1903; 2nd edn., 1921), who is followed by J. A. Stewart, *Plato's Doctrine of Ideas* (Oxford: Clarendon Press, 1909).

[11] Irwin, *Plato's Moral Theory*, 144–55; 'Plato's Heracleiteanism'.

[12] Mabbott, 'Aristotle and the *Chōrismos* of Plato', 74.

spatial and/or nontemporal;[13] yet others argue that Plato's doctrine of Anamnesis entails separation.[14]

Plato might, of course, offer more than one argument on behalf of separation. But not each of these arguments, or alleged features of forms, can be used to justify separation in each of its many guises; our estimate of how good a given argument for separation is is interdependent with our account of what separation is. (Plato might, of course, argue invalidly for separation; this, too, has been maintained.[15])

Can any order be imposed on this chaos? Since Aristotle initiated the debate, the most reasonable procedure is to decide what *he* means in saying that Plato but not Socrates separated forms; we can then fix the sense of 'separation' accordingly, and proceed to evaluate his account of the basis and plausibility of separation. What *other* claims Plato and Socrates may, or may not, make about forms may well raise interesting questions; but they should not be confused with the question of separation.

I shall argue for the following claims:

(1) The separation (*chōrismos*) Aristotle typically has in mind in connection with forms is capacity for independent existence (IE); A is separate from B just in case A can exist without, independently of, B. To say that the form of F is separate is to say that it can exist without, independently of, F sensible particulars (1086[b]4) (Section 2).

(2) Aristotle is probably correct to say that at least some forms, in some dialogues, are separate. But he and others are incorrect to suggest that Plato, beginning with the *Phaedo*, heralds separation as a new feature of forms. On the contrary, so far from this being the case, Plato never even says that forms are separate; it proves surprisingly difficult to uncover any commitment to separation; and commitment to it emerges in unexpected ways and in unexpected cases (Sections 4–10).

(3) Aristotle's account of the basis of separation is incorrect. For he argues that Plato moves from the claim (that sensibles are in flux to the claim) that forms are substances to the conclusion that they are separate. But (although he may link flux to substantiality), Plato does not link substantiality and separation in the way required by Aristotle's argument. However, Aristotle avoids the popular mistake of thinking that Plato simply confuses, or moves fallaciously between, a difference and a separation claim. Further—

[13] e.g. W. D. Ross, *Plato's Theory of Ideas* (Oxford: Clarendon Press, 1951), 232.
[14] e.g. F. M. Cornford, *Plato and Parmenides: Parmenides' Way of Truth and Plato's Parmenides*, translated with an introduction and with a running commentary (London: Routledge & Kegan Paul, 1939), 74; M. F. Burnyeat, review of Irwin, *Plato's Moral Theory*, in *New York Review of Books* (27 Sept. 1979), 56–60.   [15] See Irwin, *Plato's Moral Theory*, 154–5.

though I shall not discuss this in detail—Aristotle also correctly avoids deriving separation from Anamnesis, or from the alleged paradigmatism, nonspatiality, or nontemporality of forms (Section 3).

(4) Aristotle is probably correct to say that Socrates is uncommitted to separation. However, lack of commitment to separation in Socrates is as muted as is commitment to it in Plato (Section 11); neither Plato nor Socrates devotes the sort of attention to the issue of separation that Aristotle's account leads us to expect. Though Aristotle may well get their commitments on the question of separation correct, he is misleading to suggest that the issue is of explicit concern to them; it is not one about which they argue or to which they call attention.

(5) Finally, although this will receive considerably less attention, Aristotle ought not to view the doctrine of separation with such scorn. Although it is controversial, it has serious philosophical credentials; nor does it lead to all the difficulties Aristotle alleges.

2. Varieties of Separation

What does Aristotle mean when he says Plato separated (*echōrise*) forms? The question is not easy to answer; Aristotle uses '*chōris*' and its cognates in a variety of ways.

Thus, for example, at *Physics* 5. 3, 226^{b}21–3, he writes that 'I call things together [*hama*] in place when they are in one primary place, and separate [*chōris*] when they are in different places'. Here A and B are separate from one another when they are in different places. I shall call this sort of separation *local separation*. Aristotle sometimes indicates that he has it in mind by speaking, not of separation *tout court*, but of separation in place (*topō(i)*).[16]

Aristotle also speaks of being separate in definition (*chōriston logō(i)*) (*Metaph. H* 1, 1042^{a}29); A is definitionally separate from B just in case A can be defined without mention of (the definition of) B.[17]

Aristotle also uses '*chōris*' and its cognates to indicate capacity for inde-

[16] See e.g. *De An.* 413^{b}14, 17; *Metaph.* 1016^{b}2, 1052^{b}17, 1068^{b}26, 1092^{a}19. This is, or is close to, the sort of separation Else, for example, associates with forms; see n. 6.
[17] Aristotle also speaks of definitional separation at e.g. *De An* 432^{a}20, 433^{b}25; *Metaph.* 1030^{b}25, 1064^{a}24. Sometimes he speaks instead of definitional priority; cf. e.g. *Metaph.* 1018^{b}33, 1028^{a}32, 1077^{b}13. Definitional priority implies, but is not implied by, definitional separation. Notice that although definitional separation implies NR, the converse is not true. For NR leaves open the possibility that (definitions of) sensibles be mentioned in definitions of forms, so long as they do not exhaust such definitions; whereas definitional separation requires that no reference to (definitions of) sensibles be included in definitions of forms. See sect. 6, and nn. 7 and 37.

pendent existence (IE). At *Metaph. Z* 1, 1028^{a}31–^{b}2, for example, he says that substance is prior in three ways: in nature, definition, and knowledge.[18] He explains the natural priority of substance by saying that 'of the other categories, none is separate [*chōriston*], but only it' (1028^{a}33–4). 'Separate' is not explained; but at *Metaph. Δ* 11, 1019^{a}1–4, he writes that 'a thing is prior in respect of its nature and substance when it is possible for it to be without other things, but not them without it; this division was used by Plato' (trans. Kirwan). Here Aristotle says that A is naturally prior to B just in case A can exist without B but not conversely; in *Z* 1 he says that substance is naturally prior to other things because only it is separate. Assuming that 'natural priority' has the same sense in the two passages, it follows that A is separate from B just in case A can exist without, independently of, B. Another sort of separation, then, is *capacity for independent existence* (IE), or what I shall also sometimes call *ontological separation*.[19] This is the relevant sort of separation in connection with the natural priority of substance; it is associated with Plato (*Metaph. Δ* 4, 1019^{a}4); and it is said to be the fundamental sort of priority (1019^{a}11–12). Aristotle sometimes indicates that he has it in view by speaking of separation *haplōs*—separation without qualification. At *Metaph. H* 1, 1042^{a}28–31, for example, he contrasts being *chōriston logō(i)* with being *chōriston haplōs*, where this latter indicates IE.

It is important to note that these three sorts of separation—local, definitional, and ontological—are independent of one another. At *Metaph.*

---

[18] At 1028^{a}32–8 I read: *kai physei kai logō(i) kai gnōsei*—adding '*physei*' to, and deleting '*chronō(i)*' from, Jaeger's text. This emendation is, however, unnecessary for my argument.

[19] IE matches Hardie's account of separation; see sect. 1 and n. 5. Irwin also uses the acronym 'IE', though his account of it corresponds instead to Aristotle's notion of natural priority; see *Plato's Moral Theory*, 154, and n. 5. Morrison, 'Three Criteria of Substance in Aristotle's *Metaphysics*', objects to the claim that the sort of separation Aristotle especially associates with substance is IE; but his arguments are unconvincing. One argument he gives is that ' "*Chōristos*" just does not mean "independent" in Greek; it means "separate"' (126). One might just as well object, on this ground, to his claim that '*chōristos*', for Aristotle, means 'numerical distinctness' by claiming that no, it means 'separate'. 'Capacity for independent existence' is an effort to give content to, to explain the force of, 'separate'; and it certainly involves no mistranslation to suppose that that is its force. Morrison also argues that 'capacity for independent existence' would indicate separability, not actual separation; that '*chōristos*' indicates actual separation; and so '*chōristos*' cannot mean 'capacity for independent existence' (126). I agree that '*chōristos*', at least in connection with forms, indicates actual separation. But I think that *actual* separation is a *modal* notion; I discuss this further below. Morrison also objects that Socrates, for example, is supposed to be separate from the sun; but since he cannot exist if it does not, separation cannot be IE (127). This objection rests on the view that each substance, for Aristotle, is supposed to be separate from every other substance. But I do not think this is Aristotle's view; rather, his view is that each substance is separate from nonsubstances. This view may lead to difficulties in its turn—but they are difficulties, not for my account of separation, but for Aristotle. I discuss some of the difficulties arising here in ch. 15.

M 2, 1077^{a}30–^{b}11, Aristotle himself notes that definitional and ontological separation are independent of one another. White, he says, is definitionally prior to white man, since the definition of the former does not include that of the latter, though the converse is not true. But white is not ontologically prior to white man, since it cannot exist without it.[20] And though Aristotle does not explicitly address the question of the connection between ontological and local separation, they too are independent of one another. The quantity of matter that now constitutes me can exist independently of me; but it is not now locally separate from me. IE, then, does not imply local separation. Nor does local separation imply IE. My shadow and I are in different places; but it cannot exist independently of me.[21]

There may be other sorts of separation beyond our three;[22] but these are the ones of primary concern to us here. Which, if any, does Aristotle intend when he says Plato separated forms?

Separation, of course, is always separation *from* something. In the case of Platonic forms, Aristotle makes it clear that separation is separation from sensible particulars (*Metaph. M* 9, 1086^{b}4).[23] Hence our question is really: what does Aristotle mean when he says forms are separate from sensible particulars? (None the less, I shall sometimes follow Aristotle's lead and speak simply of the separation of forms, without troubling to add 'from sensible particulars'.)

As we shall see, Aristotle may believe forms are separate in each of our three ways—locally, definitionally, and ontologically. But when he says that Plato separated forms—when he actually uses '*chōris*' and its cognates of forms—he typically has IE in mind.

[20] Aristotle's remark is odd, however. For white surely can exist without white man, so long as something else is white. On the independence of definitional and ontological priority (separation), see also G. E. L. Owen, 'Logic and Metaphysics in Some Earlier Works of Aristotle', in I. Düring and G. E. L. Owen (eds.), *Aristotle and Plato in the Mid-Fourth Century: Papers of the Symposium Aristotelicum Held at Oxford in August, 1957* (Studia Graeca et Latina Gothoburgensia, 11; Göteborg: Elanders Bocktryckeri Aktienbolag, 1960), 163–90, esp. 170–3.

[21] Neither does either of definitional or local separation imply the other; but this need not concern us here.

[22] Thus, for example, Aristotle also speaks of priority (separation) in thought (at e.g. *Phys.* 2. 2, 193^{b}34, on which see below, this section); in knowledge (*Metaph. Z* 1, 1028^{a}31–3); in time (*De An.* 427^{a}3); in extension (*De An.* 429^{a}11, 430^{a}20, 433^{b}25). For other references, see H. Bonitz, *Index Aristotelicus* (Berlin: Reimer, 1870), 859^b–860^b. A new computer study of Aristotle's use of '*chōris*' and its cognates may be found in Morrison, 'Three Criteria of Substance in Aristotle's *Metaphysics*'.

[23] J. Stenzel, *Zahl und Gestalt bei Platon and Aristoteles* (Berlin: Teubner, 1933), 133 ff., argues by contrast that in criticizing the Platonic separation, Aristotle is criticizing Plato's account of the relation of genera to *infimae species*. For some criticism, see H. F. Cherniss, *Aristotle's Criticism of Plato and the Academy* (Baltimore: Johns Hopkins Press, 1944), n. 122.

That IE is at least one sort of separation he associates with forms is strongly suggested by the passage quoted above from *Metaphysics Δ* 11. And there is more than a suggestion of IE in the following passage from the *Eudemian Ethics*:

For they say that the good-itself is the best thing of all, and the good-itself is that to which it belongs to be both first among goods, and the cause by its presence, for other things, of their being goods. For, they say that it is of *that* object, above all, that the good is truly predicated—other things being goods through sharing in it, and similarity to it; and it is first among goods—since, if the object in which things share were taken away, with it would go all the things that share in the form, and are called (what they are called) through sharing in it; and that is the way that the first stands in relation to what comes after. And indeed, like the other forms, the form of the good is separate from the things that share in it. (1. 8, 1217^{b}2–16, trans. Woods)

Aristotle is explaining why the Platonists take the form of the good to be first among—naturally prior to—other goods. At 1217^b he suggests they do so because they believe other goods depend on, cannot exist without, the form of the good. Now if the form of the good were similarly dependent on other goods, it would not be prior to them; there would be mutual dependence instead. Hence Aristotle must be assuming that for Plato the form of the good can exist without, independently of, other goods. Nor is this merely assumed. At 1217^{b}15–16 Aristotle says that the form of the good, like other forms, is separate from (*chōriston*) its participants. It seems clear that 'separation' here indicates IE: at 1217^{b}11–13 Aristotle says that other goods depend on the form of the good; at ^{b}15–16 he says that the form of the good (like other forms) is separate from—that is, can exist without—its participants; the conjunction of these two claims gives us the natural priority of the form of the good that Aristotle is explaining.

IE is also the relevant sort of separation in the crucial passage in *Metaphysics M* 9, to be explored in detail below (in Section 3), where Aristotle explains the original impetus of the theory of forms (1086^{a}32–^{b}13). He argues that the Platonists make forms both particulars and universals. They are particulars, he claims, because they are separate. For forms are substances; substances are separate; and whatever is separate is a particular. Whatever sort of separation is at issue here, then, must be implied by substantiality and imply particularity. IE—and only IE—meets these conditions. This can be seen as follows.

In *Metaphysics Z* 1, as we have seen, Aristotle claims that all and only substance is separate; and separation, here, is IE. So substantiality implies IE.

Aristotle also believes that IE implies particularity. In *De Interpretatione* 7 he defines universals as follows: 'by universal I mean that which by its nature is predicated of many things' (17^{a}39–40). One might think he means only that universals *can* be predicated of many things; but in fact he means that universals must *actually* be predicated of many things. Universals, then, cannot exist uninstantiated—cannot, that is, enjoy IE from particulars. Hence, if something enjoys IE from (other) particulars, it cannot be a universal and so is a particular. (Aristotle assumes, not unreasonably, that everything is either a particular or a universal.[24]) Correspondingly, Aristotle repeatedly insists that no universal is separate—and it is clear he has IE in mind.

IE, then, is implied by substantiality and implies particularity. This is not so, however, for local or definitional separation. Substantiality, first of all, does not imply local separation—does not, that is, imply local separation from all (other) sensible particulars, which, as we have seen, is what separation is separation from. My desk is in the same place as its constituent matter and as its nonsubstance property instances; some of these are sensible particulars. Hence my desk is not locally separate from all other sensible particulars; and so being a substance does not imply being locally separate in the relevant way. Local separation cannot, then, be the sort of separation at work in *M* 9.

Substantiality does, on the other hand, imply definitional separation. But definitional separation does not imply particularity. On the contrary, at *Metaph. Δ* 11, 1018^{b}32–3, Aristotle claims that *universals* are definitionally prior; particulars, then, are presumably *not* definitionally prior, and so cannot be definitionally separate. And in *Metaphysics Z* 15, as well as elsewhere, Aristotle denies that particulars are definable;[25] in that case, they cannot be definitionally separate from anything. For if A is definitionally separate from B, A must, at the least, be definable. Hence definitional separation cannot be at issue in *M* 9 either.

If only IE explains the course of the argument in *M* 9, presumably it is the sort of separation to hand. Correspondingly, IE is also likely to be the relevant sort of separation in those many passages where Aristotle associates forms with separation, substantiality, and/or particularity. Given the prevalence of such passages, coupled with the centrality of *M* 9—it is Aristotle's fullest account of separation—we are justified in assuming that IE is at least one central sort of separation.

This is not to say, however, that Aristotle does not also associate defini-

---

[24] This is not to say, of course, that Aristotle does not believe that there are different sorts of universals and particulars.

[25] See e.g. *Post. An.* 1. 8; contrast *Metaph. M* 10.

tional or local separation with forms. Although neither is in view in *M* 9, or in other passages concerned with particularity and/or substantiality, or in the *Eudemian Ethics* passage considered above, perhaps they are in view elsewhere. Let us see.

One might argue that Aristotle does *not* take forms to be locally separate from sensibles, on the following ground: for A and B to be locally separate from one another, they must be in different places. But Aristotle insists that forms are 'nowhere' (*Phys.* 3. 4, 203ᵃ8–9); hence they are not in a different place from, and so are not locally separate from, sensibles. However, one might resist this argument in turn. One might argue, for example, that Aristotle would allow us to broaden the notion of local separation so that A and B are locally separate from one another just in case they are not in the same place. Forms, not being in any place, are not in the same place as, and so are locally separate from, sensibles. Alternatively, one might note that Aristotle sometimes contrasts forms that are elsewhere (*ekei*) with sensibles that are here (*entautha*);[26] if he intends this contrast literally, perhaps he at least sometimes conceives of forms as being in a place, though in a different one from sensibles, so that they are locally separate from sensibles, even on the initial account of that notion.

Aristotle may believe that forms are locally separate from sensibles, then, although this is unclear. But even if he does, I know of no place where he uses '*chōris*' or its cognates to indicate this. The passages most likely to do so are those few where Aristotle says that forms are not in (*en*) sensibles and then, in short compass, that they are separate ('*chōris*') from them.[27] It might be thought that the denial that forms are in sensibles indicates local separation, so that '*chōris*', at least in these passages, indicates it too.

But this should not be too readily assumed. First, as a quick glance at *Physics* 4. 3 reveals, 'in' need not be used locally; it can be used, for example, to indicate dependence of some sort. If 'in' is so used in those few passages where forms are said not to be in sensibles, it does not indicate local separation; correspondingly, there is no presumption that near occurrences of '*chōris*' do either. But even if 'in' is used locally, the '*chōris*' that occurs near it need not be local too—and this for two reasons. First, Aristotle never, even here, directly opposes being in and being separate. He never says that because forms are not in things, they are separate from them; or that because they are separate, they are not in them. But second, even if there were this direct contrast, and even if 'in' were local, it would not follow that

---

[26] *Metaph. M* 4, 1079ᵃ31. For '*entautha*', see also the *Peri Ideōn*, in Alexander, *In Metaph.* 83. 7 Hayduck ('*ekei*' is not used here).

[27] See especially *Metaph. M* 5, 1079ᵇ17, with 1079ᵇ35–1080ᵃ2.

'*chōris*' is local too. In *Metaphysics M* 1–2, for example, Aristotle considers two views of the relation between numbers and sensibles—that numbers are separate from, or are in, sensibles. Here 'in' seems to be local; but separation appears to be IE. So even where 'in' is used locally, and directly contrasted with being separate, separation need not be local too. And so far as I can see, in the very few passages where '*en*' and '*chōris*' appear in close proximity—though not in direct opposition—to one another, '*chōris*' might well be IE.

So even if Aristotle believes forms are locally separate, he does not use '*chōris*' to indicate this. Further, Aristotle never, in saying that forms are *chōris*, complements '*chōris*' with '*topō(i)*'. Yet one might expect him to, at least once, were local separation in view. Moreover, local separation is symmetrical; if A is locally separate from B, B is locally separate from A. But in speaking of the separation of forms, Aristotle says only that they are separate from sensibles; he never suggests that sensibles are similarly separate from forms. Indeed, in the *Eudemian Ethics* this is denied. If the relevant sort of separation is nonsymmetrical, it cannot be local.

What, now, of definitional separation? In *Physics* 2. 1 Aristotle writes:

Both the student of nature and the mathematician deal with these things; but the mathematician does not consider them as boundaries of natural bodies. Nor does he consider things which supervene as supervening on such bodies. This is why he separates them; for they are separate in thought [*chōrista tō(i) noēsei*, 193ᵇ34] from change, and it makes no difference; no error results. Those who talk about ideas do not notice that they too are doing this: they separate physical things though they are less separate than the objects of mathematics. That becomes clear if you try to define the objects and the things which supervene in each class. Odd and even, straight and curved, number, line, and shape, can be defined without change but flesh, bone, and man cannot. (193ᵇ31–194ᵃ6, trans. Charlton with minor alterations)

Here Aristotle claims that forms are separate in thought from change. One might take this to show that forms are definitionally separate from sensibles;[28] and if so, then at least here Aristotle uses '*chōris*' of forms to indicate definitional separation.

Still, three points must be borne in mind. First, this is, so far as I know, the only passage in which Aristotle uses '*chōris*' and its cognates

---

[28] On the other hand, it is not entirely clear that one ought to take separation in thought either to be or to imply definitional separation; or separation from change to be or to imply separation from sensible particulars. If one does not, then this passage is no evidence that Aristotle takes forms to be definitionally separate from sensibles. Even so, however, it would, of course, show that Aristotle associates some sort of separation other than IE with forms.

of forms to indicate definitional separation. Second, notice that, in contrast to *M* 9—indeed, in contrast to every other passage in which Aristotle associates separation (*chōrismos*) with forms—an appropriate complement (*tē(i) noēsei*) is supplied, to make it clear that IE is not in view. Once again, then, if 'separation' occurs without a complement, the natural inference is that it indicates IE.

Third, Aristotle seems to believe that definitional separation is a mistake only for *some* forms, not for all. One cannot adequately define forms of natural things without reference to change; but one can—indeed, one should—define forms of mathematicals without reference to change. Yet Aristotle typically inveighs against separation as such; it is a big mistake for *any* form. This is not so of definitional separation; but it is so, in Aristotle's view, of IE.[29] Once again, then, IE, not definitional separation, is presumably in view in most of the discussions of forms, since separation is, there, taken to be a mistake for all forms.

I conclude, then, that although Aristotle may take forms to be locally and definitionally, no less than ontologically, separate, ontological separation (IE) is the central sort of separation he associates with forms.

I shall now, then, fix the sense of 'separation' in terms of IE. When I ask whether forms are separate, I mean: do they enjoy IE from, can they exist without, sensible particulars? This, at least, is the question Aristotle—in contrast, we have seen, to many other commentators—typically has in mind; and we shall have enough work to do to evaluate his answer.

Notice that Aristotle sometimes says that forms are *chōrista*, at other times that they are *chōris* (e.g. *Metaph. Z* 16, 1040ᵇ27–8). Does anything turn on this terminological difference? To say that forms are *chōris* is to say that they are *separate*. But *-ton* endings in Greek are ambiguous; to say that forms are *chōrista* might be to say either that they are (*a*) separate, or that they are (*b*) separable. Now as *Metaphysics Δ* 11 and *Z* 1 reveal, for A to be *chōriston* from B is for A to be *able* to exist without B—a modal claim. One might then suppose that for A to be *chōriston* from B is for A to be *separable* from B, where this means to be *able* to exist without B; and that to be *chōris* from B is to be separate from B, where this means *actually* to

---

[29] There is a problem here. Aristotle suggests that definitional separation is a mistake for some forms. Yet in *Metaph. Δ* 11, 1018ᵇ32–3, discussed above, he suggests that universals (of which forms are a subclass) are definitionally prior (and so definitionally separate). It is unclear, then, why he thinks definitional separation is *ever* a mistake; for if forms are universals, they are definitionally separate. Perhaps different sorts of definitional separation are in view in the two passages, or perhaps (see n. 28) separation in thought in our *Physics* passage is not the same as definitional separation. I am inclined to think there are deep problems (not for our account but) for Aristotle lurking here; see ch. 15.

exist without B. In the case of forms, this would be to say that forms are such that nothing sensible instantiates them. If this is right, then Aristotle attributes to Plato not only the claim that forms *can* exist without anything sensible instantiating them, but also the claim that forms do so exist.

But I do not think this is correct. Aristotle seems to use '*chōris*' and '*chōriston*' interchangeably in his accounts of forms, and to use both to mean capacity for independent existence, to indicate, that is, a modal claim. Since '*chōris*' cannot easily mean 'separable', I take it that '*chōris*' and '*chōriston*' therefore both mean 'separate'; to be separate from sensibles is to be able to exist without them.

Thus, for example, we have seen that in *Metaphysics Z* 1 Aristotle says only that substance is *chōriston*; yet at *Metaph. Z* 16, 1040^{b}27–9, he commends the Platonists for making forms to be *chōris*, given that they are substances—here '*chōris*' conveys no more than capacity for independent existence. Further, a typical example of a form that is *chōris* is the form of man; but clearly this is not an example of a form that nothing sensible instantiates. Indeed, Aristotle seems to believe that the Platonists do not want forms for (sorts of) things that never exist (e.g. centaurs),[30] though he thinks they quite willingly countenance separation.

Separation, then, is a modal claim—forms can exist independently of sensible particulars. It follows that forms might be separate even if sensibles always instantiate them. If nothing sensible instantiates a given form, it follows that that form is separate; but this is only sufficient, and not also necessary, for separation. Correspondingly, to reject separation, one must reject not only the view that there are forms that nothing sensible instantiates, but also the view that it is *possible* for there to be any.[31]

At this point, if not before, a question naturally arises: why is separation so bad? If to say that forms are separate is just to say that they can exist independently of sensible particulars; and if, as Aristotle and I believe, forms are universals, then to say that forms are separate is just to say that (some) universals can exist uninstantiated (by sensible particulars). To be sure, the doctrine that universals can exist uninstantiated is a controversial one, and one Aristotle repeatedly rejects; but though controversial, it is unclear that it

[30] See e.g. the Object of Thought argument in the *Peri Ideōn*, recorded by Alexander, *In Metaph.* 81. 25–82. 7 Hayduck.

[31] Contrast M. D. Rohr, 'Empty Forms in Plato', in S. Knuutila (ed.), *Reforging the Great Chain of Being* (Boston: Reidel, 1980), 19–56. Rohr takes it as obvious that some forms are at least temporarily uninstantiated; he takes the important question to be whether any forms are *always* uninstantiated, and so concludes that forms are not separate or, rather (I suppose, on the assumption that Aristotle must be correct on this score at least), that separation does not consist in independent existence.

merits the scorn Aristotle heaps on it. How could it be thought, for example, that countenancing the possibility of uninstantiated universals turns them into particulars? It might be thought that, since Aristotle believes separation is so bad, yet IE is relatively innocuous, another account of separation is needed.

But this thought should be resisted. For though ascribing IE to universals may seem innocuous to philosophers of certain persuasions, we have seen that it does *not* seem innocuous to Aristotle: *he* believes that if universals enjoy IE, they must be particulars. For as he defines universals, they *cannot* exist independently of particulars; if something can exist independently of (other) particulars, it must itself be a particular. It is not, then, a count against IE's credentials that Aristotle believes separation is absurd—though it may well be a count against *Aristotle* that he believes this. At least, he needs to provide plausible reasons for his definition of universals; he cannot simply stipulate that they cannot exist uninstantiated.

Even if Plato separates universals, then, it is unclear that this leads to the difficulties Aristotle dockets. The real challenge may be to discover— not why or whether Plato separates universals, but—why Aristotle is so convinced that universals cannot exist uninstantiated. This is not to say, of course, that Plato's theory of forms is ultimately acceptable or even coherent; it is only to say that whatever flaws we find in it, it is not clear they stem from separation, from the claim, that is, that universals can exist uninstantiated (by sensible particulars).

Having seen what Aristotle means by 'separation', let us now see why, and with what justification, Aristotle believes Plato separates forms.

3. Aristotle's Account of the Basis of Separation

Aristotle describes the origins of the theory of forms in three passages in the *Metaphysics*: *A* 6, 987^{a}32–^{b}7; *M* 4, 1078^{b}9–1079^{a}4; and *M* 9, 1086^{a}31– ^{b}11. These are not the only passages in which he records arguments for the existence of forms; but they are the central ones.[32] I shall examine each passage in turn.

First a general point. In none of our three passages does Aristotle mention Anamnesis, or claim that forms are nonspatial, nontemporal, or paradigms. This surely suggests that he does not take these doctrines, or (alleged)

---

[32] Aristotle records other arguments for the existence of forms in, for example, the *Peri Ideōn*; but unlike the *Metaphysics* passages, these arguments do not purport to represent Plato's original motivation for introducing forms.

features of forms, to be important in understanding the origins of the theory of forms. This suggestion is reinforced by other considerations. First, so far as I know, Aristotle never even claims that forms are nontemporal; so it is unclear that he even takes them to be nontemporal. Second, although he occasionally suggests they are nonspatial, he does not do so often. Third, although he does mention Anamnesis, he does not seem to believe it is important to the metaphysics (as opposed to the epistemology) of the theory of forms. In the Argument from Relatives in the *Peri Ideōn*, for example, he omits all reference to Anamnesis, although the argument is based on a passage in the *Phaedo* which closely links Anamnesis and forms.[33] Finally, although, as the Argument from Relatives and other passages attest, Aristotle takes paradigmatism seriously, it is unclear he believes it grounds separation; separation is not mentioned in the Argument from Relatives, for example, although paradigmatism is to the fore. I shall assume, then, that whatever may be true of Plato, Aristotle—again in contrast, as we have seen, to many other commentators—does not believe that the basis of separation consists in Anamnesis, nonspatiality, nontemporality, or paradigmatism.

Flux, by contrast, is prominent in each of our three *Metaphysics* passages. This suggests that at least Aristotle takes flux to be important in understanding the origins of the theory of forms. The crucial question, correspondingly, and the one I shall focus on in this section, is what role, if any, he believes flux plays in the separation of forms.

On one familiar view, Aristotle believes Plato uses flux as an invalid argument for separation. In fact, flux only proves that forms are *different* from sensibles; but, according to Aristotle, Plato invalidly moves from their difference, to their separation, from sensibles.[34] In this section, I shall challenge some features of this view.

In *Metaph. A* 6 Aristotle writes:

The philosophies discussed were succeeded by Plato's work, which followed these in most ways; but it had special features in contrast to the philosophy of the Italians. For in his youth he first became familiar with Cratylus and with the Heracleitean beliefs, that all sensibles are always flowing and that there is no knowledge of them; and he supposed these things later too. But Socrates was concerned with ethical things, and not at all with the whole of nature; he was seeking the universal in ethical things and was the first to turn his thought to definitions. Plato agreed with him; but because of ⟨his Heracleitean beliefs⟩ he supposed that this ⟨defining⟩

---

[33] Alexander, *In Metaph.*, 82. 11–83. 17 Hayduck; cf. *Phd.* 73 A–77 A.

[34] For this view, see e.g. Irwin, *Plato's Moral Theory*, esp. 144-55, and 'Plato's Heracleiteanism'. Though he does not put the matter in just this way, I believe I correctly capture the central claim he wishes to make.

applied to different things [*heterōn*] and not to sensibles—for, he thought, it is impossible for the common definition to be of any of the sensibles, since they are always changing. These sorts of beings, then, he called 'ideas'. (987ᵃ29–ᵇ8)

The argument may be schematized as follows:

(I) (1) (x) (x is a sensible→x is always changing).
  (2) (x) (x is always changing→x is unknowable and indefinable).
∴ (3) (x) (x is a sensible→x is unknowable and indefinable).
  (4) There are definitions and knowledge.
  (5) Definitions and knowledge are of something.
∴ (6) There are objects different from (*heterōn*, 987ᵇ5) sensibles, that are the objects of knowledge and definition.
  (7) These are ideas.
∴ (8) There are ideas.

(1)–(3) rule out the possibility of knowing or defining sensibles, on the ground that they are always changing, are always in flux. I take it that sensibles (*aisthēta*) include not only sensible particulars, but also sensible properties; and that the relevant sort of flux includes not only real change through time but also relational change. It is not, or not only, that, for example, Theaetetus is constantly gaining or losing weight, but rather, or also, that, for example, three feet is both long and short—long for an ant, short for an elephant. Compresence, at least as much as succession, of opposites is relevant here, and it attaches to properties as well as to particulars.[35]

Since there are definitions and knowledge (4), however, and since they require objects (5), there must be nonsensible objects, objects different from (*heterōn*) sensibles, that are the objects of knowledge and definition (6). The Platonists called these objects 'ideas' (7)—or, as they are sometimes called, and as I shall generally call them, 'forms'. And so there are ideas (8).

(1)–(6) do not make it clear whether forms are nonsensible universals or particulars. But in later passages it is made clear that they are intended, at least in the first instance, to be universals; and though (1)–(6) do not require this, it is the natural interpretation of the passage as a whole. For Aristotle claims that Socrates was seeking universals and definitions; the suggestion is that universals are the objects of definition (and so of knowledge). And Aristotle then remarks that Plato accepted Socrates' teaching; it is just that

---

[35] See Irwin, 'Plato's Heracleiteanism', for a defence of this interpretation of Aristotle. Although I do not accept all of Irwin's account of *A* 6, I agree with his account of what flux there involves.

he proposed different objects of definition—nonsensible (sc. universals), not sensible ones.

Forms, then, are nonsensible properties or universals, universals *different* from sensible particulars or properties. But are they also separate? It is striking that Aristotle does not say so explicitly; neither '*chōris*' nor its cognates occur in the argument or, indeed, anywhere in book *A* until chapter 9 (991^{b}1). Nor does (I) use '*para*'—which can but need not import separation—of forms.[36] Furthermore, (1)–(5) only yield the claim that there are entities different from sensibles; and all (6) claims is that there are entities different from sensibles. Nor do (7)–(8) seem to license more than this; Aristotle simply remarks that Plato dubbed the entities generated by the flux argument 'ideas'. To be sure, one might argue that (I) is an invalid argument for separation; but neither is invalidity mentioned. Perhaps, then, Aristotle believes that Plato uses flux to argue not for separation, but only for nonsensible universals, for universals different, but not necessarily separate, from sensibles.[37]

This may seem unsatisfactory: surely *A* 6 purports to explain what is distinctive about Plato's theory of forms; surely separation is what is distinctive; flux is the only argument to hand; so surely (I) is meant to show that flux is the argument for separation?

We need not conclude this. First, separation is not *all* Aristotle takes to be distinctive of Plato's theory of forms; he also takes countenancing nonsensible universals to be distinctive of it, and flux is relevant here (see Section 11). Second, we shall see later that Plato does not ground separation on flux. If our account of (I) so far is correct, Aristotle sees this; on the alternative account, he does not. I conclude for now, then, that (I) is not presented as an argument for separation, but only for universals different from sensibles. Later (see the discussion of *M* 9, below) we shall in fact need to modify this conclusion—although not in the way the alternative account suggests.

I now turn to *M* 4:

---

[36] See, however, the odd use of '*para*' at 987^{b}8, and Ross's note ad loc.

[37] Does (I), however, validly show that forms are definitionally separate from sensibles? This is unclear. On the one hand, (I) involves the claim that sensibles are not definable; so definitions of them will not occur in definitions of forms. On the other hand, nothing in (I) precludes the possibility of sensibles being mentioned in definitions of forms; and if this possibility is actual, and incompatible with definitional separation, then (I) does not imply that forms are definitionally separate from sensibles. Whether or not (I) in fact implies that forms are definitionally separate from sensibles, it is not presented as an argument for definitional separation, any more than it is presented as an argument for IE. (I) does, on the other hand, show that forms enjoy NR; see above, nn. 7 and 17, and below, sect. 6.

The belief about forms came about to those who spoke about them because, as regards truth, they were persuaded by the Heracleitean arguments that all sensibles are always flowing, so that if knowledge and thought are to be of anything, there must, in their view, be some different natures, besides [*para*] sensibles, remaining; for there is no knowledge of flowing things . . . But Socrates did not make universals or definitions separate [*chōrista*]; but they (the Platonists) separated them, and they called these sorts of beings 'ideas'. (1078^{b}12–17, 30–2)

The argument is the following:

(II) (1) (x) (x is a sensible→x is always changing).
      (2) (x) (x is always changing→x is unknowable).
  ∴ (3) (x) (x is a sensible→x is unknowable).
      (4) There is knowledge.
      (5) Knowledge requires the existence of permanent natures, universals.
  ∴ (6) There are nonsensible natures, universals, besides (*para*) sensibles.
      (7) Nonsensible universals are separate.
      (8) Nonsensible universals are ideas.
  ∴ (9) There are separate ideas.

Aristotle first presents (II) (1)–(6) (1078^{b}9–17). He then breaks off to discuss Socrates. Then, at 1078^{b}30–2, he remarks that Socrates did not separate universals or definitions, whereas the Platonists did; and they called these separated universals 'ideas'. This gives us (7)–(9).

(II) (1)–(6) closely parallel (I) (1)–(6). Aristotle again begins from the Heracleitean claim that sensibles are always changing, and infers on Plato's behalf that this renders them unsuitable as objects of knowledge. Hence, since there is knowledge, there must be stable, nonsensible objects of knowledge. These, as 1078^{b}30 makes clear, are universals the Platonists call 'ideas'.

(II) (1)–(6), like (I) (1)–(6), are a valid argument for entities different, but not separate, from sensibles. Correspondingly, Aristotle uses '*heteras*' (1078^{b}15) but not '*chōris*' or its cognates. He also uses '*para*' (^{b}16), which can but need not import separation. Since it is used in connection with '*heteras*' here, presumably it means 'difference', not 'separation', here.

Still, in (II) (7), in contrast to (I), the entities generated by the flux argument are said to be separate. Does not this suggest that the flux argument is the argument for separation after all?[38]

This is not the only possibility. Notice that Aristotle again describes

[38] One might suggest that (II), even more clearly than (I), is intended to argue for definitional separation; for does not Aristotle say that Plato but not Socrates separated

the flux argument $((1)-(6) = 1079^b12-17)$ without mentioning separation; separation is not mentioned until *later*, at 1078^b30. Nor is it there said to issue from flux; Aristotle says *that*, but not *why*, Plato separated universals. Perhaps Aristotle believes, then, that Plato separates the entities generated by the flux argument—not *because* of flux, but—for other reasons not here adduced.

Let us turn, finally, to *M* 9:[39]

For they make the ideas both universal and again, at the same time, as separate [*chōristas*] and as particulars. But it has been argued before that this is impossible. The reason those who said the substances were universal combined these things ⟨universality and particularity⟩ into the same thing is that they did not make them ⟨the substances⟩ the same as sensibles. They thought that the particulars in sensibles were flowing and that none of them remained, but that the universal is besides [*para*] these things and is something different [*heteron ti*] from them. Socrates motivated ⟨this view⟩ through definitions; but he at least did not separate ⟨universals⟩ from particulars. And he was right not to separate them. This is clear from the results. For it is not possible to acquire knowledge without the universal; but separating is the cause of the difficulties arising about the ideas. But they, on the assumption that it was necessary that, if there were to be any substances besides [*para*] the sensible and flowing ones, they be separate [*chōristas*], had no others, but they set apart the substances spoken of universally; so that it followed that universal and particular ⟨natures⟩ were almost the same natures. This in itself, then, would be one difficulty for the view discussed. $(1086^a31-{}^b11)$

I take the argument to be the following:

(III) (1) Sensibles are in flux. $(1086^a37-{}^b1)$
  [(2) (x) (x) is in flux→x is unknowable and indefinable).]
  [(3) There is knowledge and definition.]
  (4) Knowledge and definition require universals. (1086^b5-6)
  [∴](5) There are nonsensible universals, universals different from (*para, heteron ti*) sensibles. (1086^b1-2)
  (6) Nonsensible universals are forms.

definitions (1078^b30-1), and is not this to say that Plato but not Socrates accepts definitional separation? But I take it that 'definitions', in 1078^b30-1, means the *objects* of definition, i.e. universals; and to say that the objects of definition are separate is to say that they enjoy IE. I do not deny that forms are definitionally separate, or that Aristotle thought this; I deny only (i) that in (II), Aristotle uses '*chōris*' to do duty for definitional separation, and (ii) that (II) is directed at definitional separation. Nor is it even clear (II) implies definitional separation; see n. 57.

[39] In the translation that follows, I use Jaeger's text. In my schematization of the argument—(III)—I have put in brackets steps or inferences I take to be implicit, but not explicit, in the text.

(7) There are nonsensible substances. ($1086^a36–7, ^b1–2$)

(8) The only candidates for nonsensible substances are nonsensible universals, the forms. ($1086^b7–10$)

(9) Nonsensible substances are separate. ($1086^b8–9$)

∴ (10) Forms are separate.

(11) (x) (x is separate→x is a particular). ($1086^a33–4, ^b9–11$)

∴ (12) Forms are both universals and particulars. ($1086^a32–4, ^b10–11$)

Aristotle is explaining why Platonic forms are both universals and particulars. The flux argument is adduced to explain why they are universals: knowledge and definition require the existence of stable, nonsensible universals, universals the Platonists call 'forms'. But why are forms also particulars? The reason, Aristotle suggests, is that the Platonists believe, correctly, that there must be some nonsensible substances. But they don't know what these nonsensible substances can be other than their forms ($1086^b9–10$). Nonsensible substances, however, are separate ($1086^b8–9$); and so forms are separate. But whatever is separate is a particular ($1086^a33–4, ^b9–11$). Hence forms are not only universals, but also particulars.

We have already questioned part of this argument: it is not clear that separation implies particularity; perhaps universals can be separate—can exist independently of sensible particulars—without thereby being particulars. But our more immediate concern is that (III) contains a subargument—indeed, a valid subargument—for the separation of forms: (5)–(10) constitute such an argument. Only in *M* 9 is the question of the basis of separation explicitly addressed; once addressed, a valid argument is adduced on its behalf; and that argument is not (just) the flux argument.

To be sure, flux is part of the story: it is used to justify (5); it explains why there must be nonsensible universals, universals *different* from sensibles. But to get to the further conclusion that they are *separate*, further considerations—considerations not explicit in *A* 6 or *M* 4—are adduced: that these universals are substances, and that substances are separate. Once these considerations are added to the flux argument, separation validly results; but flux alone does not, and is not said by Aristotle to, license it. Perhaps separation is not mentioned in *A* 6, then, because it only considers flux, and flux does not get us to separation. And although separation is mentioned in *M* 4, Aristotle does not claim that flux is its basis—perhaps because he does not believe that that is its basis.

Notice that when Aristotle records the flux argument, he again uses only '*para*' and '*heteron*' ($1086^b1–2$). It is only when he turns to forms as substances, as at 1086^{b}9, that he uses '*chōris*' and its cognates. This is as it should be. For flux only yields a claim of difference; separation issues instead from the substantiality of forms.

I conclude so far, then, that, in contrast to the familiar view sketched at the beginning of this section, Aristotle does not suggest that Plato fallaciously slides from the fact, licensed by flux, that forms are different from sensibles, to the conclusion, seemingly not licensed by flux, that they are separate from them. Rather, he suggests that Plato uses flux as a valid argument for forms different from sensibles; their separation is then validly inferred by adding to this conclusion the twin claims that forms are substances and that substances are separate.

If all the evidence we had to hand were (I)–(III), our conclusion would, I think, be the right one to draw. There is, however, further evidence to consider; and it requires some modification in our account. We can approach this modification by noting that although (III) (5)–(10) are a valid argument for separation, Aristotle would of course deny that it is sound. To be sure, he accepts (5) and (7). He also accepts (9); indeed, as we have seen, he accepts the stronger claim that all substances are as such separate. Nor is (6) troubling; it simply tells us what forms are. Aristotle rejects (8), however. Although he agrees that there are both nonsensible substances and nonsensible universals, he resists identifying the two sorts of entities. For no universal, in his view, can be a substance, since none can be separate, yet substances must be. Aristotle's alternative candidates for nonsensible substances are the prime and planetary movers which, being particulars, are, from his point of view, nonproblematically separate.

(8) is the culprit, then. But why does Aristotle believe Plato accepts it? In *M* 9, he seems to imagine Plato reasoning as follows: 'There must be some nonsensible substances; nonsensible universals are at least nonsensible; and anyway, what other candidates are there?' Obviously, this line of reasoning is unsatisfactory; and elsewhere Aristotle is more generous.

At *Metaph. H* 1, 1042^{a}15–16, he says that forms are thought to be substances for the same reason genera and universals are. Although he does not say here what this reason is, he is presumably thinking of their key role in knowledge and definition. It is because universals (and so genera and forms) are thought to be basic to knowledge and definition that some take them to be substances. So Aristotle's ultimate explanation of why Plato accepts (8)—or, at least, the weaker (8′) forms are substances—is that Plato infers it from the key role forms play in knowledge and definition.

Now Aristotle does not in fact believe that this inference is legitimate. To be sure, he concedes that priority in knowledge and definition are necessary for substantiality; but he does not seem to believe they are sufficient. In addition, substances must be separate; and priority in knowledge and definition do not guarantee separation.[40] So although in *M* 9 Aristotle gives Plato a valid argument for the separation of forms—(III) (5)–(10)—he in fact seems to believe that Plato's argument on behalf of one of its key premisses—(8)—is invalid.

Not only that, but we can also see how this alleged invalidity is lurking in the flux argument. At least, as Aristotle records it, the flux argument involves the claim that forms are the only objects of knowledge and definition; and this guarantees what Aristotle takes to be the crucial premiss grounding the substantiality of forms.

We must, then, modify our initial account. Earlier I suggested that Aristotle claims only that flux is a valid argument for universals different from sensibles; their separation is then inferred from adding to this conclusion the twin claims, that universals are substances and that substances are separate. Now it emerges, however, that Aristotle believes that Plato derives the substantiality of forms (universals) from the flux argument; and he also believes that that derivation is invalid. For, in his view, all the flux argument shows is that universals are different from sensibles, and are basic to knowledge and definition; but this does not guarantee their substantiality. So the flux argument is, in Aristotle's view, invalid after all—if its conclusion is taken to be that forms are (not only different from sensibles but are also) substances.

There are still three important differences between my account and the familiar one sketched at the outset. First, it is still true that Aristotle does not explicitly claim either that the flux argument is invalid or that it grounds the substantiality of forms. In order to find these further claims in Aristotle, we need to venture beyond *A* 6, *M* 4, and *M* 9, and piece together an account he nowhere himself explicitly presses. Our initial account is still the best reading of arguments (I)–(III), considered in isolation. Second, on the familiar account, the invalidity Aristotle dockets consists in the move from difference to separation—a crude mistake. On our alternative, the mistake Aristotle finds consists in the move from 'basic to knowledge and

---

[40] Here I retract a claim made in my 'Plato and Aristotle on Form and Substance' (below, ch. 15), where I argued that Aristotle takes each of definitional and epistemic priority to be sufficient for substance. Notice that if the claim there is correct, Aristotle must concede that the flux argument is a valid argument for separation; for it ensures that forms are prior in knowledge and definition, and so are substances and so, since substances are separate, that they are separate. This result, however, is perhaps a good reason to deny that each of definitional and epistemic priority is sufficient for substance—although Aristotle could, of course, still argue that the flux argument is unsound.

definition' to 'substance'. Although Aristotle regards this move as invalid, it is also a move with which he has some sympathy; it is not simply a crude mistake. And third, it may be misleading to speak of invalidity here at all. To be sure, *Aristotle* believes the move is invalid, because he believes that priority in knowledge and definition are insufficient for substantiality. But as we shall see, it is far from clear that Plato agrees; he may believe that being basic to knowledge and definition in the way forms are *is* sufficient for substantiality. That is to say, what we have here may not be a case of Aristotle detecting an invalid move on Plato's part, but rather a confrontation between two competing conceptions of substance: Aristotle believes priority in knowledge and definition are not enough, but Plato disagrees.

To summarize my account of Aristotle on separation. If we look only at *Metaphysics A* 6, *M* 4, and *M* 9, it looks as though Aristotle suggests that Plato only uses flux as a valid argument for nonsensible universals; and that their separation is then validly derived from the addition of two premises, that forms are substances and that substances are separate. So far, separation issues as the conclusion of a valid argument—in striking contrast to the familiar view.

If, however, we look further afield, we can see that Aristotle believes that Plato's argument for the claim that forms are substances is invalid. And, moreover, the seeds of the alleged invalidity are in the flux argument, though Aristotle does not himself point this out. Still, this is not to embrace the familiar view. For at the very least, the alleged invalidity is importantly different from the one the familiar view claims to detect. Indeed, as we have seen, it is unclear we should even speak of invalidity here. What we may have instead is a disagreement between Plato and Aristotle about the criteria for substance. This is a point I return to later, in looking at Plato's notion of substance.

Having seen what Aristotle means in saying that forms are separate, and having looked at his account of the basis of their separation, let us now turn to Plato. Does he separate forms? And if so, what are his reasons?

4. Plato's Use of '*Chōris*'

Aristotle claims that Plato, but not Socrates, separated forms or universals. Commentators have often accepted his verdict. Ross, for example, writes that it is in the *Phaedo*—allegedly the first thoroughly Platonic, as opposed to Socratic, dialogue—'that Plato first expresses a clear belief in the separate existence of the Ideas'.[41] Cornford claims that 'The separation (*chōrismos*) of the forms is explicitly effected in the *Phaedo*.'[42]

If by 'explicit' Cornford means—as his parenthetical use of '*chōrismos*' might lead us to expect—that in the *Phaedo* Plato applies '*chōris*' or its cognates to forms, his claim is false. Indeed, it is quite striking that *nowhere* in the middle dialogues, even allowing that the *Timaeus* is a middle dialogue, does Plato use '*chōris*' or its cognates of forms. The soul is often enough said to be *chōris* or *chōristē* from the body; and in the *Timaeus*, knowledge and belief are said to come to be *chōris* from one another (51 E 1–2). But '*chōris*' and its cognates are never, in the middle dialogues or *Timaeus*, used of forms. Given Aristotle's tendency to use '*chōris*' and its cognates for the allegedly distinctive Platonic claim, this is striking and suggestive.

It is true that in two later dialogues, the *Parmenides* and *Sophist*, Plato applies '*chōris*' to forms, or to form-like entities. But it is not clear this involves commitment to IE.

At *Sophist* 248 A, in the famous 'friends of the forms' passage, the Eleatic Stranger says: 'You speak of becoming [*genesis*], on the one hand, and of substance [*ousia*], on the other, dividing them separately [*chōris*], I suppose' (248 A 7). This one brief mention of '*chōris*' does not clearly convey the sense of 'capacity for independent existence'; it need mean no more than that *genesis* and *ousia* constitute disjoint classes. Indeed, it is unlikely that '*chōris*' does indicate IE here. For separation seems to be symmetrical: *genesis* and *ousia*—sensibles and forms—are separate from one another. But sensibles cannot exist independently of forms. To be sure, Socrates need not participate in the form of white; but he could not exist unless he had some complexion or other, and so he is not independent of colour forms generally. And if there is a form of man, as there clearly is at least by the time of the *Timaeus*, then Socrates is not independent of *that* form.

In any case, it is not even clear that Plato is committed to the views of the friends of the forms; certainly he is not speaking *in propria persona*. So even if '*chōris*' indicates IE here, we cannot assume that Plato accepts it.[43]

At *Parmenides* 129 D 6–8 Plato writes: 'but, as I said just now, if someone first distinguishes the forms separately [*chōris*], themselves by themselves [*auta kath' hauta*] . . .'. As in the *Sophist*, so here, '*chōris*' need indicate no more than difference; forms and sensibles are disjoint. This is reinforced by the fact that '*chōris*' is again used to indicate a symmetrical relationship (see e.g. 130 B 2–5). Since sensibles cannot exist independently of forms as

[41] Ross, *Plato's Theory of Ideas*, 125.   [42] Cornford, *Plato and Parmenides*, 74.
[43] See, most recently, J. Malcolm, 'Does Plato Revise his Ontology in *Sophist* 246c–249d?', *Archiv für Geschichte der Philosophie*, 65 (1983), 115–46.

such, '*chōris*' should not be IE here.[44] (Or, if it is, it is not a thesis Plato ever accepted.)

Further, Plato goes on to raise various difficulties for the theory of forms just adumbrated; yet none of these difficulties seems to involve the assumption that forms are separate (enjoy IE). In 132 A–B, for example, he sets out a regress argument that came to be known as the Third Man Argument. Although a separation assumption figures prominently in Aristotle's version of the argument (though it is difficult to figure out why),[45] none occurs explicitly in, nor is any tacitly required by, Plato's version. This is unsurprising if the difficulties being aired here are not directed against a theory of separate forms; but if they are, then it is surprising.

But again, even if the difficulties aired do affect a theory of separate forms, we cannot assume Plato ever accepted such a theory. First, we cannot infer that whatever theory he accepts in the *Parmenides* is also in play elsewhere. And second, even if a theory of separate forms is in play in the *Parmenides*, it is unclear Plato accepts it, even there. The *Parmenides* is dialectical and aporetic; it explores objections to different positions and espouses no final views. Plato could as well be telling us what he does *not* believe, is not committed to, as setting out difficulties for a theory he ever accepted.

Of course, even if '*chōris*' is not applied to forms in the middle dialogues or *Timaeus* (or when applied to them, or to entities like them, in later dialogues, does not indicate IE), this does not show that Plato is not committed to separation. It blocks one route to that destination; but there might be other routes to it.

5. Other Terminological Evidence of Separation

We might, for a start, look at other terminological evidence of separation. Cherniss, for example, cites various passages from the *Timaeus* (51 B–52 C), and remarks that they involve 'statements of the transcendence of

[44] Contrast R. E. Allen, *Plato's* Parmenides: *Translation and Analysis* (Minneapolis: University of Minnesota Press, 1983), who takes '*chōris*' here to indicate IE, and accepts the implication that here, in contrast to elsewhere, separation is symmetrical; much of his commentary on the first part of the *Parmenides* is predicated on this view. Irwin, *Plato's Moral Theory*, 320 n. 37, also thinks '*chōris*' here indicates IE, though the matter is not pursued.

[45] Aristotle's most detailed account of the Third Man Argument is in his *Peri Ideōn*, recorded by Alexander, *In Metaph.* 84. 22–85. 3 Hayduck. I discuss Plato and Aristotle on the Third Man Argument in 'Aristotle and the More Accurate Arguments', in M. Schofield and M. Nussbaum (eds.), *Language and Logos* (Cambridge: Cambridge University Press, 1982), 155–77; and in 'Owen, Aristotle, and the Third Man', *Phronesis*, 27 (1982), 13–33. See now also my *On Ideas: Aristotle's Criticisms of Plato's Theory of Forms* (Oxford: Clarendon Press, 1993), chs. 15–16.

the ideas that no impartial judge could overlook or sophisticate away. It would have been impossible for the question to be put more concisely and unambiguously.'[46] To highlight the allegedly unambiguous statements of 'transcendence', Cherniss underlines three key phrases: '*einai ti*', '*para*', and '*auto kath' hauto*'. But in fact, none of these phrases unambiguously indicates separation.

'*Einai ti*' means 'is something'. But forms could 'be something' without being separate from sensibles. At *Prt.* 330 c 1 Socrates asks Protagoras whether justice is something or nothing; Protagoras agrees that it is something. It is not usually supposed that he has agreed that justice is a separate form. Or again, at *Phd.* 64 c 2 Socrates asks Simmias 'Do we suppose that death is something?' Simmias agrees that we do; but he has not yet agreed to any analysis of *what* it is. As it turns out, death is agreed to involve the separation of the soul from the body. But this agreement goes beyond the agreement that death is something. '*Einai ti*', then, is not unambiguous evidence of separation.

Nor is '*para*', as Cherniss well knows. As he himself points out, Aristotle, for example, uses '*para*' sometimes to indicate separation—but sometimes to indicate mere difference.[47] So the mere use of the word creates no presumption in favour of separation. Of course, we might discover that in a particular context, '*para*' indicates separation, not difference. But this would have to be decided by close attention to the argument to hand; the use of the word, on its own, does not decide the issue, and in fact, later we shall find that the contexts in which '*para*' is embedded do not require it to mean 'separation'.

What of '*auto kath' hauto*'? One might argue that in the *Phaedo*, Plato speaks interchangeably of the soul's being *chōris* from the body, and its being *autē kath' hautēn*, so that when he speaks of forms being *auta kath' hauta*, this indicates separation. But I do not think this is right. To be sure, when the soul is *chōris* from the body, it exists without it; and it is also then *autē kath' hautēn*. But although being *chōris* implies being *auto kath' hauto*, the converse is not true. Thus, for example, Plato speaks of the soul of the philosopher trying to be *autē kath' hautēn* so far as possible (65 c 7); I do not think he means that the philosopher is trying to exist without his body (even though, to be sure, he regards philosophy as a preparation for death). Rather, he means that the philosopher tries to be uninfluenced by the body so far as possible; he tries to reason without being influenced by sense perception, which is misleading in the search for truth. To be *auto kath' hauto*, that is, is to be uninfluenced by, unmixed with, anything

---

[46] Cherniss, *Aristotle's Criticism of Plato and the Academy*, 209.   [47] Ibid., n. 56.

alien. Given the ways of the world, it might be the case that the soul of the philosopher cannot be *autē kath' hautēn* while incarnate; but it does not follow that the two conditions—being *auto kath' hauto* and separate—are the same.

In the case of forms, to be *auta kath' hauta* is also to be uninfluenced by, unmixed with, anything alien. This involves two things. First, as Owen has argued, each form is *auto kath' hauto* in that each excludes its opposite; the form of equal, for example, is *auto kath' hauto* in that it is equal but not also unequal—in contrast to sensibles, which are commingled with their opposites.[48] But to say that forms exclude their opposites is not to say that they can exist independently of sensibles. So forms can be *auta kath' hauta* in this way, without being separate.

Second, forms are also *auta kath' hauta* in that each is unmixed with anything sensible. But neither does this require separation. All that is required is that forms be nonsensible; their nature involves nothing sensible. Consider, by way of analogy, the example of drink at *Rep.* IV, 437 A–438 E: in so far as one is thirsty, one desires drink, itself by itself—just drink, and not any particular sort of drink. It does not follow that there can be drinks that are not of any particular sort, but only that the sort of drink a drink is is irrelevant to it *qua* relatum of thirst. '*Auto kath' hauto*' serves to focus attention on the thing itself; it does not indicate that anything enjoys IE.

Turning to other terminological evidence, one might note that, in the middle dialogues, Plato speaks of sensibles participating in forms; and one might then argue that to say that A participates in (*metechei*) B 'does not imply the presence of B itself in A or rather would deny such a presence'.[49] But to say that A participates in B surely is *not* to deny that B is 'present in' A. As has often been noted, participation language as such implies 'nothing technical or metaphysical';[50] it can be used quite neutrally. Indeed, Ross, in his survey of the terminology of the theory of forms, counted participation language as evidence of *immanence*—not as evidence of separation.[51] Ross may well be wrong to have done so; but the fact remains that the use of such language does not by itself imply separation.

But does not Plato, unlike Socrates, deny that forms are in (*en*) sensibles,

---

[48] G. E. L. Owen, 'A Proof in the *Peri Ideōn*', *Journal of Hellenic Studies*, 77 (1957), 301–11; repr. in R. E. Allen (ed.), *Studies in Plato's Metaphysics* (London: Routledge & Kegan Paul, 1965), 293–312 (latter pagination), esp. 305–11.

[49] N. Fujisawa, '*Echein, Metechein*, and Idioms of "Paradeigmatism" in Plato's Theory of Forms', *Phronesis*, 19 (1974), 30–58 at 32.

[50] R. Hackforth, *Plato's* Phaedo (Cambridge: Cambridge University Press, 1955), 143 n. 1 (cited by Fujisawa, '*Echein, Metechein*, and Idioms of "Paradeigmatism" in Plato's Theory of Forms', 44).   [51] Ross, *Plato's Theory of Ideas*, ch. XVII.

and does not this imply that they are separate from them? It is not in fact entirely clear that Plato does—or does consistently—deny that forms are in sensibles. At *Phd.* 100 D (cf. *Rep.* 476 A), for example, he leaves open the possibility that forms are present in (*parousia*) or commune with (*koinōnia*) their participants. But in the *Timaeus*, Plato characterizes each form as being 'ungenerated, indestructible, neither receiving anything else into itself from elsewhere nor itself going into anything else anywhere', in contrast to sensibles, which 'come to be in some place' (52 A 1–6); so let us concede for the sake of argument that forms are not in sensibles.[52]

Still, what follows? It all depends on what 'in' means. As we saw in looking at Aristotle, 'in' is quite elastic; on some uses, to say that x is not in y is not to say that x can exist independently of y.

In the *Timaeus*, 'in' seems to be local; forms are not located where sensibles are. But it does not follow that forms are separate from—can exist independently of—sensibles. My shadow does not exist where I do, but it cannot exist independently of, and so is not separate from, me. The denial that forms are in sensibles, then, does not imply that they can exist without them.

One might protest that Plato means to deny, not just that forms are where sensibles are, but also that they are in any place; they are not in sensibles, in the sense that they have no location at all. But anything that lacks location is separate from sensibles.

I am unsure what to say here; intuitions seem to vary. Some would deny that lack of location implies separation. Mental states, as the epiphenomenalist conceives of them, for example, might be held to have no location, but to be dependent on various physical states; if so, lack of location does not imply separation. But even if it does, we could at most infer that if forms lack location, they are in fact separate. We could not also infer that *Plato* would agree; perhaps he would deny that nonspatiality as such implies separation.

What of the alleged eternality of forms? I am unsure whether eternality implies separation; intuitions seem to vary here too. However, even if it does, this is of limited use to us. To be·sure, forms may be eternal in the *Timaeus*; so if—if—eternality implies separation, forms are separate in the *Timaeus*. But it is important to be clear about two things. First, Plato never mentions any such inference; so even if we, looking at the *Timaeus*,

---

[52] It is not entirely clear one ought to concede this, even for this passage in the *Timaeus*. To say that forms 'do not go into anything else anywhere' need not be to say that forms are nowhere or are not in anything; they don't 'go into anything' because they don't move or change. But they might, for all that, *be* in something. I explore the possibility of forms being in things in ch. 12. Still, let us waive this possibility for the sake of argument.

would say that because forms there are eternal, they are separate, it is
unclear Plato would agree. But second, and perhaps more important, even
if forms are eternal in the *Timaeus*, it is unclear they are eternal elsewhere.
To be sure, Plato often enough characterizes forms as being *aei onta*; but
this need imply no more than that forms are everlasting, sempiternal—
and sempiternality does not imply separation. Even if eternality implies
separation, then, this will at best explain separation in the *Timaeus*—and
perhaps not even there.[53]

What of the fact that forms are *aitiai*, causes or explanatory entities? Do
not causes temporally precede their effects, so that forms, being the causes
of sensibles, must have existed before, and so are separate from, them? If,
as Aristotle believes, forms are efficient causes, this might seem reasonable.
But Aristotle is wrong about that; and anyway, even on his view, efficient
causes need not precede their effects.

What of the language of models and copies? It is important to note,
first of all, that such language is not as prevalent as one might suppose. It
is not, for example, used to describe the relation of forms to sensibles in
the *Phaedo*, where separation is often thought first to occur. On the other
hand, in the *Euthyphro* (6 E 3–6), where separation is thought *not* to occur,
it is suggested that forms are models (*paradeigmata*). So the mere fact that
'*paradeigma*' is used of a form is insufficient to guarantee that it is separate;
one needs to see precisely how the term is being used.

And even if—what I doubt—Plato means that forms are literally models
of which sensibles are copies, separation does not ensue. To be sure, if A
is a model for B, perhaps A needs to exist before B. But it does not follow
that A existed, or could exist, in the absence of any copies of it. If time is
infinite, and if each sensible is a copy of a model form, all that follows is
that for any *given* sensible, its form existed before it.

Of course, if time is finite, and if creation takes time, then if each sensible
is a copy of a model form, there was a time when at least some models,
but no copies of them, existed. But this derives separation, not from the
model–copy account on its own, but from that account *coupled with* a
particular temporal claim. (I shall ask later whether or not Plato accepts
the temporal claim.) The fact remains that the model–copy relation, on
its own, does not require separation. To be sure, we might find it natural
to assume otherwise; but whether Plato's intuitions match ours is another
question. It is worth noting too that Aristotle at least once suggests that
being a model is *incompatible* with separation. A model, he says, requires

[53] On the alleged eternality of the forms, see J. Whittaker, 'The "Eternity" of the Platonic
Forms', *Phronesis*, 13 (1968), 131–44.

copies; nothing is a model unless it has copies. Since forms are essentially models, they are essentially dependent on, and so are not separate from, their copies (Alexander, *In Metaph*. 86. 13–23 Hayduck). To be sure, Aristotle is criticizing Plato here. But the point remains that merely to say that forms are models does not guarantee separation. We need to explore the contexts in which that characterization occurs, to see what arguments it is intended to elucidate.

What of the perfection of forms? Surely forms, being perfect, cannot depend on mundane sensibles? But what does the perfection of forms consist in? It has been plausibly argued that to say that the form of F is perfect is only to say that, unlike F sensibles, it is F and not also not-F; it is not commingled with its opposite. And, in contrast to sensibles, the form of F is always F, both in the sense that so long as it exists, it is F—it cannot lose its F-ness—and also in the sense that it always exists. But if this is all that is involved in the perfection of forms, separation does not follow.[54]

One might concede that no single word or phrase or metaphor requires separation, yet argue that the general *tenor* of the dialogues at least strongly suggests it. For surely it is incredible that Plato could have believed that forms—those objects of such great reverence—are dependent on mundane sensibles? But perhaps other features of forms than IE are sufficient to explain Plato's attitude to forms. He believes, for example, that forms are perfect, everlasting, and unchanging, the basic objects of knowledge and definition, objects suitable for a discarnate soul's reflection. None of these features requires separation;[55] but they might be sufficient to explain Plato's attitude to forms. IE might provide an additional reason; but it is unclear that it is needed. Indeed, if separation is just IE, it is unclear it is so grand a property anyway. Certainly many philosophers have believed that universals can exist uninstantiated, without also according them any special importance. So IE appears to be neither necessary nor sufficient for explaining Plato's attitude to forms. Separation may seem a natural accompaniment; but surely we need stronger evidence than that to commit him to it.

The terminology and tenor of the theory of forms, then, do not require separation; separation may seem a natural part of the package, but it is not

---

[54] On the perfection of forms, see J. C. B. Gosling, 'Similarity in *Phaedo* 73b *seq*.', *Phronesis*, 10 (1965), 151–61; followed by A. Nehamas, 'Plato on the Imperfection of the Sensible World', *American Philosophical Quarterly*, 12 (1975), 105–17.

[55] We have already suggested that neither perfection nor everlastingness implies separation, Later I suggest that neither does being unchanging; and our discussion of the flux arguments, in sect. 3, shows that neither does being basic to knowledge and definition (see also sect. 6 below). I consider separation and the soul in sect. 8.

required (or excluded) by the evidence we have examined so far. Perhaps, however, if we turn to Plato's arguments, we shall be led to re-evaluate that evidence.

6. Plato on Flux and Separation

On one familiar view Plato separates forms because of some sort of flux in sensibles. Is this view correct?

There is, of course, considerable dispute as to the precise nature of Plato's flux arguments. Some believe he is primarily concerned with flux in sensible particulars, in the sense that they undergo constant and radical change through time; just as forms are altogether exempt from change, so sensible particulars lack stability in every respect.[56]

Now Plato does, of course, believe that sensible particulars change through time; he may even believe they change in *some* respect all the time. But he does not believe they change in every respect all the time, or are not self-identical through time. Indeed, in the *Phaedo* he claims that a corpse

although liable to be dissolved and fall apart and to disintegrate, undergoes none of these things at once, but remains as it is for a fairly long time—in fact, for a very considerable time . . .; and even should the body decay, some parts of it, bones and sinews and all such things, are still practically immortal. (80 c 2–d 4; cf. 86 c–d)

Nor are these claims contradicted by Plato elsewhere in the dialogues.[57]

Furthermore, although sensible particulars do of course change through time, and although Plato often adverts to this in characterizing the differences between forms and sensibles, he does not rely on this fact in arguing for the existence of forms. As Owen and others have pointed out, here 'it is with the compresence and not the succession of opposites that he is expressly concerned'.[58] It is relational, not real, change that chiefly concerns Plato in arguing for forms—that what is large, for example, is also small, or that what is heavy is also light. Such change, moreover, attaches not only to sensible particulars—Theaetetus is tall (in relation to Socrates) and short (in relation to Milo)—but also, and primarily, to sensible properties—the action type of standing firm in battle is both brave and cowardly, in that it has some brave, and some cowardly, tokens. The flux of sensibles on

---

[56] See e.g. R. Bolton, 'Plato's Distinction between Being and Becoming', *Review of Metaphysics*, 29 (1975), 66–95.

[57] For a defence of this claim, see Irwin, 'Plato's Heracleiteanism'.

[58] Owen, 'A Proof in the *Peri Ideōn*', 307.

which Plato focuses attention in arguing for forms, then, is compresence of opposites as it attaches to sensible particulars and, more especially, to sensible properties.

But does consideration of such flux license separation? Whatever Plato may think, it does not do so in fact. Consider, for example, the famous argument of *Phaedo* 74:[59]

> (1) Equal sticks and stones, sometimes, being the same, appear equal to one, unequal to another. (74 B 7–10)
> (2) The equals themselves never appeared unequal to you, nor equality inequality. (74 C 1–3)
> ∴ (3) These equals (sc. the equal sticks and stones) and the equal itself are not the same (*ou tauton*). (74 C 4–5)

This argument has been examined in detail by numerous commentators; for our purposes here, I can be brief. Plato assumes that there is something properly called 'equality' or 'the equal itself'. The question he raises concerns its nature: is it the same as, or different from, sensible equals? (1)–(3) argue that it is different from them, on the ground that sensible equals have a property that anything properly called 'the equal itself' lacks: the property of appearing equal to one, unequal to another. 'Appears', in Greek, can function veridically, to mean 'manifestly is', and, I take it, so functions here. Hence the differentiating property is that of being both equal and unequal. Sensible equals have this property; that is to say, they suffer the compresence of opposites, and so are in flux. Since the equal itself escapes such compresence, it is different from sensible equals. Let us call this nonsensible equal itself 'the form of equal'.[60]

Is the form of equal separate from sensible equals? The argument proves no such thing; it proves only that the form is different from, nonidentical to, sensible equals. Does Plato think the argument proves more than difference? He does not say so. He introduces the argument to show that equality is *para, heteron* from sensibles (74 A 11); his use of '*para*' interchangeably with '*heteron*' suggests his argument is directed to difference, not separation. And the argument's conclusion asserts only difference, not separation: the equal

---

[59] I follow Burnet's text of *Phd.* 74 B–C. At 74 B 8, I take '*tō(i) men . . . tō(i) d' ou*' to be masculines, not neuters. For detailed discussion of the passage see D. Gallop, *Plato:* Phaedo (Oxford: Clarendon Press, 1975), along with my review in *Philosophical Review*, 86 (1977), 101–5; and K. W. Mills, 'Plato's *Phaedo* 74b7–c6', *Phronesis*, 2 (1957), 128–47, and 3 (1958), 40–58.

[60] Somewhat strikingly, Plato does not call it so here; '*eidos*' and '*idea*' are not used of forms in the *Phaedo* until 102 B.

itself and sensible equals are *ou tauton* (74 c 4–5)—not the same. Neither the language nor the logic of the argument suggests separation.

Other passages relying on flux admit of the same analysis: they are valid arguments for difference, but not for separation; nor does Plato say they prove more than difference. Consider, for example, the famous argument at the end of *Republic* V, where Plato distinguishes knowledge from belief. He argues that knowledge entails truth and an adequate explanation, and that such explanations are forthcoming only by reference to nonsensible forms. We cannot, for example, define beauty in terms of a certain colour or shape; for some things are beautiful that lack that colour or shape, and its addition to something does not always enhance the thing's beauty. Sensibles, that is (at least in a certain range of cases), suffer the compresence of opposites, and so are in flux; reference to them therefore cannot provide adequate explanatory accounts; knowledge, however, requires such accounts, and so cannot be won by reference to sensibles alone, and so must go beyond sensibles to nonsensible forms.[61]

The flux arguments, then, are valid arguments for forms different, but not separate, from sensibles; if Plato believes they license separation, he is wrong. But neither the language nor the logic of his arguments requires us to ascribe this error to him. This is not to say, of course, that forms are *not* separate; it is only to say that the flux arguments do not show, and are not thought by Plato to show, that they are. Other arguments might, of course, yield different conclusions. Before turning to other arguments, however, let us explore the point of the flux arguments further.

When Plato says that forms are different from sensibles, he means not only that they are different from sensible objects such as Theaetetus, but also that they are different from sensible properties such as redness; forms are nonsensible properties, properties irreducible to sensible properties. Beauty, for example, is not identical or reducible to any sensible properties such as bright colouring or circular shape. Though such properties might constitute or realize beauty in a particular case, none is what beauty is. This is the thesis Irwin, in *Plato's Moral Theory*, calls nonreducibility (NR):[62]

NR: ... forms ... are not definable through sensible properties alone, and not iden-

---

[61] I discuss this argument in detail in ch. 3, although the question of separation is not there considered; see also ch. 4. Notice that on my account, Plato does not rule out knowledge of sensibles. Aristotle, however, appears to think Plato does preclude knowledge of sensibles. In at least this respect, then, his account of the flux argument seems incorrect.

[62] Irwin, *Plato's Moral Theory*, 154. I have slightly modified his definition. The quote from Irwin in the next paragraph is also from p. 154.

tical with these properties, or with sensible objects as described by their sensible properties.

As Irwin shows, 'NR is a legitimate conclusion from Plato's arguments.' And it is important to note that NR is neither a trivial nor an obvious claim. It is the claim that not all properties are observable properties; it involves rejecting a version of empiricism according to which everything can ultimately be explained in terms of, or reduced to, sensible features of the world. Plato is right, then, to think NR requires argument. But those arguments do not show, and are not thought by Plato to show, that forms are separate from sensibles.

Notice that on our account of Aristotle, he agrees that Plato uses flux to argue for NR. The express conclusion of argument (I), for example, is that forms are different from sensibles—and we have seen that means that forms are different not only from sensible particulars, but also from sensible properties. And it also follows from (I) that forms are not definable through sensible properties alone. Indeed, this follows trivially, since (I) claims that forms, but not sensibles, are definable.

Irwin argues, however, that although flux in fact only implies NR, Plato fallaciously infers IE from NR.[63] Why? He sketches an invalid argument leading from NR to IE. But he does not suggest Plato actually used this argument; he says only that Plato '*could* argue' in the suggested way. Irwin believes Aristotle's testimony suggests Plato infers separation from NR. I have suggested that this is not so; but even if it is, Aristotle could of course be wrong. Irwin also suggests that Plato accepts separation. This may well be correct; but it does not follow that he accepts it because of flux. Indeed, it is somewhat surprising that Irwin believes Plato accepts IE at all. For not only does he show that flux does not imply IE, but he also notes— correctly, as we are in the course of seeing—how difficult it is to uncover any commitment to IE in the dialogues.

7. Substance and Separation[64]

We have seen that Aristotle probably believes that Plato infers from flux that forms are substances. And whether or not he believes that, he certainly claims that the substantiality of forms—however arrived at—grounds their

[63] See especially Irwin, *Plato's Moral Theory*, 154–5. The brief quote that follows is from his p. 154 (emphasis added).
[64] Some of the matters discussed in this section are considered in more detail in ch. 15.

separation. Does Plato believe forms are substances? If so, is this because of flux? Does Plato infer from the substantiality to the separation of forms?

If all that is meant here by 'substance' is 'fundamental entity', then it seems uncontroversial that forms are Plato's substances; they are the basic entities in his ontology. And Plato may well believe that flux grounds their substantiality, explains their being the fundamental entities. At least, he believes that the flux of sensibles, coupled with considerations about knowledge and definition, requires the existence of nonsensible, unchanging, and everlasting entities suitable for a discarnate soul's reflection, entities the knowledge of which is necessary for any knowledge at all, and entities the definition of which is necessary for definitions of other things. And when he characterizes the realm of forms—the realm of *ousia*, of substance—it is to such features that he appeals. This suggests that Plato moves from the claim, licensed by flux, that forms are basic to knowledge and definition, to the claim that they are basic beings just as, in *Metaphysics H* 1, Aristotle indirectly suggests.

Aristotle protests, arguing that even though being basic to knowledge and definition are necessary for being a substance, they are not sufficient; separation is required as well. Since flux does not license separation, it does not license the substantiality of forms. If Plato moves from flux to substantiality, he reasons invalidly.

Aristotle's criticism is justified—given his account of substance. That is, one of Aristotle's criteria for being a substance is being separate; since flux fails to show that forms are separate, it fails to show that they are substances—as Aristotle understands the notion of substance. But Aristotle's criteria for substance are controversial, and it is not clear Plato accepts, or is committed to, them. To be sure, there is overlap between their critiera; both, for example, link *ousia* to knowledge and definition. But unlike Aristotle, Plato never makes it a defining feature of *ousia* that it be separate. Whenever he characterizes the realm of *ousia*, he mentions— not separation but—changelessness, everlastingness, inaccessibility to sense perception, being basic to a knowledge and definition, and the like. As we have seen, none of these features requires separation.

Flux, then, may well fail to guarantee substantiality as Aristotle understands that notion; but it does guarantee substantiality as Plato seems to understand it. To be sure, flux does not ensure separation; but since, for Plato, separation is not a defining feature of *ousia*, that does not matter.

Aristotle would be right, then, to argue that Plato grounds the substantiality of forms on flux; and whether or not he argues this, he is correct to claim that forms are Plato's substances. But he is incorrect if he believes

Plato links separation and substance. Correspondingly, he would also be incorrect were he to argue that Plato *invalidly* infers the substantiality of forms from flux. For that argument would be legitimate only if Plato accepted Aristotle's account of substance; and for that we have seen no evidence.

Aristotle's account of separation in *M* 9, then, seems to rest on the incorrect assumption that Plato, like Aristotle, believes that substance is as such separate. Forms are Plato's substances; and they may well be separate. But there is no evidence that for Plato separation issues from substantiality. We have not yet, then, found a route to separation.

8. Anamnesis, Affinity, and Separation

The main other argument appealed to, to commit Plato to separation, stems from his doctrine of Anamnesis, the doctrine that all so-called learning is really recollection of things previously known by discarnate souls. Cornford, for example, claims that separation 'is entailed by the belief in Anamnesis. . . . Anamnesis, the separate existence of the soul before birth, and the separation of forms from sensible things, all stand or fall together.'[65] Similarly, Burnyeat criticizes Irwin's account of separation, according to which Plato slides fallaciously from NR to IE, saying: 'So Plato's great metaphysical vision rests on nothing more than an unclarity or confusion? I would find that the hardest paradox of all'; and he suggests we look instead at Anamnesis as the source of Plato's belief in separation.[66]

The passage just cited from Burnyeat leads us to hope that we can derive a valid argument for separation from Anamnesis, one that rests on something 'more than an unclarity or confusion'. But as Burnyeat ultimately concedes, this expectation is disappointed. Here is his account of the argument:

Anamnesis entails that:

(1) Our knowledge of (e.g.) equality is independent of our empirical existence.

Plato's realist assumptions about knowledge also lead him to believe that:

[65] Cornford, *Plato and Parmenides*, 74. The argument Cornford sketches and attributes to Plato is, however, invalid, although he does not call attention to the fact.
[66] Burnyeat, review of Irwin, *Plato's Moral Theory* (for the reference, see n. 14). All quotations from Burnyeat are from this review. I discuss the review in some detail because, among other things, it is the only review of Irwin's book that deals with his account of separation.

(2) Knowledge is of something which exists independently of the knowing mind.

From (1) and (2) it follows that:

∴ (3) Our knowledge of equality is knowledge of something which exists independently of the knowing mind.

Burnyeat suggests that Plato then infers that:

∴ (4) Equality (the thing known) exists independently of all empirical reality.

But (1)–(3) obviously do not entail (4). Burnyeat seems to concede as much: 'I do not, however, claim that the epistemological premise is sufficient justification for the Theory of Forms. Here, if anywhere, Plato's vision outruns the resources of his argument.' But now notice: Burnyeat rejected Irwin's account, because it involved the paradox that the doctrine of separation rests on a mistake. The same is true of the argument Burnyeat attributes to Plato. Why is the invalid argument he attributes to Plato less paradoxical than the one Irwin attributes to him?

Perhaps it is less paradoxical because Plato offers it. As Burnyeat says, Plato claims that 'the Theory of Forms and the pre-existence of the soul stand or fall together (*Phd.* 76e)'. To be sure; but *how*—in virtue of what features—do they stand or fall together? All Anamnesis requires is that there be, prior to the soul's bodily existence, perfect, nonsensible entities suitable for a discarnate soul's reflection. This does not even require that forms be everlasting, let alone that they be separate; nor do I see that Plato thought otherwise. He compares forms to souls with respect to many of their features—for example, their nonsensible nature, their everlastingness; it is then quite striking that although, in talking of the soul in the *Phaedo*, he often says that it is *chōris* or *chōristē* from the body, he never says that forms are *chōris* or *chōrista* from sensibles. It would have been quite easy for him to have done so, had he wished to press the point that separate souls go hand in hand with separate forms.

The real reason Burnyeat seems to find Anamnesis less puzzling than flux as a basis for, or correlate to, separation is that, allegedly like separation, it is part of a 'cosmic vision', part of Plato's 'transcendent, otherworldly dimension'. It is not so much that Plato invalidly inferred separation from Anamnesis, as that both are parts of an otherworldly vision that naturally, if not logically, go hand in hand. But if separation is just IE, then it is unclear that separation is so 'otherworldly'. If—as Burnyeat may believe: I am unsure—separation were some *other* property, then it might go naturally with Anamnesis. But if our account has been correct, this is less clear.

One might argue that although Anamnesis does not require separation, the ensuing Affinity argument does.[67] For Plato goes on to say that souls, like forms, are in some sense simple and partless; they cannot be dispersed or scattered or broken into bits; and they cannot change. Does not this show that forms are separate? For if forms really cannot change, then, no matter what happens, even if the sensible world ceases to exist, forms continue to exist; for to cease to exist would be a change in, or of, them. But if forms would exist even if no sensibles did, then they are separate.

But this line of thought involves a confusion. Even if it is true that forms cannot fail to exist, it does not follow that they are separate; it might only follow that then sensibles must exist too. If forms cannot fail to exist, then the world is such that they cannot fail to exist; and one of the conditions of the world this might necessitate is that sensibles cannot fail to exist either. (I do not mean, of course, that each, or any given, sensible necessarily exists, which Plato clearly disbelieves, but that it might be necessary that there always be some sensibles or other—a claim Aristotle accepts. I shall ask later whether Plato too accepts this claim. My point here is only that the Affinity argument does not require him to reject it, and so does not, in that way, at least, ensure separation.)

Nor does partlessness imply separation; why cannot an entity without parts be dependent on something with parts? And we in any case need to be careful in interpreting the partlessness of forms and souls. Neither have physical parts, of course; but both have many properties true of them. Once the relevant sort of partlessness is made clear, that partlessness implies separation is correspondingly less clear.

I conclude, then, that although Anamnesis and Affinity are compatible with separation, neither requires it. Nor do I see reason to suppose that Plato failed to see this.

9. Artefacts and Separation

Are the middle dialogues—leaving the *Timaeus* to one side for now—then uncommitted to separation? This may be the right conclusion to draw. But I offer for consideration the following, not often travelled, route to separation.

A given form is separate if it is ever uninstantiated. (This is, recall, suf-

[67] This was first suggested to me by M. M. McCabe.

ficient but not necessary for separation.) If there are examples of forms that are ever uninstantiated, those forms, at least, are separate, even if Plato does not call attention to the fact. Are there such examples?

The most likely candidates—quite surprisingly—are forms of artefacts.[68] In both the *Cratylus* and *Republic* X, Plato acknowledges forms of artefacts—of shuttle (*Cra.* 389) and of bed or couch (*Rep.* 596 B)—and as we shall see, a good case can be made for their being separate.

One might not wish to hear the case, however, on the ground that it introduces irrelevant evidence. It is unclear, for example, that the *eidē* of the *Cratylus* are the same entities as the *eidē* of the (other) middle dialogues. And *Republic* X is certainly odd; only here, for example, does Plato say that forms were created by a god—elsewhere, he insists that they have always existed.[69] And outside of the *Cratylus* and *Republic* X, forms of artefacts are neither mentioned in the middle dialogues nor sanctioned by their arguments. One might also dispute the suggestion that the *Cratylus* and *Republic* X are middle dialogues: some place the *Cratylus* early, others place it late; and G. Else has argued that *Republic* X is later than the rest of the *Republic*.[70]

Odd as the *Cratylus* and *Republic* X might be, however, I am reluctant to rule appeal to them out of court. Certainly Aristotle feels free to appeal to *Republic* X—although I doubt he had it in mind in committing Plato to separation.[71] For at least in the Arguments from the Sciences in the *Peri Ideōn*, he claims that the Platonists did not want forms of artefacts.[72]

---

[68] I thank Richard Sorabji for first getting me to consider forms of artefacts in connection with separation.

[69] The two claims are consistent if creation does not take time. I doubt, however, that this is Plato's view. And in the *Timaeus*, at least, it is quite clear that forms are not created by the Demiurge; and it is difficult to see who else would have done so. I take it to be tacit in the *Phaedo* and (rest of) the *Republic* that forms are uncreated, though I know of no place where this is explicitly said or required. Forms are often said to be deathless, but that is compatible with their being created; so too is the claim that they have always existed if, again, creation takes no time.

[70] A late (i.e. post-*Parmenides*) date for the *Cratylus* is urged by e.g. G. E. L. Owen, 'The Place of the *Timaeus* in Plato's Dialogues', *Classical Quarterly,*, NS 3 (1953), 79–95, repr. in Allen (ed.), *Studies in Plato's Metaphysics*, 313–38, see esp. 323 n. 3. An early (i.e. Socratic) date is urged by A. E. Taylor, *Plato: The Man and his Work* (New York: The Dial Press Inc., 1936), 75 ff., and by J. V. Luce, 'The Date of the *Cratylus*', *American Journal of Philology*, 85 (1964), 136–54. On the date of *Republic* X, see G. F. Else, *The Structure and Date of Book X of Plato's* Republic (Heidelberg: C. Winter, 1972).

[71] He seems to have it in mind, for example, in his criticism of the One over Many in the *Peri Ideōn*; see Alexander, *In Metaph.* 80. 8–81. 10 Hayduck. I discuss the One over Many in connection with *Republic* X in my 'The One Over Many', *Philosophical Review*, 89 (1980), 197–240.

[72] Alexander, *In Metaph.* 79. 3–80. 6 Hayduck.

Although this claim is surprising in turn, it suggests that Aristotle does not rest his case, for committing Plato to separation, on his account of artefacts.

But if we admit the evidence of the *Cratylus* and *Republic* X, then I think we must conclude that at least artefact forms are separate. It seems reasonable to assume that shuttles, for example, have not always existed. And even if, according to *Republic* X, a god created (some) forms, they seem to have existed prior to the creation of actual artefacts by human artisans. Thus, in both dialogues the craftsman looks to forms in fashioning his creation; and it is unclear how he could do this unless the forms existed prior to his creation. But if the form of bed, for example, existed prior to the creation of any actual physical bed, and if there have not always been physical beds, then whether time is finite or infinite, the form of bed must have existed prior to any actual beds.[73] If so, it is separate. Similarly, although the *Cratylus* does not claim—or deny—that the form of shuttle has always existed, it seems clear that the form of name, which is mentioned in the same context, existed prior to any actual languages. And at the end of the *Cratylus*, it is suggested (although Plato does not explicitly endorse the suggestion) that some entities, of which the form of shuttle may or may not be one, have always existed. But even if not, the account of craftsmanship again yields the conclusion that at least artefact forms are separate.

Perhaps we should conclude, then, that at least artefact forms are separate in the middle dialogues. Can we tell the same story about other forms? That is, can we tell a plausible story that shows that they, too, were once uninstantiated and so are separate?

I am unsure. Consider, for example, moral forms. I take it that for a moral form to be instantiated, there must be souls. Now in the middle dialogues, souls have always existed; so one cannot point to a time when moral forms are uninstantiated, by pointing to a time when no souls exist.

Still, this need not be too daunting. Separation is separation from sensible particulars. So, what we really want to know is whether there have always been embodied people and, if so, if at least (an action of) one of them always instantiates virtue—appeal to virtuous souls in Hades may be ruled out as irrelevant, since they are not, in the relevant way, sensible.

Now so far as I can tell, in the middle dialogues Plato is uncommitted, one way or the other, on the question of whether or not there are always embodied people. If there are not always embodied people, virtue is at some point uninstantiated in the relevant way, and so is separate; but the middle dialogues seem uncommitted to the antecedent of this conditional.

---

[73] One might, I suppose, hold that the form of bed and the first bed came into existence simultaneously; but I doubt that this is Plato's view.

Still, even if there are always embodied people, there might be a time when none of them instantiated virtue.

One might argue that there is such a time, as follows: for Plato, knowledge is necessary for virtue;[74] and it seems likely that at some time, no one has the requisite knowledge. So at some time, (probably) no one is virtuous. Furthermore, for a virtuous (or just) city to exist, there must be virtuous (or just) people. So it seems that there is probably a time when no virtuous people or cities exist. Does not this show, then, that even if there are always embodied people, virtue is (probably) at some point uninstantiated?

I do not think so. For even if there is a time at which there are no virtuous embodied persons, and so no virtuous cities either, there might still be virtuous *actions*; Plato seems to allow that a nonvirtuous person—one who, for example, lacks the knowledge necessary for virtue—can perform a virtuous action; and virtuous actions surely instantiate virtue. I do not say that Plato is *committed* to the claim that at every point in time, there is at least one virtuous action or person; all I have argued is that his claim that knowledge is necessary for virtue cannot be used to show that there is a time when virtue is uninstantiated.

One might argue that it seems natural to allow that at least there *could* be a time when no virtuous people or actions exist, and so virtue can be uninstantiated and so is separate. I agree that this seems natural; but that does not seem a strong enough consideration to commit Plato to separation. Certainly some—of whom we have seen Aristotle is one—would argue that virtue, like other universals, cannot exist uninstantiated. I do not mean to say that virtue forms are *not* separate. All I have done is to reject certain arguments for showing that they are separate.

A plausible case can be made, then, for the claim that Plato is committed to the separation of artefact forms. But none of the evidence we have examined so far commits him to the separation of any other forms. Plato may, for all I have shown, believe that other forms are separate. But if so, he never argues for, or even mentions, the claim. Nor does he say things from which separation for nonartefact forms follows.

If he accepts separation, perhaps he believes it is an obvious feature of forms, standing in need of no argument or attention. Whereas Aristotle

---

[74] It is sometimes argued that Plato rejects the Socratic 'knowledge is necessary for virtue' thesis; but I do not think he does. For a defence of the claim that it is retained at least in the *Meno* and *Republic*, see Irwin, *Plato's Moral Theory*, ch. vi, §§ 6.3 and 11.4, and ch. vii, § 8.1 (esp. n. 26). For a defence of the claim that it is rejected, see G. Vlastos, 'Justice and Happiness in the *Republic*', in G. Vlastos (ed.), *Plato: A Collection of Critical Essays*, ii. *Ethics, Politics and Philosophy of Art and Religion* (Garden City, NY: Doubleday Anchor, 1971), 66–95.

believes it is incoherent to separate universals, perhaps Plato believes it is
an obvious fact about the world that universals can exist uninstantiated. I
have suggested that Aristotle's charge of incoherence is unjustified; Plato's
assumption of obviousness would be too. The question of whether or not
universals can exist uninstantiated is a difficult and controversial one; arguments can be, and have been, brought to bear on both sides of the dispute.

10. Separation in the *Timaeus*

So far I have left the *Timaeus* to one side; but it repays our attention. For
here Plato seems committed to separation for more than artefact forms, and
on the basis of deeper considerations than those issuing from the *Cratylus*
and *Republic* X.

In the *Timaeus* (27 D 5–31 A 1), Plato argues that the cosmos was created;
for it is sensible, and everything sensible is created. Creations require causes;
and so there is a cause of the coming to be of the cosmos. This is the
Demiurge, who is powerful (though not omnipotent) and good. Creation
requires attention to a model; what model did the Demiurge look to? There
are just two possibilities: he looked either to forms or to features of the pre-
existing chaos. Since the Demiurge is good and so free from jealousy, he
wished his creation, the cosmos, to be as good as possible. He must, then,
have looked to the best available model, the forms.

If this account of creation is taken literally, as Aristotle takes it, then
it seems to follow that at least some forms were at some point uninstantiated.[75] For on this account, forms have always existed, but there is a time
at which no sensibles exist; and from this it follows that there is a time
at which some forms are uninstantiated by sensibles. But if any form was
ever *actually* uninstantiated by sensibles, obviously it *can* so exist, and
so is separate. For separation, again, is just the capacity for independent
existence, i.e. the ability to exist uninstantiated. We can schematize the
argument for separation as follows:[76]

[75] Whether or not to take the account literally—or how much of it to take literally—is
disputed. For some discussion, see e.g. G. Vlastos, 'The Disorderly Motion in the *Timaeus*',
Classical Quarterly, 33 (1939), 71–83, repr. in Allen (ed.), *Studies in Plato's Metaphysics*,
379–99; and 'Creation in the *Timaeus*: Is it a Fiction?', in Allen (ed.), 401–19. It is not clear
Aristotle took every feature of the account literally; but he seems to have taken the claim
that time and the sensible world have not always existed literally. See e.g. *De Caelo* 279[b]ff.,
Physics 251[b].

[76] I speak here as though forms are everlasting, rather than eternal, for the sake of
simplicity. If we take seriously the eternality of the forms, then it is no longer clear that the

(1) (∀t) (Forms exist at t).
(2) (∃t) (No sensibles exist at t).
∴ (3) (∃t) (Forms exist at t but no sensibles exist at t).
∴ (4) (∃t) (Forms are uninstantiated by sensibles at t).
∴ (5) Forms are separate (can exist independently of sensibles).

This argument shows that all forms are separate, in the sense that all did, and so all can, exist uninstantiated by sensibles: that is, by articulated sensibles such as tables and chairs, or natural kinds as we know them, or sensible fire as it exists in our world. However, the above argument does not show that all forms were at some point actually uninstantiated *tout court*. For example, though the form of fire was at one point uninstantiated by sensible fire as we know it (since there was a time at which the form of fire, but not sensible fire as we know it, existed), it is not clear that it was ever uninstantiated as such. For prior to the creation of sensible fire, chaos contained traces (*ichnē*, 53 B 2) of fire, and that seems sufficient for the form of fire always to have been instantiated by something, even if not by sensible fire as we know it. What about moral forms? The original chaos contained no embodied people or individual human souls; and so moral forms were not always instantiated by them. However, the Demiurge seems always to have existed; and he is just and good. Hence the forms of justice and goodness were always instantiated, at least by the Demiurge. Hence they were never uninstantiated *tout court*, though they were uninstantiated by articulated sensibles and presumably by chaos.

If separation is separation from articulated sensible particulars, then the above argument shows that all forms are separate, since (if the account of creation is taken literally) they all existed before there were any articulated sensibles. If, however, separation is the ability to exist uninstantiated as such, then the above argument, taken together with other things Plato believes, shows only that some forms are separate. It doesn't show that the form of goodness, for example, was ever uninstantiated as such, since the Demiurge always instantiated it.

Although the argument just sketched is a valid argument for the separation of at least some forms, it is once again important to note that Plato does not explicitly offer it; though separation follows from claims he makes, if those claims are taken literally, he does not, even here, explicitly argue

argument for separation I here construct for Plato goes through. If it does not, then either the *Timaeus* is not committed to separation after all or, if it is, then it is so committed because forms are eternal, rather than because of the argument I consider—if, that is, eternality implies separation, which is, as noted above, unclear.

for separation. Furthermore, if the account of creation is *not* taken literally, then we lose the argument for separation just rehearsed. For it rests on the claim that there was a time when forms but not sensibles existed: a claim a nonliteral account of the creation story might eschew.

On one controversial reading of the *Timaeus*, then, Plato is committed to, even if he does not directly argue for, the separation of at least some forms. Further, the considerations leading to separation are, on this reading, rooted in Plato's teleological vision of the cosmos, and they lead to the separation of key examples of forms. Here, then, is a more satisfying route to separation than that we found in the middle dialogues, even if Plato does not signpost it as such.[77]

Can we use the *Timaeus'* account of separation to show that (nonartefact) forms are separate in the middle dialogues after all? I do not think so. Plato may there believe that forms and sensibles stand in the model–copy relation, which is part of the *Timaeus'* account of creation; but that, on its own, is insufficient for separation. Plato does often enough say that forms have always existed, whereas sensibles come to be and cease to be. But this claim about sensibles seems to mean only that no *given* sensible always exists; whereas the argument in the *Timaeus* involves the stronger claim that there was a time at which *no* (articulated) *sensibles whatever* existed. And of course the *Timaeus'* claim that souls were created appears to conflict with the middle dialogues' claim that souls have always existed. Though the middle dialogues may well accept separation, then, they do not clearly do so for the *Timaeus'* reasons.

Our account of the *Timaeus* partially helps, and partially hurts, Aristotle. It helps in that, given his belief that the account of creation is to be taken literally, he is justified in concluding that at least some forms are separate, at least in the *Timaeus*. And given his further apparent belief that Plato's views about forms did not change significantly between the middle and late dialogues, he is also justified in finding separation in the middle dialogues.[78]

It hurts, however, in that the argument for separation we have uncovered is not the one Aristotle articulates; he never suggests that separation is grounded in facts about the creation of the cosmos. Although the *Timaeus*

---

[77] With my account of the *Timaeus* contrast the interesting account offered by Rohr, 'Empty Forms in Plato'.

[78] I do not mean to suggest, what is false, that Aristotle believes Plato never changes his mind about *anything*. But he does not seem to believe Plato changed his mind about separation. See e.g. *Metaph.* 987[a]34–987[b]1. Further support for this claim consists in the fact that the *Peri Ideōn* arguments draw freely on later dialogues, even when separation is at issue.

provides evidence in support of Aristotle, it is unclear it is the evidence he relies on; and the evidence he relies on—the substantiality of forms—serves him less well.

Further, even in the *Timaeus*, commitment to separation has to be teased out; so it is misleading of Aristotle to suggest that separation is a key feature of forms, one Plato argues for, beginning with the *Phaedo*. Though forms may well be separate, even in the *Phaedo*, neither Aristotle's account of separation, nor his belief that it is a matter of explicit concern to Plato, should be accepted.

11. Socrates on Separation

I turn, finally, to a brief account of Socrates. How does Aristotle distinguish Socrates from Plato, and is his account correct? One central difference Aristotle points to is that Plato, but not Socrates, separated universals from particulars. We have seen that Aristotle is probably correct to say that Plato separated (some) forms (in at least some dialogues); is he also correct to say that Socrates did not separate universals?

Before answering this question, there is a prior one: What exactly does Aristotle mean in claiming that Socrates did not separate universals? Allen suggests Aristotle means 'that Socrates did not distinguish Forms from their instances at all':[79] Socrates, in Aristotle's view, is a nominalist; he does not admit universals, as entities distinct from sensible particulars.

This view, if correct, would certainly distinguish Socrates from Plato; for whether or not Plato separates universals, he certainly believes there are universals as well as particulars; he is clearly a realist of some sort about universals.[80] But Allen's interpretation is not correct. His argument for it, first of all, rests on a misunderstanding. Citing *Metaph.* 987^{b}4 ff. (translated above, in Section 3), he claims that it 'implies that Socrates identified the objects of definitions with sensibles, which is another way of saying that he did not distinguish Forms from their instances'.[81] But it is not another way of saying this. Allen thinks it is, because he takes sensibles (*aisthēta*) to include only sensible *particulars*. We have seen, however, that for Aristotle, sensibles also include sensible *properties*. In suggesting that Socrates, unlike Plato, identified universals with sensibles, Aristotle is suggesting, not that

---

[79] Allen, *Plato's* Euthyphro *and the Earlier Theory of Forms*, 136.

[80] Contrast D. Brownstein, *Aspects of the Problems of Universals* (Lawrence, Kan.: University of Kansas Press, 1973), ch. 4, who suggests that forms are (not universals but) particulars, so that Plato is a nominalist—he countenances particulars but not universals.

[81] Allen, *Plato's* Euthyphro *and the Earlier Theory of Forms*, 134.

Socrates somehow reduced universals to sensible particulars, but rather that he believed that all universals were sensible or observable properties. Aristotle's identification of Socratic universals with sensibles, then, does not support a nominalist reading.

Furthermore, in M 9 (1086^b3–7) Aristotle clearly says that Socrates recognized universals; he sees, on Aristotle's view, that universals are necessary for knowledge. It is just that Socrates did not ascribe IE to them—this is a further, and to Aristotle disastrous, move of Plato's.

In saying that Socrates did not separate universals, then, Aristotle does not mean that Socrates did not acknowledge universals. There are still, however, three possibilities as to what he does mean: (*a*) Socrates is uncommitted to separation; (*b*) Socrates says things that imply a rejection of separation; or (*c*) Socrates explicitly denies separation.

If Aristotle means (*c*), his claim is false; the issue of separation is not broached in the Socratic dialogues any more than it is broached in the middle or later dialogues. But I see no reason to assume Aristotle means (*c*).

Let us assume, then, that Aristotle means (*a*) or (*b*). Is his claim, so interpreted, correct? Allen, for one, argues that it is not. For, Allen argues, Socratic universals *are* separate. They are 'independent of and prior to their instances'.[82] Allen's arguments for this claim, however, are unsuccessful. He writes, for example, that

Ontologically, the priority of Forms is implied by the fact that they are essences and causes by which things are what they are; their existence is a condition for the existence of their instances. That priority implies existential independence. If Euthyphro's action in prosecuting his father is holy, its existence as holy depends upon the existence of the Form of holiness, by which it is holy; it would be merely queer to think that the Form of holiness depends for its existence on Euthyphro's action in prosecuting his father being holy.[83]

To be sure, the form of holiness can exist independently of Euthyphro's act of prosecuting his father, and so it is separate from that act; but to show that the form of holiness is separate in Aristotle's (and so in our) sense, it must be shown that the form is separate from sensible instances as such. And even if the existence of forms is 'a condition for the existence of their instances', it does not follow that forms are separate from their instances; there could be mutual dependence.[84]

Allen also offers other arguments designed to show that Socratic forms

[82] Ibid. 136. [83] Ibid.
[84] Allen, however, seems to think separation involves distributive, not collective, independence; so that, as he construes separation, at least the independent-existence part of separation (he believes that more than a claim about independent existence is involved in

are separate; but none of them succeeds. One might, however, appeal instead to an argument similar to one suggested earlier in connection with Plato: Socrates, like Plato, believes that knowledge is necessary for virtue; he also believes (perhaps unlike Plato) that no one has the requisite knowledge. Hence for Socrates, no one is virtuous. So is not virtue uninstantiated, and so separate?

Against this it might be argued, as it was before in connection with Plato, that even if no one is virtuous, there can none the less be virtuous actions; a nonvirtuous person—a person lacking the knowledge necessary for virtue, for example—can still perform a virtuous action; and virtuous actions instantiate virtue. So even if no one is virtuous, virtue might none the less be instantiated. Of course, this is not to say that virtue is *not* separate; it is only to say that the suggested route to separation is a dead end. There might, of course, be other routes to it. I myself cannot discover any, however, and so am inclined to believe, against Allen, that Socrates is not committed to separation. This suggests that, if Aristotle intends only claim (*a*), he is correct.

What, however, if Aristotle intends the stronger claim (*b*)? One might argue that there is terminological evidence in favour of (*b*). For example, Socrates says that courage—which I take to be a Socratic form—is *in* courageous people.[85] Does not this imply rejection of separation? Well, it all depends on what 'in' means here. When Plato, in the *Phaedo*, allows that the soul is sometimes in the body, he does not mean that it is not separate from it—not capable of existing without it. Similarly, even if Socratic forms are in sensibles, perhaps they can exist independently of them. Socrates does not explicate 'in' for us; but I see no reason to suppose that his use of it is incompatible with separation. He sometimes seems to mean no more than that universals are 'had by', characterize, sensibles. But this is compatible with separation; to say that my car is red does not imply that redness cannot exist uninstantiated. Socrates sometimes seems to mean that forms are *where* sensibles are; and Plato, at least in the *Timaeus*, may deny this. But, as we have seen, to say that forms are where sensibles are does not imply that they cannot exist independently of sensibles. The water in this jug is where the jug is, but it can exist without it. Socrates' use of 'in', then, provides no evidence, one way or the other, about his views on separation; neither, so far as I can tell, do other features of his terminology, or any of his arguments.

separation) follows from the considerations he adduces. But this is just to say that he is wrong about what separation is. See above, sect. 1 and n. 4.

[85] See e.g. *La.* 191 E–192 B; cf. *Chrm.* 158 E–159 A; *Euphr.* 5 D 1–5; *Meno* 72 E 1, 7.

I am inclined to reject (*b*), then, as well as (*c*). But (*a*) seems correct: Socrates is uncommitted to separation. Since Plato, at least sometimes in some cases, is committed to separation, Aristotle is correct to say that Socrates and Plato differ over the issue of separation. But this does not entirely vindicate Aristotle. For he writes as though separation is the big differentiator between Plato and Socrates, and this is not true; commitment to separation is as muted in the middle dialogues as lack of commitment to it is in the Socratic dialogues. Though separation may indeed divide Plato from Socrates, it does not play the central role in their contrasting views that Aristotle suggests.

Separation is not, however, the only feature Aristotle points to in differentiating Plato from Socrates; and perhaps other of his claims are on firmer ground. Aristotle also claims, for example, that for Socrates, unlike Plato, all universals are sensible, that is, are sensible properties. Now Plato, as we have seen, accepts NR; forms are nonsensible properties, properties irreducible to, and indefinable in terms of, sensible properties. Socrates, by contrast, does not argue for, and does not seem committed to, NR; more strongly, he may believe that all properties can be defined in sensible terms alone.[86] Here, then, is an important difference between Socrates and Plato, and one Aristotle detects. Indeed, this vindicates Aristotle in spending so much time on the flux arguments. For though they do not prove, and are not thought by Plato to prove, separation, they do prove NR; and it is NR, not separation, for which Plato repeatedly, but Socrates never, argues.

Further features of Aristotle's account of Socrates are also worth noting. Aristotle may attribute to Socrates, not only the view that universals are

---

[86] That Socrates rejects, and Plato accepts, NR is a major theme of Irwin's *Plato's Moral Theory*, one defensible independently of Irwin's claim that Plato fallaciously infers IE from NR. I agree with Irwin that Plato argues for NR; and it is some support for Irwin's interpretation of Socrates that Aristotle, in claiming that Socrates identified universals with sensibles (i.e. with sensible properties), commits Socrates to a rejection of NR. But I am unsure how far one ought to press Socrates here. As Irwin argues, Socrates identifies moral forms, at least, with states of soul; it is unclear in what sense these are observable or sensible. Further, like Plato in the middle dialogues, Socrates rejects at least those observable accounts that fall prey to the F and not-F problem; and his rejection of behavioural accounts also betrays some dissatisfaction with at least some sorts of observable accounts. Irwin must argue—and does argue—that Socrates believes an observable account is available, though as yet unattained; whereas Plato gave up the search for such an account. But it may be more accurate to say only that Socrates failed to diagnose their failure to find satisfactory accounts, whereas Plato offers a diagnosis; their difference then would be that whereas Plato argues for NR, Socrates is uncommitted, one way or the other, on the issue. If this is correct, then Irwin and Aristotle overstate the difference between Plato and Socrates on NR, just as they overstate their difference on separation. None the less, they are right to claim that there is a difference between Plato and Socrates here, and one to which the flux argument is relevant, in a way in which it is not relevant to the issue of separation.

sensibles, but also the view that they are sensible *substances*. At least, he says that it was a mistake of Plato's not to make sensibles substances (*Metaph.* 1086ª35–7),[87] suggesting, perhaps, that Socrates did make sensibles substances. If he means that Socrates' substances are not (just) sensible particulars but (also) sensible properties, then Socrates, like Plato but unlike the Aristotle of the *Metaphysics*, admits universal substances. Since he denies, or does not accept, separation, he also then believes, or does not deny, that there are nonseparated substances—again in striking contrast to Aristotle but in agreement with Plato, in so far as Plato, unlike Aristotle, does not require that substances be separate. On this reading of Socrates, then, Socrates is closer to Plato, and further from Aristotle, than Aristotle admits.

It is unclear, however, that Aristotle intends this reading. He does ascribe to Socrates the view that universals answer the 'What is F?' question, tell us what things are; for Socrates as for Plato, universals are the essences of things. But Aristotle does not believe that *ousia* as essence must be separate; only *ousia* as (primary) substance must be.[88] Now Aristotle believes that forms are Plato's primary substances; and he links their separation to their substantiality. But it is less clear that he thinks that Socrates' (primary) substances are universals. If he does not claim this, then even if he claims that Socrates' universals are essences, their nonseparation does not drive a wedge between Socrates and Aristotle, at least on that score. Rather, both allow that some universals are essences even though they are not substances or separate.

Even if Socrates and Aristotle agree on this score, however, they differ on another. For Socrates, on this reading, completely severs the connection between substance and essence; substances and essences constitute disjoint classes. For Aristotle in the *Metaphysics*, however, although some universals are essences, and no universal is a substance, it is also the case that substances—individual forms—are essences. Indeed, here is another point of contact between Plato and the Aristotle of the *Metaphysics*: both believe that some one sort of entity—something properly called 'form'—is at once substance and essence. To be sure, they have different conceptions of what candidates fit the bill, Plato promoting his forms or universals, Aristotle promoting individual forms such as Socrates or his soul or the prime and planetary movers. But they agree in linking substance, form, and essence in a way Socrates, on this reading,[89] does not. Whether Socratic universals are or are not substances, then, Aristotle differs from Socrates—either over

---

[87] The remark is odd, however; for Aristotle himself believes there are nonsensible substances. See above, sect. 3. [88] I discuss this matter further in ch. 15.
[89] Again, see ch. 15.

the connection between substance and separation, or over the connection between substance, essence, and form. And in the latter case, Aristotle's affinities lie with Plato. But Aristotle carefully keeps these issues in the background—perhaps because they are in tension with his effort to portray Socrates as the hero, Plato as the villain, in the story of the introduction of universals into Western thought.[90]

[90] Earlier versions of this chapter were read at the Cambridge Philological Society, the Institute of Classical Studies in the University of London, and a seminar in Oxford conducted by Lesley Brown and Lindsay Judson; I thank the audiences on these occasions—especially Lesley Brown, M. F. Burnyeat, M. M. Mackenzie, and Richard Sorabji—for a number of helpful comments. I also wish to thank J. L. Ackrill, Julia Annas, Norman Kretzmann, Jennifer Whiting, M. J. Woods, and—as always, and especially—T. H Irwin for helpful written and oral comments. The research for the paper was supported by a fellowship from the National Endowment for the Humanities, sabbatical leave from Cornell University, and a visiting fellowship at Brasenose College, Oxford.

12

Immanence

une interprétation tout à fait scandaleuse de la théorie des idées.

(L. Robin[1])

1. Introduction

Aristotle claims that Platonic forms are not in things, and that this is just as well, since 'it is easy to collect many absurdities against such a theory' (*Metaph. A* 9, 991^{b}18–19; cf. *M* 5, 1079^{b}22–3). He records some of the absurdities in the *Peri Ideōn*, portions of which are preserved by Alexander in his commentary on *Metaphysics A* 9. Many of the alleged absurdities were aired earlier by Plato in the *Parmenides*.

In Section 2 I ask what immanence is. In 3 I argue that, at least in the *Phaedo*, forms are in things in the relevant way. In 4 and 5 I explore Plato's *Parmenides* objections to immanence. In 6 I explore Aristotle's *Peri Ideōn* objections.

Plato and Aristotle seem to believe that a form is in its participants if and only if either the whole (W) or a part (P) of the form is in each of its participants. I shall explore their objections to both W and P, arguing that they are not so decisive as they may at first appear to be.

2. What Immanence Is

Aristotle articulates a number of sorts of immanence;[2] and he may well believe that forms cannot be in sensibles in any of them. For our purposes here, however, we only need to know what sort of immanence is at issue in *Metaphysics A* 9 (*M* 5) (and so in the *Peri Ideōn*, which records the

---

[1] Attributed to L. Robin by D. J. Allan, 'Aristotle and the *Parmenides*', in I Düring and G. E. L. Owen (eds.), *Aristotle and Plato in the Mid-Fourth Century: Papers of the Symposium Aristotelicum Held at Oxford in August, 1957* (Studia Graeca et Latina Gothoburgensia, 11; Göteborg: Elanders Bocktryckeri Aktienbolag, 1960), 133–43 at 143.

[2] See e.g. *Phys.* 4. 3; *Cat.* 1^{a}24–5; *Metaph. Δ* 23.

absurdities *A* 9 alludes to). The fuller context of Aristotle's allegation of absurdity is as follows (I insert letters for ease of reference):

(*a*) But neither are ⟨forms⟩ any help towards knowledge of the other things (they are not their substance, or they would have been in them) nor towards their being ⟨what they are⟩, not being present in their participants. (*b*) If they were, they might perhaps seem to be causes, as white is of a thing's being white, (*c*) by being mixed in. But this account, given first by Anaxagoras and later by Eudoxus and some others, is very simple to upset; it is easy to collect many absurdities against such a theory. (991ᵃ12–19; cf. 1079ᵇ15–23)

(*a*) suggests that the relevant sort of immanence is one such that, if x is the essence of y, x is in y in that way; since forms are not in sensibles in that way, they are not their essences.

(*c*) tells us that for Anaxagoras and Eudoxus, but not for Plato, white is in white things by being mixed in them—that is, it is a physical part or ingredient of things.³ So for Plato, according to Aristotle, forms are not in things by being physical parts or ingredients of them. This is uncontroversial, for forms are not physical entities at all. (*c*) thus gives us one clear sort of immanence forms noncontroversially lack; but it cannot be all Aristotle has in mind. For being a physical part of something is not a necessary condition for being the essence of something—being a physical part of is not the sort of immanence intended in (*a*).

(*b*) forges the link between (*a*) and (*c*): if forms were in things, they would be in them as white is in white things. For Anaxagoras and Eudoxus, apparently that is to say that white is a physical part or ingredient of white things; but this is just one account of how white is in white things—an account Aristotle rejects. In *Physics* 4. 3, for example, he says that white is a part (though presumably not a physical part) of white things (210ᵃ25–ᵇ 8); and he then says that hot—which is presumably analogous to white—is in body as properties (*pathē*) are in things (210ᵇ25–7). Aristotle, that is, agrees with Anaxagoras and Eudoxus that the white of a white thing is a part of it; but he disagrees with them about what sort of part it is—for them it is a physical part, for Aristotle a property.

Now although the essences of things surely need not be physical parts of them, it is reasonable to suppose they must be some sort of part of them—a

³ In various places Aristotle insists that, strictly speaking, only bodies (*sōmata*) can mix; see e.g. *GC* 1. 10, 327ᵇ20–2; *Top.* 149ᵃ38–ᵇ3; *Metaph. N* 5, 1092ᵃ24–6. He is not always so strict (see e.g. *De Caelo* 1. 9, 277ᵇ33–4, 278ᵃ14–15), but the *Peri Ideōn* makes it plain that he is speaking strictly here; see below, sect. 6 (i and ii). I shall assume without argument here that Aristotle interprets Eudoxus correctly, and that Eudoxus held a theory of immanent Platonic forms. See below, n. 24.

property of them, or perhaps some other sort of part: Aristotle recognizes many sorts of parts, as a glance at *Metaphysics Δ* 25 makes clear. (*a*) and (*c*) are thus both determinate versions of a generic sort of immanence, being in by being a part of. This is the first of the eight sorts of immanence discussed in *Physics* 4. 3, 210ª15–16.

I suggest, then, that when Aristotle says in *Metaphysics A* 9 (*M* 5) (and so in the *Peri Ideōn*) that forms are not in things, he means at least that they are not parts of them, where this includes the claim that they are not properties of them.[4]

3. The Immanence of Forms

Now that the relevant sense of 'in' has been fixed, we need to know whether forms are in things in that sense. I shall begin by arguing for a different claim, however: namely that, at least in the *Phaedo*, forms are in sensibles in *some* sense—that is, Plato *says* that forms are, in some sense, in things. Only after arguing for this claim shall I argue that this involves forms being in things as properties of them. Until then, I intend 'in' to be neutral, when I argue that Plato believes forms are in things.

In the *Phaedo* (100–6) Plato offers two explanatory schemata of why things are as they are and come to be as they do, the so-called safe and clever answers (SA, CA).[5] According to the SA:

What makes a thing beautiful is nothing other than the presence or communion of that beautiful itself (or whatever the manner and nature of the relation may be; as I don't go so far as to affirm that, but only that it is by the beautiful itself that all beautiful things are beautiful). Because it seems to me to be the safest answer to give both to myself and to another, and if I hang on to this, I believe I'll never fail: it's safe to answer both to myself and to anyone else that it's by the beautiful that beautiful things are beautiful. (100 D 4–E 3)

The SA states, that is, that:

---

[4] To deny that forms are parts of things by being properties of them need not be to deny that forms are properties; forms could be properties that are not parts (properties) of things. On this view, either sensibles have different properties from forms, or else have instances of forms as parts, rather than forms themselves. Although Aristotle's denial that forms are in things as properties does not commit him to denying that forms are properties, he none the less does deny that forms can consistently be properties. I explore his reasons below: see esp. sect. 6 (viii).

[5] I discuss the SA and CA in more detail in ch. 14. Many of the claims dogmatically asserted here are defended there.

(SA) x is, or comes to be, F, just in case x is, or comes to be, suitably
      related to the form of F.

Though Plato disclaims knowledge of the precise relation, he offers some
suggestions: it might be presence or communion or, as he also suggests
(100 c 5, 101 c 3–6), participation. As the *Parmenides* (131 A 4–6; see below)
makes clear, W and P are at least two possible accounts of participation;
and presence and communion certainly seem immanentist. Perhaps, then,
although Plato is vague about the details of immanence, he is sure that the
relevant relation is some sort of immanence.

That Plato intends an immanentist reading seems suggested by 102 A
11–B 6, where Phaedo says:

As I recall, when these points had been granted him, and it was agreed that each of
the forms was something, and that the other things, partaking of them, took the
name of the forms themselves, he next asked: 'If you say that that is so, then whenever you say that Simmias is larger than Socrates but smaller than Phaedo, you
mean then, don't you, that both things are in Simmias, largeness and smallness?'

As the beginning of Phaedo's remarks makes clear, largeness and smallness are forms. So, Socrates next asks whether (and gets immediate agreement that) forms are in things; when Simmias is large, for example, the
form of largeness is in him. Further, at 105 B–C Plato refers back to the SA
in the following terms:

⟨I shall no longer offer⟩ the old, safe, ignorant answer, that it's hotness ⟨whose
presence in a body makes it hot⟩, but a cleverer answer now available, that it's fire.
And again, if you ask what it is by whose presence in a body that body will ail, I
shan't say that it's illness, but fever.

The SA, that is, claims that x is, or comes to be, F, just in case the form of
F is, or comes to be, in it; immanence just is the suitable relation binding
sensibles to forms.

The CA also sounds immanentist. In the passage just cited, for example,
the CA says—not (just) that it's the hotness in a body that makes it hot,
but—that it's the fire in a body that does; or again, the CA says—not (just)
that it's the illness in a body that makes it ill, but—that it's the fever in a
body that does. Fire and fever supplement hotness and illness as the relevant immanent explanatory entities. For, as Plato explains, fire 'brings on'
(*epipherei*, 104 E 10) the form of hot, and fever brings on the form of illness.
The form of hot, or illness, is in a body through the causal agency of fire or
fever, which are in it.

Now it may well be uncontroversial to say that fire and fever are in hot

and ill bodies; but, it may be objected, they are not forms but physical entities, and so do not support immanent forms. I agree that fire and fever are
not, here, forms. But some of the entities that play the same role in the CA
as fire and fever do are forms. The CA states quite generally that:

(CA) x is, or comes to be, F, if it is, or comes to be, occupied by something, G, that brings on the form of F.

Fire and fever occupy the G-slot and are not forms; but some substituends for 'G' are forms. Plato says, for example, that whatever the form
of three occupies is not only three but also odd (104 D 4–7); here the G-slot
is occupied by the form of three, which is, therefore, in three.[6] Both the SA
and CA thus seem to countenance immanent forms.

One might concede that Plato often speaks as though forms are in things,
but argue that he is then speaking loosely or elliptically. For in addition to
forms and sensibles, the *Phaedo*, it is often thought, acknowledges a third
sort of entity, the so-called immanent characters; and, it is sometimes argued, it is immanent characters, not forms, that are in things. When Plato
speaks as though a form is in something, what he really means is that the
corresponding immanent character is in it. Thus, for example, at 103 B 5–6
Plato speaks both of the opposite in us and of the opposite in nature; at
102 D 6–7 he speaks both of the form of largeness (*auto to megethos*) and of
the largeness in us (*to en hēmin megethos*). Surely, it is sometimes urged, it is
immanent characters—e.g. the largeness in us—that are, strictly speaking,
in sensibles, and not forms themselves.

But what exactly are these 'immanent characters'? Those who believe that
immanent characters are a distinct ontological category from forms generally suppose that immanent characters are either properties corresponding
to forms (which are not themselves properties but, say, perfect particulars
instead), or property instances of forms (which are properties). But it is also
sometimes argued—and I shall argue here—that the so-called immanent
characters are not a distinct ontological category from forms, but (parts of)
forms themselves, when they are in things. Immanent characters—e.g. the
largeness in us—are just immanent forms, i.e. (parts of) forms, when they

---

[6] Thus, even though D. Gallop, for example, on the whole denies that Plato countenances
immanent forms in the *Phaedo*, he concedes that at 104 D 5–6 the form of three is said to
occupy something; see his *Plato: Phaedo* (Oxford: Clarendon Press, 1975), 206. He suggests
that elsewhere, where Plato uses similar language, he is speaking instead of the number
three. I agree with A. Nehamas, 'Predication and Forms of Opposites in the *Phaedo*', *Review
of Metaphysics*, 26 (1973), 461–91 at 478 ff., however, that probably for Plato the number
three just is the form of three.

are in things.[7] On this view, talk of immanent characters does not replace or rival talk of immanent forms; rather, it explicates the manner in which forms are in things.

There are, I think, three main reasons people deny that immanent characters are (parts of) immanent forms: (1) Plato says that immanent characters can 'retreat or perish' (e.g. 103 A 1); the largeness in us, for example, retreats or perishes when smallness advances towards it (e.g. 102 D 5 ff.). But, it is believed, forms can neither retreat nor perish; hence immanent characters cannot be immanent forms. (2) There are or can be, it is believed, many immanent characters, but only one form of F. (3) Forms but not immanent characters are thought to be separate from sensibles.[8]

Since Aristotle in effect raises (3), I defer discussion of it until we turn to his objections; (1) and (2), however, can be dealt with here.

If Plato accepts P, then (2) is obviously not troubling; there is, in this case, one form with many parts.[9] On W the reply to (2) is to deny that there are many immanent characters of a given form; there is just the one form, which, as a whole, can be in many places at once. What may seem to be numerically distinct immanent characters are just many appearances of the same form, in its entirety.[10]

(1) is the more troubling objection, but it too can be met. Plato tells us that at the approach of coldness, both the hotness in us and also fire either retreat or perish. Or, in general, at the approach of (what is) not-F, the F in us, or whatever is essentially F, retreats or perishes (102 D–103 A; 103 C 10 ff.). At 106 A 3–6 Plato says that if something is necessarily imperishable,

[7] F. M. Cornford, for example, *Plato and Parmenides: Parmenides' Way of Truth and Plato's Parmenides*, translated with an introduction and with a running commentary (London: Routledge & Kegan Paul, 1939), 78, describes immanent characters as instances of forms; see also Gallop, *Plato: Phaedo*, 195; Nehamas, 'Predication and Forms of Opposites in the *Phaedo*', 475. G. Vlastos seems to favour the view that immanent characters, but not forms, are properties; see 'Reasons and Causes in the *Phaedo*', *Philosophical Review*, 78 (1969), 291–325. Those who believe immanent characters are just forms when they are in things include C. Stough, 'Forms and Explanation in the *Phaedo*', *Phronesis*, 21 (1976), 1–30; and D. O'Brien, 'The Last Argument of Plato's *Phaedo*', *Classical Quarterly*, NS 17 (1967), 210–13. Some believe that immanent characters are a special class of forms, immanent as opposed to transcendent ones. This is *not* my suggestion; my suggestion is rather that there is just one class of forms, and they can be in things. In suggesting that immanent characters are (not instances but) (parts of) forms, I challenge the view assumed in 'Relational Entities' (below, ch. 13), and 'Separation' (above, ch. 11).

[8] Gallop, *Plato: Phaedo*, 198, presses (1); G. Vlastos, 'The Third Man Argument in the *Parmenides*', *Philosophical Review*, 63 (1954), 319–49, repr. in R. E. Allen (ed.), *Studies in Plato's Metaphysics* (London: Routledge & Kegan Paul, 1965), 231–64 (latter pagination) at 253 n. 1, presses (3).

[9] But would not this conflict with the partlessness of forms? So Aristotle alleges; I consider his allegation below, in sect. 6.   [10] *Rep.* 476 A might, I think, be read this way.

then it retreats but does not perish at the approach of its opposite, or at the approach of something having a property opposite to one of its essential properties. Thus the soul, for example, retreats but does not perish at the approach of death; for the soul is necessarily immortal, and so cannot perish. Similarly, if the hotness in us is a form, then it retreats but does not perish at the approach of coldness. But there is no difficulty in understanding how forms can retreat from what they are in; the form of hot retreats from something when that thing ceases to have or exemplify it. This may involve a genuine change in what the form was in; a body, for example, ceases to be hot. But it involves no genuine, but only a mere Cambridge, change in the form; and although forms are exempt from various sorts of genuine change, they can undergo mere Cambridge changes.[11] Immanent forms, then, can retreat; hence they can retreat or perish; and so the fact that Plato says that immanent characters can retreat or perish does not show that immanent characters are not forms.[12]

Even if the hotness in us does perish, however, that at most precludes W and not also P.[13] To see why this is so, I need to say what forms would be like on P. The best account, I think, is that forms would then be something like nonmaterial stuffs with different bits (immanent characters) in each of its possessors. Each bit (immanent character) is dependent on its owner, and numerically distinct from every other bit. But unlike material

---

[11] I thus disagree with Owen's suggestion that prior to the *Sophist*, Plato disallows even mere Cambridge change in the case of forms. For Owen's suggestion, see his 'Plato and Parmenides on the Timeless Present', *Monist*, 50 (1966), 317–40. For the distinction between genuine and mere Cambridge change, see P. T. Geach, *God and the Soul* (London: Routledge & Kegan Paul, 1969), 71.

[12] One might object to the suggested interpretation that at 106 c 3 Plato says that 'the uneven is not imperishable'; and at c 5–7 he suggests that similarly, 'fire, hot, and the rest' are not imperishable. Does not this suggest that the hot and the rest are not forms? But I take it that Plato's point is only that it does not follow from the fact that something is uneven (hot), as it does from the fact that something is immortal, that it is imperishable. He does not mean to suggest that everything (considered here) that is uneven (hot) is perishable, but only that, to show that something uneven (hot) is imperishable, one needs to point to some fact about it other than its being uneven (hot)—e.g. to its being a form. That's why Plato says that 'another argument would be needed' (106 D 1) to show that the immortal is imperishable, if being immortal did not imply being imperishable—i.e. another argument could perhaps be given to show that something uneven is imperishable; but that argument would need premises other than that the thing is uneven.

[13] One might, however, attempt to reconcile W with the perishing of immanent characters by developing Gallop's account of perishing and withdrawing. Perhaps the F in x withdraws from x when x is considered in a different context, but perishes from x when x ceases to be F. On this view, perishing and withdrawing are both mere Cambridge changes in immanent characters (forms), corresponding to two different sorts of change (one genuine, one mere Cambridge) in the case of particulars. For Gallop's account, see *Plato: Phaedo*, 196 ff. Although I find his account attractive, it does not seem to sit well with 106 A 3–6.

stuffs, no form is exhausted by such bits. Rather, each consists in an infinite nondepletable amount of nonmaterial stuff.[14]

If forms satisfy P in this way, then there is no difficulty in allowing immanent characters to be perishable parts of forms. First, even if all the immanent characters of a given form cease to be, the form itself does not cease to be. For, as we have just seen, no form consists solely in its parts that are had by various objects; each consists in an infinite nondepletable amount of nonmaterial stuff. Second, even if the perishing of a part is not quite a mere Cambridge change, neither is it any sort of change Plato is concerned to disallow forms. All he means, in emphasizing the changelessness of forms, is that forms cannot change in any way that would jeopardize their remaining the very forms they are; the form of beauty, for example, cannot cease to be, or cease to be perfectly beautiful.[15] But losing a part (immanent character) does not put any form thus in jeopardy. For since each form consists in an infinite nondepletable amount of stuff, gaining or losing a part makes no real difference. P, so construed, is thus compatible with both the separation and the changelessness of forms.

So far I have argued that the standard arguments against construing immanent characters as (parts of) forms fail. This does not, of course, unequivocally establish that immanent characters are (parts of) forms; but, in conjunction with other evidence adduced above, it constitutes a prima facie case for that claim. I shall, in any case, from now on assume that, at least in the *Phaedo*, Plato countenances immanent forms.[16] If Plato is not committed to the perishability of immanent characters, then W and P are both viable options; if he is committed to their perishability, then W is precluded, but P remains open.

But immanent in what sense? When Plato says that forms (or fire, or the soul) are in (*en*) things, I think he probably means that they are where those things are (although this does not, of course, imply that they are

---

[14] Others have also suggested that forms are analogous to stuffs. The version of that view suggested here owes most to J. Levinson, 'The Particularisation of Attributes', *Australasian Journal of Philosophy*, 38 (1980), 102–15.

[15] On the perfection of forms, which includes their changelessness, see J. C. B. Gosling, 'Similarity in *Phaedo* 73b *seq.*', *Phronesis*, 10 (1965), 151–61; and A. Nehamas, 'Plato on the Imperfection of the Sensible World', *American Philosophical Quarterly*, 12 (1975), 105–17.

[16] One might, however, cite *Smp.* 211 A–B and *Ti.* 52 (cf. also *Parm.* 133 C 3–5, though I take this passage to be aporetic, and not to express Plato's considered views) as places where Plato denies immanence. I am not certain that these passages deny the sort of immanence I believe the *Phaedo* has; but even if they do, that does not show that in the *Phaedo* Plato did not flirt with immanence. Immanence, on the other hand, seems suggested at various places in the *Republic* (e.g. 476 A 4–7, 509 B 6–10); and I believe Plato develops P in the *Philebus*. Obviously these claims are controversial; but I do not have the space to defend them here.

extended). But I take it that for forms to be where their participants are is for them to be properties of things; this is how they are where their participants are, what it is for them to be where their participants are. Thus, I argued, immanent characters just are (parts of) forms, when forms are in things. It is generally agreed that immanent characters are either properties or property instances. Those who believe they are property instances do so because they believe forms are properties that are not in things. Once it is agreed that immanent characters are (parts) of forms, the temptation to view them as property instances rather than as properties fades. But at the same time, the temptation to view forms as properties becomes irresistible. And if forms are both where their participants are, and are also properties, then they are in things by being properties of them. I shall assume from now on, then, that forms are properties of things, and argue that this does not lead to the difficulties Plato and Aristotle docket.

One might raise the following objection: I have suggested that forms are properties of things; and also that they might satisfy P. But if forms satisfy P, are they not scattered particulars, rather than any sort of property or universal? However one answers this question, all I need for my purposes is the following: that Plato takes length, for example, to be a form, which he in turn analyses as W or P; the form of length just is length, not a peculiar entity corresponding to length. When I say that forms are universals or properties, that is all I mean.

To allow that forms are properties even if they satisfy P does not, at any rate, beg any questions against Aristotle; for he believes that W and P are rival conceptions of universals.[17] He argues that forms cannot nonproblematically be properties of particulars, not because he believes they satisfy P (and so cannot be properties at all), but rather because he believes they cannot nonproblematically satisfy W or P (which they must do in order to be universals). It is this argument I shall address, leaving to one side the further question of whether Aristotle is right to view P as an account of universals.

4. Plato's Objections: W

Plato objects that on W, 'a form which is one and the same will, at the same time, as a whole, be in a number of things which are separate, and so will be separate from itself' (*Parm.* 131 B 1–2). 'Separate', here, seems to

---

[17] In fact, G. E. M. Anscombe, *Three Philosophers* (Ithaca, NY: Cornell University Press, 1961), 31–2, suggests that Aristotle rejects W in favour of P as an account of universals. Whether or not she is correct, Aristotle's claim that a universal is in many places at once (at e.g. *Metaph. Z* 16, 1040^{b}25–7) seems to count things that satisfy P as universals.

mean 'in different places'; at least some participants in a given form are in different places. So, consider two chairs, each of which participates in the form of hard; each is in a different place—one is in my dining room, the other in my study. This raises no difficulty. But if the form of hard is, in its entirety, simultaneously in my two chairs, then it must, in its entirety, be in my dining room and my study. But surely nothing can be in a different place from itself? Hence W leads to absurdity.

There is a famous rejoinder to this objection to W: it is of course true that no physical object, such as my chair, can, in its entirety, be in two places at once. But properties or universals are not like physical objects; and one crucial difference between them just is that, unlike physical objects, they can, in their entirety, simultaneously be in different places.[18] Plato's objection is plausible only if we wrongly view forms (properties) as though they were particular physical objects.

Something like this rejoinder may be suggested by Plato in our passage. For having offered his objection to W, he immediately replies:

No, it would not, replied Socrates, if it were like one and the same day, which is in many places at once and nevertheless is not separate from itself. Suppose any given form is in them all at the same time as one and the same thing in that way. (131 в 3–6)

If forms are like days, perhaps W is plausible after all. But how are days being construed? There are at least two possibilities: (*a*) the light of day; (*b*) a period of time, e.g. 20 July 1985. On (*a*), Plato's point is presumably that the light of day is not separate from itself, because it is spatially continuous, in contrast to my chairs, which are spatially discontinuous. But this, of course, is no defence of W; for the light of day is not, as a whole, in different places at once. Hence on (*a*), Plato does not make the relevant point.

On (*b*), however, something more like the relevant point is made. At least, 20 July (unlike the light of day) does not seem to be any sort of physical object; and it may well seem plausible to suppose that it is 20 July simultaneously both in Ithaca and Chicago. To be sure, it is not clear that 20 July is a universal; it seems to be an abstract particular—so Plato is not clearly contrasting the distinctive ways in which particulars and universals exist. Still, on (*b*) he does point out that not everything exists in the way in which particular physical objects do; and that at least anticipates the rele-

---

[18] For this rejoinder, see e.g. D. M. Armstrong, *Universals and Scientific Realism* (2 vols.; Cambridge: Cambridge University Press, 1978), i. 108.

vant point. The point is not pressed, however; instead, Parmenides matches analogy with analogy:

I like the way you make out that one and the same thing is in many places at once, Socrates. You might as well spread a sail over a number of people and then say that the one sail as a whole was over them all. Don't you think that is a fair analogy? (131 B 7–9)

Since this is just the right objection against the day analogy construed in way (*a*), one might conclude that Plato so construed it and simply failed to see option (*b*). But this is not the only possibility. Perhaps Plato deliberately offers us a crude model for W, to highlight the fact that W cannot, at any rate, be defended in *that* way. Perhaps he sees option (*b*), and means us to infer that it is more plausible. Or perhaps he sees (*b*), but finds it implausible; certainly not all who countenance universals accept W.

I am inclined to believe that, for whatever reason, Plato, by the time of the *Parmenides*, does reject W. For at 144 D he remarks that 'unity, being one, cannot be in many places at once as a whole'; and in the later *Philebus* W 'seems absolutely impossible' (15 B 7)—in both places, Plato suggests that W is not just problematical, but impossible; in contrast to many later defenders of universals, Plato does not favour W. None the less, the crucial points remain: that even if Plato came to reject W, he might once have accepted it; and that no one who accepts W need be worried by Plato's objection to it.

5. Plato's Objections: P

Plato begins his criticism of P by raising two questions:

Are you, then, prepared to assert that we shall find the single form actually being divided? Will it still be one? (*Parm.* 131 C 9–10)

These two questions embody two different but related objections. The objection embodied in the first question seems to be that if a form is divided, it cannot be numerically one object. If, with Aristotle, we both take numerical oneness to imply particularity and also deny that there are scattered particulars, then it's true that if a form is scattered, it cannot be numerically one.[19] One might, however, reply that this is an objection to P only if forms are particulars; if, as I have suggested, they are properties instead, then

---

[19] *Cat.* 1^{b}6–7 and elsewhere suggest that something is a particular if and only if it is one in number; at *Metaph. Z* 16, 1040^b ff., Aristotle says that what is one in number cannot be in

that they are not numerically one is no defect, but necessary. Even if forms are particulars, one could still evade the present objection by rejecting Aristotle's claim that there are no scattered particulars; forms, though scattered, can still be numerically one in so far as that only requires particularity.

The objection embodied in the second question seems to be that if a form is scattered, its parts cannot be what Aristotle calls *hen eidei*, one in form—they cannot all share a single form.[20] It is not initially clear why this should be so. Surely each of the bits of the world's water, for example, satisfies some one description—of what it is to be water—such that each bit is one in form? Perhaps; but not all cases can be treated in this way. If I scatter the parts of my chair across the room, the parts are not one in form—one part is a leg, another a seat, and these are different in form. Water, we might say, is homoeomerous; it and its parts are all water. But chairs are not homoeomerous; parts of chairs are not chairs. If parts of forms are homoeomerous, then they can be one in form, and so evade the present objection; otherwise not.

I think this is Plato's suggestion too. For he goes on to raise various paradoxes of self-predication (SP); and I think part of his point is that, given SP, parts of forms cannot be homoeomerous and so cannot be one in form. He also suggests that, given SP, parts of forms cannot do their explanatory work; and that SP requires forms and/or their parts to suffer compresence of opposites. Indeed, it is in part because of the compresence of opposites that forms are debarred from doing their explanatory work, and from being homoeomerous.

Consider first the form of large. Presumably each of its parts is smaller than it. But if so, then sensible large things will be made large by something small, and 'will not that seem unreasonable?' (131 D 2). This is unreasonable, I take it, because it violates one of the *Phaedo*'s constraints on adequate explanations, that nothing can be made F by something that is not F (*Phd.* 101 A 8–B 2). But if, to avoid this objection, we insist that the parts of the form of large are all large, then they will be both large and small (since smaller than the form of large); the effort to preserve homoeomerity leads to the compresence of opposites.

Consider next the form of small. Given SP, it is small; and presumably its parts are smaller than it (so *Parm.* 131 D 9–E 1 seems to assume). But

more than one place at a time. The conjunction of these claims seems to preclude scattered particulars. Simiarly, in *Top.* 1. 7 Aristotle seems to suggest that different bits of water are the same only in species (form)—i.e. they do not constitute a single object; all the world's water, for Aristotle, is a universal. See also n. 18.

[20] *Top.* 1. 7; *Metaph.* Δ 6, 1016^{a}17 ff. For Aristotle, a species is one in form if its members are; however, the species does not itself have its form and so it is not homoeomerous with its members.

then the form is both small (given SP) and large (in so far as it is larger than each of its parts); and so suffers compresence of opposites. Moreover, anything to which a part of smallness is added will become smaller; for, on P, something is made F by having in it a part of the form of F. But this violates our intuition that adding something to a thing cannot make it smaller. Once again, parts cannot do their explanatory work; parts of the form of small cannot make something small. But neither can they make something large; for they are small, and what is small cannot make something large, since, as Plato explains in the *Phaedo*, what makes something F cannot itself be not F.

Consider finally the form of equal. Its parts are smaller (*smikron*, 131 D 4) than it. But then they are less than (*elatton*, 131 D 5) it, and so are not equal to it, and so are unequal (since unequal to something). But if they are unequal, they cannot explain why things are equal because, again, the *Phaedo* precludes explaining something's being F by appeal to something that is not F.

The conjunction of SP, P, and the *Phaedo*'s constraints on explanation thus leads to difficulty. Or so Plato suggests—but his suggestions are resistible.

Let's first reconsider the sort of compresence at issue here. Plato argues that sometimes forms or their parts suffer some sort of compresence. There are, however, different sorts of compresence; and perhaps the only sort he has argued for here is an untroubling sort. In the middle dialogues, Plato argues that length, for example—what it is to be long—cannot consist in any observable property such as three inches since, although some three-inch things are long, others are short. Three inches, that is, suffers the compresence of opposites, in that it makes some things long, others short. If so, it cannot be what length is; for length as such always makes the things that have it long, never short. Length, then—that is, the form of length—must be a nonobservable property, a property definable in nonobservational terms; only in this way can it escape the troubling sort of compresence.[21]

So the form of F escapes one sort of compresence—it only makes what has it F; it never makes what has it not-F. It might, however, quite compatibly with this, suffer some other sort of compresence. In the *Sophist*, for example, Plato insists that every form both is and is not (e.g. 256 E 5–6). Each is (in so far as each is the same as itself and has many predicates true of it), and each also is not (in so far as each is nonidentical to everything else, and fails to have many predicates true of it). This sort of compresence, however, is neither avoidable nor troubling. Indeed, even the form of being both is and is not (257 A 4–6)—so not only is every form of F both G and

---

[21] I discuss this argument in more detail in 'The One over Many', *Philosophical Review*, 89 (1980), 197–240.

not-G, for some predicates 'G'; but also, some forms of F are also not-F. None the less, although the form of being, for example, both is and is not, even in the *Sophist* it only explains what it is for something to be; it never explains what it is for something not to be. That is to say, even though some forms of F are F and not-F, no form of F ever explains what it is for something to be not-F, or ever makes things not-F. Even in the *Sophist*, then, forms are exempt from the sort of compresence of opposites that was of concern in the middle dialogues.

Perhaps, then, the only sort of compresence Plato can argue for here is of the nontroubling sort. But is this clear? Suppose the form of large and its parts have determinate sizes. Then, it seems, they would make some of the things that have them large, others small. To avoid the troubling sort of compresence, then, Plato must deny that the form or its parts has any determinate size. Intuitively, however, only things with determinate sizes can be large. So it may look as though Plato can avoid the troubling sort of compresence only by rejecting SP.

But this is not in fact the case. Let us distinguish between two versions of SP: narrow and broad. According to narrow SP (NSP), 'large' has its intuitive, preanalytic sense according to which, among other things, only things with determinate sizes can be large. But of course, intuitive, preanalytic beliefs can be wrong; most Platonic dialogues are devoted to showing just this, to revising our beliefs into a more cohesive explanatory whole. In so doing, however, Plato does not assign predicates new meanings; he uncovers what was meant all along, and puts it in more perspicuous fashion. At the same time, though, this procedure may alter our beliefs about what counts as being within the extension of a given predicate. Thus, for example, *Laches* apparently arrives at the seemingly surprising belief that lions are not courageous; the *Republic* tells us that a certain sort of psychic harmony is justice. Plato thus revises our beliefs about the extensions of predicates; and he also alters some of our beliefs about what is involved in the senses of various predicates. But he can thus refine or revise our beliefs without assigning predicates new meanings. He is not telling us that we gave the wrong sense to 'justice'; he is telling us what the correct core of our beliefs about justice is. This is what I mean by 'broad SP' (BSP): predicates retain their original senses but that sense needs to be refined and, with the refinement, we will alter some of our beliefs about the extensions of predicates. One of the discoveries we will make is that things can bear predicates for more reasons, or in more ways, than we preanalytically supposed. In particular, the form of F can be F in virtue of making its possessors F; the form of large is large, not because of its size (not being extended, it has no size), but because it is the property that makes things large. This is not to say that 'large' has a different sense from what we supposed; nor is it to say that 'large' is ambiguous or homonymous. It is only to say that more sorts of things than we supposed can all be large. We all quite easily call persons, actions, institutions, and laws 'just'; yet these are very different sorts of things. Plato suggests that in just the same way, we can call the property (form) of F 'F'. He is simply extending a practice found in ordinary usage.[22]

On NSP, neither forms nor their parts can avoid the troubling sort of compresence. BSP, however, holds out more hope here. First, it allows us to say that the form of large is large, even though it has no size. It is large because it makes the things that have it large; this is one way of being large—so our practice of dialectic reveals. Since it is genuinely large, it still enjoys SP; but since it is the property that makes things large, and since it never makes things not-large, it also avoids the troubling sort of compresence. We can, then, retain SP—if it is understood as BSP—and yet avoid the troubling sort of compresence.

Not only that, but we can also preserve homoeomerity. The form of large is large, in so far as it is the property that makes things large. It does so (on P) by having parts in different things, parts that make the things that have them large. Both the form and its parts are large, then, for the same sorts of reasons; and both escape the troubling sort of compresence. This seems adequate to preserve homoeomerity. To be sure, there are some different descriptions true of the form and its parts; the form is not, in its entirety, in a given place at once, though each of its parts is. None the less, this does not compromise homoeomerity. Consider again the water example: every bit of the world's water is water, although each also differs from the whole and from every other bit in some ways—they are in different places, of different sizes, of different degrees of purity. None the less, water and its parts are homoeomerous in virtue of satisfying the same relevant descriptions, of all alike being water. In just the same way, although the form and its parts do not share all and only the same properties, they do share the relevant ones, of being large, and of escaping the troubling sort of compresence.

With BSP, then, we can allow the form of F and its parts to be F; and we can do so without having the form or its parts suffer the troubling sort of

---

[22] What I call 'broad self-predication' has obvious affinities with the version of self-predication defended by S. Peterson in 'A Reasonable Self-Predication Premise for the Third Man Argument', *Philosophical Review*, 82 (1973), 451–70. More precisely, she describes a general strategy, called reinterpretation, which comes in two versions, conservative and expansive. She seems to favour the conservative version, whereas I am developing the expansive version.

compresence. Homoeomerity is also preserved; and forms can fulfil their explanatory role.

I have suggested that, if forms are properties and enjoy only BSP, they escape Plato's objections to immanence. None the less, there is some point to his raising them. They are not, to be sure, devastating objections; as Plato remarks later, they are objections an able person could refute (*Parm.* 133 B 4–C 1; 135 A 7–B 2). But they serve the heuristic purpose of warning us against one way of reading the dialogues—a way Plato is not careful to block, but one he is not committed to, either.

Such at least is Plato's verdict. Aristotle, however, disagrees; he rejects Plato's easy optimism, and suggests that in fact Plato cannot accommodate immanence—Plato's objections are not soluble puzzles, but irresoluble difficulties; and there are further objections too.

6. Aristotle's Objections[23]

In the *Peri Ideōn*, Aristotle raises various objections to immanent forms; I explore them in turn.

(i) if the ideas are mixed with the other things, then first, they would be bodies; for mixture is of bodies. (ii) Further, they will have contrariety towards each other; for mixture is according to contrariety. (97. 30–98. 2)

Here Aristotle considers a particular version of immanence—that it is mixture—and derives two allegedly unwelcome results: that forms are bodies, and that they are contraries. This is supposed to be unwelcome because forms are supposed to be incorporeal; and because, Aristotle assumes, Plato does not want forms of contraries.

I think Aristotle is simply wrong to believe that Plato disallows forms of contraries.[24] But the more interesting question for our purposes is why Aristotle should construe immanence in terms of mixture.

[23] Aristotle objects to immanent forms elsewhere than in the *Peri Ideōn*, but I restrict myself here to his *Peri Ideōn* objections. It is disputed whether Alexander, *In Metaph.* 97. 27–98. 24 Hayduck, accurately records arguments to be found in the *Peri Ideōn*; I shall assume without argument here that he does. Commentators divide the number of arguments differently; neither shall I defend my numbering or divisions here. For some discussion, see H. F. Cherniss, *Aristotle's Criticism of Plato and the Academy* (Baltimore: Johns Hopkins Press, 1944), appendix VII; and W. Leszl, *Il 'De ideis' di Aristotele e la teoria platonica delle idee* (Florence: Olschki, 1975), ch. XXI. I discuss these and related issues in *On Ideas*; see, to begin with, p. 31. Although Aristotle's arguments here are ostensibly aimed against Eudoxus, not Plato, I assume Eudoxus held a theory of immanent Platonic forms; for the sake of simplicity, I shall write as though Aristotle is criticizing Plato directly.

[24] In his criticism of the Argument from Relatives, Aristotle also seems to deny that the

I think the culprit, in Aristotle's view, is NSP: since the form of man is a man, it must consist of flesh and bones and the like; and perhaps such a form could be in Socrates only by being mixed in him. At least, NSP might well yield the result that many forms are bodies—the form of man must be a body, for example, since all men have bodies; and so too must the form of large be, since only bodies can be large.[25]

If Plato accepts or is committed to NSP, Aristotle's objection seems reasonable. I have suggested, however, that he is committed only to BSP. Why does Aristotle disagree?

I think he has two main reasons. One is this: NSP is, surely, one intuitive account of Plato's use of self-predicational language—an account Plato does nothing to qualify or soften along the lines of BSP. Aristotle feels no compulsion to offer philosophers distinctions or qualifications they do not themselves trouble to formulate; so he commits Plato to NSP and sees what results.[26]

This procedure is no doubt useful in highlighting what distinctions and qualifications are necessary to save a thesis; but Aristotle is uncharitable if he assumes Plato is unclear or confused simply because he fails to draw them explicitly. A philosopher can observe distinctions, or assume qualifications, he does not trouble to spell out; and I see no evidence of confusion on Plato's part here, but only the sort of lack of precision and literal explanation that is likely to irritate a philosopher like Aristotle.

It is just as well, then, that Aristotle has a second, and philosophically more satisfying, reason for committing Plato to NSP: he believes that Plato's commitment to separation commits him as well to NSP. I explore this second reason below (in 6 (viii)).

Further, ⟨each idea⟩ will be mixed in each of the things with which it is mixed either (iii) as a whole or else (iv) as a part. But if (iii) as a whole, then what is numerically one will be in many things (for the idea is numerically one). (iv) While if as a part, (*a*) a man will be what participates in a part of man-itself, not what participates in

Platonists want forms of contraries (Alexander, *In Metaph*. 83. 28–30 Hayduck). Perhaps he conflates that (incorrect) denial with the (correct) denial that Plato denies forms of negations (of the not-beautiful, as opposed to of the ugly). I discuss forms of negations in 'The One over Many', and in *On Ideas*, ch. 8, § 6.

[25] Ross, in his commentary on the *Metaphysics* (2 vols.; Oxford: Clarendon Press, 1924), i. 198, offers an alternative suggestion: that for Eudoxus, forms are substances and so bodies. But Aristotelian forms are substances too, and they are not bodies and do not mix with things.

[26] See G. E. L. Owen, 'Dialectic and Eristic in the Treatment of Forms', in G. E. L. Owen (ed.), *Aristotle on Dialectic: The Topics* (Symposium Aristotelicum, 3; Oxford: Clarendon Press, 1968), 103–25 at 111.

the whole of man-itself. (*b*) Further, ideas will be divisible and partible, although they are impassive. (*c*) Further, each will be homoeomerous if all the things which have some part from ⟨a form⟩ are like each other. But how can the forms be homoeomerous? For a part of a man cannot be a man, as a part of gold is gold. (98. 2–9)

Like Plato in the *Parmenides*, Aristotle suggests that if forms are in things, either W or P obtains; since each is problematical, forms cannot be in things.[27]

Aristotle's objection to W is that since forms are numerically one—and so are particulars—they cannot, in their entirety, be in more than one place at a time.[28]

As Aristotle understands numerical oneness, it is indeed incompatible with W. But I reject Aristotle's suggestion that forms are numerically one; I believe they are properties or universals instead. I do not mean to suggest, however, that Aristotle simply misinterprets Plato in claiming that forms are numerically one; he believes Plato's commitment to separation requires forms to be particulars (see 6 (viii)).

Aristotle levels a triple objection against P (iv*a–c*). (iv*a*) and (iv*c*) together constitute a dilemma against P, one anticipated in the *Parmenides*. The parts of forms are either (*a*) anhomoeomerous or (*c*) homoeomerous. If they are anhomoeomerous, they cannot do their explanatory work. But if they are homoeomerous, the resultant conception of forms is incoherent.

Consider the first horn first: Socrates and Callias are both men in virtue of having in them parts of the form of man—Socrates has its leg, say, and Callias its arm. But having a leg or an arm in one is neither necessary nor sufficient for being a man. Nor can we explain why Socrates and Callias are both men by appealing to the fact that Socrates has a leg in him, Callias an arm. If, then, the parts of forms are anhomoeomerous, they cannot do their explanatory work. But neither are matters any better if the parts of forms

[27] Although Aristotle's objection parallels Plato's, he uses 'man' rather than, for example, 'large' as his sample predicate. I take it he has two main reasons for doing so. First, it is more difficult to see how something could be a man in virtue of having a (part of a) man in it than it is to see how something could be large in virtue of having something large in it. Second, Aristotle argues elsewhere that if there are any forms at all, there are at most forms corresponding to substances; so in focusing on the form of man, he focuses on a case where there ought to be a form if there are any forms at all—but it then turns out that such forms are vulnerable to yet more devastating objections than forms of nonsubstances would be, most notably the Third Man Regress. See *On Ideas*, chs. 15–16.

[28] Aristotle's objection to W in *Metaphysics Z* 14 more nearly parallels the *Parmenides*' objection than does the present objection, which does not repeat the claim that on W, the form is separate from itself.

are homoeomerous. How could the form of man consist of lots of men? Perhaps gold is homoeomerous; but the form of man surely cannot be.

Once again, Aristotle's objection is reasonable if Plato is indeed committed to NSP. On BSP, however, there is no difficulty in seeing how the form of man can be homoeomerous, or how something can be a man by having in it a part of the form of man. For on BSP, the form of man is a man (not in virtue of having legs, or flesh and bones, but) in virtue of being the property whose parts (assuming P) make things men. Unless Aristotle has good reasons for committing Plato to NSP, his dilemma can be evaded. Above I suggested that one of his reasons may be uncharitable; I explore his second reason below (6 (viii)).

Aristotle's third objection to P (ivb) is that it requires forms to be divisible, which conflicts with the impassivity of forms. Now it is true that in the *Symposium* (211 B 4–5) Plato claims that forms are impassive; and it is also true that P requires some sort of division into parts; so Aristotle raises at least a good prima facie objection. But is it more than that? I suggested above that the only sorts of changelessness Plato ascribes to forms are those sorts that would jeopardize a form's remaining the form it is; and the same is true, *mutatis mutandis*, for being impassive. But having parts in different objects in the way explained above (as immanent characters that are finite parts of an infinite nondepletable amount of nonmaterial stuff) does not put forms thus in jeopardy; yet this is the only sort of division P requires. Once we spell out precisely what sorts of impassivity forms have, and what sort of division P requires, the apparent tension between impassivity and division dissolves. To be sure, Plato does not trouble to spell this out for us explicitly; and Aristotle would be justified in pointing that out. But to criticize Plato for lack of care or explicitness is not to deal a deadly blow, or to uncover an irresoluble contradiction.

Perhaps, however, Aristotle reasons as follows: since forms are separate, they enjoy NSP; if NSP is true of them, they are mixed in—are physical parts of—things; and if so, P would involve physical divisibility, which Plato is, of course, concerned to disallow. Once again, for this line of argument to succeed, Aristotle must be able to show that Plato is committed to NSP; I consider his argument below.

in each thing there will be not one idea mixed but many; for if there is one idea of animal and another of man, and a man is both an animal and a man, he would participate in both ideas. And man-itself, the idea, in so far as it is also an animal, would also itself participate in animal; and consequently (v) the ideas would no longer be simple but composed from many, and (vi) some of them will be primary,

others secondary. But if it is not an animal, surely it is absurd to say that man is
not an animal? (98. 10–16)

SP requires the form of man to be both a man and an animal. But then it
participates in the form of animal and so is no longer simple. Moreover,
the form of animal will then be prior to the form of man; yet no form is
supposed to be prior to any other.

It is true that Plato says that each form is uniform, pure, itself by itself,
incomposite, and the like (cf. e.g. *Phd.* 78 ff.); so Aristotle once again detects
a prima facie tension. But once again, we need to ask whether it is more than
that. If, as was once fashionable, one took such (or other) claims to suggest
that forms are 'simple nameables' analogous to the simples of logical atomism, then his objection is telling. But Plato never accepted this 'logical atomist' view.[29] To be sure, no form has physical parts; but then, for one form
to participate in another does not require it to have such parts. And Plato
always allowed that forms have 'logical' parts, at least in the sense that each
has many properties true of it. Each form is, and is one form, for example,
and so has the properties of being, and of being one. When Plato insists on
the uniformity and purity of forms, he means only that each is one form,
that unlike sensibles, each is free from compresence of opposites, and the
like; he does not mean to preclude one form's participating in another, or
having various properties or some internal structure. But Aristotle's reason
for suggesting otherwise is by now familiar: Plato does not explicitly tell us
this, and Aristotle is under no compulsion to assume clarity where matters
are not explicitly spelt out; further, Plato's commitment to NSP, via his commitment to separation, does not easily allow the relevant caveats to be made.

Aristotle also claims that if forms participate in one another, some forms
are prior to others; yet, he suggests, no form ought to be prior to any
other.[30] I think Aristotle is right to say that some forms turn out to be prior
to others, wrong to say that the Platonists would not accept this result. They
want forms to be prior to sensibles; but they recognize priority rankings
among forms. In the *Republic*, for example, the form of the good is clearly
recognized as being in some way prior to other forms (cf. e.g. 509 B 6–10).

Perhaps Aristotle sees that Plato recognizes priority rankings among
forms, but believes he ought not to do so, in view of their status as first

---

[29] For 'logical atomist' interpretations of middle Plato, see e.g. G. E. L. Owen, 'Notes
on Ryle's Plato', in O. P. Wood and G. Pitcher (eds.), *Ryle: A Collection of Critical Essays*
(London: Macmillan, 1971), 341–72. For some criticism, see ch. 10.

[30] Aristotle also discusses the priority of forms earlier in the *Peri Ideōn*; see Alexander, *In
Metaph.* 85. 15–88. 2 Hayduck. On this passage, see the excellent article by J. Annas, 'Forms
and First Principles', *Phronesis*, 19 (1974), 257–83.

principles. But all Plato means by the priority of forms as principles is their priority to sensibles; and Aristotle too recognizes that some substances are prior to others. In the *Categories*, for example, primary substances are prior to secondary ones; and in the *Metaphysics*, form is prior to matter and compound, though all three count, in the end, as substance. Once again, however, Aristotle would no doubt insist that since Plato does not spell all of this out explicitly, he is under no onus to assume clarity on Plato's part.

(vii) And further, if they are mixed with the things that are relative to them, how could they still be paradigms, as they say they are? For it is not in this way, by being mixed, that paradigms are causes of the similarity that their likenesses have to them. (98. 16–19)

Aristotle seems to make two quite different points in the passage just cited. In its first sentence, he suggests that immanence and paradigmatism are incompatible. But its second sentence, which is ostensibly introduced to explain the first sentence, suggests a weaker point: that, although immanence and paradigmatism may be compatible, the former cannot explain the latter.

'*Paradeigma*' can be used in many different ways, but Aristotle seems to have the following account in mind: x is a paradigm for y's being F just in case x and y are both F; x, but not y, is perfectly F; and y is F in virtue of its relation to x, but not conversely.[31] I think this account of paradigmatism corresponds to Plato's; but, again, it is an abstract formulation that admits of both a narrow and broad reading.

On the narrow construal, which Aristotle predictably assumes, the only sorts of things that can stand in the paradigm–copy relation are, for example, Socrates and his picture. On this account, Aristotle is surely correct to insist that sensibles are not F in virtue of having paradigms in them as parts—Socrates is not a part of his picture.

On the broad construal, however, which I predictably favour, there is no tension. On this construal, the property of F is F (given BSP); it is perfectly F, because it is everlasting and escapes the troubling sort of compresence (because, as explained above, it makes things F but never makes anything not-F); and sensibles, which are not perfectly F, are F in virtue of having in them (parts of) the form of F. That is to say, the broad construal allows forms to be paradigms, even given Aristotle's abstract account of paradigmatism; but it does so compatibly with immanence. Indeed, immanence

---

[31] That this is Aristotle's understanding of Platonic paradigmatism seems clear from his account of the Argument from Relatives. I discuss Aristotle and the Argument from Relatives in *On Ideas*, chs. 10–13.

partially explains paradigmatism, in so far as it just is the relevant relation between sensibles and forms—sensibles are F by having in them (parts of) forms as properties of them.

Aristotle favours the narrow construal for by now familiar reasons: that Plato calls forms paradigms, after all; that narrow paradigmatism is an intuitively correct account of what paradigmatism consists in, and one Plato does not trouble to guard against; and one need not assume clarity in a philosopher who does not so trouble. Moreover, Aristotle probably believes that Plato is in any case hard pressed to avoid narrow paradigmatism. For, as I explain below (in 6 (viii)), he believes that given separation, forms must be objects—and what sort of paradigmatic objects could forms be other than the sort countenanced by NSP?

(viii) Further, they would be destroyed along with the destruction of the things they are in. Nor would they be separate themselves by themselves, but ⟨they would exist only⟩ in their participants. (98. 19–20)

Here Aristotle alleges that immanence is incompatible with separation. He is echoed by Vlastos, who concludes that therefore immanent characters are not (parts of) forms. And many others too have viewed immanence and separation as exclusive options.[32]

But are they? I have argued elsewhere that separation is the capacity for independent existence; the form of F is separate just in case it can exist independently of sensible particulars.[33] Immanence in our context, I suggested, is being a part of; the form of F is in x just in case F is in some sense a part of x. If this is correct, then separation and immanence are not definitionally incompatible; one cannot infer from the fact that x is separate from y that x is not a part of y, or from the fact that x is a part of y that x is not separate from y. Indeed, Aristotle spends a great deal of time in *Metaphysics Z* asking what sorts of parts are, and are not, separate from what they are parts of.

Presumably Aristotle's point, then, is that although immanence and separation are not definitionally incompatible, they are incompatible in the special case of forms. Here is one explanation of why Aristotle might think that this is so: forms, I have suggested, are parts of things by being properties of them. Aristotle, however, believes that properties—universals—cannot exist uninstantiated. Hence forms cannot both be parts of things by being properties of them and also be separate from the things whose parts they are.

If this is Aristotle's argument, however, it clearly rests on a controversial

[32] Vlastos, 'The Third Man Argument in the *Parmenides*', 253 n. 1.
[33] In 'Separation' (above, ch. 11).

philosophical assumption many would reject: that universals cannot exist uninstantiated. If we reject this assumption, then there is no bar to forms being both separate (capable of independent existence) and immanent (parts of things, as properties of them).

This is important. For many people, seeing that Aristotle argues that since forms are separate they cannot be immanent, simply assume that Plato must, in consistency, reject immanence. They would be right, if separation and immanence were definitionally incompatible. But I have suggested that, as Aristotle understands the terms, they are not; he believes that separation precludes immanence, not as a matter of definition, but as a matter of controversial metaphysics. No one who, unlike Aristotle, admits the possibility of uninstantiated universals ought to be worried about acknowledging separate immanent forms—there is nothing 'scandaleuse' in doing so.

Aristotle's controversial assumption—that universals cannot exist uninstantiated—does yet further work for him in his criticism of Plato; not only does it ground his claim that forms cannot be both separate and immanent, but it also grounds other important claims. If forms are separate, then, Aristotle believes, they must be particulars (they cannot be universals, since universals cannot, in Aristotle's view, be separate); Aristotle sees that Plato intends forms to function as universals but he believes that separation precludes their fulfilling that function. Hence, as in the objection to W explored above, Aristotle sometimes writes as though forms are particulars, numerically one—although elsewhere he is quite clear that Plato intends them to be properties. Again, if we believe that universals can exist uninstantiated, then we ought not to cavil at separated forms that are properties.

Aristotle's controversial assumption also seems to ground his belief that Plato is committed to NSP. Given separation, Aristotle believes, forms must be particulars; moreover, Plato also subscribes to some sort of self-predication assumption. If the form of man, however, is both a particular and also a man, surely it must be a particular man; and surely all particular men have legs, arms, and the like?

The assumption also seems to ground Aristotle's suggestion that Plato is committed to narrow paradigmatism. For again, separation, on his view, makes forms particulars; and the conjunction of forms being particulars, and enjoying NSP, makes narrow paradigmatism seem irresistible.

At *Metaphysics M* 9, 1086^{b}6–7, Aristotle remarks that 'separating them is responsible for the resulting difficulties with forms'. I have explored several difficulties Aristotle seems to believe separation results in: it makes forms particulars; it commits Plato to NSP and to narrow paradigmatism; and it precludes immanence. But if I have been right, these difficulties result only if we agree with Aristotle that universals cannot exist unin-stantiated; without such agreement, separation—capacity for independent existence—does not result in any of the alleged difficulties.

Earlier I suggested that one reason Aristotle commits Plato to NSP and the like is that Plato is not careful to guard against them; and I suggested that this reason, though salutary in making clear what qualifications Plato needs to invoke, is ultimately uncharitable. I have now suggested that Aris-totle's second reason for committing Plato to NSP and the like is at least suspect, in so far as it rests on the controversial philosophical assumption that universals cannot exist uninstantiated. None the less, this second rea-son is more interesting and satisfying than the first. For first, it engages Plato at a philosophical level, rather than merely cavilling at his impreci-sion and carelessness; and it is surely altogether appropriate for Aristotle to see what happens to Platonism once his own philosophical assumptions are brought to bear. And second, it puts us in the happy position of being able to have our cake and eat it too. For now we need not say either that Aristotle simply misinterprets Plato, nor yet that Plato is obviously vul-nerable to his objections. Aristotle interprets Plato correctly and rejects his views for philosophical reasons.

(ix) And in addition to these objections, the ideas will no longer be immovable. (92. 21)

Here Aristotle alleges that immanence is incompatible with the immo-bility of forms. He gives no reason for the claim here, but he does give one in the *Topics* (113^a24–32; cf. also *Top.* 148^a14–22, *Metaph. B* 2, 998^a14–15): forms move when their possessors do.[34]

Now in *Physics* 224^b5–7, 11–16, Aristotle insists *in propria voce* that properties are immovable. But in *Physics* 211^a he distinguishes two ways something can move: in itself or coincidentally. Properties, he says, do not move in themselves; but he allows that they do move coincidentally, in so far as the bodies they are parts of move in themselves. Hence when Aristotle later says that properties do not move, he means only that they do not move in themselves, though they do move coincidentally.

If forms are in things, perhaps they move coincidentally; but they need not move in themselves any more than Aristotle believes properties do. What, then, shall we make of Aristotle's objection? He might mean that Plato, unlike himself, disallows even coincidental motion for forms. Or he might mean that since Plato is not careful to distinguish between coinci-

---

[34] My account of the ninth objection is indebted to Owen's, 'Dialectic and Eristic in the Treatment of Forms', 109–12.

dental and in-itself motion, he cannot invoke Aristotle's distinction and so avoid the objection. I see no evidence that Plato disallows coincidental motion for forms. For, as I suggested above, the only sorts of changelessness he is concerned to ascribe to forms are those sorts forms need to remain the forms they are; but coincidental motion (as opposed, say, to various sorts of alteration) is not one of those sorts. Nor, again, is Aristotle charitable in disallowing Plato distinctions, if his sole reason for doing so is Plato's failure to draw them explicitly.

Perhaps, however, Aristotle also reasons that if forms are in things at all, they are mixed in things, and so physical parts of them; and perhaps he believes that in that case, they would have to move in themselves when the things whose parts they are move.

7. Conclusion

I have explored a number of objections to immanent forms, and argued that none succeeds—if, that is, forms are properties that enjoy broad but not narrow SP, and if we allow Plato distinctions he does not trouble to formulate. Moreover, we can endorse this reading of the dialogues without having to conclude that Aristotle simply misinterprets Plato. Rather, Aristotle interprets Plato correctly, and then attacks him on two fronts: first, he disallows Plato distinctions he does not explicitly formulate; and second, he believes Plato is not entitled to such distinctions in any case, given his commitment to separation. We may or may not be sympathetic to Aristotle's criticisms; but whatever their faults, misinterpretation of Plato is not among them. We can grant this, however, without needing to agree with Aristotle's conclusion that immanent forms are absurd.[35]

[35] I am indebted to Cynthia Freeland and Terry Irwin for helpful written comments, and to Julia Annas and Michael Woods for helpful discussion. It is a pleasure to record a more general debt to Professor Ackrill, who has been generous in his help ever since I first studied with him as a graduate student in Oxford in 1973–4.

13

Relational Entities

Aristotle's theory of universals is sometimes thought to differ from Plato's in being nonrelational; it does not hold that Socrates' being a man, or being rational, consists in or involves his standing in some relation to the universal man, or to the universal rationality. Thus G. E. M. Anscombe, for example, writes that Aristotle was concerned 'to attack the doctrine of the Platonists whereby if Socrates is a man, then Socrates stands in some relation to what he is said to be'.[1] Matthews and Cohen, in their provocative article 'The One and the Many', agree: 'In place of Plato's relational account Aristotle's doctrine of primary and secondary substance offers a nonrelational way of understanding what it is for Felix to be a cat.'[2]

This alleged difference between Plato and Aristotle is sometimes thought to go with another: that for Plato, but not for Aristotle, universals are, or are associated with, transcendent or separated forms. Separation is thought to be responsible for the relational character of Plato's theory; and Aristotle's rejection of separation is thought to make his account nonrelational.

The allegedly nonrelational character of Aristotle's theory is thought to be an advantage. David Armstrong, for example, in *Universals and Scientific Realism*, criticizes Plato's theory of universals for being relational; and he praises Aristotle for seeing 'that although particularity and universality are inseparable aspects of all existence, they are neither reducible to each other, nor are they related. Though distinct, their union is closer than relation.'[3]

---

[1] G. E. M. Anscombe and P. T. Geach, *Three Philosophers* (Ithaca, NY: Cornell University Press, 1961), 26.

[2] G. B. Matthews and S. Marc Cohen, 'The One and the Many', *Review of Metaphysics*, 21 (1968), 630–55 at 635. Further references to this article will be cited parenthetically in the text.

[3] D. M. Armstrong, *Universals and Scientific Realism* (2 vols.; Cambridge: Cambridge University Press, 1978), ii. 3. I discuss Armstrong's views in more detail in 'Armstrong on Relational and Nonrelational Realism', *Pacific Philosophical Quarterly*, 62 (1981), 262–71. Further references to Armstrong's book will be cited parenthetically in the text. I focus here on Matthews and Cohen and Armstrong as especially clear and interesting exponents of this general view; but they are not idiosyncratic. Others who discuss these issues in Plato include: R. E. Allen, 'Participation and Predication in Plato's Middle Dialogues', *Philosophical Review*,

Indeed, Aristotle too seems to believe that one of the many advantages of his philosophy over Plato's is that it offers a nonrelational account of property possession.[4]

Why should a nonrelational account be preferred? Matthews and Cohen suggest that Plato's relational theory is vulnerable to an awkward dilemma: either particulars are 'bare particulars', or else they are 'mere relational entities' that owe their identity and continued existence to the relations they bear to other things. Aristotle's allegedly nonrelational theory is thought to go between the horns of this dilemma.[5]

I am sympathetic to some features of this general view. I agree that, on some accounts of relationality, Plato has a relational theory of universals. I also agree that Plato, but not Aristotle, separates universals. I agree too that relational accounts are vulnerable to Matthews and Cohen's dilemma. But I do not agree that Aristotle's theory of universals is nonrelational. Or, at least, the arguments used to commit Plato to a relational account seem to me to commit Aristotle to one as well. Nor do I conclude that Plato's and Aristotle's theories are therefore both hopelessly misguided; for I do not find both horns of the dilemma unattractive. Although I reject bare particulars, I accept relational entities.[6] If it is a consequence of Plato's or

69 (1960), 147–64; E. N. Lee, 'On the Metaphysics of the Image in Plato's *Timaeus*', *Monist*, 50 (1966), 341–68; K. W. Mills, 'Some Aspects of Plato's Theory of Forms: *Timaeus* 49c ff.', *Phronesis*, 13 (1968), 145–70; N. P. White, *Plato on Knowledge and Reality* (Indianapolis: Hackett, 1976), esp. 70–1. Others who suggest that Aristotle's account is nonrelational include: A. Donagan, 'Universals and Metaphysical Realism', *Monist*, 47 (1963), 211–46; G. E. L. Owen, 'The Platonism of Aristotle', *Proceedings of the British Academy*, 51 (1965), 125–50; M. J. Woods, 'Substance and Essence in Aristotle', *Proceedings of the Aristotelian Society*, 75 (1974–5), 167–80. There are important differences among these authors, but I obviously cannot discuss all of them here.

[4] This is surely one moral the *Categories* intends; ch. 7 is at pains to argue that no substance is a relative. I do not discuss Aristotle's argument here; an adequate account requires another paper.

[5] See e.g. pp. 634–5, 643–4. Matthews and Cohen also suggest another difficulty with relational accounts or, at least, with Plato's holding one; see pp. 633–4. It is also often objected that relational accounts are vulnerable to a regress. See e.g. Armstrong, vol. i, pt. 2, *passim*; P. F. Strawson, *Individuals* (London: Methuen, 1959), esp. 168–81; F. H. Bradley, *Appearance and Reality*, 2nd edn., 9th impression (Oxford: Clarendon Press, 1930), ch. 3. Plato considers a regress argument, the Third Man Argument, at *Parm.* 132 A–B. I do not discuss the TMA or regress arguments here; but see my 'Aristotle and the More Accurate Arguments', in M. Schofield and M. Nussbaum (eds.), *Language and Logos* (Cambridge: Cambridge University Press, 1982), 155–77, and my 'Owen, Aristotle and the Third Man', *Phronesis*, 27 (1982), 13–33; and *On Ideas*, chs. 15–16.

[6] As I shall use the phrase, a relational entity is an entity that possesses at least one essential property relationally. This is to be distinguished from Bradley's doctrine of internal relations, according to which all of a thing's relational properties are essential to it; I do not discuss Bradley's views in this paper. For Bradley, see esp. chs. 2–3.

Aristotle's theory that particulars are relational entities, that is a desirable consequence.

I ask first what a relational analysis is (Section I). I then turn to Matthews and Cohen's dilemma (Section II). In subsequent sections I ask whether Plato and Aristotle are vulnerable to their dilemma and, if so, whether that is an undesirable consequence of their views.

I

What is a relational analysis? Unfortunately, not all of the authors I'll discuss explicitly address this issue. Armstrong does, however, and I'll take his account as my starting point. He defines a relational analysis as:

> Any doctrine which gives a reductive account of a particular's having properties or relations in terms of further *relations* between the particular and some further entity or entities. (*Universals and Scientific Realism*, i. 139)

If I explain x's being F by saying that x stands in some relation to some entity or entities other than x, I give a relational analysis of x's being F. Now this account may seem unilluminating, since it elucidates a relational analysis in terms of having relations. What, we may ask, is involved in having a relation?

On one familiar view, x's being F is a relational state of affairs just in case it is a polyadic state of affairs. If *two things* are involved in x's being F—x and something other than x—they are related. Let us call this the *crude* or *unrefined* relational analysis. I shall argue that on the crude analysis, both Plato and Aristotle have relational analyses.

Some, however, reject the crude analysis; it is sometimes argued that just as not every one-place predicate denotes a genuine property or universal, so not every many-place predicate denotes a genuine relation. On this view, the mere fact that x's being F is or involves a polyadic state of affairs does not make it relational. Let us call this a *refined* relational analysis.

Different refined relational analyses are possible, since different accounts of genuine relations are possible. In this paper I discuss just one—in-fluential—refined analysis. According to it, if x is F by being related to something, x is accidentally F; if x is essentially F, it is not the case that x is F by being related to something.[7] Relations involve accidental connections. I shall argue that this notion of a relational account is unsatisfactory.

---

[7] In sect. II below I suggest that Matthews and Cohen endorse this view. In 'Armstrong on Relational and Nonrelational Realism' I argue that Armstrong accepts a variant of it. (The variation does not matter for present purposes; I mention it in sect. VII.) Although I cannot

I shall also argue that given this refined relational analysis, the alleged contrast between Plato and Aristotle again collapses; for both espouse essentialism. I do not deny, of course, that it is possible to formulate a different relational analysis, such that, given it, Plato, but not Aristotle, has a relational analysis. But this result is not forthcoming either on the crude account or on the refined analysis to be considered here.

With this rough account in mind, let us ask why relational analyses are thought unattractive.

II

Matthews and Cohen suggest that a relational account—or, at least, Plato's version of one—leads to an awkward dilemma: 'either Felix is what he is independent of participating in cathood (and is therefore a bare individual, whatever that might be thought to be) or else he is a mere relational entity (like a shadow or a reflection, or, to use an Aristotelian example, a threshold (1042b26)) that owes its identity and continued existence to the relation it bears to something else' (pp. 643–4).

Take the first horn of this dilemma first. Matthews and Cohen suggest we assume the following principle:

(P) For x to be able to bear any relation R to something else y, x must be something in its own right, independently of its bearing R to y. (p. 633)

(P) entails that, if Felix is related to cathood, he must be something in his own right, independently of his relation to cathood. But, Matthews and Cohen ask, 'What would Felix be . . . apart from cathood?' (p. 633). The intuition seems to be that since Felix is essentially a cat, he cannot be a cat in virtue of his relation to anything. More generally, if x is related to y, it cannot be essential to x that it be related to y; there are no essential relations. As Matthews and Cohen say later, for example, Callias is not related to rationality, because 'rationality is essential to a man's being a man' (p. 636).[8] It is clear from this that Matthews and Cohen offer a refined

defend the claim here, Allen, Lee, and Mills (above, n. 3) also seem to accept it. White, *Plato on Knowledge and Reality*, 70–1, by contrast, seems to assume the crude view. Strawson, *Individuals*, 168–81, draws the line between what he calls relational and nonrelational ties in yet another way.

[8] It is not in fact entirely clear that (P) entails that there are no essential relations. This seems, however, to be the way Matthews and Cohen intend (P), and I shall assume here that it does have this result.

relational analysis of the sort mentioned in Section I. Their idea is that if x is essentially F, x is not F in virtue of being *related* to anything.

Suppose now that we accept (P), and also insist that particulars possess all of their properties relationally. It follows that particulars are bare particulars in this sense: they are what they are independently of any of their properties; they have no essential properties.[9] For suppose that Socrates possesses each of his properties in virtue of a relation to something. Given (P), it follows that Socrates is what he is independently of any of his properties. He need not be a man, or be rational, to be Socrates; he might have been a teapot, or a prime number, instead.

Here, then, is one reason to reject a relational analysis: it threatens to make particulars bare particulars. But we reached this result only by pressing (P). Yet, as Matthews and Cohen note, one might reject (P); one might insist that if x is related to y, it just does not follow that x must be something in its own right, independently of its bearing R to y. Shadows, they suggest, are related to what they are the shadows of; a shadow is always the shadow of someone or something. But at the same time, shadows are also essentially related to what they are the shadows of. 'A dark spot that stays put after Schubert has gone home is not Schubert's shadow' (p. 634).

Other counter-examples to (P) come readily to mind. Surely numbers, for example, are essentially related to one another; the number three 'owes its identity and continued existence to the relation it bears to something else'—to its place in the number series. There are also counter-examples involving sensible particulars. Socrates, for example, is surely related to his parents. But, as Kripke plausibly argues, the origins of things are essential to them;[10] Socrates essentially has the parents he has. But then Socrates is essentially related to his parents; he would not be who he is had he, *per impossibile*, had different parents.

[9] For this understanding of 'bare particulars', see e.g. R. Stalnaker, 'Anti-Essentialism', *Midwest Studies in Philosophy*, 4 (1979), 343–55; M. J. Loux, *Substance and Attribute* (Dordrecht: Reidel, 1978), ch. 8. Matthews and Cohen do not say how they understand 'bare particulars', but this seems to be what they have in mind; at least, their argument does not require more than this. 'Bare particular' is sometimes defined as a particular which lacks properties, or which lacks both properties and relations; for this account, see Armstrong, i. 136. Later I consider arguments purporting to commit Plato to bare particulars in this sense; but the body of the paper considers bare particulars in the weaker sense, of having no essential properties. Notice that if one rejects the view that there are essential properties— as, of course, many do—then one might well believe that countenancing bare particulars, in the sense of particulars with no essential properties, is nonproblematic; if so, accepting the first horn of Matthews and Cohen's dilemma would be attractive. I do not pursue that possibility here, largely because it does not seem to be Plato's or Aristotle's position.
[10] S. Kripke, *Naming and Necessity* (Cambridge, Mass.: Harvard University Press, 1980); see also C. McGinn, 'On the Necessity of Origin', *Journal of Philosophy*, 73 (1976), 127–35.

Suppose, then, that we reject (P), yet still insist that particulars possess their properties relationally. Then, Matthews and Cohen urge, one is vulnerable to the second horn of their dilemma: Socrates, if not a bare particular, is a mere relational entity; he is what he is in virtue of the relations in which he stands. One may readily concede that shadows are mere relational entities. But the concession looks less happy for entities like Socrates, for what Aristotle calls 'primary substances.' Surely primary substances, unlike shadows, cannot be essentially relational entities. If Schubert, like his shadow, 'is nothing independent of bearing a certain relation' to something else (p. 634), he loses the sort of priority and independence we are inclined to ascribe him. Hence we should insist that Schubert, Felix, and the rest are not relational entities; 'Felix must be what he is independent of any relations he may stand in' (p. 635). Or so the reasoning goes; I shall ask later about its plausibility.

Relational analyses are to be avoided, then, because they are vulnerable to the dilemma just rehearsed: particulars are reduced either to bare particulars or to relational entities. Since neither option is attractive, relational analyses are to be rejected. So argue Matthews and Cohen, at least, and they are followed in large measure by others. But are both horns of the dilemma so unattractive? And is Plato, but not Aristotle, vulnerable to it? In what follows, I urge negative answers to both questions.

III

Consider the following two sentences:

(1) Socrates is white.
(2) Socrates is [a] man.

We might wish to distinguish (1) from (2) by saying that (1) is an accidental predication, (2) an essential predication; Socrates is accidentally white, essentially a man. But (1) and (2) have similar surface grammatical structures—all the more so in Greek, which enjoys no indefinite article. It may then be tempting to suppose that their grammatical similarity mirrors an underlying ontological similarity; and many believe that Plato supposes this. Thus Armstrong, for example, suggests that Plato accepts the following analysis of property possession:[11]

[11] Armstrong, however, wisely does not suppose that Plato offered this account simply because of the grammatical similarity between (1) and (2). It is one of the many virtues of his book that it separates questions about syntax and semantics from questions about properties.

a has the property, F, if and only if *a* 'participates' in the transcendent Form, the F. (ii. 2; cf. i. 64)

(1) and (2) then become:

(1a) Socrates participates in the transcendent form of white.
(2a) Socrates participates in the transcendent form of man.

But, Armstrong argues, this analysis is relational; Plato thus has a relational account of property possession. Further, the analysis makes him vulnerable to the dilemma's first horn: particulars are bare particulars; they have no essential properties.[12] Plato cannot, then, hold on to our intuition that (1) and (2) are importantly different. For him, each attributes an accidental property to Socrates, a property he might fail to have.

This line of reasoning has three stages: first, that Plato accepts the proposed analysis; second, that it is relational; and third, that it makes particulars bare particulars. Each stage requires questioning.

Armstrong's first claim—that Plato accepts the proposed analysis—requires that there be transcendent forms corresponding to every property. But it is far from clear that Plato believes this.[13] Armstrong's first claim also requires that particulars and forms always be related by participation; it is not clear that Plato believes this either.[14] None the less, for the purposes of this paper, I shall simply concede the first claim.

Armstrong's second claim is that the proposed analysis is relational. Is this claim correct? On the crude relational analysis it obviously is. Socrates' being white, for example, involves not only Socrates, but also the transcendent or separated form of white; Socrates' being white involves at least two things, Socrates and the form. On the refined analysis favoured by Armstrong and others, however, it is not immediately clear whether the analysis is relational or nonrelational; we need first to determine whether the two things are essentially, or accidentally, connected. If Plato denies that par-

---

[12] Armstrong seems to commit Plato to this view at e.g. i. 69; see 'Armstrong on Relational and Nonrelational Realism'. Cf. also Woods, 'Substance and Essence in Aristotle', 178; R. Turnbull, 'Aristotle's Debt to the "Natural Philosophy" of the *Phaedo*', *Philosophical Quarterly*, 8 (1958), 131–43; and there are many others.

[13] I discuss this issue in 'The One over Many', *Philosophical Review*, 89 (1980), 197–240, and in *On Ideas*, chs. 4 and 8. Armstrong defines transcendent realism as the view that 'universals exist separated from particulars' (ii. 140). Below, I distinguish two accounts of separation, and call just one of them 'transcendence'. I discuss Armstrong's (possibly different) accounts of separation and transcendence in 'Armstrong on Relational and Nonrelational Realism'.

[14] See e.g. *Phd.* 100 D, where Plato expresses reluctance to commit himself on this score.

ticulars have essential properties, then he has a relational account; if he accepts essential properties, he does not have a relational account.

This brings us to Armstrong's third claim: that Plato is committed to bare particulars. Once we explore this claim, we shall be in a better position to assess whether Plato's account is relational on the refined view. Why should Plato be thought to be committed to bare particulars? On one view, separation ensures this result. Indeed, it is sometimes supposed that separation makes particulars bare particulars, not only in the weak sense that they lack essential properties, but also in the strong sense that they lack properties altogether. Let us explore this issue.

What separation is is a disputed matter. On the view I favour, separation, in connection with forms, is the capacity for independent existence.[15] More precisely, the form of F is separate just in case it can exist whether or not the corresponding sensible particulars exist. The form of justice, for example, can exist whether or not there are, or ever have been or ever will be, any just people, actions, or institutions. If, as I believe, forms are universals, then this interpretation of separation says that there can be uninstantiated universals.[16]

On this view of separation, Plato is obviously not committed to bare particulars in the strong sense that particulars lack all properties; to say that a form F can exist whether or not any F particulars do is not to say that particulars are never F. Nor does this interpretation of separation imply that particulars are bare particulars in the weak sense that they lack essential properties; to say that forms can exist whether or not any particulars do is not to say that particulars can exist without forms. That is to say, this interpretation of separation leaves open the possibility that particulars possess essential properties, and so cannot exist unless the corresponding forms do.

To be sure, one might appeal again to principle (P) and insist that there are no essential relations; since particulars have properties only in virtue of being related to forms, they have no essential properties. But the point is that separation by itself does not entail this; it leaves open the possibility that things have essential properties. If, then, we construe separation as the capacity for independent existence, separation does not preclude

---

[15] For a detailed account of separation, and a defence of my interpretation of it, see ch. 11 above.

[16] Strictly speaking, this interpretation says that there can be universals that are uninstantiated by sensible particulars, which is weaker than the claim that there can be uninstantiated universals. Sometimes Aristotle speaks of separation *tout court*, sometimes of separation from sensible particulars. The difference doesn't matter for present purposes, and so I shall largely ignore them. (I discuss this briefly in the Introduction, pp. 31–3.)

things having essential properties, and so does not commit Plato to bare particulars.

Separation is, however, sometimes thought to involve more than the capacity for independent existence. Not only can forms exist independently of particulars, but also they are not the properties of particulars at all; they exist, not as the properties of things, but in splendid isolation, in a special Platonic heaven.[17] Call this second interpretation of separation 'transcendence'. If (contrary to my view) forms are transcendent, is Plato committed to bare particulars in either the weak or the strong sense?

He might seem to be, if we also assume that all properties are transcendent forms. This further assumption is often rejected.[18] But let us concede for present purposes both that forms are transcendent and that all properties are transcendent forms. It is then important to note that forms and particulars do not exhaust Plato's ontology. There are also what are sometimes called 'immanent characters'.[19] In the *Phaedo* (102 ff.), for example, Plato speaks not only of Simmias and the form of tallness, but also of the tallness in Simmias. In the later *Parmenides*, he mentions not only you and me and the form of similarity, but also 'the similarity we possess'

[17] For this view, see e.g. W. F. R. Hardie, *A Study in Plato* (Oxford: Clarendon Press, 1936), 44; G. Vlastos, 'The Third Man Argument in the *Parmenides*', *Philosophical Review*, 63 (1954), 319–49, repr. in R. E. Allen (ed.), *Studies in Plato's Metaphysics* (London: Routledge & Kegan Paul, 1965), 231–64 (latter pagination), esp. 252–4.

[18] P. T. Geach, for example, in 'The Third Man Again', *Philosophical Review*, 65 (1956), 72–8, takes up Wittgenstein's suggestion that forms are standards and so not properties at all; see also C. Strang, 'Plato and the Third Man', *Proceedings of the Aristotelian Society*, suppl. 37 (1963), 147–64. I. M. Crombie, *An Examination of Plato's Doctrines* (2 vols.; London: Routledge & Kegan Paul, 1962–3), ii. 278–84, suggests that forms are properties, but not the properties of particulars; forms are 'pure properties', whereas sensibles have 'impure' ones. This seems to be the view of those who defend what A. Nehamas, 'Plato on the Imperfection of the Sensible World', *American Philosophical Quarterly*, 12 (1975), 105–17, calls the 'approximation' view.

[19] For some discussion of Plato on immanent characters, see G. Vlastos, 'Reasons and Causes in the *Phaedo*', *Philosophical Review*, 78 (1969), 291–325, esp. 298–301; A. Nehamas, 'Predication and Forms of Opposites in the *Phaedo*', *Review of Metaphysics*, 26 (1973), 461–91 at 475–7; Turnbull, 'Aristotle's Debt to the "Natural Philosophy" of the *Phaedo*'; D. Gallop, *Plato: Phaedo* (Oxford: Clarendon Press, 1975), 195–6. In ch. 12, I argue that so-called immanent characters are forms, or parts of forms, when they are in things. If that view is correct, then various of the difficulties I raise for Plato in this chapter dissolve. For example, I go on to ask whether Plato takes particulars to be bare particulars, in the sense that they have no properties in them. If forms are properties, and they, or parts of them, are in particulars, then obviously particulars are not bare particulars in the sense of having no properties in them. Here, however, I am considering the view that forms are transcendent. If (contrary to my view) they are transcendent, then immanent characters can't be forms (or parts of forms) when they are in things. My suggestion is that an alternative account of immanent characters from the one defended in ch. 12 is available, and it allows Plato to avoid bare particulars, even if he accepts transcendent forms.

(130 B). There is no agreed analysis of immanent characters. But on one view, they are unit properties, like those countenanced by Aristotle in the *Categories*; each is an individual, nonrecurrent unit property, proprietary to its owner.[20] On this view, if Simmias is tall, there is an instance of tallness in him, an instance that ceases to exist if he ceases to be tall. If two things are white, each has its own numerically distinct particular whiteness; but there is also, in addition, the universal whiteness of which these particular whitenesses are instances. The universal is not 'in' things; but instances of it are.[21]

On this view, even if, for Plato, particulars 'have' no properties 'in' them, they have property instances in them. It is then misleading to say that the second interpretation of separation (i.e. as transcendence) entails that things have no properties. In whatever sense that is true, it is a sense compatible with their having property instances in them. Hence, even if all properties are transcendent forms, it does not follow that particulars are bare particulars in the strong sense of lacking properties.

Does it entail that they are bare particulars in the weaker sense of lacking essential properties? One might argue that a property instance is in a particular just in case the particular is suitably related to the corresponding form; and that if it has property instances only in virtue of being related to forms, no property, or property instance, is essential to it. But this again appeals to (P). Without that appeal, transcendence does not imply that particulars lack essential properties.

Whether we construe separation as capacity for independent existence or as transcendence, then, and whether or not we agree that all properties are separated forms, separation does not commit Plato to the view that particulars are bare particulars in either the strong or the weak sense.

I have not yet argued that Plato rejects bare particulars; I have argued only that separation by itself does not commit him to them. Is he committed to them for other reasons? One might argue that the way in which sensibles and forms are connected—by participation—has this result. Let us briefly consider this possibility.

---

[20] I discuss this interpretation of Aristotle briefly below; see sect. VI.

[21] In Armstrong's terminology, this combines particularism and transcendent realism. Armstrong discusses particularism in ch. 8, transcendent realism in ch. 7. At i. 85 he writes: 'I know of no Particularist who has appealed to transcendent Forms' (contrast i. 78 n. 1). Plato is such a particularist if he takes forms to be transcendent, and takes immanent characters to be unit properties. For other discussions of particularism see, *inter alios*, G. F. Stout, 'On the Nature of Universals and Propositions', *Proceedings of the British Academy*, 10 (1921–3), 157–72. D. C. Williams, 'On the Elements of Being, I, II', *Review of Metaphysics*, 7 (1953), 3–18, 171–92; see also N. Wolterstorff, *On Universals* (Chicago: Chicago University Press, 1970), ch. 6.

Plato is unfortunately little help here; he never tells us in any detail what participation is—whence Aristotle's complaints of 'empty metaphor' (*Metaph. A* 9, 991ᵃ20–3). Once, however, Plato suggests that 'this participation they have in the forms is nothing but their being made in their image' (*Parm.* 132 D 3–4). And elsewhere sensibles are said to be like, indeed likenesses or imitations of, forms; forms are models of which sensibles are but imperfect copies.[22]

How to interpret such claims is disputed. Are sensibles literally copies of model forms, as a picture or statue of me might be said to be a copy of me? Are forms models as I might be a model for sculpture students? Or as a blueprint or design might be said to be a model? Or are such claims metaphorical, designed only to highlight the deficiency and dependency of sensibles? Plato uses different metaphors and examples; they do not all suggest the same answers to our questions.

Let us, however, look at one example of a copy and a model.

Consider two paintings, both of which look rather like Ronald Reagan. Suppose one of the paintings was commissioned by Ronald Reagan; I painted it in the Oval Office, watching Reagan eat jelly beans. This picture is of Ronald Reagan, not because it looks like him (I might not be a very good painter), but because it bears an appropriate causal connection to him. The other picture, let us suppose, was painted by a chimpanzee (not Bonzo) who had never met or heard of Ronald Reagan. Even if his picture looks very much like Reagan, it is not of him, because it lacks an appropriate causal connection to him. Indeed, although the chimpanzee painted a picture, it is not a copy of anything. A painting is a copy, then, only if it bears an appropriate causal connection to that of which it is a copy. This suggests that being a copy involves being *essentially* connected to something.[23] If the connection is relational, then my picture of Reagan

---

[22] It is important to bear in mind, however, that this language is not as prevalent as some suggest. For example, although Plato uses mimesis to refer to the relationship between sensibles and forms at *Ti.* 48 D 2, he does not use it in this sense in *Republic* X, where one might expect it. (I owe this point to Alexander Nehamas.) Similarly, in the *Phaedo* he says that sensibles are like, and fall short of, forms (see e.g. *Phd.* 74 E); but he does not say that sensibles are copies or images of forms. For other discussions of these issues, see Allen, Lee, and Mills (above, n. 3); see also Crombie, *An Examination of Plato's Doctrines*, ii. 271–319; and J. C. B. Gosling, 'Similarity in *Phaedo* 73b *seq.*', *Phronesis*, 10 (1965), 151–61.

[23] John Boler has objected to me that I need to show, not only that *being a copy* involves being essentially related to something, but also that *the thing which is a copy* is essentially related to something. I am inclined to think that the thing which is a copy, in my example, is essentially a picture of Ronald Reagan, and so is essentially a copy. If this is right, then the thing which is a copy *is* essentially related to something, and so is an essentially relational entity. But even the claim that being a copy involves being essentially related to something is difficult to square with (P).

is an essentially relational entity; it has an essential property relationally.[24] The model–copy metaphor thus does not commit Plato to bare particulars.

We are now in a position to return to an issue left to one side before. We saw before that Plato clearly has a relational account on the crude view. But does he have a relational account on the refined view? It seems clear that Armstrong and others believe he does, because they assume something like principle (P). If x is F by being related to something, x is accidentally F; if x is essentially F, x is F nonrelationally. The thought then is that separation or participation makes particulars bare particulars, at least in the sense that particulars have no essential properties. Since no essential properties are involved, the account is relational. That is to say, it is *because* separation or participation is thought to commit Plato to bare particulars that he is thought to have a relational account. But if I have been right, neither separation nor participation commits Plato to bare particulars; they are compatible with essentialism. If this is so, Plato has not yet been shown to be committed to a relational account on the refined view. Alternatively, if it is taken to be *obvious* that Plato has a relational account, one should reject (P), and conclude that he accepts relational entities.

IV

Neither separation nor participation commits Plato to bare particulars, then. Does he none the less accept them? The evidence here is unfortunately thin, but I believe it supports an essentialist reading. In the *Phaedo*, for example, Plato implies that although Simmias only happens to be tall, he is Simmias by nature (102 c) ; and in the later *Philebus* (14 D) he remarks that although Protarchus is in a way many, in virtue of having many limbs, he is by nature one—one person by nature. Or again, Plato insists that snow cannot exist and be hot, nor can fire exist and be cold; being cold is essential to snow, being hot essential to fire (*Phd.* 103 c 10–E 1). Nor can three be even; it is odd 'by nature' (*Phd.* 104 A 3, A 7).[25]

One might argue, however, that even if the dialogues just mentioned

[24] Lee distinguishes between what he calls substantial and insubstantial images; examples of the first include paintings and statues, of the second shadows. He argues that there are important differences between these two sorts of images. I agree, although I do not agree with the ways in which he distinguishes them or with his account of their relevance to Plato; I cannot pursue this issue here. Here the crucial point is that both sorts of images—so I believe, although I suspect Lee would not—are essentially relational entities in my sense. (I discuss shadows briefly above, in sect. II.)

[25] These passages are well discussed by Gallop, *Plato*: Phaedo. Turnbull, 'Aristotle's Debt to the "Natural Philosophy" of the *Phaedo*', 137, agrees that the *Phaedo* 'seems to require

countenance essential properties, the *Timaeus* does not; there, at least, Plato is committed to bare particulars. How does the *Timaeus* thus allegedly differ? Perhaps the thought is that in the *Timaeus*, but not in the dialogues just mentioned, Plato countenances separated forms of, say, man and fire. In the *Phaedo* sensible fire can have essential properties precisely because there is no separated form of fire. In the *Timaeus* there is a separated form of fire; correspondingly, sensible fire is a bare particular.[26] But if the argument of the preceding sections is correct, this view is untenable—at least without appeal to (P). For I have already argued that neither separation nor participation commits Plato to bare particulars—*no matter what the range of forms*. Even if there are more forms in the *Timaeus* than elsewhere, this does not by itself carry with it any commitment to bare particulars.

The *Timaeus* also introduces the receptacle of all becoming (49 c 5–6), that in which sensibles come to be as imitations (50 c 5) of forms. Perhaps the expanded range of forms does not on its own commit Plato to bare particulars. But is he not so committed given the receptacle as well? Here two views are possible: (1) that the receptacle is a bare particular; and (2) that sensible particulars like Socrates or fire are bare particulars. But neither (1) nor (2) is true.

As against (1): it is true that Plato says that the receptacle is characterless (50 d 7; cf. 50 e 4). But this has to be set against the claim—made more than once—that the receptacle has a nature (51 b 3; cf. 50 b 7–8). These remarks are consistent. For what Plato means, I believe, is that the receptacle does not essentially possess any of the properties that come to be instantiated in it by sensibles (cf. esp. 50 d 7–8). This is perfectly compatible with its possessing *other* properties essentially.[27] Plato's scent (50 d 4–51 e 2) and gold (50 a 5–b 5) analogies suggest this. The base from which various scents are made must be as odourless as possible; but even if it is entirely odourless, it has other properties, and some essential properties. A liquid base, for example, might be essentially liquid, even if it is not essentially

that some (or all) individuals are, as it were "natured" individuals'; but he believes that this is 'inconsistent with the main drift of the dialogue'. On my account, there is no inconsistency; nor do I find Turnbull's reasons for finding one persuasive.

[26] This argument should appeal to Nehamas. He argues that in the *Phaedo*, for example, Plato does not recognize separated forms of, for example, man, precisely because whatever is a man is so essentially, and things cannot possess their essential properties relationally. See his 'Predication and Forms of Opposites in the *Phaedo*', esp. pt. II, and 'Plato on the Imperfection of the Sensible World', esp. 108.

[27] This assumes that even in the *Timaeus*, there are not forms corresponding to every property. Even if there are, however, this would not, *on its own*, make the receptacle a bare particular.

sweet-smelling, and indeed even if it lacks odour altogether. Or again, gold is not essentially triangular or any other shape; but it is essentially gold, and it is essentially such that it can be moulded into various shapes. Similarly with the receptacle. It does not essentially possess any of the properties instantiated by sensibles. But it essentially has traces (*ichnē*, 53 B 2), and is essentially such that it can receive the properties it does.[28]

I turn then to (2). If Socrates were reducible to the receptacle, and if the receptacle were a bare particular, Socrates would be a bare particular. I have already argued, however, that the receptacle is not a bare particular. Nor, in any case, is Socrates reducible to it, or even to it and forms. Sensibles are a *third* sort of thing, beyond the receptacle and forms (49 A 7, 50 C 7, 52 A 8, 52 D 4); they are not reducible to, eliminable in favour of, anything else.[29]

To be sure, Plato insists that no sensible bit of fire is pure fire; each such sample is mixed with the other elements (49 C 7–E 7). Nor is any sensible bit of fire permanent; each is transient, and turns into its opposite. It is for these reasons that one should not say, pointing at any sensible sample of fire, 'Fire is *that*' (49 D–C)—thinking that one has pointed to something that tells us what fire is, as though one has a pure sample of fire from which one can abstract what it is to be fire. The sensible world offers no such easy route to definitions. Instead of saying 'Fire is *that*', one should say 'Fire is *that sort of thing*' (49 D–E). This avoids the implication that there are pure samples of fire in the sensible world.[30] But even if no bit of sensible fire

[28] F. M. Cornford, *Plato's Cosmology: The* Timaeus *of Plato*, translated with a running commentary (London: Routledge & Kegan Paul, 1937), vacillates on this matter. On p. 183 he says that the receptacle 'has a nature of its own from which it never departs'. But on p. 185 he writes that 'the Receptacle has no characters of its own "before" the qualities enter it, unlike the gold, which has its own sensible properties'. The gold analogy is also discussed by E. Lee, 'On the "Gold-Example" in Plato's *Timaeus* (50a5–b5)', in J. Anton and G. Kustas (eds.), *Essays in Ancient Greek Philosophy* (Albany, NY: State University of New York Press, 1971), 219–35. H. F. Cherniss discusses the relevant portions of the *Timaeus* in a number of articles. See e.g. 'A Much Misread Passage in Plato's *Timaeus* (*Timaeus* 49c7–50b5)', *American Journal of Philology*, 75 (1954), 113–30. Many of Lee's and Cherniss's views are well criticized by D. Zeyl, 'Plato and Talk of a World in Flux: *Timaeus* 49a6–50b5', *Harvard Studies in Classical Philology*, 79 (1975), 125–48.

[29] Cherniss and Lee, by contrast, seem to find four, not three, sorts of things in the *Timaeus*; their view is criticized by N. Gulley, 'The Interpretation of Plato, *Timaeus* 49d3', *American Journal of Philology*, 81 (1960), 53–64, esp. 63–4.

[30] So I read the controversial passage 49 A 6–50 B 5. On this reading, Plato is essentially extending what I elsewhere call the 'imperfection argument' to predicates like 'fire' in order to generate separated forms corresponding to them. In the middle dialogues, by contrast, the imperfection argument is restricted to 'incomplete' predicates and their ilk. See my 'The One over Many', and *On Ideas*, ch. 7, § 8, and ch. 16, §§ 2–3. For accounts very different from mine, see Cherniss, Lee, Gulley, and Zeyl (above, nn. 28–9). Zeyl's criticisms of Cherniss, Lee, and Gulley seem to me effective, although I do not endorse all of his positive suggestions.

is purely fire or permanent, it does not follow that none is *essentially* fire, or hot.

Plato also says that the 'safest' answer (50 B 1), when asked the 'what is it?' question of a sensible, is 'the receptacle' and not, for example, 'fire'. But this is not to say that sensible fire is reducible to the receptacle or that, as is sometimes said, sensible fire does not really exist.[31] The point, again, is only that no bit of sensible fire is purely fire or permanent, whereas the receptacle never ceases to be, never changes into anything else. Even if no sample of fire is pure or permanent, however, it is still something more than the receptacle, and still has essential properties. To be sure, it may have such properties only in virtue of being suitably connected to forms. But without (P), this is compatible with the essentially relational view; it does not require bare particulars.

I conclude, then, that Plato is not committed to, and does not countenance, bare particulars; although he is not as detailed or explicit as one could wish, he seems to assume that things have essential properties. If one accepts (P), one then ought to conclude that Plato has a nonrelational account of property possession. For reasons already adduced, I prefer to reject (P) ; and I am happy to admit that Plato has a relational account. But if particulars have essential properties, and have all of their properties in virtue of relations to forms, then their essential properties are possessed relationally. And that is just to say that they are relational entities; they are what they are in virtue of their relations to forms.

V

Of course, one might argue, as Matthews and Cohen do, that it is no more attractive to view particulars as relational entities than as bare particulars. If Felix is really a primary substance, he 'must be what he is independent of any relations he may stand in'.

But what does this mean? The claim may be that primary substances cannot possess their essential properties relationally; but this assumes (P) again.

Alternatively, the claim may be that 'a particular is a substance, logically capable of independent existence. It could exist although nothing else existed' (Armstrong, i. 115). It is a necessary condition of something's being a substance that it not be dependent on anything else. But how are we to interpret this claim? Suppose one is a realist about universals; universals exist

---

[31] By Lee and Cherniss, for example.

and are irreducible to particulars. Does the independent-existence criterion then tell us that a particular could exist even if no universals or properties did? It might seem to. For no particular is identical with any property, or with any sum of properties. So, if particulars can exist even if nothing else does, they must be able to exist even if no properties do. But if particulars can exist whether or not any properties do, they are bare particulars, at least in the sense of lacking essential properties. If the independent-existence criterion is pressed too far, it leads us back to bare particulars (or, in another tradition, to God) as the only genuine substances.

Sensible particulars like Socrates, then, do not satisfy the strong independent-existence criterion for substantiality; they are not such that they could exist although nothing else existed, for they are dependent at least on various properties (and, if Kripke is right, on some other particulars as well). I do not mean that Socrates is not a substance. I suggest instead that we reject the strong independent-existence criterion of substantiality. Socrates is a substance, not because he can exist independently of everything else, but for other reasons. He exists independently of at least many other particulars. He is a roughly independently identifiable spatio-temporal continuant. He is a bearer of properties, and not himself a property. Such factors, rather than complete independent existence, should determine what are substances.

I agree, then, that Plato has a relational account of property possession. But I hope to have shown that his account is not vulnerable to all of the objections that have been levelled against it. In particular, neither his account of separation nor his account of participation implies that particulars are bare particulars. He can perfectly well allow—and, if I have been right, does allow—that particulars possess essential properties. To be sure, this may commit him instead to the view that particulars are essentially relational entities. But I hope to have suggested too that this result is not as unattractive as some suppose.

We need now to see whether, as many allege, Aristotle rejects a relational account and, if so, if his account is, on that score, to be preferred to Plato's.

VI

In the *Categories*[32] Aristotle offers the following analyses of (1) and (2):

(1b) White is in Socrates.

[32] Following Matthews and Cohen's lead, I here discuss only the *Categories*. Some believe that the *Metaphysics* has a quite different view of some of these matters; I do not believe it does, but discussion of the *Metaphysics* is beyond my scope here.

(2b) Man is said of Socrates.

The 'said of'–'in' distinction is the focal point around which pivots the *Categories*' fourfold division of *onta*, of beings or things that are: (*a*) *primary substances* (*prōtai ousiai*), such as an individual man or horse, are neither said of nor in anything; they are the subjects which everything else is either said of or in; (*b*) *secondary substances*, the species and genera of primary substances, are said of primary substances (and of lower secondary substances) but are not in anything;[33] (*c*) individual nonsubstances, such as an individual, nonrepeatable, instance of a colour, are in substances but are not said of anything;[34] (*d*)*nonsubstance species and genera*, such as white or colour, are said of individual nonsubstances (and of lower universal nonsubstances) and are in substances.

(*a*)–(*d*) draw two distinct but overlapping contrasts: that between universal[35] and particular, and that between substance and nonsubstance. The 'said of' locution ties universals to particulars and to lower universals in the same genus; if x is said of y, x is a universal and y is either a lower universal or an individual in the same genus as x. For example, animal is said both of man and of Socrates; man is said of Socrates but not of animal. Similarly, colour is said both of white and of an individual instance of white; white is said of an individual instance of white but not of colour. The 'said of' locution applies within every category; the crucial factors concern only the relative universality of x and y, which must, in addition, be in the same genus. But they could be substances or nonsubstances. The 'in' locution, by contrast, ties nonsubstances to substances. If x is in y, x is a nonsubstance and y is a substance. Every nonsubstance is in a substance, but no substance is in anything.

So much is relatively clear; but a more detailed understanding of 'said of' and 'in' is difficult to come by. For our purposes here, the following brief remarks must suffice. If x is said of y, both the name and the definition of x

[33] Here I simplify. Substance differentiae are also said of, but are not in, substances. Similarly, (*d*) collects nonsubstance differentiae as well as nonsubstance species and genera. I do not consider differentiae here, but I do not believe they raise any special difficulties for my view.

[34] What individual nonsubstances are is disputed. On one account, they are nonrecurrent unit properties, proprietary to their owners: Callias' bit of white, Socrates' bit, and so on; for this view, see, e.g. J. L. Ackrill, in his notes on the *Categories* and *De Interpretatione* (Oxford: Clarendon Press, 1963). On an alternative view, individual nonsubstances are (for example) most determinate shades of colour; for this view see G. E. L. Owen, 'Inherence', *Phronesis*, 10 (1965), 97–105. I accept Ackrill's view.

[35] Aristotle does not in fact call species and genera 'universals' here; but *De Int.* 17ᵃ38–ᵇ1 licenses the appellation. I do not beg any questions in importing it here; I ask later precisely what sort of analysis species and genera should receive.

are predicated of y (2^a19–21). Further, if x is said of y, then x 'reveals' what y is; it answers the 'What is it?' question with respect to y (2^b7–10, 29–37). Both the name and the definition of the species man, for example, are predicated of Socrates; what Socrates is is a man. It is then tempting to say that if x is said of y, y is essentially an x. At any rate, (2b)—or rather (2): the 'said of' terminology is later dropped—is the sort of predication Aristotle elsewhere calls an essential predication, and I shall for convenience speak that way here.[36]

Notice that if Aristotle believes that primary substances have essential properties, he rejects bare particulars in both of the senses discussed above: primary substances do have properties, and they have essential properties.

The 'in' locution, by contrast, is connected to nonessential predication.[37] At least, (1b) is an accidental predication; Socrates is only accidentally white. It does not follow, of course, that Socrates could exist with no colour; but he is independent of any given colour.

Aristotle claims that all universals, and all nonsubstance particulars, are ultimately said of or in primary substances (2^a34–5); primary substances are the basic subjects which everything else is either said of or in. This partially explains the sense in which individual substances like Socrates are first or primary.

Aristotle infers that if 'the primary substances did not exist it would be impossible for any of the other things to exist' (2^b3–6). Or again, 'if everything were healthy, health would exist but not sickness; and if everything were white, whiteness would exist but not blackness' (14^a7–10). This shows that Aristotle rejects separation, in the sense of the capacity for independent existence; universals cannot exist uninstantiated. Indeed, he often criticizes the Platonists for separating universals (e.g. *Metaph. M*, 1078^b ff., 1086^a30 ff.).

VII

Aristotle, then, rejects separation; there can be no uninstantiated universals. He also rejects bare particulars. For the 'said of' locution, we suggested, indicates essential predication. So either Aristotle agrees with Plato and

---

[36] See e.g. *Metaph.* 1029^b13–16; *Z* 6. Not all agree, of course, that Aristotle believes that individuals—as opposed to their kinds—have essential properties. I cannot discuss this issue here. If (2b) *does* leave open the possibility that Socrates has no essential properties, then the case for attributing a nonrelational account to Aristotle is considerably weakened; here I give myself the harder case, and assume that Aristotle intends to preclude that possibility.

[37] Although it is not identical to *accidental* predication. *Idia*, for example, are *in* substances, but are not accidental properties. See J. M. E. Moravcsik, 'Aristotle on Predication', *Philosophical Review*, 76 (1967), 80–96.

views particulars, not as bare particulars, but as relational entities; or else he rejects a relational account, and thereby avoids our dilemma—Socrates is neither a bare particular nor a relational entity. Which option is correct?

Divergent readings of Aristotle have produced different answers. Some argue that Aristotle is a nominalist, and that nominalism avoids a relational account. What sort of nominalism?[38] Perhaps Aristotle is what Armstrong calls a predicate nominalist: to say that a is F is to say that the predicate 'F' is true of a. Or perhaps Aristotle is a class or aggregate nominalist: to say that a is F is to say that a is a member of the class of Fs, or that a is a part of the aggregate of Fs. In these cases, to say that a is F is not to say that there is some genuine universal, F-ness, out there in the world to which a is somehow related; for there is no universal, F-ness, at all. Hence, nominalism avoids a relational account by denying that there are properties or universals.

Matthews and Cohen seem, at least sometimes, to intend this view. They suggest, for example, that Aristotle denies 'that we need, or should, make reference to F-ness to understand what it is for x to be F' (p. 643). Or again, 'there being the secondary substance cat is a matter of there being individual cats—Fenimore, Felix, Felicia, and the rest' (p. 632).[39] If they mean to suggest that the existence of cat is somehow reducible to the existence of individual cats, this is a version of nominalism, in one sense of that word;[40] and perhaps it too would avoid a relational account.

Now one might argue that even if Aristotle is a nominalist in any of these ways, he does not thereby avoid a relational account. At least, Armstrong has argued that each of these accounts is relational.[41] If one is a predicate nominalist, for example, then one believes that a is F because the predicate 'F' applies to a. But then one explains a's being F in terms of a's *relation*

[38] For the purposes of this chapter, I follow Armstrong in speaking of class and aggregate (he uses 'mereological') nominalism, as well as of predicate nominalism (see i. 12–17). As he notes, 'nominalism' is sometimes restricted to what he calls 'predicate nominalism'. Nothing turns on this terminological issue, and following Armstrong here serves the purpose of separating off these three accounts from the account of Aristotle I favour, according to which universals are (not predicates or classes or aggregates, but) properties irreducible to, though dependent on, particulars.

[39] The next sentence reads: 'There would not be cat without there being some individual cat or other.' This expresses the dependence of universals on particulars, and is compatible with universals not being reducible to particulars. The sentence quoted in the text, however, seems to press for this stronger claim.

[40] It might, however, be a different version of nominalism from the three just mentioned. For this version, see M. J. Creswell, 'What is Aristotle's Theory of Universals?', *Australasian Journal of Philosophy*, 53 (1975), 238–47; Armstrong, i. 16. I do not consider this view separately here; but if the arguments I adduce against Aristotle's being a nominalist in the other senses are correct, they tell against this view too.

[41] In chs. 2–5; cf. ii. 2.

to the predicate 'F'; there are still two things involved, *a* and the predicate 'F'. One might prefer Aristotle's relational nominalism to Plato's relational realism; but then one is choosing between relational accounts, not between a nonrelational and a relational account. Even if one rejects Armstrong's argument, however, one might with reason insist that, if this is Matthews and Cohen's view, it might be phrased more usefully in terms of nominalism and realism, than in terms of nonrelational and relational accounts of property possession.[42]

But in any case, Aristotle is not a nominalist, at least not in the *Categories*. Certainly his talk of 'being said of' cannot be used to press him in any such direction; 'being said of' is an ontological, not a linguistic, notion. It is man—not the word 'man'—that is said of Socrates; colour—not the word 'colour'—is said of white.[43] These are species and genera, among the kinds of *onta* or beings that there are; they are not any sort of linguistic entity.

Nor are Aristotelian universals aggregates. In the *Peri Ideōn* Aristotle insists that *koina*, universals, are different from (although not separate from) any or all particulars (79. 15–19). Particulars are *apeira*, infinite or indefinite, and so *ahorista*, indefinable. But universals are limited and definable (79. 10). Or again, 'each science does its work with reference to some one identical thing, and with reference to none of the particulars' (79. 5–6).

Nor are Aristotelian universals sets. Sets are identical just in case their members are; but Aristotelian universals are not identical just in case all and only the same things exemplify or instantiate them. Sets necessarily or essentially have just the membership they do;[44] but Aristotelian universals do not necessarily or essentially have just the instantiations they do. Aristotelian universals are best construed as properties or kinds, irreducible to any or all particulars.

Aristotle, then, is not a nominalist, but a realist. But is he a relational or

---

[42] Perhaps Matthews and Cohen assume that any realist account would be relational; and, since they accept (P) and reject bare particulars, they embrace nominalism. Armstrong attempts to defend a nonrelational account that is also realist, but it is unclear how far he is successful; see 'Armstrong on Relational and Nonrelational Realism'.

[43] That 'said of' is not linguistic is argued by, *inter alios*, Ackrill, *Aristotle's* Categories *and* De Interpretatione, 75–6. That it is linguistic is argued by, *inter alios*, D. Sachs, 'Does Aristotle Have a Doctrine of Secondary Substance?', *Mind*, NS 57 (1948), 221–5; Chung-hwan Chen, 'On Aristotle's Expressions *kath' hupokeimenou legesthai* and *en hupokeimenō(i) einai*', *Phronesis*, 2 (1957), 148–59. Some argue that in the *Categories* Aristotle is confused on this point: see B. Jones, 'Introduction to the First Five Chapters of Aristotle's *Categories*', *Phronesis*, 20 (1975), 146–72; and also R. M. Dancy, 'On Some of Aristotle's First Thoughts about Substances', *Philosophical Review*, 84 (1975), 338–73 at 340.

[44] For some discussion of this point, see Wolterstorff, *On Universals*, 173–81.

a nonrelational realist? Let us look first at the 'in' and 'said of' locutions, to see if they suggest an answer.

Does the 'in' locution avoid a relational account? The question may not seem pressing. At least, Matthews and Cohen suggest that, since Socrates is only accidentally white, 'there will not be the same worry about what (or whether) [Socrates] is supposed to be whatever [he] is independent of [whiteness]'[45] (p. 644).

I am quite happy to allow that the 'in' locution is relational. But Matthews and Cohen's reason for the claim bears scrutiny. They clearly advert again to (P): since Socrates is only accidentally white—and so is what he is independently of whiteness—he may be related to whiteness. Again the assumption is that relational ties are accidental ties.

Let us agree, in any case, that the 'in' locution is relational, and turn instead to the more controversial case: is the 'said of' locution relational?

Matthews and Cohen—despite their sympathy for a nominalist reading of Aristotle—suggest one reason for a negative answer to our question:

The question may arise, what is the relation between a particular bit of pink and pink in general? . . . Concerning this question, it would be a mistake to think of a given color-individual as being something independent of the shade of color it exemplifies, such that it could bear a relation to it. (p. 642)

Since an individual bit of pink is essentially pink, it is not related to pink; similarly, since Socrates is essentially a man, he is not related to man. The suggestion, again, is that things do not possess their essential properties relationally. But this again relies on (P). Why not say instead that, since Socrates is essentially a man, and is a man in virtue of having the secondary substance man said of him, he is essentially related to man? It is only if we accept (P) that we would not say this; but (P), as we have seen, is questionable. Without (P), then, neither the 'said of' nor the 'in' locution points to a nonrelational account.

One might argue that Aristotle's rejection of separation avoids a relational account;[46] but I cannot see that this is so. The secondary substance man is still different from any or all particular men. Further, it is independent of any given man; the secondary substance exists whether or not Socrates does, just as Platonic forms do. The secondary substance is sepa-

---

[45] Anscombe agrees that 'in' is relational; see *Three Philosophers*, 13. Armstrong does not explicitly discuss the 'in' locution; but he presumably would say that it is nonrelational. At least, he insists that particulars are related to none of their properties; and although he insists this *in propria voce*, he also believes that Aristotle shares his view; see i. 109. See 'Armstrong on Relational and Nonrelational Realism'.

[46] So Armstrong argues; see 'Armstrong on Relational and Nonrelational Realism'.

rate from Socrates, even if it is not separate from particular men generally. Why should the fact that for Aristotle the secondary substance requires the existence of some men or other imply that it is not related to Socrates when it is, after all, independent of him? Of course, one might simply stipulate that this is what makes the difference between a relational and a nonrelational account; but this is implausible. Indeed, it rests on a variant of (P): since the secondary substance is necessarily instantiated, it and its instantiations are not related.

Plato and Aristotle agree that Socrates cannot exist unless man exists; and they agree that man is independent of Socrates. They differ in that Aristotle believes that man cannot exist uninstantiated. But surely what is crucial is that man is different from, and independent of, Socrates. If Socrates is related to the form, he is related to the secondary substance.

Of course, Aristotle rejects more than separation; he also rejects paradigmatism. His universals are not models of which sensibles are but imperfect copies. One might argue that it is this fact that makes Aristotle's account nonrelational. But although this shows that Aristotle rejects *one* version of a relational account, I cannot see that it shows that he rejects the versions we have been discussing.

One might insist that Aristotle's account *must* be nonrelational. After all, he accords sensible particulars a privileged status not accorded them by Plato; they are the primary substances or basic realities. Earlier we noted that part of what this means is that universals are dependent on particulars. But if this is *all* that is meant, if particulars are equally dependent on universals, it would be unclear why Aristotle should call them *primary*. Must he not also mean that they enjoy independent existence? He does, in the *Metaphysics*, claim that substance enjoys independent existence; indeed, one might argue that it is definitory of substance that it enjoy independent existence.[47] And if so, surely no primary substance is a relational entity.

It is important to note, first of all, however, that nowhere in the *Categories*, at least, does Aristotle say that primary substances could exist if nothing else did; perhaps their privileged status does not consist in existential independence from everything else. Certainly that is not the only sort of priority Aristotle recognizes.[48]

And we need to ask once again what it means to say that substances enjoy independent existence. On Armstrong's view, as we have seen, it means that a particular 'could exist although nothing else existed'. But if

[47] For lucid discussion, see Dancy, 'On Some of Aristotle's First Thoughts about Substances', 346–8.

[48] For discussions of priority, see *Cat.*, ch. 12; *Metaph. Δ* 11; *Z* 1.

Socrates could exist although nothing else existed, he could exist even if the secondary substance man did not exist. He is then independent of the secondary substance, and so is not essentially a man. Yet we suggested that Aristotle believes that Socrates is essentially a man. If the independent-existence criterion is pressed too far, it makes particulars bare particulars; and this is incompatible with Aristotle's essentialism. It is difficult to see how we can have it both ways. Either Socrates is what he is independently of everything else, and so is a bare particular; or else he is essentially a man, and so is not independent of the secondary substance man.

But we need not conclude that Socrates is just a shadow and not a substance. Platonic particulars are copies of model forms; but they are also roughly independently identifiable spatio-temporal continuants. In just the same way, Aristotelian primary substances are roughly independently identifiable spatio-temporal continuants—even if they bear essential connections to other things, and so do not exist independently of everything else.

VIII

If we now compare Plato and Aristotle, the similarities are striking. On the crude view, Plato has a relational analysis; for two things are involved—Socrates, say, and the form of man. But Aristotle's account is relational on the crude view too; for there are still two things involved—Socrates, say, and the secondary substance man. On Plato's account, Socrates is a man by participating in the form of man; on Aristotle's account, Socrates is a man in virtue of having the secondary substance man said of him.

One might appeal to the refined view, and argue that since Aristotle clearly recognizes essential properties, he does not have a relational account; since Socrates is essentially a man, he is not related to the secondary substance man. But if this argument shows that Aristotle has a nonrelational account, it equally well shows that Plato does. For Plato can perfectly well allow, indeed *does* allow, that things have essential properties. In any case, the suggested argument relies again on (P). Why not say instead that both Plato and Aristotle have essentially relational accounts?

To be sure, there are also important differences between Plato and Aristotle. Aristotle rejects separated forms; his universals are all dependent on particulars, by being either said of or in them. He elaborates a system for explaining different sorts of predications that is not set out by Plato; and it is a system more attuned to important differences between various descriptions of things than is Plato's notion of participation. Further, Aristotle accords sensible particulars a more exalted status than Plato does; and he rejects Plato's view that particulars are copies of model forms. But if I have been right, none of these differences shows that Plato, but not Aristotle, has a relational account—not, at least, as we have understood that notion.

One might, of course, articulate a different sort of relational account, according to which Plato, but not Aristotle, has a relational account. I do not deny that this can be done. But if my argument here has been correct, there should be less urgency to do so. For one central reason for attempting to do so has been the view that without such an account, particulars are either bare particulars or relational entities. And while I have not questioned this claim, I hope to have suggested that the view that particulars are relational entities is not so unattractive as some suppose. Perhaps the conclusion to draw is not that some version of a nonrelational account must be true, but that substances can be essentially related to other things.[49]

[49] Earlier versions of this chapter were read at Cornell University, at Franklin and Marshall College, and at Pittsburgh University; I thank the audiences on these occasions for a number of helpful comments. I am especially indebted to conversations with Alexander Nehamas, Michael Roth, and Leon Galis; and to John Boler, Sydney Shoemaker, and Norman Kretzmann for detailed written comments.

14

Forms as Causes: Plato and Aristotle

1. Introduction

'One might be especially puzzled', Aristotle muses in *Metaph. A* 9 (991[a]8–10 = *M* 5, 1079[b]12–14), 'about what forms contribute either to everlasting sensibles or to those that come and cease to be.' If forms are to 'contribute' to sensibles, they must be some sort of *aitia*—explanatory factor—of them.[1] There are, Aristotle believes, just four sorts of explanatory factors—material, formal, efficient, and final. Platonic forms, he argues, are explanatory of sensibles in none of these ways; hence they contribute nothing to sensibles. Since we have reason to believe something exists only if it serves some explanatory purpose, we have no reason to believe forms exist. At least, they are explanatorily useless so far as the sensible world goes, although perhaps they are required elsewhere—say, in the realm of logic or mathematics.

Aristotle expects Plato to agree with some of this. For, he believes, Plato did not himself intend forms to be efficient, material, or final, but only formal, *aitiai*. But this, of course, just masks a further difficulty; for perhaps part of the reason Plato failed to put forms forward as efficient or final *aitiai* is simply that he had no—or at least no systematic and well-worked-out—account of efficient and final *aitiai* to offer. Not only, then, are forms explanatorily useless; but also, Plato had an inadequate account of *aitiai* in general.

How, and how well, does Aristotle prosecute his case? In order to answer

---

[1] I shall generally leave *aitia* untranslated. Sometimes, however, especially in connection with the E-*aitia*, I shall translate *aitia* as 'cause'; at other times, I shall translate it as 'explanatory factor'. It is important to bear in mind that most of Aristotle's 'explanatory factors' are not any sort of linguistic entity, but real features of the world. (Sometimes, of course, an explanatory factor is a linguistic entity: e.g. the premisses of a syllogism. But this is not the sort of case Aristotle usually has in mind.) Moreover, I take causes to be among the explanatory factors there are; so in translating *aitia* as 'explanatory factor', I do not mean to suggest that *aitiai* are always noncausal. I provide a more detailed account of my understanding of Aristotle's *aitiai* in sect. 2. See also the Introduction, pp. 37–8 n. 77.

these questions, we need an account of Aristotelian *aitiai*; accordingly, I begin by providing one (Section 2). I next look at Aristotle's criticisms of Plato on *aitiai*, focusing on some of the arguments he levels in *Metaph. A* 9 (=in part *M* 5) (Sections 3–5). Finally, I turn to the *Phaedo*—the main focus of Aristotle's attack—and try to assess the damage (Sections 6–11).

2. Aristotle on *Aitiai*

In *Physics* 2. 3 Aristotle tells us that we can properly answer 'Why?' questions in four ways; these give us Aristotle's four sorts of *aitiai*: the material (M), formal (F), efficient (E), and final (T, for 'teleological'). The M-*aitia* of a thing is what it comes from and consists of—bronze, for example, is the M-*aitia* of a bronze statue; the premisses are the M-*aitia* of a syllogism.[2] The F-*aitia* of a thing is the shape, order, or arrangement of its parts, and reference to it specifies the thing's essence;[3] one of Aristotle's examples is the ratio 2:1 of an octave. The E-*aitia* is explained as 'the primary source of the change or the staying unchanged' (*Phys.* 2. 3, 194^{b}29–30); the father, for example, is the E-*aitia* of his child. The T-*aitia* is what something is for, its end or goal; as such, it is a good or apparent good (195^{a}24–6). Health, for example, might be the T-*aitia* of walking.

Aristotle's account of the four *aitiai* is sometimes said to be his account of causation.[4] It is nowadays often objected, however, that this is misleading; for not all of Aristotle's examples of *aitiai* can nonproblematically be causes. As Annas writes, 'we cannot have the bronze producing the statue, or the goal exercising ghostly causal tugs from the future'.[5] If, however, we instead understand his *aitiai* as explanatory factors, then the difficulty dissolves.

[2] Strictly speaking, Aristotle should speak of propositions, rather than of premisses; once 'premiss' is introduced, so too is order, and hence form. I take it, however, that this is, if anything, a difficulty for Aristotle, and not for my interpretation of him. Since, however, some sorts of form include some sorts of matter, and since some sorts of matter include some sorts of form, it is unclear that there is any deep difficulty here.

[3] Aristotle also, of course, recognizes material essences; I shall ignore this complication here.

[4] Or so, at least, it is nowadays often said; and '*aitia*' is quite often translated as 'cause'. But it is in fact surprisingly difficult to find anyone who actually holds the offending view. M. Hocutt, for example, in 'Aristotle's Four Becauses', *Philosophy*, 49 (1974), 385–99 at 386, chastises Ross and Santayana for holding the offending view. However, when their claims are carefully read, it is not in fact clear that they hold that view; they might more charitably be read as holding that M-, F-, and T-*aitiai* are sometimes causally relevant, in the way I go on to defend.

[5] J. Annas, 'Aristotle on Inefficient Causes', *Philosophical Quarterly*, 32 (1982), 311–26 at 319.

In saying that there are four sorts of *aitiai*, Aristotle, on this view, is not saying that there are four sorts of causes, but only that there are four ways in which one might explain why something is so.[6] Defenders of this view sometimes hasten to add that it does not follow that Aristotle has no concern with causality: 'the material, formal, and final *aitiai* explain in non-causal fashion, but the efficient *aitia* is the source of *kinēsis*, movement or change'.[7] The E-*aitia*, that is, is, or is close to, a cause in 'our' sense, even if the M-, F-, and T-*aitiai* 'explain in non-causal fashion'.

Now it is certainly true that at least some of Aristotle's M- and F-*aitiai* range outside the area we would label 'causal'. The premises of a syllogism and the ratio 2:1 may be explanatory of certain phenomena; but they are not causes in 'our' sense. Hence at least some M- and F-*aitiai* are not causes and so '*aitia*' is, at least sometimes, better translated as 'explanatory factor' than as 'cause'. At least, this is so if 'explanatory factor' is construed ontologically, not linguistically; even if some of Aristotle's examples of *aitiai* are not causes, they are still real entities, existing out there in the world. His explanatory factors are not (usually) sentences describing things, but real features of the world.

But is it true that only the E-*aitia* is a cause in our sense, and that M-, F-, and T-*aitiai* always explain in noncausal fashion? Here much depends, of course, on how one understands causation. Suppose first one takes causation to be a relation between spatially and temporally contiguous events, the first of which brings about or produces the second.[8] Then it certainly

---

[6] So Annas, 'Aristotle on Inefficient Causes'. See also e.g. J. M. E. Moravcsik, 'Aristotle on Adequate Explanations', *Synthese*, 28 (1974) 3–17; Hocutt, 'Aristotle's Four Becauses'; G. Vlastos, 'Reasons and Causes in the *Phaedo*', *Philosophical Review*, 78 (1969), 291–325; and there are many others as well.

[7] 'Aristotle on Inefficient Causes', 319. Actually, Annas argues that Aristotle's E-*aitia* is a causal explanation, not a cause, so that if it is cited in a nonexplanatory way, it no longer counts as an E-*aitia*. I believe, by contrast, that Aristotle's E-*aitiai* can be cited in nonexplanatory fashion, and still be E-*aitiai*. (I also believe, more generally, that Aristotle believes that each of his *aitiai* can be cited in nonexplanatory fashion, and still count as an *aitia*. I take it, that is, that explanation, for Aristotle, can be construed extensionally.) E-causes, on my view, are *causes*; and they are also explanatory factors, in so far as one way in which to explain something is to cite its cause. Vlastos, 'Reasons and Causes in the *Phaedo*', 294, also claims that Aristotle's E-*aitia* is a cause.

[8] Something like this account of cause is, I think, fairly common. However, whether causes are necessary and/or sufficient for their effects, or are INUS conditions of their effects, or something else is disputed, as is the precise analysis of events, and even the claim that causation relates events (as opposed, for example, to states of affairs or facts). I intend here simply to state a relatively common and noncontroversial account of cause—something it is surprisingly difficult to do. Vlastos, 'Reasons and Causes in the *Phaedo*', 294, seems to assume something like this account of cause in suggesting that Aristotle's E-*aitia*, alone of the *aitiai*, is a cause.

seems true that M-, F-, and T-*aitiai* are not causes. Bronze, for example, is not an event and so not a cause, if causes are restricted to events.

If one restricts causes to events, however, then one might object that not even Aristotle's E-*aitia* is a cause. For Aristotle is just as, or more, likely to cite substances than events as examples of E-*aitiai*. The father, for example, is the E-*aitia* of his child, the builder of a building.

But there is an obvious reply to this objection in turn: in *Phys.* 2. 3 ($195^b4–$ 6) Aristotle distinguishes two ways of specifying E-*aitiai*: as actual or as potential. The builder is the potential E-*aitia* of the building; its actual E-*aitia* is the builder actually building. We can usefully explain this distinction if, following Jaegwon Kim, we speak of the constituents of events. Events are complex entities with different sorts of constituents. Kim, for example, suggests that an event consists in an object, a property, and a time. Thus, if at 2:00 I put pen to paper, I am a constituent object of that event, 2:00 is its constituent time, and the relation of putting is a constituent property of it.[9] Applying this back to Aristotle, we can say that his actual E-*aitiai*—e.g. the builder building—are events, whereas his potential E-*aitiai*—e.g. the builder—are constituent objects of events. Strictly speaking, Aristotelian E-*aitiai* are events; when Aristotle speaks of substances as E-*aitiai*, he is speaking elliptically, of the constituent objects of events. Hence, at least actual E-*aitiai* are, or are close to, causes in 'our' sense.

I agree that actual—if not potential—E-causes are, or are close to, causes in 'our' sense. (Hence, I shall from now on speak of 'E-causes', rather than of 'E-*aitiai*', when the efficient *aitia* is in view; and by 'E-cause' I shall mean the actual E-cause.) I also agree that M-, F-, and T-*aitiai* are not causes, if causes are restricted to events. If, however, causes are construed more broadly—as they sometimes are, even in contemporary philosophical literature—as entities one cites in explaining change, then, I think, each of the four *aitiai* can, in suitable circumstances, be a cause.[10] And even if

---

[9] J. Kim, 'Causation, Nomic Subsumption, and the Concept of Event', *Journal of Philosophy*, 70 (1973), 217–36. Although I borrow the notion of constituents of events from Kim, I have a more generous notion of what count as constituents of a given event than he does. The properties that explain why I put pen to paper do not, for Kim, count as constituent properties of the event of my putting pen to paper (though they are of course constituent properties of other events). On my usage, however, those properties do count as constituents of that event. If I am a constituent of an event e_1, and my properties are a 'part' of me, then I see no reason not to count my properties as equally being constituents of e_1. (No doubt I differ from Kim here because, although I agree that events have constituents, I accept different criteria for individuating events: I take it there is no difficulty in accepting Kim's notion of events having constituents, yet rejecting his account of how one ought to individuate events.) If one dislikes my broader use of 'constituent', however, one can translate my talk of constituent properties into talk of properties of the constituent object.

[10] For this broader account of cause, see e.g. L. Wright, *Teleological Explanations: An*

we restrict causes to events productive of change, still, each of the four *aitiai* can be—if not a cause, at least—causally relevant, by being a factor one cites in explaining change; they will still be referred to in, be parts of, causal explanations. (To avoid begging any questions, I shall from now on generally restrict 'cause' to event productive of change, and argue only that each of the M-, F-, and T-*aitiai* can be causally relevant, by being a factor one cites in explaining change. For those who favour a broader use of 'cause', my argument may be taken to show that each of the four *aitiai* can, in suitable circumstances, be a cause.) In particular, M- and F-*aitiai*, even if not E-causes, can, like the builder, be constituents of E-causes; and T-*aitiai*, even if not always constituents of events, are none the less still causally relevant, at least by being goals aimed at.

Thus, consider an example of an M-*aitia*: the bronze of a statue. The bronze of course does not *produce* the statue it constitutes; it is not a producing cause or an E-cause. None the less, it is a constituent of various events explaining the history—the *causal* history—of the statue. That the statue discolours, for example, is to be *causally* explained by reference to a series of events, some of which contain the bronze as a constituent. As Vlastos explains:[11]

We could hardly speak of bronze as the 'cause' of the weight of a bronze statue; bronze scarcely causes itself to be heavy. What we have here is a natural kind—that is to say, a cluster of properties regularly conjoined, among which is its characteristic specific gravity. Though the laws of the conjunction of these properties are not themselves causal, they have a network of connections with causal laws by means of which we are able to make relevant causal predictions, such as that a bronze statue will outweigh several wooden ones of the same dimensions.

Though Vlastos agrees with me that the M-*aitia* is sometimes causally relevant, he disagrees with my suggestion that so too is the F-*aitia*. He says

Etiological Analysis of Goals and Functions (Berkeley, Calif.: University of California Press, 1976), 25. Interestingly enough, Annas also invokes this account of cause at 'Aristotle on Inefficient Causes', 319, when she writes that 'The use to which Aristotle puts [the efficient cause] makes it clear that it is recognisably a cause in our sense: it is the kind of item cited in the explanation of why a particular change occurred.' Yet Annas also argues that M-, F-, and T-*aitiai* are noncausal explanations. M-, F-, and T-*aitiai* are noncausal on some accounts of cause; but not, I think, on the broad account of cause now under consideration (or, more exactly, there are examples of M-, F-, and T-*aitiai* that are causal in the broad sense, even if there are other examples of at least the M- and F-*aitiai* that are not). When Annas says (p. 315) that Plato's account of teleology is causal, she seems to have the broad account of cause in mind; but when she argues that M-, F-, and T-*aitiai* are noncausal explanations, she seems to have the narrower account in mind.

[11] Vlastos, 'Reasons and Causes in the *Phaedo*', 294.

that 'here the gap between *aitia* and cause is unbridgeable by any ancillary device that will stand up under investigation'.[12]

Vlastos's defence of this claim is, however, unsatisfactory. It rests on considering a mathematical example: the F-*aitia* of the angle at the semicircle being a right angle is that the angle is equal to the half of two right angles. Now as I said before, I agree that *some* M- and F-*aitiai* range outside the area where 'we' would speak of causes; and the F-*aitia* of the angle at the semicircle being a right angle is one such case. But if this disqualifies the F-*aitia* from ever being causally relevant, it should by the same token disqualify the M-*aitia* from ever being causally relevant—for, as Vlastos agrees, not *all* M-*aitiai* are causally relevant. Yet Vlastos correctly acknowledges that the M-*aitia* is sometimes causally relevant. The question he does not explicitly address, but to which his remarks seem to mandate a 'no' answer, is whether the F-*aitia* is *ever* causally relevant. And it is not too difficult to see that, contrary to Vlastos, the answer to this question is 'yes'.[13] Just as matter can be a constituent of an event, so too can form be. Sometimes we explain a change in an object by saying—not that it is so much wood, but—by saying, for example, that it is an apple tree. That an object grows leaves in a certain season is to be explained—*causally* explained—by reference to its form, to the fact that it is an object of a certain sort, with certain sorts of interlocking, mutually supportive capacities. Of course, the claim that some changes should be so explained is controversial. It would be rejected, for example, by Aristotle's Presocratic materialist reductionist opponents. But the fact remains that at least in Aristotle's view, natural objects have (or are) forms which are not reducible to configurations of matter, and which are causally relevant.

Aristotle brings these points out especially well in *Physics* 2. 1, where he asks what the nature of a natural object is. By the nature of a natural object, he explains, he means its inner source of change. His claim is that natural objects have two natures, their matter and their form; that is to say, their matter and their form are two inner sources of change. Some of a thing's behaviour is due to, is to be causally explained by, its matter;

---

[12] Ibid. 295. It is especially odd that Vlastos denies that Aristotelian forms can be causally relevant in the way in which matter is, in the light of the fact (which is also surprising, given the main ostensible aim of his paper) that he eventually concedes that Platonic forms, though not causes, are causally relevant in just the way he allows that matter is; it is difficult to see why he should allow Platonic forms, but not Aristotelian forms, this sort of causal relevance. See n. 67 below.

[13] Here, and in the ensuing account of teleology, I am indebted to J. Cooper, 'Aristotle on Natural Teleology', in M. Schofield and M. Nussbaum (eds.), *Language and Logos* (Cambridge: Cambridge University Press, 1982), 197–222.

some of its behaviour is due to, is to be causally explained by, its form. So the matter and form of a natural object are causally relevant, though they are not themselves E-causes. Aristotle captures this difference by saying that matter and form are inner sources of change, whereas the E-cause is the 'primary source of the change'. E-causes, that is, are events which may, however, include matter or form as constituents; matter and form are, then, causally relevant.

We have yet to consider the T-*aitia*. I agree that the T-*aitia* does not operate by exercising 'ghostly causal tugs from the future'. But it does not follow that it is irrelevant to causality. Though not itself a cause, in the sense of 'event productive of change', the T-*aitia* too is causally relevant.

There is some evidence that Aristotle would agree. For he says that in natural objects, formal and final *aitiai* 'coincide' (*Phys.* 2. 7, 198ᵃ24–5). If the formal *aitia* is causally relevant, so too should the final *aitia* be.

Thus, I said above that an apple tree grows leaves in a certain season because of its form—because it is an apple tree. But, as Cooper puts it, 'this explanation will be expressed more fully by saying it does this in order to protect the fruit'.[14] 'To protect the fruit' is a T-*aitia*, a goal the action of growing leaves aims at. One understands the action only if, among other things, one understands the goal it aims at. The goal is, then, causally relevant; it is a factor one cites in explaining change. To be sure, the goal does not E-cause the apple tree to grow leaves; nor, perhaps, is the goal most naturally said to be a constituent of the event of growing leaves (though it is, of course, a constituent of other events, e.g. of the event of the goal's actually being now achieved). None the less, the goal is still causally relevant.

Or again, an immature apple tree is growing into a mature specimen of its species. That is, it is acquiring its form, that of an apple tree. One explains how the apple tree grows by reference to the form it is acquiring; this form is also the goal of its growth. Once again, appeal to form coincides with appeal to the T-*aitia*; and both are causally relevant, by being factors one cites in explaining change.

In explaining how teleology is, for Aristotle, causally relevant, I have deliberately focused on examples of natural teleology, rather than of intentional action. This is because, as Aristotle puts it, 'it is absurd to suppose that a goal is not present, (just) because we do not see the mover deliberating' (*Phys.* 2. 8, 199ᵇ26–8). Teleology, that is, is not restricted to agents, or to creations of agents, with deliberative capacities.

I conclude, then, that even if M-, F-, and T-*aitiai* are not causes, in the sense of being events productive of change, they are causes in the broader

---

[14] Cooper, 'Aristotle on Natural Teleology', 200.

sense of being the sorts of factors one cites in explaining changes. If this broad sense of 'cause' strikes some as too broad, it is still true that M-, F-, and T-*aitiai* can all be causally relevant, by being factors one cites in explaining change. M- and F-*aitiai* are constituents of events; and T-*aitiai* are sometimes constituents of events, sometimes goals aimed at.

Now the following dilemma is sometimes posed: Aristotle, it is alleged, claims that forms are intended to be E-causes. Either he is correct, in which case the theory of forms is absurd—for surely eternal, immutable entities such as forms cannot be E-causes. Or else he is incorrect, in which case forms are merely noncausal explanations, and so the theory of forms is 'saved', at least on this score—at least, there is less difficulty in assuming that forms are noncausal explanations than in assuming they are E-causes.[15]

Our account suggests that this dilemma is not exhaustive. For it would not follow from the fact that forms were not E-causes that they were mere noncausal explanations; they might be causally relevant factors instead. I shall argue that this is in fact the case: though not themselves E-causes, forms are causally relevant, both by being constituents of events and also by being goals aimed at.

3. Aristotle on Forms and E-Causes

Having glanced at Aristotle's account of *aitiai*, let us now turn to his criticisms of Plato. I begin with his criticism of Plato on E-*aitiai*.

Aristotle is often thought to have chastised Plato for—either intentionally or unintentionally—making forms E-causes.[16] I shall argue that Aristotle levels no such allegation. His charge is rather that Plato put forward no candidates for E-causes; he ignored, failed to see the importance of, E-causes altogether.[17]

Aristotle is certainly unlikely to believe that Plato intended forms to be E-

[15] The first horn of the dilemma is endorsed by e.g. R. Hackforth, *Plato's* Phaedo (Cambridge: Cambridge University Press, 1955), 144. The second horn is endorsed by e.g. Vlastos, 'Reasons and Causes in the *Phaedo*'; see also H. F. Cherniss, *Aristotle's Criticism of Plato and the Academy* (Baltimore: Johns Hopkins Press, 1944), 383 ff. Annas's view is somewhat more nuanced. She does not believe that Plato intentionally put forms forward as E-causes; but she believes that he is committed to their being E-causes, because of unclarity on his part about differences between different sorts of *aitiai*. I address this sort of view below, in n. 66.

[16] See e.g. Hackforth, *Plato's* Phaedo; and there are many others as well. The person who comes closest to advancing the alternative view I favour, though he does not develop it in any detail, is W. D. Ross, in *Plato's Theory of Ideas* (Oxford: Clarendon Press, 1951), 233–4.

[17] At least, this is Aristotle's usual view, and certainly the view in the passages under consideration here. However, in *GC* 315^{a}22–33 he allows that for Plato (actions of) the great and the small function as E-causes; and in *Metaph. Λ* 7, 1072^a, he allows that actions of soul

causes. For in *Metaph. A* 9 he says that 'we [sc. Platonists] say nothing about the *aitia* from which change begins' (992ᵃ25–6). Plato, that is, does not say that forms—or anything else—are E-causes; he does not speak about the E-cause at all. Further, in *A* 7 Aristotle says that those who believe in forms[18]

do not suppose either that the Forms are the matter of sensibles, and the one the matter of the Forms, or that they are the source of movement (for they say these are *aitia* rather of immobility and of being at rest), but they furnish the Forms as the essence of every other thing, and the one as the essence of the Forms. (988ᵃ35–ᵇ6, trans. Ross (emphasis added))

Plato, that is, does not suppose that forms are M- or E-causes, but only that they are F-*aitiai*.

If we take these two passages *de re*, then Aristotle claims that Plato did not—even unintentionally—make forms E-causes. If we take them *de dicto*, then it is left open whether Aristotle believes that Plato is unintentionally committed to treating forms as E-causes. But even the *de dicto* reading rules out the possibility that Aristotle believes Plato intended forms to function as E-causes.

A passage in *Metaph. A* 6 might be taken to suggest, more strongly, that Plato does not even unintentionally put forms (or anything else) forward as E-causes. For here Aristotle says that Plato 'used [*kechrētai*] only two *aitiain*, the essential and the material' (988ᵃ9–10). If, as I think, 'used' is *de re*, then this passage implies that Plato did not even unintentionally make forms (or anything else) E-causes.

One might argue, however, that in charity to Aristotle, one ought to take all three of the preceding passages *de dicto*. For it is often thought that in two *other* passages—one from *Metaph. A* 9 and one from *GC* 2. 9—Aristotle argues that Plato is at least unintentionally committed to treating forms as E-causes; and this would conflict with the *de re*, but not with the *de dicto*, reading of our three passages. I do not believe, however, that either the

so function. All of these passages are consistent if Aristotle means that Plato has no worked-out conception of an E-cause, although he sometimes, perhaps somewhat unreflectively, describes soul, or the great and the small, in such a way that they in fact function as what Aristotle calls E-causes. In any case, the crucial point for our purposes is that Aristotle never suggests that Plato furnishes forms as E-causes—not even in the passages where he allows Plato some rudimentary E-causes.

[18] One might object that here Aristotle does suggest that Plato put forms forward as E-causes, on the grounds that he says that, for Plato, forms are the *aitiai* of being at rest; and, in *Physics* 2. 3, he says that the E-cause is the *aitia* of change and of rest. I take it, however, that the *Physics* passage means that E-causes are causes of things so constituted by nature as to be able both to change and to rest; whereas the present *Metaphysics* passage means that forms are *aitiai* of things that are by nature immobile.

Metaph. A 9 or the *GC* 2. 9 passage argues or assumes that Plato is even unintentionally committed to thinking forms are E-causes; and the passage in *De Generatione et Corruptione* in fact favours the *de re* reading.

In *Metaph. A* 9 Aristotle writes:

> In the *Phaedo* it is put this way: forms are *aitia* both of being and of coming to be. Yet even if forms exist, there is still no coming to be unless there is something to start things moving; and many other things come to be, such as a house or a ring, of which they say there are no forms. So clearly those things of which they say there are forms can also be and come to be because of *aitiai* like those just mentioned, and not because of forms. (991^{b}3–9 = 1080^{a}2–8, trans. Annas, with minor alterations)

Aristotle's argument, I take it, is the following:[19]

(1) Forms are *aitiai* of change.

(2) If x is an *aitia* of change, its existence is either a necessary or a sufficient condition for change.

(3) Houses, for example, come to be even though there is no form of house.

(4) Therefore, the existence of forms is not a necessary condition for change.

(5) Change requires something to start things moving, i.e. an E- cause.

(6) Forms do not start things moving.

(7) Therefore, the existence of forms is not a sufficient condition for change.

(8) Therefore, forms are not *aitiai* of change $(= \neg (1))$.

Aristotle begins by claiming that Plato believes (1). This, by itself, does not imply that Plato is committed to treating forms as E-causes; as Aristotle agrees, there are other sorts of *aitiai* involved in change—M, F, and T. If forms are *aitiai* of change, however, then, Aristotle assumes, their existence is either a necessary or a sufficient condition for change (2). Aristotle then

---

[19] The argument of *Metaph. A* 9 also discusses forms as *aitiai* of being; I shall ignore this issue here. With my account of the *Metaph. A* 9 argument, contrast that offered by Annas in her commentary on *Metaphysics M and N* (Oxford: Clarendon Press, 1976). She writes that 'Aristotle thus clearly takes the *Phaedo* to claim that Forms are necessary and sufficient, or necessary, or sufficient, conditions for coming into being, i.e. causally operative in the modern sense' (162). But if, as Annas here allows, Aristotle leaves open the possibility that forms are only necessary conditions for change, then he need not be taking the *Phaedo* to be committed to treating forms as causes; for as Aristotle agrees, not all necessary conditions for change are E-causes (though they may be constituents of E-causes). I agree with Annas that Aristotle here leaves open this possibility, and so reject her claim that he here clearly takes forms to be causes.

argues that the forms cannot be *aitiai* of change, since their existence is neither a necessary nor a sufficient condition for change.

Aristotle's argument against the claim that the existence of forms is a necessary condition for change (3, so 4) seems two ways wrong. First, even if there is no form of house, it does not follow that no forms are involved in the production of houses; perhaps forms of various shapes, for example, are involved. Second, even if no forms are involved in *some* cases of coming to be, it does not follow that no forms are *ever* involved in coming to be. That would be like arguing that since '*phlogiston*' doesn't name a genuine property, there are no genuine properties. But independently of the apparent invalidity of this part of Aristotle's argument, it does not suggest he assumes that forms are E-causes. To be sure, he suggests that the Platonists take forms to be necessary for change. But that doesn't imply that he thinks they take them to be E-causes; for not all necessary conditions for change are E-causes.

What about Aristotle's argument against the claim that the existence of forms is a sufficient condition for change (5–7)? (5)–(6) imply (7), and Aristotle believes both (5) and (6). So far as I can see, however, Aristotle is mute about Plato's attitude or commitments here; he neither says nor implies that Plato accepts or rejects (7). His point is only that since (5)–(6) are in fact true, the existence of forms can't be a sufficient condition for change; so, if they were *aitiai* of change, their existence would be a necessary condition for change—but we have just seen that it is not. This leaves open the possibility that Plato accepts (7), believing only that the existence of forms is a necessary condition for change. It also leaves open the possibility that Plato rejects (7)—and so rejects at least *one* of (5) and (6). But nothing in Aristotle's argument requires Plato to reject (6) rather than (5). Hence, even if Plato rejects (7), it does not follow that he rejects (6); he might reject (5) instead. Perhaps he viewed the existence of forms as a sufficient condition for change, in part because he did not see that the existence of E-causes is a necessary condition for change. This, we shall see, is just what Aristotle suggests in *GC* 2. 9.

I conclude, then, that nothing in the argument just considered commits Plato to treating forms as E-causes. What, however, of *GC* 2. 9?

To these, however, must be added the third cause, which every philosopher dreams of but none actually mentions. On the contrary [*all(a)*], some thought the nature of forms an adequate cause for coming to be. This is the view of Socrates in the *Phaedo*. (He, you remember, after blaming everyone else for saying nothing to the point, adopts the hypothesis that, of things that are, some are forms and some participate in the forms, and that everything is said to be in virtue of the form, to come to be in virtue of participating in it and to perish in virtue of losing it; so if this is true, the forms, he thinks, are necessarily causes of coming and ceasing to be.) . . . But if the forms are causes, why do they not always generate things continuously, rather than sometimes doing so and sometimes not, since both the forms and the things that participate in them are always there? Furthermore, in some cases we observe something else being the cause: it is the doctor who induces health and the knowledgeable man knowledge, despite the existence of both health itself and knowledge and those who participate in it; and it is the same in all the other cases where something is performed in virtue of capacity. (*GC* 2. 9, 335^{b}7–16,18–24, trans. Williams, with minor revisions)

Aristotle seems to argue as follows:[20]

(1) If x comes or ceases to be F, it comes or ceases to be F in virtue of coming or ceasing to participate in the form of F.
(2) Therefore, forms are the sole *aitiai* of coming and ceasing to be.
(3) Forms and participants always exist.
(4) Therefore, forms generate continuously.
(5) ¬(4).
(6) Therefore, ¬(2).
(7) The existence of E-causes is a necessary condition for change.
(8) The doctor, not the form of health, is the E-cause of health.
(9) Therefore, ¬(2).

One initial objection to this argument is that it is invalid, since (1) does not imply (2). (1) at best implies—not (2), but—(2′): Coming and ceasing to participate in forms is the sole *aitia* of coming and ceasing to be. But since coming and ceasing to participate in a form involves more than the form itself, (2) does not follow. I take up this argument below (in Section 9); here, however, I shall grant Aristotle (2), and ask what follows from it.

One might suppose that if, as (2) says, forms are the sole *aitiai* of change, they are E-causes; for surely the existence of E-causes is a necessary condition for change? Well, *Aristotle* certainly believes that the existence of E-causes is a necessary condition for change; but whether or not (he thinks) Plato agrees is of course another question. Aristotle's introduction to the argument suggests he believes Plato does *not* agree. For he begins by saying that none of his predecessors mentioned the E-cause, and then goes on to

---

[20] There is actually nothing in the text corresponding to premiss (2) to indicate 'sole'. However, if it is not supplied, Aristotle's arguments collapse; so I give him the better argument in supplying 'sole'. In his introduction to the argument, Aristotle does claim that, for Plato, forms were *hikanon*, suggesting that they are at least sufficient conditions; and I take it as fairly uncontroversial that (Aristotle believes that) for Plato, forms are, at least in some cases, necessary for change.

say that Plato, *on the contrary* (*all(a)*), invoked forms *instead*. Aristotle's suggestion is not that Plato mistakenly furnished forms as E-causes; it is rather that Plato *ignored* E-causes in his accounts of change, did not see that the existence of E-causes is a necessary condition for change. Neither forms nor anything else functioned for Plato as E-causes.

Aristotle's criticisms of (2) certainly allow this reading. His first argument is (3)–(6). Here his thought seems to be the following. Suppose forms are the sole *aitiai* of change. In that case, the relevant changes ought always to be going on. For if no other factors are necessary for change, there is no reason for change to occur at one time, but not at another. But the relevant changes are not always going on; and so forms cannot be the sole *aitiai* of change.

This argument assumes, as the argument of *Metaph. A* 9 did not, that the existence of forms is both a necessary and a sufficient condition for change. But as we have seen, this does not require Plato to believe that forms are E-causes; he might instead believe that the existence of E-causes is not a necessary condition for change. This is just what Aristotle's introduction to the argument suggests he thinks Plato believes.

(3)–(6) argue quite generally that forms cannot be the sole *aitiai* of change. (7)–(9) argue more specifically that they cannot be E-causes in particular. (7)–(9) thus give content to (3)–(6), by telling us what role in particular forms cannot fulfil. But once again, the argument does not suggest that Plato is committed, even unintentionally, to treating forms as E-causes. Perhaps he accepts (2) (if he does: we shall need to see) because he rejects, or does not acknowledge, (7). Once again, this appears to be Aristotle's view in the introduction to the argument.

Neither the *GC* 2. 9 nor the *Metaph. A* 9 argument suggests, then, that Aristotle believes Plato is, even unintentionally, committed to treating forms as E-causes. The *Metaphysics* argument does not even imply that Plato thought that the existence of forms was a sufficient condition for change. And though the argument of *De Generatione et Corruptione* does suggest this, it does not suggest Plato accepted this claim in such a way as to make forms E-causes. Aristotle's complaint is rather that Plato ignored E-causes in his accounts of change, wrongly thought change could take place without E-causes. The existence of forms is a sufficient condition for change, not because forms are E-causes, but because E-causes are bypassed.

I shall ask later (in Section 9) whether Plato makes forms E-causes or, alternatively, whether he bypasses E-causes altogether; I shall argue that neither charge is justified. First, however, let us investigate Aristotle's other charges.

4. Aristotle on Forms as Formal *Aitiai*

Although Aristotle does not believe that Plato put forms forward as E-causes, he does believe Plato put forms forward as F-*aitiai*. Here his complaint is—not that Plato ignored F-*aitiai*, but—that his candidates are inadequate. Aristotle has a variety of reasons for this claim; here I consider just three, all of which are aired in *Metaph. A* 9 (=*M* 5).

The first objection I shall consider is the following:[21]

> But neither are they any help towards knowledge of the other things (they are not their essence or they would have been in [*en*] them) nor towards their being, not being present in [*enuparchonta*] their participants. If they were, they might perhaps seem to be causes, as white is of a thing's being white, by being mixed in. But this account, given first by Anaxagoras and later by Eudoxus in his discussions, and by some others, is very simple to upset; it is easy to collect many absurdities against such a theory. (991ᵃ12–19 = 1079ᵇ15–21, trans. Annas, substituting 'essence' where she has 'reality')

To know something is to know its essence; and a thing's essence is its form. So, if forms are no help towards knowledge of sensibles, they are not part of their essence either, and so cannot be their F-*aitiai*. Forms cannot be the F-*aitiai* of sensibles, because they are not in them; and, Aristotle assumes here, the essences (forms) of things, must be in them. This assumes the following principle:

(P) If F is the essence of x, F is in x.

How exactly is (P) to be unpacked? Aristotle seems to accept (P) here, and to argue that forms cannot satisfy it with respect to sensibles. So, we need a sense of 'in' such that Aristotle both believes that the essences (forms) of things are in them in that sense, and that forms cannot be in them in that sense. Aristotle often articulates a number of ways in which one thing can be in another;[22] none of them seems apposite here. Instead, he seems to mean 'in' relatively nontechnically, simply to mean 'is a property of', in some sense of 'property'.

In what sense? In the *Categories* Aristotle acknowledges both universal

---

[21] There are further interesting points made in this passage that I shall not discuss here. For example, in addition to objecting that forms are not in things, Aristotle also says that they could not nonproblematically be in them. He does not tell us his reasons here, but he does do so in the *Peri Ideōn*. See Alexander, *In Metaph.* 97. 27–98. 24 Hayduck. I discuss his reasons and their cogency in ch. 12.

[22] See e.g. *Phys.* 4. 3; *Metaph. Δ* 3; *Cat.* 1ᵃ24–5.

and particular properties.[23] There is both the universal property whiteness, common to milk and to snow; and there is also the unit property whiteness, e.g. Socrates' whiteness, which, even if it is exactly the same shade of white as Callias' white, is numerically distinct from it. Whiteness construed the first way is independent of Socrates in particular (although, in Aristotle's view, it must be had by something to exist); Socrates' particular whiteness, however, is dependent on him in particular. So far as I can see, nothing in our passage allows us to choose between these two accounts of properties, and so I shall assume that both are left open.

Why does Aristotle claim that forms fail (P)? He must be assuming that they cannot be either universal or particular properties of sensibles. And in fact it is not difficult to see why he believes this. For Aristotle believes that forms are separate from sensibles, in that they can exist whether or not any sensibles ever do; the form of justice can exist whether or not any just people ever do.[24] Aristotle also believes that both universal and particular properties are dependent on particulars, though in different ways: Socrates' whiteness is dependent on him; the universal white is dependent on there being some white particulars or other. Forms are dependent on particulars in neither of these ways, and so cannot be the properties of sensibles. The separation of forms thus precludes their satisfying (P).

A second objection Aristotle raises to forms as F-*aitiai* is the following: 'it would seem impossible for a thing's essence to exist separately from the thing whose essence it is; so how could forms exist separately, if they are the essence of things?' ($991^b1-3 = 1079^b35-1080^a2$). This assumes (Q):

(Q) If F is the essence of x, F cannot exist separately from x.

(Q) requires that, if F is the essence of x, F be dependent on x in particular; Socrates' essence depends on, cannot exist without, separately from, Socrates. Since forms are separate, they are not dependent on any given sensible particular, and so cannot be their F-*aitia*.

It is natural to assume that (P) and (Q) state the same principle.[25] It is certainly true that the same fact about forms—their separation—disqualifies them from satisfying either. None the less, I think (P) and (Q) are different principles. (P) requires that the essence of x be a property of x. But it allows the essence of x to be either a universal or a particular property. Suppose

---

[23] Here I follow the interpretation defended by J. L. Ackrill, in his Clarendon edition of the *Categories* and *De Interpretatione* (Oxford: Clarendon Press, 1963), rather than the rival interpretation put forward by G. E. L. Owen, in his 'Inherence', *Phronesis*, 10 (1965), 97–105.

[24] For my account of what Aristotle means in speaking of separated forms, see ch. 11.

[25] So e.g. Annas in her commentary, 162.

that, as (P) allows, Socrates' essence is general or shared; it is, let us suppose, the species man or its form. The species man or its form is not dependent on Socrates. It cannot, then, be the essence of Socrates, so far as (Q) is concerned; but it can be the essence of Socrates, so far as (P) is concerned. Since (P) leaves open a possibility (Q) precludes, (P) and (Q) are different principles.

Why does Aristotle accept (P) and (Q)? All that motivates (P), I think, is the intuition that the essences of things must be somehow predicable of them, where 'being predicable of' is construed broadly enough to allow essences (a subclass of properties) to be universals or particulars. But what about (Q)? Arguably, Aristotle rejects (Q) in the *Categories*. For there, Socrates' essence seems to be, or to be given by, his species and genus, man and animal (2^b7–10, 29–31). And although Aristotle insists that substance species and genera cannot exist independently of primary substances as such—if there are no individual men, neither does the species man exist (2^b3–6)—he does not believe that the existence of the species man is dependent on Socrates in particular. So the *Categories* seems to reject (Q) (though it is compatible with (P)).

But Aristotle seems to have changed his mind about Socrates and his essence by the time of the later *Metaphysics*; and some of these changes support (Q). In *Metaph. Z* 4–6 Aristotle argues that each primary thing is identical to its essence. On the interpretation I favour of this claim, Aristotle means that the species man is identical to its essence—the species form or properties; and Socrates is identical to his essence. But Socrates' essence is not, as in the *Categories*, his species or its form, but an individual or particular essence, one proprietary to him. Socrates and the species man are each identical to their respective essences; but their respective essences are not identical to one another.[26] This reading saves Aristotle from the absurdity, sometimes attributed to him, that Socrates is identical to the species or its form;[27] and it also secures (Q). For if each thing is identical to its essence, clearly no essence is separate from what it is the essence of; nothing is separate from itself.

I shall ask later (in Section 8) whether forms fail (P) and (Q) and, if so, whether that is to their discredit. But here let us explore a third objection Aristotle levels against forms as F-*aitiai*.

[26] I discuss this interpretation in somewhat more detail, though still briefly, in 'Owen, Aristotle, and the Third Man', *Phronesis*, 27 (1982), 13–33.

[27] This view is attributed to Aristotle by e.g. M. J. Woods, 'Substance and Essence in Aristotle', *Proceedings of the Aristotelian Society*, 75 (1974–5), 167–80; he (to my mind, unconvincingly) argues that the view is not in fact absurd. See also G. E. L. Owen, 'The Platonism of Aristotle', *Proceedings of the British Academy*, 51 (1965), 125–50.

Not only do the Platonists say *that* forms are the F-*aitiai* of sensibles; but they also attempt to say *how* this is so. Aristotle believes the attempt fails: 'our account of the way in which they are the substances of sensibles is empty talk; for "participation", as we said before, is nothing' (992ᵃ26–9). To say that the form of F is the F-*aitia* of x involves saying that x participates in the form of F.[28] But participation, Aristotle claims, 'is nothing'. For his reasons, he refers us to an earlier passage (surely 991ᵃ20–2 = 1079ᵇ24–6), where he says: 'Saying that they ⟨forms⟩ are paradigms and that other things participate in them is to use empty words and poetic metaphor.' Sometimes, that is, the Platonists attempt to say what it is for something to participate in a form: x is F by participating in the form of F just in case the form of F is a paradigm or model of which x is a copy or likeness.[29] But, Aristotle protests, their attempt so to explain participation fails.

What is it for one thing to be a paradigm or model of which another thing is a copy or likeness? The account Aristotle has in mind seems to be the following: if x is a paradigm or model of which y is a copy or likeness, then x and y are like, resemble, one another in some relevant respect. In addition, there must be a particular causal connection between x and y: either y must be designed or created in the image of x; or else y must somehow strive to imitate, emulate, or embody x. Thus—to use one of Aristotle's favourite examples—Socrates and a picture or statue of him stand in the model–copy relation.[30] Or, to take another sort of case, if I aim to be F by

---

[28]   Actually, Aristotle seems to say something stronger here than merely that participation is *involved* in a form functioning as an F-*aitia*; he seems to say that F's being the F-*aitia* of x *consists* in x's participating in F. This would mean that there are no cases of x's being accidentally F that involve participation—in striking contrast to the view of some (to be considered below) that participation is restricted to accidental predication. In fact, I believe participation includes both accidental and essential predication; and I think this is Aristotle's usual view too.

[29]   Many people have objected to me that 'paradigm' and 'copy' are not correlative. I agree that as we use the English word 'paradigm', it is not correlative with the way in which we use 'copy'. This is partly because we sometimes use 'paradigm' in a weak epistemological sense, as something one might look to in deciding whether or not something has a given property. But I take it that as Plato uses *paradeigma*, more than this weak epistemological sense is in view. In addition, there must be an appropriate causal connection between the paradigm, and what it is a paradigm of; if x is a paradigm of y, then y is as it is because of its relation to x. If we so understand 'paradigm', then I think there is less difficulty in treating paradigms and copies as correlatives—though I perhaps think this because I understand the notion of copy somewhat more broadly than is usual. In any case, it seems clear to me that Aristotle believes Plato takes *paradeigma* and *eikōn* to be correlative; and though he faults Plato's paradigmatism on several fronts, he never objects to it on that score. If one is still unhappy, then I suggest reading 'model' where I have 'paradigm', and/or 'likeness of' where I have 'copy of'. I do not think this terminological matter should affect any substantive claim I wish to make.

[30]   See e.g. *Peri Ideōn*, in Alexander, *In Metaph*. 82. 11–83. 17 Hayduck.

trying to emulate something that is F, that thing is a paradigm or model I seek to copy. In this latter case, the paradigm functions as a goal I aim at. If, however, I merely take a sample of blue paint and try to find another like it, the two bits of blue paint do not stand in the model–copy relation; for the appropriate causal connection is lacking. Or again, although a VW Rabbit is a copy of a VW design, a car designed on a desert island by an ingenious engineer entirely ignorant of VWs is not a copy of a VW design, no matter how much it looks like a VW; for once again, the appropriate causal connection is lacking.

Why does Aristotle object that Plato's paradigmatism is empty and metaphorical? If sensibles are copies of model forms, they must be designed or created in their image, or must strive to emulate them. But, Aristotle asks, 'what is it that works, looking towards forms?' (991^{a}22–3 = 1079^{b}26–7).

Part of Aristotle's complaint is no doubt that forms are not in fact paradigms, that no one in fact uses them in the appropriate manner. Thus, in *NE* 1. 6 he objects that even if the form of the good exists, no one uses it (or, by parity, other forms) in directing their work; forms are too remote to be paradigms for human beings, at least.

But Aristotle says not only that forms are not in fact paradigms, but also that Plato's paradigmatism is empty and metaphorical. He must then also be suggesting that Plato does not himself specify a worker—or at least, he does not do so clearly and intelligibly—so that on Plato's own account, forms are not literally paradigms.

Aristotle has other objections to Plato's paradigmatism too. Suppose we waive the objection that even on Plato's own account paradigmatism turns out to be empty and metaphorical. As already noted, Aristotle also objects that forms are not in fact paradigms. Further, he also says that 'anything can both be and come to be without having been copied ⟨from something else⟩, so that someone like Socrates could come to be whether or not Socrates exists; and clearly it is the same even if Socrates is everlasting' (991^{a}27–30 = 1079^{b}27–30). I take the point of this remark to be the following. The Platonists take sensibles to be copies of forms. But, Aristotle objects, anything (*hotioun*) can be or come to be F without having been copied from something else.

Now if *anything* can be or come to be F without having been copied from something else, then this very object—which, let us suppose, is in fact a statue of Socrates—could exist without being a copy of Socrates. But if this very object—as opposed to another lump of bronze of the same shape and size—could exist without being a copy of Socrates, then it cannot be essential to it that it be a copy of Socrates. Aristotle seems to assume, then, that nothing is essentially a copy. It follows that if sensibles are copies of forms, they are not essentially copies of forms. But if so, then forms cannot be the F-*aitiai* of sensibles in the way Plato says they are, by being paradigms or models of which sensibles are copies.

Paradigmatism is, then, even on Plato's own showing, a hopeless metaphor. But matters are no better if we construe paradigmatism literally. For no one in fact uses forms in the appropriate way; and anyway, it cannot be essential to sensibles that they be copies of forms, since nothing is essentially a copy.

5. Aristotle on Forms as Teleological *Aitiai*

Aristotle claims, then, that Plato puts forms forward as F-*aitiai*, but not as E-causes. What of the T-*aitia*? Does Aristotle believe Plato put forms forward as T-*aitiai*?

He seems not to. Thus we have seen that in *Metaph*. A 6 he says that Plato used only two *aitiai*, the formal and material—not then the teleological. To be sure, in *Metaph*. A 7 (988^b6–16) he allows that for Plato 'the one or being is the good' and 'the *aitia* of substance'; still, the one or being (that is, I take it, the form of one) is not an *aitia* as being good. That is to say, Plato invokes as an *aitia* something that is in fact good; but its being good is incidental (*kata sumbebēkos*, 988^b15) to its being an *aitia*—it does not function as a T-*aitia*. Similarly, in *Metaph*. A 10 (1075^a38–$^b1$) Aristotle remarks that 'The school we first mentioned ⟨the Platonists⟩ is right to say that it ⟨the good⟩ is a principle; but how it is a principle they do not say—whether as end or as mover or as form'. The Platonists make goodness an *aitia*, that is, but not clearly a T-*aitia*.

It is true that, as we have seen, Aristotle says that according to Plato, forms are paradigms; and if forms are literally paradigms, and in the sense of being goals aimed at, then they are T-*aitiai*. For, as Aristotle says, one sort of T-*aitia* is 'something action aims at' (*Metaph*. A 7, 1072^b2–3). Aristotle seems to believe, however, that Plato's talk of paradigmatism is empty and metaphorical, in which case forms are not goals aimed at and so not T-*aitiai*, at least not in that way. If that suggestion is correct, then Aristotle does not, in admitting that Plato calls forms 'paradigms', accord forms a T-role. I know of no other passages in which Aristotle seems to accord forms a T-role; and so the weight of the evidence suggests that, in Aristotle's view, they have none; indeed, it suggests more strongly that Aristotle believes

Plato has no—or, at least, no clear and worked-out—account of teleology at all.

Whether or not Aristotle believes that forms, for Plato, are T-*aitiai*, he clearly believes they are inadequate to play that role. In *Metaph. A* 9 (992ª29–31) he says: 'Nor have the forms any connection with what we see to be the *aition* in the case of the sciences, that for whose sake both all mind and the whole of nature work.' Forms, that is, are T-*aitiai* neither for human beings nor in nature. Aristotle provides no reasons for his claim here, but they are not difficult to discern: the objections he levels against forms as paradigms apply here as well. As he objected in *NE* 1. 6, for example, no one in fact uses forms in the appropriate manner. In any case, later we shall need to see whether or not Plato intends forms literally to be paradigms or to be in some other way teleologically relevant.

Aristotle argues, then, that forms for Plato are not E-causes—indeed, that Plato has no E-causes to offer at all. He also seems to believe that Plato has no—at least no clear—account of teleology so that neither does he put forms forward as T-*aitiai*—which is just as well, since they cannot be T-*aitiai* any more than they can be E-causes. Aristotle does allow that forms for Plato are F-*aitiai*; but, he objects, they are inadequate to play that role too. Plato may believe forms are of some explanatory value. But since they cannot be *aitiai* of any sort (of sensibles at least), that claim is called into jeopardy. Perhaps Plato partially believed forms were *aitiai* because of his inadequate account of *aitiai*.

Is Aristotle right to say that Plato ignores E- and T-*aitiai*? Or, are others right to say that forms function for Plato as E-causes? Does Plato put forms forward as F- or T-*aitiai*? And if so, are they inadequate to play those roles?

It seems clear that Aristotle, in pressing his charges, has primarily the *Phaedo* in mind: it is the only dialogue he cites by name in the passages we have explored, and there are clear echoes of its language and doctrine. I shall, correspondingly, focus primarily on it in attempting to answer our questions.

6. Socrates' Early Materialism, and its Fall from Favour

Socrates begins, in the relevant part of the *Phaedo* (96 A 6), by recalling his 'youthful infatuation'[31] with the *aitiai* offered by natural science (96 A 8) of 'why each thing comes to be and why it perishes and why it is' (96 A 9–10). Such explanations include the following:

[31] Vlastos, 'Reasons and Causes in the *Phaedo*', 297.

(1) Living creatures develop whenever the hot and cold give rise to putrefaction.
(2) We think with blood.
(3) A small person becomes large by eating and drinking.

(1)–(3) seem to state M-, or M- and E-, *aitiai* of various phenomena. But it is then initially surprising that Socrates assimilates or associates such cases with the following:

(4) One person is larger than another by a head.
(5) Ten is more than eight by the addition of two.

Socrates apparently believes that each of (1)–(5) is similarly deficient, and is to be replaced by an alternative sort of *aitia*, one covering them all alike.

Vlastos suggests that Socrates' youthful mistake had been to confuse[32]

the arithmetical operation of addition with a physical process—that of taking things which were 'apart' to begin with and putting them 'close to each other'. And he had been supposing that the feasibility of this material process was the *aitia* of the logico-mathematical truth that the same items which count as units, if taken disjointly, will count as a pair, if taken conjointly.

Or again:

Socrates was confusing physical *aitiai* with logical ones: he was assuming that a material factor, like a head, or the material presence of two units, or the material projection of part of one thing beyond another could account for the respective statements, all of which are true *a priori*, and could only be accounted for by referring to the meaning of the terms they use.

We might put Vlastos's point by saying that Socrates, early on, believed there were only material *aitiai*, and this, it turns out, is doubly wrong: for cases like (1)–(3), material *aitiai*, even if necessary, are insufficient; for cases like (4)–(5), they are unnecessary as well—for (4)–(5) are logical, not empirical, cases, and so are to be explained in entirely different terms. Socrates, early on, wrongly assimilated logical to empirical cases; and he gave the wrong account of both of them.

Now it is true that Socrates *associates* (1)–(3) with (4)–(5). But I do not think he *confuses* them—any more than Aristotle is confused when he says not only that bronze is the material *aitia* of the statue it constitutes, but also that the premisses of a syllogism are its M-*aitia*. There is no reduction of the logical to the empirical; nor yet is there a confusion of them.

---

[32] Ibid. 311–12. The quote that follows is from p. 314.

Rather, both are instances of a more general phenomenon, of one thing's constituting another: bronze constitutes a statue; premisses constitute a syllogism. But different sorts of things constitute and get constituted. (1)–(5) are all instances of a more general phenomenon; but (4)–(5) are not thereby reduced to, or confused with, cases like (1)–(3).[33]

One important difference between the constitution relations involved should be noted: in (1)–(3), facts about constitution are causally relevant, or have causal implications, whereas in (4)–(5) they do not. In looking at Aristotle's account of his four *aitiai*, we saw that the M-*aitia* does not always have causal import, though sometimes it does. Similarly here, some constitutive factors—such as those mentioned in (1)–(3)—have causal force, whereas others—such as those mentioned in (4)–(5)—do not. This betrays no confusion. There is a general concern with constitution; some specific instances carry causal import.

If this is right, then we need not say, with Vlastos, that Socrates confuses the logical and the empirical, nor yet that he reduces the former to the latter. Nor need we choose between saying that Socrates is *either* interested in causality *or* in explanation. He is, at least at this early stage, concerned with material *aitiai* in a broad sense; sometimes this has causal implications.[34]

Why did Socrates come to be dissatisfied with M-accounts? He offers two reasons. The first (96 E 6–97 B 3) is that they allow *something* to be explained in opposite ways, which violates a general condition on adequate explanations. Being two cannot be explained by saying: the addition of one to one. For one thing's being divided could equally well be adduced to explain something's being two.

Vlastos objects that there is no genuine contradiction here, since addition and division would be adduced to explain different phenomena.[35] Annas, taking up this point, adds that 'This underlines the point that this problem is not really about the explanation of the occurrence of particular events; the solution to it will be the form solution that explains the possession of twoness by anything, without regard for the causal history of how the two particular items came to possess twoness.'[36]

---

[33] In explaining Socrates' general concern with constitution, which is sometimes causally relevant (and also in my later account of real definition), I am indebted to a paper by Philip Gasper.

[34] Annas, 'Aristotle on Inefficient Causes', 313, says, by contrast, that 'the *Phaedo*'s initial puzzles are, in fact, puzzles about *causal* explanation'; and she then berates Plato for shifting, without warning, to non-causal explanations like (4)–(5). On my account, Plato need not be berated here. In any case, 96 D 8 seems to signal awareness that (4)–(5) are in some way different from, if also aligned in some other way to, (1)–(3): cf. '*tade eti*'.

[35] Vlastos, 'Reasons and Causes in the *Phaedo*', 312 n. 57.

[36] Annas, 'Aristotle on Inefficient Causes', 314 n. 8.

I agree that Socrates' claim is meant to be applicable to more than causal explanations; and I also agree that he is not—directly, at least—concerned to offer causal histories of particular token events. But I think that what he says is meant to contribute to that project (if to others as well). Socrates focuses on types (rather than tokens) of states of affairs and events; he insists that none can be explained by opposites. If being F ever explains something's being G, not being F can never explain something's being G. This general constraint on explanation is meant to apply to noncausal explanations. But it is also meant to apply to causal explanations. To say that no type of event can be explained by opposites is shorthand for—or at any rate also involves—the claim that no tokens can be so explained either; if being F ever explains x's coming to be G, not being F can never explain y's coming to be G. We may well reject this constraint on causal (and noncausal) explanations. But it may not seem entirely unreasonable to those who believe that causal (or other sorts of) explanation import generality.

Socrates' second reason (97 B 8–99 D 2) for dissatisfaction is that none of (1)–(5) is teleological; none says why it is best that things happen as they do. To illustrate this objection, he cites two accounts of why he stays in prison, rather than fleeing to Megara or Boeotia:

(6) Socrates stays in prison, because his body consists of bones and sinews and the like.
(7) Socrates stays in prison, because he judges it best to stay.

But, Socrates says:

to call such things [as (6)] *aitia* is quite absurd. It would be quite true to say that without possessing such things as bones and sinews, and whatever else I possess, I shouldn't be able to do what I judged best; but to say that it's because of these things that I do what I do, rather than by my choice of what is best, and that too though I act with intelligence, would be a thoroughly loose way of talking. Fancy being unable to distinguish two different things: the *aition* proper, and that without which the *aition* would never be an *aition*. Yet it's this latter that most people call an *aition* . . . (99 A 4–B 5, trans. Gallop, somewhat revised)

'Most people'—including Socrates' earlier self—take accounts like (6) to specify the only *aitiai*. (6), I take it, specifies M-factors. So, most people believe that the only sort of *aitia* there is is the M-*aitia*. Socrates now rejects this view. In the case to hand—Socrates' staying in prison—(6), so far from being the only *aitia*, is not an *aitia* at all; it merely states necessary conditions for there being an *aitia*. The *aitia* of Socrates' staying in prison is—not (6), but—(7). So, M-*aitiai* are not the sole *aitiai*; at least sometimes, accounts like (7) state *aitiai*.

(7), I take it, states an E-cause with a T-constituent.[37] Socrates' staying in prison is E-caused by his decision to stay. That decision includes his belief that it is best to stay; and that it is best to stay is a teleological constituent of his decision. So, Socrates now believes that sometimes the *aitia* is—not an M-account, but—an E-cause with a T-constituent.

Socrates may indeed go further than this; he may claim that M-accounts *never* qualify as *aitiai*, and that the *only aitiai* there are are E-causes with T-constituents. Thus, for example, he says approvingly that according to Anaxagoras, *nous* is the cause of all things; and he adds that if this is so, *nous* ought to order all things for the best. *Nous* ordering all things is an E-cause; its ordering all things *for the best* is the T-constituent of that cause. So perhaps Socrates now suggests that there is an E-cause with a T-constituent for everything. And indeed, he adds that 'On this theory, then, one should consider nothing else . . . but the best, the highest good' (97 D 1–3); or again, 'I never supposed that, having said they were ordered by intelligence, he'd bring in any *aitia* for them other than its being best for them to be just the way they are' (98 A 4–B 1). All of this might suggest that Socrates now believes, or at least hopes, that there is an E-cause with a T-constituent for everything; and that, indeed, there is no other sort of *aitia*—although, as he is careful to point out at 98–9, there are necessary conditions for there to be an *aitia*.

On the other hand, perhaps the range of 'all things', in his account of teleology, is restricted to natural phenomena; if so, his belief or hope is at most that all natural phenomena have E-causes with T-constituents. Further, at 112 B 1 Plato says that 'the *aitia* of all the streams flowing out there, and flowing in, is that this liquid has neither bottom nor resting place'. Here M-accounts are reinstated. Either Plato is speaking loosely or else the earlier passage on teleology is not intended to claim anything as strong as that M-accounts never qualify as *aitiai*. Perhaps, then, Socrates suggests only that M-accounts in fact have narrower scope than most people believe, and that E-causes with T-constituents have correspondingly wider scope.

However we resolve this matter, it is important to be clear about two further points. First, Socrates, as we have seen, distinguishes between the

---

[37] Alternatively, one might prefer to say that (7) specifies both a T-*aitia* that is E-causally relevant and an E-cause. I do not think it matters much which way we choose to describe (7), so long as it is agreed that both a T-*aitia* and an E-cause are involved, and that the T-*aitia* is causally relevant, by being a factor one cites in explaining what the cause is. I speak of (7)'s involving an E-cause with a T-constituent for the sake of simplicity.

aitia and conditions necessary for there being *aitiai*. This suggests that on his view, *aitiai* are not always sufficient conditions; for, in addition to the *aitia*, there are, at least sometimes, certain conditions necessary for there being that *aitia*. An *aitia*, for Plato (as often for Aristotle), seems to suggest saliency rather than sufficiency.

Second, Socrates suggests that at least a wide range of phenomena have, or ideally ought to have, E-causes with T-constituents. Sometimes, however, he speaks as though the *aitia* were—not the E-cause, but—its T-constituent (e.g. at 97 D 1–3 and 98 A 4–B l, both cited above). But I take it that such remarks are elliptical for the fuller formulation encapsulated in statements like (7). Strictly speaking, the *aitia* is the E-cause with the T-constituent; sometimes Socrates speaks elliptically, as though the T-constituent were itself the *aitia*. This does not mean that the T-constituents themselves function as E-causes, or that E-causes are bypassed; it is just that Plato, like Aristotle, sometimes cites an E-cause by reference to its salient constituent.

So far, then, we have seen nothing to justify Aristotle's charge that Plato ignores or bypasses E- or T-*aitiai*. On the contrary, E-causes with T-constituents are singled out as his preferred sort of *aitia*. Plato goes on to say, however, that he was unable to find such causes generally; and so he embarked on a 'second voyage in quest of the *aitia*' (99 D 1–2). Perhaps this second voyage forsakes E- and/or T-*aitiai* in such a way as to sustain Aristotle's charges.

7. The Second Voyage[38]

What is the second voyage and where is it headed? There are, as is well known, two basic answers: (*a*) that Plato is embarked on a new route to the *original* destination; and (*b*) that he is embarked on a new route to a *different* destination. (*a*) and (*b*), however, conceal a variety of further

---

[38] I take it that the second voyage, or some portion of it, signals a shift from Socrates to Plato: the material and teleological accounts are Socratic; the shift to forms is Platonic. I intend my use of 'Socrates' and 'Plato' to reflect this view. However, the shift is not precise. For example, Socrates also invokes forms of some sort; and both Plato and Socrates practise dialectic, and favour teleological accounts. In addition to the question of where the second voyage is headed, there are two further important questions to be considered: (i) what is the first voyage? and (ii) does 'second voyage' indicate an inferior voyage? As to (i), I think the first voyage is concerned directly with *ta onta*, as opposed to *hoi logoi*. As to (ii), I do not think 'second voyage' conveys the notion of inferiority but, at best of a longer, possibly more arduous, journey. Obviously Plato does not view dialectic as inferior to natural science. If, however, one believes 'second voyage' does convey the notion of inferiority, one need not reject my answer to (*a*); Plato could, of course, be speaking ironically, as he so often does.

differences—over what, for example, the original and different destinations are; and over what the new route, wherever it is headed, involves.[39]

With many commentators, I favour (*a*); Plato is embarked on a new route to the original destination. But what is that destination? The best answer, I think, is the following: At 95 E 9 Socrates says that, to answer Cebes' worries about the immortality of the soul, they must seek 'the *aitia* of coming and ceasing to be'. More generally, he wants to know why 'each thing comes to be, why it perishes, and why it is ⟨as it is⟩' (96 A 9–10). Initially Socrates sought the *aitia* of coming and ceasing to be, and of being, through natural science and M-accounts. He then hoped E-causes with T-constituents would do; and though that remains an attractive possibility, Plato is unsure whether it can be realized. So, he embarks on a new route to the same destination—of specifying the *aitia* of coming and ceasing to be, and of being. This new voyage may discover E-causes with T-constituents for a wide range of phenomena; but Plato does not commit himself to that here. In fact, as the *Timaeus* makes clear, Plato does eventually discover E-causes with T-constituents for many phenomena: desires of the Demiurge to create the best possible world. But at this stage, the scope of such causes is left open.

At the same time, however, if Plato does not provide, or at least point to there being, E-causes of *some* sort for many phenomena, we may well conclude that Aristotle's charge—that Plato bypasses or ignores E-causes—is justified. For surely the *aitiai* of coming and ceasing to be, and of some cases of being, include E-causes, even if not T ones. I take it, then, that the fact that Plato is embarked on a new journey does not license us to forget about E-causes. For given the destination of the second voyage, E-causes are required. Further, although the announced destination of the second voyage does not require it to uncover T-*aitiai*, it certainly does not preclude their discovery either. And given Plato's (Socrates') profession of favour for them, we might well expect the second voyage at least to point us towards them, for at least some cases.

The new method for discovering the *aitiai* of coming and ceasing to be, and of being, turns away from *ta onta* to *hoi logoi*—from natural science to dialectic. And in particular, it offers us two answers to questions about why things are as they are and come to be as they do: the 'safest answer' (*asphalestaton*, 100 D 8–9; cf. E 1–2; SA) and a 'cleverer answer' (*kompsoteran*

---

[39] (*a*) is favoured by D. Gallop, *Plato: Phaedo* (Oxford: Clarendon Press, 1975), 176–7, and my account closely follows his. (*b*) is favoured by e.g. N. R. Murphy, *The Interpretation of Plato's Republic* (Oxford: Clarendon Press, 1951), 145–6; Hackforth, *Plato's Phaedo*, 132; and Vlastos, 'Reasons and Causes in the *Phaedo*', 297–8, esp. n. 15.

*apokrisin,*105 c 1–2; CA). In response to the question 'Why is something beautiful', the safest answer (SA) replies:

It seems to me that if anything else is beautiful besides the beautiful itself, it is beautiful because of nothing else at all than that it participates in that beautiful; and the same goes for all of them. (100 c 4–6)

Or again:[40]

what makes a thing beautiful is nothing other than the presence or communion of that beautiful itself (or whatever the manner and nature of the relation may be; as I don't go so far as to affirm that, but only that it is by the beautiful that all beautiful things are beautiful). Because it seems to be the safest answer to give both to myself and to another, and if I hang on to this, I believe I'll never fall: it's safe to answer both to myself and to anyone else that it is by the beautiful that beautiful things are beautiful. (100 d 4–e 3)

And in response to the question 'How did this come to be beautiful?', the SA replies:[41]

you know no other way in which each thing comes to be, except by coming to participate in the peculiar being of any given thing in which it comes to participate ... (101 c 2–4)

The SA says, then, that:

(SA) x is, or comes to be, F, if and only if x participates, or comes to participate, in the form of F.[42]

---

[40] Here, and in other translations of the *Phaedo*, I generally follow Gallop. In the passage just cited, however, Gallop's translation is misleading; he makes it sound as though Plato says that the form of F itself makes something to be F, when in fact Plato rather says that the presence (or whatever) of F in x is what makes it to be F. At 100 d 6 I retain the MS *prosgenomenē(i)*, and so assume that what Socrates leaves open is the question of what exactly the relation between sensibles and forms is, not what it is to be called (though he is imprecise about that too, of course).

[41] Gallop's translation is again misleading; he has Plato say that x comes to be F only by participating in the form of F, when what Plato says is that x comes to be F by coming to participate in the form of F. It is important to preserve Plato's distinction between the present *methexis* and the aorist *metaschesis*; the former concerns property possession, the latter property acquisition. That there is this distinction supports my view that Plato is concerned to distinguish between events, which involve causation, and noncausal states of affairs. Forms are relevant to both sorts of cases; but that is perfectly compatible with there also being important differences between the two sorts of cases. (Of course, some states of affairs involve causes too; I do not mean to suggest that all states of affairs are noncausal. It is just that some are, whereas this is not so clearly true of events.)

[42] Actually, I do not believe that Plato intends the SA as a general account of property possession, since I do not think he believes there are forms corresponding to every property. I shall ignore this complication here, however.

In response to the question why something is, for example, hot, the CA says—not (just) that x is hot if and only if it participates in the form of hot, but—that it is hot if fire is in it; for fire 'brings on' (*epipherei*, 104 E 10) the form of hot. Or again, instead of (or as well as) saying that someone is ill because he participates in the form of illness, the CA says he is ill if fever is in him; for fever brings on the form of illness. Similarly, three is odd, according to the CA, if the form of three is in it; for the form of three brings on the form of odd.

And in response to the question 'how did this come to be hot?', the CA says that something comes to be hot if fire, which brings on the form of hot, approaches it (cf. esp. e.g. 105 D, 106 A). Or, in general:

(CA) x is, or comes to be, F if it is, or comes to be, occupied by something, G, that brings on the form of F.

Exactly what sorts of entities does the CA invoke? As my formulation of it makes clear, I believe it invokes forms: the hot, the odd, and illness—substituends for 'the form of F' in my formulation—are all forms. But what of fire, fever, and three—substituends for 'G' in my formulation? I believe that fire and fever are 'physical' entities, not forms; fire, for example, is the familiar stuff in our fireplaces in winter, not the form of fire. Three, however, may well be a form.[43] If so, what occupies the 'G' slot can, but need not, be a form. This betrays no confusion. It is just that different sorts of entities can satisfy constraints placed on substituends for 'G'.

What is so safe about the SA? And what is the 'different ⟨kind of⟩ safety' (105 B 7–8) enjoyed by the CA?

Vlastos suggests that the safety of the SA lies in the fact that 'The *aitia* we are given is a logical one':[44]

it is the logical function of the metaphysical entity [the Form] that does the *explanatory* work of the 'safe' *aitia*. When I want to know what makes this figure a square rather than a pentagon, what answers my question is not the *existence* as such of the Form, Square—countless other Forms also exist which do not help to answer my question—but the logical content of its definition.

This is, I think, two ways wrong. First, the content of the definition of the form of F is at best a partial explanation of why x is, or comes to be, F; x's

---

[43] I do not mean to imply that there is no form of fire in the *Phaedo*—only that, if there is, it is not invoked here. For some discussion of this matter, and also on the issue of whether or not three is here a form, see Gallop, *Plato: Phaedo*, 197 ff.; A. Nehamas, 'Predication and Forms of Opposites in the *Phaedo*', *Review of Metaphysics*, 26 (1973), 461–91, esp. pt. II.

[44] Vlastos, 'Reasons and Causes in the *Phaedo*', 305. The quote that follows is from pp. 306–7.

participating, or coming to participate, in the form of F is also explanatory, but involves reference to more than the content of the definition of the form of F. I take up this point in more detail below.

Second, although I agree with Vlastos that the content of the definition of the form of F is at least partially explanatory of why x is, or comes to be, F, I disagree with his suggestion that this content must be 'logical'. The definitions Plato favours are real definitions, definitions specifying the real natures or essences of things; and not all real definitions are 'logical'. The real definition of beauty, for example, cannot be specified in purely logical terms.[45]

This point is analogous to one made before, in connection with Socrates' early materialism. Earlier I criticized Vlastos for suggesting that Socrates, early on, conflated the logical and the empirical, or reduced the former to the latter; I suggested that Socrates was interested in a more general phenomenon, that of material constitution in a broad sense, that both sorts of cases can instance. Vlastos now suggests that Plato, so far from reducing the logical to the empirical, reduces the empirical to the logical; all explanations are purely logical. Hence he later speaks of 'Plato's reduction of physical to logical necessity'.[46] I again dissent, and in a similar way. Plato is now interested in real definitions in general; but not all such definitions can be expressed in logical terms. There is no reduction of the empirical to the logical; there is a general interest in real definition, though of course such definitions may be offered in both logical and empirical cases.

What, then, does the safety of the SA consist in, if not the ' "safety" of analytic inference'?[47] The answer, I believe, is one several commentators have provided: that the new answer satisfies various constraints Plato imposes on adequate explanations.[48] Thus, for example, we saw before that each of (1)–(5) allows one to invoke opposites in explaining what it is to be or to have some property. Plato's SA disallows this; something is, or comes to be, F just in case it is, or comes to be, suitably related to the form of F, and no form (Plato assumes) consists of opposites. Similarly, the rejected accounts allow that some one thing, A, can explain the opposites, F and not-F; the

---

[45] If Kripke is correct, all real definitions may express some sort of necessity; but the necessity need not be logical. See S. Kripke, *Naming and Necessity* (Cambridge, Mass.: Harvard University Press, 1980) (originally published 1972).

[46] Vlastos, 'Reasons and Causes in the *Phaedo*', 321. Notice that even if Vlastos were correct to say that Plato is concerned here with logical necessity, it would not follow that he was not also concerned with causal necessity; on some views, causal necessity is a species of logical necessity. Just this is argued by, for example, Sydney Shoemaker, in an article discussed below (see n. 63).

[47] Vlastos. 'Reasons and Causes in the *Phaedo*', 309.

[48] See e.g. 'Aristotle on Inefficient Causes', 315, and the references cited there.

SA disallows this too (100 E 8–101 C 8). Or again, the failed accounts allow one to explain why something is, or comes to be, F by invoking something that is the opposite of F—someone is or becomes large, for example, by a head, which is small (101 A–B). But the form of F is, at the least, not the opposite of F; it is either large (assuming Self-Predication) or neither large nor small. Finally, the SA, unlike the rejected material accounts, seems to specify necessary and sufficient conditions for something to be, or to become, F.

The SA is safest, then, not because it is 'logical', but because it, unlike the rejected answers, satisfies Plato's constraints on adequate explanations, and because it purports to specify necessary and sufficient conditions. We may, of course, reject Plato's criteria for adequate explanations; but that is another matter.

It is worth asking in a bit more detail precisely how the SA, but not the rejected accounts, satisfies these constraints. Earlier I contrasted M-accounts, explicated in terms of constitution, with real definitions; but this contrast itself requires further explication, explication it is not easy to provide.

Contrast the following two accounts of why something is beautiful: (*a*) because it is brightly coloured; and (*b*) because it participates in the form of beauty. (*a*) is the sort of account Socrates initially favoured but now rejects. For, not all brightly coloured things are beautiful, and appealing to something's bright colour does not always explain its beauty. But saying that something participates in the form of beauty is alleged to be explanatory. It must, then, be being assumed that features like bright colour will not be mentioned in the real definition of beauty. We might construe bright colour as a (broadly speaking) material constituent, in that it might realize or constitute something's beauty in a particular case; but it is not what beauty is, since not all beautiful things have it, and since some things that have it are not beautiful—bright colour is neither necessary nor sufficient for being beautiful.

What sorts of features figure in real definitions, if not material constituents like bright colour? Let us, following Aristotle, contrast a list of ingredients (again broadly construed!) and their arrangement (see e.g. *Metaph. Z* 17). The real nature of a property consists not in the various features that constitute it on different occasions, but in more abstract features, such as structure or arrangement, that any such features must conform to. The distinction is not precise because, once we range outside of simple agreed cases, the distinction between form and matter is not precise; but there is an intuitive distinction here, and I think it is the one Plato is trying to capture in contrasting materialism with the second voyage.

What, then, of the different kind of safety enjoyed by the CA? Whereas the SA specifies necessary and sufficient conditions, the CA need specify no more than sufficient conditions. Further, the CA allows some explanations involving opposites. Fever, for example, is adduced to explain illness; but, as Gallop notes, the opposite of fever—hypothermia—can also explain illness.[49] None the less, the CA is still safe because it does at the least provide sufficient conditions, as the rejected material accounts do not (having a head is not sufficient for being tall). Further, the CA disallows some explanations involving opposites. Fever, for example, can only explain illness and not also health. Though some one phenomenon can now apparently be explained in opposite ways, no one (sort of) thing can be adduced to explain opposite phenomena.

Having looked, in a general way, at the nature of the SA and CA, and at what sort of safety they enjoy, let us now return to our central questions: what sorts of *aitiai* are forms here? Are forms E-, F-, or T-*aitiai*? And if so, do they fall prey to Aristotle's and others' objections? I look first at forms in connection with the F-*aitia*.

8. Forms as Formal *Aitiai* in the *Phaedo*

Are forms F-*aitiai* in the *Phaedo*? Let us first distinguish between a broad and a narrow conception of form. The broad use is illustrated in *Physics* 1. 7, where any (positive) property a thing may acquire or lose counts as a form; when Socrates becomes tan or musical, tan and musical count as his forms. The narrow use is illustrated in *Physics* 2. 3, where a form is said to be 'the account of what the being would be'; form in the narrow sense is the essence or nature of a thing. In this sense, neither tan nor musical is a form of Socrates', though his soul is. When Aristotle asks whether form is substance, it is form in the narrow sense that concerns him; and in exploring Aristotle's objections to forms as F-*aitiai*, we focused primarily on the narrow use.

It seems clear that forms are F-*aitiai* in the broad sense. Plato explains Socrates' coming or ceasing to be large, for example, by reference to his coming or ceasing to participate in the form of large—just as, in *Physics* 1. 7, being large is a form in such a change. Socrates is not essentially

---

[49] Gallop, *Plato: Phaedo*, 211.

large; here we are simply explaining the acquisition or loss of an accidental property.

But are forms also, as Aristotle assumes, F-*aitiai* in the narrow sense? Some would argue that, at least in the *Phaedo*, forms are *not* the narrow F-*aitiai* of sensibles at any rate.[50] For there, it is sometimes argued, there are forms only corresponding to the accidental properties of sensibles. We invoke the form of large to explain Socrates' being large; but we do not invoke the form of man to explain his being a man. Socrates is a man 'by nature' (102 c 1), in virtue of himself, and there is no form of man, at this stage, at all. Indeed, on one version of this view, the denial of a form of man is motivated by (allegedly) Aristotelian worries. The thought is that if Socrates were a man in virtue of being related to the form of man, he would only be accidentally a man; since he is essentially a man, he cannot be what he is in virtue of being related to anything, and so no form of man is needed. One is present, of course, by the time of the *Timaeus*; but by then, Plato has abandoned the claim that Socrates is essentially a man—perhaps precisely because he has come to believe that Socrates is a man in virtue of being related to something.

I do not think this view is correct, however. Even in the *Phaedo*, as we have seen, Plato at least recognizes forms of hot and cold; and fire and snow are hot and cold in virtue of being related to them. Similarly, three is odd in virtue of being related to the form of odd. Yet fire is essentially hot, snow essentially cold; and three is essentially odd—so Plato is concerned to argue here. So even in the *Phaedo*, some things have at least some of their essential properties in virtue of being suitably related to forms. Perhaps the *Phaedo* is uncommitted to forms of man or fire; but if so, this is not to be explained by saying that there are, in general, no forms corresponding to any of the essential properties of sensibles. For there is a form of hot, and some sensibles—e.g. fire—are essentially hot; and there is a form of cold, and some sensibles—e.g. snow—are essentially cold. Even in the *Phaedo*, then, forms are invoked to explain at least some of the essential properties of some sensibles—just as Aristotle, in contrast to some contemporary commentators, says.[51]

---

[50] This line of argument is developed by A. Nehamas in several recent articles; see esp. 'Plato on the Imperfection of the Sensible World', *American Philosophical Quarterly*, 12 (1975), 105–17. In an earlier article, however, Nehamas seems to allow that there are forms corresponding to at least some of the essential properties of some sensibles; see 'Predication and Forms of Opposites in the *Phaedo*'.

[51] M. F. Burnyeat has suggested to me that even if Plato invokes forms to explain at least some of the essential properties of some sensibles, the relation, in this case, is not that of participation; participation, he suggested, is restricted to accidental predication, even if there

One might insist that this is not enough to show that forms are the narrow F-*aitiai* of sensibles. Annas, for example, says that 'instead of Aristotelian substantial forms we find only qualities that can have opposites'.[52] But we must be careful to distinguish between criteria and candidates for formal causation. According to Aristotle in *Physics* 2. 3, the criterion for being a formal *aitia* is 'the account of what the being would be'. Plato believes forms satisfy this criterion; he explains what the beings of things are by relating them to forms. Aristotle rejects forms as formal *aitiai* and proposes other candidates. But Plato and Aristotle—here as often elsewhere—are disagreeing about candidates, not criteria.

I believe, then, that Aristotle is perfectly correct when he says that Plato intends forms to be F-*aitiai*. But what of his objections to their candidacy? We examined three of them: that forms fail (P); that they fail (Q); and that Plato fails to explain how forms could be the F-*aitiai* of sensibles.

(Q) states that if F is the essence of x, F cannot be separate from x. If, as I believe, forms are universals, then forms indeed fail (Q). For (Q) requires the essence of a given particular to be dependent on it; but no universal is dependent on any given particular. Aristotle is thus perfectly correct to say that forms fail (Q).

But is (Q) itself reasonable? The answer depends, in part, on one's conception of essence. If one believes with Aristotle in the *Metaphysics* that Socrates has an essence proprietary to him, then (Q) seems reasonable (though not required). If one believes with Aristotle in the *Categories* that all essences are general, then (Q) is more likely to seem false. I don't know which position is correct; philosophical intuitions go both ways here. But that in itself is interesting. It is too often assumed that either Plato or Aristotle is obviously correct, to the inevitable detriment of the former. I am more inclined to see a serious debate, with intelligent considerations mounted on both sides.

What about (P)? (P) states that if F is the essence of x, F is in x—that is, is a property of x. Aristotle argues that since forms are separate, they cannot be the properties of sensibles or, therefore, their F-*aitiai*. I agree that forms are separate from sensibles. But unlike Aristotle, I do not believe

are other sorts of ties between sensibles and forms as well. I am inclined to think, however, that Plato is willing to speak of participation in connection with essential predication, no less than in connection with accidental predication; but I shall not try to defend that claim here.

[52] 'Aristotle on Inefficient Causes', 318 n. 18. See also C. C. W. Taylor, 'Forms as Causes in the *Phaedo*', *Mind*, 78 (1969), 45–59. Taylor spends some time asking how close Plato's forms are to Aristotle's formal *aitiai*; but even if they are unlike them, it does not follow that they are not Plato's candidates for filling the same role.

it follows that forms are therefore not properties of sensibles; for with Plato I believe that universals can exist uninstantiated. So, the separation of forms does not prevent their being the properties of sensibles; nor, therefore, does it prevent their satisfying (P). Aristotle's argument that forms fail (P) is valid; but, because it rests on the false belief that universals cannot exist uninstantiated, it is unsound.

The third objection we considered was that Plato fails to explain how forms could be the F-*aitiai* of sensibles. To be sure, Aristotle allowed that Plato sometimes appeals to paradigmatism. But paradigmatism, Aristotle objected, is, even on Plato's own showing, metaphorical; and matters are no better if we construe it literally. For forms are not in fact paradigms; nor can sensibles be essentially copies of forms, since nothing is essentially a copy.

Several difficult and important points are at issue here; and I cannot possibly discuss them all in detail. So I shall restrict myself to a few brief— and regrettably dogmatic—assertions.

I believe, first of all, that Aristotle's crucial assertion, that nothing is essentially a copy, is false. A statue of Socrates is essentially a statue of Socrates; if it does not bear an appropriate causal relation to Socrates, it cannot be a statue of him.[53] If we reject the claim that sensibles are essentially copies (as we no doubt in general do), it should not be because we believe that nothing is essentially a copy.

But does Plato believe that sensibles are essentially copies of forms? In contrast to the *Timaeus* and, to a lesser extent, the *Republic*, the *Phaedo* never calls sensibles copies, or forms paradigms—though, of course, neither the presence nor the absence of these words is decisive.[54] Plato does compare Simmias to his picture, and then forms to sensibles (73 E 9–10 ff.). But the only point of comparison he seems to have in mind is that just as pictures are like, but inferior to, what they are pictures of, so sensibles are like, but inferior to, forms; and that point of contrast does not require sensibles to be copies of forms. Nor does Plato explicitly invoke a worker who looks towards forms. He does say that sensibles strive but fail to be like forms; but this, again, seems to be a metaphor for the claim that sensibles are like, but inferior to, forms.[55]

---

[53] I discuss this and some related matters in somewhat more detail in ch. 13.

[54] Thus, for example, Plato's use of *paradeigmati* at *Euphr.* 6 E 4–5 is often thought to be hygienic, in contrast to later, allegedly less hygienic, uses. Cf. e.g. *Rep.* 500 C–E, 511 A, 520 C, 596 B ff.; *Ti.* 28 A ff., 48 D 2. I am well aware that the precise interpretation of these passages is disputed, and that the interpretation I am assuming is controversial; unfortunately, I do not have the space to defend it in any detail here.

[55] Contrast R. Turnbull, 'Aristotle's Debt to the "Natural Philosophy" of the *Phaedo*',

Furthermore, at 100 D (cited above) Plato explicitly declines to tell us precisely what the relation between sensibles and forms is. He is convinced, he says, that x is F by being somehow connected to the form of F; but he declines to say what the connection is.

If we focus on such passages in the *Phaedo*, Aristotle seems to be to some extent justified in his third criticism: Plato is quite openly vague and inexplicit; he does use the metaphor of striving, if not the language of paradigm and copy. It is, however, perhaps somewhat uncharitable to construe relative silence and lack of commitment as 'empty talk'; and later we shall see that the *Phaedo* at least contains hints—though no explicit or detailed account—of how forms might literally be paradigms, in the sense of being goals aimed at (see Section 9).

Whether or not one is impressed by Aristotle's objections to forms as F-*aitiai*, one might argue that Plato still faces various problems. In particular, in turning to F-*aitiai*, has he not left T- and E-*aitiai* far behind? And is not that problematical? As Annas writes:[56]

But whatever the merits of Plato's theory, two facts are clear about it. One is that it is not teleological. The Form F explains an F instance by its guaranteed freedom from being the opposite of F; this is the safest kind of explanation, but goodness does not enter into it, in however weak a form. The other is that it is not a causal explanation. What is being explained, is why a thing has a quality F; the Form explains this with no reference to any particular processes or events of things' coming or ceasing to be F. Plato, in fact, has changed the subject.

Let us see whether this is so.

9. Forms and Efficient Causes in the *Phaedo*

Are forms efficient causes in the *Phaedo*? One might argue as follows that the SA makes forms E-causes. Plato says that (1) Forms are the only *aitiai*. It follows that (2) The existence of forms is a necessary and sufficient

Philosophical Quarterly, 3 (1958), 131–43 at 134, who interprets the talk of striving literally. Actually, Plato does not even explicitly compare Simmias and his portrait to forms and sensibles; both sorts of cases are mentioned, but they are not explicitly compared. Aristotle, however, seems to think Plato at least intends the contrast, and intends it in such a way as to suggest that just as a picture of Simmias is a copy of him, so sensibles are copies of forms; see esp. the Argument from Relatives in the *Peri Ideōn*, in Alexander, *In Metaph.* 82. 11–83. 17 Hayduck.

[56] Annas, 'Aristotle on Inefficient Causes', 318.

condition for change. But since (3) The existence of E-causes is a necessary condition for change, it follows as well that (4) Forms are E-causes.[57]

But I do not think this argument succeeds. First, (1) does not imply (2). For, as we have seen, as Plato understands *aitiai*, they can involve saliency rather than sufficiency. If this is so, (1) implies—not (2) but—(2′): Forms are the salient factors in change. I think Plato believes (2′), and I shall discuss it further below. But it does not make forms E-causes.

Second, Plato does not, in any case, strictly speaking say (1), but at best (1′) Participation, or coming to participate, in a form provides the only *aitia*. When he suggests (1), he is speaking elliptically, of the salient constituent of the *aitia*. This, again, mirrors Aristotle's strategy of sometimes identifying an *aitia* in terms of its salient constituent. But (1′) does not imply (2), since participating, and coming to participate, in forms obviously involves more than forms themselves. Participating in a form is a state of affairs that includes a form as a constituent; coming to participate in a form is an event that includes a form as a constituent. But it is such states of affairs and events that are the *aitiai*, not forms all by themselves; forms are constituents of these *aitiai*, but they are not themselves, strictly speaking, the *aitiai*.

Neither (1) nor (1′) implies (2), then; and I do not think Plato believes, or is committed to, (2). He may, to be sure, accept not only (2′) but also (2″) Coming to participate in a form is a necessary and sufficient condition for change—though it is unclear that (1′) implies (2″) since, as we have seen, as Plato understands *aitiai*, they need not involve sufficiency. But even if Plato accepts (2′) and (2″), (4) need not follow. First, Plato might reject (3), and so accept—not (4), but—(4′) The existence of E-causes is not a necessary condition for change; this is Aristotle's interpretation. But even if Plato accepts (3), (4) does not follow. All that follows is that (4″) Coming to participate in a form involves E-causes. But to say that the event of something's coming to participate in a form involves an E-cause is not to say or imply that forms are themselves E-causes. To be sure, if the E-cause is an event or state of affairs, it may follow that a form is a constituent of the E-cause; but forms can obviously be constituents of E-causes, without themselves being E-causes.

I conclude, then, that the SA does not put forms forward as E-causes. What, however, of the CA? It states, recall, that:

---

[57] Some believe, of course, that this is just what Aristotle argues in *Metaph. A* 9 and *GC* 2. 9; but I have argued that he does not in fact argue in this way.

x is, or comes to be, F if it is, or comes to be, occupied by something, G, that brings on the form of F.

What is the 'bringing on' relation? Gallop suggests that it may be 'causally imparting';[58] Vlastos suggests it is entailments between forms (unlike me, he restricts substituends for 'G' to forms).[59]

If Gallop's account of 'bringing on' were correct, and if I am also correct to say that substituends for 'G' can (though they need not) be forms, then it looks as though the CA makes forms E-causes. For it then tells us that the form of three, for example, causally makes something odd. But I do not think we need to accept Gallop's suggestion; nor yet need we endorse Vlastos's. Rather, I suggest, 'bringing on' is the generic relation of sufficiency; sometimes the sufficiency to hand is causal sufficiency, sometimes not. Thus, actions of fire causally impart heat to something; they E-cause Socrates to become hot. But the form of three, though its possession by something is sufficient to make it odd, does not causally make anything odd. As before so here: Plato focuses on a general phenomenon, which sometimes but not always has causal implications. If this is correct, we need not say that the CA makes forms E-causes. For 'bringing on' is not causal in the cases where substituends for 'G' are forms.

I have argued so far that neither the SA nor the CA requires forms to be E-causes. But is Aristotle's alternative charge—that Plato bypasses E-causes—justified? Let's consider the SA first.

The SA is, to be sure, quite general and abstract; and it includes more than E-causal cases. It is meant to be applicable to all events and states of affairs, to the natural and the mathematical alike. And although it distinguishes between states of affairs and events—between participating, and coming to participate, in a form—it does not specify E-causes for the events it considers. The SA instead has a different concern: to tell us what states of affairs and events consist in. The state of affairs of x's being F consists in x's participating in the form of F; the event of x's coming to be F consists in x's coming to participate in the form of F. This specifies no E-causes; it merely tells us what states of affairs and events consist in. To this extent, Aristotle is justified: the SA does not specify E-causes, and in that sense it 'bypasses' them.

But we ought not to infer from this that Plato therefore believes that change can take place without E-causes, or that he is uninterested in, or fails to see the importance of, E-causes. For though the SA does not itself specify E-causes, neither is it irrelevant to their specification. Read in context, it

<hr/>

[58] Gallop, *Plato:* Phaedo, 208.   [59] Vlastos, 'Reasons and Causes in the *Phaedo*', 317.

contributes to, even if it does not exhaust, the project of providing E-causes. Plato began by telling us that E-causes with T-constituents were his favoured sort of *aitiai*. But, since he could not discover such *aitiai* directly, he embarked on a second voyage. That second voyage includes the discovery of E-causes in its ultimate destination. The SA is one stop in this voyage. If the ultimate destination of Plato's voyage includes the discovery of E-causes, then the SA is quite an appropriate temporary resting place; it is not an irrelevant detour. For, as many have urged, an adequate specification of E-causes requires an adequate account of causation which, in turn, requires an adequate analysis of events.[60] Causation relates events; and we can hope to understand what causation involves only if we are clear about its relata, events. The SA takes up this latter task, en route to the discovery of E-causes. The SA is thus relevant to the project of specifying E-causes, even if it does not itself provide them. Its focus on the analysis of events and states of affairs does not justify or support the charge that Plato has changed the subject, or is headed towards a new ultimate destination; on the contrary, that focus is perfectly appropriate for one journeying to E-causes.

Moreover, the SA is just one stop along the way. There is also the CA and it, I think, goes somewhat further towards specifying E-causes. For it tells us that, at least in some cases, x comes to be F in virtue of an intermediary entity G, which brings on the form of F, acting on x; the CA introduces intermediary entities, the causal actions of some of which impart properties to things. Actions of fire, for example, E-cause Socrates to become hot. This, I take it, is a forerunner of the familiar, if now discredited, idea that a cause must be like, and at least as great as, its effect.[61] Actions of fire E-cause Socrates to become hot. That cause contains fire as a constituent; and fire is, of course, itself hot. So, Plato claims that, at least in some cases, the cause of x's coming to be F includes as a constituent something which is itself F. (This, of course, is only to be expected, given Plato's earlier constraint on explanation, that x's coming to be F must be explained by something which is itself F; this eliminates some explanations involving opposites.) The CA, then, provides at least a framework for specifying E-causes.

One might object that, if Plato really has E-causes still in mind, it is rather odd that he spends so much time on forms. But I think this objection fails; and the reply to it shows how forms, though not themselves E-causes, are E-causally relevant. The SA, we said, provides an analysis of events and states

[60] Kim, 'Causation, Nomic Subsumption, and the Concept of Event', is again useful here (although, as noted above, I reject his criteria for individuating events).

[61] See e.g. A. C. Lloyd, 'The Principle that the Cause is Greater than its Effect', *Phronesis*, 21 (1976), 146–56; Annas, 'Aristotle on Inefficient Causes', 316.

of affairs, according to which forms are constituents of events and states of affairs. The CA provides a framework for specifying E-causes; and forms are involved in the E-causes it points us to. Actions of fire, for example, E-cause Socrates to become hot. They do so in virtue of the fact that fire, a constituent of that event, has the property of heat—and heat, for Plato, is a form: forms just are (a subclass of) properties or universals. Forms are constituents of events and causes; they are the properties in virtue of which substances act, and what substances acquire in change. Forms, then, are E-causally relevant, by being constituents of events.

Now anyone who is interested in causation has reason to be interested not only in the analysis of events, but also in the analysis of properties. For properties are among the salient constituents of events; and we can fully provide an analysis of events only when we have an account of their salient constituents. On Plato's view, we lack a proper account of properties. We believe, for example, that they are definable in purely observational or material terms, when they are not. In fact, a proper account of properties requires understanding that properties are forms.[62] Plato focuses on forms, then, because he believes we cannot adequately specify E-causes until we understand that properties are forms. He has not changed course, away from E-causes; he is taking a longer, more laborious route to a destination that includes them—a route that includes, perfectly appropriately, an analysis of events and of properties. This reflects no neglect or misunderstanding of E-causes; only an insistence on some necessary preliminaries.

To be sure, Plato's position is controversial. Not all would agree that properties are forms; Plato's metaphysical analysis of events is open to debate. And there is a further point of controversy too. Sydney Shoemaker writes that it is a 'now familiar point that in claiming to know the truth of a singular causal statement one is not committed to knowing the laws in virtue of which it holds'.[63] I think Plato rejects this 'now familiar point'. On his view, to know anything about some sensible object, one must know its connections to various forms; indeed, knowledge of forms is necessary for knowledge of anything.[64] It follows that, for Plato, to know the truth of a singular causal statement—to know how particular events in the world are related—one must know the causal laws they instance; and these laws essentially refer to forms. For, as Shoemaker also remarks:[65]

---

[62] For further discussion of this issue, see my 'The One over Many', *Philosophical Review*, 89 (1980) 197–240.

[63] S. Shoemaker, 'Causality and Properties', in his *Identity, Cause and Mind* (Cambridge: Cambridge University Press, 1984), 206–33 at 232.

[64] I discuss Plato's view that knowledge requires knowledge of forms in chs. 3 and 4.

[65] Shoemaker, 'Causality and Properties', 232.

If I assert that one event caused another, I imply that the constituent objects of the cause event had properties which always contribute in certain ways to the causal powers of the things that have them, and that the particular episode of causation at hand was an actualization of these potentialities.

Causal laws make reference to properties; so, knowing those laws involves knowing the properties they refer to. But those properties are, in turn, constituents of particular events. Plato's claim is that one cannot know—in his strict sense of 'know'—anything about events unless one knows their constituent properties. Not only, then, does Plato have a controversial metaphysical analysis of events, according to which properties are constituents of events and are to be identified with forms; but he also offers us a controversial epistemological claim, according to which one must know the properties involved in the cause of an event in order genuinely to know that it is the cause of that event. But though Plato's focus on forms is rooted in controversial metaphysical and epistemological claims, that should not obscure the fact that his focus is perfectly appropriate for a journey that includes the discovery of E-causes: it is not a new direction, a change of subject, but a more careful and exacting way of reaching the same destination.

If my general account so far is correct, we can also defuse a second objection. One might wonder why, if Plato is indeed interested in E-causation, he should spend so much time articulating a general framework that encompasses more than causal cases. Does not this suggest that he is unclear about differences between causal and noncausal explanations?[66] I do not think so.

---

[66] Annas, by contrast, does see evidence of confusion here. She writes that 'Socrates does start from problems about causal explanation. And although he goes on to yearn for another kind of explanation, and ends up providing a third, there are no indications at all that he is aware of changing the subject. He does, of course, see that offering Forms is second-best to offering teleological explanations; he is going some way to distinguishing, in Aristotle's terms, between formal and final explanation. But there is no recognition that offering either of these kinds is something totally different from offering causal explanations' ('Aristotle on Inefficient Causes', 324–5). As against this: I have suggested that the *Phaedo*'s initial problems are not solely concerned with causal explanation, but also with constitution in a broad sense; so right from the start, Plato's concern is broader than, though it includes, causal explanation. And anyway, he does distinguish between the causal and noncausal cases he considers (see n. 34). Further, his conception of teleology is, as we have seen, causal; he offers E-causal accounts with T-constituents (as Annas seems to say on p. 315: 'The desired teleology is a special kind of causal explanation, not a rejection of the latter'). Nor are the SA and CA 'totally distinct' from causal explanations. To be sure, like the M-accounts with which Socrates began, they include more than E-causal cases; but, again like them, they include E-causal cases, and the difference is again signalled, this time by distinguishing between participating, and coming to participate, in forms. To be sure, Plato is not as explicit or detailed as one could wish; but failure to mark distinctions explicitly and in detail need

Plato has just told us that to understand causation, we need to understand the properties in virtue of which substances act. But a proper understanding of properties is necessary in other sorts of cases too. For properties are constituents of various noncausal states of affairs too. Once we see the importance of properties—both metaphysically, as constituents of various events and states of affairs, and epistemically, in so far as knowledge of them is necessary for knowledge of the events and states of affairs of which they are constituents—then we can see that it is useful to provide a general account of properties. This account will contribute to our understanding of, and to the metaphysical analysis of, causal and noncausal contexts alike. That Plato's sweep is grander than that of some contemporary philosophers who discuss causation should come as no surprise to those familiar with his broad vision of things.[67]

10. A Challenge[68]

I have argued that although forms are not E-causes, they are causally relevant, by being constituents of events. One might challenge this claim in the

not betray confusion; and if my reading of the *Phaedo* is correct, we need not see any confusion lurking. Annas seems less sympathetic to the observing/explicitly formulating distinction. She suggests that 'So charitable a mode of interpretation, would make it hard to prove that any philosopher was ever confused in his or her use of a key term' (325). I disagree: one needs to read the text carefully and decide point by point whether any claim is motivated by tacit confusion or can be otherwise explained; sometimes one verdict is required, sometimes another. I quite agree, of course, that (as Annas has suggested to me in private communication) the mere fact that Plato mentions what are in fact different sorts of *aitiai* does not show that he is clear about differences between them. But then, I do not think that I am reasoning in that way.

[67] Interestingly enough, one of my crucial points in the foregoing—that forms, though not themselves E-causes, are causally relevant—is in effect conceded by even so ardent a defender of the 'logical' interpretation of Plato on *aitiai* as Vlastos. Vlastos insists, as we have seen, that the SA has 'strictly noncausal import' (307). Yet early on, in n. 49, he warns us that 'a certain qualification is needed'. He refers us to n. 78; but in fact the needed qualification is mentioned earlier, on pp. 319–20, where Vlastos writes: 'To be sure, none of the entailments holding between the relevant Forms are being credited with causal agency. But they are expected to *have causal implications.* That the occurrence of fever is the cause of the occurrence of sickness would be a textbook example of a cause in Greek medicine.' And in n. 78 Vlastos writes: 'Even the safe *aitia*, though expressed in a tautological formula, has farreaching substantive implications for the causal order of the universe; for as I remarked above, the regular concomitance of the properties which make up that natural kind [bronze] has causal implications.' In these passages, Vlastos seems to allow that forms are, after all, causally relevant.

[68] In this section, I am especially indebted to conversations with David Brink and Sydney Shoemaker. A similar worry was also raised by Cynthia Freeland.

following way. In the *Phaedo*, Plato distinguishes between (for example) the form of large, and the large in us, between forms and what are sometimes called immanent characters (see e.g. 102 B ff.). On one interpretation of this distinction, forms are properties, and immanent characters are property instances.[69] If this interpretation is correct, then, one might argue, it is property instances, not properties, that are constituents of events; and if so, perhaps forms are not causally relevant after all.

I shall leave to one side the question of whether or not this interpretation is correct, and instead argue only that even if it is, the alleged results do not follow. Suppose first that property instances, not properties, are constituents of events. It need not follow that forms are not causally relevant. For though being a constituent of an event may well be sufficient for being causally relevant, it is not clear that it is necessary. Forms might be metaphysically necessary factors in change, even if they are not themselves constituents of events. Even if this were denied, forms would still be at least epistemologically, if not metaphysically, relevant. For it would still be the case that, to know singular causal statements, one needs to know the causal laws they instance; and knowledge of causal laws requires knowledge of forms.

But *does* it follow, if we distinguish between properties and property instances, that properties are not constituents of events? It all depends, I suppose, on how generously one counts constituents; and no doubt different philosophers have different intuitions here. If we count constituents generously—allowing, for example, that whatever is necessary for the event to occur is a constituent—then forms remain constituents of events. For there would be no property instances without properties; and property instances are necessary for events. Even if we are somewhat less generous, forms remain constituents of events. Suppose, for example, that we allow that if x is a constituent of an event, and y is definitionally prior to x, y is also a constituent of the event. Then, once again, forms are constituents of events. I do not know precisely how generous to be here, or how generous Plato would be (though I suspect that he is fairly generous here). But there are reasonable accounts of the constituents of events on which forms are constituents of events, even if we acknowledge property instances.[70]

---

[69] Gallop, *Plato: Phaedo*, 195. I discuss this interpretation of immanent characters in ch. 13. I provide a more detailed account of immanent characters in ch. 12, where I argue that, at least in the *Phaedo*, immanent characters are forms (or parts of forms) when they are in things. If that view is correct, then forms are nonproblematically constituents of events. Here I give myself the harder case.

[70] This may, however, be yet another source of dispute between Plato and Aristotle. Aristotle may believe that a universal does not exist unless it has a plurality of instances:

Furthermore, there are of course questions about how precisely to under-stand property instances. If, for example, property instances are simply exemplifications of properties at given times—rather than, for example, Russellian unit properties—then forms seem clearly to be constituents of events, even if property instances are too.[71]

Even if Plato believes there are property instances as well as properties, then, forms can still be constituents of events. But even if this is false, they can still be metaphysically or, at the very least, epistemically, causally relevant. And however we decide this matter, we need not conclude that Plato bypasses E-causes or makes forms E-causes.

11. Forms and Teleology in the *Phaedo*

I return, finally, to the question of teleology. Aristotle, recall, seemed to suggest that Plato had no, or at least no explicitly worked-out, account of teleology. He also objected that forms could not, in any case, be T-*aitiai*, since no one works, looking towards them; they are not goals aimed at, or any sort of paradigm.

We have already seen, in exploring Plato's (Socrates') objections to mate-rialism, that he seems to have a conception of teleology; indeed, he (at least at one point) favoured E-causes with T-constituents over all other sorts of *aitiai*. At that point, however, forms were not on the horizon. I want now to ask whether Plato, in embarking on the second voyage with the aid of forms, makes forms T-*aitiai* or, at least, believes they are somehow relevant to teleology.

One might hope that he does not do so. Vlastos, at least, suggests that it is[72]

after all, he defines the universal as that which by its nature is such as to be predicated of many things (*De Int.* 17ᵃ39–40). In that case, perhaps he would argue that no single property instance in fact requires the existence of a property; only groups of instances do. If so, he might argue that although property instances are constituents of causes, properties themselves are not, nor are they even necessary for there being any single property instance. I am not sure that this is Aristotle's view; but if it is, I confess to being more sympathetic to Plato's view that property instances require properties, so that properties are metaphysically necessary for causation.

[71] For some discussion of 'particularist' conceptions of properties, see D. M. Armstrong, *Universals and Scientific Realism* (2 vols.; Cambridge: Cambridge Univeristy Press, 1978), vol. i, ch. 8.

[72] Vlastos, 'Reasons and Causes in the *Phaedo*', 303. As I hope the discussion below makes clear, I also disagree with Vlastos's suggestion that forms are irrelevant to the teleology of the *Timaeus*. On the contrary, the world is as it is because of the Demiurge's desire to embody

unnecessary to inquire how Plato could have assigned, without grave confusion, to his Forms—entities whose most conspicuous feature is their absolute immutability—the teleological function which, both in this dialogue and in the *Timaeus*, pertains exclusively to mind or soul.

This, however, reflects a mistake. It may well be true that for Plato—in striking contrast to Aristotle, as we have seen—the only sorts of E-causes that operate in teleological contexts pertain 'exclusively to mind or soul'. But it does not follow that nothing but actions of mind or soul are involved in teleological contexts. There are also the goals aimed at by minds or souls and it is they, not minds or souls themselves, that are T-*aitiai*. So even if teleology, for Plato, always requires the E-causal agency of mind, it does not follow that there is no T-role for forms, or that assigning them one somehow turns them into E-causes, or usurps or conflicts with any role for E-causes; forms might be among the goals aimed at by minds. Further, to say that forms play such a role would of course not imply that they exercise any ghostly causal tug from the future. The only causal tugs there are are E-causes, which precede the attainment of goals and are not forms.

But does Plato put forms forward as T-*aitiai*? Well, in the *Republic* he tells us that the existence and essence of other forms—indeed of everything—depends on the form of the good (505 A 1–10; 509 B 6); to know anything fully, one must relate it to the form of the good. This, however, is not decisive. Aristotle allows that Plato put goodness forward as an *aitia*; but he objected that it was not clear what sort of *aitia* it was—'as end or as mover or as form' (*Metaph.* 1075ᵃ38–ᵇ1). Is his claim justified?

Actually, it is rather puzzling. We have seen that Aristotle rightly does not believe that forms are E-causes; so presumably he does not think the form of the good, for Plato, is an E-cause. And he believes that forms, for Plato, are F-*aitiai*; so presumably the form of the good is an F-*aitia*. Still, the crucial question here is whether it is also a T-*aitia*; it is not clear that merely to say that it is an *aitia* shows that it is a T-*aitia*.

forms; and that makes forms T-*aitiai*. To be sure, later in the *Timaeus* Plato offers some teleological explanations that do not explicitly mention forms; but a reference to forms is, I take it, required for a full teleological account of why things are as they are. Forms are ultimate, if not always proximate, teleological *aitiai*. One might argue that even if Vlastos is wrong to say that it would be confused to treat forms as T-*aitiai*, it would be unnecessary to do so: one perhaps needs to appeal to the belief that forms exist; but why need one refer to forms themselves? (This objection was raised to me by Nicholas Sturgeon.) I think the answer to this question is that, at least in the case of philosophers and the Demiurge (to be discussed below), not just belief, but also knowledge, of forms is relevant; and in this case, it is less clear that reference to forms can cancel out. Furthermore, given Plato's belief that forms exist, it is reasonable of him to believe that they figure in the explanation of action even more broadly.

If, however, someone or something works, looking towards the form of the good, then it is a T-*aitia*. So, does the *Republic* specify such a worker? I think so. For Plato tells us that philosophers know and love forms; and this causes them to embody forms in the sensible world. The philosopher attempts to make the world as just a place as possible; and he does so, in part, by looking to the form of justice and trying to get people and institutions to approximate to it so far as possible. So at least the virtue forms—including, of course, the form of the good—are goals the philosopher aims at.[73]

In the *Timaeus* the teleological role of forms is extended to the natural world. For there Plato introduces the Demiurge as the creator of the cosmos (28 A ff.). The Demiurge is good, and free from jealousy, and so he wishes his creation to be as good as possible. He must, then, have looked to the best possible model to guide his creating; and these are the forms. To understand the Demiurge's actions in creating the cosmos, one needs to refer to the forms he attempts to embody. Once again, then, forms are paradigms, or goals aimed at, and so are T-*aitiai*. As Aristotle puts it in the *Metaphysics*, 'The final cause moves, then, by being loved' (1072[b]). To be sure, forms may be too remote for ordinary people to look towards them, at least as we are now constituted. But all Plato needs, to defend the claim that forms are literally paradigms, is the claim that someone, sometimes looks towards forms. And he makes this claim; for in his view, philosophers and the Demiurge, if not ordinary people, so use forms.

Forms in the *Republic* and *Timaeus*, then, function as T-*aitiai*. And the way in which they are T-*aitiai* provides another sense in which forms, though not themselves E-causes, are E-causally relevant. For forms are the goals aimed at by various agents; in order to understand their actions, we need to refer to the goals of those actions, i.e. to forms. Forms, as Aristotle put it, move by being loved.

Now Aristotle asked, 'What is it that works, looking towards forms?' I have suggested that the answer to his question, for the *Republic* and *Timaeus*, is: philosophers and the Demiurge. One might wonder why Aristotle does not offer the same reply. But I think that perhaps he does, at least with respect to the Demiurge. For Aristotle's laconic question might be seen—not as neglect of the Demiurge, but—as a veiled reference to it.[74]

---

[73] This sort of account also emerges, of course, in the *Symposium*'s and *Phaedrus*' accounts of the ascent of desire. But I take it that it is present in the *Republic* too. For the philosopher has the virtue of wisdom or knowledge; and that involves not merely a cognitive, but also an affective, attitude towards forms, that of love and desire.

[74] Contrast Annas, in her commentary, p. 161, who believes Aristotle dismisses the Demiurge as mythical. Certainly Aristotle takes other features of the *Timaeus*—such as its account of the creation of time—quite literally. I do not mean to suggest that Aristotle has only the

Perhaps Aristotle sees well enough that Plato introduces the Demiurge as a worker; and perhaps he even believes Plato intends the reference literally. Still, the force of Aristotle's question might well be: what is this being? Plato has no coherent account to offer; and the appeal to the Demiurge is anyway unnecessary and *ad hoc*. Unnecessary, because not even global teleology requires conscious agency; as Aristotle puts it in *Physics* 2. 8, it is absurd to require conscious agency for genuine teleology. And *ad hoc*, because Plato's only reason for dragging in the Demiurge is the bad one that he falsely believes that teleology requires conscious agency. From this point of view, we need not say that Aristotle curiously neglects to mention the Demiurge, nor yet that he takes Plato's reference to it to be metaphorical; it is just that Aristotle finds the Demiurge deeply unsatisfying.

What, however, if we focus on the *Phaedo*? Are forms intended to be T-*aitiai* there too? There are, I think, hints of this—though, I freely grant, no more than hints. Still, they are worth considering.[75]

If there is a worker looking towards forms in the appropriate manner in the *Phaedo*, then forms are T-*aitiai* in the *Phaedo*. So, does Plato specify a worker? Well, at 105 D 3–4 he says that soul brings life to whatever it occupies; and at 106 D 5–7 he mentions an imperishable god and the form of life. Though he does not say so explicitly, perhaps god—like the Demiurge of the *Timaeus*—brings life to the cosmos. If god brings life to the cosmos, presumably it orders things in the cosmos—that's just what bringing life to the cosmos would consist in. In discussing Anaxagoras, Plato insisted that if mind orders things, it ought to do so for the best; so, if god orders things in the cosmos, it ought to do so in the best possible way. To do so, he must look to the form of the good; for to know what is good or best, one must know the form of the good; something's being good consists in its being suitably related to the form of the good.[76] To order things for the best by looking to the form of the good is to operate teleologically, and in such a way that forms figure as T-*aitiai* which are, moreover, E-causally relevant. If, as in

Demiurge in mind; as I suggested in sect. 4, he also believes that no ordinary person looks towards forms. But I do think he has the Demiurge, as well as other possible workers, in mind; and he ought to. For to rebut the claim that forms are paradigms, he needs to show that no one looks towards forms, not merely that no ordinary person does.

[75] In thinking about teleology in the *Phaedo* (indeed, in thinking about Plato's teleology generally), I have benefited from a paper by Susan Sauvé Meyer. Some of the suggestions that follow are also made by Gallop, *Plato:* Phaedo, 221–2.

[76] As *Phd.* 100 B 6 makes clear, the *Phaedo* recognizes the form of the good. And the SA tells us that x is F just in case x participates in the form of F; so, something is good just in case it participates in the form of good. And to know that x is F, one must know the form of F.

the *Republic*, the form of the good is not just one form among others, but something more like the system of forms suitably interrelated, then looking to the form of the good in effect involves looking to forms generally; and so all forms turn out to be T-*aitiai* which are causally efficacious, by being goals aimed at.[77]

Obviously none of this is spelt out in any detail in the *Phaedo*. But surely that is only to be expected. Plato tells us that he wants to discover, but lacks, causal teleological accounts; he embarks on his second voyage, which makes crucial use of forms, in order to discover such accounts. The most we can reasonably expect from the *Phaedo* is that it point us in the right direction, hint at how forms might figure in causal teleological accounts. And this much, if I have been right, the *Phaedo* may well do.

I think, then, that even in the *Phaedo* there is the suggestion that forms are goals aimed at, or are at least somehow teleologically relevant; and this gives us yet another way in which forms, though not themselves E-causes, are E-causally relevant or figure in causal explanations.[78]

[77] For this account of the form of the good, see T. H. Irwin, *Plato's Moral Theory* (Oxford: Clarendon Press, 1977), 223 ff.

[78] An earlier version of this chapter was presented at the Xth Symposium Aristotelicum, held in Sigriswil, Switzerland, in September 1984; a shorter version was read at the Cornell Philosophy Discussion Club, in November 1984, and at the Pacific APA, held in San Francisco, in March 1985. I am indebted to a number of people for helpful comments on one or the other version, and especially to the following: Julia Annas, David Brink, Myles Burnyeat, S. Marc Cohen (my commentator in San Francisco, who, among other things, rescued me from an invalid argument), Cynthia Freeland, David Gallop, Terence Irwin, Alexander Nehamas, Susan Sauvé Meyer (my commentator at Cornell), Sydney Shoemaker, Gisela Striker (my chairperson in Sigriswil), and Michael Woods.

15

Plato and Aristotle on Form and Substance

1. Introduction

Plato and Aristotle give different answers to the question 'What are the substances [*ousiai*]?' One way Aristotle defends his answer is by arguing that his candidate substances—particulars such as Socrates or Callias—better satisfy the criteria for substance than do Plato's candidates—eternal, unchanging, nonsensible universals called 'forms'.[1] This defence goes along with another. For Aristotle disagrees with Plato, not only about the candidates, but also about the criteria, for substance: one reason Plato fastens on to the wrong candidates is that he focuses on some of the wrong criteria.

Aristotle mounts his defence in different ways in the *Categories* and *Metaphysics*. In both works he defends the priority of particulars. In the *Categories*, however, their nature is left unanalysed; and their priority is defended largely by appeal to un-Platonic criteria. In the *Metaphysics*, by contrast, Aristotle analyses (sensible) particulars into compound, form, and matter. Socrates, for example, may be viewed as a compound of his form (his soul) and his matter (his body); or he may be viewed as his form or soul. Further, Aristotle now invokes additional, Platonic criteria for substance; and this leads him to argue that it is Socrates as form that counts as primary substance; the primary substances are individual forms.[2]

---

[1] Some dispute that forms are, or are only, universals; with Aristotle, I assume that forms are at least universals. Though all forms are universals, the converse is not true: forms appear to be a subclass of universals—nonsensible ones. (I assume that not all universals are nonsensible—redness, for example, is not.) I discuss various features of forms in more detail in chs. 11–14; see also *On Ideas*.

[2] I thus align myself with those who believe that in the *Metaphysics* Aristotle acknowledges individual forms, and counts them as his primary substances. This view is, of course, highly controversial; and my defence of it here is at best partial. The view that the primary substances of the *Metaphysics* are individual forms is defended by, *inter alios*, E. Hartman, *Substance, Body, and Soul* (Princeton: Princeton University Press, 1977), esp. ch. 2; and W. Sellars, 'Aristotle's *Metaphysics*: An Interpretation', *Philosophical Perspectives* (Springfield, Ill.: Thomas, 1959), 73–124, and T. Irwin, *Aristotle's First Principles* (Oxford: Clarendon Press, 1988), esp. ch. 12. If this view is rejected, then many of the things I say about Aris-

By the time of the *Metaphysics*, then, Aristotle agrees with Plato that the primary substances are forms; but Platonic and Aristotelian forms are quite different. Platonic forms are universals; Aristotelian forms are particulars. Where there can be at most one Platonic form corresponding to a given predicate, there may be several Aristotelian forms. And many Aristotelian forms, though no Platonic ones, are sensible, perishable, and changeable.

Why, and with what justification, does Aristotle prefer his candidates and criteria to Plato's? Is he right to believe that his candidates (ASs, for 'Aristotelian substances') fare better than do Platonic forms (PFs)? And are his criteria plausible? I shall suggest that where Plato's and Aristotle's criteria converge, PFs if anything fare better than do ASs; Aristotle can defend his candidates only by significantly weakening his own criteria, a weakening Plato need not countenance. Where their criteria diverge, PFs fare badly; but this is not obviously to PFs' discredit, since such criteria are not plausible necessary conditions on substance.

2. Substance and Essence

First we need a more detailed account of what substances (*ousiai*) are, and of Plato's and Aristotle's candidates for that role; so let me begin with that.

'*Ousia*' is a verbal noun from the Greek verb 'to be'. As Aristotle uses the word, it occurs in two distinct grammatical constructions. We can say that x is an *ousia*—a being, reality, or substance; or we can say that the *ousia* of x is F, where 'F' answers the 'What is it?' question about x. In the first construction, we are talking about substances, full stop; in the second, about the substances *of* things—here '*ousia*' carries a dependent genitive.[3]

On the first use, *ousiai* are the basic beings there are, whatever these turn out to be. To call something an *ousia*, in this sense, is to confer basicness; but there is no antecedent restriction on what sort of thing fits the bill. Let us call this sort of *ousia*: *primary substance*. Any entities one takes as basic or fundamental are one's primary substances. For the Presocratics, the primary substances are various sorts of material stuff—water or air or

tle's criticism of, and alternative to, Plato would need to be revised. On the other hand, if I sketch Aristotle's criticisms correctly, that supports the picture I paint of his alternative. I do not deny, by the way, that Aristotle countenances forms (or entities called '*eidē*') other than individual forms (see esp. n. 7). But unless otherwise noted, whenever I speak of Aristotelian forms, I shall mean the individual forms that count as primary substances.

[3] D. R. Cousin, 'Aristotle's Doctrine of Substance', *Mind*, ns 42 (1933), 319–37; 43 (1935), 168–85; R. Dancy, *Sense and Contradiction: A Study in Aristotle* (Dordrecht: Reidel, 1975), 95 ff.

fire; for Plato, they are eternal, unchanging, nonsensible universals called 'forms'; for Aristotle they are particulars such as Socrates or Callias.

In its second use, Aristotle often identifies a thing's *ousia* with its essence or nature (e.g. *Metaph.* 1017^b21-2; 1031^a18); so let us call this sort of *ousia*: *essence*. If you think everything is essentially watery, you think water is the *ousia*, essence, of things; if you think living a certain sort of life is the human essence, you think living that sort of life is the *ousia* of human beings.

It is natural, but not necessary, to identify these two sorts of *ousiai*—to believe, that is, that the essences of things are the primary substances. That, I take it, is Plato's view: his primary substances are his forms; and he takes forms to be the essences of things. We specify a thing's essence, say what it is, by suitably relating it to the relevant form or forms. It is, indeed, in part *because* he believes that forms provide answers to the 'What is F?' question—are the essences of things—that he takes them to be the primary substances.[4]

In the *Categories*, by contrast, Aristotle resists the Platonic identification of primary substance and essence. There he argues that the primary substances are not universals of any sort, but such entities as an individual man or horse or tree. He does not say that such entities are primary substances because they are essences; indeed, they do not appear to *be* essences at all, although they *have* essences. Their essences are their species and genera—universals in the category of substance; and these are Aristotle's secondary substances. Hence, although no universal is a *primary* substance, Aristotle concedes to Plato that at least some universals—the species and genera of primary substances—are *secondary* substances. One reason they count as secondary substances is that they tell us what the primary substances are—that is, are their essence.[5] Aristotle thus sees *some* connection between being a substance and being an essence. But what the *primary* substances are is not determined by appeal to essence; and essences are demoted to the status of (at best) secondary substances.[6]

In the *Metaphysics*, on the other hand, Aristotle is newly sympathetic to Plato's identification of primary substance, form, and essence. He now argues that each primary thing is identical to its essence (*Z* 6), and that the form of each thing is its essence, and so is primary substance (1032^b1-2).

---

[4] It is, of course, sometimes disputed that Plato accords sensibles essences or that, if he does, their essences are forms. For a partial defence of the view assumed here, see ch. 13.

[5] *Cat.* $2^b7-14, 29-37$. A second reason they count as secondary substances is that they are the second best subjects. I discuss both reasons further below, in sects. 3 and 5.

[6] I say 'at best' because not all essences count as secondary substances; only the essences of primary substances do. Redness, or colour, are the essences of various nonsubstances; but they are not substances at all.

This claim is liable to misinterpretation, however, so let me say a bit more about the *Metaphysics*' view of things before proceeding further.

In the *Categories* some entities called '*eidē*'[7]—substance species—are allowed to be secondary substances and essences. When Aristotle, in the *Metaphysics*, argues that *eidē*—forms—are primary substances, is he arguing that the *Categories*' secondary substances (or their universal forms or essences) are primary substances after all—that, as for Plato, certain universals are the primary substances? So it is sometimes thought. G. E. L. Owen, for example, in 'The Platonism of Aristotle', writes that in *Metaphysics Z* Aristotle argues that:[8]

if we take any primary subject of discourse and say just what it is, we must be producing a statement of identity, an equation which defines the subject. And this in turn helps to persuade him that the primary subjects of discourse cannot be individuals such as Socrates, who cannot be defined, but species such as men. In the *Categories*, on the other hand, the primary subjects are still the individual man or horse or tree. Aristotle seems at this early stage to be much more hostile than he later becomes to Plato's treatment of the species as a basic and independent subject of discourse. So it becomes tempting to think of this element in *Metaphysics* VII as a return to, or a renewal of sympathy with, Plato.

But I believe that the *eidē* that now count as primary substances are not species, or universals of any sort, but individual forms; it is, for example, Socrates' individual form or essence, his soul, that now counts as a primary substance. This goes beyond the *Categories*, in so far as the *Categories* does not analyse particulars; it does not invoke the notions of compound, form, and matter, nor does it argue that individual forms are the primary substances. But Aristotle still maintains the *Categories*' view that particulars are the primary substances. Hence, when he suggests that Socrates is identical with his form, he does not, as is sometimes said,[9] mean that he is

---

[7] '*Eidos*' is one word Plato uses for PFs. Aristotle uses '*eidos*' in at least the following ways: (*a*) for individual forms (e.g. Socrates' soul); (*b*) for species (e.g. man); and (*c*) for the universal form or essence of that species (e.g. rationality). This multiple usage need not import any confusion. The distinction between (*b*) and (*c*) is made much of by J. Driscoll, 'EIDE in Aristotle's Earlier and Later Theories of Substance', in D. J. O'Meara (ed.), *Studies in Aristotle* (Washington: Catholic University of America Press, 1981), 129–59. He argues that in the *Metaphysics* the primary substances are *eidē* of sort (*c*); I favour (*a*). Driscoll is right to argue that (*a*) is not the only alternative to (*b*), which he agrees is not primary substance in the *Metaphysics*; but there are other reasons for preferring (*a*) to (*c*).

[8] G. E. L. Owen, 'The Platonism of Aristotle', *Proceedings of the British Academy*, 51 (1965), 125–50 at 136–7. In a later article, 'Particular and General', *Proceedings of the Aristotelian Society*, 79 (1978–9), 1–21, esp. 14–15, however, he seems to have retracted this view in favour of individual forms, though the claim is not pressed.

[9] By e.g. M. J. Woods, 'Substance and Essence in Aristotle', *Proceedings of the Aristotelian*

identical with the species man (or with the universal form of that species), but that he is identical with his soul, which is proprietary to him. Aristotle's promotion of form and essence, then, is not a concession to Plato about the priority of universals; there is no 'renewal of sympathy with' Plato on this score. Indeed, the *Metaphysics* is, if anything, more hostile to universals than is the *Categories*; for it revokes the *Categories*' concession that at least some universals are secondary substances. In the *Metaphysics* no universal is a substance at all (see esp. Z 13, at e.g. 1038^b8–16, $^b34$–1039^a2). Though Plato is right to identify primary substance, form, and essence, he proposes the wrong candidates for playing these roles. The claim that the primary substances of the *Metaphysics* are individual forms is, to say the least, highly controversial, and I shall not mount anything like a complete defence of it here. But in the next section I argue that Aristotle's criteria for substance require that all substances be particulars; and in subsequent sections I argue that Aristotle can escape his criticisms of Plato only if his substances are particulars. Aristotle may, of course, be inconsistent, and other evidence might pull us in a different direction. But if we focus on his criteria for substance, and on his criticism of Plato, we are pulled towards individual forms. To defend individual forms is not, however, the main purpose of this paper; the main purpose is to assess the plausibility of Aristotle's criticisms of the claim of PFs to substancehood, and his success in defending his alternative. The first stage in such an analysis must be consideration of Aristotle's criteria for substance, so I turn next to that.

3. Criteria for Substance

Although criteria can be culled from many sources, I shall focus on criteria Aristotle commends in the *Categories* and *Metaphysics*.

(1) *Substances persist through change*. In the *Categories* Aristotle proposes the following *idion*—special feature or distinguishing mark—of substance: 'It seems most distinctive of substance that what is numerically one and the same is able to receive contraries. In no other case could one bring forward anything, numerically one, which is able to receive contraries' (4^a10–13). Although (1) is proposed as distinctive of substance, strictly speaking it is distinctive only of primary substance. Aristotle is concerned, not with the fact that, for example, the species man can be pale and dark—that there can be pale and dark men—but with the fact that an individual man can be

Society, 75 (1974–5), 167–80; cf. also C. Kirwan, *Aristotle's* Metaphysics: *Books Γ, Δ, and E* (Oxford: Clarendon Press, 1971), esp. 100–1.

pale at one time, dark at another. (1) thus requires of (primary) substance that it be able to sustain change through time; (primary) substances are the basic subjects of change.[10]

(1) is necessary and sufficient for being a *primary substance*. But it is not necessary for being a *substance*, since there are secondary substances, and they do not satisfy (1) (except, of course, in so far as their members do).

(2) *Substances are (basic) subjects.* In the *Categories* something is a *subject* just in case something can be predicated of it; and something is a *basic* subject just in case it is a token of a type such that tokens of that type are not predicated of anything, but all other sorts of things are ultimately predicated of tokens of that type. In the *Metaphysics*, by contrast, Aristotle explicates the notion of a *subject* (and not just of a basic subject) in terms reminiscent of the *Categories'* notion of a *basic subject*. In *Z* 3, for example, he says that a subject is 'that of which other things are predicated, while it itself is no longer ⟨predicated⟩ of anything' (1028^{b}36–7; but cf. *Δ* 8, 1017^{b}23–4, *to th' hupokeimenon eschaton*).

In the *Categories* being a subject is necessary but not sufficient for being a substance; and being a basic subject is both necessary and sufficient for being a primary substance (2^{a}11–14; ^{a}34–5; ^{b}36–3^{a}1). Correspondingly, in the *Categories* particulars such as Callias count as basic subjects; but one reason secondary substances are adjudged substances is that they are the next best subjects—they are secondary subjects (2^{b}15–22; ^{b}36–3^{a}6).

In the *Metaphysics*, by contrast, being a subject (that is, being one of the *Categories'* basic subjects) is apparently both necessary and sufficient for being a substance *tout court* (1029^{a}1–2, 17–19; 1038^{b}15). Since every universal is, in Aristotle's view, necessarily predicated of something (e.g. 1038^{b}15–16), no universal (and so no secondary substance) is a subject. (2) thus requires that the *Metaphysics'* substances all be particulars.

(3) *Substances are thises (tode ti).* In the *Categories* (3^{b}10–18) Aristotle takes it to be both necessary and sufficient for being a this that something be a particular. Thus he first claims that whatever is indivisible and one in number—that is, is a particular—is a this (3^{b}10–13); he then argues that secondary substances are not thises, because they are said of many things (3^{b}13–18)—that is, are universals. This leaves open the possibility that nonsubstance particulars are thises, and so the *Categories* seems to allow. In the *Categories*, then, being a this—that is, a particular—is necessary but not sufficient for being a primary substance; but it is neither necessary nor sufficient for being a substance.

---

[10] Cf. J. L. Ackrill, *Aristotle's* Categories *and* De Interpretatione (Oxford: Clarendon Press, 1963), 89–90. The translation is also Ackrill's; all other translations are my own.

In the *Metaphysics* the status, explication, and application of the this-ness criterion change. First, it is now necessary and sufficient for being a substance;[11] in contrast to the *Categories*, there are no longer any nonsubstance thises. Second, thisness is no longer explicated in terms of particularity. In truth, Aristotle never provides a clear explanation of the notion; but it seems to convey the idea of determinateness, perhaps of countability, and of being a stable object of reference. And at 1030^a4 he suggests that a this must not essentially involve one thing's being said of another. Third, although thisness is no longer explicated in terms of particularity, it still applies only to particulars—though not to *all* particulars, at least not in the primary way. Now every universal, in Aristotle's view, is necessarily said of something; hence none is a this (1038^b15-16; $^b34-1039^a2$). If no universal is a this, but every substance must be, then, once again, it follows that Aristotle's substances in the *Metaphysics* are all particulars.

Aristotle uses the notion of thisness, not only to exclude universals from the ranks of substance, but also to restrict the range of particulars that so count. In *Z* 4, for example, he argues that a white man is not a this, since it essentially involves one thing's being said of another—white of the man. Aristotle also seems to believe (a point which perhaps emerges most clearly in *Z* 11) that a man considered as a compound is not a this, since his form is essentially said of his matter. It is individual forms that count as thises in the primary way, and so they are the primary substances.

(1)–(3) are all present in the *Categories;* and at least (2)–(3) are present in the *Metaphysics* as well, though they are there handled differently and used to different ends.[12] In particular, they are all used to show that all substances are particulars. The *Metaphysics* also highlights further criteria, either absent or muted in the *Categories*:

(4) *Substances are separate (chōris, chōriston).*[13] In *Metaphysics Z* 1 Aris-

---

[11] Thus, in *Z* 4 (1030^a5-6) he says that *only* substances are thises; and in *Z* 3 matter is ruled out as (the sole) substance on the grounds that, *inter alia*, it is not a this (1029^a28-30). The notion of a *tode ti* is difficult, and has been explicated in many different ways. Cf. e.g. J. A. Smith, 'TODE TI in Aristotle', *Classical Review*, 35 (1921), 19; Owen, 'Particular and General', 2; J. Barnes, *Aristotle* (Oxford: Clarendon Press, 1982), 43. Barnes remarks that *tode ti* is 'an unorthodox phrase which Aristotle nowhere explains'.

[12] I am unsure whether (1) is tacit in the *Metaphysics*. Perhaps it plays a role in the restriction Aristotle sometimes makes of substances to natural substances, i.e. to those with internal sources of change. In any case, I shall largely ignore (1) when speaking of the *Metaphysics*.

[13] I take both '*chōris*' and '*chōriston*', as used in connection with substance and PFs, to indicate *actual*, and not merely possible, separation; and I take actual separation to be the *capacity* for independent existence. That is, x is separate from y just in case x can exist without y. Most of the claims I make in this chapter about separation are defended in detail in ch. 11.

404 _Plato and Aristotle on Form and Substance_

totle says that substances are naturally prior to nonsubstances, because only they are separate (1028ᵃ33–4).[14] 'Separate' is not explained here; but in Δ 11 Aristotle says that substances are naturally prior to other things because they 'can be without the other things, while the others cannot be without them' (1019ᵃ1–4). A is separate from B, then, just in case A can exist without B. Aristotle believes that substances are separate from other things, though not conversely. Like (2)–(3), (4) appears to be a necessary and sufficient condition for substance in the _Metaphysics_. Since only substance is separate, it is sufficient; and since all substances must be separate, it is necessary.

In both the _Categories_ (2ᵇ3–6) and _Metaphysics_ (e.g. 1086ᵇ3–5) Aristotle denies that universals (and so the _Categories'_ secondary substances) are separate.[15] In the _Categories_ the species and genera of substance, though not separate, are none the less allowed to be secondary substances. In the _Metaphysics_, however, the fact that universals are not separate debars them from the ranks of substance altogether. Once again, then, the substances of the _Metaphysics_ must all be particulars.

Notice that although the _Categories_ denies that universals are separate, it does not say that (primary) substance is separate. In contrast to the _Metaphysics_, the _Categories_ contents itself with the weaker claim that everything else is dependent on the primary substances; but this leaves open the possibility that primary substances are similarly dependent on, and so are not separate from, other things. In the _Metaphysics_ the separation of substance is stressed, and used against universals.

(5) _Substances are prior in definition._ In _Z_ 1 Aristotle says that substances are prior in definition because 'in the definition of each thing there must be a definition of the _ousia_' (1028ᵃ35–6). The force of (5) might be:

(5a) For all x, to define x, one must define its essence.

Or it might be:

---

[14] At 1028ᵃ32–3 I read: _kai physei kai logō(i) kai gnōsei_—adding '_physei_' to, and deleting '_chronō(i)_' from, Jaeger's text. This emendation is not essential to my view.

[15] I say that in the _Categories_ Aristotle denies that universals are separate. To be sure, this follows from his remark that universals are ultimately dependent on primary substances; but it is interesting to note that Aristotle does not use '_chōris_' or its cognates in pressing this claim. Notice, in this connection, the account of natural priority in _Cat._ 14ᵇ10–22. Here, in striking contrast to _Metaph. Z_ 1, A can be naturally prior to B without being separate from B; indeed, separation is actually precluded, since natural priority is defined so as to obtain only between items that reciprocate as to existence. In general, the _Categories_ has considerably less to say about separation than the _Metaphysics_ does. '_Chōris_' and its cognates occur only once, at 1ᵃ25.

(5b) For all x, to define x, one must include a definition of a relevant substance.

Aristotle believes that definitions state essences (e.g. 1017^{b}21–2; 1036^{a}6–7); so he believes (5a). But (5) is a criterion for *substance* only if read as (5b). These two readings are connected, however, since Aristotle argues that to state the essence of anything, one must state the definition of (or at least mention) a relevant substance; hence (5a) implies (5b). Aristotle also argues (in *Z* 4) that the primary substances are the primary definables; and that the primary definables are identical to their essences (*Z* 6). Hence the essences mentioned in (5a) will be identical with the substances mentioned in (5b), in the case where x is a primary substance. Notice that one result of this is that primary substances are essences.

Commitment to (5) is at best muted in the *Categories*; but in so far as it is present, it appears to favour secondary over primary substances. For one reason secondary substances are adjudged substances is that they answer the 'What is it?' question about primary substances—they tell us what they are, are their essences (2^{b}7–14, 29–37). (Some) definitions state, or are of, secondary substances; though the content of such definitions applies to, or is true of, primary substances, primary substances are not themselves definable nor, though they have essences (their secondary substances), are they themselves essences.

In the *Metaphysics*, by contrast, (5) is explicit; and it too now appears to be necessary and sufficient for substance.[16] Now if, in the *Metaphysics* as in the *Categories*, (5) favours universals, then Aristotle is in difficulty. For as the discussion in (2)–(4) reveals, Aristotle now denies that there are any universal substances; yet (5) is supposed to determine substance. To be consistent, then, he must argue that (5) determines particular substances.

(6) *Substances are prior in knowledge*. In *Z* 1 Aristotle argues that substances are prior in knowledge because 'we think we especially know each thing when we know what it is—what man or fire is—rather than when we know ⟨what⟩ quality or quantity or where ⟨it is⟩; since we also know each of these ⟨only⟩ when we know what the quantity or quality is' (1028^{a}36–^{b}2).

---

[16] Such, at any rate, appears to be the implication of *Z* 1. Even if (5) is only necessary, however (and it is clearly at least that), the problems I raise for Aristotle over (5) would remain (see below, sect. 5 (5)). One might find it tempting to weaken (5) so that it requires only that *ousiai* be mentioned (as opposed to defined) in every definition. I know of no place where priority in definition is explicated in this weaker way, however. But even if it is, neither would this remove the difficulties canvassed below; for substance must still be definable, even if its definition need not actually occur in definitions of other things, and that is sufficient for the worries I later air. Analogous remarks to those made in this note apply to (6).

Aristotle does not explicitly use '*ousia*' in stating (6), and his use of '*ti estin*' suggests he is making a point analogous to (5a): to know something is to know what it is, i.e. its essence. This point is relevant to the epistemological priority of substance, however, since Aristotle argues that to know the essence of anything, one must know a relevant substance. For to know something is to know its definition; and we saw, in discussing (5), that an adequate definition of anything must include a definition of a substance. Hence to know anything, one must know a definition of a substance. This again suggests that primary substances are essences. For presumably the primary knowables are the primary definables; and the primary definables, as we have seen, are essences.

In the *Categories* commitment to (6) is muted; but in so far as it is present, it, like (5), appears to favour secondary over primary substances. In the *Metaphysics*, by contrast, (6), like each of (2)–(5), is a necessary and sufficient condition for substance; and, again, since universals no longer count as substances, Aristotle must, to avoid contradiction, show how particular substances satisfy it.

Our survey of criteria has brought to light some interesting differences between the *Categories* and *Metaphysics*. The *Categories* uses fewer criteria, at least explicitly; and different criteria enjoy different statuses—some are necessary but not sufficient for being a primary substance, some are necessary and sufficient, and so on. Further, different criteria favour different candidates: (1)–(3) favour certain particulars as the primary substances; (5)–(6) (in so far as they are present) favour certain universals as secondary substances—though the favour is not so great as to challenge the primacy of particulars. (4) is not used at all.

In the *Metaphysics*, by contrast, each of (2)–(6) (where some of these are now explained differently) is apparently both necessary and sufficient for being a substance *tout court*. Moreover, all substances are now particulars; there are no longer any universal substances.

Contrary to Owen and others, then, the *Metaphysics* does not display increased sympathy with Plato on the status of universals; it is if anything more hostile to them. For it revokes the *Categories*' concession that at least some universals count as secondary substances; the criteria for substance debar all universals from the ranks of substance.

In other respects, however, the *Metaphysics* is more sympathetic to Plato. For the particulars that now count as primary substances are individual forms; Aristotle, like Plato, now promotes forms and essences (though non-Platonic ones) as primary substances. Further, his use of criteria owes something to Plato too. (1)–(3), the criteria highlighted in the *Categories*, are un-Platonic; in the *Categories* Aristotle fights Plato on foreign territory. But (4)–(6) are Platonic criteria (or so at least Aristotle believes): the battle now moves to home turf; the *Metaphysics* engages in a dialectical debate absent in the *Categories*. But though this in a way displays increased sympathy with Plato, in a way it does not. For Aristotle argues that even if we give Plato his criteria, PFs do not qualify as substances. Let us see how well he prosecutes his case.

4. Platonic Substances

(1) Since PFs cannot sustain change through time, they obviously fail (1)— just as the *Categories'* secondary substances do. But I doubt that Plato would be much worried; he would challenge the criterion. To be sure, he might argue, it might be reasonable to insist that the basic entities in the universe be stable, persist from one moment to the next. But of course PFs are stable, indeed, eminently so. If (1) is weakened to stability, it is plausible; but then PFs satisfy it. If it is strengthened in Aristotle's way, it is not plausible.

Aristotle might reply that stability is not enough; the stable entities must explain changes objects in the world undergo—yet PFs cannot explain change (*Metaph.* 991^{a}8–11; 991^b). Now it might be reasonable to require explanatory relevance to change; but I think Plato could fairly insist that PFs are explanatorily relevant to change. To be sure, they do not *initiate* change; they are not efficient causes of change. But as Aristotle should be the first to agree, efficient causes are only one sort of explanation of change. Nor would Aristotle be reasonable to require that whatever explains change must itself change; indeed, his own prime mover explains at least some changes but does not itself change. PFs, being properties, are relevant—indeed necessary—to explaining some changes, even though they themselves do not change; for explanations of change require reference to the properties involved; and PFs are among the properties there are.[17]

Aristotle may be right, then, to require that substances be stable and explanatorily relevant to change; if (1) is so weakened, it is at least a reasonable necessary condition on substance—but one PFs satisfy. If, however, it is strengthened so as to require that substances be capable of sustaining change through time, then it is not a reasonable necessary condition on substance, and so PFs' failure to satisfy it is not to their discredit.

Aristotle might, however, fairly protest (though Plato would no doubt

---

[17] I discuss Plato and Aristotle on forms as causes in ch. 14.

reject the protest) that (1) is a reasonable sufficient condition for sub-stance—for it seems reasonable to assume that among the entities explana-torily relevant to change are those that undergo and sustain change. PFs' failure to satisfy a sufficient condition for substance does not show that they are not substances at all; but if other entities than PFs satisfy (1), that would show that PFs are not the *only* substances.

(2) Just as Aristotle denies that PFs satisfy (1), so he denies they satisfy (2); PFs are not basic subjects. Indeed, in the *Metaphysics* they are not subjects at all.

Plato would probably agree that PFs are not basic subjects; in the *Timaeus* he seems to accord the receptacle that role (see e.g. 49 E 7 ff., 50 B 5 ff.). But Plato would again simply reject the criterion. To be sure, he might argue, it might be reasonable to insist that the basic entities be subjects in the following sense: 'those subjects of discourse to which all our descriptions of the world must, at any rate when properly analysed in canonical form, make direct or indirect reference'.[18] But PFs are basic subjects in this weakened sense; for to call something a basic subject in this sense is only to call it a fundamental explanatory entity. It is only by tightening (2) up and restricting it to (basic) subjects of properties that Aristotle can use it against Plato; but since (2) so construed is an implausible criterion for substance, this does not harm Plato.

I think Plato would be right to protest against (2), construed as a ne-cessary condition on substance. What, after all, makes subjects prior to their properties? Perhaps Aristotle would say, appealing back to (1): the fact that subjects can sustain change of property through time. But even if this is so, I have suggested that properties are equally necessary to explain-ing change—we should not be forced to choose between them. Or perhaps Aristotle would say that subjects are favoured over properties because pro-perties depend on, cannot exist without, their subjects. But it is far from clear that properties are dependent on their subjects; perhaps they can exist uninstantiated.[19] It is difficult to see, however, how subjects can exist with-out properties; do not properties then have the edge? Or are not properties and their subjects at least mutually dependent? (See further Sections 4 (4) and 5 (4).) Or perhaps Aristotle would say that we invoke properties to

---

[18] Owen, 'Particular and General', 2. This is Owen's explication of what Aristotle means by 'subject'. If Owen is right, then PFs are subjects in Aristotle's sense; but I doubt that Owen is right.

[19] The issue is disputed; but for one plausible defence of the possibility of uninstantiated universals, see P. Butchvarov, *Resemblance and Identity: An Examination of the Problem of Universals* (Bloomington, Ind.: Indiana University Press, 1966), 186–97.

explain particulars, and that explananda are prior to explanantia. But why are not explanantia at least as basic or fundamental as explananda?

(2), then, is not a plausible necessary condition on substance. But Aristotle might with more reason defend its sufficiency—for subjects, no less than their properties, seem necessary to explaining change; explananda seem as fundamental as explanantia. And although this would not dislodge PFs as substances, it would show, if other things satisfy (2), that PFs are not the only substances.

(3) In contrast to (1)–(2), Aristotle seems to believe that PFs satisfy (3). At least, he insists that Plato treats PFs as thises (*SE* 22; *Metaph. Z* 13). This might be thought an advantage of PFs; but in Aristotle's view, it is not. He argues that because PFs are thises, they are vulnerable to the TMA—a vicious infinite regress. Though PFs satisfy (3), this leads to severe difficulties; satisfaction of (3) is thus no boon.

Aristotle in effect levels a dilemma against Plato: either (*a*) PFs are thises, and so are vulnerable to the TMA; or else (*b*) they are not thises, and so cannot be substances. On the face of it, this is an odd criticism for Aristotle to press. For (3) is an Aristotelian criterion. If PFs are vulnerable to this dilemma, how can Aristotle escape it?

The answer, in brief, is as follows. PFs are not vulnerable to the TMA merely because they are thises, but because (so Aristotle believes) they are *also* universals; it is because they are allegedly universals and particulars at once that the TMA threatens. Aristotle can avoid the dilemma, then, if ASs are thises but not also universals. Here is one reason to doubt that ASs are universals of any sort—for if they were, they would succumb to Aristotle's dilemma.[20]

Whether or not Aristotle can escape his dilemma, I believe Plato can: he would protest against both (*a*) and (*b*). As to (*a*): if we think of the *Categories'* account of thisness, in terms of particularity, then I doubt that PFs are thises; they are universals but not particulars.

Why does Aristotle disagree? Later (pp. 411–12) I shall sketch an argument of Aristotle's, according to which the separation of PFs implies their particularity; but this argument fails. Of course, even if separation does not imply particularity, PFs might none the less be particulars. Some (perhaps including Aristotle) believe that self-predication has this result; but this is unclear. At least, as I understand self-predication, it does not imply particularity. In my view, self-prediction says that any form of F is F (that is, is a member of the class of F things)—though in a very different way from

---

[20] See Owen, 'Particular and General', 14; contrast the passage cited above from 'The Platonism of Aristotle'.

the way in which 'ordinary' F things are F (though not in different sense of 'F'). The form of large, for example, is a member of the class of large things: not, however, because it exceeds other things in size (being incorporeal, it has no size at all), but because it is the property of largeness in virtue of which everything that is large is so.[21] At least self-predication, then, does not turn forms into particulars, and so we do not yet have any reason to suppose that forms are thises, in the *Categories*' sense of that term.

If we turn, on the other hand, to the *Metaphysics*' account of thisness, in terms of one thing's not being essentially predicated of another, and determinacy, then I think Plato would say that PFs are thises, and so satisfy (3): for since they can exist uninstantiated, they are not what they are in virtue of being said of anything; and they can also be stably referred to.[22] But this does not, *pace* Aristotle, turn them into particulars; not only particulars satisfy (3), understood in the *Metaphysics*' way. Since I am sympathetic to the possibility of uninstantiated universals, this reply seems reasonable to me.

Either, then, PFs fail (3), construed in terms of particularity; or else they satisfy it, construed in the *Metaphysics*' way, but they do so without thereby becoming particulars.

If PFs are not thises, are they not vulnerable to (b)? Here I think Plato would follow a by now familiar ploy: (3), construed in terms of particularity, is not a plausible criterion for substance, and so PFs' failure at (3), so construed, does not impugn their status as substances. And since even Aristotle does not believe that (3), so construed, is a sufficient condition for substance, the fact that other sorts of entities than PFs satisfy (3) would not even lead us to question PFs' status as *the* substances.

[21] I defend this interpretation of self-predication in ch. 12, where I call it 'broad self-predication', in contrast to 'narrow self-predication'. Broad self-predication is a variant on the interpretation of self-predication defended by S. Peterson, 'A Reasonable Self-Predication Premise for the Third Man Argument', *Philosophical Review*, 82 (1973), 451–70. On narrow self-predication, the form of F is also a member of the class of F things, but in roughly the same way in which 'ordinary' F things are F. The form of large, for example, is itself large by exceeding other things in size. It's worth noting that even on narrow self-predication, not all forms are thereby particulars. The form of immobility, for example, can be immobile without thereby being a particular; the form of oneness is one form, but it is not thereby a particular.

[22] Indeed, the *Metaphysics* account of thisness has Platonic antecedents: cf. *Cra.* 439 c 6–440 c 1; *Tht.* 181–3; *Sph.* 261–3; *Ti.* 48 E 2–52 D 1 . For some discussion, see D. Zeyl, 'Plato and Talk of a World in Flux', *Harvard Studies in Classical Philology*, 79 (1975), 125–48, esp. 146–8; J. Driscoll, 'The Platonic Ancestry of Primary Substance', *Phronesis*, 24 (1979), 253–69. Interestingly, Plato never seems explicitly to say that PFs are thises, so conceived; and like Aristotle he at least sometimes uses similar phrases of sensible particulars. But his notion of being a this is not defined in terms of sensible particulars; and PFs satisfy his notion, even if he does not himself explicitly make the point.

If, on the other hand (3) is instead construed in the *Metaphysics'* way, then, as Aristotle believes, it may well be at least a plausible necessary condition for substance; for we expect substances to be determinate, stable objects of reference. But as we have seen, PFs (despite Aristotle's view to the contrary) satisfy (3) so construed.

PFs fail (3), then, only if it is implausible; they satisfy (3) on its more plausible reading—but they do so without being particulars, or succumbing to the TMA.

(4) Just as Aristotle insists that PFs are thises, so he insists that they are separate (see e.g. *Metaph.* $1078^b30–1$; $1086^a32–^b13$); and he appears to be correct. At least, in the *Timaeus* Plato seems committed to the separation of at least some PFs. For there (if the account of creation is taken literally) he commits himself to the following two claims:

(*a*) Forms have always existed.
(*b*) Sensibles have not always existed.

(*a*) and (*b*) imply:

(*c*) There was a time at which forms, but no sensibles, existed.

(*c*) implies that all forms are separate, in the sense that all did, and so all can, exist uninstantiated by sensibles: that is, by articulated sensibles such as tables and chairs, or natural kinds as we know them, or sensible fire as it exists in our world.[23]

Although Aristotle is probably correct to say that Plato is committed to the separation of at least some PFs, he is wrong to suggest, as he seems to, that Plato explicitly mentions separation as a criterion for substantiality that PFs satisfy. Indeed, Plato never even explicitly says that forms are separate; and it is surprisingly difficult to find any commitment to separation in the dialogues (though as we've just seen, commitment to separation can, on one controversial reading, be teased out of the *Timaeus*).

Although Aristotle thinks that Plato takes PFs to be separate, he argues that being separate is not to their credit, since severe difficulties then ensue.

---

[23] (*a*)–(*c*) don't, however, imply that all forms were at some point uninstantiated *tout court*. For example, the Demiurge always existed, and he always instantiated various moral forms. Moreover, though (*a*)–(*c*) imply that the form of fire was at some point uninstantiated by sensible fire as we know it, they do not imply that the form of fire was ever uninstantiated *tout court*. For prior to the existence of sensible fire as we know it, chaos contained traces of fire, and they instantiated the form of fire. Hence, if separation is the capacity to exist uninstantiated as such, the argument described in the text does not imply that all forms were at some point uninstantiated, though, given other things Plato believes, it implies that some forms were at some point uninstantiated. I discuss separation further in ch. 11.

For if PFs are separate, they are thises, and so particulars; but since they are also universals, they are incoherent entities—both universals and particulars at once.[24] This charge, however, fails; for the separation of PFs does not imply their particularity. (Notice, however, that since *Aristotle* believes that separation implies particularity, and since he insists that his substances are separate, he presumably believes that his substances are particulars.) If separation is just the capacity for independent existence, and if PFs are universals, then to say that they are separate is just to say that they can exist uninstantiated; and this does not turn them into particulars.

Why does Aristotle disagree? I can think of only one explanation. In *De Int.* 7 Aristotle defines universals as follows: 'by universal I mean that which by its nature is predicated of many things' (17ᵃ39–40). One might suppose he means only that universals *can* be predicated of many things; but he seems to mean instead that they must *actually* be predicated of many things. If, then, one countenances the possibility of uninstantiated universals, one countenances the possibility of something that can exist that is not actually predicated of many things. This cannot, by definition, be a universal; what else can it be, then, but a particular? Hence allegedly separate universals must actually be particulars.

This is not, however, so much an argument against separate universals as a definitional fiat that they cannot exist. Unless Aristotle can provide plausible reasons for his definition—and I cannot find any—his argument simply begs the question against the Platonist. And since I am myself sympathetic to the possibility of uninstantiated universals, I am inclined to believe that PFs can be separate, while still retaining their status as universals. I conclude, then, that PFs nonproblematically satisfy (4).

(5)–(6) I believe Plato would argue that PFs satisfy (5)–(6). In the *Meno* he argues that knowledge is true belief bound by an explanatory account (an *aitias logismos*) (98 A). In *Phaedo* 100 he argues that PFs are *aitiai*, basic causes or explanatory entities. Hence, adequate accounts must refer to PFs; all definitions, and so all knowledge (since knowledge requires definitions, *logoi*), involves reference to PFs. Similarly, in *Republic* V Plato argues that knowledge involves appropriate reference to PFs. To know or define PFs, however, one need not—indeed, one cannot—first know or define other things; knowledge and definition of PFs is a precondition for knowledge and definition of anything. Hence, PFs are prior in knowledge and definition.

Further, Plato presumably believes that PFs are thus prior because he accepts the connection between knowledge, definition, and essence; it is be-

24 See, for example, *Metaph. M* 9; I discuss the passage in detail in ch. 11.

cause he believes that PFs are the essences of things, and that knowledge and definitions are of essences, that he believes that PFs are prior in knowledge and definition. Hence, for Plato as for Aristotle, constraints on knowledge and definition suggest that the primary substances are essences.

We have seen that Aristotle allows that PFs satisfy (4). Does he also believe they satisfy (5)–(6)? Since he rejects the existence of PFs, he does not believe they are really thus prior. But does he believe Plato has a plausible case here?

One might believe he should. First, he agrees that PFs are at least universals; and he sometimes says that universals are prior in definition—perhaps, more strongly, that they are the only objects of knowledge and definition (see e.g. *Metaph. Δ* 11, 1018^b32–3; *Z* 15; *Post. An. passim*). Second, he agrees that PFs are at least intended to be the essences of things (e.g. *Metaph. A* 9, 991^b1–3 = *M* 5, 1079^b35–1080^a2); and so again he should concede that they are plausibly said to be prior in knowledge and definition.

Aristotle sometimes seems to suggest that Plato would reason in this way. In *Metaph. A* 6, *M* 4 and 9, for example, he suggests that Plato introduced PFs as stable objects of knowledge and definition; the possibility of knowledge and definition requires the existence of unchanging, non-sensible universals that the Platonists call 'forms'. And in *H* 1 he says that PFs are thought to be substances for the same reasons that universals and genera are (1042^a15–16)—presumably because they are all thought to be the essences of things, and so basic objects of knowledge and definition.

But Aristotle protests that this line of thought is implausible; he argues that, to the contrary, PFs are unknowable and indefinable. If so, they are not prior in knowledge and definition. Thus, in *Metaph. Z* 15 he argues that definitions are of universals and so PFs, being particulars, cannot be defined. In *M* 10 a parallel point is pressed for knowledge: since knowledge is of universals, and PFs are particulars, PFs are unknowable.

We have already seen why Aristotle believes PFs are particulars: because they are separate, and separation, Aristotle believes, implies particularity. Aristotle thus in effect now levels the following dilemma against Plato: (*a*) if PFs satisfy all of (4)–(6), they are incoherent entities, both universals and particulars at once—for satisfaction of (4) requires particularity, whereas satisfaction of (5)–(6) requires universality; (*b*) if PFs satisfy only (4) (and so are particulars), or only (5)–(6) (and so are universals), they fail to satisfy at least one necessary condition for substance. Either way, PFs cannot be the primary substances.

Once again, it is puzzling to see Aristotle levelling this dilemma. For (4)–(6) are not just criteria Plato, perhaps confusedly, commends; they are Aristotle's own criteria. If Plato is vulnerable to this dilemma, is not

Aristotle vulnerable to it as well? Later we shall need to ask whether Aristotle escapes this dilemma and, if so, if he does so in a way that leaves intact his criticism of Plato.

For now it is worth noting that Plato has an easy escape route: he would simply reject (*a*). Separation does not imply particularity; hence PFs can satisfy all of (4)–(6), without incoherence, as universals. Since Aristotle believes that separation implies particularity, however, the same escape route is not open to him.

Aristotle might argue that even if all of this is so, there is another way in which the separation of PFs is incompatible with their being prior in knowledge and definition. If PFs are separate from sensible particulars, they cannot be their essences; and if they are not their essences, they are 'no help towards knowledge of them' (*Metaph.* $991^a12–13 = 1079^b15–16$). Even if PFs can be known, then, such knowledge would be useless; and so, again, they are not prior in knowledge and definition.

Thus in *Metaph. Z* 6 Aristotle argues that the essence of a primary thing is identical with that thing; if PFs are separate from sensible particulars, they cannot be identical to them and so, if sensible particulars are primary things, PFs cannot be their essences. Further, in *Z* 13 Aristotle insists that the essence of x must be peculiar to x; but the PF of man, for example (if there is one), is not peculiar to Socrates and so cannot be his essence. (Notice that these arguments again pull us in the direction of individual forms. At least, if Socrates has an essence at all (and he seems to), his essence must be peculiar to him; since no universal is peculiar to any particular, his essence must be a particular. But since essences are forms, there are individual forms; and they must be Aristotle's primary substances.)

Neither of these arguments depends on the dubious claim that separation implies particularity. None the less, Plato is not without his resources. To the argument in *Z* 6, he would no doubt reply that sensible things are not primary things, and so need not be identical to their essences. On the other hand, PFs are primary things, and they are identical to their essences. Either way, Plato can accept the claim in *Z* 6—that primary things are identical to their essences—without abandoning the claim that PFs are the essences of sensibles.

The argument of *Z* 13 is in effect an argument for individual essences; whereas Plato, in putting forth PFs as the essences of things, opts for general or universal essences—as had Aristotle in the *Categories*. Since I do not know whether there are individual essences, I do not know who has the better position here; certainly both views have serious philosophical credentials. But even if Aristotle is right on this score, it shows only that

PFs cannot be the whole essence of any sensible; it does not show that they cannot be part of their essence,[25] or that they are not knowable or definable. Indeed, unless we agree with Aristotle about the primacy of particulars, it does not even show that PFs are not prior in knowledge and definition.

If we accept the view Aristotle himself often advocates—that universals are prior in knowledge and definition—and agree, against Aristotle, that PFs are universals but not particulars, then PFs fare quite well on (5)–(6). The most Aristotle can persuade us of is that PFs cannot be the whole essence of any sensible; but that falls short of showing failure at (5)–(6).

To summarize so far: Aristotle is correct to say that PFs fail (1)–(2); but this does not impugn their status as substances, since (1)–(2) are not plausible necessary conditions on substance. The most Aristotle can fairly argue is that (1)–(2) are plausible sufficient conditions, so that if other things satisfy them, PFs are not the only substances. Aristotle is probably wrong, on the other hand, to argue that PFs satisfy (3) (if, that is, (3) involves particularity); but this does not even disqualify them as *the* substances, since (3) so construed is not, even by Aristotle's lights, a necessary or sufficient condition on substance. PFs do, however, satisfy (3) construed in the *Metaphysics'* way.

Aristotle believes PFs satisfy (3) because he believes they satisfy (4). They do satisfy (4); but this does not turn them into particulars—PFs can satisfy (4) as universals. Aristotle argues that PFs fail (5)–(6), again largely on the grounds that they are particulars; this argument fails, since PFs are universals, not particulars—and Aristotle himself (sometimes) believes universals satisfy (5)–(6). Perhaps PFs are inadequate as the whole essence of particulars; but this is insufficient to show failure at (5)–(6).

PFs, then, fail the un-Platonic criteria (1)–(3)—the only criteria pressed in the *Categories*; but this does not disqualify them as substances. On the other hand, they fare quite well on the allegedly Platonic criteria (4)–(6) highlighted in the *Metaphysics*. Though the dialectical project of the *Metaphysics* is more impressive than is the quick attack in the *Categories*, it too fails to dislodge PFs from the ranks of substance.

Aristotle's offensive attack thus fails: he has not succeeded in persuading us that PFs are not substances. But a defensive strategy might still be successful: for perhaps Aristotle can persuade us that even if PFs are substances, they are not the only substances. And this might be accomplished in a variety of ways. If, for example, (1)–(2) are plausible sufficient conditions on substance, and if ASs satisfy them, this should persuade us to add ASs to the list of substances. Or if ASs do at least as well on (4)–(6) as PFs

[25] Aristotle may, however, intend to foreclose this possibility in *Metaph. Z* 13.

do, that too should persuade us to accept ASs along with PFs—if, that is, (4)–(6) are plausible criteria for substance.

5. Aristotelian Substances

(1) Aristotle is surely correct to say that the *Categories'* primary substances can persist while changing;[26] and since PFs do not satisfy (1), ASs fare better here. Since (1) is only plausible construed as a sufficient condition, this should not lead us to prefer ASs to PFs; but it does give us some reason to add ASs to the list of substances.

It is worth noting, however, that although the *Categories'* primary substances fare better on (1) than PFs do, various difficulties none the less arise. For example, Aristotle claims that *only* his primary substances satisfy (1). Yet by the time of the *Physics,* he acknowledges that matter appears to satisfy it as well—a lump of bronze, for example, can sustain the change of shape that results in its constituting a ring. Perhaps this is one reason why (1) is muted in the *Metaphysics*.

(2) To be a (basic) subject, recall, is to be a token of a type none of whose members is predicated of anything, and is such that all other sorts of things are predicated of tokens of that type. We have seen that PFs (in common with all universals) fail (2). But, again, this is not to their discredit, since (2) is not a plausible necessary condition on substance. Still, we have agreed that (2) is a plausible sufficient condition on substance; if Aristotle's substances satisfy it (in which case they must be particulars), then once again we have reason to add them to the list of substances.

In the *Categories* Aristotle claims that his primary substances are basic subjects; everything else is predicated of (said of or in) them, and they are not predicated of (said of or in) anything. But unlike the *Metaphysics,* the *Categories* does not wrestle with the notions of form and matter; and in the *Metaphysics,* where Aristotle wishes to promote individual form as primary substance, it appears that forms are predicated of matter. How, then, can they satisfy (2)? Indeed, it looks as though matter (or prime matter) is the only subject. For only matter is not predicated of anything; and everything else is ultimately predicated of it (*Z* 3, 1029^{a}7–27). (2) thus threatens to dislodge not only PFs, but also Aristotle's favoured candidates. (Notice, though, that the threat is from *matter*, not universals.) Plato is unmoved; he rejects the criterion, perhaps because of the difficulties just adverted to. But Aristotle retains the criterion; so he needs to confront the difficulties.

[26] I assume mereological essentialism is false.

And of course he does. He attempts to resist the descent to matter by arguing that, for example, matter does not do so well on other criteria for substance, such as separation and thisness (*Z* 3, 1029ᵃ28–30). This is not to the present point, however, which is that Aristotle's alleged primary substances do not do as well as he would like on the subject criterion.

A better argument is this one: that the *way* in which form is predicated of matter is importantly different from the way in which other things are predicated of form. To be a (basic) subject is to be a token of a type (i) none of whose members is predicated of anything but matter; and (ii) such that all other sorts of things than matter are predicated of tokens of that type.

This may allow individual forms to be (basic) subjects. But it does so by modifying the criterion. That might look like cheating—altering the criterion so that it picks out the desired candidates. But it is not cheating if Aristotle can produce a good argument to show that his modified subject criterion is preferable to the initial one—preferable, that is, not just because it yields the candidates he would like, but for reasons of general appeal. Perhaps Aristotle means to signal that this is his justification for the revision when he remarks (*Z* 3, 1029ᵃ9–10) that the initial criterion is inadequate and unclear. Whether or not Aristotle has a good argument here is, of course, another question, and not one I shall try to answer here. Here the main point is that, although PFs fail (2), so too may Aristotle's favoured candidates; but however well ASs fare here, this does not give us a reason to prefer them to PFs, since the criterion is not a plausible necessary condition on substance. In so far as ASs satisfy (2), however, and in so far as it is a plausible sufficient condition, that gives us reason to believe that ASs, as well as PFs, are among the substances.

(3) We have seen that PFs are not thises, as the *Categories* conceives of thises, but are thises—though not particulars—as the *Metaphysics* conceives of them. Are ASs thises? They certainly are on the *Categories'* construction; for they are particulars. This, however, is no reason to count ASs as substances, since (3) so construed is not a plausible necessary or sufficient condition for substance.

Are ASs thises on the *Metaphysics'* understanding of that notion? So Aristotle claims (1030ᵃ3 ff.), and I am not concerned to dispute the point. Though many individual forms are predicated of some matter, they are not what they are in virtue of being so predicated—in contrast to compounds, or to such accidental unities as a white man: here no doubt is one reason for opting for individual forms over compounds as the particulars that count as primary substances. And it is also, as we have seen, a reason for preferring them to universals since, in Aristotle's view, universals are necessarily predicated of many things.

Notice, though, that the fact that ASs are thises does not render them vulnerable to the TMA, as Aristotle urged PFs would be, if they were thises—for ASs are only particulars, and not also universals. Here is another reason to believe that Aristotle acknowledges individual forms; for the forms that are thises (and so primary substances) cannot be universals, on pain of the TMA.

ASs, then, do better on (1)–(2), and on (3) construed in terms of particularity, than do PFs. The best Platonic defence in the face of this fact—and I have argued that it is a good one—is to argue that (1)–(2), and (3) so construed, are not plausible necessary conditions on substance, so that ASs' success over PFs does not impugn PFs' status as substances. On the other hand, in so far as at least (1)–(2) are plausible sufficient conditions, Aristotle can fairly insist that PFs are not the only substances; ASs qualify as well. This is, to be sure, a more hospitable conclusion than Aristotle wishes to endorse; but it none the less involves a significant criticism of Plato, for whom PFs appear to exhaust the ranks of substance.

What, now, of (4)–(6)? I shall suggest that PFs satisfy (4)–(6) at least as well as, perhaps better than, ASs—as Aristotle himself should (in some moods) agree (at least in the case of (5–6)). Of course, this gives us no reason to prefer PFs to ASs, unless (4)–(6) are plausible criteria for substance; so that too needs to be investigated.

(4) In the *Categories* Aristotle wisely does not insist that his primary substances are separate, though he less wisely insists that no universals are—less wisely because, as we have seen, universals may well be able to exist uninstantiated. In the *Metaphysics* Aristotle retains his belief that universals are not separate; but he now insists that substance is separate. This insistence, however, is not clearly justified.

Consider compounds first—say Socrates, considered as a compound of form and matter. Socrates, on Aristotle's view, cannot exist and fail to be a man. But then, the secondary substance or species man must exist if Socrates does. (This is so even in the *Metaphysics*, where man no longer counts as a secondary substance.) But if Socrates cannot exist unless man does, he is not independent of, and so is not separate from, man. Similar remarks apply in other cases. For example, although Socrates can of course exist even if he is not tan, he cannot exist if he is not coloured in some way; hence he is not independent of colour or, therefore, of nonsubstance generally. Nor are individual forms separate. Just as the compound Socrates cannot exist unless man does, so no individual form of man can exist unless man (the universal, however conceived) does. PFs, however, are separate from particulars; and so they, but not ASs, satisfy (4).[27]

One might argue that this is no reason to prefer PFs to ASs, since (4) is not a plausible condition on substance. All that is plausible is the weaker claim of ontological basicness, that the basic entities in the universe be such that other things depend on them. (This claim is weaker because it allows mutual dependence.)

This is a reasonable claim: separation may be sufficient for basicness; but it does not seem to be necessary. It does seem reasonable, however, to suppose that basicness involves other entities being dependent on the basic ones; indeed, this seems constitutive of ontological basicness.

Weakening (4) in this way turns it into a plausible condition on substance. But does this help Aristotle? Notice first that Plato would of course argue that PFs satisfy not only (4) but also the weaker claim of ontological basicness; sensibles depend on PFs.[28] But do ASs also satisfy our new version of (4)? Can Aristotle plausibly argue that they are ontologically basic? If, as I have suggested, universals are separate, then of course they are not dependent on ASs, and so ASs are not ontologically basic with respect to

[27] Notice that this problem for ASs is not alleviated by claiming that they are universals, not particulars; for as we have seen, Aristotle consistently denies that universals are separate, and he consistently associates separation with particularity. On the other hand, T. H. Irwin has suggested to me that ASs—conceived as individual forms—are, contrary to my suggestion, separate, at least from universals: whenever Aristotle defines universals, he defines them in terms of being predicated of *many* things. Suppose that only Socrates—one man—exists. Then the universal, man, does not exist; its existence requires the existence of *many* men. But if Socrates exists, and the universal, man, does not, then Socrates is separate from man. A parallel argument shows that Socrates is separate from all universals. He is not, of course, independent of, for example, his individual pallor or height; but perhaps these are not *other* than him, and so he need not be separate from them. (An analogous argument might be used to show that neither is he separate from his matter; for he is not other than it in the requisite way.) But if Socrates is separate from all universals, so, too, is every other man and, analogously, every other AS. (Irwin has now developed this argument in *Aristotle's First Principles*; see esp. chs. 4 and 10.) I am unpersuaded by this argument, however. Even if it is accepted, it gives us no reason to prefer ASs to PFs; it shows at most that universals and particulars are on an equal footing.

[28] This might actually be disputed. Suppose, as is sometimes believed, that there are forms corresponding only to the accidental properties of things. Then even if Socrates is, for example, tan, in virtue of participating in the form of tan, he is not dependent on the form, since he can exist without it; he would of course then cease to be tan, but that would not impugn his continued existence. However, at least in the *Timaeus* there are forms corresponding to some of the essential properties of things (there is, for example, a form of man), and so at least there sensibles do depend on (some) forms: Socrates could not exist if he were not a man; hence he is dependent on the form of man, since he can be a man only by participating in it. I discuss this issue more fully in ch. 13.

them. But if other sorts of things are dependent on ASs, ASs might none the less count as ontologically basic. One might argue, for example, that individual nonsubstances (Callias' whiteness, as opposed to the universal, whiteness) or events depend on ASs; if so, ASs are ontologically basic at least in that *some* other sorts of things depend on them. This is, however, a weaker version of ontological basicness than Aristotle himself defends for ASs in the *Categories* (2^b3–6), where he claims that *all* (and not just some) other sorts of things depend on ASs. Still, this weaker version of ontological basicness gives a reasonable sense to the notion, and allows ASs to satisfy it. Hence both PFs and ASs can be allowed to satisfy the new version of (4).

Aristotle himself seems to see the need to modify (4)—though not in the way I have suggested, in terms of ontological basicness. In *H* 1 (1042^a28–31) he distinguishes between being separate without qualification (*haplōs*) and being separate in definition (*logō(i)*). He claims that although compounds are separate without qualification—that is, can exist without other things— some forms are separate only in definition—that is, can be defined without reference to other things. It is now apparently sufficient for satisfying (4), then, that something be separate in definition.

This suggestion, however, involves at least four difficulties. First, Aristotle in effect concedes that some of his own substances do not satisfy (4), but at best a weakened or modified version of it. To be sure, we earlier urged, on Plato's behalf, that Aristotle's criteria (1)–(3) are plausible only if modified or weakened. But this involved Plato rejecting Aristotle's criteria; whereas now Aristotle is rejecting his own criteria.

Second, Aristotle still insists that compounds are separate without qualification; but that seems false.

Third, if to define other things one needs to include a definition of substance, then the modified version of (4) collapses into (5); but as we shall shortly see, it is unclear that Aristotle's primary substances satisfy (5). If this is so, then the retreat from (4) to (5) is of no help.

Fourth, the retreat threatens to undermine one of Aristotle's criticisms of Plato. We saw before that Aristotle argues that PFs cannot satisfy all of (4)–(6) without incoherence—for (4) requires particularity, whereas (5)– (6) require universality. Yet if Aristotle now collapses (4) into (5), he can no longer argue that joint satisfaction of (4) and (5) is incoherent; for to satisfy (5), now, just is to satisfy (4). (To this, I suppose Aristotle could reply that although satisfaction of (5) is sufficient for satisfying (4), PFs are in fact separate without qualification, so incoherence still threatens. But we have seen that Plato has an effective reply to this argument.)

PFs, then, fare better on (4) than ASs do. If, however, (4) is altered to a weak version of ontological basicness—which yields a more plausible condition than (4)—then PFs and ASs both satisfy it. Aristotle, however, apparently modifies (4), not in terms of ontological basicness, but in terms of being separate in definition. Let us see, then, how well ASs fare on (5), and its close companion (6).

(5)–(6) Aristotle begins *Metaph. M* 10 by raising a dilemma that, he says, threatens both himself and the Platonist: substances must be separate; whatever is separate is a particular; particulars are unknowable; but substances must be knowable. This is just the dilemma we earlier saw Aristotle force on Plato (Section 4 (5–6)); now he acknowledges that he faces it as well. How does he avoid the dilemma? And does he do so in such a way as to leave intact his criticism of Plato?

Aristotle's solution is to insist that substances must be separate, and so particulars;[29] but he insists that particulars—or at least some particulars—are knowable after all. Hence Aristotle, like Plato, rejects (*a*) of the dilemma (see Section 4 (5–6)); but he rejects it by insisting that particulars can be known and defined, whereas Plato rejects it by insisting that universals are separate, but not thereby particulars. We have seen that Plato's response is effective; is Aristotle's?

He distinguishes between actual and potential knowledge; he then claims that actual knowledge, being definite (*hōrismenon*), is of something definite—a particular; whereas potential knowledge, being universal and indefinite, is of what is universal and indefinite, or indefinable (*ahoriston*, 1087ª17). One sees colour coincidentally, by seeing this token colour; or studies the letter A by studying a particular token of the letter-type A.

Aristotle is claiming at least that one can recognize individual objects as tokens of types, or as instances of universals. If this were all he were arguing, one might protest that this recognitional ability is not sufficient to make particulars prior in knowledge or definition; indeed, it is not even sufficient to make them knowable or definable, as Aristotle normally understands those notions. But Aristotle seems to go further, and to insist that particulars are definite or definable, universals indefinite or indefinable (1087ª16–18). This stronger claim allows particulars to be knowable and

---

[29] Notice that if separation here is *definitional* separation (and not IE), then Aristotle appears to believe that even definitional separation implies particularity. And at least one line of thought does yield this result: in *Z* 1 Aristotle argues that every definition must include a definition of *ousia*. If all *ousiai* are substance particulars, then definitions of everything else, including universals, must include definition of them. But then no universal can be definitionally separate; each must include a definition of a substance particular. Hence if something is definitionally separate, it is a particular. I rather suspect, however, that separation here is IE.

definable; but it is inconsistent with other claims Aristotle makes, such as the claim in *Z* 15, that particulars are indefinable. The claim in *M* 10 thus seems to be either too weak, or else to contradict other central Aristotelian claims.

Even if this could be resolved, is there a point against the Platonist here? Has Aristotle argued that his own substances satisfy (5)–(6), but that PFs cannot? If we focus on the weak point about recognition, then perhaps Aristotle would argue as follows: we can come to know various universals, or acquire general concepts, only by first learning to recognize and identify various particulars. But these must be this-world particulars, such as compounds and their forms, and not otherworldly particulars, such as PFs. Hence forms and compounds are prior in learning and recognition, whereas PFs cannot be.

In reply, I think Plato would appeal to his doctrine of Anamnesis, and argue that PFs are prior in learning; we can identify objects in this world only because we knew PFs in another world. Aristotle seems to believe that there are two neatly separable stages in learning, as though one first identifies particulars, and only later acquires general concepts.

Though I think Aristotle is right to attack parts of the doctrine of Anamnesis, as he does, for example, in the *Posterior Analytics*, Plato at least sees that we do not first identify particulars, and only later apply general concepts to them; to identify anything, one must already possess general concepts. That is the core of truth in the doctrine of Anamnesis that Aristotle's simple account of concept acquisition ignores.[30]

To learn about properties, however, it is not clear that we need first, or as well, to have access to sensible particulars. Certainly, as even Hume agrees, we can form the idea of a shade of blue we have never seen; so we can at least form ideas of properties independently of particulars that instantiate those very properties.[31] But perhaps, as Leibniz may believe, we need experience of *some* particulars to become aware even of our innate ideas.[32] If so, perhaps the best conclusion to draw, in the case of learning and recognition, is the hospitable one we have suggested in other cases: neither sensible particulars nor PFs (universals) are prior to the other; both are necessary to learning and recognition, to the way we view the world.

[30] This is, of course, a controversial account of Aristotle that I do not have the space to defend here.
[31] D. Hume, *A Treatise of Human Nature*, ed., L. A. Selby-Bigge, rev. P. Nidditch (Oxford: Clarendon Press, 1978), bk. 1, pt. 1; *Enquiry concerning Human Understanding*, ed. L. A. Selby-Bigge, rev. P. Nidditch (Oxford: Clarendon Press, 1982), § 2.
[32] G. W. Leibniz, *New Essays on Human Understanding*, ed. and trans. P. Remnant and J. Bennett (Cambridge: Cambridge University Press, 1981), bk. 1, ch. 1, *passim*.

What, however, if we turn from learning and recognition to a higher-level sort of knowledge (*epistēmē*) and definition? If we explicate these notions as Aristotle usually does, such that there is knowledge and definition only of universals, then PFs, but not ASs, satisfy (5)–(6); for PFs, but not ASs, are universals.

One might again argue that this is no reason to prefer PFs to ASs, since (5)–(6) so construed are at best plausible sufficient conditions for substance. That may well be true, and I shall shortly consider various modifications of (5)–(6). But notice first that there is a difficulty in *Aristotle's* pressing this argument; for it involves conceding that his substances do not satisfy his own criteria but, at best, modified versions of them.

Still, how might (5)–(6) be modified so as to yield more plausible criteria? One might argue that the best sort of knowledge and definition must at least concern permanent features of the universe. From this point of view, PFs, being eternal or everlasting, are better off than many Aristotelian forms, which are perishable. But perhaps Aristotle could insist that at least the prime mover, or god, or the stars, fare as well as do PFs; for they too are imperishable.

One might argue that (5)–(6) are still too strong to be reasonable criteria for substance. Surely the best sort of knowledge and definition will refer, not just to universals or to permanent features of the universe, but also to various sublunar phenomena, not all of which are permanent? After all, we are concerned to understand the world around us, and hence definitions and knowledge must in some sense be about it. If we weaken (5)–(6) in this way, then they constitute plausible criteria for substance; but they are then also ones both PFs and ASs satisfy.

PFs and ASs, then, fare equally well on (5)–(6), if they are construed in terms of learning and recognition. If (5)–(6) are instead interpreted in terms of knowledge and definition, then PFs fare better than ASs do— unless Aristotle significantly weakens his usual views about the nature of the best sort of knowledge and definition. Such modification might yield a more plausible conception of such knowledge and definition; but it is noteworthy that it is required, not to argue against Plato, but to allow his own candidates to satisfy (5)–(6). In any case, none of the interpretations of (5)–(6) that we have considered favours ASs over PFs.

It is worth noting, however, that Aristotle's new focus on (5)–(6) is probably one reason for his advocacy of individual forms. First, forms are identical to their essences, as primary substances must now be. Second, though individual forms, being particulars, may not be knowable or definable in the strictest sense, they are closer to being knowable and definable than are such particulars as compounds. At least, since they do not include matter as compounds do, they are 'purer' instances of universal laws, and so subject to fewer vagaries. This goes along with a point noted before (Section 5 (3)): that individual forms, in the *Metaphysics*, are better thises than are compounds; for they are not what they are in virtue of one thing's being predicated of another, and so are more determinate objects of secure reference.

It is also worth noting that although Aristotle may not easily be able to defend his claim that individual forms satisfy (5)–(6), he does try to argue this; he does not, at this point, slide back to the *Categories'* view according to which universals better satisfy (5)–(6). (5)–(6) may indeed raise difficulties for Aristotle; but he does not attempt to resolve them by turning to universal substances.

6. Conclusion

What can we say, by way of conclusion, about the debate between Plato and Aristotle on what the substances are?

In the *Metaphysics* Aristotle argues that PFs cannot be substances, because they satisfy none of (2)–(6)—at least, they satisfy none of them nonproblematically: no universal can be a subject or a this; none can be separate; none is the essence of any particular; none is prior in knowledge or definition. Though Plato would protest against most of these claims, Aristotle believes the protest is implausible and, in some cases, that it leads to incoherence, making PFs both universals and particulars at once. ASs, on the other hand, nonproblematically satisfy (2)–(6), and so are the substances. As we have seen, the details of his argument require that his (primary) substances be individual forms.

If our argument has been correct, a different verdict should be returned. Though PFs are not subjects or (*Categories*) thises, this does not impugn their status as substances, since these are not plausible necessary conditions on substance; and PFs do satisfy associated weaker, and more plausible, conditions. On the other hand, PFs satisfy (4)–(6) (in Plato's view; but also, he appears to have a reasonable view here); nor does this require them to be universals and particulars at once. If we focus on (2)–(6), then, we have been given no reason to reject PFs, and some reason to look on them favourably.

Though Aristotle goes too far in barring PFs from the ranks of substances, he can reasonably press a weaker claim: that ASs belong in the ranks as well. To be sure, ASs satisfy (4)–(6) only if Aristotle significantly weakens them—a weakening Plato need not countenance. But such weakenings may be welcome, since they yield more plausible criteria for substance than do the initial strong readings. Further, ASs also satisfy (1)–(2), which, I have conceded to Aristotle, are at least plausible sufficient conditions on substance; and they also satisfy (3), on both of its interpretations.

Our argument suggests that the question with which I began—'What are *the* substances?'—is not legitimate, if it is taken to suggest that there is some one sort of entity that alone has privileged status, that alone satisfies all the criteria for substance. For different sorts of entities—both universals and particulars—are indispensable features of the way the world is, and so of our understanding of the world.[33]

[33] An earlier version of this chapter was read at the Oxford Philosophical Society in November 1982; I thank the audience on that occasion for a number of helpful comments. I especially wish to thank my commentator, Professor J. L. Ackrill, for generous and helpful written and oral comments; and also Terry Irwin, M. M. McCabe, and Jennifer Whiting. I am also grateful to the National Endowment for the Humanities for awarding me a fellowship for 1982–3, and to the Principal and Fellows of Brasenose College, Oxford, for electing me to a visiting fellowship for 1982–3.

WORKS CITED

ACKRILL, J. L., *Aristotle's* Categories *and* De Interpretatione (Oxford: Clarendon Press, 1963).
—— 'Plato on False Belief: *Theaetetus* 187–200', *Monist*, 50 (1966), 383–402.
—— 'Language and Reality in Plato's *Cratylus*', in his *Essays on Plato and Aristotle* (Oxford: Clarendon Press, 1997), 33–52; repr. in Fine (ed.), *Plato 1*, 125–246.
ADAM, J., *The* Republic *of Plato*, ed. with critical notes, commentary and appendices, 2nd edn., intr. D. A. Rees (2 vols.; Cambridge: Cambridge University Press, 1963).
ALLAN, D. J., 'Aristotle and the *Parmenides*', in Düring and Owen (eds.), *Plato and Aristotle in the Mid-Fourth Century*, 133–44.
ALLEN, R. E., 'Participation and Predication in Plato's Middle Dialogues', *Philosophical Review*, 69 (1960), 147–64.
—— 'The Argument from Opposites in *Republic* V', *Review of Metaphysics*, 15 (1961), 325–35.
—— (ed.), *Studies in Plato's Metaphysics* (London: Routledge & Kegan Paul, 1965).
—— *Plato's* Euthyphro *and the Earlier Theory of Forms* (London: Routledge & Kegan Paul, 1970).
—— *Plato's* Parmenides: *Translation and Analysis* (Minneapolis: University of Minnesota Press, 1983).
ANNAS, J., 'Forms and First Principles', *Phronesis*, 19 (1974), 257–83.
—— 'On the Intermediates', *Archiv für Geschichte der Philosophie*, 57 (1975), 146–66.
—— *Aristotle's* Metaphysics Books M and N (Oxford: Clarendon Press, 1976).
—— *An Introduction to Plato's* Republic (Oxford: Clarendon Press, 1981).
—— 'Aristotle on Inefficient Causes', *Philosophical Quarterly*, 32 (1982), 311–26.
ANSCOMBE, G. E. M., and GEACH, P. T., *Three Philosophers* (Ithaca, NY: Cornell University Press, 1961).
ANTON, J. P., and KUSTAS, G. L. (eds.), *Essays in Ancient Greek Philosophy* (Albany, NY: State University of New York Press, 1971).
ARMSTRONG, D. M., *Belief, Truth and Knowledge* (Cambridge: Cambridge University Press, 1973).
—— *Universals and Scientific Realism* (2 vols.; Cambridge: Cambridge University Press, 1978).
—— *Universals: An Opinionated Introduction* (Boulder, Colo.: Westview Press, 1989).
BAMBROUGH, R. (ed.), *New Essays on Plato and Aristotle* (London: Routledge & Kegan Paul, 1965).

BARNES, J., *The Presocratic Philosophers* (2 vols.; London: Routledge & Kegan Paul, 1979).

—— 'Socrates and the Jury: Paradoxes in Plato's Distinction between Knowledge and True Belief', *Proceedings of the Aristotelian Society*, suppl. 54 (1980), 193–206 (= reply to Burnyeat's article of the same title in the same volume).

—— *Aristotle* (Oxford: Clarendon Press, 1982).

BARNEY, R., *Names and Natures in Plato's* Cratylus (New York: Routledge & Kegan Paul, 2001).

BARTON, T., 'The *Theaetetus* on How We Think', *Phronesis*, 44 (1999), 163–80.

BENSON, H., 'Why is There a Discussion of False Belief in the *Theaetetus*?', *Journal of the History of Philosophy*, 30/2 (1992), 171–99.

BERTI, E. (ed.), *Aristotle on Science: The* Posterior Analytics (Padua: Editrice Antenore, 1981).

BETT, R., 'The Sophists and Relativism', *Phronesis*, 34 (1989), 139–69.

BEVERSLUIS, J., 'Socratic Definition', *American Philosophical Quarterly*, 11 (1974), 331–6.

BLUCK, R. S. (ed.), *Plato's* Meno (Cambridge: Cambridge University Press, 1961).

BOBONICH, C., *Plato's Utopia Recast* (Oxford: Clarendon Press, 2002).

BOLTON, R., 'Plato's Distinction between Being and Becoming', *Review of Metaphysics*, 29 (1975), 66–95.

BONITZ, H. *Index Aristotelicus* (Berlin: Reimer, 1870).

BONJOUR, L., *The Structure of Empirical Knowledge* (Cambridge, Mass.: Harvard University Press, 1985).

BOSTOCK, D., *Plato's* Phaedo (Oxford: Clarendon Press, 1986).

—— *Plato's* Theaetetus (Oxford: Clarendon Press, 1988).

BRADLEY, F. H., *Appearance and Reality*, 2nd edn., 9th impression (Oxford: Clarendon Press, 1930).

BRANDWOOD, L., 'The Dating of Plato's Works by the Stylistic Method: A Historical and Critical Survey' (diss. Ph.D., University of London, 1958).

—— 'Stylometry and Chronology', in Kraut (ed.), *Cambridge Companion to Plato*, 90–120.

BRENTLINGER, J., 'Particulars in Plato's Middle Dialogues', *Archiv für Geschichte der Philosophie*, 54 (1972), 116–52.

BROWN, L., 'Connaissance et réminiscence dans le Ménon', *Revue philosophique*, 181 (1991), 603–19.

—— 'Understanding the *Theaetetus*', *Oxford Studies in Ancient Philosophy*, 11 (1993), 199–224.

—— '*Theaetetus*: Knowledge and Definition, Parts, Elements, and Priority', *Proceedings of the Aristotelian Society*, 94 (1994), 229–42.

—— 'The Verb "to be" in Greek Philosophy: Some Remarks', in Everson (ed.), *Language*, 212–37.

BROWNSTEIN, D., *Aspects of the Problems of Universals* (Lawrence, Kan.: University of Kansas Press, 1973).

BURNYEAT, M. F., 'The Simple and the Complex in the *Theaetetus*' (1970; unpublished).

—— 'The Material and Sources of Plato's Dream', *Phronesis*, 15 (1970), 101–22.

—— 'Protagoras and Self-Refutation in Later Greek Philosophy', *Philosophical Review*, 85 (1976), 44–69.

—— 'Protagoras and Self-Refutation in Plato's *Theaetetus*', *Philosophical Review*, 85 (1976), 172–95; repr. in Everson (ed.), *Epistemology*, 39–59.

—— 'Examples in Epistemology: Socrates, Theaetetus, and G. E. Moore', *Philosophy*, 52 (1977), 381–98.

—— 'Conflicting Appearances', *Proceedings of the British Academy*, 65 (1979), 69–111.

—— review of T. Irwin, *Plato's Moral Theory*, in *New York Review of Books* (27 Sept. 1979), 56–60.

—— 'Aristotle on Understanding Knowledge', in Berti (ed.), *Aristotle on Science*, 97–139.

—— 'Socrates and the Jury: Paradoxes in Plato's Distinction between Knowledge and True Belief', *Proceedings of the Aristotelian Society*, suppl. 54 (1980), 173–91.

—— 'Idealism and Greek Philosophy: What Descartes Saw and Berkeley Missed', *Philosophical Review*, 91 (1982), 3–40.

—— 'Wittgenstein and Augustine *De Magistro*', *Proceedings of the Aristotelian Society*, 61 (1987), 1–24.

—— *The* Theaetetus *of Plato*, trans. M. J. Levett, rev. and intro. M. F. Burnyeat (Indianapolis: Hackett, 1990).

BUTCHVAROV, P., *Resemblance and Identity: An Examination of the Problem of Universals* (Bloomington, Ind.: Indiana University Press, 1966).

CHAPPELL, T. D. J., 'Does Protagoras Refute Himself?', *Classical Quarterly*, NS 45 (1995), 333–8.

CHEN, C., 'On Aristotle's Expressions *kath' hupokeimenou legesthai* and *en hupokeimenō(i) einai*', *Phronesis*, 2 (1957), 148–59.

CHERNISS, H. F., 'The Philosophical Economy of the Theory of Ideas', *American Journal of Philology*, 57 (1936), 445–56.

—— *Aristotle's Criticism of Plato and the Academy* (Baltimore: Johns Hopkins Press, 1944).

—— 'A Much Misread Passage in Plato's *Timaeus* (*Timaeus* 49c7–50b5)', *American Journal of Philology*, 75 (1954), 113–30.

CHISHOLM, R., *Theory of Knowledge* (Englewood Cliffs, NJ: Prentice Hall, 1966).

COOPER, J., 'Aristotle on Natural Teleology', in Schofield and Nussbaum (eds.), *Language and Logos*, 197–222.

—— Introduction to *Plato: Complete Works* (Indianapolis: Hackett, 1997).

COOPER, N., 'Between Knowledge and Ignorance', *Phronesis*, 31 (1986), 229–42.

CORNFORD, F. M., *Plato's Theory of Knowledge: The* Theaetetus *and the* Sophist *of Plato*, translated with a running commentary (London: Routledge & Kegan Paul, 1935).

—— *The* Republic *of Plato*, translated with introduction and notes (Oxford: Clarendon Press, 1941).

—— *Plato's Cosmology: The* Timaeus *of Plato*, translated with a running commentary (London: Routledge & Kegan Paul, 1937).

—— *Plato and Parmenides: Parmenides' Way of Truth and Plato's* Parmenides, translated with an introduction and with a running commentary (London: Routledge & Kegan Paul, 1939).

—— 'Mathematics and Dialectic in the *Republic*, VI–VII', in Allen (ed.), *Studies in Plato's Metaphysics*, 61–95.

COUSIN, D. R., 'Aristotle's Doctrine of Substance', *Mind*, NS 42 (1933), 319–37; 43 (1935), 168–85.

CRESWELL, M. J., 'What is Aristotle's Theory of Universals?', *Australasian Journal of Philosophy*, 53 (1975), 238–47.

CROMBIE, I. M., *An Examination of Plato's Doctrines* (2 vols.; London: Routledge & Kegan Paul, 1962–3).

CROSS, R. C., and WOOZLEY, A. D., *Plato's* Republic: *A Philosophical Commentary* (London: Macmillan, 1964).

DANCY, R. M., 'On Some of Aristotle's First Thoughts about Substances', *Philosophical Review*, 84 (1975), 338–73.

—— *Sense and Contradiction: A Study in Aristotle* (Dordrecht: Reidel, 1975).

—— 'Theaetetus' First Baby: *Theaetetus* 151e–160e', *Philosophical Topics*, 15 (1987), 61–108.

DENYER, N., *Language, Thought and Falsehood in Ancient Greek Philosophy* (London and New York: Routledge & Kegan Paul, 1991).

DESCARTES, R., *Rules for the Direction of the Mind*, in *The Philosophical Writings of Descartes*, trans. J. Cottingham, R. Stoothoff, and D. Murdoch (2 vols.; Cambridge: Cambridge University Press, 1985).

DEVEREUX, D., 'Separation and Immanence in Plato's Theory of Forms', *Oxford Studies in Ancient Philosophy*, 12 (1994), 63–90; repr. Fine (ed.), *Plato 1*, 192–214.

DIMAS, P., 'True Belief in the *Meno*', *Oxford Studies in Ancient Philosophy*, 14 (1996), 1–32.

DONAGAN, A., 'Universals and Metaphysical Realism', *Monist*, 47 (1963), 211–46.

DRISCOLL, J., 'The Platonic Ancestry of Primary Substance', *Phronesis*, 24 (1979), 253–69.

—— 'EIDE in Aristotle's Earlier and Later Theories of Substance', in O'Meara (ed.), *Studies in Aristotle*, 129–59.

DUMMETT, M., 'Frege's Distinction between Sense and Reference', in his *Truth and Other Enigmas* (Cambridge, Mass.: Harvard University Press, 1978), 116–44.

DÜRING, I., and OWEN, G. E. L. (eds.), *Aristotle and Plato in the Mid-Fourth Century: Papers of the Symposium Aristotelicum Held at Oxford in August, 1957* (Studia Graeca et Latina Gothoburgensia, 11; Göteborg: Elanders Bocktryckeri Aktienbolag, 1960).

ELSE, G. F., 'The Terminology of the Ideas', *Harvard Studies in Classical Philology*, 47 (1936), 17–55.

—— *The Structure and Date of Book X of Plato's* Republic (Heidelberg: C. Winter, 1972).

EMILSSON, E., 'Plato's Self-Refutation Argument in *Theaetetus* 171 AC Revisited', *Phronesis*, 39 (1994), 136–49.

EVERSON, S. (ed.), *Epistemology* (Companions to Ancient Thought, 1; Cambridge: Cambridge University Press, 1990).

—— (ed.), *Language* (Companions to Ancient Thought, 3; Cambridge: Cambridge University Press, 1994).

FINE, G., 'Plato and Acquaintance' (unpub. diss. Ph.D., Harvard, 1975).

—— review of D. Gallop, *Plato:* Phaedo, in *Philosophical Review*, 86 (1977), 101–5.

—— 'The One over Many', *Philosophical Review*, 89 (1980), 197–240.

—— 'Armstrong on Relational and Nonrelational Realism', *Pacific Philosophical Quarterly*, 62 (1981), 262–71.

—— 'Aristotle and the More Accurate Arguments', in Schofield and Nussbaum (eds.), *Language and Logos*, 155–77.

—— 'Owen, Aristotle and the Third Man', *Phronesis*, 27 (1982), 13–33.

—— 'Separation: A Reply to Morrison', *Oxford Studies in Ancient Philosophy*, 3 (1985), 159–65.

—— 'The Object of Thought Argument', *Apeiron*, 21 (1988), 105–45.

—— 'Plato on Perception', *Oxford Studies in Ancient Philosophy*, suppl. vol. (1988), 15–28.

—— 'Owen's Progress: *Logic, Science, and Dialectic: Collected Papers in Greek Philosophy.* By G. E. L. Owen, ed. by M. Nussbaum', *Philosophical Review*, 97 (1988), 373–99.

—— 'Vlastos on Socratic and Platonic Forms', in Irwin and Nussbaum (eds.). *Virtue, Love and Form*, 67–83.

—— *On Ideas: Aristotle's Criticisms of Plato's Theory of Forms* (Oxford: Clarendon Press, 1993).

—— 'Nozick's Socrates', *Phronesis*, 41 (1996), 233–44.

—— 'Relativism and Self-Refutation in Plato's *Theaetetus*: Plato, Protagoras, and Burnyeat', in Gentzler (ed.), *Method in Ancient Philosophy*, 138–63.

—— (ed.), *Plato 1: Metaphysics and Epistemology* (Oxford: Oxford University Press, 1999).

FRANKLIN, L., 'The Structure of Dialectic in the *Meno*', *Phronesis*, 46 (2001), 413–19.

FREDE, D., 'The Philosophical Economy of Plato's Psychology: Rationality and Common Concepts in the *Timaeus*', in Frede and Striker (eds.), *Rationality in Greek Thought*, 29–58.

FREDE, M., and STRIKER, G. (eds.), *Rationality in Greek Thought* (Oxford: Clarendon Press, 1996).

FUJISAWA, N., '*Echein, Metechein,* and Idioms of "Paradeigmatism" in Plato's Theory of Forms', *Phronesis,* 19 (1974), 30–58.

FURTH, M., 'Elements of Eleatic Ontology', *Journal of the History of Philosophy,* 6 (1968), 111–32.

GALLOP, D., 'Image and Reality in Plato's *Republic*', *Archiv für Geschichte der Philosophie,* 47 (1965), 113–31.

—— 'Dreaming and Waking in Plato', in Anton and Kustas (eds.), *Essays in Ancient Greek Philosophy,* 187–220.

—— *Plato: Phaedo* (Oxford: Clarendon Press, 1975).

GEACH, P. T., 'The Third Man Again', *Philosophical Review,* 65 (1956), 72–8.

—— 'Plato's *Euthyphro*: An Analysis and Commentary', *Monist,* 50 (1966), 369–82.

—— *God and the Soul* (London: Routledge & Kegan Paul, 1969).

GENTZLER, J., 'Knowledge and Method in Plato's Early through Middle Dialogues' (diss. Ph.D., Cornell University, 1991).

—— (ed.), *Method in Ancient Philosophy* (Oxford: Clarendon Press, 1998).

GILL, C., and McCABE, M. M. (eds.), *Form and Argument in Late Plato* (Oxford: Clarendon Press, 1996).

GLIDDEN, D., 'Protagorean Relativism and the Cyrenaics', in Rescher (ed.), *Studies in Epistemology,* 113–40.

GOLDMAN, A., *Epistemology and Cognition* (Cambridge, Mass.: Harvard University Press, 1987).

GONZALEZ, F., 'Propositions or Objects? A Critique of Gail Fine on Knowledge and Belief in *Republic* V', *Phronesis,* 41 (1996), 245–75.

GOSLING, J. C. B., '*Republic* V: *Ta Polla Kala,* etc.', *Phronesis,* 5 (1960), 116–28.

—— 'Similarity in *Phaedo* 73b *seq.*', *Phronesis,* 10 (1965), 151–61.

—— '*Doxa* and *Dunamis* in Plato's *Republic*', *Phronesis,* 13 (1968), 119–30.

—— *Plato* (London: Routledge & Kegan Paul, 1973).

GOTTLIEB, P. L., 'Aristotle and the Measure of All Things' (diss. Ph.D., Cornell, 1988).

GULLEY, N., 'The Interpretation of Plato, *Timaeus* 49d3', *American Journal of Philology,* 81 (1960), 53–64.

HACKFORTH, R., *Plato's* Phaedrus (Cambridge: Cambridge University Press, 1952).

—— *Plato's* Phaedo (Cambridge: Cambridge University Press, 1955).

HARDIE, W. F. R., *A Study in Plato* (Oxford: Clarendon Press, 1936).

HARMAN, G., *Change in View* (Cambridge, Mass.: Bradford Books, 1986).

HARTMAN, E., *Substance, Body, and Soul* (Princeton: Princeton University Press, 1977).

HINTIKKA, J., 'Knowledge by Acquaintance—Individuation by Acquaintance', in Pears (ed.), *Bertrand Russell,* 52–79.

—— 'Knowledge and its Objects in Plato', in Moravcsik (ed.), *Patterns in Plato's Thought,* 1–30.

HOCUTT, M., 'Aristotle's Four Becauses', *Philosophy,* 49 (1974), 385–99.

HUME, D., *A Treatise of Human Nature*, ed. L. A. Selby-Bigge, rev. P. Nidditch (Oxford: Clarendon Press, 1978).

—— *Enquiry concerning Human Understanding*, ed. L. A. Selby-Bigge, rev. P. Nidditch (Oxford: Clarendon Press, 1982).

IRWIN, T. H., 'Aristotle's Discovery of Metaphysics', *Review of Metaphysics*, 31 (1977), 210–29.

—— 'Plato's Heracleiteanism', *Philosophical Quarterly*, 27 (1977), 1–13.

—— *Plato's Moral Theory* (Oxford: Clarendon Press, 1977).

—— *Aristotle's First Principles* (Oxford: Clarendon Press, 1988).

—— *Plato's Ethics* (Oxford: Oxford University Press, 1995).

—— 'The Theory of Forms', in Fine (ed.), *Plato 1*, 143–70.

—— and NUSSBAUM, M. (eds.), *Virtue, Love and Form* (Edmonton, Alberta: Academic Printing and Publishing, 1992).

JONES, B., 'Introduction to the First Five Chapters of Aristotle's *Categories*', *Phronesis*, 20 (1975), 146–72.

JOSEPH, H. W. B., *Knowledge and the Good in Plato's* Republic (Oxford: Clarendon Press, 1948).

KAHN, C. H., *The Verb Be in Ancient Greek* (Dordrecht: Reidel, 1973).

—— 'Language and Ontology in the *Cratylus*', in Lee, Mourelatos, and Rorty (eds.), *Exegesis and Argument*, 152–76.

—— 'Some Philosophical Uses of "to be" in Plato', *Phronesis*, 26 (1981), 119–27.

KAPLAN, D., 'Quantifying In', in Linsky (ed.), *Reference and Modality*, 112–44.

KERFERD, G., 'Plato's Account of the Relativism of Protagoras', *Durham University Journal*, 42 (1949), 20–6.

KETCHUM, R., 'Plato's "Refutation" of Protagorean Relativism: *Theaetetus* 170–171', *Oxford Studies in Ancient Philosophy*, 10 (1992), 73–105.

KEYT, D., 'Plato on Falsity: *Sophist* 263b', in Lee, Mourelatos, and Rorty (eds.), *Exegesis and Argument*, 285–305.

KIM, J., 'Causation, Nomic Subsumption, and the Concept of Event', *Journal of Philosophy*, 70 (1973), 217–36.

KIRWAN, C., *Aristotle's* Metaphysics: *Books Γ, Δ, and E* (Oxford: Clarendon Press, 1971).

KNUUTILLA, S. (ed.), *Reforging the Great Chain of Being* (Boston: Reidel, 1980).

KOSTMAN, J. P., 'False Logos and Not-Being in Plato's *Sophist*', in Moravcsik (ed.), *Patterns in Plato's Thought*, 192–212.

KRAUT, R., *Socrates and the State* (Princeton: Princeton University Press, 1984).

—— (ed.), *Cambridge Companion to Plato* (Cambridge: Cambridge University Press, 1992).

KRETZMANN, N., 'Plato on the Correctness of Names', *American Philosophical Quarterly*, 8 (1971), 126–38.

KRIPKE, S., *Naming and Necessity* (Cambridge, Mass.: Harvard University Press, 1980) (originally published 1972).

LEE, E. N., 'On the Metaphysics of the Image in Plato's *Timaeus*', *Monist*, 50 (1966), 341–68.

—— 'On the "Gold-Example" in Plato's *Timaeus* (50a5–b5)', in Anton and Kustas (eds.), 219–35.

—— MOURELATOS, A. P. D., and RORTY, R. M. (eds.), *Exegesis and Argument: Studies in Greek Philosophy Presented to Gregory Vlastos* (Assen: Van Gorcum, 1973).

LEIBNIZ, G. W., *New Essays on Human Understanding*, ed. and trans. P. Remnant and J. Bennett (Cambridge: Cambridge University Press, 1981).

—— 'Meditations on Knowledge, Truth, and Ideas', in *Philosophical Essays*, trans. R. Ariew and D. Garber (Indianapolis: Hackett, 1989), 23–7.

LESHER, J. H., '*Gnōsis* and *Epistēmē* in Socrates' Dream in the *Theaetetus*', *Journal of Hellenic Studies*, 89 (1969), 72–8.

LESZL, W., *Il 'De ideis' di Aristotele e la teoria platonica delle idee* (Florence: Olschki, 1975).

LEVETT, M. J., *The* Theaetetus *of Plato*, rev. M. F. Burnyeat (Indianapolis: Hackett, 1990).

LEVINSON, J., 'The Particularisation of Attributes', *Australasian Journal of Philosophy*, 38 (1980), 102–15.

LEWIS, F. A., 'Two Paradoxes in the *Theaetetus*', in Moravcsik (ed.), *Patterns in Plato's Thought*, 123–49.

LINSKY, L. (ed.), *Reference and Modality* (London: Oxford University Press, 1971).

LLOYD, A. C., 'The Principle that the Cause is Greater than its Effect', *Phronesis*, 21 (1976), 146–56.

LOCKE, J., *An Essay concerning Human Understanding*, ed. P. Nidditch (Oxford: Clarendon Press, 1975).

LORENZ, K., and MITTELSTRASS, J., 'On Rational Philosophy of Language: The Programme in Plato's *Cratylus* Reconsidered', *Mind*, 76 (1967), 1–20.

LOUX, M. J., *Substance and Attribute* (Dordrecht: Reidel, 1978).

LUCE, J. V., 'The Date of the *Cratylus*', *American Journal of Philology*, 85 (1964), 136–54.

MABBOTT, J. D., 'Aristotle and the *Chōrismos* of Plato', *Classical Quarterly*, 20 (1926), 72–9.

McDOWELL, J. H., 'Identity Mistakes: Plato and the Logical Atomists', *Proceedings of the Aristotelian Society*, 70 (1970), 181–96.

—— *Plato:* Theaetetus, trans. with notes (Oxford: Clarendon Press, 1973).

McGINN, C., 'On the Necessity of Origin', *Journal of Philosophy*, 73 (1976), 127–35.

—— *The Subjective View* (Oxford: Clarendon Press, 1983).

McPHERRAN, M. (ed.), *Recognition, Remembrance and Reality* (Apeiron, 32; Kelowna, BC: Academic Printing and Publishing, 1999).

MALCOLM, J., 'Does Plato Revise his Ontology in *Sophist* 246c–249d?', *Archiv für Geschichte der Philosophie*, 65 (1983), 115–46.

MATTHEN, M., 'Perception, Relativism, and Truth: Reflections on Plato's *Theaetetus* 152–60', *Dialogue*, 24 (1985), 33–58.

MATTHEWS, G. B., and COHEN, S. MARC, 'The One and the Many', *Review of Metaphysics*, 21 (1968), 630–55.

MATTHIAE, A. W., *A Copious Greek Grammar*, trans. E. V. Blomfield, 2nd edn. (2 vols.; Cambridge: Murray, 1820–1).

MEILAND, J., 'Concepts of Relative Truth', *Monist*, 60 (1977), 568–82.

MILLS, K. W., 'Plato's *Phaedo* 74b7–c6', *Phronesis*, 2 (1957), 128–47; 3 (1958), 40–58.

—— 'Some Aspects of Plato's Theory of Forms: *Timaeus* 49c ff.', *Phronesis*, 13 (1968), 145–70.

MORAVCSIK, J. M. E., 'Aristotle on Predication', *Philosophical Review*, 76 (1967), 80–96.

—— 'Learning as Recollection', in Vlastos (ed.), *Plato*, i. 53–69.

—— (ed.), *Patterns in Plato's Thought: Papers Arising out of the 1971 West Coast Greek Philosophy Conference* (Dordrecht: Reidel, 1973).

—— 'Aristotle on Adequate Explanations', *Synthese*, 28 (1974), 3–17.

MORRISON, D. R., 'Three Criteria of Substance in Aristotle's *Metaphysics*: Unity, Definability, and Separation' (diss. Ph.D., Princeton, 1983).

—— 'Separation in Aristotle's *Metaphysics*', *Oxford Studies in Ancient Philosophy*, 3 (1985), 31–89.

—— 'Separation: A Reply to Fine', *Oxford Studies in Ancient Philosophy*, 3 (1985), 167–73.

MORROW, G. R., 'Plato and the Mathematicians', *Philosophical Review*, 79 (1970), 309–33.

MURPHY, N. R., *The Interpretation of Plato's* Republic (Oxford: Clarendon Press, 1951).

NATORP, P., *Platos Ideenlehre*, 2nd edn. (Leipzig: Meiner, 1921).

NEHAMAS, A., 'Predication and Forms of Opposites in the *Phaedo*', *Review of Metaphysics*, 26 (1973), 461–91.

—— 'Plato on the Imperfection of the Sensible World', *American Philosophical Quarterly*, 12 (1975), 105–17; repr. in his *Virtues of Authenticity*, 138–58; and in Fine (ed.), *Plato 1*, 171–91.

—— '*Epistêmê* and *Logos* in Plato's Later Thought', *Archiv für Geschichte der Philosophie*, 66 (1984), 11–36; repr. in his *Virtues of Authenticity*, 224–48.

—— 'Meno's Paradox and Socrates as a Teacher', *Oxford Studies in Ancient Philosophy*, 3 (1985), 1–30; repr. in his *Virtues of Authenticity*, 3–26.

—— 'Socratic Intellectualism', *Proceedings of the Boston Area Colloquium in Ancient Philosophy*, 2, ed. J. J. Cleary (Lanham, Md.: University Press of America, 1987), 275–316; repr. in his *Virtues of Authenticity*, 27–58.

—— *Virtues of Authenticity* (Princeton: Princeton University Press, 1999).

O'BRIEN, D., 'The Last Argument of Plato's *Phaedo*', *Classical Quarterly*, NS 17 (1967), 210–13.

O'MEARA, D. J. (ed.), *Studies in Aristotle* (Washington: Catholic University of America Press, 1981).

Owen, G. E. L., 'The Place of the *Timaeus* in Plato's Dialogues', *Classical Quarterly*, ns 3 (1953), 79–95; repr. in Allen (ed.), *Studies in Plato's Metaphysics*, 313–38; and in his *Logic, Science and Dialectic*, 65–84.

—— 'A Proof in the *Peri Ideôn*', *Journal of Hellenic Studies*, 77 (1957), 103–11; repr. in Allen (ed.), *Studies in Plato's Metaphysics*, 293–312; and in his *Logic, Science and Dialectic*, 165–79.

—— 'Logic and Metaphysics in Some Earlier Works of Aristotle', in Düring and Owen (eds.), *Aristotle and Plato in the Mid-Fourth Century*, 163–90; repr. in his *Logic, Science and Dialectic*, 180–99.

—— 'Inherence', *Phronesis*, 10 (1965), 97–105; repr. in his *Logic, Science and Dialectic*, 252–8.

—— 'The Platonism of Aristotle', *Proceedings of the British Academy*, 51 (1965), 125–50; repr. in his *Logic, Science and Dialectic*, 200–20.

—— 'Plato and Parmenides on the Timeless Present', *Monist*, 50 (1966), 317–40; repr. in his *Logic, Science and Dialectic*, 27–44.

—— (ed.), *Aristotle on Dialectic: The* Topics (Symposium Aristotelicum, 3; Oxford, Clarendon Press, 1968).

—— 'Dialectic and Eristic in the Treatment of Forms', in Owen (ed.), *Aristotle on Dialectic*, 103–25; repr. in his *Logic, Science and Dialectic*, 221–38.

—— 'Plato on Not-Being', in Vlastos (ed.), *Plato*, i. 223–67; repr. in his *Logic, Science and Dialectic*, 104–37.

—— 'Notes on Ryle's Plato', in Wood and Pitcher (eds.), *Ryle*, 341–72; repr. in his *Logic, Science and Dialectic*, 85–103; and in Fine (ed.), *Plato 1*, 298–319.

—— 'Particular and General', *Proceedings of the Aristotelian Society*, 79 (1978–9), 1–21; repr. in his *Logic, Science and Dialectic*, 279–94.

—— *Logic, Science and Dialectic: Collected Papers in Greek Philosophy*, ed. M. Nussbaum (Ithaca, NY: Cornell University Press, 1986).

Pears, D. (ed.), *Bertrand Russell: A Collection of Critical Essays* (Garden City, NY: Doubleday Anchor, 1972).

Penner, T., 'The Unity of Virtue', *Philosophical Review*, 82 (1973), 35–68.

Peterson, S., 'A Reasonable Self-Predication Premise for the Third Man Argument', *Philosophical Review*, 82 (1973), 451–70.

Putnam, H., 'The Meaning of "Meaning"', in *Philosophical Papers* (2 vols.; Cambridge: Cambridge University Press, 1975), ii. 215–71.

Quine, W. V., *Methods of Logic* (New York: Holt, 1950).

Railton, P., 'Facts and Value', *Philosophical Topics*, 14 (1986), 5–31.

Rescher, N. (ed.), *Studies in Epistemology* (Oxford: Clarendon Press, 1975 = *American Philosophical Quarterly* Monograph Series, 9).

Robinson, R., 'Forms and Error in Plato's *Theaetetus*', *Philosophical Review*, 59 (1950), 3–30; repr. in his *Essays in Greek Philosophy*, 39–73.

—— *Plato's Earlier Dialectic*, 2nd edn. (Oxford: Clarendon Press, 1953).

—— *Essays in Greek Philosophy* (Oxford: Clarendon Press, 1969).

ROHR, M. D., 'Empty Forms in Plato', in Knuutilla (ed.), *Reforging the Great Chain of Being*, 19–56.

ROSS, W. D., *Aristotle's* Metaphysics (2 vols.; Oxford: Clarendon Press, 1924).

—— *Plato's Theory of Ideas* (Oxford: Clarendon Press, 1951).

RUNCIMAN, W. G., *Plato's Later Epistemology* (Cambridge: Cambridge University Press, 1962).

RUSSELL, B., 'Knowledge by Acquaintance and Knowledge by Description' (1910–11), repr. in *Mysticism and Logic, and Other Essays* (London: Allen & Unwin, 1917), 202–24.

—— 'Logical Atomism' (1924), repr. in his *Logic and Knowledge*, 321–43.

—— *The Problems of Philosophy* (New York: Oxford University Press, 1912).

—— 'The Philosophy of Logical Atomism' (1918), repr. in his *Logic and Knowledge*, 177–281.

—— *Logic and Knowledge: Essays 1901–1950*, ed. R. C. Marsh (London: Allen & Unwin, 1956).

RYLE, G., 'Plato's *Parmenides*', *Mind*, NS 48 (1939), 129–51 and 302–25; repr. in Allen (ed.), *Studies in Plato's Metaphysics*, 97–147.

SACHS, D., 'Does Aristotle Have a Doctrine of Secondary Substance?', *Mind*, NS 57 (1948), 221–5.

SANTAS, G., 'Hintikka on Knowledge and its Objects in Plato', in Moravcsik (ed.), *Patterns in Plato's Thought*, 31–51.

SAYRE, K. M., *Plato's Analytic Method* (Chicago: University of Chicago Press, 1969).

SCHIAPPA, E., *Protagoras and Logos: A Study in Greek Philosophy and Rhetoric* (Columbia, SC: University of South Carolina Press, 1991).

SCHOFIELD, M., 'A Displacement in the Text of the *Cratylus*', *Classical Quarterly*, NS 22 (1972), 246–53.

—— and NUSSBAUM, M. (eds.), *Language and Logos* (Cambridge: Cambridge University Press, 1982).

SCOTT, D., 'Platonic Anamnesis Revisited', *Classical Quarterly*, NS 37 (1987), 346–66.

—— *Recollection and Experience* (Cambridge: Cambridge University Press, 1995).

SEARLE, J., 'Proper Names', in Strawson (ed.), *Philosophical Logic*, 89–96.

SEDLEY, D. N., 'Three Platonist Interpretations of the *Theaetetus*', in Gill and McCabe (eds.), *Form and Argument in Late Plato*, 79–103.

SELLARS, W., 'Aristotle's *Metaphysics*: An Interpretation', in his *Philosophical Perspectives* (Springfield, Ill.: Thomas, 1959), 73–124.

SHIELDS, C., 'The Logos of "Logos": The Third Definition of the *Theaetetus*', in McPherran (ed.), *Recognition, Remembrance and Reality*, 107–24.

SHOEMAKER, S., *Identity, Cause and Mind* (Cambridge: Cambridge University Press, 1984).

—— 'Causality and Properties', in his *Identity, Cause and Mind*, 206–33.

SILVERMAN, A., 'Flux and Language in the *Theaetetus*', *Oxford Studies in Ancient Philosophy*, 18 (2000), 109–52.

—— 'The End of the *Cratylus*: Limning the Real', *Ancient Philosophy*, 21 (2000), 25–43.

SMITH, J. A., 'TODE TI in Aristotle', *Classical Review*, 35 (1921), 19.

STALNAKER, R., 'Anti-Essentialism', *Midwest Studies in Philosophy*, 4 (1979), 343–55.

STENZEL, J., *Zahl und Gestalt bei Platon und Aristoteles* (Berlin: Teubner, 1933).

STEWART, J. A., *Plato's Doctrine of Ideas* (Oxford: Clarendon Press, 1909).

STICH, S. P. (ed.), *Innate Ideas* (Berkeley: University of California Press, 1975).

STOKES, M., 'Plato and the Sightlovers of the *Republic*', *Apeiron*, 25 (1992), 103–32.

STOUGH, C., 'Forms and Explanation in the *Phaedo*', *Phronesis*, 21 (1976), 1–30.

STOUT, G. F., 'On the Nature of Universals and Propositions', *Proceedings of the British Academy*, 10 (1921–3), 157–72.

STRANG, C., 'Plato and the Third Man', *Proceedings of the Aristotelian Society*, suppl. 37 (1963), 147–64; repr. in Vlastos (ed.), *Plato*, i. 184–200.

STRAWSON, P. F., *Individuals* (London: Methuen, 1959).

—— (ed.), *Philosophical Logic* (London: Oxford University Press, 1967).

STURGEON, N. S., 'Moral Disagreement and Moral Relativism', *Social Philosophy and Policy*, 11 (1994), 80–115.

TAYLOR, A. E., *Varia Socratica* (Oxford: J. Parker & Co., 1911).

—— *Plato: The Man and his Work* (New York: The Dial Press Inc., 1936).

TAYLOR, C. C. W., 'Plato and the Mathematicians: An Examination of Professor Hare's Views', *Philosophical Quarterly*, 17 (1967), 193–203.

—— 'Forms as Causes in the *Phaedo*', *Mind*, 78 (1969), 45–59.

—— *Plato*: Protagoras, 2nd edn. (Oxford: Clarendon Press, 1991).

TIGNER, S., 'The "Exquisite" Argument at *Theaetetus* 171a', *Mnemosyne*, 4th series, 24 (1971), 366–9.

TURNBULL, R., 'Aristotle's Debt to the "Natural Philosophy" of the *Phaedo*', *Philosophical Quarterly*, 3 (1958), 131–43.

VLASTOS, G., 'The Disorderly Motion in the *Timaeus*', *Classical Quarterly*, 33 (1939), 71–83, repr. in Allen (ed.), *Studies in Plato's Metaphysics*, 379–99.

—— 'The Third Man Argument in the *Parmenides*', *Philosophical Review*, 63 (1954), 319–49; repr. in Allen (ed.), *Studies in Plato's Metaphysics*, 231–64.

—— 'Introduction', in *Plato*: Protagoras (Indianapolis and New York: Bobbs-Merrill, 1956).

—— '*Anamnesis* in the *Meno*', *Dialogue*, 4 (1965), 143–67.

—— 'Creation in the *Timaeus*: Is it a Fiction?', in Allen (ed.), *Studies in Plato's Metaphysics*, 401–19.

—— 'Degrees of Reality in Plato', in Bambrough (ed.), *New Essays on Plato and Aristotle*, 1–20; repr. in Vlastos, *Platonic Studies*, 58–75.

—— 'Reasons and Causes in the *Phaedo*', *Philosophical Review*, 78 (1969), 291–325; repr. in Vlastos (ed.), *Plato*, i. 132–66; and in his *Platonic Studies*, 76–110.

—— (ed.), *Plato*, i. *Metaphysics and Epistemology*; ii. *Ethics, Politics and Philosophy of Art and Religion* (Garden City, NY: Doubleday Anchor, 1971).

438   *Works Cited*

—— 'Justice and Happiness in the *Republic*', in Vlastos (ed.), *Plato*, ii. 66–95.

—— *Platonic Studies*, 2nd edn. (Princeton: Princeton University Press, 1981).

—— 'The Unity of the Virtues in the *Protagoras*', in his *Platonic Studies*, 221–65.

—— 'The Socratic Elenchus', *Oxford Studies in Ancient Philosophy*, 1 (1983), 27–58.

—— 'Socrates' Disavowal of Knowledge', *Philosophical Quarterly*, 35 (1985), 1–31; repr. in Fine (ed.), *Plato 1*, 64–92.

—— 'Elenchus and Mathematics', *American Journal of Philology*, 109 (1988), 362–96.

—— *Socrates, Ironist and Moral Philosopher* (Ithaca, NY: Cornell University Press, 1991).

WATERFIELD, R., *Plato:* Theaetetus (Harmondsworth: Penguin Books, 1987).

WATERLOW, S., 'Protagoras and Inconsistency', *Archiv für Geschichte der Philosophie*, 59 (1977), 19–36.

WEDBERG, A., *Plato's Philosophy of Mathematics* (Stockholm: Almquist & Wiskell, 1955).

—— 'The Theory of Ideas', in Vlastos (ed.), *Plato*, i. 28–52.

WHITE, N. P., 'Inquiry', *Review of Metaphysics*, 28 (1974), 289–310.

—— *Plato on Knowledge and Reality* (Indianapolis: Hackett, 1976).

—— *A Companion to Plato's* Republic (Indianapolis: Hackett, 1979).

—— 'Plato's Metaphysical Epistemology', in Kraut (ed.), *Cambridge Companion to Plato*, 277–310.

—— 'Plato on the Contents of Protagorean Relativism' (unpublished).

WHITTAKER, J., 'The "Eternity" of the Platonic Forms', *Phronesis*, 13 (1968), 131–44.

WIGGINS, D., 'Sentence Meaning, Negation, and Plato's Problem of Non-Being', in Vlastos (ed.), *Plato*, i. 268–303.

WILLIAMS, B., Introduction to *Plato:* Theaetetus (Indianapolis: Hackett, 1992).

WILLIAMS, C. J. F., 'Referential Opacity and False Belief in the *Theaetetus*', *Philosophical Quarterly*, 22 (1972), 289–302.

WILLIAMS, D. C., 'On the Elements of Being, I, II', *Review of Metaphysics*, 7 (1953), 3–18, 171–92.

WOLTERSTORFF, N., *On Universals* (Chicago: Chicago University Press, 1970).

WOOD, O. P., and PITCHER, G. (eds.), *Ryle: A Collection of Critical Essays* (London: Macmillan, 1971).

WOODRUFF, P., 'Plato's Early Theory of Knowledge', in Everson (ed.), *Epistemology*, 60–84.

WOODS, M. J., 'Substance and Essence in Aristotle', *Proceedings of the Aristotelian Society*, 75 (1974–5), 167–80.

WRIGHT, L., *Teleological Explanations: An Etiological Analysis of Goals and Functions* (Berkeley, Calif.: University of California Press, 1976).

ZEYL, D., 'Plato and Talk of a World in Flux: *Timaeus* 49a6–50b5', *Harvard Studies in Classical Philology*, 79 (1975), 125–48.

INDEX LOCORUM

Alexander of Aphrodisias
In Metaph. (*Peri Ideōn*)
79. 3–80. 6: 289 n. 72
79. 5–6: 345
79. 8–11: 94 n. 16
79. 10: 345
79. 15–19: 345
80. 8–81. 10: 289 n. 71
81. 25–82: 263 n. 30
82. 11–83. 17: 265 n. 33, 366 n. 30, 383–4 n. 55
83. 7: 260 n. 26
83. 28–30: 316–17 n. 24
84. 22–85. 3: 275 n. 45
85. 15–88. 2: 320 n. 30
86. 13–23: 280
92. 21: 324
97. 27–98. 24: 316 n. 23, 363 n. 21
97. 30–98. 2: 316
98. 2–9: 318
98. 10–16: 320
98. 16–19: 321
98. 19–20: 322

Aristotle
Categories
1^a24–5: 301 n. 2, 363 n. 22
1^a25: 404 n. 15
1^b6–7: 311 n. 19
2^a11–14: 402
2^a19–21: 343
2^a34–5: 343, 402
2^b3–6: 343, 365, 404, 420
2^b7–14: 399 n. 5, 405
2^b7–10: 343, 365
2^b15–22: 402
2^b29–37: 343, 399 n. 5, 405
2^b36–3^a6: 402
2^b36–3^a1: 402
3^b10–18: 402
3^b10–13: 402
3^b13–18: 402
4^a10–13: 401

14^a7–10: 343
14^b10–22: 404 n. 15
De interpretatione
17^a38–$^b1$: 29 n. 63, 342 n. 35
17^a39–40: 259, 391–2 n. 70, 412
Topics
113^a24–32: 324
148^a14–22: 324
149^a38–$^b3$: 302 n. 3
Sophistici elenchi
183^b6–8: 50
Physics
193^b31–194^a6: 261
193^b34: 257 n. 22, 261
194^b29–30: 351
195^a24–6: 351
195^b4–6: 353
198^a24–5: 356
199^b26–8: 356
203^a8–9: 260
210^a15–16: 303
210^a25–$^b8$: 302
210^b25–7: 302
211^a: 324
224^b5–7: 324
224^b11–16: 324
226^b21–3: 255
251^b: 292 n. 75
De caelo
277^b33–4: 302 n. 3
278^a14–15: 302 n. 3
279^b ff.: 292 n. 75
De generatione et corruptione
315^a22–33: 357 n. 17
327^b20–2: 302 n. 3
335^b7–16: 361
335^b18–24: 361
De anima
413^b14: 255 n. 16
413^b17: 255 n. 16
427^a3: 257 n. 22
429^a11: 257 n. 22
430^a20: 257 n. 22

De anima (*cont.*):
432^{a}20: 255 n. 17
433^{b}25: 255 n. 17, 257 n. 22
Metaphysics
911^{a}22–3: 367
987^{a}29–^{b}8: 30, 266
987^{a}32–^{b}7: 264
987^{a}34–987^{b}1: 294 n. 78
987^{b}4 ff.: 295
987^{b}5: 266
987^{b}8: 267 n. 36
988^{a}9–10: 358
988^{a}35–^{b}6: 358
988^{b}6–16: 368
988^{b}15: 368
991^{a}8–11: 407
991^{a}8–10: 350
991^{a}12–19: 302, 363
991^{a}12–13: 414
991^{a}20–3: 336
991^{a}20–2: 366
991^{a}22–3: 367
991^{a}27–30: 367
991^b: 407
991^{b}1: 267
991^{b}1–3: 364, 413
991^{b}3–9: 359
991^{b}18–19: 301
992^{a}25–6: 358
992^{a}26–9: 366
992^{a}29–31: 369
998^{a}14–15: 324
1005^{b}25–6: 211 n. 85
1008^{a}28–30: 209 n. 61
1009^{a}7–12: 209 n. 61
1016^{a}17 ff.: 312 n. 20
1016^{b}2: 255 n. 16
1017^{b}21–2: 399, 405
1017^{b}23–4: 402
1018^{b}32–3: 259, 262 n. 29
1018^{b}33: 255 n. 17
1019^{a}1–4: 256, 404
1019^{a}4: 256
1019^{a}11–12: 256
1028^{a}31–^{b}2: 256
1028^{a}31–3: n. 257
1028^{a}32–8: 256 n. 18
1028^{a}32–3: 404 n. 14
1028^{a}32: 255 n. 17
1028^{a}33–4: 256, 404
1028^{a}35–6: 404
1028^{a}36–^{b}2: 405

1028^{b}36–7: 402
1029^{a}1–2: 402
1029^{a}9–10: 417
1029^{a}17–19: 402
1029^{a}28–30: 403 n. 11, 417
1029^{b}13–16: 343 n. 36
1030^{a}3 ff.: 417
1030^{a}4: 403
1030^{a}5–6: 403 n. 11
1030^{a}25: 255 n. 17
1031^{a}18: 399
1032^{b}1–2: 399
1036^{a}6–7: 405
1038^{b}8–16: 401
1038^{b}15–16: 403
1038^{b}15: 402
1038^{b}34–1039^{a}2: 30 n. 66, 401, 403
1040^b ff.: 311 n. 19
1040^{b}25–7: 309 n. 17
1040^{b}27–8: 262
1042^{a}15–16: 271, 413
1042^{a}28–31: 256, 420
1042^{a}29: 255
1052^{b}17: 255 n. 16
1064^{a}24: 255 n. 17
1068^{b}26: 255 n. 16
1072^a: 357 n. 17
1072^b: 394
1072^{b}2–3: 368
1075^{a}38–^{b}1: 368, 393
1077^{a}30–^{b}11: 257
1077^{b}13: 255 n. 17
1078^b ff.: 343
1078^{b}9–1079^{a}4: 264
1078^{b}9–17: 268
1078^{b}12–32: 30
1078^{b}12–17: 268
1078^{b}15: 268
1078^{b}16: 268
1078^{b}30–2: 268
1078^{b}30–1: 252, 268–9 n. 38, 411
1078^{b}30: 268, 269
1079^{a}27: 416
1079^{a}31: 260 n. 26
1079^{b}12–17: 269
1079^{b}12–14: 350
1079^{b}15–23: 302
1079^{b}15–21: 363
1079^{b}15–16: 414
1079^{b}22–3: 301
1079^{b}24–6: 366
1079^{b}26–7: 367

1079^{b}27–30: 367
1079^{b}35–1080^{a}2: 260 n. 27, 364, 413
1080^{a}2–8: 359
1081^{b}32–3: 413
1086^{a}30 ff.: 343
1086^{a}31–^{b}11: 264, 269
1086^{a}32–^{b}13: 30, 30 n. 66, 258, 411
1086^{a}32–4: 270
1086^{a}35–7: 299
1086^{a}37–^{b}1: 269
1086^{b}1–2: 269, 270
1086^{b}3–7: 296
1086^{b}3–5: 404
1086^{b}4: 252, 257
1086^{b}5–13: 30 n. 66
1086^{b}5–6: 269
1086^{b}6–7: 252, 323
1086^{b}7–10: 270
1086^{b}8–9: 270
1086^{b}9–11: 270
1086^{b}9–10: 270
1086^{b}9: 271
1086^{b}10–11: 270
1086^{b}32–5: 252
1086^{b}36–7: 270
1087^{a}16–18: 421
1087^{a}17: 421
1092^{a}19: 255 n. 16
1092^{a}24–6: 302 n. 3
Eudemian Ethics
1217^b: 258
1217^{b}2–16: 258
1217^{b}11–13: 258
1217^{b}15–16: 258

Diogenes Laertius
Lives
9. 51: 132 n. 1, 161 n. 2, 184 n. 1, 186 n. 6
9. 53: 189 n. 15

Heracleitus
DK A 6: 132 n. 2, 162 n. 8
DK B 91: 132 n. 2, 162 n. 8

Plato
Charmides
158 E–159 A: 297 n. 85
159 C 1: 48 n. 12
160 E 6: 48 n. 12
Cratylus
385: 130

385 B–D: 17 n. 39
385 B 2–D 1: 17, 124
385 C 5–6: 124 n. 14
385 D 2: 124 n. 15
385 E–386 D: 185
385 E 6–386 A 3: 132 n. 1, 161 n. 2, 184 n. 1
385 E 7–8: 124 n. 15
385 E 10: 124 n. 15
386 A 1–3: 133 n. 5, 161 n. 2
388 B 10–11: 125
389: 289
392–3: 121
392 B–393 B: 126
393 B–C: 126
394 D: 126
393 D 1–4: 127
394 E 3: 127
394 E 7–8: 127
395 B 6: 127
395 B 7–C 5: 127
396 E 5: 127
402 A 8–10: 132 n. 2, 162 n. 8
412 E 6–413 D 2: 127
421 D–E: 122
422 C–D: 128
422 D–E: 121
424 B: 128
424 C ff.: 237
425 B: 128
428 E: 121
429 E 8–9: 129
430 A 4–5: 129
430 D: 124
430 E 5–7: 130
431: 124 n. 17
431 B: 124, 124 n. 17
431 B 5–C 7: 122
432 B–433 B: 127
435 E–440 A: 16 n. 38
436 C–D: 111
437 D 5–6: 17 n. 39
438 D 7–8: 17 n. 39
439 C 6–440 C 1: 410 n. 22
Euthydemus
286 B–C: 184 n. 2, 189 n. 15
286 C 3–5: 184 n. 2
Euthyphro
5 D 1–5: 297 n. 85
6 E 3–6: 279
6 E 4–5: 383 n. 54
11 A–B: 46 n. 6

Gorgias
454 D: 71, 224
454 D 6–7: 89
488 A 4: 80–1 n. 21
488 D 9: 80–1 n. 21
Hippias Maior
289 C–D: 78 n. 17
294 C 4: 80–1 n. 21
Laches
191 E–192 B: 297 n. 85
192 C 5–7: 48 n. 12
196 E: 82
196 E 1–197 C 4: 60
Meno
70 A 1–2: 45
71 A–B: 2
71 A: 23–4 n. 53
71 A 5–7: 45 n. 4
71 A 7: 45, 52 n. 21, 56–7 n. 29
71 B: 2, 86 n. 4, 93 n. 15
71 B 3–4: 45, 45 n. 4, 52 n. 21, 56–7
    n. 29
71 B 4–7: 63 n. 42
71 B 4–6: 45 n. 4
71 B 5: 52 n. 21, 56–7 n. 29
72 A ff.: 2 n. 3
72 C 6: 8–9 n. 19
72 C 7: 28 n. 62
72 C 8: 2, 28, 39 n. 81
72 D 8: 8–9 n. 19, 28 n. 62
72 E 1: 297 n. 85
72 E 5: 8–9 n. 19, 28 n. 62
72 E 7: 297 n. 85
75 C 8–D 7: 226, 248 n. 29
75 D: 9, 87, 106–7 n. 38
77 A 6: 29 n. 63
79 C 8–9: 226
80 D: 3
80 D 5–8: 51
80 D 5–6: 45 n. 4
80 D 6: 52 n. 21
80 E 1–6: 51
81 A 5–6: 64
81 A 10–B 2: 64
81 C 5–D 5: 54
81 C 6–7: 55 n. 26
81 C 9: 61 n. 40
81 D 1: 55 n. 26
81 D 4–5: 55 n. 26
81 E 3–5: 55
82 B–85 D: 55
82 B 2–4: 4 n. 8

82 B 2: 55
82 C–E: 55
82 E: 55
83 D: 58
84 A–B: 55
84 B–C: 56
84 D–85 B: 56
85 B–D: n. 61
85 B 8–D 1: 4
85 C: 104 n. 34
85 C 2–8: 56
85 C 6–7: 57
85 C 9–D 1: 49
85 C 10–D 1: 56
85 D–86 C: 55
85 D 1: 61 n. 40
85 D 3–4: 5 n. 9, 61 n. 40
85 D 6: 61 n. 40
85 D 9: 5 n. 9, 61 n. 40
85 E 2–3: 56
86 A 8: 61 n. 40
86 B: 65
86 B 1: 61 n. 40
86 C: 56
87 E 1–3: 48 n. 12
97 A ff.: 6 n. 12, 7, 8
97 A–98 C: 58
97 A–98 B: 71
97 A 9–B 7: 86 n. 4
97 A 9–B 3: 63–4 n.42
98 A: 5, 5 n. 11, 7, 39 n. 81, 50, 50 n.
    19, 50 n. 20, 55 n. 26, 66, 73 n. 12,
    85, 89, 93, 104, 107, 224, 225, 412
98 B 1–5: 65
99 C: 65
Parmenides
129 D 6–8: 274
130 B: 335
130 B 2–5: 34 n. 71, 274
131 A 4–6: 304
131 B 1–2: 309
131 B 3–6: 310
131 B 7–9: 311
131 C 9–10: 311
131 D 2: 312
131 D 4: 313
131 D 5: 313
131 D 9–E 1: 312
132 A–B: 275
132 D 3–4: 336
133 B 4–C 1: 316
133 C 3–5: 308 n. 16

135 A–C: 81 n. 22
135 A 7–B 2: 316
144 D: 311
157 C 4–E 2: 239 n. 20
Phaedo
64 C 2: 276
65 C 7: 276
66 A: 78 n. 17
73 A–77 A: 265 n. 33
73 A: 5 n. 9
73 E 9–10 ff.: 383
74: 282
74 A 11: 282
74 B–C: 282 n. 59
74 B: 78 n. 17
74 B 7–10: 282
74 B 8: 282 n. 59
74 C 1–3: 282
74 C 4–5: 282, 283
74 E: 336 n. 22
75 D 4: 69 n. 8
76 A 4: 69 n. 8
76 B: 93, 107, 228
76 C 15: 69 n. 8
76 E: 287
78 ff.: 320
78 D: 228
80 C 2–D 4: 281
86 C–D: 281
95 E 9: 375
96 ff.: 85
96 A 6: 369
96 A 8: 369
96 A 9–10: 369, 375
96 E 6–97 B 3: 371
97 A 8–99 D 2: 372
97 D 1–3: 373, 374
98–9: 373
98 A 4–B 1: 373, 374
99 A 4–B 5: 372
99 D 1–2: 374
100 ff. : 106 n. 38
100–6: 303
100: 33 n. 69, 412
100 B 6: 395 n. 76
100 C 4–6: 37, 376
100 C 5: 304
100 C 9–E 3: 37
100 D: 10, 278, 332 n. 14
100 D 4–E 3: 303, 376
100 D 6: 376 n. 40
100 D 8–9: 375

100 E 1–2: 375
100 E 8–101 C 8: 379
101 A–B: 379
101 A 8–B 2: 312
101 C 2–4: 376
101 C 3–6: 304
102 ff.: 334
102 A 11–B 6: 304
102 B ff.: 391
102 B: 282 n. 60
102 C: 337
102 D–103 A: 306
102 D 5 ff.: 306
102 D 6–7: 305
103 A 1: 306
103 B 5–6: 305
103 C 10 ff.: 306
103 C 10–E 1: 337
104 A 3: 337
104 A 7: 337
104 D 4–7: 305
104 D 5–6: 305 n. 6
104 E 10: 304, 377
105 B–C: 304
105 B 6–C 6: 37
105 B 7–8: 377
105 C 1–2: 376
105 D: 377
105 D 3–4: 395
106 A: 377
106 A 3–6: 306, 307 n. 13
106 C 3: 307 n. 12
106 C 5–7: 307 n. 12
106 D 1: 307 n. 12
106 D 5–7: 395
112 B 1: 373
Philebus
14 D: 337
15 B 7: 311
17 E 4–6: 249–50 n. 30
18 B–D: 237
18 C: 243
37 A: 69 n. 8
58 E–59 C: 13 n. 31, 67 n. 3
61 D 10–E 4: 67 n. 3
62 A 2–D 7: 67 n. 3
Politicus
277 B 7–8: 249–50 n. 30
281 A 12–B 1: 123 n. 13
Protagoras
330 C 1: 276
349 E 3–5: 48 n. 12

Protagoras (*cont.*):
359 E 4–7: 48 n. 12
Republic
331: 60
331 C: 80
435: 106
437 A–438 E: 276
472 A 1–7: 87
473 C 6–E 5: 87
473 C 11–480 A 13: 67
475 D 2: 68
476 A: 278, 306 n. 10
476 A 4–7: 308 n. 16
476 A 10: 68
476 B 4: 68
476 C 2–7: 68
476 C 9–D 3: 67 n. 4
476 E 4–8: 68
476 E 7–9: 68
476 E 10–11: 68
477 A: 224
477 A 2–4: 68
477 A 6–7: 68
477 A 9–10: 68, 87, 87 n. 6
477 A 10–B 1: 68
477 B–478 B: 90
477 B 3–6: 71
477 B 7–8: 71
477 B 10–11: 71
477 C 1–4: 72
477 C 6–D 5: 72, 90
477 D 7–9: 72
477 E 1–3: 72
477 E 6–7: 72, 91
478 A 3–4: 72
478 A 6: 72
478 A 8: 72
478 A 12–B 2: 72, 91
478 B 3–5: 72
478 B 9–10: 74
478 B 12–C 1: 74
478 C 3–4: 75
478 C 6: 75
478 C 8: 76
478 C 10–14: 76
478 D: 9 n. 22
478 D 1–4: 76
478 D 5–9: 77
478 D 12: 10
478 E: 91
478 E 1–4: 77
478 E 5–479 B 8: 77

478 E 7–479 B 2: 68
479 A ff.: 10, 91
479 A 4: 92
479 B 9–10: 77, 206 n. 54
479 C 6–D 1: 77
479 D 3–5: 78, 92
479 D 7–9: 78
479 D 7–8: 78
479 D 10–480 A 4: 78
479 E 1–5: 78, 92
479 E 7–480 A 5: 94
479 E 10–480 A 4: 70
480 A 1: 94
484 D 2: 80–1 n. 21
493 A 6–C 8: 103
500 C–E: 383 n. 54
504 C 9–E 3: 98, 106
505 A: 97
505 A 1–10: 393
506 C: 66, 86, 95
506 E: 97
507 A 7–B 10: 96
507 B 9–10: 96 n. 18
507 C–508 D: 96
507 D 11–E 2: 97 n. 22
508 A 5: 97
508 B 12–C 2: 96
508 D 8: 92–3 n. 14
508 E 3: 97 n. 22
509 B 6–10: 98, 308 n. 16, 320
509 B 6: 393
509 B 7–8: 96 n. 19
509 B 9–10: 98
509 D 1–510 A 3: 97 n. 22
509 D 6: 99
509 E 1–510 A 3: 102
510 A 9: 99 n. 27
510 B: 95, 105
510 B 4–9: 105
510 C 2–D 3: 105
510 C 7: 109
510 D: 105 n. 35
510 D 5–8: 105
511 A: 383 n. 54
511 A 3–C 2: 105
511 A 3: 99 n. 27
511 B–C: 113
511 B: 100
511 B 3: 99 n. 27
511 D: 105, 112
514 A: 100
515 A 5: 100, 102

515 B 4–C 2: 103
517 B: 101 n. 30
517 D 4–E 2: 102, 103 n. 33
520 C: 66, 67 n. 4, 86, 102, 383 n. 54
520 C 1–D 1: 102, 103 n. 33
520 C 2: 97
520 C 4: 13 n. 31
520 C 7–D 1: 103
522 E: 107
525 B–C: 107
525 C: 107
525 D–E: 112
525 E: 112
526 A 1–7: 112
526 D: 107
531 C 6–E 5: 115
531 E: 93, 107
533 A–D: 113
533 C: 100, 108 n. 43, 111
533 C 1–5: 109
533 C 8: 100, 112
533 D 7–E 2: 99 n. 27
533 E 2: 99 n. 27
533 E 8–534 A: 99 n. 27
534 B: 13 n. 33, 93, 107, 115, 228
534 B 3–6: 114
534 C 2: n. 113
537 B 8–C 7: 115
537 C: 115
589 A 7: 80–1 n. 21
596 B ff.: 383 n. 54
596 B: 289
623–4: 78 n. 17
Sophist
202 B 4–5: 122
225 E: 121
237 D 2: 121 n. 10
248 A: 274
248 A 7: 274
252 C: 249–50 n. 30
253 B 10: 249–50 n. 30
256 E 5–6: 313
257 A 4–6: 313
261–3: 410 n. 22
261 D 4 ff.: 230
261 E 5: 121
262 A 4: 119
262 A 6: 119
262 B 9–C 7: 230
262 D 2–6: 119
262 E 5–6: 119
263 A 8: 130

263 B 7–13: 219
Symposium
211 A–B: 308 n. 16
211 B 4–5: 319
Theaetetus
146 D: 248 n. 29
147 B: 248 n. 29
147 B 2–5: 226
151–60: 136 n. 12, 186, 189
151 E–186 E: 132, 162
151 E 1–3: 18, 132, 162
151 E 8–152 A 1: 135 n. 10
152 A–169 D: 134, 162
152 A 2–4: 132, 161, 184
152 A 6–8: 19, 133, 161
152 B–C: 144 n. 28, 185
152 B 1–C 3: 188
152 B 1–7: 141
152 B 9–12: 135–6 n. 10
152 C–153 D: 173
152 C 1–2: 135 n. 9, 162 n. 7
152 C 8–E 10: 141
152 C 10: 135 n. 10, 163 n. 9
152 D 8–E 1: 142
152 E 8: 142
153–4: 154, 169, 170 n. 24, 178
153 D ff.: 144 n. 28
153 D–154 B: 19, 147, 153, 154 n. 53,
    160, 165, 170, 175–6 n. 36, 180 n.
    43, 181–2 n. 46
153 D 9–E 1: 171
153 E: 165
153 E 4–5: 172 n. 29, 181
153 E 5: 165
154: 165, 167
154 A 2: 144 n. 28
154 A 3–8: 157 n. 62, 182–3 n. 48
154 A 5: 165
154 A 6–8: 152
154 B: 165, 166, 166 n. 14, 170 n. 25,
    171, 172, 172 n. 29, 176 n. 37, 178,
    179, 179 n. 41, 180, 181
154 B 1–2: 165–6 n. 13
154 B 3: 165–6 n. 13
154 B 5: 165
154 B 6–8: 174, 177
154 C 1: 175
154 C 2–4: 175
154 C 6: 177
154 C 7–9: 175
155 D–156 A: 178 n. 40
155 D 5–8: 177

Theaetetus (*cont.*):
155 D 5–7: 177
155 D 9–E 1: 177
156: 178
156 A ff.: 178 n. 40
156 A 1–3: 154
156 A 2 ff.: 177
156 A 3–5: 135 n. 10, 163 n. 9, 177
156 A 5: 178 n. 39
156 B 4–6: 189 n. 13
156 E: 171 n. 28
156 E 5–7: 171
158 A: 185
158 E 5–160 D: 144 n. 28
159 A–160 C: 189 n. 14
160 D 5–E 2: 135 n. 10
160 D 6: 18, 162
160 D 7–8: 18, 132, 162
161 C 2–3: 185–6 n. 5
161 D 5–7: 185–6 n. 5
162 A 1: 185–6 n. 5
166 B 5–C 2: 209 n. 61
166 C–167 C: 185
167 A 8: 136 n. 11, 163 n. 10
167 B 1: 185–6 n. 5
167 C 2: 185–6 n. 5
169–71: 18, 20, 20–1 n. 48
169 D–171 D: 134, 136 n. 12, 162, 184
169 E 7–8: n. 184
170–1: 201–2 n. 45
170 A–C: 190, 193 n. 19
170 A: 185
170 A 3–C 5: 191
170 A 3: 193 n. 21
170 A 6–9: n. 196
170 A 7: 193 n. 21
170 B 5–6: 193 n. 21
170 C: 201
170 C 5–E 6: 190
170 C 5–D 2: 197 n. 34
170 C 5–8: 193 n. 21, 196
170 C 5–7: 207
170 C 9: 196
170 D 1–2: 196
170 D 4–E 6: 197, 199 n. 40
170 D 5–6: 199
170 D 5: 199 n. 39
170 D 6–8: 198
170 D 8–9: 200
170 E 4–5: 199, 199 n. 39
170 E 7–171 D 8: 190
170 E 7–171 C 7: 202

170 E 7–171 A 2: 203 n. 49
170 E 7–171 A 1: 203
170 E 8: 203 n. 49
170 E 9: 204 n. 50
171 A: 185, 203, 203 n. 49
171 A 1–3: 203
171 A 4–5: 203, 203 n. 48
171 A 6 ff.: 190
171 A 6–C 7: 198–9 n. 37
171 A 6–8: 203, 204
171 A 6: 190, 204 n. 50
171 A 8–9: 203
171 B 1–2: 204
171 B 4–5: 202 n. 46
171 B 4: 203 n. 49, 204
171 B 6–7: 204
171 B 9–10: 203 n. 49, 210
171 B 9–C 2: 204
171 B 10–C 5: 210
171 C 2: 204
171 C 5–7: 193 n. 20, 204, 210
171 C 5: 204
171 E–172 A: 185
171 E: 135 n. 9, 162 n. 7
172 B 6: 185–6 n. 5
177 C 6–179 D 2: 18, 136 n. 12
178 B 5: 135 n. 9, 162 n. 7
179 B–D: 185–6 n. 5
179 C 2: 185–6 n. 5
179 C 4: 185–6 n. 5
181–6: 137 n. 14
181–3: 18, 21, 21 n. 49, 136 n. 12, 157
    n. 62, 157 n. 63, 201 n. 43, 201–2 n.
    45, 410 n. 22
183 A 2–3: 135 n. 10, 163 n. 9
184–6: 18, 21, 21 n. 49, 21 n. 50, 23,
    136 n. 12, 164, 201 n. 43
187 B: 213
188 A–C: 53 n. 24, 214
188 B 3–5: 215, 219
188 B 6–C 4: 215
188 C 9–189 B 8: 214 n. 4
189 C 1–4: 217
189 C 5–6: 217
189 E 1–2: 220
189 E 6–7: 220
190 B 2–8: 219
199 A: 121 n. 10
200 D: 213–14 n. 3, 222
201 A–C: 23, 66, 71, 86 n. 4, 213, 223
201 B: 227
201 C 9–D 1: 227

201 E 1: 228
202 A 7: 232, 240
202 A 8–B 2: 230
202 B–C: 122
202 B: 122
202 B 6–7: 230
202 B 7: 228
202 B 8–C 5: 232
202 D 6–7: 237
202 D 8–E 1: 237
202 D 10–E 1: 236
203 B 2–7: 237
203 B 7: 237
203 C: 241
204 A 7–8: 238
205 B 8–13: 239 n. 21
205 D 7–E 4: 241
206 A–C: 241
206 A 10–B 3: 241
206 B 9–11: 241
206 C 1–2: 242
206 D–E: 122, 232
206 D: 122
206 D 1–5: 243
206 D 7–E 2: 243
206 E 6–207 A 1: 232, 243
207 A: 239
208 C 7–8: 25, 244
208 D 1–3: 244
209 B 8: 244
209 C 4–9: 245
209 E 6–210 A 9: 25
210 A 3–5: 248
210 A 7–9: 248
Timaeus
27 D ff.: 99
27 D 5–31 A 1: 292
28 A ff.: 383 n. 54, 394
28 A–29 C: 67 n. 3
28 A 1–2: 23 n. 53

33 A 6: 5 n. 11
48 D 2: 336 n. 22, 383 n. 54
48 E 2–52 D: 410 n. 22
49 A 6–50 B 5: 339 n. 30
49 A 7: 339
49 C 5–6: 338
49 C 7–E 7: 339
49 D–E: 339
49 D–C: 339
49 E 7 ff.: 408
50 A: 121 n. 10
50 A 5–B 5: 338
50 B 1: 340
50 B 5 ff.: 408
50 B 7–8: 338
50 C 5: 338
50 C 7: 339
50 D 4–51 E 2: 338
50 D 7–8: 338
50 D 7: 338
50 E 4: 338
51 B–52 C: 275
51 B 3: 338
51 D: 81 n. 22
51 E 1–2: 274
51 E 3: 23 n. 53
52: 308 n. 16
52 A 1–6: 278
52 A 8: 339
52 D 4: 339
53 B 2: 293, 339

Sextus Empiricus
Adversus mathematicos
7. 60–4: 186 n. 6
7. 60–1: 132 n. 1, 161 n. 2, 184 n. 1
7. 389–90: 184 n. 2
Pyrrhoneae hypotyposes
1. 216–19: 144 n. 28, 186 n. 6